The DE ORCHI Portrait of COLUMBUS.

(Reputed to be the original once in the Jovian Gallery at Como.)

The Four Voyages
of Columbus

A HISTORY IN EIGHT DOCUMENTS,
INCLUDING FIVE BY
CHRISTOPHER COLUMBUS,
IN THE ORIGINAL SPANISH,
WITH ENGLISH TRANSLATIONS

Translated and Edited
with Introduction and Notes
by
CECIL JANE

TWO VOLUMES BOUND AS ONE

Dover Publications, Inc.
New York

Published in Canada by General Publishing Company, Ltd., 30 Lesmill Road, Don Mills, Toronto, Ontario.

Published in the United Kingdom by Constable and Company, Ltd., 3 The Lanchesters, 162-164 Fulham Palace Road, London W6 9ER.

This Dover edition, first published in 1988, is a slightly altered and corrected republication in one volume of Nos. LXV and LXX of the Second Series of works published by The Hakluyt Society, London, in 1930 and 1933 respectively (issued for 1929 and 1932 respectively), under the title *Select Documents Illustrating the Four Voyages of Columbus: Including those Contained in R. H. Major's "Select Letters of Christopher Columbus."* The foldout maps are here presented as two-page spreads, in which red lines have been replaced with gray.

Manufactured in the United States of America
Dover Publications, Inc., 31 East 2nd Street, Mineola, N.Y. 11501

Library of Congress Cataloging-in-Publication Data

Columbus, Christopher.
The four voyages of Columbus.

"Slightly altered and corrected republication in one volume of nos. LXV and LXX of the second series of works published by The Hakluyt Society, London, in 1930 and 1933, respectively, under the title Select documents illustrating the four voyages of Columbus."
Bibliography: p.
Includes index.
1. Columbus, Christopher—Correspondence. 2. America—Discovery and exploration—Spanish. 3. America—Early accounts to 1600. 4. Explorers—America—Correspondence. 5. Explorers—Spain—Correspondence. I. Jane, Lionel Cecil, 1879-1932. II. Title.
E114.J36   1988   970.01'5   87-33201
ISBN 0-486-25626-X (pbk.)

VOLUME I

The First and Second Voyages

PREFACE

IN 1847 Mr. R. H. Major edited for the Hakluyt Society the *Select Letters of Columbus*. This volume, a second edition of which appeared in 1870, contained the Spanish text and an English translation of the letters of Columbus relating to his first, third and fourth voyages; the letter to the Nurse; the letter of Dr. Chanca; the De Torres Memorandum, and extracts from the will of Diego Mendez. In 1892 the same Society issued an English translation, but not the Spanish text, of Las Casas' précis of the *Journal* of the first voyage, in a volume which was edited by Sir Clements R. Markham and which contained also materials relating to the voyages of John Cabot and Gaspar Corte Real. Both Mr. Major and Sir Clements Markham were compelled to rely mainly upon the Spanish text of the documents which had been printed in 1825 by Martin Fernandez de Navarrete, in his *Colección de los Viages y Descubrimientos*.

Since the volumes ·in question were published, however, the folio version of the *Letter* describing the results of the first voyage has become known, and a far more accurate text of the most important documents has been published by Cesare de Lollis in his *Scritti di Colombo*.

The first volume of the present collection of documents contains the material relating to the first and second voyages which was contained in Mr. Major's *Select Letters*, with the addition of the account given by Andrés Bernáldez of the exploration of the coasts of Cuba and Jamaica in 1494. Subsequent volumes will contain the remainder of the material edited by Mr. Major, the text and a translation of the précis of the *Journal*, and other materials.

I wish to take this opportunity of expressing my thanks to those who have assisted me in the preparation of this volume, and more especially to the staff of the Reading Room of the British Museum and to Mr. F. P. Sprent, Honorary Secretary of the Hakluyt Society.

CECIL JANE

May 1930.

CONTENTS OF VOLUME I

LIST OF ILLUSTRATIONS

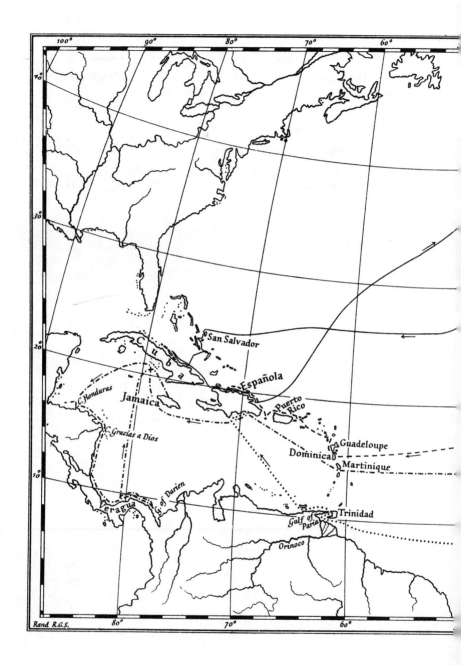

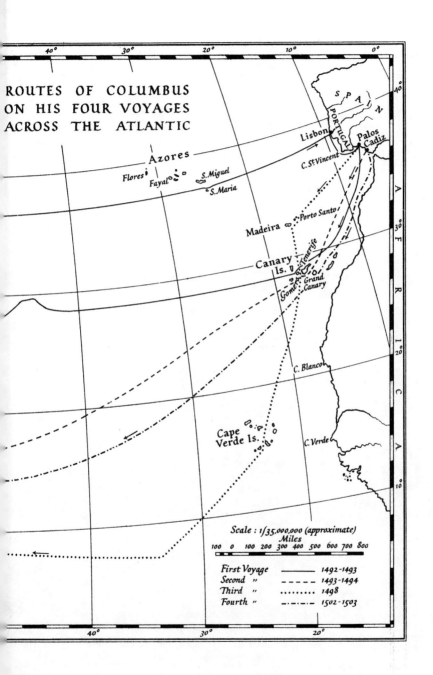

ROUTES OF COLUMBUS
ON HIS FOUR VOYAGES
ACROSS THE ATLANTIC

Azores

Flores   Fayal   S. Miguel
              S. Maria

Lisbon
C. St Vincent

S P A I N
PORTUGAL
Palos
Cadiz

Madeira   Porto Santo

Canary
Is.   Tenerife
Gomera   Grand
         Canary

C. Blanco

Cape
Verde Is.   C. Verde

A F R I C A

Scale : 1/35,000,000 (approximate)
Miles
100   0   100 200 300 400 500 600 700 800

First Voyage   ————————   1492-1493
Second „   – – – – –   1493-1494
Third   „   1498
Fourth „   –·–·–·–   1502-1503

INTRODUCTION

THE OBJECTIVE OF COLUMBUS

1

THE discovery of America by Columbus is one of the few events in the history of mankind of which the importance can scarcely be overestimated. In its most obvious aspect, indeed, the achievement of Columbus cannot be justly described as unique, since it is not to be supposed that no European had ever before crossed the Atlantic and since it is impossible to reject as mere inventions all the stories of a pre-Columbian discovery.[1] It is true that among those stories there are some of which the absurdity is so palpable as hardly to require demonstration. For one, there is no better evidence than the testimony of a fifteenth-century poem and of a six-teenth-century fabrication; the philological arguments which have been advanced to prove its truth are more ingenuous than rational. The narrative of another pre-discovery is alleged to have been contained in documents which have since been conveniently destroyed; their authenticity may be gauged from the fact that they claimed for the hero, whose exploits they recounted, the honour of having anticipated not only Columbus, but also Vasco da Gama and Cabral.[2] Greater credence might, perhaps, be given to certain other stories, were it not that they are marred by the appearance in them of gross improbabilities. In one, the inhabitants of the newly found lands spoke Latin; in another, the king of these lands had with him an interpreter who understood Arabic; it may be safely concluded that if either of these statements be true, the country concerned did not lie beyond the Atlantic. In one story, a type of civilization is found which certainly

[1] For the stories of a pre-Columbian discovery, cp. Major, *Select Letters of Columbus*, Introduction; Harrisse, *The Discovery of North America*.

[2] Cp. Gaffarel, *Les Découvertes françaises du XIVme au XVIme siecle*: and *Études sur les Rapports de l'Amérique et de l'ancien continent*. Perhaps the most effective criticism of this story is contained in Fernandez Duro, *Pinzón en el descubrimiento de las Indias* (Appendix IV, *Pinzón en las Indias ante Colón*): 'No concibiendo el envidiable genio francés que cosa grande, noble ó provechosa, ... haya tenido iniciativa fuera de Francia.'

never existed in America at any time; in all these narratives, there is so obvious an element of falsehood, that it becomes questionable whether there is also any element of truth, and there is generally so much obscurity that no conclusions can be confidently based upon them. The very most that can be asserted is that, before the date of the first voyage of Columbus, attempts had been made to reach lands which were believed to exist in the west and that it is not improbable that some measure of success attended one or other of these attempts.

The expeditions of the Norsemen, however, fall into a different category.[1] There is no doubt that these expeditions were actually made or that those adventurous sailors, voyaging by way of Iceland and Greenland, did reach the coast of North America. To them must be accorded the somewhat barren honour of having been the first Europeans known to have set foot on the American continent and to have, moreover, established settlements on its shores. Their exploits, however, were far more romantic than important. After having been maintained for a considerable period, communications between Scandinavia and America were interrupted; the settlements which had been founded were abandoned or destroyed, and such accounts of them as have been preserved suffice to prove that the memory of their existence soon became both vague and confused. In Europe generally the story of the voyages of the Norsemen was apparently little known and less regarded; if it did serve to induce Prince Henry the Navigator to conceive of the possibility of a north-west passage to India, there is no evidence to show that it inspired either the fifteenth-century efforts to cross the Atlantic or the final attempt of Columbus. It was, indeed, with considerable justice that the discoverer declared that until he had made his first voyage there was no knowledge, but merely vague conjecture, concerning the western hemisphere.

It was the achievement of Columbus to convert conjecture

[1] On the Northmen, there is a vast literature. Valuable bibliographies will be found in Lucas, *Annals of the voyages of the brothers Nicolo and Antonio Zeno*; and in Nansen, *The Northern Mists*. A new work on the subject by Mr. T. D. Kendrick, *History of the Vikings*, is about to appear.

into certainty, to substitute knowledge for hypothesis, and to open a way across the Atlantic which has never since been closed. He thereby gave a new world, not so much to Castile and Leon, as the oft-quoted phrase declares him to have done, as to Europe and to European civilization. Of the momentous character of this achievement there can be no question; it is not the less momentous because its accomplishment sooner or later was in reality inevitable.[1] The importance of most events seems constantly to diminish as they recede into the background of the past. The drama of history moves on; new incidents occur to attract the attention or to excite the wonder of mankind, and that which was once of absorbing interest ceases to be even remembered save by a few. To the age in which they occurred, the invasion of Italy by Charles VIII or the sack of Rome by the troops of Charles V appeared to be events that could never be forgotten. To-day it may well seem to be strange that so great significance was ever attached to them. But in the case of the discovery of America by Columbus, the exact contrary is true. The wonder is not that it should have astonished those who then lived, but that it should have astonished them so little; not that the magnitude of the event should have been recognized, but that it should not have been recognized more fully. For its importance is not less, but more, obvious to-day than it was a hundred, two hundred, four hundred years ago. That importance appears to become constantly greater with the passage of time, with the development of those lands for the colonization and exploitation of which by Europeans Columbus paved the way. In a very well-known passage, Gomara declares the discovery of the Indies to have been the greatest event since the creation of the world, save the incarnation and death of Him who created it.[2] It might with justice be added that no event of such moment can ever occur again, unless, perhaps, the tracts of space be bridged and communication established between the Earth and her sister planets.

[1] So much may be legitimately argued from the fact that only eight years after the first voyage of Columbus, Cabral accidentally reached the coast of Brazil.

[2] Gomara, *Historia General de las Indias*, vol. I, p. 4 [ed. 1922]. The passage occurs in the epistle dedicatory, addressed to Charles V.

2

While the importance of the Columbian discovery of America hardly admits of doubt and has indeed been never seriously denied, the degree of credit which should in justice be accorded to the discoverer has always been and still is a matter of dispute. On this point, there was diversity of opinion even during the lifetime of Columbus; the question was debated in the course of the lawsuit brought by his son against the crown, and the controversy is reflected in the pages of the earliest historians of the event. In the sixteenth century, the point primarily at issue was that of the extent and situation of the lands actually discovered by Columbus, a matter of supreme importance both to his heir, who was naturally anxious to control or at least to draw revenue from as wide an area as possible, and to the king, who was as naturally anxious to limit that area and to prevent the emergence in the New World of 'an overmighty subject'. When, however, a compromise on this point had been accepted by the third admiral, Luis Columbus,[1] this aspect of the question was no longer of practical importance. In due course, the fuller exploration of the coast of the continent solved such problems as that of the geographical relationship between Veragua and Paria, the general outline of the New World became known, and eventually nothing in this connexion remained to be determined save the identification of certain points within a limited and well-defined area. For all practical purposes, the territorial extent of the discoveries of Columbus was settled; that which remained to be decided was of no more than academic interest and gave rise to no very serious debate.

But the question of the degree of credit due to Columbus was not thereby also settled. It was still disputed whether he could justly be regarded as having been ultimately responsible for all the discoveries made in the New World, whether he had conceived of the project, which he carried out, as a result of his own thought and experience, whether he was

[1] Cp. *infra*, vol. ii, p. 112, note 1.

indeed a man of exceptional intelligence, whether he had indeed, as he claimed, achieved something which no other man could have achieved. There is abundant evidence that opinion differed on these points at a very early date. It would not have been necessary for Columbus to insist, as he does insist with almost wearisome iteration in his extant writings, upon the justice of his claim and the magnitude of his services, had not that claim been seriously challenged and had not those services been seriously belittled. A conflict of opinion is very clearly indicated in the interrogatories addressed to the witnesses in the lawsuit brought by Diego Columbus and in the answers given by those witnesses.[1] Certainly as early as the first quarter of the sixteenth century, the claim of Martin Alonso Pinzón to an equal or almost equal share of the credit for the discovery had been urged; at as early a date, the story of the mysterious pilot, of whose deathbed confidences Columbus was alleged to have made unacknowledged use, was current at Santo Domingo.[2] In modern times, it has been argued that the famous letter of Toscanelli and the whole story of his correspondence with Columbus was a fabrication designed to refute those who had declared the discoverer to have been an ignorant, though fortunate, adventurer,[3] and it might possibly be urged with as great or greater plausibility that to attain the same object, the account of his early education, given by his son and

---

[1] Cp. 'Pleitos de Colón', in *Doc. Inéd*, &c. 2ᵉ serie, 7–8.

[2] The story of the pilot is given as current gossip by Las Casas (*Historia de las Indias*, i. 14), who neither affirms nor denies its truth, and by Oviedo (*Historia General y Natural de las Indias*, ii. 2), who adds: 'por mí yo lo tengo por falso.' It was related as a fact by Gomara (*Historia General de las Indias*, c. 13), and, with some elaboration of detail, by Garcilasso de la Vega (*Primera Parte de los Comentarios Reales*, c. 3). The intrinsic improbability of the story has been generally recognized by all critical scholars, and the various inconsistencies between the different versions have been indicated. The story was, however, accepted by Vignaud (*Histoire critique de la Grande Entreprise de Christophe Colomb*), and it has found some other, more obscure, advocates. Luis Ulloa (*Xristo Ferens Colom*) has recently argued that Columbus was himself the mysterious pilot, that the event occurred in 1477, and that the story as related is a somewhat vague record of a fact; the evidence which he adduces in support of his contention is hardly convincing.

[3] Cp. Vignaud, *Toscanelli and Columbus*. For a destructive criticism of the arguments of Vignaud, cp. De Lollis, *Cristoforo Colombo* (ed. 1923), *Disquisizione critica sulle genesi e sul carattere dell' impresa di Cristoforo Colombo*.

repeated by Las Casas, was invented. When Gomara[1] declared
that it was uncertain when or by whom the Indies were discovered, he was no more than expressing a doubt which had
been felt by some from the very first.

During the seventeenth, eighteenth, and early nineteenth
centuries, however, controversy on this aspect of the question
was suspended. Antonio de Herrera[2] produced a version of
the story of the discovery which, perhaps in some measure
because no material interests were now involved, was generally received as being at once authentic and complete. This
version was rendered classical by the literary genius of
Washington Irving[3] and the poetic fervour of Lamartine,[4]
and was so universally accepted that it appeared to be
established beyond the reach of criticism. It was, indeed,
not until the second half of the nineteenth century that it
was called in question. Down to that time no one was
seriously inclined to deny that Columbus was a man of out-
standing intelligence, whose genius had enabled him to
triumph over the opposition presented to him by the prejudice of an ignorant age.

It was, perhaps, the very fact that his credit stood aston-
ishingly high which ultimately led to attempts to destroy it.
He was already so far exalted that some of his more enthusiastic admirers hoped that he might be exalted still more.
Roselly de Lorgues[5] and others hailed him as a Catholic hero
and demanded that his name should be included in the
calendar of saints. This demand produced a natural reaction;
not one *advocatus diaboli*, but many, forthwith appeared.
Some were impelled by their critical spirit to expose the extra-
vagances of these panegyrists; others were, perhaps, moved
less by a passion for the truth than by religious animosity
to vilify a man who was asserted to have been a foremost
champion of a creed which they regarded with aversion.

[1] Gomara, *loc. cit.* and c. 13.

[2] Herrera, *Historia General de los Hechos de los Castellanos en las Islas í Tierra Firme del Mar Oceano.* For the history of Columbus, the work of Herrera is almost entirely based upon that of Las Casas, to whose MS. he had access.

[3] Washington Irving, *Life and Voyages of Christopher Columbus.*

[4] Lamartine, *Christophe Colomb.*

[5] Roselly de Lorgues, *Christophe Colomb* and *l'Ambassadeur de Dieu.* He was followed by Belloy, *Christophe Colomb,* and Bloy, *Le Révélateur du Globe.*

Fernandez Duro[1] subjected certain aspects of the accepted story of the discovery to a damaging critical analysis, more especially undertaking the rehabilitation of Pinzón. Aaron Goodrich[2] revived the story of the dying pilot and endeavoured to show that Columbus was a mean adventurer who merited nothing but contempt. A considered and substantial contribution to the revision of the classical account was supplied by the labours of Henry Harrisse,[3] whose profound scholarship commanded respect even from those who were unable to accept his conclusions. Finally, in the last decade of the century, the celebration of the four hundredth anniversary of the discovery was the occasion for the appearance of a flood of Columbian literature, in much of which the received version was challenged in many of its details.[4]

The essential accuracy of that version was, however, still generally accepted. As the classical story had not been discredited by the earlier researches of Muñoz[5] and Navarrete,[6] or by the critical examination of certain of its aspects by Alexander von Humboldt,[7] so it survived the publication or republication at the close of the nineteenth century of a number of original documents.[8] The reputation of Columbus as having been in the fullest sense the author of his discovery was not really assailed.

But the attention of a number of scholars had now been

[1] Fernandez Duro, *Colón y Pinzón; Colón y la Historia Póstuma; Nebulosa de Colón*; and *Pinzón en el Descubrimiento de Las Indias*.

[2] Goodrich, *History of the Character and Achievements of the so-called Christopher Columbus*.

[3] Harrisse, *Christophe Colomb*: and various other works and papers.

[4] Among the lives of Columbus which appeared at this time may be mentioned those by Sir Clements Markham, in England: Justin Winsor, in the United States; Asensio, in Spain; Sophus Ruge, in Germany; De Lollis, in Italy. A mass of monographs also appeared in various countries. One life of Columbus was distributed as an advertisement.

[5] Muñoz, *Historia del Nuevo Mundo*. Muñoz made a vast collection of materials for his history, which he was officially employed to write, but died before his work was completed.

[6] Navarrete, *Colección de los Viages y Descubrimientos*.

[7] Humboldt, *Examen critique de l'histoire de la Géographie du nouveau continent*.

[8] Especially the *Raccolta di Documenti e Studi . . . dalla R. Commissione Colombiana*; and the duchess of Berwick and Alba, *Autógrafos de Cristóbal Colón*, and *Nuevos Autógrafos de Colón*.

focussed upon the question of the reliability of the accepted version; the materials upon which any discussion of this question had necessarily to be based had been rendered more accessible and their number had been increased by the production of further documents of value, while the whole mass of material had been more carefully examined and sifted. In such circumstances, it was probably inevitable that sooner or later the classical story of the discovery would be seriously attacked, and such an attack was in fact delivered upon it in the early years of the present century. Henry Vignaud[1] endeavoured both to disprove that which had been regarded as proven and to establish a new version of the genesis and the accomplishment of the project of Columbus. To this task he brought much erudition and infinite patience, but he perhaps permitted the sobriety of his judgement to be impaired by the intensity of his convictions. His theory failed to win any very wide acceptance; the majority of critics were inclined to feel with De Lollis that Vignaud was 'fedele al proprio sistema di costruire su ciò che non esiste a distruzione di ciò che esiste.'[2]

On the other hand, the effect of the work of Vignaud was to create the impression that the accepted account of the discovery required at least fuller substantiation than it had as yet received and that the accuracy of its broad outlines, no less than that of some of its details, was disputable. Some were consequently inclined to believe that the true story had yet to be written and were led by this belief to put forward novel versions of that story. In so far as the question of the reputation of Columbus was concerned, some of these versions tended to maintain and even to enhance the credit of the discoverer, while others had an exactly contrary tendency. But neither those which were favourable nor those which were unfavourable to Columbus have secured that measure of credence which was once universally accorded to the classical account. The result of the controversy up to

---

[1] Vignaud elaborated his thesis in three main works: *Toscanelli and Columbus*; *Études critiques sur la Vie de Colomb*; and *Histoire critique de la Grande Entreprise de Christophe Colomb*. He afterwards summarized his arguments and conclusions in *Le vrai Christophe Colomb*.

[2] De Lollis, *op. cit.*, p. xvii.

the present has been rather to destroy than to construct, to suggest doubts rather than to establish certainties, and such definite conclusions as may perhaps be said to have been reached have been rather negative than positive. The question of the degree of credit justly attributable to Columbus has so far remained a matter of debate.

3

A vital point in this debate has been that of the opinions held by Columbus upon certain questions which were more or less eagerly canvassed among his contemporaries. Since the age in which he lived was one of vigorous intellectual life and since the spirit of inquiry was very active, speculation upon almost every topic was naturally rife. That speculation, while it was not always informed by any very highly developed critical faculty, was often both ingenious and daring. Despite the respect generally accorded to the writers of antiquity, there was a certain disposition to question the opinions of even the most revered masters and a certain inclination to oppose to the authority of the past the results of present experience. When Columbus, having controverted a generally received opinion, remarked that a correction of common belief need cause no surprise, 'since the farther one goes, the more one learns,'[1] he was but expressing in what Las Casas calls his 'homely language'[2] the current conviction that no blind adherence should be given to accepted dogmas and that those dogmas should be reviewed in the light of increased knowledge.

As was only natural, among the questions which were so discussed was that of the nature of the world, its exact size, the true proportion between land and water, the character of that portion of the globe which was as yet unknown. Speculation was here all the more active because the discoveries made by the Portuguese had both revealed much that was new and apparently demonstrated the falsity of some once current beliefs.[3] In this field, rather perhaps than in any other, it seemed to be altogether legitimate to appeal

[1] Cp. *infra*, vol. ii, p. 42.   [2] Las Casas, i. 127.

[3] For example, the idea that the torrid zone was uninhabitable.

to practical experience as against authority, and it was in
fact very generally agreed that there was abundant room for
a revision of opinion. The nature and extent of that revision,
however, was more debatable. While some were inclined to
disregard authority entirely and to rely solely upon experience, others were less ready to break with the past and
wished to effect a reconciliation between the views of ancient
authors whom they revered and the statements of contemporary explorers whose veracity they were not disposed to
doubt. The intellectual world was divided into those who
were radical and those who were conservative in their
attitude towards these questions.

Upon one point, indeed, both radicals and conservatives
were agreed. By the middle of the fifteenth century, the
sphericity of the globe was accepted as a fact by all, or at
the very least by almost all, educated men throughout
western Europe. There is no foundation for the assertion,
which was once credited, that in Spain a contrary view was
maintained by orthodox theologians and supported by religious prejudice.[1] On the contrary, even so simple-minded
and ingenuous an ecclesiastic as Andrés Bernáldez,[2] whose
freedom from any taint of heresy cannot be disputed, entertained no doubts at all upon this point. And as an inevitable
corollary to this belief in the sphericity of the globe, it was
equally recognized that its circumnavigation was theoretically possible. No one seriously denied that any one who
journeyed continuously eastward or westward would eventually regain his starting-point, provided that his journey
were not somehow cut short.

But upon the further question of the practicability of such
circumnavigation, there was a marked division of opinion.
Some were convinced that the undertaking was no less
practically than theoretically possible, and that for its success no more was required than that a man should have
suitable ships and reasonably good fortune, and that, as one
writer piously adds, 'God should go with him'. Others, however, and they probably a majority even of the most educated,

---

[1] On these points, cp. Vignaud, *Histoire critique*, vol. I, pp. 720 *et seq.*, and
Nunn, *Geographical Conceptions of Columbus*.   [2] Cp. *infra*, p. 118.

held on various grounds an exactly contrary view. Some argued that the distance which to the westward separated Europe from Asia was so great that it could not possibly be traversed; it was suggested that no ship could carry provisions sufficient for so extended a voyage and that, long before land was sighted, the voyagers would have perished from starvation. Some contended that in so vast a waste of waters as was supposed to lie between the two continents a ship would be infallibly lost, and believed moreover that in the midst of the Atlantic there were unknown perils, against which no provision could be made and which could not be surmounted by any human effort. Some were disposed to regard any attempt to accomplish such a journey as being in the nature of blasphemy against God; they held that it was part of the hidden purposes of the Almighty that the mysteries of the western ocean should not be penetrated and that a divine inhibition had been laid upon man, forbidding him even to seek to lift the veil behind which those mysteries lay concealed.

Neither those who believed nor those who disbelieved in the practicability of crossing the Atlantic were entirely agreed among themselves as to the length of the voyage which it would be necessary to accomplish. Concerning the Far East, there was a paucity of exact information; the conjectures which served in the place of knowledge were varied, and on the question of the eastward extension of the Asiatic continent opinion was divided. On the whole, the authority of Ptolemy appeared to prevail; his estimate of the distance by land from western Europe to the extremity of Asia was very widely accepted, and it was very generally supposed that no mainland was to be found beyond the one hundred and eightieth parallel. As a necessary consequence, it followed that half the entire circumference of the globe lay to the westward between the Canaries and Asia, and that a transatlantic voyage would thus be one of vast magnitude. Some, however, held a different view. The travels of Marco Polo and others suggested that the Asiatic geography of Ptolemy required modification, and some were inclined to prefer the earlier estimate of Marinus of Tyre and thus considerably to reduce the distance at which eastern Asia lay to the west of Spain. It did not, however, follow that those who accepted the greater, or that those who accepted the lesser, estimate of that distance, adopted also corresponding views concerning the practicability of the journey. Some belonging to both schools of thought believed that other difficulties than that of mere distance would prevent the accomplishment of such a voyage, and some belonging to both schools of thought held that no difficulties save that of distance existed, while of these last, some considered the obstacle of distance to be insurmountable, others that it could be overcome.

A similar diversity of opinion prevailed concerning that which lay to the west between Europe and Asia. From classical times, stories of lands hidden amid the mists of the Atlantic had been current and had not been wholly disbelieved; if some considered them to be the product of the lively Hellenic imagination, others were disposed to regard them as born of lost knowledge and to suppose that those voyages which were vaguely recorded had actually occurred.[1] In the fifteenth century, the existence of Antilla was widely credited; the legend of the Island of the Seven Cities was not thought to be entirely legendary. While some were convinced that when the Canaries and Azores had been left behind, no other land would be sighted until the islands off the Asiatic coast were reached, this conviction was by no means universal. Some believed that in the Atlantic there lay islands, as yet undiscovered or at most but dimly sighted, which were more or less numerous, although not possessed of any great importance, and this belief found expression on early maps. Others believed that in the ocean there were lands, insular indeed in character, but yet of great extent, wealth, and populousness, the discovery of which would be of almost incalculable value to the discoverer; so many expeditions would not have ventured out into the Atlantic had not this belief been somewhat widely held.

This opinion, however, was not universally shared even by those who refused to admit that the other hemisphere,

[1] Cp. Babcock, *Legendary Islands of the Atlantic.*

concerning which there was no certain knowledge, was a mere waste of waters. There were not a few who believed that any land which might be discovered in that hemisphere would prove to be uninhabited and uninhabitable. It is true that the explorations of the Portuguese had demonstrated that men could and did live south of the equator, and that the habitability of all the five zones was consequently admitted by very many to be a theoretical possibility. It was hardly admitted to be more. Such travellers' tales as those collected by Sir John Mandeville were somewhat readily accepted in an age which was rather inquisitive than critical and which was perhaps almost eager to credit the incredible. Many expected that if the other hemisphere were ever to be explored, it would be found to be peopled not by men, but by monstrous beings, and the degree to which this expectation had been entertained may be gathered from the fact that, when America had been discovered, there was a certain reluctance to admit that its inhabitants were human and an ever present fear or hope that sooner or later monsters would be found.

Upon no one of these points can it be asserted with confidence that there was any very settled opinion. They were all debated, and concerning each diverse conclusions were reached even by the most educated men of the age. The most that can be said is that it appears to be probable that it was more generally believed than not that the circumnavigation of the globe was a practical impossibility; that there were, however, lands of uncertain character and extent lying beyond the Canaries and between Europe and Asia, and that were it possible to reach those lands, they would be found to be both habitable and inhabited, and perhaps to be peopled by a race of men not very dissimilar from the races which were already known, and that in any case they would prove to be rich both in precious metals and in spices.

4

From his extant writings, it is abundantly clear that Columbus was well aware of the existence of debate upon these questions. It is possible, if no more than possible, that before his first voyage he had considered some at least of the points involved.[1] But neither the conclusions to which his consideration of these problems led him, nor the grounds upon which those conclusions were based, can be exactly determined; it cannot even be dogmatically asserted that he had reached any conclusions at all. It is impossible to decide absolutely whether any opinions which he may have held at the time when he embarked upon his great adventure were or were not crystallized, and it is equally impossible to estimate precisely the degree to which his views were modified, if they were modified at all, in the light of that practical experience and knowledge which he gained in the course of his four voyages.

This uncertainty is the greater because such materials as are available to assist in the determination of the views of Columbus are at once somewhat scanty and somewhat unsatisfactory in character. No secure reliance can be placed upon those indications which are to be found in the writings of Ferdinand Columbus[2] and Las Casas.[3] Their works were composed at a time when the discovery had long been an accomplished fact; they produce no documentary evidence derived from Columbus himself and dating before the event, and their value as guides on this particular point is rendered somewhat suspicious by the fact that in the account which they give of the early life of the discoverer, there appear some flagrant errors and some probable inaccuracies.

Recourse has therefore to be had to the writings of Columbus himself, and the assistance which they afford is hardly greater. Such information as they do supply is very largely contained in documents which certainly postdate the discovery and which are therefore of uncertain value where his opinion before that event is concerned. Nor can the statements or hints contained in the *Journal* be regarded with any complete confidence. It is true that it is so probable as to be

---

[1] Cp. especially, his letter concerning his third voyage (*infra*, vol. ii, pp. 1 *et seq.*).

[2] Cp. Ferdinand Columbus, *Historie*, c. 6–9.

[3] Cp. Las Casas, *op. cit.*, i. 5–14.

morally certain that Columbus kept a log-book[1] of his voyage
which was written from day to day, but the diary of his first
voyage is preserved only in the précis made by Las Casas
from a copy, and even if the substantial accuracy of the précis
be admitted, it obviously has not that authority which
would be possessed by the original were it still in existence.[2]
It is impossible to prove that entries which purport to have
been written before the discovery had been accomplished
were actually so written; it is impossible to know whether,
even if they were made at the time at which they appear to
have been made, they were or were not afterwards modified.
There is some reason for believing that Columbus himself subjected his original diary to a certain measure of editing and
that the aim of his editing was to conceal his errors and to
enhance his reputation for knowledge. But since the extent
to which the original was edited cannot be even approximately determined, the evidence of the *Journal* for the ideas
of Columbus before he reached the Indies can only be
accepted with reserve.

There remain those notes[3] which Columbus wrote in the
margins of various books, and here again the evidence supplied is of doubtful value. It is at least arguable that they
postdate the discovery, in which case they afford no surer
clues than are supplied by other documents composed after
the event. But even if it be admitted that the notes or that
some of the notes were written at an earlier period, the light
thrown by them on the question does little more than emphasize the darkness. For the most part, they serve only to
indicate those passages in the authors which made an impression upon the mind of the annotator; it remains doubtful
whether that impression was one of approval or of dis-
approval, whether the marking of a passage is to be taken
as indicating assent or dissent. It becomes a question of
choosing between two equally possible interpretations, and
the likelihood of misinterpretation in such circumstances is

---

[1] It is, however, not certain, and it is perhaps improbable, that Columbus
wrote this log-book with his own hand.

[2] Cp. further, *infra*, pp. xlv–xlvi; xcv–xcix.

[3] The notes are printed by De Lollis (*Scritti di Colombo*, ii, pp. 291–523; in
Rac. Col. I. ii).

obvious. It may be added that it is not invariably certain that Columbus was the author of the notes which have been ascribed to him. The admitted similarity between his handwriting and that of his brother, Bartholomew, creates an element of doubt, and in the most recent study of the question, his authorship of many of the annotations is denied.[1]

Even where it seems to be probable that Columbus was definitely expressing his own opinion, it would be rash to conclude that he was in actual fact doing so. There has sometimes been a tendency too readily to give to his statements that meaning which they appear most obviously to bear, and this tendency has been strongest when the statements, so interpreted, are in accord with that which is now known to be fact. It has too often been apparently forgotten that much which is now a commonplace to the most ignorant was then either unknown or mere hypothesis to the most learned. It has been still more frequently forgotten that Columbus was by nature somewhat reticent, that he often used words rather to obscure than to convey his meaning, and that he was constantly at pains rather to conceal than to reveal his ideas.

The available evidence for ascertaining his opinions, at least before the discovery, is therefore to be received with caution and must be so received even when it appears to be most satisfactory. Any conclusion which may be reached must be admitted to be no more than conjectural and to be essentially open to dispute. In such circumstances, dogmatism on the question would be entirely misplaced. To assert that, before he had discovered the New World, Columbus held any given opinion, would be to assert something wholly impossible of proof.

5

To form even a confident conjecture on this subject is the more difficult, because it cannot be certainly determined to what extent Columbus was in a position to come to an independent and reasoned judgement concerning those questions which were debated by his contemporaries. At one time it

---

[1] The most recent discussion of the handwriting of Columbus is by Streicher, *Die Kolumbus-Originale.*

was, indeed, almost taken for granted that, as an outcome of his own studies and of his own practical experience, he was fully and even exceptionally qualified to do so. He was credited with having accomplished this task and with having as a result formed opinions more just and more enlightened than those which were held by the majority even of the most educated men of his age. It was believed that it was the intellectual superiority of which he was possessed, and which he thus displayed, that enabled him to conceive of the project which he ultimately executed, and that he was indeed so far mentally in advance of his time that his views appeared to most to be heterodox and the ideas which he expressed to be the idle imaginings of a madman.

But if it would be an exaggeration to assert that this view of the intellectual equipment of Columbus has been, or indeed can be, altogether disproved, it is at least certain that it cannot be unreservedly accepted, and it is at least possible that it should be almost wholly rejected. It can be, and has been, contended, and that not without considerable plausibility, that so far from having been able to form any independent judgement, Columbus was of necessity obliged to rely, and to rely somewhat blindly, upon the judgement of others. It has been argued that he was in no position to criticize opinions advanced by his educated contemporaries and that he was even probably unable to appreciate the arguments upon which those opinions were based. It cannot be said that this view is either more or less capable of proof than is that to which it is diametrically opposed. For if the direct evidence available for the purpose of determining the attitude of Columbus be scanty and unsatisfactory, such accounts as there are of the theoretical and practical training which he had received before his first voyage are almost equally scanty and are almost more unsatisfactory.

All that concerns the origin and early life of Columbus is enveloped in a cloud of obscurity so dense that it appears to be little possible that it will ever be dissipated. That obscurity is all the greater because, to some extent, it is probably due to those who might have been supposed to have been in the best position to lighten the darkness. Ferdinand

Columbus, the son of the discoverer, and Las Casas, the friend of his family, supply approximately identical accounts of the life of Columbus down to the time of his first voyage.[1] These accounts are characterized by an absence of essential detail, by a like absence of statements which can be satisfactorily checked, and by the appearance in them of other statements, the falsity of which is either demonstrable or at least probable. With the single exception of the letter of Toscanelli, the authenticity of which has been vigorously denied, neither of these writers produce any documentary evidence to illustrate or to support the story which they tell. It is true that Ferdinand Columbus gives certain quotations alleged to have been derived from Columbus himself and that these quotations were reproduced by Las Casas, who thus may be regarded as indicating his belief that they were genuine. But since the sources from which they were drawn are not otherwise known, their accuracy cannot be described as proven and is, indeed, open to serious doubt.[2] The tendency of these quotations is to represent Columbus in a very favourable light, to suggest that he was possessed of considerable maritime skill and experience and that he was a personage of some importance long before he arrived at the court of Ferdinand and Isabella, while one at least would seem to credit him with having come of a not undistinguished line of ancestors.

It was no more than natural that Ferdinand Columbus should be ready to enhance the reputation of his father, and that it was his wish to do so is, indeed, clear from the whole tenour of the *Historie* and more especially from that passage in which he so vigorously attacks Giustiniani.[3] His account of Bobadilla[4] suffices to prove that his filial piety was greater than his passion for truth and justice, and it cannot be regarded as a wholly untenable hypothesis that he may have

---

[1] Ferdinand Columbus, *Historie*, cc. 1, 2, and 4; Las Casas, i. 2, 3, 4.

[2] This is, for example, the case with the statement, 'Io non sono il primo Ammiraglio della mia famiglia', which is said by Ferdinand Columbus (c. 2) to come from a letter to the nurse of Prince Juan, but which does not appear in the letter which has been preserved.

[3] Ferdinand Columbus, *loc. cit.*

[4] Ferdinand Columbus, cc. 84–5. Cp. Vidart, *Colón y Bobadilla.*

misinterpreted or modified statements made by his father and
that he may even have ascribed to his father statements which
he never made. It may be added that, although he was certainly the author of a life of Columbus, the original Spanish
version of that life is lost and that the *Historie*, as preserved,
is almost certainly not a faithful representation of the work
as it was written. Quite apart from those minor errors which
are always likely to appear in any translation, it is probable
that the extant version is disfigured both by additions and
omissions, and its evidence must always be received with a
certain reserve.[1] To base any positive assertion concerning
the early life of the discoverer upon the unsupported testimony of his son is at least somewhat unwise; its unwisdom
is the greater because Ferdinand Columbus himself admits
the deficiency of his information and professes to have been
unwilling to endeavour to supply that deficiency by questioning his father.[2]

It is unlikely that, even if he had not been so unwilling,
his curiosity would have been gratified. Concerning all
that related to his life before the discovery of America,
Columbus was singularly reticent. In all his voluminous
writings, he never once mentions his own name;[3] he pre-
ferred to use a curious and perhaps inexplicable cypher as a
signature even to official documents. He makes no allusion
to his father or to his mother; he alludes to his wife only in a
manner so indirect that, for all that he says, he might never
have been married.[4] His mention of Genoa as his birthplace
appears in a document which is not in his autograph and
which had no legal validity: the authenticity of this document
has, indeed, been hotly denied.[5] Such reticence concerning
his origin and his more intimate private affairs is, perhaps,
susceptible of ready explanation upon various grounds;
quite apart from other possible reasons for concealment of

---

[1] On the character of the work of Ferdinand Columbus, cp. Harrisse, *Fernand Colomb*; Vignaud, *Histoire critique*; Caddeo, *Le Historie*, Pt. I. Int. pp. xix *et seq.*

[2] Ferdinand Columbus, c. 4.

[3] Unless he be regarded as having written the Prologue to the *Journal*: on which, cp. *infra*, pp. xciii–xcv.

[4] Cp. *Journal*, 14 Feb. and *Rac. Col.* I. ii. p. 65.

[5] On the *Institución del Mayorazgo*, cp. Altolaguierre, in *Boletin de la Real Academia de la Historia* (86, p. 307, and 88, p. 330).

this kind, Columbus would not have been the first or the last
man to be ashamed of the humility of his birth, and that he
was humbly born admits of no doubt. But it is less easy to
explain his reticence upon other matters, both because it
would appear to have been to his interest to be informative
and because his reticence is that of verbosity. Columbus
makes a comparatively large number of statements concerning his early life; up to a certain point, especially if the quotations in the *Historie* be accepted as authentic, he supplies
a comparatively large amount of information. When, however, this information is examined somewhat more closely,
it becomes clear that it is in reality scanty enough and that
it is most essentially vague. He seems to have been almost
scrupulously careful to avoid making any statement of which
the accuracy could be checked, and the impression thus
created that he was anxious to hide, rather than to make
known, the truth, is enhanced by the fact that he appears to
have been no more communicative in his intercourse with his
personal friends. There is no reason for doubting the affectionate regard in which he was held by Andrés Bernáldez
and Diego Mendez, but whereas the former states that Columbus was born at Genoa,[1] the latter declared that he was born
at Savona,[2] while Bernáldez can give no more detailed description of him, before the discovery, than that he was 'a
hawker of printed books, carrying on his trade in this land
of Andalusia.'[3] Peter Martyr Angleria, who professes to have
known Columbus well and whose inquisitive mind can but
have impelled him to seek to learn everything that was to
be learned concerning him, had obviously here to allow
his curiosity to remain unsatisfied; 'Cristophorus quidam
Colonus vir Ligur' is the best account of the discoverer
which he was able to supply to Giovanni Borromeo.[4]

---

[1] Bernáldez, *Historia de los Reyes Católicos*, cc. 118, 131. The statement made
e.g. by Ulloa (*op. cit.*), that Bernáldez contradicts himself by saying in one place
that Columbus was a native of Genoa and in another that he was from the province of Milan, betrays ignorance of the fact that, at this period, Genoa was
regarded as being comprised within the duchy of Milan.

[2] Uhagon, *La Patria de Colón según los documentos de las Ordenes militares.*

[3] Bernáldez, c. 118.

[4] Peter Martyr Angleria, *Opus Epistolarum*, Ep. CXXX (ed. 1670). Such
letters of Peter Martyr as concern Columbus are printed in *Rac. Col.* (III. ii.).

If Columbus did in fact wish to throw a veil of mystery over the events of his early life, he was entirely successful in doing so. The most exhaustive modern research has done very little towards elucidating this mystery. It has rendered possible the putting forward of a number of more or less probable conjectures, but it has failed to discover any indubitably accurate information concerning those points upon which Columbus was himself thus reticent. Ample room is still left for the elaboration of the most diverse theories of his origin and early life and for producing in support of those theories of much which appears to be evidence of value until it is examined. Of these theories, it is hardly necessary to say more than that they demand the rejection of a number of contemporary statements for no better reason than that they controvert the theories, and that their authors would appear to regard reiterated assertion as sufficing to convert pure hypothesis into ascertained fact. They contribute nothing towards the establishment of an account of the life of Columbus, before the discovery, which can be regarded as being beyond dispute. It may, indeed, be asserted that no such account can be produced from such materials as are at present available.

6

While, however, it must be admitted that concerning the facts of the early history of Columbus no absolute certainty is attainable and that, upon some points in that history, it is almost dangerous even to hazard a conjecture, it is yet possible to establish a number of probabilities, of which some are perhaps no more than probabilities, but of which some may be legitimately regarded as amounting to moral certainties. It thus becomes also possible to form a reasonably just estimate of the qualifications possessed by Columbus for the task of weighing opinions put forward by his contemporaries and for arriving at an independent judgement upon the questions which they discussed. The extent of his theoretical and practical training can be determined, not indeed exactly but approximately, and some conclusion can be reached concerning the degree to which he was intellectually either no more and no less than a man of his time, or in advance of or behind his age. It is even possible to contend that both the genesis of his project and the objective which he sought can be determined with some approach to certainty.

Among the points connected with his early life which may be regarded as being established beyond all reasonable doubt is that of his Italian origin. It is true that many attempts have been made to show that he was of another nationality, but if these attempts reflect some credit upon the ingenuity, they reflect none upon the critical capacity, of their authors, and are distinguished neither by ability to estimate the value of evidence nor by any sobriety of judgement. Their futility is, indeed, obvious in view of the unanimous testimony of all those writers who were personally acquainted with Columbus and of all those who were in a position to know the truth, and in view of the coincident absence of any contemporary witness in favour of any view other than that so expressed. To suggest, as has been suggested, that all these writers were guilty of wilful fabrication or even that they were grossly ignorant, is to bring a charge for which there is no shadow of justification and of which the falsity is almost self-evident; it is to degrade the writing of history to the level of scurrilous pamphleteering.

Nor can it be seriously questioned that he was a Genoese, despite the fact that upon this point some doubt seems to have been entertained by his son.[1] Even if the positive evidence contained in the *Institución del Mayorazgo* be rejected as inadmissible, it cannot be denied that Columbus is described as a native of the territory of the Genoese republic by all those who knew him and who have made any definite statement on the point. It would appear to be certain that he was so regarded by his contemporaries and that they were not mistaken is more probable than improbable. The fact that during his lifetime he was charged with designing to hand over the Indies to a foreign prince[2] supplies some indirect evidence in favour of the same view, as perhaps does the further fact that he was regarded with antipathy by a number of Spaniards from all parts of the Iberian peninsula.

[1] Ferdinand Columbus, c. 1.   [2] Cp. *infra*, vol. iii, p. 108.

It is not absolutely certain, although it is highly probable, that he was born in Genoa itself and that he was the son of the Domenico Colombo and the Susanna Fontanarossa who figure in the notarial records of that city.[1] That his exact birthplace and his precise parentage should be doubtful can be a matter of no surprise save to those who forget that the keeping of a regular register of births, marriages, and deaths had not yet been enjoined by a council of the Church. In the absence of any statement by the individuals most immediately concerned, the parentage of those who belonged to the poorer classes was in that age always somewhat uncertain and was rarely placed on record unless it became necessary to do so for some legal reason, while the surname, Colombo, was sufficiently common in northern Italy for the identity of any one person of that name to be doubtful. That Columbus was of plebeian birth is explicitly stated by Gallo [2] and is almost angrily admitted by Ferdinand Columbus himself.[3] For the suggestion that his family had descended from wealth to poverty, or at least from eminence to obscurity, there is no more evidence than such as is continually produced to-day by those who, having attained prominence, are eager to claim a distinguished original or who, being in fact poor, are somewhat ashamed of their poverty.

There is even less foundation for the further suggestion that, in his boyhood, Columbus received a far more elaborate education than that which was normally received by those of his class.[4] All the balance of probability is in favour of the

---

[1] The relevant passages from the records are printed in *Rac. Col.* III. ii.

[2] Gallo, 'De Navigatione Columbi' (*Rac. Col.* III. ii).

[3] While Ferdinand Columbus (c. 2) denies the statement of Giustiniani (*Psalterium* in *Rac. Col.* III. ii) that Columbus was of plebeian birth, he immediately afterwards quotes the alleged comparison by his father of his case with that of David. Ferdinand Columbus had already (c. 1) declared his refusal to assert the Roman ancestry of his father. It was left for Las Casas (i. 2) to give currency to the story that Columbus was descended from 'that Colonus' mentioned by Tacitus, that in Spain he reverted to the original name of his family, &c. Oviedo states that, while he was 'hombre de honestos parientes', his family was 'antiguo é noble' (ii. 2). Columbus himself continually suggests that he was of humble origin: cp., for example, the letter prefixed to the 'Libro de las Profecías' (*Scritti*, I. ii, pp. 79–83): 'non doto en letras, de lego marinero, de hombre mundanal.'

[4] For such accounts of his early education, cp. Ferdinand Columbus, c. 4; Las Casas, i. 3; Barros, *Asia*, Dec. i. 11. 2. In the letter prefixed to the 'Libro de

view that he was no better educated than he might have been expected to be. Bernáldez describes him as a man 'of little book learning, although of great natural intelligence,'[1] and this description would seem to be not unjust. The fact that Columbus never used Italian even when corresponding with those of his own nationality argues that his literacy dates from a period when he had already left Italy.[2] The character of the notes which he wrote in the margins of books, and that parade of learning which he makes in some of his letters, suggests that such learning as he possessed had been somewhat recently acquired, and it is by no means impossible that while he was still resident in Genoa or Savona, he was unable even to read and write.[3] If this were so, it would not be surprising. The percentage of illiterates in all countries was in that age extremely high; the attainment of letters was not

las Profecías' (Rac. Col. I. ii, pp. 79–83), Columbus himself states that he possessed considerable learning, but he suggests that it was divinely implanted in him: 'á este mi deseo fallé á Nuestro Señor muy propicio, y ove d'él para ello espírito de yntelligencia: en la marineria me fiso abondoso, de astrologia mu dió lo que abastava, y asý de geometria, y arismética, y engenio en el ánima, y manos para debusar espera, y en ella las cibdades, rýos y montañas, yslas y puertos, todo en su propio sytio.' In the same letter, he remarks that he may be declared by some to be unsuited for the work that he has undertaken on the ground that he is 'non doto en letras', and suggests that the statement would not be untrue, since he adds that 'out of the mouths of babes and sucklings, hath He ordained strength', and that the apostles, 'nunca deprehendieron letras.'

[1] Bernáldez, c. 118.

[2] Three of his extant letters are addressed to Italian correspondents; they are all in Castilian, as are his notes on the Italian translation of Pliny, with the exception of one (note 23: Rac. Col. I. ii, p. 472), which is in a tongue so barbarous that it needs a certain imagination to regard it as being in Italian. It can hardly be supposed that Columbus lost a faculty which he once possessed: he was, in all probability, connected with an Italian business house after leaving Genoa; the advantage of being able to correspond with his principals in their own language is obvious, and he was never blind to his material advantage. Both in Lisbon and in Spain, he was brought into contact with Italians, by intercourse with whom he might have maintained his knowledge of his native tongue and his ability to write in it. The explanation that he did not use Italian in his letters because he had never learned to write in that language would seem to be the only rational explanation: unless, therefore, it be believed that he was not an Italian, it would seem to follow that he was unable to write when he left Genoa. It may be added that he was obviously unable to write letters in Latin: had he been able to do so, he would assuredly have used that tongue in writing to Alexander VI.

[3] These points are discussed at greater length in a paper which will appear in the Hispanic American Historical Review in the course of 1930.

infrequently postponed until manhood had been reached, and in his boyhood Columbus can have had little leisure, if he had much inclination, to engage in studies, the material value of which was not immediately apparent.

Columbus himself asserts, or is represented as asserting, that he came of a race of sailors, that he went to sea at an early age and that he made a number of voyages, including one to Chios eastward, one to a point 'a hundred leagues beyond Tile' northward, and more than one to Guinea southward. That some members of his family were sailors is likely enough; within the territory of the Genoese republic it would in that age have probably been difficult to find any family no member of which had engaged in a maritime career. His immediate relatives, however, were probably occupied in other pursuits; if his father were Domenico Colombo, it is certain that they were rather weavers and wool carders, and perhaps tavern keepers, as Gallo states them to have been. Nor is there any direct evidence in favour of the assertion, which has been frequently made, that Columbus himself was a member of the crews of the ships in which he sailed, unless, indeed, it be admitted that he did actually command a vessel in the service of King Réné.[1] It is perhaps significant that he, while showing some anxiety to insist upon his maritime experience, nowhere explicitly states that he was ever himself a sailor[2] and that he appears to claim that his nautical knowledge was the outcome rather of the study of books than of active employment at sea.[3] There is some reason for believing that at one period of his life he represented an Italian commercial house in Madeira and Lisbon,[4] and it is certain that he was always interested in the business aspect of every question and that he was by no means devoid of business acumen.[5] Since his skill as a navigator is more open to

---

[1] The story of the expedition to Tunis is accepted as true, but with some hesitation, by De Lollis (*Cristoforo Colombo*, pp. 33–5); is doubted by Harrisse (*Christophe Colomb*, i. 254–8); and denied by Vignaud (*Études critiques*, pp. 313 *et seq.*).

[2] Unless it be in the passage already cited (cp. *supra*, p. xxxv, note 3).

[3] Cp. *supra*, p. xxxv, note 4.

[4] Cp. Assereto, 'La Data della Nascita di Colombo' (*Giornale Storico e Letterario della Liguria*, v. 5–16).

[5] Cp. *infra*, pp. 92, 106, 108, *inter alia*.

question and since he seems at times to display a lack of those qualities and of that knowledge which a practical sailor might be expected to possess,[1] it is at least possible that he made such voyages as he did make before his arrival in Spain less in the capacity of a seaman than in that of a trader.

It may, therefore, be concluded that there is no evidence to show that Columbus was especially qualified, either by reason of his theoretical knowledge or by reason of his practical experience, to form a judgement upon the various questions concerning the nature of the globe which were then debated. It must, indeed, be admitted that there is no more evidence to show that he was less qualified than the majority of his contemporaries. If his education was probably somewhat defective and perhaps acquired somewhat late in life, he had yet the advantage of having travelled more extensively than had most men and of having had abundant opportunities for discovering the opinions of a number of practical seamen. The value of such opportunities and of such travels to a man 'of great natural intelligence' is obvious, and it may appear to be safe to conclude that in all probability the opinions which Columbus entertained before his discovery of America were neither more nor less just than those entertained by the majority of the educated men of his age, that he was in fact in this respect a man of his time.

7

That any views which Columbus held before the discovery of America were less the outcome of study or of any solid reasoning on his part, than of the use which he made of such advantages as he possessed, is a conclusion which wins no little support from a consideration of the probable nature of those views, so far as that nature can be ascertained. It is clear that, at this period of his life, he believed, as did the majority of his contemporaries, in the sphericity of the globe, but it may be doubted whether his belief rested upon any very solid foundations. At a later date, his conviction on

---

[1] He was always extremely alarmed in rough water, or at least represented himself as being so (cp. for example, vol. ii, pp. 74, 86, 90). His knowledge of navigation was defective (cp. *infra*, p. xli).

this point was shaken or overthrown; while he continued to admit that one hemisphere was a true hemisphere, concerning the other he propounded a somewhat fantastic theory which he claimed to have derived from his own thought upon the subject.[1] It may therefore be legitimately questioned whether his earlier belief resulted from anything more profound than the fact that it was the belief held by most of those with whom he was brought into contact. It would in any case be altogether unreasonable to allege his conviction of the sphericity of the globe as an argument in support of the view that he was a man of exceptional intellectual capacity.

It would be equally unreasonable to suggest that any such argument is supplied by his apparent attitude towards the further question of the practicability of crossing the Atlantic and of circumnavigating the world. That attitude has, perhaps, been somewhat misrepresented. At first sight, it seems to be obvious that of such practicability he must have been profoundly convinced. Had he not been so, it may seem to be hard to believe that he should ever have conceived of that project which he formed and to be still harder to believe that he should have ever ventured to attempt the accomplishment of that project. Even if it be held that he designed no more than to achieve the passage of the Atlantic to some lands which he believed to lie at a distance of three hundred and fifty leagues west of the Canaries, it may still appear to be certain that he must have believed that, as he notes on a passage in the *Epilogus Mappe Mundi*, 'omnem marem sit navigabile,'[2] and that circumnavigation was accordingly practicable, provided that no mass of land intervened. There would thus seem to be sufficient ground for including Columbus among the number of those who regarded it as being no less practically than theoretically possible to reach the east by sailing west and to regain the starting-point by means of a continuous journey in one direction. And it has been very generally supposed that such a view of his position on this question is wholly in accord with fact and that, in this respect, he was in agreement with the best opinion of his age, if, indeed, by reason

[1] Cp. *infra*, vol. ii, p. 30.
[2] Note 496 (*Rac. Col.* I. ii, p. 408). The Latin is that of Columbus.

of the strength of his conviction, he were not actually somewhat in advance of that opinion.

It would, however, appear to be possible and perhaps probable that this supposition is only just up to a certain point and that it does not supply an entirely accurate idea of the attitude of Columbus. There are some grounds for thinking that he should be included in the number of those who believed that, if the Atlantic had not yet been crossed, it was because its passage was divinely forbidden, because it had so far been the will of God that its mysteries should not be revealed, and not merely because either ships, adequate for such a voyage, or the requisite nautical skill, had been lacking. At a much later period of his life, Columbus claimed that he had achieved something which no other man could have achieved.[1] To suggest that he put forward this claim simply as a retort to those who belittled him or simply because he was inordinately vain, is perhaps to adopt a somewhat superficial or a somewhat cynical view. In the absence of any evidence to the contrary, it is hardly more than just to assume that he believed in the validity of his pretension and that he was doing no more than stating his honest conviction. It is therefore germane to any discussion of his probable opinions to consider upon what foundations he based the claim which he advanced.

It is clear enough that he cannot have intended to suggest that he was provided with ships better fitted than any other vessels could have been to accomplish so lengthy a voyage; Columbus constantly complained of the inadequacy of the means with which he was provided for the attainment of so great ends. Nor is it very probable that he wished to imply that his knowledge of navigation was such as to enable him to succeed where any other man would have failed. The age was one in which skilled navigators abounded, and Columbus can but have been aware that, in practical knowledge of maritime matters, he had many equals and perhaps many superiors even among those who sailed with him.[2] To have made any assertion to the contrary would have been to make

---

[1] 'Memorial de agravios' (*Nuevos Autógrafos*, p. 6). Cf. Las Casas, i. 38.
[2] To mention two only: Martin Alonso Pinzón and Juan de la Cosa.

a merely idle boast and to expose himself to legitimate ridicule. Nor is there much ground for supposing that he was in fact inclined to pretend to pre-eminence in this respect. It is true that upon occasion he appears to insist upon his nautical skill, but he does not do so with such emphasis as to suggest that he was also prepared to insist that his skill was so great as to enable him to do that which few or no others could have done. On the contrary, when he himself says that the method by which he determined his position upon one occasion was one 'which resembles a prophetic vision,'[1] he seems almost to admit that he was not an experienced navigator in the ordinary sense and to suggest that he was in possession of some knowledge other than maritime, of some capacity other than that which might also be possessed by any pilot. It may be added that he would seem to have placed no little reliance upon the practical skill of others; during his first voyage, he more than once sought the advice of Pinzón and appears to have deferred in some measure to his judgement; during his last voyage, he consulted the masters and pilots of his vessels concerning the course which should be followed.[2] His very assertion or boast that these same masters and pilots could not, for all their knowledge, have found again the way to Veragua, unless they had rediscovered it, reads, when taken in its whole context, like a declaration that it was not to nautical skill that he owed his success.

In the suggestion, here somewhat darkly conveyed, that he possessed something which was peculiarly his own, a clue to the basis upon which he rested his claim may perhaps be found. Columbus was undoubtedly deeply imbued with the religious spirit. It is impossible to read his extant writings without realizing that he was ever ready to perceive the finger of God in all that might come to pass. He seems to have been almost eager to convert the commonplace into the miraculous; he could divine a special dispensation of Providence in every change of weather and could see the hand of the Almighty constantly shaping the course of his

---

[1] 'á visión profética se asemeja esto' (cp. *infra*, vol. ii, p. 98). The whole of this passage, in his letter descriptive of his fourth voyage, is interesting in this connexion. [2] Cp. *infra*, vol. ii, p. 72, note 4.

life. He was very certain that nothing ever happened by
chance, that the most trivial incidents of everyday existence
had been fore-ordained from all eternity. Like St. Joan before him, he heard voices and saw visions; like Cromwell
after him, he was profoundly convinced that he enjoyed the
special protection of the Deity, that he was, as a Puritan
field preacher might have expressed it, 'a chosen vessel,'
ordained to be an instrument by means of which the high
purposes of Heaven might be accomplished.

To such a man, it was but natural that 'the enterprise of
the Indies' should appear in a somewhat different light from
that in which it might appear to others of a colder and less
enthusiastic temper. For others, that enterprise might be of
some, and even of great, economic and political importance;
for him, it was assuredly this, but it was also very much more.
It was a divine mission, and he who engaged upon it was
emphatically the servant of the Most High: he was labouring
not merely for the temporal but still more for the spiritual
welfare of mankind. As Columbus declared, in a moment of
mingled depression and exaltation, it was the revelation of the
New Heaven and the New Earth, spoken of by St. John the
Divine, and of that revelation he was himself the apostle.[1]
'The Holy Trinity moved me', he wrote to Ferdinand and
Isabella,[2] 'to come with this message into your royal presence.'
He felt himself to be the very ambassador of God, sent forth
to carry the glad tidings of salvation to those who sat in
darkness and in the shadow of death. 'When therefore',
wrote Las Casas long afterwards,[3] 'the day of the marvellous
mercies of God had dawned, in the which from those parts of
the earth, the seed or word of life having been therein sown,
there should be garnered a most abundant harvest, . . . the
divine and exalted Master chose from among the sons of
Adam, who in those our days were dwelling upon the earth,
that illustrious and great Columbus, . . . that to him He
might commit the accomplishment of a most notable and
divine enterprise.' Las Casas is here expressing that which
was indubitably the deep conviction of Columbus himself,

[1] Cp. *infra*, vol. ii, p. 48. [2] Cp. *infra*, vol. ii, p. 2.
[3] Las Casas, i. 2.

and it is reasonable to suggest that upon this conviction was based the claim of the discoverer to have rendered to the sovereigns service such as no other could have rendered. In the light of such a belief, his claim appeared to him to be no more than just. For it was to him and to him alone that God had entrusted the carrying out of an undertaking which, as he wrote at the close of his first voyage, would bring great fame to Ferdinand and Isabella and to their realms, at the success of which all Christendom should rejoice, and through which great temporal benefits would accrue to all lands and many nations be turned to the True Faith.

His claim, upon any other assumption apparently extravagant and apparently one which would have been immediately disallowed by contemporary opinion, upon this assumption becomes one which could at least not be easily refuted or ridiculed in an age in which it was akin to heresy to question that all great achievements were the outcome of a special intervention of the Divine Providence. But if so much be admitted, the explanation of the attitude of Columbus upon the question of the practicability of circumnavigating the globe becomes somewhat different from that which has been generally advanced. It is obvious that a man who believed that he was commissioned by the Almighty to carry the tidings of salvation to the other hemisphere and to reveal a new world to mankind, must also have believed that he would be enabled to reach that hemisphere. He must therefore have equally believed that he would be enabled to cross the ocean, if only by doing so could he come to the unknown parts of the world. It does not follow that he believed that any other would be so enabled. It rather follows, from the very terms of his claim, that he was convinced that a journey, which he could perform, could be performed by no one else, since he alone was the chosen ambassador of God.

His assurance that the globe could be circumnavigated thus becomes rather limited than absolute. It appears as being based less upon study and reason, less upon knowledge of any kind and whencesoever derived, than upon his further assurance that he was entrusted with a divine mission. His belief may be justly regarded as evidence of his deep religious fervour; it can hardly be regarded as evidence of deep learning. If it were the product of experience and of use of those opportunities afforded to him by the circumstances of his life, it was perhaps so in another sense from that in which some have supposed it to have been. It was rather the product of faith than of science. It was one which might have equally been entertained by a man whose only literature had been works of devotion and who had never emerged from the dim seclusion of a hermit's cell.

8

The opinions held by Columbus before his discovery of America can, however, have been determined by his belief in his mission only if he already entertained that belief when he embarked upon his first voyage, and that he did so may be disputed. All direct evidence for his conviction that he was 'a man sent from God' dates from a much later period of his life, and had any such idea been present in his mind when he set out upon his adventure, it may seem that some trace at least would be found in the *Journal* or in the letter in which he announced his return. At first sight it may appear to be a legitimate inference that the absence of any such trace proves the absence of any such belief, and it may, indeed, also appear that an idea, seemingly so fantastic, could but have been the product of a disordered brain. There is some plausibility in the suggestion that Columbus was led to imagine that he was entrusted with a mission because his mental balance had been overthrown, either as a result of excessive elation, born of success, or of excessive depression, born of adversity. When, however, the events of his life, from the date of the discovery down to that at which he is first known to have announced his belief, are considered, the validity of this suggestion becomes doubtful. It is questionable whether during that period he had enjoyed such success or suffered such adversity as would have sufficed to unbalance an originally normal mind. It is equally questionable whether his belief can be legitimately regarded as the product of his experiences during that same period or as an indication of an abnormal mental state.

At the present day, when the momentous consequences which have flowed from the adventure of Columbus can be fully appreciated, the success of the first voyage may seem to have been sufficiently astounding to induce a very delirium of joy. To those who then lived, that success was far less obvious and was, indeed, by no means so great as had been hoped and anticipated by those who had most cordially embraced the project. Official letters, dealing with the preparations for the second voyage, indicate clearly enough that among those who may be supposed to have been best informed, some at least deprecated any further expenditure.[1] Those who had declared the undertaking to be a delusion were far from having been put to silence; they were inclined to feel that their original scepticism had been justified and that the discovery of a few islands and of an unknown race of savages was an inadequate return for the investment made, especially at a time when, despite heavy taxation, the crown was in a condition of chronic financial embarrassment.

The satisfaction of Columbus himself was almost certainly somewhat mitigated. It is true that both in the *Journal* and in the letter concerning the first voyage, he insists upon the wealth, the fertility, and the populousness of the newly discovered lands, and it is obvious that he was impressed, and even profoundly impressed, by the novelty of all that he saw. But as evidence of his actual sentiments, these documents must be regarded with a certain measure of reserve; there is some reason for thinking that they do not represent those sentiments with complete fidelity. The letter is preserved only in an edited form,[2] and while the extent and nature of the editing to which it was subjected cannot be precisely determined, the tendency of that editing would appear to have been in the direction of hiding or at least of minimizing any disappointment, and of magnifying any gratification, which was felt concerning the results of the voyage. The précis of the *Journal* by Las Casas is not complete and the omissions may have been of vital importance. It must be

---

[1] Cp. the case of Juan de Soria, for which see Navarrete, ii. 89–95 (ed. 1825).

[2] Cp. *infra*, pp. cxxiii *et seq.*

remembered that Las Casas was working upon his materials long after the event and that, since he was in a position to realize the importance and the actual success of the first voyage of Columbus, he might be almost expected to imagine that Columbus himself had fully appreciated the magnitude of his achievement and hence to ignore any statement which might seem to suggest the contrary. He was, moreover, eager to show that the first discoverers of the Indies found perfection in all things, and that this desire led him to exaggerate the good and to ignore the evil is abundantly clear from page after page of the *Historia de las Indias*, to assist in the composition of which work the précis of the *Journal* was certainly made. Nor was Las Casas by any means so conscientious in his treatment of his materials as he has sometimes been represented as having been; where his deep convictions were concerned, he was capable of *suppressio veri* and of *suggestio falsi*, and he was constantly guilty of flagrant and deliberate misrepresentation.[1] In such circumstances, his version of the *Journal* cannot be accepted as conclusive evidence of the sentiments of Columbus save in so far as those sentiments were in complete accord with the ideas of Bartolomé de las Casas.

But even if the witness of these documents could be unquestioningly received, there is still enough evidence to suggest that Columbus was very far from being wholly satisfied with the results of his first voyage. He had sought in vain for that highly developed civilization, for those mighty cities and for those powerful kings that he had expected to find. Instead, he had met only with barbarians, amiable perhaps but still barbarians, living in a most primitive condition under the dominion of a host of petty chieftains, and to describe the rude huts of Guacanagarí as constituting 'a large town'[2] was to indulge in something more than poetic licence. Even as he dwells upon the wonders of these lands, even as he declares that 'Española is a marvel,' he reveals his disappointment;

---

[1] Instances are numerous, and it may be suggested that if the *Historia de las Indias* were a less unreadable work, its reputation would be very different from that which it has enjoyed. For examples of the unreliability of Las Casas, cp. 'Las Casas as an Historian' (*Times Literary Supplement*, 15 Mar. 1928).

[2] Cp. *infra*, p. 12.

'I sent two men ashore to learn if there were a king or great cities . . . they found . . . no trace of ordered society.'[1] There was here little enough to produce extreme elation. Sufficient had been found, perhaps, to justify hope that more might be found, but not to give any assurance that Ferdinand and Isabella would be inclined to afford him that 'very slight assistance'[2] for which he pleads. Joy and disappointment, hope and misgiving, were so mingled in the mind of Columbus that it may be safely assumed that there was nothing so to disturb his mental balance that he should suddenly develop a fantastic idea of his own destiny. At no subsequent period of his life, however, did he attain any success commensurate with that which, even in his own estimation, crowned his first voyage. It must, therefore, be concluded that, whatever may have been the origin of his belief in his mission, it is not to be found in the elation of victory.

Nor can that belief be with more justice regarded as the product of the opposite extreme of feeling, as having originated from intense depression, born of adversity and driving him to seek consolation in the wild flights of a disordered imagination. Columbus was undoubtedly convinced of the reality of his mission before he had suffered any crushing blows of fortune and at a time when his hopes, if their realization were still deferred, seemed none the less to be well grounded. Of his conviction, the earliest direct evidence which has been preserved is contained in a letter to Ferdinand and Isabella, describing his third voyage. 'The Holy Trinity', he writes, 'inclined your highnesses towards this enterprise of the Indies, and of His infinite goodness He made me the apostle thereof, so that, being thereunto moved, I came with His embassy into your royal presence.'[3] At that moment, his position was, or at least appeared to him to be, one full of hope for the future and was very far from giving him cause for anxiety or depression.

Columbus had returned to Spain in order to meet the attacks which had been made upon him and, if his time in Castile had been one rather of stress than of rest,[4] he seemed

---

[1] Cp. *infra*, p. 4. [2] Cp. *infra*, p. 16.
[3] Cp. *infra*, vol. ii, p. 2. [4] Cp. *infra*, vol. ii, p. 8.

to have succeeded in countering the hostility of those who had criticized him adversely. The unfavourable report upon his administration of Española, drawn up by Juan Aguado, had been rejected by Ferdinand and Isabella.[1] The sovereigns had renewed to him their expressions of continued favour and confidence, and since he was always ready to believe that which he wished to be true, it is probable that he regarded those expressions as being something more than mere courtesies.[2] He is emphatic in declaring himself satisfied with the treatment which he had received from the king and queen, and it is at least certain that he altogether failed to appreciate the strength of that hostility towards him which was presently to triumph in the appointment of Bobadilla.

If he had so found the results of his visit to Spain satisfactory, he derived still greater satisfaction from those of his voyage, which he regarded as being such as to justify the highest hopes.[3] He had discovered a land, the vast extent of which he could gauge from the magnitude of its rivers, and of which he believed the wealth to be incalculable.[4] He had found important pearl fisheries and had concluded, or at least afterwards alleged that he had concluded, an agreement with the natives, in virtue of which a constant supply of pearls for Castile would be assured. He was full of plans for the future. He proposed to send his brother to continue the work of exploration which had been begun, and he designed to establish a settlement in the neighbourhood of the pearl fisheries, perhaps as a prelude to the full exploitation of the newly discovered lands.[5] It is clear that he was very far from expecting that the internal situation of Española would absorb his attention and effectively prevent the execution of these designs. It is even clearer that he did not anticipate that Alonso de Ojeda would be granted a licence enabling him to reap some part of that harvest which he had hoped to garner. His whole letter breathes a spirit of confident optimism. It reads as the composition of a man who

---

[1] Cp. Las Casas, i. 112.   [2] Cp. *infra*, vol. ii, p. 8.
[3] Cp. *infra*, vol. ii, p. 42.   [4] Cp. *infra*, vol. ii, pp. 24, 50, 68.
[5] Cp. *infra*, vol. ii, p.46: and Las Casas, i. 177.

feels that he has triumphed over a hampering opposition, that his way is now clear for the future and that complete success is at last certain of attainment. There is in it nothing to suggest that he regarded himself as the victim of an unkind fate. For the hypothesis that he was induced to believe in his mission because he had experienced strokes, whether of good or of ill fortune, which seemed to him to be exceptional and which produced in him a state of mental exaltation, there is, indeed, no real justification.

9

No such hypothesis is actually needed to explain the fact of the belief, since that belief was by no means inconsistent with his possession of a balanced mind. At the present day, it may perhaps seem to be hardly conceivable that a man should entertain a parallel conviction unless his mental equilibrium had been destroyed; it may seem that only a madman or a saint could regard himself as being directly inspired and guided by the Almighty. But the mentality of the later fifteenth century was not that of the twentieth. In that age, many were very readily inclined to imagine that the Deity was both continually forming their thoughts and continually determining their actions.

The period was one of discovery and of re-discovery, when hitherto unknown wonders were revealed and when the half-lost memory of the glories of classical times was revived. Men received a number of new, or of at least long unaccustomed, impressions; the multiplicity of strange facts presented to them produced a fever of speculation and debate, and their minds were filled with a very welter of ideas. They were thrown into a state of mental turmoil, which to some was welcome and invigorating, but which to others was so grievous as to be altogether intolerable. Some received the revelation gladly and found in it justification for the rejection of that which had been long accepted and for the flouting of authority, however respectable. They gave free rein to their passion for inquiry and discussion; that passion grew with gratification and in many cases produced a species of intellectual intoxication. Some appeared to take a cynical delight in making a mockery of all that had been held most sacred; they appeared to be eager to burn all that they had adored and to adore all that they had burned, and to set Apollo and Aphrodite in the place of Christ and the Virgin. A wave of physical and intellectual licentiousness threatened to engulf society, and the spread of a kind of neo-paganism to render null and void the famous edict of Theodosius the Great.

By the same revelation, however, some were very differently affected; to them, it was a source not of pleasure, but of pain. If in that age there were much scepticism, there was also much credulity: superstition kept pace with enlightenment, and despite the prevalence of practical indifference and of moral laxity, the Church at no time appeared to be more secure of the obedience of her children than almost on the eve of the greatest of all revolts against her authority. There were some who, while they felt the impulse towards inquiry, were yet reluctant to yield to that impulse; moved to disbelief, they sighed for faith, and it was only slowly and sadly that they departed by one iota from that creed, religious and secular, which they had received from their fathers. 'I can do no other; God help me', is alleged to have been the agonized cry wrung from Martin Luther; the same cry might have been uttered by many who in the later fifteenth century dared, indeed, to speculate, but who, even as they did so, trembled at their own audacity. Of these, not a few sought means by which they might escape the consequences of their own daring and by which they might evade a responsibility, beneath the weight of which they dreaded lest they should be crushed. Some found the means; they attributed all their thoughts and all action resulting from those thoughts to the working of the mighty hand of God. They ascribed the ideas which they formed and by which they were distressed to divine inspiration, and the success which they attained, and by which they were not a little astounded, to some special dispensation of an overruling Providence. In effect, they conceived of themselves as so many missioners of Heaven.

Nowhere was this readiness to ascribe all to God so general and so sincere as in Spain. That readiness, natural enough in a race by temperament religious, had been confirmed by

the events of the past history of the country, of which the
long struggle against the Moors had been the central feature.
It had been further strengthened by the character of the
second half of the fifteenth century. During that period,
Castile had sunk into a condition of apparently hopeless
anarchy and weakness, from which it had been miraculously
delivered. The land had been given a degree of law and order
such as it had never before known, government had become
efficient, and national prosperity and national power had
revived. The marriage of Ferdinand and Isabella, romanti-
cally effected despite all the obstacles which threatened to
prevent it; their accession to two thrones, for neither of which
they had appeared at birth to be destined; their triumph over
a dangerous combination of foreign and domestic foes, and
the establishment of unity between Castile and Aragon in
place of age-long rivalry, were all events which seemed to
the age in which they occurred to be attributable only to the
direct intervention of the Almighty. It was, perhaps, little
wonder that the belief that God watched with peculiar care
over the Spanish race became increasingly strong. And
when the struggle with the Moors was at last victoriously
resumed, when the Sacred Office began to purge the country
from the taint of heresy, that feeling was soon converted into
a burning faith; the nation believed implicitly that it was
chosen of God, set apart to perform a sacred mission, for
which all the trials and tribulations which had been endured
in the past had been sent as a preparation, to make the race
worthy of its high destiny.

But if the race as a whole believed itself to be in a very
special sense directed by God, so individuals believed themselves to be similarly directed; if the race felt itself to be
charged with a divine mission, so individuals felt themselves
to be. It is hardly too much to say that any Spaniard of
that age who performed any notable act, civil or military,
secular or religious, was regarded by his fellows and regarded
himself as having been set apart by Heaven to achieve that
which he achieved; to Heaven he owed the conception, to
Heaven the execution, of that which he had conceived and
executed. Such was the belief of Isabella, when she undertook

the material and moral redemption of her country; it was only her living faith in her divinely ordained destiny which enabled her to thread her way through a very labyrinth of difficulties and to overcome every obstacle. Such was the belief of Torquemada, when he undertook the extirpation of the false *conversos*; he was fully convinced of the sacred character of the mission which he so ruthlessly carried out. Such was the belief of those who, even while they wept, hardened their hearts, lest they might feel compassion for the Jews whom they hurried relentlessly to the coast. It was no mere expression of a formal piety when his contemporaries hailed Gonsalvo de Córdoba as a scourge of God, sent to chastise the impiety and vices of the French, or when they declared that the successful defence of Salsés was a miracle wrought by Heaven. In the eyes of their subjects it was not only to 'the enterprise of the Indies', but to all their undertakings, that Ferdinand and Isabella were 'moved by the Holy Trinity'.

In such circumstances, there is nothing surprising in the fact that Columbus should have believed himself to have been commissioned by God to execute some great design, nor does his belief argue that his mentality was abnormal. Rather, when consideration is given to the circumstances of his early life, so far as those circumstances can be ascertained or reasonably conjectured, it becomes no more than natural that he should have entertained some such conviction from the moment when he first conceived of that project which he afterwards undertook to carry out. Columbus was a man of humble birth and of little education; it is at least possible, if not probable, that his nautical skill was small and that his interest in, and his knowledge of, the sea and maritime affairs was rather that of a trader than of a sailor. Yet he had conceived of a project which appeared to him to be, and which in fact was, magnificent, and which was, moreover, one that had at most been but vaguely conceived by any other man. He had been impelled to offer to dare that which others shrank from daring; he had been led to believe to be possible that which many, at least, believed to be altogether impossible. From the very first, he had been assured in his own mind that he would succeed where others had failed or were reputed to have failed, and that he would accomplish a voyage which skilled navigators seemed to have been unable or unwilling even to attempt. To him, those lands, concerning which others could offer no more than vague conjectures, appeared as clearly as if 'he had personally visited them'.[1] In all this, there was enough to lead any man in that age to perceive the very hand of God.

For a man possessing the special mentality of Columbus, there was far more than enough. He was wholly untainted by that indifference or scepticism which was so general in the Italy of his time; his temperament was rather that of a Savonarola than of a Leo X, and he was deeply imbued with the religious spirit, while there was in him a pronounced strain of mysticism. Las Casas bears witness to his piety, and this witness is emphatically confirmed by the testimony of his own extant writings. His mysticism appears most clearly in letters dating from the last period of his life, to which period also belongs the *Libro de las Profecias*, in the compilation of which he shared. But it is not therefore to be concluded that Columbus was converted into a mystic by the misfortunes which he suffered; on the contrary, it would seem to be certain enough that he was mystical by nature. That he was so is suggested by his marked attachment to the Franciscan Order,[2] by his especial devotion to the dogma of the Immaculate Conception,[3] by his constant invocation of the Trinity,[4] by his extreme readiness to detect the miraculous in the commonplace,[5] and perhaps also by his use of that curious cypher signature, which has so successfully baffled those who have endeavoured to interpret it.

That outlook upon life, which was thus natural to him, can but have been confirmed by his experiences down to the time when he appeared at the court of Ferdinand and Isabella. Whether he had himself been a sailor or whether,

---

[1] 'Como si en estas personalmente hobiere estado' (Las Casas, i. 5).

[2] Cp. Las Casas, i. 32.

[3] An illustration of this devotion is supplied by the names which he gave to places in the Indies.

[4] Cp. Las Casas, i. 2.

[5] This appears constantly in the *Journal* and in his letters.

as is more probable, he had been rather a trader, he had certainly been brought into contact with many sailors, and the tendency of those who are engaged in a seafaring life to be superstitious and to be inclined towards mysticism is notorious. When he passed from Portugal to Castile, he came into the midst of a people, to a very large number of whom a similar attitude of mind was habitual. He there associated, moreover, with the fathers of La Rabida, from whom he received both moral and material assistance, and with some of whom at least he was certainly in close sympathy. The very fact that he, 'a poor foreigner,' as he later described himself, should have won a hearing from such a magnate as the duke of Medinaceli, and that he should have been enabled to reach the presence of the sovereigns, was almost enough to prove to him that Heaven indeed favoured him.

In such circumstances, it would have been extraordinary if he had not regarded himself as being in some measure 'a man sent from God'. Had he not done so, he would have been far more truly exceptional than he in fact was; his mentality would have been more truly alien from that of those by whom he was surrounded and more truly abnormal for the age in which he lived. It was because he was essentially a man of his time, because he was the temperamental peer of Isabella or of Torquemada, of a majority of his contemporaries in Spain, that he was convinced that he had a mission from Heaven to perform. It is intrinsically probable that he entertained this conviction as soon as he had conceived, even dimly, of that project which he set out to execute, and that by this conviction his opinion concerning all the questions debated at that time was coloured and indeed ultimately determined.

10

This probability is the greater because there is at least some indirect evidence to suggest that, when he first laid his proposals before Ferdinand and Isabella, Columbus already regarded himself as the missioner of God. Upon that which was then in his mind, the account, given by Ferdinand

Columbus and Las Casas,[1] of his negotiations with the sove-reigns throws a certain light. From that account, it is clear that he was profoundly convinced of the transcendent im-portance of the project of which he had conceived. The rewards which he demanded in event of success were so extensive as to seem to be altogether extravagant; of those demands, he steadfastly refused to abate one iota, and upon the terms which he had propounded from the first, he insisted to the last with a degree of firmness that seemed to be an unwise obstinacy.

It is equally clear from the same accounts that he was as profoundly convinced that secrecy was essential. He invited the sovereigns to embrace an enterprise, the exact nature of which he refused to define. In effect, he required that they should countenance and that they should furnish supplies for an undertaking, for the practicability and advantages of which he offered no evidence save the mere word of an obscure foreigner who might well be nothing more than a plausible and smooth-tongued adventurer. Although he talked with the utmost assurance of the lands which he pro-posed to 'discover and gain', although he insisted that he was in no doubt concerning their existence and their value, or concerning his ability to reach them, he would not indicate with any clarity the basis of his confidence. He would appear, perhaps, to have suggested that to reach these lands it was necessary to cross the Atlantic, and it is probable that, whether intentionally or unintentionally, he conveyed the impression that they were situated in the Indies; despite the efforts of Vignaud to prove the contrary, it can hardly be questioned that such an impression was formed by Ferdinand and Isabella and by some, at least, of those to whose con-sideration the proposals were submitted.

But even if it be admitted that Columbus explicitly stated that he designed to reach the Indies, his intentions would not thereby have been made altogether clear. 'The Indies' was a vague term, covering whatever land might lie between the eastern frontiers of Arabia and Persia and the western shores of Europe and Africa and the islands lying off the coasts of

[1] Cp. Las Casas, i. 31.

those two continents. It included Catayo and, according to the opinion of some, the dominions of Prester John; it included also those mysterious and half-mythical territories and islands, concerning which there was so much conjecture and so little knowledge. It might even be taken to cover any land, concerning which there was hardly so much as conjecture, but which might conceivably exist somewhere westward of the Canaries and eastward of the Ganges. There was thus, in any case, a lack of definiteness in his statements, and their vagueness was in all probability one cause of the initial rejection of his proposals. Since he still maintained his reticence, despite the obviously prejudicial effect which it exerted upon his prospects of success in his negotiations with the sovereigns, it is clear that he must have had some strong reason for being so secretive.

That reason can hardly be found in any fear that he would be forestalled. It is true that the Portuguese are alleged to have examined him closely concerning his ideas, to have gained a measure of information and to have made use of that information to attempt to anticipate his discovery, but even if this story, the authenticity of which is questionable, be accepted, there is in this experience itself no sufficient ground for the peculiar reticence of Columbus. The warning which he had thus received might indeed suffice to put him on his guard against being over ready to explain the exact route which he proposed to follow[1] and even against specifying with much precision the arguments upon which he based his conviction that his design was practicable. But it hardly suffices to account for his refusal to supply even such information as might be legitimately demanded by those whom he invited to support his enterprise. His secretiveness, indeed, was carried to a point at which it might well seem that it was no more than a cloak for ignorance; that he was altogether indefinite because he could not be definite, that his whole proposals were based upon nothing more substantial than conjectures as vague as those which had been put forward again and again since classical times.

Nor is it really a tenable hypothesis that the magnitude and even extravagance of the rewards which he demanded were

---

[1] Cp. Las Casas, i. 29.

the outcome of extreme vanity or of vaulting ambition and that his reticence was calculated, designed to create an atmosphere of mystery which might facilitate acquiescence in his demands. That Columbus was devoid of personal vanity is a contention which can be advanced only if the evidence of his own writings be entirely ignored. That he lacked ambition is an equally fallacious suggestion. He could not have achieved that which he did achieve, had he been less full of confidence in himself or had he been diffident concerning his own capacity. He would, perhaps, have ultimately achieved more and would have been delivered from some of those misfortunes which fell to his lot, had he not been ever anxious to secure his own advancement and that of his family. That he had a certain fondness for mystery is at least suggested by the silence which he preserved concerning his own antecedents, by his cypher signature, and by a certain lack of confidence in his associates which cannot be wholly explained as the result of legitimate suspicion of their ill-will.

When, however, so much has been admitted, it remains true that Columbus was not entirely devoid of commonsense and that he was not altogether blind to practical considerations. Whatever other qualities he possessed or did not possess, he had certainly some business acumen; even in his most exalted moments, he could not forget the commercial aspect of 'the enterprise of the Indies'. He was, moreover, a Genoese, and the Genoese have notoriously never been lacking in astuteness. It is clear enough that everything must have disposed him to leave himself a margin of bargaining capacity, to set his demands higher than that point at which he was actually prepared to come to an agreement. To adopt a rigid attitude must have been almost painful to a man of his character and training. Yet, if the accounts of his negotiations with Ferdinand and Isabella can be credited, and of the substantial accuracy of those accounts there is no reasonable doubt, such was precisely the attitude which he did adopt. That he refused to effect any compromise is, indeed, almost obvious from the character of the terms ultimately granted to him; it is hardly conceivable that he should have put forward even higher demands than those which were conceded in the *Capitulations* of Santa Fé.

And if such rigidity of attitude may be regarded as surprising, the secrecy in which he enveloped his project is equally surprising. It is so probable as to be morally certain that Columbus had been for some years engaged in the buying and selling of commodities, and he must therefore have been aware of the elementary truth that it is less difficult to dispose of an article if some proof of its value be forthcoming. When, however, he laid his proposals before Ferdinand and Isabella, he seemed to be almost wholly oblivious of this commonplace of all business. Towards them and towards those who were commissioned to investigate his case, he in effect adopted the attitude of a man who demands a high price for an article, the excellence of which is guaranteed only by his unsupported assertion. It may be admitted that, in the very nature of things, absolute proof of excellence could not be produced, but Columbus appears to have made no effort to supply anything which could be regarded as evidence that his assertions were well grounded. It is true that he is represented as having exhibited to the sovereigns a map,[1] on which were indicated those lands that he proposed to discover, but even if he did in actual fact do so, it is obvious that such a map must have been conjectural and he would appear to have refrained from explaining the facts or arguments upon which his conjectures were based. His position was almost an anticipation of that of the promotor of the time of the South Sea Bubble, who invited investment in an undertaking 'but no one to know what it is'.

His conduct at this juncture, indeed, seems at first sight to have been not only alien from that which might have been expected from a man accustomed to transact business, but even alien from that which might have been expected from a man of ordinary intelligence. He asked for support in the execution of a project so indefinite that its advantages could but be dubious; he asked for a guarantee of lavish rewards in

[1] M. de la Roncière (*La Carte de Christophe Colomb*), believed that he had found this map in the Bibliothèque Nationale. His identification has been disputed and would seem to be scarcely tenable. It is, in any case, very questionable whether Columbus was, at that period, capable of drawing maps.

event of its accomplishment, but since its nature was not defined, of its accomplishment he would necessarily be the sole judge. It can hardly be supposed that Columbus failed to realize that he was thus setting in his path obstacles which might be expected to prove fatal to success, that he was putting forward a proposal which any rational man would have some difficulty in accepting. It can hardly be supposed that the unwisdom of the course which he pursued was not suggested to him by those who wished him well, or that he was not pressed to be somewhat more explicit. And since it must be believed that he desired that his propositions should be accepted, it is clear that there must have been some powerful consideration which so weighed with him as to lead him to refrain from doing what he could to render acceptance more probable.

11

This consideration must clearly have been of a somewhat unusual character, since from the material and practical point of view the attitude which Columbus adopted was one well calculated to secure his defeat. It is, however, perfectly supplied by his belief that he was the missioner of Heaven and that his project was therefore upon an entirely different plane from that upon which any human project might be supposed to be. For him, it ceased to be a scheme of his own devising; it was not the product of man's wisdom, but of divine inspiration. He had been moved to conceive of it; like David, to whom he is said to have compared himself, he was specially chosen to fulfil a special purpose. He was not a free agent, but the bondservant of the Most High; he could do only that which he was directed to do; he was no more than the ambassador of God.

But if he were no more, he was also no less. He was assured beforehand of the constant favour and guidance of Heaven; he was assured also of ultimate success, since the accomplishment of his mission was decreed by God and against the decree of God no opposition could prevail. The means by which his object would be achieved were, moreover, foreordained; they were infallibly the best means, since they were divinely selected, and they would be made known to him by God Himself, upon the revelation of Whose will he could confidently rely.

A mystic rarely, if ever, fails to receive that revelation of the divine will for which he seeks and which he expects to receive; he will always tend to interpret the promptings of his own nature as the still small voice of the very spirit of God. It was almost inevitable that Columbus, believing that he would be divinely instructed, should discover that instruction in his own heart and mind. By temperament reticent and even secretive, by temperament also ambitious, he was naturally impelled to conceal his actual intentions and to demand great and even lavish rewards. He may be supposed to have had no difficulty in convincing himself that these impulses were divinely implanted in him and that if he felt any contrary impulse, suggested by practical considerations, it should be resisted as one of those temptations to which the chosen servants of God had always been notoriously exposed.

With the disposition to do so, indeed, it was sufficiently easy for him to discover grounds upon which secrecy might be imperatively demanded. He was assured that to him, as the missioner of Heaven, some part of the hidden purposes of God had been made known. The mere fact that his proposals did not win instant acceptance was almost enough to prove that from others those purposes were still concealed. Had it been otherwise, his message would have been received with alacrity; it would not have appeared, as the very faith of Christ itself had once appeared, to be 'to the Jews a stumbling-block and to the Greeks foolishness'. But since God had willed that those to whom he preached should not at once hear, it was obligatory upon His ambassador not to go beyond the terms of his embassy. He was bound to deliver only that message which was entrusted to him; he was bound not to commit the error of 'adding here a little and there a little'. To have done so would have been to display a lack of faith; it would have been impious and also vain. It would have been to attempt to anticipate the appointed time, in which the truth would surely be made known and in which his message would be received by those whose understanding would be enlightened.

Nor could it be supposed that by reticence, the accomplishment of his mission would be in any way retarded. Had his project been of mere human devising, it might have been wise and even essential to exhibit greater candour. It might then have been advisable to produce every argument by which conviction could be carried to the incredulous, to do something more than merely insist upon the honour and glory that were to be gained and upon the spiritual and material benefits which would accrue, to propound a definite scheme in definite terms.[1] But since the enterprise was divine, and since it was the purpose of God that it should be achieved, its achievement was certain and could be neither hastened nor retarded by any human action. At the appointed time, 'the Holy Trinity would inspire' some sovereign to embrace the undertaking, that sovereign whom God had already chosen to be the recipient of His message and to reap the reward. How imperative it was that no attempt should be made to hasten that hour had, indeed, been made clear to Columbus in Portugal, if the story of the effort to appropriate his project be credited. At Lisbon, he had been illegitimately communicative and that which resulted had shown him how he had thereby incurred the displeasure of Heaven. The instinct which urged him to reticence was assuredly the whispering of the Holy Spirit, which he had momentarily allowed to be drowned by the clamorous voice of mundane wisdom. He had been mercifully warned and that warning he must not neglect, lest, like Saul, he should be rejected.

And if Columbus were thus readily able to interpret his impulse towards secrecy as being divinely implanted in him, so when he obeyed the promptings of personal ambition, he was as well able to persuade himself that he was no more than following the guidance of Heaven. For a man eager to be so persuaded, there were indeed ready to hand arguments sufficient to carry conviction. If he demanded great rewards, it was because only if such rewards were granted to him,

[1] For the arguments which he did use, cf. *infra*, vol. ii, pp. 6 *et seq.*

could the enterprise be brought to a successful conclusion. At a much later date, he protested to Ferdinand and Isabella that it was from fear lest that enterprise should be mismanaged that he was led to seek that the government of the Indies should be conferred upon himself.[1] It is probable enough that in making this protest he was altogether sincere, that he did believe that such had been his motive. It was natural enough that he should feel that he was in duty bound to endeavour to secure that the direction of the undertaking should remain in his own hands. Upon him had been laid the task of executing a great mission, the nature of which could be revealed to him alone and could not be appreciated by others. To him equally, and to him alone, would be shown the means by which the mission could be performed. In such circumstances, it was essential that he should be free to do that which he thought to be necessary and which in truth he knew to be necessary, since he was trusting not to his own judgement but to the guidance of Him Whose servant he was.

Nor could any rewards for which he might ask be justly regarded as excessive. He was the chosen means by which that monarch, who was to be moved to hear and to receive his message, was to be enabled to gain such glory and to receive such benefits as no other monarch had ever gained. It was no more than right that the man who had rendered to a sovereign services so notable should be lavishly recompensed, if only for the sake of the reputation of the sovereign himself. And by seeking a rich reward, Columbus could feel that he was also emphasizing the importance of the enterprise which he proposed and that he was avoiding the error of seeming to hold as of small price the gift of God which he offered.

Whatever he might demand, whatever he was moved to demand, would moreover be assuredly granted to him. Not only was it certain that the enterprise would be undertaken and achieved, but it was also certain that it would be undertaken and achieved by him alone, since he alone was chosen for this purpose. It was the immutable purpose of Providence that some sovereign, whether the king of Portugal or the

[1] Cp. *infra*, vol. ii, pp. 106–8.

king of England, the king of France or the king and queen of
Castile, would be moved to embrace the undertaking and to
employ the only means by which it could be carried out. The
actual or reputed failure of earlier attempts to reach the
unknown hemisphere were evidence that God had willed
that these attempts should not succeed. Despite every rebuff,
despite all opposition, Columbus could therefore feel the most
perfect confidence, assured that every obstacle would be
overcome and that his efforts would end in triumph. To
bargain, to compromise, was altogether unnecessary.

The steadfast confidence with which Columbus pursued
his design has been remarked by all who have considered his
career; it is no less obvious than the rigidity of the attitude
which he adopted in his negotiations with Ferdinand and
Isabella or than the mystery in which he shrouded his project. And it is the more notable since he was, as the witness
of his own extant writings proves, temperamentally inclined
to acute depression, temperamentally inclined to imagine
hostility where none perhaps existed and to exaggerate,
rather than to minimize, the difficulties with which he met.
Yet there was in him also a countervailing strain of optimism,
which enabled him to overcome his own nature and to entertain the brightest hopes even in his hours of darkest adversity.
Columbus was indubitably filled with an intense belief in his
own destiny, a belief which determined his conduct throughout his life. He was as indubitably convinced that his
destiny was to perform the mission entrusted to him, a conviction which filled his mind from the very moment when
he first conceived of 'the enterprise of the Indies'.

12

The suggestion that Columbus was thus filled, almost to
the point of obsession, with a conviction that such was his
destiny, implying, as it does, that he regarded his project as
being rather of divine than of human origin, may at first
sight appear to be inconsistent with those opinions which,
before his discovery of America, he would seem to have
held concerning the unknown parts of the world. It is
beyond question that he believed that it was possible to

cross the Atlantic and that, granted that no mass of land intervened to bar the way, it was also possible to circumnavigate the globe. It can hardly be doubted that he rejected the view, held by some of his contemporaries, that the other hemisphere was nothing but a waste of waters and that nothing remained to be discovered, save a certain number of relatively insignificant islands, such as those which were already known. It is at least very probable that, on the contrary, he held that lands of no inconsiderable extent were yet to be made known and that these lands would be reached as a result of a voyage beyond the Canaries and Azores. He would further seem to have been assured in his own mind that the voyage to these unknown lands would be one of reasonable duration, and that the lands were both habitable and inhabited, that so far from their climatic conditions making life impossible for man, they were peopled by a numerous, intelligent, and civilized race, possessed of great material wealth and enjoying all the benefits of a developed and ordered society.

His opinions, so far as they can be reasonably conjectured in the absence of any decisive evidence concerning them, were thus apparently in advance of those held by a large number of educated men of his time and were also in far closer accord with actual fact. It may therefore seem to be probable, if not evident, that they must have been the product of careful thought and of the exercise of trained judgement by a man of considerable intellectual capacity. It may appear to be hardly possible that he should otherwise have formed so just a view upon debated points, unless it be supposed that he was possessed of information derived from some person or persons who had already accomplished the passage of the Atlantic and who had already visited the unknown lands beyond the Ocean. It has, indeed, been argued by those who decline to believe that Columbus was actually capable of scientific reasoning, that such is the true explanation of the origin of the opinions which he held and that he merely availed himself of the knowledge and experience of others, of information received from the mysterious pilot, from Martin Alonso Pinzón and other practical seamen.

When, however, the views of Columbus are more closely examined, it becomes clear that no such explanation is necessitated by their character, even if it be admitted, as it in all probability should be admitted, that he had not 'much book learning'. They were not in actual fact at all inconsistent with the most complete lack of scientific knowledge and of capacity for scientific reasoning. They were, indeed, precisely the views which he might be expected to hold if he were convinced that he was 'a man sent from God' to perform a certain mission, for the performance of which it was necessary to reach the other hemisphere. The substantial justice of his opinions does not suffice to disprove the verdict passed upon him by Andrés Bernáldez or to invest his project with any scientific character.

It is obvious enough that, if he believed that he was chosen by God to make known that part of the world which was unknown, he would also be enabled to reach that part, and that accordingly for him the Atlantic was navigable whether or no it were navigable for others. It is hardly less obvious that his other opinions followed naturally from this initial conviction. If the ocean extended uninterruptedly from Europe to Asia, if there were no land distinct from these two continents, there was in reality nothing to be discovered, for Catayo had been already reached and if Cipangu had not been actually reached, knowledge of it had already been gained. If it were merely his mission to find a somewhat shorter route to eastern Asia, or a route other than that for which the Portuguese were seeking, then this mission could hardly be regarded as the revelation of the New Heaven and the New Earth, spoken of by St. John the Divine.

If, however, Columbus were thus, by the very nature of his conviction, almost bound to believe that land of some considerable extent was still to be discovered, he was even more bound to believe that this land was habitable and inhabited. It would have been for him almost an absurdity to suppose that God had selected him to discover some barren and desolate tracts, to carry the gospel of salvation to sticks and stones, to noxious reptiles or to horrible monsters who could hardly have been deemed to possess immortal souls and who were assuredly the very spawn of the Wicked One. He could but be assured that he would there find those 'other sheep', of whom Christ Himself had spoken and who were to be brought into the true fold. He was, indeed, the missioner of God; he was to prepare the way for the coming of that day when all mankind should confess the Saviour. His very name indicated his destiny; Las Casas was doubtless no more than expressing the idea of Columbus himself when he declared that not in vain was he called Christopher, since he was in very truth the bearer of Christ.[1] Columbus was inevitably compelled by his belief in his mission to believe also that the unknown hemisphere was peopled by intelligent beings, by men capable of eternal salvation.

And the more the apparent basis of his opinions is considered, the clearer does it seemingly become that this basis was rather religious than scientific, less rational than mystical. So far as he argued the matter, he argued from a false premise, although he arrived at a relatively just conclusion. Not only did he believe that the Atlantic could be crossed, but he was also assured that its passage would not occupy that length of time which many supposed that it must necessarily occupy. Since it was a fact that, sailing westward from Spain, land would be reached in less time than would have been needed to reach Catayo, Columbus had here formed a right opinion. But the grounds upon which he had done so were in all probability fallacious. In the notes, which he wrote on books which he had studied, he gives attention to every assertion that no great space intervened to the westward between Spain and the extreme East.[2] In a letter to Ferdinand and Isabella, he insists that the world is far smaller than the vulgar suppose, and he declares that Ptolemy was mistaken when he imagined that 'he had well corrected' Marinus of Tyre on this point.[3] It is not clear whether or no Columbus adopted the calculations of the earlier of these two writers in their entirety, but it is clear that he enter-

---

[1] Cp. Las Casas, i. 2. The same idea is found in Ferdinand Columbus (c. 2).

[2] Cp., for example, notes 23, 43 (to the *Imago Mundi*): note 486 (to the *Epilogus Mappe Mundi*), &c. The notes are numbered as by De Lollis (*Rac. Col.* I. ii.).

[3] Cp. *infra*, vol. ii, p. 82.

tained a false conception of the area of the globe and that it was as a result of this false conception that he was satisfied that the passage of the Atlantic would not occupy an impossible length of time, even were the voyage to be extended to the very shores of Catayo.

Upon an equally erroneous basis he rested his conviction that a considerable area of land was yet to be discovered. He dwells with marked insistence upon that passage in Esdras which declares that only one sixth of the globe is covered by water, and it is clear that he accepted as accurate this estimate of the proportion between sea and land. From this false estimate, he drew a conclusion which was actually in greater accord with fact than that which had been reached by many of his contemporaries, who held that little land was still unknown. But in his view, there is nothing to suggest that he was possessed of any special intellectual capacity; it rather suggests that he was inclined to place reliance upon the statements of writers who had no claim to be regarded as scientific.

So far, indeed, as there are any indications of the basis of his opinions, it would seem that it was essentially theological. These indications are certainly not very clear. No documents, illustrating his views before the date of the discovery, have been preserved, unless the notes be assigned to that period. His assertion, that he had acquired sufficient knowledge of all sciences to enable him to perform his undertaking, is really contradicted by himself and cannot be true. Even if he were equipped with the necessary preliminary education, there is no period in his life when he can have had either the opportunity to consult the necessary books or the leisure required for their study, unless, indeed, his own statements concerning his early life be rejected as inventions and such other evidence as there is for his activities down to the time of his first voyage be dismissed as false.

There is, however, definite evidence of the sources upon which he founded his opinions later in life, and in the absence of any proof to the contrary, it may be reasonably conjectured that upon these or similar sources he had always been disposed to rely. And it is significant that he exhibits a

marked preference for works of a theological character. He
does indeed refer to Ptolemy[1] and to Aristotle,[2] but he refers
to the former primarily in order to explain that he was mistaken, while as to the latter, it must be remembered that in
an earlier age Aristotle had been raised or had fallen almost
to the level of a Father of the Church. Columbus certainly
read and read with extreme care the tracts of Cardinal
Pierre d'Ailly, and more especially the *Imago Mundi*,
but while it may be admitted that this work was for him a
species of text-book, its share in determining his opinions
has perhaps been sometimes overestimated. Quite apart
from the possibility or probability that it did not come into
his hands until after his discovery of America, when his
annotations upon it are examined they will be found to be
in the main little more than a kind of analytical table of contents. They do not in general reveal either assent or dissent
on the part of Columbus; it is noteworthy that when they
do so, it is rather dissent that is indicated. Only upon one
occasion in his later writings does he make use of Pierre
d'Ailly[3] as an authority to support his own opinions, and he
then quotes him only in conjunction with other writers and
lays no special stress upon the value of his testimony. On
the other hand he does lay such stress upon the Vulgate and
upon glosses on passages in it. Esdras is his authority for the
proportion of land to water. For an explanation of the small
extent of the latter, he turns to Petrus Comestor and Nicholas
de Liria.[4] He makes use, in fact, of exactly those materials
of which a man of a religious and mystical temperament, who
believed that his ideas were divinely inspired, might be expected to make use. His employment of them certainly lends
more colour to the suggestion that he was obsessed by the
idea of his mission, than that he was a man of powerful intel-
lect and of scientific attainment.

An identical impression is conveyed by those passages in

---

[1] He explains that Ptolemy was mistaken concerning the shape of 'the other
hemisphere' (*infra*, vol. ii, p. 30), and concerning the size of the globe (*infra*,
vol. ii, p. 82).

[2] Cp. *infra*, vol. ii, p. 40. He refers also to Pliny and to Averroes (*infra*, *loc.
cit.*).

[3] Cp. *infra, loc. cit.*   [4] Cp. *infra, loc. cit.*

which he sets forth his views. These passages are confused and vague; there is a complete lack of clear and coherent argument, and there is nothing to indicate that any knowledge which he had acquired had also been digested. They read rather as the meanderings of a man who has somehow gathered a mass of unrelated information and who is anxious to display it without much regard for its relevancy. The mind of Columbus seems to be displayed in these passages as being not indeed disordered, but disorderly; it is the mind not of an educated but of an uneducated man, almost pathetically unaware that what seems to him to be something new and strange is to others perfectly familiar and ordinary. The very way in which, in one of his letters, he gives Ferdinand and Isabella an elementary lesson in the meaning of Castilian words[1] seems to betray the fact that his own knowledge was of somewhat recent acquisition.

The more the real nature of his opinions is considered, indeed, the less probable does it appear to be that they can have had any scientific basis, the less probable does it appear to be that Columbus was possessed of even a tithe of that scientific knowledge with which he is credited by his son and to the possession of which he himself laid claim. It becomes thus also questionable whether he can have conceived of any scientific project, whether he had formed any very clear idea of that which he proposed to achieve before he undertook its achievement. It becomes not unreasonable to suggest that he was led to embark upon his great adventure less by any knowledge, either theoretical or practical, which he possessed, than by his mystical temperament which caused him to feel that he had a great destiny and to discover in a vague idea of exploration a divine intimation of a mission which he was called upon to perform.

13

It must be admitted that at first sight it would appear to be hardly possible that, when Columbus passed the bar of

---

[1] ' . . . lago . . . que más de le puede llamar mar que lago, porqu'el lago es lugar de agua, y en seyendo grande, se dize mar, como se dixo á la mar de Galilea y al mar Muerto ' (*infra*, vol. ii, p. 43.)

Saltés, he had no very definite purpose in his mind and no very clear objective in view. It may seem to be little likely that he should have set out upon a lengthy and perhaps perilous voyage without having some conception of what would be the probable result of that voyage, at least if successful. If he did so, he perhaps displayed a very living faith in his own destiny, but he displayed also a degree of daring which might be more justly described as criminal rashness. His conduct was, indeed, then such as to supply no small justification to those who declared that he was a madman, carried away by the vain fancies of a disordered mind. So obvious has it seemed to be that he cannot have been so devoid of that ordinary caution which might be expected to be shown by any man, that it has been generally assumed that he was inspired by a clear idea. It has been held that, even if he had not explained his intentions with any precision, his intentions were not the less precise, and that he had set before himself an objective which may, perhaps, have been actually unattainable, but which was none the less perfectly definite.

While, however, up to this point there has been general agreement, agreement has there ended, and those who have felt assured that Columbus had a clear plan in his mind have differed widely concerning the nature of that plan. That there should be such difference of opinion is natural enough and is perhaps almost inevitable, since there is little evidence, antedating the discovery, to show what purpose was in the mind of Columbus, and such evidence as there is may be variously interpreted. It is true that before he sailed, he was granted a passport or letters of credence by Ferdinand and Isabella and that from this document it appears that he was to proceed to the Indies,[1] while from the *Journal* it further appears that he was to deliver letters from the sovereigns to the Grand Khan.[2] Inasmuch as the Grand Khan was the ruler of an Asiatic territory, it would thus seem that the

---

[1] 'Mittimus in presenciarum nobilem virum Christoforum Colon cum tribus caravelis armatis per maria oceania ad partes Indie pro aliquibus causis et negotiis seruicium Dei ac fidem ortodoxe concernentibus.' A copy of the passport is preserved in the *Registro Libro de la Corona de Aragón* (Reg. 3569, f. 136).

[2] Cp. the *Journal*: Prologue: 21 Oct. and 30 Oct.

'Indies' must be here taken to mean some part of Asia and that Columbus was therefore dispatched on a voyage to Asia. It would accordingly seem also to be no more than reasonable to assume that it was his aim to reach the east by sailing west; his objective would appear to be sufficiently defined.

This definition, however, is more apparent than real. Too much emphasis may perhaps be laid upon the fact that the title of Grand Khan had ceased to be currently used,[1] but it would seem that his personality was somewhat indistinct and that the precise situation of his dominions was really unknown; the very title was possibly rather magnificent than explicit. It would be unwise to regard the evidence of these two documents as proving that Columbus was definitely sent on a mission to the successor of that monarch whose court had been visited by Marco Polo or of him who had sent envoys to Eugenius IV. Both these events had occurred some years before; political conditions in Asia were reputed to be very unstable, and despite the amount of intercourse between west and east, western Europe was but imperfectly informed of the revolutions of the Far East. The sovereigns, with whom caution was habitual especially in foreign relations, were most unlikely to commit themselves to expressions of friendship for a monarch who might well be found to have been dispossessed of his throne or to be involved in a precarious struggle with some foreign or domestic rival. To have done so would have been needlessly to risk the alienation of some other monarch, whose good-will might prove to be advantageous; it would have been to assume a definite political attitude without previous examination of the situation, and to impose upon their envoy an unnecessary, and perhaps a prejudicial, limitation of discretion. It is more reasonable to regard the evidence of these documents as being vague rather than definite, and the title of Grand Khan as referring not to some specific ruler, but to any ruler who might seem to the envoy to be of sufficient importance and power to be entitled to receive courteous attention from the sovereigns of Castile and Aragon.

[1] This point is emphasized by Vignaud (*Toscanelli and Columbus*).

That this is the more just interpretation of the wording of the document is indicated, if it is not actually proved, by the terms of the grants which Columbus received from Ferdinand and Isabella. In that grant, if anywhere, it might be supposed that some definite statement of the objective of the voyage would be found and that the services, for the performance of which he was to be so lavishly rewarded, would be exactly specified. So far, however, is this from being the case, that the wording of the document seems to be almost studiously obscure. 'Forasmuch,' it runs, 'as you, Cristóbal Colón, are going by our command, with certain vessels of ours and with our subjects, to discover and to gain certain islands and mainland in the Ocean Sea.'[1] There is here an entire absence of definition. The lands in question are not even described as lying towards any particular point of the compass; they might be in the north or in the south, no less than in the west; they might be part of Asia or of Africa, or of some entirely unknown continent. Only by implication was it even stated that they were unknown; had they been already known, it is hardly probable that it should be said that they were to be discovered 'by command' of Ferdinand and Isabella. But the dominions of the Grand Khan of Marco Polo's travels were not unknown; they had been 'discovered' centuries before, and it would, moreover, have been at once insulting to a reputedly powerful and friendly monarch and an entirely fatuous undertaking to send three practically unarmed vessels, manned by miscellaneous crews, not selected for military capacity, to 'gain' those dominions. Unless it be supposed that, for no very obvious reason, Ferdinand and Isabella were deliberately misrepresenting the mission upon which Columbus was dispatched, that mission cannot have been merely to reach the ruler of Catayo. The evidence of the passport, of the *Journal*, and of the grant made at Granada cannot then be regarded as definite concerning the objective of Columbus, and it must therefore be admitted that for the nature of that objective there is no

---

[1] 'Por cuanto vos Cristóbal Colón vades por nuestro mandado á descobrir é ganar con ciertas fustas nuestras, é con nuestras gentes ciertas Islas, é Tierrafirme en la mar Océano' (Navarrete, ii, p. 9).

conclusive evidence dating from the period before the first voyage.

There is, however, evidence dating from a later period which, until the twentieth century, was accepted as decisive without any serious question. Ferdinand Columbus and Las Casas, both of whom were apparently in a position, if any one were in a position, to know the truth, agree in declaring that the aim of Columbus was to reach the Indies by sailing westwards. Their testimony is supported by the opinion of other early writers, no one of whom appears to have doubted that such was in fact the project which had been formed. It was regarded as being more decisively confirmed by the witness of Columbus himself, whose statements, as contained in his earliest writings or as quoted by those who had access to his papers, were held to bear out this view. It was more especially pointed out that he showed much apparent anxiety to identify those lands which he discovered with the lands which had been described by those who had journeyed from Europe to the extremity of Asia, and it was contended that, as he had set out with the intention of reaching the Far East, so he died in the belief that he had realized this intention, although he had not actually established relations with the Grand Khan or with Prester John or with any other of the actual or reputed oriental monarchs.

Upon such a basis was founded the classical version of the project of Columbus. That project was regarded as simplicity itself, and his objective was considered to have been so definite and so clear as to be beyond all question. Following the accounts given by Ferdinand Columbus and Las Casas, he was credited with having received a somewhat elaborate education, although it was admitted that these writers were mistaken in supposing that he had studied at the University of Pavia and there acquired 'the rudiments of letters'. Columbus was declared to have gained enough knowledge to be able to profit both from his intercourse with a number of learned men and from information which he later received from others of practical experience, the more so as he had himself made extensive voyages.

A gradual process has, indeed, been imagined by which

Columbus was prepared for the task which he eventually undertook. Las Casas[1] enumerates a number of reasons which, as he says, might have served to strengthen the conviction, already entertained by Columbus, that the east could be reached by sailing westward. The suggestion thus put forward, that the reasons operated to clarify and to consolidate ideas vaguely held, has been taken by some as being more than a suggestion. It has been supposed that the arguments, adduced by Las Casas, were actually present in the mind of Columbus. More especially, it has been held that he was influenced by the reading of the tracts of Pierre d'Ailly which became for him a kind of gospel and from which he drew substantial confirmation of his already existing conviction that all seas were navigable and that no great distance divided Spain from Asia across the Ocean. The fact that in the Azores and Madeira, and indeed generally among sailors who had made voyages in the Atlantic, a number of stories concerning lands to the west were current, served to support upon practical grounds a conclusion already reached upon theoretical grounds, the more so since in these stories there seemed to be evidence that the winds and currents had carried the products of the east to the shores of these African islands.

It was when his project was thus already fully formulated in his own mind that he received the powerful encouragement of the approval of Paolo Toscanelli. According to the accounts given by Ferdinand Columbus and Las Casas,[2] the Florentine philosopher was approached by Columbus through the medium of Lorenzo Giraldi and invited to deliver his opinion and advice. In reply, Toscanelli sent a copy of a letter which he had earlier written to a Portuguese canon concerning the western route to the Indies and a map which he had himself drawn and which later served as the chart for the first voyage. Since the letter deals solely with the question of reaching Asia and the dominions of the Grand Khan, and since the map would seem to have indicated that no land intervened to bar the direct passage from Lisbon to Quinsay,

---

[1] Las Casas, i. 3–14.

[2] Cp. Ferdinand Columbus, c. 7. 8: Las Casas, i. 12. The intermediary is called Lorenzo Girardi by Ferdinand Columbus; Berardo by Las Casas. For his identity, cp. Uzielli, in *Rac. Col.* V. i.

it becomes obvious that the point at issue must have been the voyage to the Indies. The character of the project of Columbus and the nature of his objective are thus clearly displayed, and no room for doubt appears to remain. This view of the question was almost universally held by those who had considered the problem until a comparatively recent date, and it would be altogether erroneous to suppose that it has been discarded. Since, indeed, Vignaud delivered his elaborate attack upon it, it has received the weighty support of that most profound Columbian scholar, the late Cesare de Lollis.[1] It is in accord with the obvious opinion of the age in which Columbus lived and of those who were personally acquainted with him. It is equally in accord with that which might seem to have been the necessary opinion of all educated men of that period. Granted that many believed that islands of greater or lesser extent lay between Europe and Asia, it can hardly be contended that any suspected the existence of the American continent, and hence, as the sphericity of the globe must be regarded as having been a recognized fact, the result of a westerly voyage could only be the eventual reaching of Asia. The debatable ground thus seems to be reduced in area; it appears to be no more than the question whether the distance to be traversed were too great to be accomplished, or whether obstacles would be encountered, such as contrary winds and currents or perils of a more obscure and fatal nature, which would effectually bar navigation, or perhaps whether the art of navigation itself were equal to the task of conducting such a voyage, in the course of which land would be so long out of sight. In such circumstances, it would seem that Columbus, if he were a man of even ordinary intelligence, could but have conceived of the project of reaching Asia and of no other, and that his objective could but have been perfectly defined. It may none the less be doubted whether the classical view is in fact just, and whether the arguments by which it has been supported are indeed as irrefutable as might appear. There is some reason for believing that, while there is in this view a con-

---

[1] Vignaud, *op. cit.*; De Lollis, *Disquisizione critica*; in his *Cristoforo Colombo* (ed. 1923.)

siderable element of truth, it does not represent the whole truth and that the objective of Columbus was not precisely that which it is thus supposed to have been, that while the classical view cannot be altogether rejected, it cannot be received without some modification.

14

It is sufficiently clear that the validity of this view depends at least to some extent upon the measure of credit which may be accorded to Ferdinand Columbus and Las Casas, whose testimony is its primary foundation. That the accounts of the early life of the discoverer given by those two writers[1] cannot be accepted without considerable reserve is admitted even by the most convinced supporters of the traditional version of the history of the discovery. No one now seriously contends that Columbus was descended from 'that Colonus, of whom Cornelius Tacitus treats', or that 'he acquired the rudiments of letters' at the University of Pavia. That he was related to the corsairs who were known in Italy as Colombo is asserted only by those who labour to justify a particular hypothesis concerning his origin.[2] The statement that he served under that admiral or pirate cannot be accepted as true. Other details in the story told by Ferdinand Columbus and Las Casas appear to be hardly less at variance with fact. The account of the manner in which he first arrived in Portugal is more romantic than it is probable, while that of his meeting with Felipa Moñiz is somewhat reminiscent of the story of Dante and Beatrice, and it is more likely that he resided at Porto Santo as the representative of a Genoese business house than as the son-in-law of Bartholomeu Moñiz Perestrello, who, indeed, was possibly not the father of the wife of Columbus.[3] Such errors, whether they were deliberate or accidental, on the part of these two writers,

---

[1] Cp. Ferdinand Columbus, c. 4: Las Casas, i. 3–4.

[2] On the Colombos, see *Rac. Col.* II. iii: Vignaud, *Études critiques*, pp. 131–193. Ulloa (*op. cit.*, pp. 272 *et seq.*) has endeavoured to show that there was actually some relationship between Columbus and the Colombo whose real name was Casenove or Coullon: his attempt cannot be regarded as successful.

[3] For the identity of the wife of Columbus, cp. Vignaud, *Études critiques* pp. 424 *et seq.* That identity is somewhat uncertain.

suffice to suggest that their account of the training which
Columbus received cannot be trusted, and when that account
is examined it becomes clear that it is consistent neither with
probability nor with that which he himself relates, or is
alleged to have related, concerning his early life, nor with the
character of his extant writings.

Aristotle justly remarks that education is never easily
acquired but must always be the result of painful effort, and
if Columbus indeed 'learned arithmetic, drawing and paint-
ing', became an expert Latinist, and acquired 'an adequate
knowledge of geometry, geography, cosmography, astronomy
and navigation', he must have spent some considerable time
upon the study of these varied branches of learning. It may
further be legitimately presumed that, despite the fact that
he was of quick intelligence and filled with a desire to learn,
he had need of some instruction, and it is questionable
whether even a Genoese instructor would have expended the
necessary time and labour without receiving some more or less
substantial payment. But Columbus was of humble parentage; his father, Domenico Colombo, was in a chronic condition of financial embarrassment, and in any case it can be
safely assumed that, for a boy in such a position in life, the
means for providing so elaborate an education would not
have been forthcoming, even if it had been the type of
education which those responsible for his upbringing would
have wished him to receive. It has, indeed, been suggested
that he may have acquired the rudiments of knowledge at the
school which the weavers of Genoa had established.[1] But the
document in which this school is mentioned dates from a
period when Columbus was already in Spain, and there is no
evidence to justify the hypothesis that any such school was
already in existence when he was still resident in Genoa. An
alternative hypothesis[2] that some learned priest taught him
is no more than an hypothesis put forward to meet the
difficulty of explaining how he acquired his alleged proficiency in various branches of knowledge. The argument

---

[1] Cp. Harrisse, *Christophe Colomb*, i, pp. 246–7. The school is first mentioned
in a document of 1486.

[2] Thacher, *Christopher Columbus*, i, pp. 287–8.

that his piety and theological knowledge prove that he had received such instruction is fallacious; the theological knowledge displayed in the *Libro de las Profecías* was more probably that of Gaspar Gorricio, while even to-day religion and business are the twin passions of the Genoese.

Even, however, had the means been available and the desire to use those means present, both in the mind of Columbus and in the minds of those who controlled him in his boyhood, it is difficult to imagine that he could have found the necessary leisure. The son of Domenico Colombo, and for that matter the son of any parents in straitened circumstances, would undoubtedly be set at the earliest possible moment to the task of contributing to the support of his family. If his own statement that he went to sea at the age of fourteen and that for years he was rarely off the sea be accepted as true, it is clear that he can have had few educational opportunities after he left Genoa. It is to the last degree improbable that he could have found an instructor among the crews of the vessels in which he sailed; it is equally improbable that those vessels were equipped with libraries or that he had purchased and that he carried with him a library of his own. Since Porto Santo and Madeira can hardly be supposed to have been at that time centres of learning, it is clear that such academic knowledge as Columbus possessed when he arrived in Spain must have been acquired by him either in early boyhood or while he was at Lisbon, engaged in urging the Portuguese king to support his project. That he should have learned all that he is alleged to have known before the age of fourteen argues an improbable degree of precocity, while if he gained his knowledge at Lisbon, it cannot have been as a result of that knowledge that he first conceived of his project.

There is, however, reason enough for believing that neither in childhood nor in early manhood nor, indeed, at any other period of his life, did Columbus attain that degree of proficiency which he is alleged by Ferdinand Columbus and Las Casas to have attained in various branches of knowledge, or to the possession of which he himself laid claim. It may be presumed that had he done so, he would have allowed the fact to become known to Toscanelli. But the famous letter to Martims, although it may have been written by a philosopher, was assuredly not designed to impress a man of intellectual capacity; it appeals to piety and cupidity, and perhaps to a spirit of adventure, but it does not appeal to learning or even to very acute intelligence. It is true that this letter was not written directly to Columbus, but that Toscanelli should have laboured to copy it out to forward to him argues that he had no very high opinion of his learning. An identical impression is conveyed by the second letter, which was directly addressed. It seems, indeed, that the Florentine, after having seen the communications sent to him by Columbus, had formed a low estimate of the scientific ability of his correspondent. So much is almost conveyed by a passage in the second letter; 'you cannot', writes Toscanelli, 'have perfect knowledge on this matter, save as the outcome of experience and discussion, such as I have had in abundance, and have received good and true information from men of magnificence and of great learning.' Columbus had certainly failed to produce the idea that he had himself read extensively and that he had enjoyed intercourse with a number of learned men, 'ecclesiastical and lay, Latins and Greeks, Jews and Moors, and many others of varying beliefs'.[1] It is true that he was habitually reticent, but it is fair to presume that, if he did not produce this idea in the mind of Toscanelli, it was because he was unable to do so, it was because any such idea would have been altogether erroneous.

Inasmuch as, at the date of his correspondence with Columbus, the Florentine was a man advanced in years, it would perhaps be unwise to insist very strongly upon the evidence supplied by his letters. He may have had little inclination to enter into any laborious discussion; he may have felt that he was no longer equal to the task of doing so. It may even be that his faculties were somewhat impaired and that he was thus led to write in a style which would hardly have been expected from a man of his great reputation and attainments, although, as has been justly pointed out, the philosophers of the later fifteenth century did not express themselves with that restraint and accuracy which is

[1] Cp. *Rac. Col.* I. ii, p. 79.

necessarily found in the philosophers of the twentieth century. The very fact that Columbus never alluded, so far as is known, to his debt to Toscanelli might, indeed, be taken to show that he did not regard that debt as being at all considerable, and that he was rather disappointed than gratified by the response made by the Florentine to his appeal for advice, that he considered that response as being something of an insult to his intelligence. In this case, so far from the evidence of the correspondence indicating that Columbus was lacking in knowledge, it would rather argue that the exact contrary was the case and that he was offended that Toscanelli appeared to have assumed that he was a mere unlettered sailor.

There is, however, other evidence to show that whatever may have been the opinion of Columbus concerning his own learning, that learning was certainly not profound and was probably almost non-existent. He was not merely incapable of that measure of clear reasoning which might be expected to be found in an educated man, even in that period of history, but he makes just that parade of learning which the unlearned always tend to make. Whatever he may have been at the time of the discovery, at a later date he was certainly not an expert navigator. Had he been so he would not have regarded the determination of his ship's position as being in the nature of a 'prophetic vision', nor would he have supposed that his vessels sailed rapidly northwards because they were going downhill.[1] His acquisition of other sciences than that of navigation would appear to have been equally imperfect.[2] His statement that La Mina lay under the equator is erroneous; his claim, if he actually put forward the claim, to have personally determined the degree cannot be admitted.[3] It is at least doubtful whether he was the first to observe the variation of the compass.[4] He further exhibited a certain preference for the more erroneous of two opinions, rejecting the estimate of the size of the world given by Ptolemy in favour of that given by Marinus of Tyre and asserting the falsity of

---

[1] Cp. infra, vol. ii, p. 98 and p. 40.
[2] Cp. Ferdinand Columbus, c. 4: Las Casas, i. 11 : notes 22, 860, to the Historia of Pius II (Rac. Col. I. ii, pp. 294, 369): notes 16 and 234–5 to the Imago Mundi (ibid., pp. 375, 390).
[3] Cp. Nunn, op. cit.
[4] Cp. Castro, Diario de Navegação de Pero Lopes de Sousa, p. 50.

the general belief in the complete sphericity of the globe, declaring that one hemisphere was disfigured by a protuberance which he compares with a woman's nipple.

A still stronger argument against the truth of the statement that Columbus had received an elaborate education is afforded by the character of his Latinity. It is obvious that, in that age, a knowledge of Latin was the necessary basis of all other knowledge, and that without Latin it was impossible to study books upon scientific topics. The number of translations into the vulgar tongues was limited, and was for practical purposes confined to such learned works as had been originally written in Greek; the number of new learned works composed in any language save Latin was extremely small. Las Casas, following João de Barros, credits Columbus with being a proficient Latinist[1]; if he were proficient, the standard of proficiency must have been excessively low. In his notes, written in what purports to be Latin, he displays a degree of ignorance of grammatical rules, or a disregard for those rules, which would almost have put Gregory of Tours to shame.[2] It is, of course, true that not every one who has been well able to read Latin has also been able to write it, and the occurrence of even elementary blunders in composition does not necessarily prove inability to understand the language. But the errors of Columbus are so numerous and so grave, his prose is so barbarous, that it becomes difficult to believe that he can have received any real education, especially in an age when the writing of Latin was so general and when ability to compose, at least respectably, in that language was so widespread as to be almost universal among educated men. His Latin is further disfigured by a number of Castilianisms,[3] which serve to suggest that his knowledge of the language was acquired in Spain or while in a Spanish atmosphere.

There are, indeed, rather more arguments in favour of the view that Columbus was illiterate when he left Italy, and even

---

[1] The same statement is made by Oviedo (ii. 2).

[2] The subject of his verbs is constantly in the accusative, the object in the nominative case; a plural subject is frequently followed by a singular verb, &c.

[3] Columbus constantly uses the Latin accusative as a nominative, when the accusative is the Castilian noun: e.g. 'fluvios' for 'fluvii', &c. He employs 'habet' in the exact sense of the Castilian 'hay', &c.

to a comparatively late period of his life, than there are in favour of any contrary view. All the balance of probability is against the truth of the assertion that his training in youth was such as to enable him to form a scientific conception of the enterprise which he projected. The account given by Ferdinand Columbus and Las Casas may be dismissed as the result of misinformation or of faulty deduction from the known fact that Columbus did cross the Atlantic and discover a 'new world'.

15

Those who have held that, when he set out upon his first voyage, Columbus did so with Asia as his clearly defined objective, have not, however, depended for the justification of their view wholly, or perhaps even principally, upon any assumption that he was equipped with some scientific knowledge. On the contrary, they have argued that, holding such opinions as he is admitted to have held, he could have had no other aim in view. It is not disputed that he believed in the sphericity, although perhaps not in the perfect sphericity, of the globe, and of this belief the natural corollary is that a continuous westerly voyage must lead back to its starting-point by way of the east. Such a journey, or, at the very least, a westerly journey of great and indeed of indeterminate length, Columbus certainly proposed to make. It would appear to follow that, granted the supposition that no mass of land intervened to bar the way, he must have necessarily contemplated reaching the extremity of the known Asiatic continent or those Asiatic countries which lay beyond that known extremity. It was merely logical that this should be his objective; it was moreover very natural, when the deep interest felt by his contemporaries in the Indies is remembered. A conviction that this was both his desire and his deliberate intention does not involve acceptance of the statements of his son and of Las Casas concerning his early training; it involves no more than the assumption that he was a man of sufficient intelligence to recognize the implications of his own ideas concerning the shape of the world and that he accepted those implications.

This argument is undoubtedly weighty; it is not, however, entirely conclusive. The operations of an untutored mind are not invariably guided by the rules of logic. They are perhaps least likely to be so guided when that mind is naturally active and when it is further assailed by a number of new facts and required to assimilate a number of strange impressions and of unaccustomed ideas. Few, if any, will deny that the mind of Columbus was active, and even extremely active; it is certain that to it were presented new facts or supposed facts, new impressions and new ideas. The age was one in which, not 'ex Africa' alone, but 'ex Asia' and even 'ex Europa', 'aliquid semper novi'. Never, perhaps, has there been a time when a greater variety of new impressions were received or when there was a greater riot of conjecture. Men were seemingly called upon suddenly to exercise faculties which, since the decline of scholasticism, had lain almost dormant; their minds were excited, amazed, confused; intellectually, 'they reeled to and fro, and staggered like a drunken man'.

If, then, it be admitted that the mind of Columbus was untutored as well as active, it is far from inconceivable that he should have been unable to grasp fully the logical consequences of opinions which he had adopted. Had he been taught to reason and to think systematically, had his views been formed as a result of such reasoned consideration, it may perhaps be true that he would have appreciated those consequences. But if he had ever been so taught, the teaching had seemingly been of little profit, if the evidence of his own extant writings may be accepted. It is only necessary to read the letter which he wrote to Ferdinand and Isabella at the end of his third voyage, to see that then at least he was so completely a prey to mental turmoil that he was unable to think clearly or to express the results of his thoughts with any coherence. There is nothing to show that the capacity, which was then lacking in him, had been possessed by him before he discovered America, and any supposition that it had been is illegitimate. Every indication of his mentality that can be found suggests that, if he were in some measure endowed with genius, that genius was on the borderland of insanity. Inasmuch, however, as his actual sanity is hardly in question, it is more reasonable to suppose that throughout his life his mental processes were somewhat confused, that they were those of an uneducated man of active mind, whose defective training made it difficult or impossible for him to set in order the ideas which he had derived from that which he had seen and heard.

When the character of the subject upon which his thoughts were concentrated is considered, it must be recognized that it is little surprising if those thoughts tended to become so riotous as to be beyond his control. At the present day, when the crossing of the Atlantic is a trivial undertaking, accomplished by thousands upon thousands every year, it is somewhat hard to realize how vague and how pregnant with mystery the western ocean appeared to be to the mind of the later fifteenth century. It was then not long since even to venture out of sight of land was to perform a feat of daring, willingly attempted only by the bravest or the most foolhardy. To sail boldly out into that vast and unknown expanse of water which lay beyond the western shores of Africa and Europe demanded an exceptional degree of courage or recklessness, or a very lively faith. The Atlantic was not uncommonly believed to conceal dangers, the very nature of which could not be even dimly comprehended, but conviction of the reality of which sufficed to make it a matter of some difficulty for Columbus to gather together the small band required to man the three vessels for his first voyage. At the present day, moreover, the world has been and is being constantly circumnavigated, and there is no room for rational doubt concerning its shape and size, but in the age of Columbus there was such room. It was not then felt to be by any means certain that circumnavigation could be accomplished. It was then possible to believe that in actual fact the globe was shaped like a pear, elongated in one part to an indeterminable extent, and it was indeed also possible to conceive that it might have any other form, consistent with the admitted sphericity of one hemisphere. The potentialities of such a voyage as Columbus proposed seemed, indeed, to that age to be not merely those which, in the light of modern knowledge, they are known to have been; they appeared to be really incalculable.

It can hardly be doubted that to Columbus himself those potentialities did appear to be vast beyond all imagining. It has been pointed out that of the passages in the Vulgate which impressed themselves upon him, there is one which seems to have been continually in his mind: 'the Heavens declare the glory of God, and the firmament sheweth His handywork.' He was prepared at all times and in all places to see that glory and to recognize that handiwork; he was ever ready to perceive marvels where others could perceive none and to believe that he was encountering the miraculous. Mystical by nature, he was carried away by the very grandeur of his own conception of a voyage which none had accomplished and which few, if any, had even dared to attempt. Profoundly assured that success awaited him, ever feeding upon those jealously guarded thoughts which burned in his untutored brain, his very reticence led him to avoid that frank intercourse with others which might have brought him to a more rational frame of mind. Convinced that in a very literal sense 'the stars in their courses fought against' the Siseras who opposed him, recognizing, in every slight advance which he made, the working of the mighty hand of God, daily becoming more certain that he was predestined to greatness, it was no more than natural that he should come to expect that he would find rather the utterly unexpected than that which might have been anticipated. Such a man, and above all such a man in such an age, was almost bound to believe that the hidden mysteries of the ocean were indeed wonderful and that when he penetrated them he would reveal to man, not a new route to the Indies, but 'the New Heaven and the New Earth, spoken of by St. John the Divine'. His belief in the sphericity of the globe was, in such circumstances, little likely to affect his conception of that which would result from his enterprise. That belief was, after all, probably no more than a modified belief, held only because others held it; he, perhaps, never found it to be incompatible with a conviction that 'the other hemisphere' was not spherical. The argument that his conception of the world must have led him to design to reach Asia, because that was what he might have been naturally supposed to have designed, ignores the peculiar mentality of the man, and its force is far more apparent than real.

If it be admitted, indeed, that Columbus was either unable to see or unwilling to accept the logical consequences of his belief in the sphericity of the globe, or that he held this belief only in a modified form and as a species of working hypothesis, much that has been adduced to support the classical version of the story of the discovery loses something of its value and even of its relevancy as evidence. It has been argued that the letters of Toscanelli prove that Columbus had formed the design of reaching the east by sailing west, and the apparent force of this argument may be gathered from the fact that Vignaud felt it necessary to counter it by endeavouring to show that the correspondence was a fabrication. But an impartial consideration of the letters suggests that their importance as an indication of the ideas of Columbus has been exaggerated. It may be questioned whether they actually supply any clear indication of those ideas.

It is of some importance to remember that in the first instance, at least, Columbus did not communicate directly with Toscanelli, but did so through the medium of a certain Lorenzo Giraldi. There is accordingly an initial possibility that his intermediary failed to represent his ideas correctly; if those ideas were inconsistent with current beliefs concerning the globe, it is obvious that Giraldi was little likely to have been able to understand them or to have realized that such ideas could be seriously entertained. Quite apart, however, from any possibility of this kind, there is an inherent improbability in the suggestion that Columbus opened his heart to his intermediary, since he would not afterwards do so to Ferdinand and Isabella when there was far greater reason for candour on his part. There is thus some ground for thinking that the first communication to Toscanelli was vague and general, amounting to no more than an expression of a belief that a westerly voyage would result in the attainment of considerable spiritual and temporal advantages. The reply of the Florentine does not in itself suggest more than that Columbus had invited his opinion on some such suggestion, since that reply is really no more than a copy of an earlier statement of his own view on the matter. Indeed, two passages in that part of the letter of Toscanelli which is not a mere transcript of his letter to Martims seem to indicate that the message from Columbus had been vague; reference is made to the land of spices, which might be taken to mean the Indies, and to 'Antilla', and it almost seems as if the writer were not sure whether Columbus desired to reach the one or the other, or perhaps that it was the opinion of the writer that he was being invited to say what would be reached by a man who had merely a vague idea of a westerly voyage.

Nor is much more light thrown upon the nature of the objective which Columbus had in his own mind by the second letter, in which, since it was written directly to him, it might be expected that such light would be found. Toscanelli states that he has received the letters of Columbus and seen that he wishes to sail westwards 'into the parts of the east', but he adds, in effect, that his correspondent cannot be expected to understand what would result from this voyage. Here again the suggestion is that the communication which the Florentine had received had been vague, to the extent of creating the impression that its author was a man of limited intelligence and of still more limited education, adventurous and enterprising and a practical sailor, perhaps, but not mentally capable of formulating any clear idea. Such an impression was not improbably the impression actually conveyed. If, as is rather more likely than not, Columbus was at this period unable to write, he must have entrusted the composition of the letter to another. Even if he were able to write, it is morally certain that he was unable to write in Latin or Italian,[1] and hence must have employed an amanuensis to conduct his correspondence with Toscanelli. His habitual reticence would assuredly have operated here to lead him to refrain from being at all explicit, with the result that the Florentine could do no more than conclude that he had some thought of possibly reaching Asia.

[1] Cp. *supra*, p. xxxvi, notes 2, 3.

That it was not this thought which was predominant in the mind of Columbus is somewhat forcibly suggested by the fact that he makes no reference to Toscanelli and that he acknowledges no debt to him. This fact has not been satisfactorily explained by those who admit that the letters are genuine and who hold that the debt was of some considerable importance. There is no justification for the suggestion that Columbus was actuated by vanity or jealousy. His extant writings prove that he was not unwilling to acknowledge such obligations, and it would seemingly have been a source of no little pride to him that he, an unknown stranger, should have aroused the interest and secured the approval of the foremost philosopher of the age. Nor could the recognition of his debt detract from his own merit. From the very evidence of the correspondence itself, the idea had been present in his mind before he placed himself in communication with Toscanelli, who did no more than confirm that idea. If, however, it were the deliberate intention of Columbus to reach the Indies, if that were his real and considered objective, he did derive assistance as well as encouragement from the Florentine, who supplied him with a map which has been declared to have served as the chart for the first voyage. His silence concerning the correspondence thus becomes either inexplicable or discreditable.

But it can be explained, and explained without any reflection upon the honesty of Columbus, if in actual fact he did not essentially design to reach Asia—if he conceived, not indeed clearly but vaguely, that something far greater would be the outcome of his voyage than the mere discovery of a new route to the Indies. In such a case, his debt to Toscanelli becomes negligible if, indeed, it does not cease to exist. He had invited the Florentine to express an opinion upon that which would be the result of sailing westwards; the answer, so far from affording encouragement, was somewhat disheartening. It appeared to show that there could be only one result, that between Europe and Asia lay nothing but water and some relatively unimportant islands, and that any hope which he might have entertained of discovering anything in the nature of 'a New Heaven and a New Earth' was, in the opinion of the greatest living philosopher, altogether illusory. Nor did a second appeal produce a more satisfactory answer; Toscanelli was convinced that the end of the projected voyage would be the attainment of those lands of which Marco Polo had written and which he and other travellers had already visited. The great mission, entrusted to Columbus by God, forthwith fades into insignificance; it is nothing more than the finding of a way to the already known. His dream becomes no more than a dream; that he had ever believed it to be rather a revelation from Heaven almost proves that he lacked experience and the necessary intercourse with men of learning. The sole result, indeed, of his reference to Toscanelli was thus to induce doubt rather than to intensify belief, to undermine rather than to increase confidence. In such circumstances, to have recalled the correspondence would have been to recall an episode, the memory of which was bitter; to have acknowledged a debt would have been to acknowledge something which he did not feel himself to owe. It is admitted that it was not to Toscanelli that Columbus owed the original conception of his project; it may be reasonably contended that he did not owe to him any confirmation of his resolve. The letters of Toscanelli cannot be regarded as affording any real support to the classical version of the story of the discovery. They indicate, indeed, that which the Florentine believed that Columbus proposed to do, but they indicate no more, and it is at least possible that the belief of the Florentine was altogether erroneous.

Nor can such arguments as are derived from the annotations written by Columbus on the tracts of Pierre d'Ailly be regarded as more conclusive. Those tracts, which are generally known by the name of the first and most important among them, the *Imago Mundi*, were printed by John of Westphalia at some uncertain date.[1] It has been held that the volume was produced some nine years before the discovery of America; it has also been held that it was not produced until some five or even until some two years before that event. Between these conflicting opinions, no certainly just choice can be made, but if the later date be accepted, it

---

[1] Cp. Thacher, *op. cit.* ii, p. 341, note 2.

becomes clear that it is improbable that the book should
have penetrated to the Spanish peninsula before Columbus
had elaborated his ideas at least sufficiently to lay proposals
before Ferdinand and Isabella, and certain that in any case it
did not serve to lead to the first conception of the project.
But however this may be, there are other reasons for
thinking that the annotations, whether upon the tracts of
Pierre d'Ailly or upon other works, do not antedate the discovery of the New World. It is true that De Lollis[1] has contended that the mere fact that in those annotations, while
there are references to the discoveries of the Portuguese,
there is no trace of any reference to those of Columbus himself proves that the latter had not yet been made. When,
however, the character of the notes is considered, an explanation of the omission appears. It is abundantly clear that they
are not intended to add to the information contained in the
texts; out of a total of more than two thousand five hundred,
only five make any reference at all to recent voyages, and of
these four were in all probability written by Bartholomew
Columbus,[2] while the fifth,[3] which mentions the frequent
journeys of Columbus to Guinea, does so only incidentally
and because it was during those journeys that he came to the
conclusion that the estimate of a degree by Alfragan was
correct. The overwhelming majority of the notes seem at
first sight to be nothing more than aids to memory or a guide
to the contents of the works annotated. But while they may
well be this, they appear to be something more.

It is clear that they should be considered in conjunction
with the other writings of Columbus, and they bear an almost
obviously close relationship to the *Libro de las Profecías*.[4]
Of that work, the intention was certainly to collect passages
which seemed to show that the discovery had been divinely
foretold, that the 'unknown hemisphere' was to be revealed,
and that great spiritual benefits would be gained by the
preaching of the Gospel to peoples hitherto sunk in the
darkness of heathendom. Upon more than one occasion,

---

[1] Cp. De Lollis, *Cristoforo Colombo*, pp. xx *et seq.*
[2] Notes 2, 6, and 860 to Pius II: note 23 to *Imago Mundi*.
[3] Note 490, to the *Epilogus Mappae Mundi*.
[4] Printed by De Lollis [*Scritti: Rac. Col.* I. ii, pp. 73–160].

Columbus insists that such benefits would accrue from 'the enterprise of the Indies' and that the support of that enterprise was accordingly a religious duty. But whenever he so insists, he insists also upon the temporal advantages which will be secured. Here would seem to lie the purpose of the numerous annotations. In the *Libro de las Profecías* the Vulgate and the Fathers of the Church were called upon to testify to the justice of his spiritual claim. In the annotations, authors of repute, and above all a Vicar of Christ and a Cardinal, were called upon to testify to the equal justice of his temporal claim, to bear witness to the incalculable riches of those same unknown lands which were to supply so wonderful a harvest of souls. 'It was necessary', Columbus tells Ferdinand and Isabella, 'to insist also upon the worldly gain;'[1] to show to those who might be indifferent to the hope of saving from eternal damnation myriads of souls, that the enterprise promised wealth beyond that of Solomon, and to ensure that those, whom piety could not move to support the prosecution of the undertaking, might be led to do so by their cupidity.

In such circumstances, however, and for such a purpose, it would have been of no avail to refer to his own discoveries, for those whom he wished to convince were already determined to disbelieve his word and had given their adherence to those who declared that he had been guilty of gross deception. Every assertion which he might make concerning the character of the lands which he had found would be countered by the assertions of those who had returned 'with faces as yellow as the gold which they sought', or who while still in Española had used as their strongest asseveration, 'As I hope that God will bring me back to Spain!' It was essential that he should call upon witnesses who could not be suspected of bias, and accordingly he laboured to find in those books which he read the evidence of which he was so greatly in need, if his undertaking were not to be abandoned. That evidence is, as it were, underlined by means of the notes, which are the materials upon which Columbus will base his answer to those who have defamed the Indies. It thus becomes

[1] Cp. *infra*, vol. ii, p. 2.

probable that these materials were prepared only when the process of defamation had begun, and that they can but dubiously be held to throw any light upon the opinions which he entertained before he set out upon his first voyage.

16

More substantial evidence for the opinions of Columbus at the time of the discovery is, however, supplied by the two documents which describe his first voyage and its results. In those passages in the *Journal*, which are declared by Las Casas to be the actual words of the admiral, there is much to suggest that Asia was the objective sought. In the prologue to that document, it is explicitly stated that Columbus was dispatched by Ferdinand and Isabella to those lands of which he had spoken to them and in which resided the Grand Khan, the successor of that monarch who had asked the Pope to send teachers of Christianity to him. Other passages indicate that when Columbus had reached the New World, he believed that he was in the neighbourhood of the Asiatic continent. On hearing of Cuba, he thought that it must be Cipangu; he interpreted the stories of Carib raids as proving that the islanders were at war with the Grand Khan. The whole of the *Journal*, indeed, suggests that he was convinced that the lands which he had reached were those of which Marco Polo had written. The evidence of the *Letter* points to precisely the same conclusion. Columbus says definitely that he has reached the Indies; he does not even hint that he has been to any other part of the world, and he does express himself as being assured that a lucrative trade can be opened by way of Española with the dominions of the Grand Khan.

These documents, in their original form, were exactly contemporaneous with the discovery. When, therefore, their evidence is considered in conjunction with that of the letters of credence granted to Columbus before his departure by Ferdinand and Isabella, it seems to be merely perverse to contend that no thought of reaching the east by sailing west was entertained by those who sanctioned, who organized, and who participated in the first voyage. It cannot really

be questioned that such a thought was in the mind of
Columbus himself. The suggestion of Vignaud that the statement that the Indies had been reached does not mean that
there was any idea of reaching them when the voyage
began appears to be hardly worthy of a writer of such
undoubted scholarship.

The *Journal* and the *Letter* may, in fact, be legitimately
regarded as proving that when he left Palos, Columbus did
consider that he might reach Asia and that, when he did find
land, he concluded that he was at least in the neighbourhood
of Cipangu, if not in that of Catayo, despite the absence of
those evidences of advanced civilization and of abounding
wealth which he had been led to expect that he would there
encounter. To this extent, they throw light upon the nature
of the objective which he set before him. That light, however,
is perhaps somewhat imperfect. It reveals something of that
which was in the mind of Columbus; it may be questioned
whether it reveals all that was in his mind. It would be
dangerous to argue that these documents prove that the aim
of Columbus was simple, clear, and determinate.

It would seem that it has sometimes been half forgotten
that neither the *Journal* nor the *Letter* exists in its original
form and that both have been subjected to editing, the extent
and nature of which cannot be really ascertained. It is,
however, clear that they do not possess that degree of
authority which would attach to the originals, and least of all
have they that degree of authority which would attach to
originals in the autograph of the discoverer. Some caution,
whether much or little, must be exercised in using these
documents; at least, their evidence has that element of
dubiety which is inseparable from a copy which is admittedly
not absolutely exact. The suspicion which must be felt should
further be perhaps felt most strongly when the documents
seem most satisfactorily to solve the problems for the
attempted solution of which they are employed.

So far as the *Journal* is concerned, the need for caution is
indeed obvious, and to some part of the evidence derived from
it very serious exception must be taken. It is only in the prologue that the purpose of the voyage is definitely stated, and

the prologue has been justly regarded as highly suspect. It is not found in the *Historie* of Ferdinand Columbus, who would appear to have been unaware of its existence. It is marked by some anachronisms and it was certainly not written at the date at which it purports to have been written. There occur in it, moreover, two peculiarly suspicious phrases. Ferdinand and Isabella are addressed as 'king and queen of the Spains', a title which formed no part of their regnal style and which they are said to have deliberately refrained from assuming. It may be argued that Columbus was a foreigner and that he was so impressed both by the victory gained over the Moors and by his own achievement, as to confer upon the sovereigns a title which seemed to him adequately to describe their greatness. This argument, however, is no more than hypothetical; it cannot be regarded as conclusive and it would appear to be somewhat unsatisfactory, since upon no other occasion does Columbus use any such title. It would seem to be more probable that the phrase is an interpolation. Even more suspicious is the appearance of the name, 'Cristóbal Colón'. Columbus makes use of his name upon no other occasion; it is extraordinary that he should do so here, and it would appear to be far more credible that the text is corrupt or falsified than that upon this solitary occasion he should have departed from a rule which he otherwise scrupulously observed.

There would, indeed, seem to be some ground for suggesting that the prologue is a fabrication, were it not that it is difficult to suggest a fabricator. The copy of the *Journal*, used by Las Casas, was possibly in the possession of Luis Columbus, who was doubtless as capable of committing forgery as of committing bigamy. It is, however, hard to believe that he, a careless polygamist and voluptuary, should have had the energy and application required for the performance of such a task, in view of the fact that no pecuniary advantage was to be gained from it. It is equally hard to believe that the copyist, whether working upon the original or upon a copy of that original, should have gratuitously added the prologue, unless it be supposed that he suffered from a species of obsession which impelled him to give a more perfect literary form to the document. The last possible fabricator would appear to be Las Casas, in whose autograph alone the prologue exists. It is, true that the explanation there given of the primary purpose of the first voyage exactly coincides with the thesis of the *Historia de las Indias*; it is also true that to the literary style of that work, the style of the prologue bears an almost unfortunate resemblance. It cannot really be denied that Las Casas was always ready to economize truth in that which he conceived to be a good cause and that he was not over scrupulous in his use of his materials. But it has yet to be shown that he was capable of deliberate forgery, and in the absence of any evidence that he was so capable it would be unjust to charge him with fabrication in this particular case. It might, indeed, be rash to assert that the prologue is not authentic, but its authenticity is certainly dubious; it can be unhesitatingly declared that it is, as De Lollis described it, 'sospettoso.' [1] But this being so, its witness is also suspect.

Even the witness of the body of the *Journal* cannot be unhesitatingly received. It is highly improbable that either Ferdinand Columbus or Las Casas ever even saw the original; they certainly did not possess it, and the précis made by the latter was from a version which had been edited and which was perhaps no more than a copy of a copy of the original. When, therefore, Las Casas states that a passage is in the exact words of the admiral, he can mean no more than that he has here copied his material verbatim; he had no conceivable means by which he could determine whether or no the version before him adhered strictly to the original. It may have so adhered; it equally may not. [2]

There is further the strong probability that the précis is coloured by the prejudices of Las Casas, as are the abstracts of documents which he gives in the *Historia de las Indias*. He may give complete texts faithfully, but he was an adept at selecting just those phrases which supported the point of view that he so earnestly laboured to elaborate. Nor is there any guarantee

---

[1] De Lollis, *Cristoforo Colombo*, p. xxvi.
[2] For a masterly discussion of the *Journal*, cp. De Lollis (*Scritti: Rac. Col.* I. i, pp. v–xxiiii).

that the 'ipsissima verba' of Columbus are preserved in the *Letter*; there are no means by which the fidelity of the editor-copyist to the original can be demonstrated.

On the contrary, there is some reason for thinking that, in their extant form, both the unabbreviated portions of the *Journal* and the *Letter* differ very markedly from the lost originals. At a much later date than that of his first voyage, Columbus declared that he had always been very conservative in his estimate of the value of his discoveries and that everything which he had said concerning them had proved to be true. It is no more than necessary to read a few sentences in either of these two documents in order to find a number of palpable exaggerations and a number of statements which are the reverse of restrained. It is possible that Columbus forgot that which he had said in the first enthusiasm of discovery; it is possible that his later statement was a deliberate lie. But if these two possibilities be dismissed, the passages in question cannot now exist in their original form. It must be supposed that some qualifying phrases have been omitted; that the vigour of some phrases has been intensified. It must be supposed that the documents have been so edited as to overstate the opinion of Columbus concerning the character of the lands which he had discovered and to exaggerate his estimate of their excellence. If, however, to this extent, these documents misrepresent his actual views, it is not unreasonable to suggest that they do so in other respects and that in general the editors exercised a somewhat wide discretion in their treatment of the materials upon which they worked.

That they did so appears to be indicated by another consideration. There is a marked difference in the literary style of the unabridged passages of the *Journal* and of the *Letter* and that of such documents as are regarded as being preserved in the exact form in which they were composed by Columbus. In the latter, the admiral is generally vague, wandering, obscure; Las Casas himself draws attention to the difficulty of understanding exactly what it was desired to convey. On the other hand, the *Letter* is almost a model of clarity; if it be admitted that the materials might have been rather more systematically arranged, there are no obscure sentences and the meaning is not open to diverse interpretations. In the Journal, there is certainly a wealth of repetition, but it is really inevitable repetition, and here again, even in the most lengthy quotations, there is no serious dubiety. This notable dissimilarity between the style of these documents and that of documents of a later date, indeed, almost suggests that they were of different authorship. It is possible, perhaps, to account for the variation by the supposition that the mind of Columbus was adversely affected by the events of his life after the discovery, that he became mentally confused and that his mental confusion was reflected in his writings. For this supposition, however, there is no substantial justification, and since it cannot be denied that the early documents have, to some extent, been edited, it is rather more reasonable to attribute their greater clarity to this fact.

It is, indeed, rather more probable than not that neither document was actually composed by Columbus. There are reasons for questioning whether he was, at that period, able to write ; if it cannot be proved that he was unable, it cannot be proved that he possessed the ability. There is no evidence at all that either the Journal or the Letter ever existed in his autograph. The statement which has been made that day by day, or night by night, he set down the occurrences of the first voyage is not supported by anything more substantial than the suggestion contained in the suspicious prologue and the fact that such was apparently the opinion of Ferdinand Columbus and of Las Casas, neither of whom was present and neither of whom makes an explicit statement to this effect. For the somewhat romantic accounts of the circumstances in which the Letter was written, there is no foundation at all.[1] It has, indeed, been merely assumed, without proof, that Columbus wrote this document with his own hand. When the variation of style is taken into account, it becomes perfectly probable that the admiral merely supplied verbally materials which were reduced to writing by a clerk.

In view of these circumstances, it is obvious that the possibility and even the probability of imperfect representation or of misrepresentation of the opinions of Columbus is very

[1] Cp. infra, pp. cxxxii et seq.

great. There is no guarantee that the copyists of the originals were accurate; since these copyists were rather editors, even the semblance of such a guarantee disappears. If even the originals themselves were the actual production of a clerk, there is a further opening for misrepresentation. In the process of giving literary form to dictated materials, changes of sense and variations of meaning would be far more likely than not to occur. If, in actual fact, Columbus gave expression to views not in accord with those generally entertained, it is clear enough that a clerk might have failed to grasp his meaning or might have deliberately abstained from incorporating such views in documents which he knew would probably come to the notice of some who were already inclined to regard Columbus as a madman. And finally, even if it be admitted that the originals were in the autograph of the admiral and that in the form in which the documents have been preserved editing has been of the slightest description, his reticence makes it very improbable that either in the *Journal* or the *Letter* he should have laid bare his soul. He had not done so when there was reason for so doing; there was now no such reason. The mere fact that he still awaited confirmation of the grants which had been provisionally made to him at Granada would serve to urge him to more than usual caution, since in all ages the word of princes has been notoriously unreliable and their ingratitude proverbial; to have revealed all, while his position was as yet insecure, would have been needlessly to have risked deprivation of the fruits of his discovery. If, as is possible, he suspected Martin Alonso Pinzón of designing to supplant him, he had, moreover, an additional reason for reserve.

The light which these two documents throw upon the question of the objective of Columbus is thus less fully illuminating than it might appear to be and than it has been regarded as being. It does indeed suffice to show that the idea of reaching the east by sailing west was present in the mind of the admiral; it does not suffice to show that this idea dominated him to the exclusion of other ideas. There is nothing to prove that Columbus set out with one clearly defined objective before him, save in so far as it was his intention to sail continuously westward until some land was reached. The classical view of his purpose is assuredly not disproved. It must be admitted to contain at least part of the truth. But it seems to be equally true that it cannot be legitimately stated with that assurance with which it has been urged. An impartial consideration of the evidence upon which it rests appears to show that some measure of revision is necessary and that dogmatism is misplaced.

17

That Columbus did not embark upon his first voyage merely with the idea of finding a new route to the Indies is clearly indicated by the terms of the two documents which embody the demands addressed by him to Ferdinand and Isabella and the grants made to him by the sovereigns. From these documents, it is evident that his purpose was not simply to reach Cipangu and Catayo, but that some other thought was in his mind. The exact nature of that thought is, indeed, not revealed; the documents do not, as they might perhaps have been expected to do, state with any approach to precision the objective of the proposed expedition. But upon the character of that objective they would seem to throw not inconsiderable light, and when they are considered in connexion with other available material, they perhaps make it possible to form a reasonably accurate view of that which was in the mind of the discoverer when he set out to discover.

It is true that the original text of the *Capitulations* of Santa Fé, the document which contains the final and probably the persistent demands of Columbus and the answers of the sovereigns to those demands, is not known to be in existence. It has been stated that this original is preserved in the *Libro-Registro de la Corona de Aragon*.[1] But it is only necessary to examine the document in question in order to see that this statement is erroneous. It opens with the following passage:

The demands made and which your highnesses give and grant

---

[1] E.g. by Ulloa (*op. cit.*, pp. 350 *et seq.*). He bases his theory of a Columbian pre-discovery of America largely upon the appearance of the past tense in the heading of this document.

to Don Christopher Columbus in some satisfaction for that which he has discovered in the Ocean Sea and for the voyage which, with the help of God, he is now to make in them in the service of your highnesses. . . .[1]

The appearance of the past tense has attracted the attention of various writers. Navarrete, somewhat arbitrarily, altered the past into the future, without noting the fact that he had so modified the text which he printed. Others, declining to accept the view that this correction was legitimate, have suggested that Columbus was so assured of the existence of the lands which he sought and so confident of success, that he regarded them as being already discovered. It has even been fancifully suggested that the past tense represents the fact, and that Columbus had already been to the New World before he made his application to Ferdinand and Isabella.

It is, however, entirely unnecessary to adopt any such explanation or to conclude with Navarrete that the text is corrupt, since it is perfectly clear that the copy in the *Libro-Registro* post-dates the first voyage. In it, Columbus is given the title of Don, which was not then a mere epithet of courtesy but implied nobility. The right to use this title, however, was not granted to him until after his return; in the grant made to him at Granada, he is not so described. Its appearance in the *Capitulations* has been explained as proof of the extreme vanity of the discoverer, but this explanation is untenable. Quite apart from the fact that Columbus is little likely to have been so unwise as to risk incurring the displeasure of Isabella, who was notoriously sensitive to any infringement of her prerogative, it is obvious that no royal clerk would have dared to confer upon him a title which he had not been granted. This particular copy of the document, moreover, is in the handwriting of Almazán, Ferdinand's alter ego, a man by temperament careful, scrupulously accurate, and even

---

[1] 'Las cosas suplicadas e que Vuestras Altezas dan é otorgan a don Xristoval de Colon en alguna satisfación de lo que ha descubierto en los mares oceanas y del viaje que agora con el ayuda de dios ha de hacer por allas en servicio de Vuestras Altezas.' The text of the *Capitulations* is printed in Navarrete (ii, pp. 7–8), and in *Rac. Col.* (II. ii, pp. 23–4): it is also given by Las Casas (i. 32), &c.

punctilious.[1] It is wholly inconceivable that he should have been guilty of so gross a breach of etiquette. It may be added that he was not concerned with the negotiations at Santa Fé, and that the royal assent to the demands of Columbus was witnessed not by him but by Juan de Coloma. The nature of the copy in the *Libro-Registro* thus becomes clear. After the return of Columbus, the grant made to him at Granada was confirmed at Barcelona; a record of the demands of Columbus and of the reply to them was obviously prepared by Almazán for the use of the sovereigns in the work of preparing the confirmatory grant. The past tense is thus accurately used in the preliminary statement of the nature of the document which follows, as the future tense is used with equal accuracy in the body of the document itself. Since Ferdinand and Isabella had already addressed Columbus as Don in their letter summoning him to the court to give an account of his voyage, the royal secretary naturally gives him that title.

But while the extant version of the *Capitulations* is not the original, there is no reason to suppose that it does anything but accurately represent the demands made by Columbus and the replies given to those demands. The exactness of the copy is, indeed, demonstrated by a certain variation between it and the text of the formal grant made at Granada. In the *Capitulations*, Columbus asks to be made viceroy and governor-general of the islands and *tierra firme* which he shall 'discover or gain', and to this request the sovereigns signify their assent. In the actual grant, he is promised this position in the islands and *tierra firme* which he shall 'discover and gain'. The sovereigns thus did not actually grant that which Columbus had asked and which they had at first promised. He sought to obtain a certain position in such territories as he might either discover or annex to the crown of Castile; he was promised eventually that he should receive this position in such territories as he might both discover and annex. Ferdinand and Isabella

---

[1] Bergenroth, *Calendar of Letters, Despatches, and State Papers: England and Spain: Vol. I, Henry VII*: Int., pp. xvii–xix; cxxxv.

[2] Cp. the text in Navarrete, ii, pp. 9–11, &c.

insisted upon the fulfilment of two conditions, instead of upon the fulfilment of one only.

Nor is it probable that this modification was due to some mere oversight, that it was anything but deliberate. Careless drafting was not characteristic of official documents in the reign of Ferdinand and Isabella, and in this case there is an apparently obvious reason for the change. In laying his proposals before the sovereigns, Columbus had undoubtedly been somewhat economical of exact detail; if there were no other reason for believing this to be so, it would seem to be sufficiently indicated by the fact that when he set out on his first voyage, he was expressly forbidden to go to La Mina da Ouro or to the coast of Guinea, where he might come into conflict with the Portuguese.[1] It is probable enough that he had not explained whether he intended to sail to the north, to the south, or to the west; 'in the Ocean Sea' is a somewhat vague description of the situation of the 'islands and *tierra firme*', especially when it is remembered that Columbus laid down that all seas are one, and it may be with some assurance asserted that Ferdinand and Isabella were not given any more accurate description. On the other hand, Columbus had insisted upon the value of the discoveries which he proposed to make; it may be legitimately presumed that he had at least allowed it to be understood that he was going to lands from which gold, precious stones, and spices might be obtained. The unanimous opinion of that age was that such lands could be found only in the south and east, and since Columbus had apparently offered no objection to the inhibition laid upon any expedition to the former, it was natural to assume that his design was to reach the latter.

To Ferdinand and Isabella, it must have therefore seemed to be almost palpably obvious that Columbus intended to find a new route to Asia; this conviction is expressed in the wording of the passport granted to him; it is declared that he

---

[1] 'con tanto que vos, ni el dicho Cristóbal Colón, ni otros algunos de los que fueren en las dichas carabelas, no vayan á la Mina, ni al trato de ella que tiene el Serenisimo Rey de Portugal, nuestro Hermano, porque nuestra voluntad es de guardar é que se guarde lo que con el dicho Rey de Portugal sobre esto tenemos asentado é capitulado:' *Royal provision addressed to Palos*, 10 Apr. 1492: Navarrete, ii, pp. 11–13). Cp. also the *Journal*, 9 Mar. 1493.

is going 'cum tribus caravelis armatis per maria oceania ad partes Indie'. It was not less obvious to them that this attempt would bring him to Cipangu and Catayo. Between Spain and those lands, it was supposed that there lay nothing more important than some islands, in all probability similar in character and extent to the Canaries and the Azores. The sovereigns were thus able more readily to accede to the demands of Columbus, when they felt assured that this was his design; they could feel that they were making no grant of any great moment. They would, perhaps, have felt far less hesitancy in acceding to his requests, had it not been that he himself obviously attached so great importance to the grants for which he asked.

At the eleventh hour, it would seem that Ferdinand and Isabella were assailed by a certain misgiving and were led to wonder whether, after all, they had not promised more than they were really prepared to grant. In any case, it was at the eleventh hour that they safeguarded their position by the substitution of a conjunctive for a disjunctive, thereby to all seeming rendering their concession innocuous. For if they were correct in their supposition that Columbus proposed to sail to Cipangu and Catayo, they were in reality granting him nothing at all. It would be impossible for him to claim that he had discovered Catayo, a land which had been visited and described by Marco Polo and from which ambassadors had come to Pope Eugenius IV. It would be hardly possible for him to allege that he had discovered Cipangu. It might, indeed, be urged that this land had never been visited by any one from Europe, but its position was known or was supposed to be known, a Grand Khan had attempted its conquest, and there were in existence accounts of its golden palaces and rich cities. Even, however, if Columbus could claim to have discovered these lands, it would assuredly be impossible for him to 'gain' them. He was setting out with three vessels, two of which were small; although in the passport they are described as 'armed', they were not actually equipped for warlike operations, nor were they so manned as to be fitted to engage in such operations. The expedition could obviously effect nothing against powerful and organized states, such as Cipangu and Catayo were reputed to be. It might, indeed, be apparently assumed with some certainty that it would be altogether ineffective for the purpose of 'gaining' any lands of importance. In the view of Ferdinand and Isabella, it might well seem that they had guarded against the danger that Columbus would become 'an over-mighty subject' as a result of the agreement which they had concluded with him.

It is hardly conceivable that Columbus should have imagined that with the means placed at his disposal he could 'gain' rich kingdoms in Asia. Even if he had been so optimistic, or if he had supposed that initial success would induce the sovereigns to accord him greater support, he must yet have been aware that hostile operations against monarchs in eastern Asia would be entirely contrary to the consistent policy of Ferdinand and Isabella. It was always their aim to cultivate friendly relations with all those oriental rulers who might be induced to oppose the Ottoman Turks. When the sultan of Egypt protested against the treatment of his co-religionists in Spain, Peter Martyr Angleria was sent on a mission to conciliate him and to negotiate, if possible, an alliance against the Ottoman.[1] Efforts were made to establish cordial relations with the Grand Khan and to secure the aid of the half-mythical Prester John, with the same idea of attacking the Turks from the east. Unless it be supposed that Columbus took the word 'ganar' to mean no more than 'gain the friendship', it cannot be supposed that he hoped to gain eastern Asia, and even were he to secure the friendship of the rulers of those lands, he would not thereby become a viceroy and governor-general.

On the other hand, Columbus would seem to have been perfectly satisfied with the grant made to him. He declares that the means supplied were generally adequate, although he does complain that smaller vessels would have been better suited for the work of exploration. After his discovery had been achieved, and when he is contemplating a second expedition, he does not seek to be given a large armament; it is for 'muy poquita ayuda' that he asks. It thus seems to

[1] Cp. Martyr, *De Legatione Babylonica.*

be obvious that the known or relatively known Asiatic lands cannot have been in his mind when he sought to be appointed viceroy and governor-general, that it was something else that he proposed to discover and gain.

Vignaud urged that this something was Antilla and that it was of the island or islands in the Atlantic that Columbus was thinking. But this view does not accord either with the terms of the *Capitulations* or with such indications as there are of the estimate formed by Columbus concerning the character of his own undertaking. For, however extensive it may have been supposed to be, however wealthy, Antilla was still an island; it was not *tierra firme*. And if the idea of reaching this island had been really predominant in the mind of Columbus, it is curious that he should never have mentioned it and that he should apparently have so easily abandoned his original intention, making no effort to discover it after his first voyage. Nor can it be readily supposed that he was content with the hope that he might win something equivalent to the Canaries or the Azores. That he was ambitious, and that he was even inordinately ambitious, can hardly be doubted; that he regarded his enterprise as something far greater than any which had been accomplished by a Bethencourt or a de Lugo is certain enough. That it was with him no question of some island which he might discover is proved by the inclusion of the term *tierra firme*.[1] It is, indeed, sufficiently clear that Columbus believed that he would discover and that he would be able to gain something of extreme importance and that this something was neither the eastern shores of Asia nor the islands which figured vaguely on maps of the Atlantic Ocean.

His objective, then, becomes uncertain. It may be admitted that he contemplated the possibility of reaching Cipangu and Catayo; so much is proved by the evidence of

[1] It may be suggested that the inclusion of the term *tierra firme* was merely due to the desire of Columbus to guard against the possibility that there might be some doubt whether land discovered was or was not insular. But this explanation of the terms of the demands is hardly consistent with the fact that Columbus was obviously anxious to reach something that was not an island. It is clear that he hoped that Cuba would prove to be *tierra firme* (cp. *infra*, pp. 116 *et seq.*; and the questionnaire which he addressed to the crews of his vessels, 12 June 1494: Navarrete, ii, pp. 143–9).

the passport, of the *Journal*, and of the *Letter*. It may be equally admitted that he contemplated the possibility of reaching Antilla or other islands in the Ocean; the evidence so laboriously collected by Vignaud may be taken to show this. But in his mind there was something more; there was something which he was to discover and gain and which was of sufficient moment to justify every claim which he put forward. To fix the exact position of the islands and *tierra firme* of which he thought is, however, impossible. No more can be asserted than that it can hardly have been in the known east or in the midst of the Atlantic, and that the hypothesis that he was already at least dimly aware of the existence of the American continent is hardly tenable. It may, perhaps, be suggested with some confidence that Columbus himself was without any clear conception of that which he hoped to discover and gain, that his objective was altogether vague and that his purpose, when he set out on his first voyage, was not to reach any very definite point. It was to perform a mission, the precise nature of which he did not know, although he might suspect that which would in due course be made known to him.

18

At the present day, for a man to embark upon a voyage with no more than the very vaguest conception of the destination to which that voyage will conduct him is in reality impossible. The form and the extent of the globe have been accurately determined; it can no longer be imagined that its shape is anywhere distorted by a protuberance, stretching for an unknown distance into the very infinity of space. The limits of the area of possible exploration are definitely fixed; no 'new world' remains to be discovered, nor can it be supposed that any great 'mysteries' are still to be solved. So true is this that it is not altogether easy to realize that in the later fifteenth century the position was radically different, that much which is now certain was then wholly uncertain, and that those who set out to explore did in very truth set out to penetrate the unknown. In that age, scientific knowledge was no more than in its infancy, or, it may be, in the process of rebirth; geographical conceptions were vague and somewhat fluid, and a great deal that is now realized to be utterly impossible was then held rather to be altogether within the bounds of probability. To the area of discovery there were then no recognized limits; the 'pear stalk', of which Columbus wrote, might even prove to be an isthmus uniting the known world with some celestial twin.

In such circumstances, the objective of any explorer, even of one whose temper was somewhat cold and practical, could hardly be more than provisional. He might set out with the deliberate intention of reaching a particular point; he was yet almost bound to admit that, for all that he could know, he might be carried to some entirely different goal, of the existence of which he had never dreamed. To a man of imagination, and it can hardly be denied that the majority of explorers were men of imagination, it was perhaps inevitable that the greatest doubt concerning the outcome of an expedition should seem to be merely rational. His objective might be ostensibly definite enough; it was so no more than ostensibly. The very quality which impelled him to seek to discover impelled him also to set no limits in his own mind upon that which he might reveal; he was almost bound to feel that it might be his destiny to reach a new world. The greater his imaginative gifts, the stronger was, of necessity, his conviction that the potentialities offered to him were incalculable.

In the special case of Columbus, it would seem that almost everything conspired to make this conviction exceptionally strong and accordingly to incline him to set before himself an objective so vague as hardly to be an objective at all. His imagination was at once vivid and untutored. He had in a marked degree the poetic temperament, which he reveals in his delight in the song of birds, in the scent of flowers, in every vision of natural beauty. 'All was so delightful,' he writes on one occasion, 'that nothing was lacking save the voice of the nightingale.' The *Journal* again and again reveals the spirit of the poet, and here, at least, it may be safely concluded that the true feelings of Columbus are preserved, since no one could suspect Las Casas of a secret addiction to poetry. But while he was thus imaginative,

Columbus was also a man of no more than imperfect education; whatever practical or theoretical knowledge he had gained, he had not acquired the power, and he had perhaps no great desire to possess the power, of cold and systematic reasoning. He was, moreover, credulous, even if he did not actually believe such stories as that of the tailed men in Cuba, which Bernáldez unhesitatingly rejected as either a jest or a fable.

Above all he was deeply religious and his religion was at once personal and mystical. He was fully assured that he was under the special care of the Almighty; again and again, he declares that God always guided and guarded him, and in his very trials, he saw the hand of Providence so forming his character and so shaping his ends that he might be the better fitted to fulfil that purpose which Heaven had decreed that he should fulfil. To him, moreover, signs were vouchsafed; he set out on his third voyage in the name of the Holy Trinity, and it was no mere coincidence that the first land sighted was the three peaks of Trinidad; here was a clear promise of success.

Yet, despite his limitations, Columbus undoubtedly possessed abilities above the ordinary, and of this he was himself fully aware. His mind was active and his intelligence acute, even if his learning were small and his judgement very imperfect. Others might have greater capacity of one kind or another; it was his special gift to appreciate the hidden importance of that of which they were merely aware, to understand that which they merely knew. He was profoundly convinced of his ability to perform great deeds; in his self-confidence there is, indeed, something of the sublime. It was thus impossible for him to believe that he was to pass all his days as a mere weaver or carder of wool, or as a subordinate in an Italian business house. It can hardly be doubted that even as a boy he resented the position of inferiority to which he was condemned by the obscurity and poverty of his family. That resentment is, indeed, revealed by his very ambition, by his earnest desire to wield authority, by his otherwise somewhat sordid anxiety to acquire wealth.

Nor was his revolt against his environment the vain complaining of a mean soul. It was rather that fruitful indignation which forces a man to endeavour to master his fate and which fills him with faith that his endeavour will not be barren of result. If any reliance can be placed upon the imperfect accounts of his early life, Columbus was still young when he resolved to escape from the hampering restrictions which circumstances imposed upon him. He did that which a Genoese of ambition and of an adventurous temper might naturally be expected to do; he turned to that career which had in the past proved to be the avenue to wealth and power for so many of his compatriots, and aspired perhaps to become, as they had become, a great merchant prince. It is hardly fanciful to suggest that he turned to the west, rather than to the east, because while eastern fields were already well tilled, those in the west were as yet almost virgin soil. It may be safely asserted that he embarked upon a new career with the more confidence because his mysticism convinced him that his intention was not his own, but the result of divine inspiration, because he felt that he was taking the first step on the path which would enable him to reach that goal which it was the will of God that he should reach.

While, however, so much was clear to him, perhaps no more was clear. He could not foresee to what goal he would be led, nor, it may be, did he wish to foresee it; for him, as for another mystic of more modern times, one step was enough; he did not ask to see the distant scene. He was content to wait upon that Providence in Whose care he was; more than once, he rebukes his own impatience and lack of faith, hearing the divine voice chiding him with his unbelief. But it was inevitable that he should expect a revelation to come, and it may be conjectured that it was in Madeira and the Azores that he felt that it had been given to him. There he heard stories, some of which are faithfully recorded in the *Journal*, in the pages of his son and of Las Casas, stories of mysterious islands dimly seen through the morning and evening mists; stories of bodies of men, belonging to some unknown race, which had been cast upon the shore, of pieces of wood, curiously carved, of branches of unfamiliar trees, borne to the

1 Cp. *Journal*, 9 Aug.: Ferdinand Columbus, c. 9: Las Casas, i. 13.

coast by the winds and currents of the Ocean. He heard also of
those who had ventured out in search of that which lay
hidden beyond the western horizon, of how some had returned, after having been tossed by storms and almost over-
whelmed by waves, their quest unfulfilled, of how others had
never come back. In all this there was enough to fire a mind
less imaginative than that of Columbus; its effect upon one
who was of such a temper as was he can only have been profound. When it is remembered that he was also reticent, con-
stitutionally disposed to feed upon his own thoughts and to
hide them from others, it is not extravagant to suppose that
all which he heard assumed a peculiar importance in his
mind and that in it he found that revelation of the divine will
for which his mysticism impelled him to look. Believing that
he had a mission to perform, always expecting that the
nature of this mission would be made known to him, it was
natural enough that he should here find it, that he should be
sure that it was the will of God that he should succeed where
all others had failed and that he should at last penetrate the
mystery of the Atlantic.

19

There seems to be little doubt that one marked characteristic
of the proposals which Columbus laid before the rulers of
Portugal and Castile was their vagueness; such is, at least, the
impression derived from such accounts as exist of his negotiations with Ferdinand and Isabella. He would appear to have
deliberately refused to admit into his confidence those for
whose assistance he was pleading, despite the fact that by
such refusal he could hardly fail to prejudice his chances of
securing that which he sought. To some extent, an explanation of his conduct may be found in his habitual reticence.
He was by nature so cautious as to be somewhat suspicious;
it is not unreasonable to suggest that he dreaded lest his
ideas, of the greatness and value of which he was profoundly
convinced, might be appropriated by others and he himself
thus cheated of the reward which he so earnestly coveted. To
some extent also, an explanation is perhaps to be found in
his belief that his project was not of mere human devising;

that it was not permissible for him to anticipate or to attempt to anticipate a divine revelation.

But there is a further and more obvious explanation. If it were his primary purpose to solve the mystery of the Atlantic, it is clear that he could not be anything but somewhat vague; he was himself obviously unaware of the exact nature of that mystery. He might be convinced that the result of its solution would be wonderful, that it would entail the discovery of new lands, rich and populous. Of this, he might be so assured that he could speak of those lands as if he had already visited them, or as if he had in some way gained certain knowledge concerning them. He could not, however, describe their exact situation, even if he had desired to do so. They were to be reached by the path of a voyage into the Atlantic; of so much he might be sure. Of more than this he could not be sure. All else constituted part of that very mystery which it was his purpose and his destiny to solve.

Looking back at the present day upon his first voyage, knowing what were the actual results of that voyage and realizing that its issue was bound to be the discovery of the continent which is interposed between western Europe and eastern Asia, it is somewhat hard to appreciate even the possibility that Columbus had no clear conception of that which was to follow from his expedition. It is, perhaps, easy to conceive that he should have fancied that he would reach not a new world, but the farthest extremity of the old; or that he should have imagined that his voyage would bring him to the half-mythical islands of the west. It is far from easy to picture him as having perhaps neither Asia nor Antilla primarily in his mind, although so much is very forcibly suggested by the very nature of the demands which he made. That it was upon the west, which, as Bernáldez puts it, was in truth the east, that the mind of Columbus was fixed, has indeed been regarded as almost axiomatic.

Despite the consensus of opinion in favour of this view, however, its absolute justice is yet open to doubt. It is true enough that it was upon a westerly course that he steered; it is true enough that upon more than one occasion he insisted that no great distance parted the shores of Spain from those of Catayo, and that his conviction upon this point almost certainly played a very important part in encouraging him to embark upon his enterprise. It cannot be denied that he was assured that to the west across the Atlantic there lay land which could be reached or that to reach this land was his deliberate purpose; nor is it really contestable that he believed that he would thus arrive, if not at the dominions of the Grand Khan, at least at some point adjacent to those dominions. But it may be questioned whether this was his whole purpose, whether when he at last sighted Guanahani he felt that he had done more than complete an initial step, whether he would have felt that he had done more even if that island had proved to be Cipangu, even if he had found in the West Indies great cities, mighty sovereigns, and a vast and civilized population.

It has been noted as an apparently curious fact that Columbus did not follow the precise course which would seem to have been suggested in the letter of Toscanelli and which might have been expected to lead him directly to Quinsay. In place of steering immediately westwards, he turned at first somewhat to the south, proceeding to the Canaries and only setting out upon his actual voyage from those islands. This circumstance has, indeed, been taken to indicate that he owed nothing to the Florentine philosopher; it has been taken also to show that Columbus had some special knowledge of the prevailing winds in the Atlantic and of the ocean currents. A simpler and a more rational explanation of his action is afforded by the reflection that the Canaries were the most westerly possession of the Castilian crown. Upon every ground, it was obviously wise to make them the starting-point of the actual voyage of discovery. Columbus thus gave himself the opportunity of taking in at the last possible moment requisite supplies; casks could be filled with water, the stock of wood could be replenished and provisions taken on board. It was possible also for his vessels to be refitted; in actual fact, the rig of the *Niña* was there changed and the rudder of the *Pinta* repaired.[1] Upon psychological grounds,

---

[1] *Journal*, 9 Aug.

his deviation from the direct course westward was equally advisable. It had been a matter of some difficulty to find crews prepared to brave the dangers of a voyage into an unknown sea;[1] there is no doubt that every reduction in the length of time during which they would be out of sight of land was a gain, lessening the possibility of disaffection among the men and minimizing the ever-present danger of panic terror. When, however, all this has been admitted, it is still possible that a certain significance does attach to the fact that Columbus steered somewhat to the south, and it is, indeed, possible that he would have done so even if considerations of expediency had not been operative. For it is at least possible that it was upon the potentialities of the south, rather than upon those of the west, that his hopes were really fixed, and that to turn somewhat southward from the due westerly course was really in accord with his conception of the ultimate purpose of his enterprise.

If the evidence of the *Journal* may be accepted on this point, Columbus, before he set out on his first voyage, was instructed to avail himself of Portuguese harbours and to apply to the Portuguese authorities for such supplies as he might need. At the same time, he was expressly forbidden to go to Mina da Ouro or to the coast of Guinea. An obvious reason for this inhibition is to be found in the desire of Ferdinand and Isabella to avoid the danger of friction with the Portuguese, the African coast having been recognized as the preserve of Portugal since the treaty which ended the War of Succession. If, however, it had been clear that the design of Columbus was to proceed due west and that the west alone was in his mind, the prohibition would seem to have been somewhat superfluous. It would, perhaps, have been rather worse than superfluous. The dangers of the projected voyage were undoubtedly dreaded by the crews of the three vessels; it was obviously wise to avoid doing anything which might serve to increase that dread. But to proclaim 'in all the ports of Andalusia' that the route to be followed would not lie along the African shore and that it would therefore lead into the trackless expanse of the ocean was assuredly calculated to

[1] Las Casas, i. 24.

excite alarm amongst those who were disposed to feel terror and to anticipate disaster. There must, therefore, have been some good reason for the issue of the order. It is possible, indeed, that this reason may be found in the desire of the sovereigns to discover the actual intentions of Columbus, and that they forbade him to sail along the African shore in order to find whether he had any wish to do so.

To this explanation of the order, however, there is the obvious objection that it would have been a somewhat elaborate method of securing information, which when secured would be no more than negative and in no sense precise. It is equally possible and more probable that the prohibition was designed to guard against a danger, in the existence of which Ferdinand and Isabella had some reason to believe; it may be reasonably supposed that Columbus had somehow created the impression that he was looking towards the south rather than towards the west. If he had produced any such impression, it was obviously advisable and even essential to warn him that he must not so act as to infringe the stipulation, formal or implied, of the agreements between Castile and Portugal. It would be illegitimate to assert with any approach to dogmatism that this is the true explanation. It is, after all, an incontrovertible fact that Columbus sailed west across the Atlantic and it would be a somewhat wild hypothesis that he had not originally intended to do so. At the same time, there is some reason for thinking that, while Columbus proposed to reach the opposite shore of the ocean, his deeper purpose, or if not his purpose at least his hope, was to attain other lands than those which, whether Asiatic or non-Asiatic, lay directly to the west of Spain beyond the Atlantic.

There is a curious characteristic of the notes, on the *Imago Mundi* and other works, which has, perhaps, not received the attention which it deserves and which may serve to elucidate the problem of his actual design. In those notes, it is true enough that Columbus, or their author if he were another than Columbus himself, marks the various references to eastern Asia, but it may be added that he marks also references to the characteristics of lands which were certainly not Asiatic. It cannot be said that he lays any particular emphasis upon those passages which concern Asia beyond the Ganges, as opposed to such as refer to Asia within the Ganges. There is, however, a particular type of passage to which he does seem to wish to draw very special attention. If he may be said to underline every reference to Catayo, he may be said to underline doubly every reference to that which lay south of the Equator.[1] It is curious that whereas in general the notes do not reveal any personal opinion, those which refer to the south do contain such revelation. He marks every statement to the effect that in this part of the world the climate is very temperate and that the lands there are populous, and he adds with almost obvious satisfaction that the discoveries of the Portuguese have proved the truth of the conjectures of early writers. He notes that some have regarded the south as the highest and therefore as the most excellent part of the globe, and it is clear that with this opinion he is in agreement, rather than with the contrary opinion that the north was the region nearest the heavens. He accepts also the view that in the south, and not in the east, lies the Earthly Paradise, as he afterwards found there that distortion which he conceived to characterize 'the other hemisphere' and of the importance of which he was so deeply convinced.

This insistence upon the south is the more remarkable if it be admitted that the intention of the notes was to produce witness to the great material wealth of the lands which he had discovered. For whatever else might be supposed to be true concerning those lands, it was certain that no part of them lay to the south of the equator; so far as they were concerned, it was of no interest whether the south was or was not temperate or inhabited. If his attention were really fixed on the west, whether as the west or as the gateway to the east, his peculiar interest in something which was neither west nor east can be explained only by the supposition that he was indulging idle curiosity. That supposition, however, hardly accords with his intensity of interest, and it so accords the less because Columbus, throughout his life, would appear to have been possessed of the power of concentration and to have

---

[1] Cp. notes 22, 24, 29, on Pius II (*Rac. Col.* I. ii, pp. 293–4): and notes 16, 18, 20, 23, 33, and 40, on the *Imago Mundi* (*Rac. Col.* I. ii, pp. 275, 376, 378, 379).

been little disposed to concern himself with anything which did not seem to be germane to his great purpose. It would appear to be more probable that the explanation of this characteristic of the notes is to be found in the fact that the south was prominently in his mind and that he looked to the south for that which he hoped to find.

It would seem to be also probable that it was not only in later life that this was the case. It is true that the annotations would appear rather to postdate than to antedate the discovery, despite the contrary view held by no less an authority than De Lollis, and that they cannot therefore be taken necessarily to represent the opinions of Columbus at the earlier period. It is further reasonable to suppose that his opinions developed with the passage of time and as a result of the experience gained upon his voyages. On the other hand, there is no evidence of fundamental change in his ideas. So far as can be judged, the views which he entertained at the time of his last were in essentials those which he entertained at the time of his first voyage; he would seem to have found reasons rather to confirm than to correct his conceptions. When, therefore, in the notes he shows a special interest in the south, it is not unfair to presume that this interest was no new thing and that he had felt it from the first. But if this were so, it almost necessarily follows that his ultimate objective lay there.

That it did so would appear to be confirmed by his conduct on his first voyage. After he had effected his landfall at Guanahani, he made his way to Cuba, to the southward. On reaching the shore of that island, he very soon turned to the eastward; having come to the strait which divides Cuba from Española, he did not pass through it, but continued in the same direction, until the wreck of the *Santa Maria* brought further exploration to a close. He thus constantly failed to aim directly westward, as he might have been expected to do if the ultimate west were his goal, and still more if he had seriously wished to reach the dominions of the Grand Khan, since he was convinced that they lay at no great distance to the westward.[1] To some extent, the course

---

[1] Cp. *Journal*, 28 Oct., 1 Nov., and *infra*, p. 12.

which he followed may be explained by a wish to verify the information which he had received from the natives whom he had taken; to some extent, it may be explained by the direction of the wind and by the condition of his ships, to the somewhat unsatisfactory state of which there are references in the *Journal*. But it may be questioned whether it can be fully so explained. He declares that, if his vessels had been better suited for the purpose, or if Pinzón had not parted company with him, he would have continued the work of exploration,[1] but it is noteworthy that he would have done so apparently not to the westward but to the southward. So far as he states his desire in this respect, it was to go to the Carib Islands and to the island of women.

This same tendency to steer always to the south, rather than to the west, as soon as the actual passage of the Atlantic had been achieved, appears equally in his later voyages. On his second voyage, instead of following the course which he had previously taken, he steered much farther to the south; on his third voyage, his course was still more southerly. That this variation cannot be wholly explained on the supposition that he wished to avail himself of favourable winds, is really proved by his own account of his unhappy experiences on the third voyage, and by the whole tenour of his letter to the sovereigns.[2] In the case of his last voyage, his aim appears even more clearly. It has often been remarked that it almost seems as if some perverse fate prevented Columbus from anticipating Grijalva and Cortés, that he was so near to the discovery of Mexico that it appears to be bitterly ironical that he failed to make the discovery. On his first voyage, if, after reaching Cuba, he had sailed west instead of east, he would almost certainly have reached Florida, and by this initial discovery he might easily have been led to penetrate farther into the Gulf of Mexico, to explore its northern coast and hence to reach its western extremity. On his last voyage, having sighted Cape Honduras, instead of following the coast of the gulf towards the modern Guatemala, he turned southward, with the result that in place of reaching those rich and civilized lands at the door of which he was, he discovered

[1] Cp. *Journal*, 3 Jan., 8 Jan.   [2] Cp. *infra*, vol. ii, pp. 2 *et seq.*

Darien and Nombre de Dios. That he adopted that course which he did adopt was no doubt because he was in search of some strait, but it may be reasonably urged that the strait which he wished to find was one which should lead him not west but south. There is, indeed, at least some ground for arguing that the aim of Columbus has been imperfectly appreciated and that he conceived the islands and mainland, of which he aspired to be viceroy and governor-general, from which he hoped to win wealth beyond that of Solomon, to lie not at the extremity of the east, but in the unknown south.

20

When the conception which Columbus would appear to have formed concerning the nature of his enterprise is considered, the suggestion that it was in the south that he hoped to find the goal of his desire acquires a somewhat greater probability. It is certain that at a later date he believed himself to be the missioner of God, destined to reveal a new Heaven and a new Earth; it is at the very least arguable that from the very first he entertained this belief, and that even before he had formed any idea of the project which he ultimately undertook to execute, he regarded himself as having been chosen by God to do some great thing. There is at least some reason for thinking that, when he sailed from Palos, he was convinced that he was setting forth to make a discovery more momentous than any which had hitherto been made, and that he was destined to penetrate to those parts of the globe to which none had as yet penetrated, which until then had been hidden from the knowledge of mankind because God had decreed that they should so remain hidden.

At the same time, it is hardly questionable that he was fully assured that his enterprise would be productive both of honour and of material gain, and that in this honour and gain he would himself share to the full. The very terms of the demands which he made proves beyond doubt that in the accomplishment of his undertaking he saw the means by which he was to be rescued from obscurity and poverty and to win fame and wealth, by which he was to be enabled to exchange his humble for a noble status. If he believed that God

willed that through him many souls should be saved, Christendom enriched and the Holy Places rescued,[1] it was
assuredly also his belief that God would not forget His servant or deny to him that recompense which was the just due
of one who was to labour so fruitfully in the service of Heaven.
Over the lands which he was to discover, he was to be ruler;
from those lands, he was to derive riches; in them, he was to
find the fullest satisfaction for an ambition which was not to
be appeased by a little.

It would thus seem to be also true that his real objective
must have lain in some quarter of the globe in which he might
find territories to acquire, which should supply him with the
means of satisfying his utmost desire for power and wealth.
But, if so much be admitted, it is hardly possible to believe
that his true goal was either the islands of the Atlantic or the
Far East. The former were, after all, no more than islands;
even the fabled Antilla could not be regarded as the *tierra
firme* of the *Capitulations* or be held to constitute a territory
of such importance that its discovery could be described as
the revelation of a new Heaven and a new Earth. Cipangu
and Catayo, so far as their wealth and their populousness
were concerned, might seem to constitute a more worthy
objective, and by opening a new route to them, many souls
might be won for Christ and a vast increase of wealth secured
for Christendom and more especially for Castile. Here also
Columbus might hope to find riches for himself, but he could
not hope to find that for which he seems to have cared more
than for riches, that power and position for which he so
carefully stipulated. Even in his most optimistic moments,
he can hardly have anticipated that he would ever become
viceroy and governor-general of the dominions of the Grand
Khan, or that he would 'gain' Cipangu which the Grand
Khan himself had failed to subdue.

And if his true objective can thus hardly be supposed to
have been the islands of the Ocean or the Far East, it can
still less be supposed that it was some vast, unknown land

---

[1] 'que así . . . protesté á Vuestras Altezas que toda la ganancia d'esta mi
empressa se gastase en la conquista de Hierusalem, y Vuestras Altezas se rieron
y dixeron que les plazia ' (*Journal*, 26 Dec.).

lying between the shores of Spain and those of Catayo. Such a supposition is precluded by the very nature of those cosmographical views which Columbus undoubtedly held. He was convinced that the distance which divided west from east across the Ocean was small; in the intervening space, it could not be believed that anything of greater moment than some islands was situated. It is true that the mere fact that such is the logical consequence of his conceptions does not in itself prove that it was accepted by Columbus; it would be illegitimate to argue that he necessarily reasoned so clearly. There is, however, evidence enough that in this case his conclusions followed from his premises. The *Journal* and the *Letter* show that he believed the islands which he discovered to be Asiatic; Cuba, to him, was undoubtedly Cipangu, and the natives of Guanahani were almost certainly at war with the Grand Khan. Nor did this belief in any wise distress him; if he experienced disappointment, it was rather because he failed to meet with conclusive proof that his belief was just.[1] If, however, he had anticipated that before reaching Asia, he would arrive at that *tierra firme*, to the government of which he had stipulated that he should be appointed, it would seem that so far from being anxious to prove that he had attained Cipangu and the neighbourhood of Catayo, he would have been anxious to find the exact contrary. It would thus appear to be also obvious that Columbus cannot have done other than accept the logical consequences of his cosmographical ideas in this respect, and hence have hoped to find his objective in some quarter other than in the space which intervened, according to those ideas, between Spain and the Far East.

Since, however, that quarter cannot have been the north, from which it was universally believed that no great riches could be derived, it seems to follow that it must have been in the south that he expected to find his ultimate goal. And if he did so, it was no more than natural. For it was in the south that Marco Polo had placed those innumerable islands, of which he had dimly heard; it was of islands in the same quarter than Mandeville had collected such marvellous stories. In the south also lay that *Terra Australis*, which

[1] Cf. *infra*, p. 4.

could be justly regarded as *tierra firme*, which figured in ancient maps, and which it is obvious that Columbus regarded as being anything but a desolate land of ice and snow. On the contrary, it was the stalk end of the pear, a region of infinite potentialities, a veritable 'new earth' and perhaps the gateway to a 'new heaven'. It was further assuredly a *terra incognita*, to which man had never penetrated, and filled with peoples who had never heard of the Gospel of Christ. In it might indeed be expected to be found all that should enable Columbus to realize his most ambitious dreams.

If this were actually his ultimate purpose, the reticence which he displayed in his negotiations with Ferdinand and Isabella becomes immediately understandable. It was very generally believed that the extreme south was both uninhabited and uninhabitable, a region of ice and snow, whence nothing of value could be derived. To have declared openly that he sought help in order to make an expedition to that quarter of the globe would have been almost to court a contemptuous refusal. The voyage which he proposed in his own mind, if such were indeed his aim, was, moreover, one so novel in conception and for so vast a distance, that its accomplishment would have appeared to be altogether impossible. Those who were to form the crews of his vessels were terrified at the thought of endeavouring to cross the Atlantic; they would have been far more terrified, had it been suggested to them that when the Atlantic had been crossed, no more than the first and perhaps the easier part of their voyage would have been achieved. For Columbus to allow it to be believed that the distance to be traversed was at least calculable was no more than necessary prudence.

Nor can it be held that the course which he actually followed is inconsistent with the supposition that his true objective was neither the extreme west nor the Far East. It was advisable and it was perhaps essential so to steer as to be as far as possible in constant touch with land. To follow the African coast would have been the most obvious route, but that route was closed to him. It was thus necessary to find some other coast which might be followed, and it might well be expected that across the ocean Africa was paralleled by

Asia. To sail west until land was reached and then to turn southward along its shore would be the method which would naturally suggest itself, and it is at least certain that when he had reached the Indies, Columbus does seem to have adopted such a course until the wreck of the *Santa Maria* prevented further exploration.

It may, therefore, be suggested that there is some justification for the view that it was in the south that the true objective of Columbus lay. To assert dogmatically that this was so would be, indeed, illegitimate. Neither before, nor during, nor after, his first voyage, did he ever declare his aim in unequivocal terms; he sought 'the Indies', but the exact application of that term in his mind cannot be determined. It is, however, a fact that he sought to establish relations with the Grand Khan and to deliver to that potentate the letters of which he was the bearer, and it would seem to be therefore idle to deny that to reach the eastern shores of Asia was at least part of his purpose. At the same time, it is difficult, if it be not impossible, to maintain that this was his whole purpose. The suggestion that it was appears to be inconsistent both with the terms of the *Capitulations* of Santa Fé and with the course which he followed after he had reached Guanahani. There is thus a possibility that his real purpose has hitherto been no more than partially understood, and that to cross the Atlantic to the shores of Asia was no more than a means to an end. However this may be, it is hardly questionable that, whereas in the Far East Columbus could scarcely have expected to make the revelation of 'a New Heaven and a New Earth', in the south he could expect to do so; there, in less grandiloquent language, he could hope to find the means by which he might acquire riches, fame, and honour, and by which 'the poor stranger' might be transformed into 'Don Cristóbal Colón', a viceroy and governor-general, taking rank among the mightiest princes of the earth.

NOTES ON THE DOCUMENTS

1. *Letter of Columbus: on the First Voyage*[1]
(pp. 2–19)

THE original of the letter of Columbus, describing the general results of his first voyage, is not known to be now in existence. Several versions of it, however, have been preserved, and while no one of them can be regarded as an exact copy of the original, it is possible from them to reconstruct with some approach to certainty the text of the lost document. The materials for such reconstruction are four Spanish and three Italian versions, and a Latin version, extracts preserved in the *Historia de los Reyes Católicos* of *Andrés Bernáldez*, and the metrical Italian rendering made by Giulano Dati.

Of the different versions of the letter, the position of primary importance must obviously be assigned to the four Spanish. These are:

(A) [2] The folio.

This consists of two leaves, the text on a full page measuring 9 inches by 6 inches (246 mm. × 169 mm.). The recto of folio 1 and that of folio 2 both contain forty-seven lines; the verso of folio 1 contains forty-eight lines and that of folio 2 sixteen lines. The extra line on the verso of folio 1 is partially obliterated and is imperfectly repeated as the first line of the recto of folio 2, which suggests that each full page was intended to consist of forty-seven lines and that the forty-eighth line of the verso of folio 1 was due to faulty printing, or that the work of printing the letter was entrusted to two persons working simultaneously. The letter begins with an initial 'S' in a woodcut. No date or place of printing is given, but it is universally agreed that the date should be April–May 1493.

Only one copy of this edition is known. It was reproduced in facsimile by Maisonneuve of Paris in 1889,[3] and having

---

[1] By far the most valuable and masterly discussion of the various questions concerning this letter is that by De Lollis, *Scritti di Colombo* (*Rac. Col.* I. i, pp. xxv–lxvii), upon which this note is mainly based.

[2] The letters used to distinguish the different versions are adopted from De Lollis (*Rac. Col.* I. i, pp. xxv–xxvi).

[3] *La Lettre de Christophe Colomb annonçant la découverte du Nouveau Monde.*

been purchased by Bernard Quaritch, was again reproduced in facsimile in London in 1891, an English translation, an introduction and notes being added by 'M.K.' (Michael Kerney).[1] The unique copy is now in the Lenox Collection of the New York Public Library.[2]

(B) The quarto.

This consists of four leaves, the text on a full page measuring 6 inches by 4 inches (150 mm. $\times$ 100 mm.). Each page contains thirty-two lines, except the verso of leaf 4, which contains twenty-five lines. The letter begins with an initial 'S' in a woodcut. No date or place of printing is given, but it is agreed that the date must be 1493.

Only one copy of this edition is known. It was left in 1852 by Baron Pietro Custodi to the Ambrosian Library at Milan, where it now is. A copy of this version was made by hand for the marquis Girolamo d'Adda in 1866 and lithographic examples were published. Some years later, five examples were fabricated by hand from the lithographic copy and were sold as newly discovered originals, by a native of Bologna, who confessed his fraud to De Lollis in 1892. In the interval, one of these fabrications was bought in London and there published,[3] being afterwards sold in the United States; the fraud was detected and a lawsuit followed.[4] There is no doubt that the only extant copy of the quarto is that in the Ambrosian Library.

(C) The MS. copy from the Archives of Simancas.

In 1818 Tomás Gonzalez, the custodian of the archives at Simancas, made a copy of a MS. of the letter which was then in his care. This MS. was then in a very damaged condition and it no longer exists. From the copy made by Gonzalez, Navarrete printed his version of the letter in 1825.[5]

---

[1] *The Spanish Letter of Colombus to Luis de Sant' Angel.*

[2] Both the folio and the quarto are reproduced in facsimile in Thacher, *Christopher Columbus* (ii, pp. 17–20, 33–40). An English translation of the letter is also given (pp. 21–26).

[3] The *Letter in Spanish of Christopher Columbus to Luis de Sant' Angel* (London, 1889). This volume must, of course, be distinguished from the volume with somewhat similar title published by Quaritch in 1891 (cp. *supra*).

[4] Cp. Thacher, *op. cit.*, ii, p. 41, note 1.

[5] Navarrete, *Colección de los Viages* &c., i, pp. 167–175.

(D) The MS. copy from the Colegio mayor of Cuenca.

This MS. was contained in a small quarto MS. volume, endorsed as having belonged to Don Juan de Sanfélices, Colegio mayor of Cuenca. The volume began with extracts from the *Ceremonial del Consejo de las Indias* and ended with other documents relating to the New World. It was bought at Valencia by Varnhagen, and the letter of Columbus was printed by him, but not in facsimile, in 1858.[1] After the discovery of B, Varnhagen published a revised edition of his volume in 1869,[2] supplying a critical consideration of D in the light of the discovery of the quarto. The MS., printed by Varnhagen, is known only through his account of it, and it has now disappeared.

When Varnhagen first printed D, he was of opinion that it was an accurate copy of the original letter ; after the discovery of B, he frankly admitted that his estimate had been erroneous. It is uncertain whether the MS. was in a sixteenth or a seventeenth century hand, but the later date is the more probable, having regard to the other contents of the volume and to the fact that the Cuenca copy of the letter of Columbus of 1502 undoubtedly dates from the seventeenth century.[3] It is not unlikely that D should be regarded as an attempt to construct an accurate version of the letter, the printed Spanish text or some MS. copy being revised in the light of the Latin translation and of the *Historie* of Ferdinand Columbus and the *Historia General* of Herrera. In any case, the value of D is dubious, and its apparently greater accuracy cannot be regarded as proving that it was in reality made from the lost original or that it exactly reproduces that original.

Such exact reproduction is, in fact, not found in any of the four versions. It was at one time supposed that the Simancas MS. from which C was copied was the actual letter sent by Columbus. This supposition, however, was certainly due to a misunderstanding. When he made his copy, Gonzalez

---

[1] Under the pseudonym, Genaro H. de Volafan: *Primera epistola del Almirante D. Cristóbal Colón.*

[2] El Seudomino de Valencia: *Carta de Cristóbal Colón.*

[3] De Lollis (*op. cit.*, I. i, p. lii).

appended to it a note to the effect that it was made from 'the original document' in the Archives of Simancas,[1] and this note was taken to be an assertion on his part that the MS. was the original letter. There is, however, no doubt that it should not be taken to mean more than that the copy made was accurate; the document was only 'original' as opposed to the copy made by Gonzalez. The subsequent discovery of B, and afterwards of A, sufficed to show that C could not be regarded as an entirely faithful reproduction of the letter.

Nor is that character possessed either by B or by A. The final word upon the inter-relationship of A B C and upon the relationship between each of these and the original has been written by De Lollis. He has shown that while B is an edition of A, it is an edition made with reference to the source of A. That source, in the opinion of De Lollis, was x_1, a copy of x, which in turn was a copy of the original, both x and x_1 being now lost. On the assumption that D must be given some value, De Lollis described the relationship of these four copies as being:

If, however, the final estimate apparently reached by Varnhagen concerning his own possession be accepted, the greater accuracy of D ceases to necessitate the supposition of the intervention of x_1 between A(B)C and x, the lost copy of the original letter. In this case, the relationship of the four versions would, perhaps, be more accurately represented as:

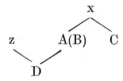

---

[1] The note reads: 'Está copiada literalmente del documento original que obra en este Real Archivio de Simancas; en el Despacho y correspondencia general Interior de Estado al número 1⁰' (Navarrete, i, p. 175).

z representing the materials also used by the compiler of D, the Latin translation of the letter and the information contained in Ferdinand Columbus and Herrera. On the other hand, the very doubt which exists concerning the actual character of D makes it as impossible entirely to ignore it as it is impossible confidently to rely upon it.

The fact that no one of the extant versions can be regarded as exactly representing the original has made it possible to advance a hypothesis concerning that original which, although untenable, must be noticed. In his catalogue[1] of his books, Ferdinand Columbus includes the entry:

'Christoforo Colon—Letera enviada al escribano deracion —1493—En catalan.—4643⁰.'

The German translation of the letter, dating from 1497, is said to have been made from Catalan and Latin.[2] With these facts as a basis, it has been suggested that the original letter of Columbus was written in Catalan.[3] It is pointed out that there are said to be forty-two Catalanisms in A, a number reduced to twenty-two in B.[4] It is added that De Lollis, while arguing that some of the so-called 'Catalanisms' are in reality 'Italianisms', was so impressed by the appearance of Catalanisms in A and B, as to put forward as a possible explanation the suggestion that A B were prepared from an editio princeps printed at Barcelona.[5] It is then contended that a more rational explanation is that the copy from which the printed versions were made was a translation into Castilian of a Catalan original, certain Catalan words remaining untranslated. It is urged that the style of the extant letter, which is admittedly different from that of the other letters of Columbus, is due to the fact of translation by someone very familiar with Castilian.

To this hypothesis, the ingenuity of which may be admitted,

---

[1] The catalogue has been printed in facsimile by Mr. A. M. Huntingdon. The Catalan version of the letter of Columbus has disappeared.

[2] *Eyn schon hubsch lesen von etlichen insulen die de in kuntzen zyten funden synd durch de konig von hispania, und sight vo grossen wonderlichen dingen die in deselbe insulen synd. Getuetschet uss der katilanischen zungen unduss dem latin zu Ulm. Barlomero kustler: strassburg,* 1497.

[3] Ulloa, *Xristo-Ferens Colom*, pp. 64–79.

[4] The list is given by 'M.K.', *Spanish letter of Columbus*, p. 29.

[5] De Lollis (*op. cit.*, I. i, p. lxi).

there would seem, however, to be a number of sufficiently weighty objections. Of the forty-six alleged 'Catalanisms' in A, only ten can be legitimately regarded as such; of the twenty-two in B, only seven. Even of these, two, *mugers* for *mugeres*, and *quals* for *quales*, might be reasonably explained as mere printing errors. Others, such as the final *-es* for *-as* and the final *-t* for *-d*, would seem not to supply any very convincing argument in favour of the idea of a Catalan original; they might rather be an argument in favour of the supposition that the compositor was a Catalan. The conclusions drawn from the 'Catalanisms' in A B appear to become rather more fanciful when it is remembered that C, which was certainly derived from the same original as A B, contains only two examples of possibly Catalan words and these are both place-names.

Even were the suggestion that the 'Catalanisms' may be explained as the result of faulty printing to be rejected, it must be remembered that Columbus was not so well educated as to have been likely to have been free from the use of dialect words and forms. There is no doubt that the spoken language of Genoa at that time was very similar to that of Barcelona, and hence words which are apparently Catalan, such as *calavera* for *caravela*, may equally well be Genoese. If Columbus wrote the letter with his own hand, blunders in spelling and the appearance of words in common use among the sailors of the Mediterranean ports would be very probable. If it be supposed rather that he dictated the letter, it is doubtful whether, in view of the character of his crew, he could find a very highly educated amanuensis; it is the more doubtful because Rodrigo de Escovedo had been left at La Navidad.

It may be admitted that the style of the letter is unlike that of the other letters of Columbus, but this is no very strong argument in favour of the idea of a translation. It is certain that the letter, as preserved, has been subjected to editing; it is feasible to suggest that before it was printed, it was revised in such a way as to give its style that 'official' character which it was noted by Varnhagen as possessing.[1]

[1] *La carta de Cristóbal Colón.*

A further objection to the hypothesis that Columbus wrote the original letter in Catalan is found in the fact that there is no trace of evidence that he was acquainted with that language. It is true that here and there in his other writings words can be found which may perhaps be Catalan. This, however, is no more than might be expected in the case of a man, not very well educated, who had long associated with sailors; the words may be most reasonably be regarded as examples of the *lingua franca* which has always been current in Mediterranean ports.

Nor is it difficult to find an explanation for the appearance of a Catalan version of the letter in the library of Ferdinand Columbus. The date which he gives in his entry is not necessarily to be regarded as that of the production of the copy; the Catalan edition may have been produced at a much later period. That the progress of discovery between the date of the first voyage of Columbus and that of the compilation of his son's catalogue should have aroused interest in a port such as Barcelona can hardly be regarded as surprising. If this interest led to the production of a version of the first account of the discovery in the language of that port, that might be expected. It is far less astonishing that there should be a Catalan, than that there should be a German version. No great importance need be attached to the statement in the Strassburg edition that it was translated from 'Catalan and Latin'. That statement may be explained as due to ignorance on the part of the translator, who associated the letter with Barcelona and therefore supposed that a language with which he was not very perfectly acquainted was Catalan; his imperfect knowledge of Castilian may be gathered from the fact that he had recourse to the Latin version.

The place at which A and B were printed cannot be exactly determined. It has been very generally held that A was printed in Spain and probably at Barcelona, while B was printed in Italy and probably at Naples. Spanish printing of A is strongly suggested by the appearance of the initial rr, and if A were printed in Spain at all, Barcelona becomes the most probable place of printing, since the letter was received, and a press was in existence there. The 'Catalanisms' may be urged as an additional argument in favour of this view. On the other hand, De Lollis has pointed out that various hypotheses are possible.[1] It may be that A and B were both printed in Italy and perhaps from an editio princeps printed at Barcelona. A may be a Catalan version of an Italian edition and B an Italian version of A, in which some Catalanisms and Italianisms were omitted and other Italianisms inserted. The fact that the typically Italian 'stimabile' appeared in the undoubtedly Spanish C may argue that the Spanish text returned to Spain from Italy infected with Italianisms, the result of printing in Italy.

In addition to the four Spanish versions of the letter, some assistance for the reconstruction of the original text may be derived from:

(E) The material contained in Bernáldez.[2]

The account which Bernáldez gives of the first voyage of Columbus is somewhat sketchy and is cast into narrative form. It is, however, clear, as De Lollis has pointed out, that he had access to some version of the letter of Columbus which was not A B C, which gives a certain value to his account.

Of obviously less importance than the Spanish versions, but still of considerable importance, are the three Italian translations of the letter, all of which have been printed by De Lollis.[3] They are:

(F) MS. in the Ambrosian Library.[4]

This version is incomplete, ending with the description of the unwarlike character of the natives of the islands, and thus consisting of something near one half of the letter.

(G) MS. in the National Library at Florence.[5]

This version is practically complete, but there are some gaps, due in the opinion of De Lollis to inability on the part of the translator to read the original MS.

---

[1] De Lollis (op. cit., I. i, pp. lvi–lx).
[2] Bernáldez, Historia de los Reyes Católicos, c. 118.
[3] De Lollis (op. cit., I. i, pp. lxviiii–lxxiiii).   [4] Vol. R. 113.
[5] In the Codice gia Strozziano. It bears the title: Posteriori di Galileo, tomo 33, Accademia del Cimento, parte III, Carteggio, vol. 18, Miscellanee scientifiche, I. cc. 132–134.

(H) MS. in the National Library at Florence.[1]

This version omits the postscript added at Lisbon and ends with a summary of the last sentence of the letter proper. It is also marked by gaps similar to those in G.

De Lollis showed that more than one copy of the Spanish version of the letter was circulating in Italy, and that the translations were made from MSS. and not from A or B. These translations are therefore in a similar relationship to the lost copy of the original as are A and B.

Considerable importance also attaches to the Latin translation (I),[2] although it is no longer believed to be possible that the original letter was composed in that language. The translation was made by Leonardo de Cosco, an Aragonese, from a MS. and not from A or B. Leonardo (Berardo) de Carminis, bishop of Monte Peloso, in the Basilicate, caused the version to be printed, and nine editions appeared in Italy, at Paris, Basle and Antwerp in the course of the years 1493–1494.[3] The question of the priority among these editions has been very exhaustively discussed;[4] the balance of probability appears to be in favour of the order L (printed by Planck), S (printed by Silber), T (printed by Planck). It is, of course, obvious that the editions produced at Rome must have antedated those printed outside Italy.

There is finally:

(K) A metrical version in Italian.[5]

This was made by Giuliano Dati at Florence in 1493. He would seem to have been imperfectly acquainted with Spanish, and therefore utilized a Latin translation, which, however, was not that of Cosco. Certain peculiarities in the poem indicate that the MS. translated was one otherwise unknown.

In addition to the letter which has been preserved,

---

[1] Codice gia Strozziano, cc. 135–136.

[2] Printed by De Lollis (op. cit., I. i, pp. 120–134), below the Spanish text of the letter.

[3] The various editions are enumerated by De Lollis (op. cit., I. i, pp. lx–lxi), by whom they are distinguished by the letters L to T.

[4] Major dealt with the question in his Select Letters of Columbus: it is discussed also by Harrisse, Notes on Columbus; by 'M.K.' (op. cit.); by Thacher (op. cit. ii. 46 et seq.); and by De Lollis (loc. cit.).

[5] Printed by Major (op. cit.), and in Rac. Col. (III. ii, pp. 8–25).

Columbus also sent a letter to Ferdinand and Isabella, the original of which is lost and no copy of which exists. Varnhagen,[1] indeed, held that the extant document was in reality sent to the sovereign. He argued that Isabella objected to being known as the recipient of a letter in which allusion is made to the nudity of women and that she therefore caused the letter to be printed as if it had been sent to a royal official, the necessary changes of phraseology being made in it. This hypothesis, however, would appear to be incompatible with the wording of the first sentence of the extant document and with the postscript to that document. It is, indeed, somewhat fanciful. It is true that 'maidenly modesty' is noted by Pulgar as having been a marked characteristic of the queen, and that her possession of this quality is attested by others, but there is no reason to believe that it served to produce in her such an extreme of bashfulness. It may be added that of the extant versions, A B C bear an endorsement[2] which indicates that the letter which has been preserved either contained or was contained in a letter to the sovereigns. Between the two documents, while there was not identity, there was probably a strong similarity; it may be reasonably conjectured that the communication sent to the sovereigns was a general summary of a rather more detailed character than that which is extant. The reply of Ferdinand and Isabella to the letter has been preserved.[3]

It was long believed that a distinction should be drawn between the letter endorsed as having been sent to the 'escribano de racion' and that endorsed as having been sent to Gabriel Sanchez, the treasurer of Aragon. There was a very general opinion that the latter should be regarded as a revised version of the former. De Lollis, however, showed that any such distinction is fallacious, and that there is no ground for supposing that Columbus sent more than two letters.

There has been considerable controversy concerning the date at which the letters were composed, and the question cannot be regarded as settled beyond dispute. It has been

[1] *Carta de Cristóbal Colón*, p. xix.

[2] This endorsement reads: '*contenida a otra de Sus Altezas*' in A, B; '*e otra de Sus Altezas*' in C. It has been suggested that for *a* or *e*, *en* should be read.

[3] Printed in Navarrete, ii, pp. 21–22.

urged that the letter to Ferdinand and Isabella was written at Lisbon,[1] the other letter having been already prepared. It is true that in the postscript, added after the *Niña* had entered the Tagus, Columbus seems to express his intention of writing to the sovereigns.[2] It is, however, hardly possible to believe that he prepared an account of his voyage for a royal official before he had drawn up a report for that official's master and mistress; it is still less possible to believe that if he had been guilty of such a breach of courtesy, he should have mentioned the fact in writing, and that in a document which might well reach the royal eye. The phrase in the postscript must apparently be taken in a somewhat less literal sense, meaning no more than that Columbus resolved at Lisbon to forward a letter to Ferdinand and Isabella, in place of waiting until he should be again in a Castilian port.

Nor can it be well believed that the letters were not prepared until Columbus had reached the Tagus. It must be remembered that the rough weather experienced after leaving the Azores caused an entirely unexpected delay, and that when he left those islands, Columbus obviously anticipated that he would soon reach a Spanish harbour. There is every reason for supposing that he was anxious to send a report on his voyage at the earliest possible moment after that voyage was completed, and hence it must also be supposed that he had the report ready for dispatch as soon as he should arrive at a point from which it could be sent. This supposition becomes practically a certainty in view of the fact that the extant letter is dated 15 February and that it is only in the postscript that any reference is made to the stormy weather which had been experienced on the return voyage.

It follows that the letter must have been written either during the storm which began on 12 February and which reached its height on 14 February, or in that period of fair weather which prevailed from 17 January to 12 February. The later of these two possible periods has been very generally accepted as that of the composition of the letter.[3] It is stated

[1] Thacher, *op. cit.* ii, p. 7.   [2] Cp. *infra*, p. 18.

[3] Thacher (*loc. cit.*, note 2) is in error when he says that: 'The *Journal* distinctly states that it was written then.'

in the *Journal* that the occurrence of the storm of 12–14 February determined Columbus to compose a brief account of his voyage, in order that if the *Niña* were to be lost, and if the *Pinta* were also to fail to reach Spain, the success of his expedition might still become known to the sovereigns. This account is said to have been written on parchment, to have been placed in a sealed barrel and thrown overboard.[1] It is obvious enough that the document here mentioned cannot be identical with the extant letter; it can have been no more than the very briefest report. But it has been suggested that the danger in which he then found himself and his resultant fear that he might never reach port, led Columbus to write an account of his voyage. A somewhat picturesque description[2] has been given of the manner in which he spent his sleepless nights in writing, presumably consoling himself for his present distress by recalling to his mind the delights of the Indies. It is urged that this view of the date of composition accords with the opening sentence of the extant letter and with the date at its close.

On the other hand, to this view there are weighty objections. It is somewhat hard to discover in his expectation that he might not reach Spain a motive for the preparation of a report which would have presumably been lost with him if he had been wrecked. It must be supposed that during the storm Columbus was somewhat preoccupied; even if he were not directing the navigation and personally responsible for the safety of his vessel, the alarm which seems invariably to have filled his mind in a rough sea[3] would almost certainly have deterred him from attempting literary composition. It may be suggested, although it would be unwise to insist upon this point, that in a ship of the type of the *Niña*, and in the midst of a violent storm, writing would have been almost

---

[1] This barrel has been periodically washed ashore or picked up by a passing vessel, and will doubtless continue to be so. One story of its finding deceived, or perhaps rather delighted, Lamartine (*Christophe Colomb*, pp. 194–196); another deceived Asensio (*Cristóbal Colón*, i, pp. 388–389). The thousand ducats, which, according to Ferdinand Columbus (c. 36), were to be paid to the finder of the barrel, have still to be earned.

[2] Cp. 'M.K.' (*op. cit.*, p. 6).

[3] Cp. *infra*, vol. ii, pp. 16–18, pp. 74–76, *inter alia*.

a physical impossibility. The idea that it was not until the occurrence of the storm that Columbus thought of preparing a report on his voyage is little probable. It is hardly credible that he should have proposed to appear before Ferdinand and Isabella without having first announced his return; it may be added that, in actual fact, he did not proceed to their court until he had been invited or commanded to do so, and that for this invitation or command he would certainly seem to have waited with some anxiety. To deliver a formal report on his mission was his obvious duty, and it is improbable that he can at first have designed that full account, which is represented by the *Journal*, to be such a report.

The arguments which can be advanced in favour of the view that the date of composition should rather be placed in the period of fair weather would appear to be of some force. It is obvious that during this period there was abundant leisure for the composition of an account of the voyage, while that period was also the first opportunity for the discharge of a duty. The style of the letter suggests mental calm, disturbed only by pleasurable excitement. It is true that the extant version has been edited, but when every allowance has been made for this fact, it is still hard to believe that the original was prepared at a time when its author was in imminent peril of death. If, as is not unlikely, the actual writing of the letter was not the work of Columbus himself, but of an amanuensis, it becomes perhaps still more probable that it was composed in the fair weather period. On the whole, indeed, it seems that the view of De Lollis should be accepted, that the letter was written between 17 January and 11 February, and that the appearance of the date, 15 February, at its close merely indicates that the document was then sealed up.

The postscript, if Navarrete's explanation of the meaning of the word 'anima' be accepted,[1] was written on a separate sheet and inserted in the letter after it had been closed. From its contents, it is clear that it was written at Lisbon. The remark concerning the peculiarly stormy winter corresponds

---

[1] '*Anima* llamában al papel escrito que se introducia en la carta despues de cerrada' (Navarrete, ii, p. 174, note 2).

very closely with an entry in the *Journal* which refers to the
time when the *Niña* was in the Tagus.[1] The words, 'I ran here
to-day into this port of Lisbon', equally indicate the same
place of composition. The appearance of 14 March as the date
of the postscript in A B C G H I would therefore seem to be
an error; the date should be 4 March, since on 14 March
Columbus was off Cape St. Vincent.[2]

The date at which the letters were dispatched has also been
matter of dispute. That they were sent at the same time is
indicated by the endorsement, 'contenida a otra de Sus Altezas', but it has been held that the place of dispatch was not
Lisbon but Palos or Seville. It has been urged, in support of
this view, that the true date of the postscript should be
14 March and that the sea route to Barcelona was faster than
that by land. But it seems to be morally certain that the
postscript should be dated 4 March, and it may be suggested
that the recent experiences of Columbus had not been such
as to suggest that it was wise to go by sea to Barcelona; he
would appear to have intended at one time to do so, but
to have abandoned that intention. It has further been
urged that Columbus would have been unwilling to allow such
a communication to pass through Portuguese territory. It is
true that he had no reason to feel any very great confidence
in Portuguese professions of goodwill;[3] his distrust of Portuguese intentions is perhaps indicated by his rejection of the
offer made by the king[4] to allow him to proceed directly
from Lisbon to the Spanish court. The extant letter, however,
was not a document of such a character that knowledge of its
contents would have been of value to the Portuguese or have
added anything material to the information which they must
have already gained from the crew of the *Niña*. It gives no
indication of the route followed by Columbus or of the dis-

---

[1] The *Journal* (4 March) says: '. . . donde supo de la gente de la mar que
jamás hizo invierno de tantas tormentas, y que se avían perdido .25. naos en
Flandes, y otras estavan allí que avía quatro meses que no avían podido salir.'
The postscript (*infra*, p. 19) says: 'dizen aquá todos los hombres de la mar que
jamás ovo tan mal yvierno ni tantas pérdidas de naves.'

[2] *Journal*, 14 March.

[3] Cp. *Journal*, 19 February, 5 March.

[4] Cp. *Journal*, 12 March.

tance travelled or even of the general direction of his voyage. There is no reason to suppose that the lost letter to Ferdinand and Isabella was more explicit, and hence it is hardly likely that there was in the mind of Columbus any objection to sending the documents by land from Lisbon. It has also been argued that Columbus could not have known where the sovereigns were residing, but the court had been at Barcelona since the previous May[1] and the recent attempt on the life of Ferdinand[2] would certainly have conveyed the news that he was in that city to all quarters of the peninsula. A somewhat stronger argument in favour of the view that the dispatch of the letters was delayed until the *Niña* arrived at Palos is supplied by the date of the reply of the sovereigns to the letter sent to them. The fact that this reply is dated 30 March led De Lollis to suggest that Columbus may have delayed to send his letters until 12 March, the time of his departure from Lisbon. If, however, he sent them from Lisbon at all, there seems to be no reason for supposing that he did not send them at the earliest possible moment, and the delay in the answer of the sovereigns would appear to be readily explicable. There was no need for their reply to be sent immediately; it would, indeed, have been useless to send it while Columbus was still at sea and while it could not be known to which Castilian port he would proceed, since even if he had announced his intention of making for Palos, stress of weather might well have driven him into some other harbour. That the sovereigns should have waited until they knew that the *Niña* had reached port, and even until they were sure that Columbus was not coming to Barcelona by sea, appears to be natural enough. It may be objected that even so the interval from 15 March, the date at which Columbus once more passed the bar of Saltes, and 30 March, the date of the answer of the sovereigns, can still hardly be explained except on the assumption that the letters were not sent until Palos had been reached. But the length of time which would have been occupied in the transmission of news from an obscure Andalusian port to Barcelona can be no more than approxi-

---

[1] Galindez Carvajal, in *Doc. Inéd. para la Historia de España*, vol. xviii, p. 280.

[2] The attempted assassination occurred on 6 December (Carvajal, *loc. cit.*).

mately estimated; a messenger sent by Columbus would perhaps not have secured the facilities which a royal messenger might have enjoyed or have travelled with that haste which the occasion might seem to demand. Nor, perhaps, was the reply of Ferdinand and Isabella hurriedly prepared; the fact that in it, for the first time, Columbus is accorded the title of admiral and given the style of Don suggests that the terms of the answer were somewhat carefully considered.

The alternative view that the letters were sent from Lisbon on the day on which the postscript is dated is supported by various considerations. The letter of Trotti[1] shows that the news of the return of Columbus reached Barcelona at an early date. The postscript is obviously hastily written, which suggests that it was composed at the moment of dispatch. It contains the statement that Columbus decided to write to the sovereigns from Lisbon. It may be further suggested that, quite apart from the fact that it was his duty to send a report as soon as possible, Columbus would have been naturally anxious to announce his success at once. He was by temperament ambitious and eager to acquire both fame and honours; every delay in making known his triumph meant delay also in his receipt of the promised rewards. There were also special circumstances to impel him to send his report at once. He had entered Lisbon, and his action in doing so was likely to be unwelcome to the sovereigns; to explain, as he does in the postscript, that he had been the victim of circumstances was advisable, in order to meet possible insinuations against his loyalty, insinuations which were, in fact, made.[2] An even stronger motive for sending his announcement immediately was supplied by his doubt concerning the attitude of Pinzón. While still in the Indies, Columbus had become suspicious of his lieutenant;[3] during the storm, the *Pinta* had parted company with the *Niña* and since then he had heard nothing of her. To a man with the mentality of Columbus it would undoubtedly have seemed to be very probable that if Pinzón could gain the ear of the

---

[1] Cp. *Rac. Col.* III. i, p. 141.   [2] Cp. *infra*, p. 18, note 4.
[3] Cp. *Journal*, 21 Nov., 31 Dec., 3, 6, 8, and 10 Jan.

sovereigns first, he would endeavour to appropriate the fruits of the voyage, and to guard, as far as possible, against this was a natural effort to make. It may, therefore, with some assurance be concluded that the letters were sent from Lisbon on 4 March. The character of the extant letter has, perhaps, not been hitherto justly appreciated. It has been assumed that it was a private communication sent by Columbus to a personal friend or to two personal friends, but in actual fact it was probably nothing of the kind. Varnhagen pointed out that the style of the letter is not that of a private, but of an official document; the note, 'contenida a otra a Sus Altezas', presents a difficulty which has not so far been satisfactorily solved, although that note perhaps suggests the true nature of the document. For the determination of that nature, it is important to remember that the extant letter does not bear the name of any addressee. All the texts, how-ever, except H, carry endorsements,[1] added by the recipients, the copyists or the translators, descriptive of the document. A B C are thus described as having been sent to the 'escribano de racion', that is, to Luis de Santangel;[2] D and I as having

---

[1] These endorsements read as follows: (i) A B C. 'Esta carta embio Colom (B, Colon) al escrivan de racion de las islas halladas en las Indias contenida a otra (C, e otra) de Sus Altezas.' (ii) D.' Carta del Almirante á Gabriel Sanchez. (iii) F. 'Copia de una letra scritta dal armiralgio Colon del signor re de spagna laqual scrive ala corte regal as certi consieri del signor re, mandata del grane Tresorir del ditto signor in fiorenza al fratello Zoane Sanzio.' (iv) G. 'Copia della letera venuta di Spagna.' (v) I. 'Epistola Christofori Colom: . . . . ad Magnificum dominum Raphaelem Sanxis (*in other editions*, Gabrielem Sanches): eiusdem serenissimi Regis Tesautarium missa. . . .' No real importance can be attached to the error in the name of Sanchez in some of the Latin editions. At that period it was by no means uncommon to find the names Raphael and Gabriel confused, while Cosco, as an Aragonese, not unnaturally used the Aragonese form, Sanxis, for the Castilian, Sanchez.

[2] Luis de Santangel was a member of a family of *conversos*, originating from Zaragoza, who had adopted the name Santangel in place of their original name, Chinillo, upon their conversion from the Jewish faith. He was the son of another Luis de Santangel, a merchant, who had important financial dealings with Juan II of Aragon, the father of Ferdinand the Catholic. Luis de Santangel him-self was probably born at Calatayud, but removed to Valencia, of which city he is described as a native, and later to Barcelona, where he was in charge of a branch of the business founded by his father. In 1478 he relinquished his mercantile career and entered the royal service, becoming *escribano de ración* three years later. The duty of this official was to keep a register of the names and salaries of

been sent to Sanchez,[1] the treasurer of Aragon; F as the copy
of a letter 'ad certi consieri,' and G as a copy 'della letera
venuta di Spagna.' The identity of the addressee is thus not
really revealed by the endorsements, since it cannot be supposed that Columbus sent three letters in addition to that to
Ferdinand and Isabella.

There is nothing intrinsically improbable in the idea that
Columbus should have written early news of his success to
Santangel, to whom he was greatly indebted, but there seems
to be no reason why he should at the same time and in the
same manner have written to Sanchez. The suggestion of
Varnhagen[2] that the treasurer was acting as escribano de
racion *ad interim* cannot be entertained, nor is it possible to
suppose that the name of the treasurer should have appeared
without any warrant for doing so. The statement in the
endorsement on F that the letter was sent by him to his
brother[3] in Florence is sufficiently explicit to show that at an
early date a copy of the letter was certainly in the possession
of the treasurer. A further difficulty lies in the fact that
Columbus is not likely to have been guilty of so great a
breach of etiquette as that involved in the dispatch of news of

all persons employed in the royal palace; an inventory of jewels, arms, clothes,
and other contents of the palace; a book giving the daily expenditure of the
royal household, and a record of the salaries paid and of gifts made from the
royal purse. While holding this office, Santangel continued to engage in financial
business on his own account and seems to have amassed a considerable fortune.
The exact date of his death appears to be unknown, but he was still *escribano de
ración* in 1498. His share in securing the acceptance of the proposals of Columbus
is well known. He is not to be confused with another Luis de Santangel, who was
involved in a charge of heresy in 1449. (Cp. Serrano y Sanz, *Origines de la
Dominación Española en América*, vol. i, pp. lxv–cli).

[1] Gabriel Sanchez was also of *converso* origin. His uncle is said to have been
named Alazar Usuf; his father, who, on baptism, assumed the name of Pedro
Sanchez, was a notary at Calatayud. His mother was a converted Jewess of
Tortosa. Luis Sanchez, his elder brother, became treasurer of Aragon in 1474,
and Gabriel became his deputy in the following year, succeeding to the office of
treasurer at some date between 1479 and 1481. Some of his relatives were concerned in the murder of St. Pedro Arbués, inquisitor of Aragon, in 1485, and for
a time the position of Gabriel Sanchez was one of peril. Although cleared of any
suspicion of complicity in the murder, he withdrew from court and took up his
residence at Zaragoza, although he continued to be treasurer until his death
at Segovia in 1505. He was succeeded in his office by his son, Luis. (Cp. Serrano
y Sanz, *op. cit.*, pp. clii–cxcvi).

[2] *Carta de Cristobal Colón*, p. xx. [3] Juan Sanchez, a merchant.

his discovery to a royal official at the same time as to that official's master and mistress; it is, indeed, very unlikely that he would have sent that news to anyone until he had been authorized by the sovereigns to do so.

In view of these, and of other similar considerations, it may be suggested that the truth is most nearly stated in the endorsement to F, and that the letter was really a draft semi-official dispatch, enclosed in the letter to Ferdinand and Isabella, for publication by them if they so desired. They caused copies to be made which were distributed both in Spain and Italy. This view of the character of the document is borne out both by its 'official' style and by the fact that it so studiously abstains from supplying any information which could be of service to any who might wish to encroach upon an area which Ferdinand and Isabella proposed to maintain as their own preserve. It removes the difficulty created by the varying endorsements, all of which appear to be equally authentic, and it accounts for the rapid dissemination of the news of the discovery.[1]

It is certain that in the process of copying, and before it was printed, the letter was subjected to some editing, the exact extent and nature of which cannot be determined. There is, however, reason to believe that this revision was made by explicit royal command, since to the original there was one addition which can hardly be otherwise explained. In A B C the signature 'El Almirante' appears, a signature which is somewhat unintelligently elaborated in the Latin translation.[2] Columbus, however, could not have described

---

[1] For the elaboration of the argument here summarized, cp. *The Letter of Columbus, announcing the results of his First Voyage*, in the *Hispanic American Historical Review* (Feb. 1930).

[2] 'Christoforus Colom, oceanee classis prefectus.' This 'signature' is obviously no more than an addition by the translator. Columbus never used his name in signing any letter or document, or, indeed, upon any other occasion, so far as is known. He could not have described himself as 'admiral' at a date earlier than that at which he received the royal letter of 30 March 1493, and by that time the MS. from which Cosco translated was, in all probability, already in Italy. Even if it be supposed that it was not, and that Columbus sent it himself to Italy, he could not have described himself as 'admiral' of a 'fleet'. A Castilian admiral of the period was not the admiral of a fleet, but of an area; as Fadrique Enriquez was 'almirante de Castilla', so Columbus became 'almirante del mar oceano'. It cannot be supposed that Cosco translated 'mar' by 'classis'.

himself as 'El Almirante' in February 1493, in a letter which was in any case intended to reach a royal official and which would probably come to the notice of the sovereigns themselves. For the title was not his to use. In the *Capitulations* of Santa Fé he had asked that he should be created admiral in those islands, lands, and seas which he was setting out to discover, and in the grant made at Granada he was promised that he should receive this position in event of success. But the title was not formally conferred upon him until the grant was confirmed at Barcelona in 1493, although it was implicitly granted to him when he was addressed by it in the letter of the sovereigns of 30 March 1493. It cannot be supposed that Columbus should have risked incurring royal displeasure by assuming a style before that style had been accorded to him, and it follows that the signature to A B C and also to the MS. from which I was translated must have been inserted either after 30 March 1493 or if at an earlier date, then by royal command. The fact that copies of the latter were in print perhaps as early as April 1493, and still more the fact that versions were so soon circulating in Italy, makes it highly probable that the work of copying was undertaken as soon as the letter was received at Barcelona. That it should have been is more likely than not, since there was no reason for delay. The style of the letter generally also suggests revision by an editor; it is not improbable that the work was performed by Santangel, whose Aragonese origin would account for the appearance or retention of a certain number of 'Catalanisms'.

It has been generally assumed that the lost original of the letter was in the autograph of Columbus, but the validity of this assumption may be questioned. While there is no evidence that he actually wrote the letter with his own hand, there are reasons for believing that he did not. Its style is unlike that of his undoubted compositions; on the whole, the Castilian is purer and more fluent. Editing may, indeed, account to some extent for this, but it seems hardly to account for it entirely. It is, however, impossible to suppose that

Thacher (*op. cit.*, ii, p. 14 and note 3) allowed his sense of the dramatic to carry him away, when he regarded this 'signature' as authentic.

Columbus at the time of his first voyage was capable of writing in a clear and fluent style, while by the time of his third voyage he could express himself only in what Las Casas calls his 'homely language'. It is rather more likely that the reverse was the case, while it is by no means certain that in 1493 he was able to write in any language. If it would be dangerous to assume that the original letter was not a holograph, it would be perhaps more dangerous to assume that it was.

The letter has been frequently reprinted and has been many times translated. It was included, with a translation, by Major in his *Select Letters of Columbus*, edited for the Hakluyt Society. At that date, A had not yet been discovered and Major based his text upon B, corrected by reference to D, F, and K. For the present edition, the text printed by De Lollis, in the *Scritti di Colombo*, has been adopted and the letter has been newly translated.

2. Letter of Dr. Chanca

(pp. 20–72)

Ferdinand Columbus[1] states that his father kept journals of each of his voyages and Bernáldez[2] refers to 'a book' made by the admiral and describing, if not the whole of the second voyage, at least the exploration of the coasts of Cuba and Jamaica. No trace of these records, however, is to be found, and the account of the second voyage must be drawn from sources other than Columbus himself. It is narrated by Ferdinand Columbus,[3] by Las Casas,[4] by Peter Martyr Angleria,[5] and by Bernáldez,[6] as well as by Nicolo Syllacio[7] and Michele de Cuneo.[8] There is finally an account written by Dr. Diego Alvarez Chanca, who was physician to the fleet.

This letter was first printed by Navarrete,[9] who appended to it the following note:[10]

'Copied from a codex which is in the possession of the Royal

---

[1] Ferdinand Columbus, c. 87.
[2] Cp. *infra*, p. 158.
[3] Ferdinand Columbus, cc. 44–69.
[4] Las Casas, i. 84–99.
[5] Peter Martyr Angleria, Decades, i. Bk. 2–3.
[6] Bernáldez, cc. 119–131.
[7] *Rac. Col.* III. ii, pp. 83–94.
[8] *Rac. Col.* III. ii, pp. 95–107.
[9] Navarrete, i, pp. 198–224.
[10] Navarrete, i, p. 224.

Academy of History. It was written in the middle of the sixteenth century and was part of a collection of papers, relating
to the Indies, formed by Fray Antonio de Aspa, a Jeronomite
of the monastery of la Mejorada, near Olmedo. The codex
consists of thirty-three leaves; the first seventeen contain the
first and second books of the *Decades* of Peter Martyr
Angleria, translated into Castilian. In the first book various
additions have been interpolated by the translator who wrote
between the years 1512 and 1514. The second book is an
almost literal translation. From the seventeenth leaf to the
thirty-first comes the earlier account by Dr. Chanca; the
document has not been previously edited. Don Manuel
Avilla made a copy of it which is found in the collection of
Don J. B. Muñoz, and which I have had before me to compare with the original in Madrid, 12 June 1807.'

To the letter, as printed by Navarrete, there is prefixed the
following note, presumably written by Aspa:[1] 'Concerning
this second voyage, Peter Martyr wrote to Rome in Latin,
and as a certain doctor, called Chanca, a native of Seville,
went on the voyage and in the fleet by command of the
Catholic sovereigns, and from there wrote to the lords of
the cabildo of Seville that which happened there and that
which he saw, I place below this the copy of his letter,
although the two accounts are almost identical. But the one
relates that which he heard and he of Seville that which he
saw, and the two accounts are not contradictory, and one
omits to relate some small matter which the other records,
and since some are more pleasing in their manner of telling
a story than are others, there follows the letter of the said
Dr. Chanca which he wrote to the city of Seville concerning
this second voyage in the manner following.'

At the end of the letter, a further note, also no doubt
written by Aspa, is appended:[2]

'So far is the copy of that which refers to news from those
parts and Indies. The remaining contents of the letter is not
to the point, since it deals with personal matters which the
said Dr. Chanca, as a native of Seville, asked and gave as a
commission to the members of the cabildo of Seville, relating

[1] Navarrete, i, p. 198. [2] Navarrete, i, p. 224.

to the property and people that he had left in the said city, and this arrived at Seville in the month of ... in the year one thousand four hundred and ninety-three.'

The Spanish text of Navarrete and an English translation of the letter were included by Major in his *Select Letters of Columbus*. For the present edition, the text printed by Major has been utilized and newly translated.

3. Memorandum of Columbus, sent to Ferdinand and Isabella, by Antonio de Torres

(pp. 74–113)

Allusion is made to the memorial concerning Española, which Columbus sent to Spain by Antonio de Torres, in the *Historie* of Ferdinand Columbus[1] and by Las Casas.[2] It was utilized by Oviedo.[3] De Torres was the bearer of other documents as is proved by the contents of this memorandum and by the letter of the sovereigns to Columbus, 14 August 1494.[4]

Only one MS.[5] of the memorial is known to exist; it is in the Archives of the Indies at Seville. The replies of Ferdinand and Isabella appear in the margin. From the inventory of the contents of the chest at Las Cuevas, made at the request of Baldassare Colombo by the Council of the Indies, it would appear that the original was still in existence at the close of the sixteenth century, or at least an early copy of the original. In the inventory, it is stated that the document was signed with the cypher of Columbus and the words 'El Almirante', in a manner similar to that which appears at the end of the letter to Gorricio, 26 February 1501, also in the chest at Las Cuevas. De Lollis argues that the fact that the memorial was so signed proves that Columbus used his cypher as early as 1494, but to this argument it may be objected that the document at Las Cuevas may have been no more than a copy of the original. The fact that it is stated to have been signed in a manner not otherwise adopted by Columbus, except in the

[1] Ferdinand Columbus, c. 51.
[2] Las Casas, i. 89.
[3] Oviedo, ii. 48.
[4] Navarrete, ii, p. 152.
[5] Cp. De Lollis, *op. cit.* (*Rac. Col.* I. i, pp. ciiii–cvi).

case of documents of no earlier date than 1498, suggests that to that period the Las Cuevas copy of the memorial should be assigned. It further seems to be improbable that Ferdinand and Isabella should have returned the memorandum to Columbus; it would more naturally have been retained in the royal archives. De Lollis holds that the original was in the autograph of Columbus, but the entry concerning the document at Las Cuevas in the inventory seems rather to suggest that it was in the handwriting of a clerk.[1] In any case, it cannot be definitely asserted that the original was a holograph of the admiral. The style of the document rather favours the view that it was prepared from dictated materials.

The memorandum was first printed by Navarrete.[2] Major included the Spanish text of Navarrete and an English translation in his *Select Letters of Columbus*. For the present edition, the text printed by De Lollis has been used and the document newly translated.

4. Andrés Bernáldez, 'Historia de los Reyes Católicos', c. 123–31

(pp. 114–167)

Dr. Chanca's account of the second voyage ends with the foundation of Isabella, and he supplies no information concerning the exploration of the coasts of Cuba and Jamaica, on which Columbus entered 24 April 1494 and from which he returned to Española on 29 September 1494. Accounts of this expedition are given by Ferdinand Columbus,[3] Las Casas,[4] and Peter Martyr Angleria,[5] and by Andrés Bernáldez.

Such knowledge as is possessed concerning the life of Bernáldez is almost entirely derived from his own work. The

---

[1] The entry in question reads: 'Ay una instrución, que suena ser dada por el almirante don Christoval, á Antonio de Torres capitan de la nao Marigalante y alcayde de la ciudad Isabela, fecha en la Isabela a .30. de enero de .94. ay una firma en ella con unas cifras, y, por letra, el almirante' (Memorial del Pleyto, c. 57 A–). The fact that in this copy the title of alcaide of Isabella is given to le Torres may also suggest that it was not the original document, since he did not receive that position officially until the provisional appointment by Columbus had been confirmed by Ferdinand and Isabella: that confirmation was later than the memorandum (cp. *infra*, p. 96).

[2] Navarrete, i, pp. 225–241.   [3] Ferdinand Columbus, c. 53–59.
[4] Las Casas, i. 94–99.   [5] Peter Martyr Angleria, Dec. i. Bk. 2.

date of his birth is unknown, but he was a native of Fuentes in Leon and the grandson of a notary public. In 1488 he became cura of Los Palacios, near Seville, a position which he still held in 1513. He was also chaplain to Diego de Deza, who was archbishop of Seville, confessor to Ferdinand the Catholic, a member of the royal council, and grand inquisitor. He was on friendly terms with Rodrigo Ponce de Leon, marquis of Cadiz, one of the heroes of the Moorish war, and had for him a whole-hearted admiration; his character sketch of the marquis might be justly described as 'the portrait of a Castilian gentleman'.[1] Bernáldez was also on friendly terms with Juan Rodriguez de Fonseca and with Columbus, both of whom were at one time his guests;[2] he would seem to have known the future admiral in the period immediately following his arrival in Spain from Portugal.[3] The date of his death is unknown, but it was perhaps 1513, in which year his history ends abruptly.

In his own pages, Bernáldez clearly reveals his personal character. He was a man of simple mind and ingenuous, delighting in pomp and ceremony,[4] and with some appreciation of beauty. He was kind-hearted and discharged the duties of his office as a parish priest with commendable zeal.[5] His kindliness, however, was not proof against the intolerant spirit of his age; he was filled with a lively hatred for the false conversos, for Jews and for Moors;[6] he gloried in the revival of the Inquisition,[7] and rejoiced to think that Ferdinand and Isabella had 'delivered the heretics to the flames, in which with good cause and by the decision of the Church, they have been burned and do burn and shall burn, in living flames until they be no more'.[8] As might be expected he had a firm belief in the miraculous and loved to hear of marvels; he had obviously devoured with enthusiasm the pages of Mandeville. He was sufficiently credulous, recording, as sober fact, the birth of a remarkable monstrosity at Ravenna. The extent of his intellectual attainments may be gathered from his remark that, since the eclipse of the sun on 29 July

[1] Cp. c. 104.   [2] Cp. infra, p. 116.   [3] Cp. c. 118.
[4] Cp. cc. 32, 33, 80.   [5] Cp. c. 200.   [6] Cp. cc. 43, 110–114.
[7] Cp. c. 44.   [8] Cp. c. 7.

1478, 'the sun has never regained its full brightness nor have days ever been so fine as they were before'.[1]

His *Historia de los Reyes Católicos* extends from the accession of Ferdinand and Isabella to the year 1513. He has placed on record the circumstances in which he was led to undertake its composition.

'I who write these chapters of memories,' he says,[2] 'being then twelve years of age, was reading a register which had belonged to my dead grandfather, who was a notary public of the town of Fuentes, in the encomienda mayor of Leon, where I was born. In that book, I found some entries describing notable events which had occurred in his time, and my widowed grandmother, his wife, being almost in extreme old age, hearing me read them, said: "Child, why do not you so write the events of this present time, as they are? For to do so would be no idle task. If you write of the good things that come to pass in your days, those who come after will know of them and, marvelling as they read of them, will give thanks to God." And from that day, I undertook to do this, and when I had come to a riper understanding, I many times told myself, "If God give me life and health, and I live, I will write until that day which shall see the kingdom of Granada become pasturage for the herds of the Christians." And that I had always hope of seeing, and I have seen it as those who are now alive have seen it and heard it; to the Lord Jesus Christ be great thanks and praise given.'

His history is unpretentious both in style and matter. Bernáldez assuredly was not inclined 'to exercise himself in great matters which were too high for him', and it would be vain to search his pages for any account of the constitutional development of the reign of the Catholic sovereigns. In general, he narrates events without commenting upon them, save when his feelings are strongly aroused; he is moved to something akin to real emotion by the death of Ponce de Leon and by that of Isabella,[3] while his anger is kindled by the thought of the villainy of the *conversos*. His history is obviously most valuable for events which were within his

---

[1] Cp. c. 34.   [2] Cp. c. 7.
[3] For his appreciation of Isabella, see c. 201.

personal knowledge or of which he had heard accounts from
his friends; it is a most important source for the narrative of
the Moorish war, concerning some events in which he undoubtedly received information from Ponce de Leon, and of
some incidents in which he was certainly an eyewitness.[1] He
makes little use of documents, although at the close of his
history he gives some letters addressed by Ferdinand to
Diego de Deza. His honesty is undoubted; he frankly reveals
his likes and dislikes, his contempt and his admiration, and
he never conceals his prejudices, but he never wilfully distorts
the truth.

His account of Columbus is uneven.[2] He sketches the first
voyage somewhat hurriedly, although he supplies some
details not found elsewhere; his description of the third and
fourth voyages is perfunctory. On the second voyage, however, he is very full, his account of it being derived, as he says,
partly from Dr. Chanca and others who had been present on
it, and partly from Columbus himself, who left with him
'certain papers'.[3] For that part of the voyage which closed
with the foundation of Isabella, Bernáldez in essence reproduces the letter of Dr. Chanca;[4] his account of the exploration
of the coasts of Cuba and Jamaica,[5] however, is independent,
although very similar to that given by Peter Martyr Angleria.

To this account a special interest attaches. Of the other
writers who describe the voyages of Columbus, men like
Chanca and Peter Martyr were frequenters of courts; Cuneo
was the reverse of unsophisticated; Ferdinand Columbus, Las
Casas and Oviedo wrote at a time when the value of the discoveries and their nature were much better understood. It
is only from the pages of Bernáldez that it is possible to
gather the impression made by the discovery upon an ordinary man, of simple mind and simple tastes and habits. To
Bernáldez, the interest of the events of which he heard is
analogous to that of Pigafitta in those which he saw. He cares
little for the increase of knowledge of the surface of the globe,
for the wealth to be won from the newly found lands, for the

---

[1] E.g. the siege of Malaga (c. 83).
[2] His account of Columbus is contained in cc. 118–131.
[3] C. 118.   [4] C. 131.   [5] Cc. 119–131.

political advantages that may be gained. Despite his religious character, he is not deeply interested in the work of conversion. It is the wonder and strangeness of everything in this new world that excites him; it is in curious customs and incidents that he takes delight. To him also, the beauty of nature made a strong appeal, and it may be reasonably conjectured that here he found himself in the fullest accord with Columbus and that those passages in which the loveliness of the islands is described are almost reports of the table talk of the admiral. As the account of the later part of the second voyage is read, it is easy to picture the scene in the house at Los Palacios, to see Columbus eagerly descanting upon that which so fired his poetic nature, to see Bernáldez eagerly listening and at moments encouraging the narrator to continue, perhaps to see also Fonseca in the background, listening with a somewhat cynical smile. If it were only because Bernáldez so represents one, and that perhaps the most attractive side of the character of Columbus, his account of the second voyage would be well worth reading.

Seven MSS. of the *Historia de los Reyes Católicos* are in existence; six are apparently derived from one which is in the possession of the Biblioteca Colombiana, with which the contents of the others agree, although the chapters are differently numbered.[1] The work was printed at Granada in 1856, at Seville in 1870, and at Madrid in 1878.[2] So much of it as deals with the later part of the second voyage of Columbus was printed by De Lollis in the *Scritti di Colombo*.[3] In 1838 the Massachusetts Historical Society published an English translation of the chapters concerning Columbus;[4] this translation would appear to have been made from a very faulty copy of the MS. since it is disfigured by numerous blunders. No other English version of Bernáldez would seem to have appeared. For the present edition, the text printed by De Lollis has been utilized and it has been newly translated.

---

[1] Cp. Ballester, *Fuentes Narrativas de la Historia de España durante la Edad Moderna*, i, pp. 49–50.

[2] The text of the 1870 edition is marred by numerous blunders in transcription; that of 1878, in the *Colección Rivadeneira*, is somewhat better, but poorly printed.

[3] De Lollis, *op. cit.* (*Rac. Col.* I. i, pp. 235–265).

[4] *Collections*, series 3, vol. 8.

LIST OF WORKS CITED

THIS list is in no sense intended to be a complete bibliography for the voyages of Columbus; it contains only the titles of such works as are mentioned in the Introduction and notes.

AILLY, CARDINAL PIERRE D'. Imago Mundi. (*In* RACCOLTA COLOMBIANA, SCRITTI DI COLOMBO, *q.v.*)

ALTOLAGUIRRE Y DUVALE, ANGEL DE. Declaraciones hechos por D. Cristóbal, D. Diego y D. Bartolomé Colón acerca su nacionalidad (in Boletín de la Real Academia de la Historia, vol. lxxxvi, pp. 307 *et seq.*): Madrid, 1925.

—— La real confirmación del Mayorazgo (in Boletín de la Real Academia de la Historia, vol. lxxxviii, pp. 330 *et seq.*): Madrid, 1926.

ANGLERIA, PETER MARTYR. *See* MARTYR.

ASENSIO Y TOLEDO, JOSE MARIA, Cristóbal Colón. Barcelona, 1891 (2 vols.).

ASSERETO, UGO. La Data della Nascita di Colombo (in Giornale Storico e Letterario della Liguria, vol. v, pp. 5 *et seq.*): Spezia, 1904.

BABCOCK, WILLIAM H. Legendary Islands of the Atlantic (American Geographical Society: Research Series, No. 5). New York, 1922.

BALLESTER Y CASTELL, RAFAEL. Las Fuentas Narrativas de la Historia de España durante la Edad Moderna. Valladolid, 1927.

BARROS, JOÃO DE. Decades de Asia. Lisbon, 1628.

BELLOY, MARQUIS DE. Christophe Colomb et la Découverte du Nouveau Monde. Paris, 1865.

BERGENROTH, G. A. Calendar of Letters, Despatches and State Papers: England and Spain: Henry VII. London, 1862. (2 vols.)

BERNÁLDEZ, ANDRÉS. Historia de los Reyes Católicos Don Fernando y Doña Isabel. (Sociedad de los Bibliófilos Andaluces.) Seville, 1869. (2 vols.)

BERWICK Y ALBA, MARIA DEL ROSARIO STUART, DUCHESS OF. Autográfos de Cristóbal Colón y papeles de América. Madrid, 1892.

—— Nuevos Autógrafos de Colón. Madrid, 1902.

BLOY, LÉON. La Révélateur du Globe. Christophe Colomb et sa Béatification Future. Paris, 1884.

BOUREL DE LA RONCIÈRE, CHARLES. *See* RONCIÈRE.

CASAS, BARTOLOMÉ DE LAS. *See* LAS CASAS.

CASTRO, EUGENIO DE. *See* LOPES DE SOUSA.

Colección de Documentos Inéditos relativos al descubrimiento, conquista y organización de las Antiguas Posesiones Españoles de Ultramar. (2ª serie.) Madrid, 1892, etc.

COLUMBUS, CHRISTOPHER. The Letter in Spanish of Christopher Columbus to Luis de Sant' Angel. London, 1889.

COLUMBUS, CHRISTOPHER. The Spanish Letter of Columbus to Luis de Sant' Angel. (Edited: 'M.K.'.) London, 1891.

COLUMBUS, FERDINAND. Le Historie della Vita e dei Fatti di Cristoforo Colombo. (Edited, Rinaldo Caddeo.) Milan, 1930. (2 vols.) (The Italian translation of the 'Historie' by Alfonso Ulloa was first published at Venice in 1571.)

CRONAU, RUDOLF. The Discovery of America and the Landfall of Columbus. New York, 1923.

CUNEO, MICHELE DE. Lettera (in Raccolta Colombiana, part iii, vol. ii, pp. 95 et seq.). Rome, 1892.

ENGLISH PILOT, THE. The Fourth Book, describing the West Indian Navigation from Hudson's Bay to the River Amazonas. London, 1749.

FERNÁNDEZ DE NAVARRETE, MARTIN. See NAVARRETE.

FERNÁNDEZ DE OVIEDO Y VALDES. See OVIEDO.

FERNÁNDEZ DURO, CESAREO. Colón y la Historia Postuma. Madrid, 1885.

—— Nebulosa de Colón. Madrid, 1890.

—— Pinzón en el Descubrimiento de las Indias. Madrid, 1892.

—— Colón y Pinzón (Mémorias de la Real Academia de la Historia, vol. x, pp. 161 et seq.). Madrid, 1893.

FITA Y COLOMER, FIDEL. Fray Bernald Buyl y Cristóbal Colón: Nueva colección de Cartas reales, etc. (in Boletín de la Real Academia de la Historia, vol. xix, pp. 173 et seq.). Madrid, 1891.

—— Fray Bernal Buyl o el primer apóstol del Nuevo Mundo. Colección de documentos inéditos relativos a este varón ilustre. Madrid, 1884.

GAFFAREL, PAUL. Études sur les Rapports de l'Amérique et de l'ancien continent. Paris, 1869.

—— Les Découvertes françaises du XIVme au XVIme siècle. Paris,1888.

GALINDEZ CARVAJAL, LORENZO. Anales Breves del reinado de los Reyes Católicos D. Fernando y Doña Isabel. (Edited: Miguel Salva and Pedro Sainz de Baranda.) (Documentos Inéditos para la Historia de España, vol. xviii.) Madrid, 1851.

GALLO, ANTONIO. De Navigatione Columbi (in Raccolta Colombiana, part iii, vol. ii, pp. 188 et seq.). Rome, 1892.

GARCÍA DE LA RIEGA, CELSO. Colón, español. Madrid, 1908.

GARCILASO DE LA VEGA, INCA. Comentarios Reales. Madrid, 1825.

GIUSTINIANI, AGOSTINO. Psalterium (in Raccolta Colmbiana, part iii, vol. ii, pp. 245 et seq.). Rome, 1892.

GOMARA, FRANCISCO LÓPEZ DE. Historia general de las Indias. Madrid, 1922. (2 vols.)

GOODRICH, AARON. A History of the Character and Achievements of the so-called Christopher Columbus. New York, 1874.

GOULD Y QUINCY, ALICE. Nueva Lista Documentada de los Tripulantes de Colón (in Boletín de la Real Academia de la Historia, vols. lxxxvi, lxxxvii, lxxxviii, xc, and xcii). Madrid, 1925-8.

HARRISSE, HENRY. Fernand Colomb. Paris, 1872.

—— Christophe Colomb, son Origine, sa Vie, ses Voyages, sa Famille et ses Descendants. Études d'Histoire Critique. Paris, 1884. (2 vols.)

—— The Discovery of North America. Paris, 1892. (2 vols.)

HERRERA, ANTONIO DE. Historia General de los Hechos de los Castellanos en las Islas í Tierra Firme del Mar Oceano. Madrid, 1730. (3 vols.)

HUMBOLDT, ALEXANDER VON. Examen critique de l'histoire de la Géographie du nouveau continent. Paris, 1836. (3 vols.)

IRVING, WASHINGTON. Life and Voyages of Christopher Columbus. London, 1885. (3 vols.)

KENDRICK, T. D. History of the Vikings. London, 1930.

KEYSERLING, M. The First Jew in America (in H. B. Adams and Henry Wood, Columbus and his Discovery of America: John Hopkins University Studies, Series 10, No. 10). Baltimore, 1892.

LAMARTINE DE PRAT, M. L. A. DE. Christophe Colomb. Paris, 1863.

LAS CASAS, BARTOLOMÉ DE. Apologética Historia de las Indias. (Edited M. Serrano y Sanz.) (Historiadores de Indias, vol. i.) (Nueva Biblioteca de Autores Españoles, vol. xiii.) Madrid, 1909.

—— Brevissima relación de la destrucción de las Indias. (Documentos Inéditos para la Historia de España, vol. lxxi.) Madrid, 1842.

—— Historia de las Indias. (Edited Gonzalo de Reparaz.) Madrid, 1927. (3 vols.)

LOLLIS, CESARE DE. Cristoforo Colombo nella Legenda e nella Storia. Rome, 1923.

—— Scritti di Cristoforo Colombo. See RACCOLTA COLOMBIANA.

LOPES DE SOUSA, PERO. Diario da Navegação (1530–2). (Edited: Eugenio da Castro.) Rio de Janeiro, 1927. (2 vols.)

LUCAS, F. W. The Annals of the Voyages of the brothers Nicolo and Antonio Zeno in the North Atlantic about the end of the fourteenth century and the claim founded thereon to a Venetian discovery of America. A criticism and an indictment. London, 1898.

MANDEVILLE, SIR JOHN. Travels. (Edited: A. W. Pollard.) London, 1900.

MARKHAM, SIR CLEMENTS R. Christopher Columbus. London, 1892.

MAJOR, R. H. Select Letters of Christopher Columbus, with other original documents relating to his Four Voyages to the New World. (Hakluyt Society.) London, 1870.

MARTYR, PETER (ANGLERIA). Opus Epistolarum. Amsterdam, 1670.

—— Legatio babylonica. Seville, 1511.

—— De Orbe Novo Petri Martyris Angolerii mediolanensis, protonotarii et Caroli quinti Senatoris, decades octo, diligente temporum observatione et utilissimis annotationibus illustratae, suoque nitore restitute labore et industria Richardi Hakluyti Oxoniensis, Angli. Paris, 1587.

MILLARES, AGUSTIN. Historia general de las Islas Canarias. Las Palmas, 1893–5. (10 vols.)

MUÑOZ, JUAN BAUTISTA. Historia del Nuevo Mundo. Madrid, 1793.

NANSEN, FRÌDTJOF. In Northern Mists: Arctic Exploration in Early Times. (Translated: Arthur G. Chester.) London, 1901. (2 vols.)

NAVARRETE, MARTIN FERNÁNDEZ DE. Colección de los Viages y Descubrimientos que hicieron por mar los Españoles desde fines del siglo xv. Madrid, 1825. (3 vols.)

NUNN, GEORGE E. The Geographical Conceptions of Columbus. New York, 1924.

OVIEDO Y VALDES, GONZALO FERNÁNDEZ DE. Historia General y Natural de las Indias, Islas y Tierra-Firme del Mar Oceano. (Edited: José Amador de los Rios.) Madrid, 1851. (4 vols.)

PESCHEL, O. Das Zeitalter der Entdeckungeng Geschichte. Stuttgart, 1858.

PIZARRO Y ORELLANA, FERNANDO. Varones Ilustres del Nuevo Mundo. Madrid, 1639.

PLEITOS DE COLÓN, DE LOS. (Edited Cesareo Fernández Duro.) (Colección de Documentos Inéditos . . ., vols. 7 and 8.) Madrid, 1892–4. (2 vols.)

RACCOLTA COLOMBIANA. Raccolta di documenti e studi pubblicati dalla Regia Commissione Colombiana pel quarto centenario della scoperta dell' America. Rome, 1892–4:

Part I. Vols. i and ii. Scritti di Cristoforo Colombo (edited Cesare de Lollis).

Part I. Vol. iii. Autografi di Cristoforo Colombo.

Part II. Vol. i. Documenti relativi a Cristoforo Colombo e alla sua famiglia.

Part II. Vol. ii. Codice del privilegi di Cristoforo Colombo.

Part II. Vol. iii. Questioni colombiane. C. Colombo e i corsari Colombo. I ritratti di C. Colombo. Le medaglie di C. Colombo.

Part III. Vols. i and ii. Fonti Italiane per la Storia della Scoperta del Nuevo Mundo.

Part IV. Vol. i. La costruzione navali e l' arte della navigazione al tempo di Cristoforo Colombo.

Part IV. Vol. ii. La declinazione magnetica e la usa variazone nella spazia, scoperta da Cristoforo Colombo.

Part V. Vol. i. Paulo del Pozzo Toscanelli.

Part V. Vol. ii. Peter Martyr, Vespucci, John Cabot, etc.

Part V. Vol. iii. Pigafita. Benzoni.

Part VI. Bibliografia degli Scritti Italiani e Stampati in Italia sopra Cristoforo Colombo.

RIVAS PUIGCERVER, F. Los Judíos en el Nuevo Mundo. Mexico, 1891.

RONCIÈRE, CHARLES BOUREL DE LA. La carte de Christophe Colomb. Paris, 1924.

—— Une Carte de Christophe Colomb. Bordeaux, 1925.

ROSELLY DE LORGUES, COUNT. L'Ambassadeur du Dieu et le Pape Pie ix. Paris, 1874.

—— Christophe Colomb; histoire de sa vie et de ses voyages. Paris, 1856.

—— Histoire posthume de Christophe Colomb. Paris, 1885.

RUGE, SOPHUS. Christoph Columbus. Dresden, 1892.

SERRANO Y SANZ, MANUEL. Orígines de la Dominación Española en América. Estudios Históricos. Madrid, 1916.

STREICHER, FRITZ, S. J. Die Kolumbus-Originale (Eine Paleographische Studie). Munich, 1928.

THACHER, JOHN BOYD. Christopher Columbus: his Life, his Work, his Remains. New York, 1903. (3 vols.)

ULLOA, LUIS. Xristo-Ferens Colom, Fernando el Católico y la Cataluña Española. Paris, 1928.

—— La Genèse de la Découverte de l'Amérique. Paris, 1927.

VARNHAGEN, FRANCISCO ADOLFO DE, VISCONDE DE PORTO SEGURO. Primera Epistola del Almirante D. Cristóbal Colón. (By 'Genaro H. de Volafan'.) Valencia, 1858.

—— Carta de Cristóbal Colón. (By 'El Seudónimo de Valencia'.) Vienna, 1869.

VIDART, LUIS. Colón y Bobadilla. Madrid, 1892.

VIGNAUD, HENRI. Toscanelli and Columbus. London, 1902.

—— Études critiques sur la Vie de Christophe Colomb avant ses découvertes. Paris, 1905.

—— Histoire critique de la Grande Entreprise de Christophe Colomb. Paris, 1911. (2 vols.)

—— Le vrai Christophe Colomb et la légende. Paris, 1921.

WINSOR, JUSTIN. Christopher Columbus. Boston and New York, 1891.

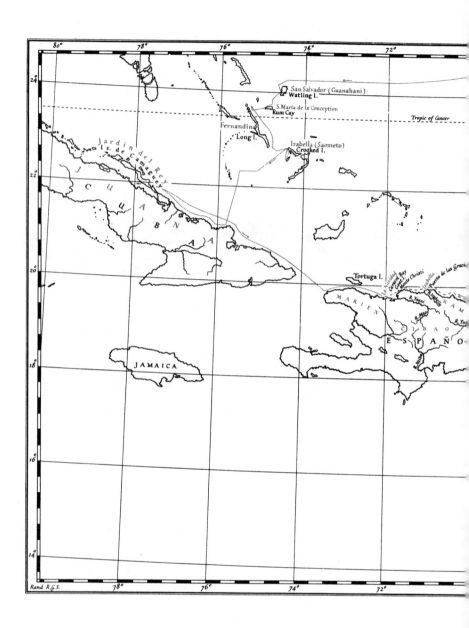

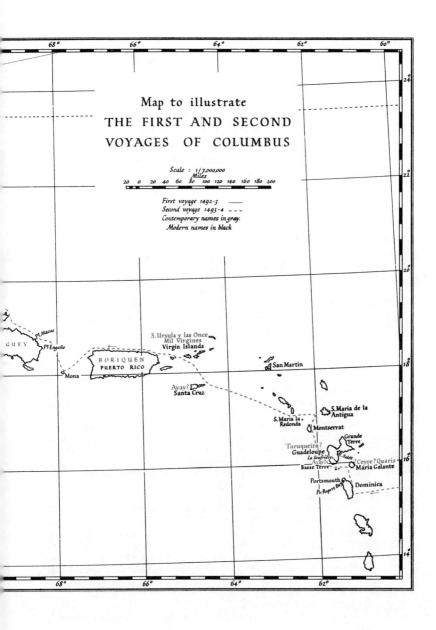

Map to illustrate

THE FIRST AND SECOND
VOYAGES OF COLUMBUS

Scale : 1/7,000,000
Miles
20 0 20 40 60 80 100 120 140 160 180 200

First voyage 1492-3 _____
Second voyage 1493-4 _ _ _
Contemporary names in gray.
Modern names in black

Pt Macao

GUEY   Pt Engaño

BORIQUEN
PUERTO RICO

Mona

S. Ursula y las Once
Mil Virgines
Virgin Islands

San Martin

Ayay?
Santa Cruz

S. Maria la
Redonda

S. Maria de la
Antigua

Montserrat

Turuqueira?
Guadeloupe
La Soufrière   Salée
Ayay?
Basse Terre

Grande
Terre

Ceyre? Quaris
Maria Galante

Portsmouth
Pt. Rupert Bay

Dominica

FIRST VOYAGE OF COLUMBUS

Letter of Columbus.[1]

SIR, As I know that you will be pleased at the great victory with which Our Lord has crowned my voyage, I write this to you, from which you will learn how in thirty-three days,[2] I passed from the Canary Islands[3] to the Indies[4] with the fleet which the most illustrious king and queen,[5] our sovereigns, gave to me. And there I found very many islands filled with people innumerable, and of them all I have taken possession[6] for their highnesses, by proclamation made and with the royal standard unfurled, and no opposition was offered to me.[7] To the first island which I found, I gave the name *San Salvador*,[8] in remembrance of the Divine Majesty, Who has marvellously bestowed all this; the Indians call it 'Guanahani'.[9] To the second, I gave the name *Isla de Santa María de Concepción*;[10] to the third, *Fernandina*;[11] to the fourth, *Isabella*;[12] to the fifth, *Isla Juana*,[13] and so to each one I gave a new name.

[1] Cp. Introduction, p. cxxiii *et seq.*

[2] 'twenty' in the folio letter, an error no doubt due to illegible handwriting in the original, 'xxxiii' being read as 'veinte'. He left Gomera on 6 Sept., but was becalmed from 6 Sept. to 8 Sept., only beginning the final stage of his voyage on the latter date. Thirty-three days thus represents the period between leaving the Canaries and reaching Guanahani.

[3] Inés Peraza and her husband, Diego de Herrera, had recognized the suzerainty of Ferdinand and Isabella over the Canaries in 1477, and in the same year the Portuguese renounced all claims to the islands. The conquest of Grand Canary for Castile was begun in 1479 and completed in 1483; Palma had just been subdued by Alfonso de Lugo when Columbus reached the Canaries. Teneriffe was not acquired for Castile until 1496.

[4] Cp. Introduction, p. lxix *et sqq.*

[5] In the first Latin translation of the letter of Columbus, the admiral is described as having been sent by the king, the queen not being mentioned. Harrisse (*Christophe Colomb*, ii. 18) found in this an attempt on the part of the translator, Leandro Cosco, to secure the credit of the discovery for Aragon alone, but it is more probable that it was either the result of hasty printing or the outcome of that reluctance to admit the equality of Isabella, which is found even in so patriotic a Castilian as Andrés Bernáldez (cp. especially, *Historia de los Reyes Católicos*, c. 87).

[6] Cp. *Journal*, 11 Oct. 1492.

[7] For a description of the standards borne by Columbus, see *Journal*, 11 Oct. 1492.

[8] The landfall of Columbus has been variously placed at Cat Island, Grand Turk, Mariguana and Watling Island; the last identification is now generally

PRIMER VIAGE DE COLÓN

Carta de Colón

SEÑOR, porque sé que avréis plazer de la gran vitoria que Nuestro Señor me ha dado en mi viaje, vos escrivo esta, por la qual sabréys como en .xxxiii. días pasé de las islas de Canaria á las Indias con la armada que los ilustrísimos rey é reyna nuestros señores me dieron, donde yo fallé muy muchas islas pobladas con gente sin número; y d'ellas todas he tomado posesión por Sus Altezas con pregón y vandera real estendida, y no me fué contradicho. á la primera que yo fallé puse nombre 'San Salvador', á comemoración de Su Alta Magestad, el qual maravillosamente todo esto ha dado; los Indios la llaman 'Guanahaní'; á la segunda puse nombre 'la isla de Santa María de Concepción'; á la tercera 'Fernandina'; á la quarta 'la Ysabela'; á la quinta 'la isla Juana', é así á cada una nombre nuevo.

accepted (cp. Cronau, *The Discovery of America and the Landfall of Columbus*, pp. 1–31). For the motives which led Columbus to select the names which he gave to these islands, see Las Casas, *Historia de las Indias*, i. 44. García de la Riega (*Colón, español*, p. 129 et seq.) argued that, while in this instance the motive for giving the name 'Salvador' was religious, that name was afterwards given, as were many others, in memory of Galicia.

⁹ Rivas Puigcerver (*Los Judios en el Nuevo Mundo*) declared that this was not really the native name of the island, but was thought to be so owing to a misunderstanding of a dialogue conducted in Hebrew between Rodrigo de Triana (more accurately Juan Rodriguez Bermejo) and another Jewish sailor. His statement was based on a story which first appeared in Mexico in the seventeenth century. Rodrigo de Triana was not a Jew, nor did the Spanish Jews of the period talk Hebrew (cp. Serrano y Sanz, in *Revista de Archivos, Bibliotecas y Museos*, 30, pp. 326–31).

¹⁰ Identified with Rum Cay (Cronau, pp. 32–3). Ulloa (*Xristo-Ferens Colom y Fernando el Católico*, p. 95 et seq.) finds in this name an illustration of the influence of 'Lullism' on Columbus and a reference to the probable name of his mother.

¹¹ Identified with Long Island (Cronau, pp. 39–42).

¹² Identified with Crooked Island (Cronau, pp. 39–42). The name appears as 'la Isla Bella' in the folio letter, but there is no reasonable doubt that the island was named in honour of the queen, as Fernandina had been named in honour of the king, and as Juana was named in honour of prince Juan.

¹³ Cuba. Ulloa (*La Genèse de la Découverte de l'Amérique*, p. 27) argues that Columbus in so naming Cuba really wished to perpetuate his own name, Juan Baptista; he finds in the later attempt of Ferdinand to change the name to Fernandina the outcome of the king's fear that the real name and true origin of Columbus might be recalled (cp. *Geographical Journal*, Jan. 1929).

When I reached Juana, I followed its coast to the westward, and I found it to be so extensive that I thought that it must be the mainland, the province of Catayo.[1] And since there were neither towns nor villages on the seashore, but only small hamlets, with the people of which I could not have speech, because they all fled immediately, I went forward on the same course, thinking that I should not fail to find great cities and towns. And, at the end of many leagues, seeing that there was no change and that the coast was bearing me northwards, which I wished to avoid, since winter was already beginning and I proposed to make from it to the south, and as moreover the wind was carrying me forward, I determined not to wait for a change in the weather and retraced my path as far as a certain harbour known to me. And from that point, I sent two men inland to learn if there were a king or great cities. They travelled three days' journey and found an infinity of small hamlets and people without number, but nothing of importance. For this reason, they returned.[2]

I understood sufficiently from other Indians, whom I had already taken, that this land was nothing but an island. And therefore I followed its coast eastwards for one hundred and seven leagues to the point where it ended.[3] And from that cape, I saw another island, distant eighteen leagues from the former, to the east, to which I at once gave the name 'Española'.[4] And I went there and followed its northern coast, as I had in the case of Juana, to the eastward for one hundred and eighty-eight great leagues in a straight line.[5] This island and all the others are very fertile to a limitless degree, and this island is extremely so. In it there are many harbours on the coast of the sea, beyond comparison with others which I know in Christendom, and many rivers, good and large, which is marvellous. Its lands are high, and there are in it very many sierras and very lofty mountains, beyond comparison with the island of Teneriffe.[6] All are most

---

[1] Columbus, despite his statement later in this letter (cp. *infra*, p. 12, etc.), long remained in doubt concerning the character of Cuba, and was not convinced that it was an island until some time in 1494 (cp. *Geog. Journal*, March 1929).

[2] Rodrigo de Xerez and Luis de Torres. The latter was a Jew and understood Hebrew, Chaldee, and a little Arabic (*Journal*, 4 Nov. 1492). Keyserling (*The First Jew in America*) is in error in supposing that de Torres afterwards

Quando yo llegué á la Juana, seguí yo la costa d'ella al
poniente, y la fallé tan grande que pensé que sería tierra
firme, la provincia de Catayo. y como no fallé así villas y
lugares en la costa de la mar, salvo pequeñas poblaciones,
con la gente de las quales no podía haver fabla, porque
luego fuýan todos, andava yo adelante por el dicho camino,
pensando de no errar grandes ciudades ó villas; y, al cabo
de muchas leguas, visto que no havía innovación, y que la
costa me llevava al setentrión, de adonde mi voluntad era
contraria, porque el yvierno era ya encarnado, y yo tenía propósito de hazer d'él al austro, y también el viento me dió
adelante, determiné de no aguardar otro tiempo, y bolví
atrás fasta un señalado puerto, de adonde enbié dos hombres
por la tierra, para saber si havía rey ó grandes ciudades.
andovieron tres jornadas, y hallaron infinitas poblaciones
pequeñas y gente sin número, mas no cosa de regimiento; por
lo qual se bolvieron.

Yo entendía harto de otros Indios, que ya tenía tomados,
como continuamente esta tierra era isla; é así seguí la costa
d'ella al oriente ciento y siete leguas fasta donde fazía
fin. del qual cabo ví otra isla al oriente, distante d'esta diez
é ocho leguas, á la qual luego puse nombre la 'Española', y
fuí allí, y seguí la parte del setentrión, así como de la Juana
al oriente, .clxxxviii. grandes leguas por linia recta; la qual y
todas las otras son fertilísimas en demasiado grado, y esta en
extremo. en ella ay muchos puertos en la costa de la mar,
sin comparación de otros que yo sepa en cristianos, y fartos
rios y buenos y grandes, que es maravilla. las tierras d'ella
son altas, y en ella muy muchas sierras y montañas altísimas,
sin comparación de la ysla de Teneryfe; todas fermosísimas,

settled in Cuba. He was one of those killed at La Navidad (cp. Gould y Quincy,
*Nueva Lista Documentada de los Tripulantes de Colón, Boletin de la Real Academia
de la Historia*, 90, p. 541).

[3] Ulloa (*La Genèse*, &c., p. 17) supposes that Columbus refrained from
prosecuting the exploration of Cuba because he was anxious to reach Española,
to which island he had already been in 1477.

[4] Española was first sighted 5 Dec. 1492.

[5] Presumably leagues of four miles each, making the total distance 702 miles.
The greatest length of the island is actually 400 miles (cp. *infra*, p. 12, note 2).

[6] The highest peak in the island has an altitude of 10,300 feet; the peak of
Teneriffe has an altitude of 12,200 feet.

beautiful, of a thousand shapes, and all are accessible and
filled with trees of a thousand kinds and tall, and they
seem to touch the sky. And I am told that they never lose
their foliage,[1] as I can understand, for I saw them as green
and as lovely as they are in Spain in May, and some of them
were flowering, some bearing fruit, and some in another
stage, according to their nature. And the nightingale was
singing and other birds of a thousand kinds in the month of
November there where I went. There are six or eight kinds
of palm, which are a wonder to behold on account of their
beautiful variety, but so are the other trees and fruits and
plants. In it are marvellous pine groves, and there are very
large tracts of cultivatable lands, and there is honey, and
there are birds of many kinds and fruits in great diversity.
In the interior are mines of metals, and the population is
without number.[2] Española is a marvel.

The sierras and mountains, the plains and arable lands and
pastures, are so lovely and rich for planting and sowing, for
breeding cattle of every kind, for building towns and villages.
The harbours of the sea here are such as cannot be believed
to exist unless they have been seen, and so with the rivers,
many and great, and good waters, the majority of which contain gold.[3] In the trees and fruits and plants, there is a great
difference from those of Juana. In this island, there are many
spices and great mines of gold and of other metals.

The people of this island, and of all the other islands which
I have found and of which I have information, all go naked,
men and women, as their mothers bore them, although some
women cover a single place with the leaf of a plant or with a
net of cotton which they make for the purpose.[4] They have
no iron or steel or weapons, nor are they fitted to use them,
not because they are not well built men and of handsome
stature, but because they are very marvellously timorous.
They have no other arms than weapons made of canes,

---

[1] Oviedo (*Historia General y Natural de las Indias*, ix. 21) says that there
were only four or five trees in the Indies which lost their leaves, and regards it
as one of the most notable characteristics of the trees in that part of the
world.

[2] For the botany of Española, see Oviedo, Bks. vii–xi. Oviedo says that the
pine cones were valueless (ix. 2). For the mines, see Oviedo (vi. 8). Las Casas

de mill fechuras, y todas andables, y llenas de árboles
de mill maneras y altas, y parece que llegan al cielo; y tengo
por dicho que jamás pierden la foja, según lo puedo comprehender, que los ví tan verdes y tan hermosos como son por
mayo en España, y d'ellos estavan floridos, d'ellos con fruto,
y d'ellos en otro término, según es su calidad; y cantava el
ruiseñor y otros paxaricos de mill maneras en el mes de
noviembre por allí donde yo andava. ay palmas de seis ó de
ocho maneras, que es admiración verlas, por la diformidad
fermosa d'ellas, mas así como los otros árboles y frutos é yervas. en ella ay pinares á maravilla é ay campiñas grandísimas,
é ay miel, y de muchas maneras de aves, y frutas muy diversas. en las tierras ay muchas minas de metales, é ay gente
in estimable número. la Española es maravilla; las sierras y
las montañas y las vegas y las campiñas, y las tierras tan fermosas y gruesas para plantar y sembrar, para criar ganados de
todas suertes, para hedeficios de villas é lugares. los puertos de
la mar aquí no havría creencia sin vista, y de los rios muchos
y grandes, y buenas aguas, los más de los quales traen oro.
en los árboles y frutos é yervas ay grandes diferencias de
aquellas de la Juana. en esta ay muchas especierías, y
grandes minas de oro y de otros metales.

La gente d'esta ysla y de todas las otras que he fallado y
he avido noticia, andan todos desnudos, hombres y mugeres,
así como sus madres los paren, aunque algunas mugeres se
cobijan un solo lugar con una foja de yerva ó una cofia
de algodón que para ellos fazen. ellos no tienen fierro, ni
azero, ni armas, ni so(n par)a ello, no porque no sea gente bien
dispuesta y de fermosa estatura, salvo que son muy te(merosos)
á maravilla. no tienen otras armas salvo las armas de las
cañas, quando est(án) con la simiente, á (la) qual ponen al cabo

(ii. 18, 42) estimated the population of Española at some three or four millions.
The most probable estimate is rather under than over two hundred thousand
(cp. Peschel, *Das Zeitalter der Entdeckungen*, p. 430).

[3] This statement, made at this time, was pure conjecture, as is the case with
many other statements in the letter.

[4] Bernáldez (c. 118), probably expressing the opinion of Columbus himself,
suggests that only pregnant women covered themselves. Oviedo (v. 3) says that
virgins went entirely uncovered, and this statement is confirmed by Peter
Martyr (*Opus Epistolarum*, Ep. 156), where the words 'mulieres corruptas' are
clearly not used in their ordinary sense.

cut in seeding time, to the ends of which they fix a small sharpened stick. And they do not dare to make use of these, for many times it has happened that I have sent ashore two or three men to some town to have speech, and countless people have come out to them, and as soon as they have seen my men approaching they have fled, even a father not waiting for his son. And this, not because ill has been done to anyone; on the contrary, at every point where I have been and have been able to have speech, I have given to them of all that I had, such as cloth and many other things, without receiving anything for it; but so they are, incurably timid. It is true that, after they have been reassured and have lost their fear, they are so guileless and so generous with all they possess, that no one would believe it who has not seen it. They never refuse anything which they possess, if it be asked of them; on the contrary, they invite anyone to share it, and display as much love as if they would give their hearts, and whether the thing be of value or whether it be of small price, at once with whatever trifle of whatever kind it may be that is given to them, with that they are content. I forbade that they should be given things so worthless as fragments of broken crockery and scraps of broken glass, and ends of straps, although when they were able to get them, they fancied that they possessed the best jewel in the world. So it was found that a sailor for a strap received gold to the weight of two and a half *castellanos*,[1] and others much more for other things which were worth much less. As for new *blancas*,[2] for them they would give everything which they had, although it might be two or three *castellanos'* weight of gold or an *arroba*[3] or two of spun cotton. . . . They took even the pieces of the broken hoops of the wine barrels and, like savages, gave what they had, so that it seemed to me to be wrong and I forbade it. And I gave a thousand handsome good things, which I had brought, in order that they might conceive affection, and more than that, might become Christians and be inclined to the love and service of their highnesses and of the whole Castilian nation, and strive to aid us and to give us of the things which they have in abundance and which are necessary to us. And they do not know any creed and are not idolaters;[4]

un palillo agudo; é no osan usar de aquellas; que m(uchas)
vezes me (a a) caescido embiar á tierra dos ó tres hombres
(á) alguna villa, para haver fabl(a, y) salir á (ellos d'ellos) sin
número; y después que los veýan llegar fuýan, á no aguardar
padre á hijo; y esto no porque á ninguno se aya hecho mal,
antes, á todo cabo adonde yo aya estado y podido haver
fabla, les he dado de todo lo que tenía, así paño como otras
cosas muchas, sin recebir por ello cosa alguna; mas son así
temerosos sin remedio. verdad es que, después que se aseguran y pierden este miedo, ellos son tanto sin engaño y tan
liberales de lo que tienen, que no lo creería sino el que lo
viese. ellos de cosa que tengan, pidiéndogela, jamás dizen de
no; antes, convidan la persona con ello, y muestran tanto amor
que darían los corazones, y, quier sea cosa de valor, quier sea
de poco precio, luego por qualquiera cosica, de qualquiera
manera que sea que se le dé, por ello se an contentos. yo
defendí que no se les diesen cosas tan civiles como pedazos de
escudillas rotas, y pedazos de vidrio roto, y cabos de agugetas,
aunque, quando ellos esto podían llegar, les parescía haver la
mejor joya del mundo; que se acertó haver un marinero,
por una agugeta, de oro peso de dos castellanos y medio, y
otros, de otras cosas que muy menos valían, mucho más; ya
por blancas nuevas davan por ellas todo quanto tenían,
aunque fuesen dos ni tres castellanos de oro, ó una arrova ó dos
de algodón filado. . . . fasta los pedazos de los arcos rotos, de
las pipas tomavan, y davan lo que tenían como bestias; así
que me pareció mal, é yo lo defendí, y dava yo graciosas mill
cosas buenas, que yo levava, porque tomen amor, y allende
d'esto se fazan cristianos, y se inclinen al amor é servicio de Sus
Altezas y de toda la nación castellana, é procuren de ayuntar
é nos dar de las cosas que tienen en abundancia, que nos son

---

[1] The weight of gold in the coin which, in the time of Ferdinand and Isabella,
was worth 490 silver maravedis, calculated to be equivalent to $6\frac{1}{4}$ pence. The
weight has been estimated at 46 decigrammes.

[2] A copper coin, worth half a maravedi, i.e. ·125 of a halfpenny.

[3] 25 lb. at 14 oz. to the lb.: 11 kil. 522 gr.

[4] Las Casas (i. 40) bases upon this testimony of the admiral his comparison
of the Indians with the Seres, described by Pliny and others, and his belief that
they were perhaps even free from the taint of original sin. Their mythology
is described by Fray Ramón, who was sent by Columbus to investigate their
beliefs and whose report is preserved by Ferdinand Columbus (*Historie*, c. 183).

only they all believe that power and good are in the heavens, and they are very firmly convinced that I, with these ships and men, came from the heavens, and in this belief they everywhere received me, after they had overcome their fear. And this does not come because they are ignorant; on the contrary, they are of a very acute intelligence and are men who navigate all those seas, so that it is amazing how good an account they give of everything, but it is because they have never seen people clothed or ships of such a kind.

And as soon as I arrived in the Indies, in the first island which I found, I took by force some of them,[1] in order that they might learn and give me information of that which there is in those parts, and so it was that they soon understood us, and we them, either by speech or signs, and they have been very serviceable.[2] I still take them with me, and they are always assured that I come from Heaven, for all the intercourse which they have had with me; and they were the first to announce this wherever I went, and the others went running from house to house and to the neighbouring towns, with loud cries of, 'Come! Come to see the people from Heaven!' So all, men and women alike, when their minds were set at rest concerning us, came, so that not one, great or small, remained behind, and all brought something to eat and drink, which they gave with extraordinary affection. In all the island, they have very many canoes,[3] like rowing *fustas*,[4] some larger, some smaller, and some are larger than a *fusta* of eighteen benches. They are not so broad, because they are made of a single log of wood, but a *fusta* would not keep up with them in rowing, since their speed is a thing incredible. And in these they navigate among all those islands, which are innumerable, and carry their goods. One of these canoes I have seen with seventy and eighty men in her, and each one with his oar.

In all these islands, I saw no great diversity in the appearance of the people or in their manners and language. On the

---

[1] Las Casas (i. 46) argues that the forcible taking of these natives was wholly unjustifiable, and finds in this incident the beginning of the maltreatment of the Indians.

[2] On his return journey to Spain, Columbus took with him several Indians, of whom only seven survived the voyage. One of these acted as interpreter on the second voyage. (Cp. Las Casas, i. 77, Peter Martyr, i. 1, and *infra*, p. 122.)

necesarias. y no conocían ninguna seta nin idolatría: salvo
que todos creen que las fuerças y el bien es en el cielo, y creían
muy firme que yo con estos navíos y gente venía del cielo, y
en tal catamiento me recebían en todo cabo, después de haver
perdido el miedo. y esto no procede porque sean ignorantes,
salvo de muy sotil ingenio y hombres que navegan todas
aquellas mares, que es maravilla la buena cuenta qu'ellos dan
de todo; salvo porque nunca vieron gente vestida ni semejantes navíos.

Y luego que legué á las Indias, en la primera isla que hallé
tomé por fuerça algunos d'ellos, para que deprendiesen y me
diesen noticia de lo que avía en aquellas partes, é así fué que
luego entendieron, y nos á ellos, quando por lengua ó señas;
y estos han aprovechado mucho. oy en día los traigo que siempre están de propósito que vengo del cielo, por mucha conversación que ayan avido conmigo; y estos eran los primeros
á pronunciarlo adonde yo llegava, y los otros andavan corriendo de casa en casa y á las villas cercanas con bozes altas:
'venid, venid á ver la gente del cielo'; así, todos, hombres
como mugeres, después de haver el corazón seguro de nos,
venían que no quedavan grande ni pequeño, y todos trayan
algo de comer y de bever, que davan con un amor maravilloso. ellos tienen en todas las yslas muy muchas canoas, á
manera de fustas de remo, d'ellas mayores, d'ellas menores;
y algunas son mayores que una fusta de diez é ocho bancos.
no son tan anchas, porque son de un solo madero; mas una
fusta no terná con ellas al remo, porque van que no es cosa de
creer. y con estas navegan todas aquellas islas que son in-
numerables, y tratan sus mercaderías. alguna d'estas canoas he
visto con .lxx. y .lxxx. hombres en ella, y cada uno con su remo.

En todas estas islas no vide mucha diversidad de la fechura
de la gente, ni en las costumbres ni en la lengua; salvo
que todos se entienden, que es cosa muy singular para lo que

---

³ Cp. *Journal*, 26 Oct. and 22 Dec. 1492. For the significance probably
attached by Columbus to the number of canoes in the islands, cp. his notes on
Marco Polo (especially Nos. 213–16, 220, 221–3) (in *Raccolta Colombiana*,
I. ii. 446 et seq.).

⁴ A *fusta* was a light-oared vessel of not more than three hundred tons. Some
fustas had one or two masts, lateen rigged. The Spaniards occasionally fixed
masts to the native canoes (cp. *infra*, vol. II, p. 130).

contrary, they all understand one another, which is a very curious thing, on account of which I hope that their highnesses will determine upon their conversion to our holy faith, towards which they are very inclined.[1]

I have already said how I have gone one hundred and seven leagues in a straight line from west to east along the seashore of the island Juana, and as a result of that voyage, I can say that this island is larger than England and Scotland together,[2] for, beyond these one hundred and seven leagues, there remain to the westward two provinces to which I have not gone. One of these provinces they call 'Avan',[3] and there the people are born with tails; and these provinces cannot have a length of less than fifty or sixty leagues, as I could understand from those Indians whom I have and who know all the islands.

The other, Española, has a circumference greater than all Spain,[4] from Colibre,[5] by the sea-coast, to Fuenterabia in Vizcaya, since I voyaged along one side one hundred and eighty-eight great leagues in a straight line from west to east. It is a land to be desired and, seen, it is never to be left. And in it, although of all I have taken possession for their highnesses and all are more richly endowed than I know how, or am able, to say, and I hold them all for their highnesses, so that they may dispose of them as, and as absolutely as, of the kingdoms of Castile, in this Española, in the situation most convenient and in the best position for the mines of gold and for all intercourse as well with the mainland here as with that there, belonging to the Grand Khan, where will be great trade and gain, I have taken possession of a large town, to which I gave the name *Villa de Navidad*,[6] and in it I have made fortifications and a fort, which now will by this time be entirely finished, and I have left in it sufficient men [7] for such a purpose with arms and artillery and provisions

---

[1] Columbus afterwards discovered that there was much diversity of language (cp. *infra*, p. 88). For his remark that it was curious that they should understand one another, cp. his note 319 on Pierre d'Ailly, *Imago Mundi* (*Rac. Col.* I. ii. p. 398).

[2] The estimated area of Cuba is 43,000 square miles: that of England alone is 50,874 square miles.

[3] Cp. *infra*, p. 138. The district was otherwise known as Magón, and seems to have stretched across the narrow part of the island from the north coast to the

espero que determinarán Sus Altezas para la conversión d'ellos á nuestra santa fe, á la qual son muy dispuestos. Ya dixe como yo havía andado .cvii. leguas por la costa de la mar por la derecha liña de oçidente á oriente por la isla Juana, según el qual camino puedo dezir que esta isla es mayor que Inglaterra y Escocia juntas; porque, allende d'estas .cvii. leguas, me quedan de la parte de poniente dos provincias que yo no he andado, la una de las quales llaman 'Avan', adonde nasçe la gente con cola; las quales provincias no pueden tener en longura menos de .l. ó .lx. leguas, según pude entender d'estos Indios que yo tengo, los quales saben todas las yslas.

Esta otra Española en cierco tiene más que la España toda, desde Colivre, por costa de mar, fasta Fuenterravia en Viscaya, pues en una quadra anduve .clxxxviii. grandes leguas por recta línea de occidente á oriente. esta es para desear, é, v (ista), es para nunca dexar; en la qual, puesto (que de to) das tenga toma(d)a posesión por Sus Altezas, y todas sean más abastadas de lo que yo sé y puedo dezir, y todas las tengo por de Sus Altezas, qual d'ellas pueden disponer como y tan complidamente como de los reynos de Castilla, en esta Española, en el lugar más convenible y mejor comarca para las minas del oro y de todo trato así de la tierra firme de aquí como de aquella de allá del gran can, adonde havrá gran trato é ganancia, he tomado posesión de una villa grande, á la qual puse nombre la 'villa de Navidad'; y en ella he fecho fuerza y fortaleza, que ya á estas horas estará del todo acabada, y he dexado en ella gente que abasta para semejante fecho, con armas y artellarías é vituallas por más de un año, y

south. 'Avan' suggests Havana, which was the native name of a province (cp. Las Casas, iii. 31).

⁴ The estimated circumference of Española is c. 1500 miles: the coastline of Spain and Portugal is c. 1,900 miles.

⁵ Collioure, in Rousillon; modern department of Pyrénées-Orientales. Ulloa, (*Xristo-Ferens Colom*, p. 101) suggests that this comparison proves that Columbus was intimately acquainted with the coast of Cataluña.

⁶ On Puerto Real, the modern bay of Caracol. (Cp. *Journal*, 26 Dec., 28 Dec., and 2 Jan.)

⁷ The number of men left by Columbus at La Navidad is given as 38 by Peter Martyr (*Decades*, i. 1, 2) and Oviedo (ii. 6, 12); as 39 in the *Journal* (2 Jan. 1493), Las Casas (i. 64), and Ferdinand Columbus (c. 52); and as 40 by Bernáldez (c. 118). Navarrete (*Colección de los Viajes*, ii. 18–20) printed what

for more than a year, and a *fusta*, and one, a master of all sea-craft, to build others, and great friendship with the king of that land,[1] so much so, that he was proud to call me, and to treat me as, a brother. And even if he were to change his attitude to one of hostility towards these men, he and his do not know what arms are and they go naked, as I have already said, and are the most timorous people that there are in the world, so that the men whom I have left there alone would suffice to destroy all that land, and the island is without danger for their persons, if they know how to govern themselves.[2]

In all these islands, it seems to me that all men are content with one woman, and to their chief or king they give as many as twenty.[3] It appears to me that the women work more than the men. And I have not been able to learn if they hold private property; what seemed to me to appear was that, in that which one had, all took a share, especially of eatable things.[4]

In these islands I have so far found no human monstrosities, as many expected,[5] but on the contrary the whole population is very well-formed, nor are they negroes as in Guinea, but their hair is flowing, and they are not born where there is intense force in the rays of the sun; it is true that the sun has there great power, although it is distant from the equinoctial line twenty-six degrees. In these islands, where there are high mountains, the cold was severe this winter, but they endure it, being used to it and with the help of meats which they eat with many and extremely hot spices. As I have found no monsters, so I have had no report of any, except in an island 'Quaris',[6] the second at the coming into the Indies, which is inhabited by a people who are regarded in all the islands as very fierce and who eat human flesh. They have many canoes with which they range through all the islands

he imagined to be a list of those left in the island, making the total 43: but he was in error in his idea of the document which he used, and the real number is 39 (cp. Gould y Quincy, *B.A.H.* vol. 85, p. 151). In the list given by Navarrete, an Irishman, Guillermo Ires, 'natural de Galney, en Irlanda', and an English-man, Tallarte de Lajes, appear, but they do not figure in any authentic records of the companions of Columbus on his first voyage. It is probable that the loss of the *Santa María* made it necessary to leave some men behind, but there is no reason to suppose either that those left were the crew of the lost vessel or that their number corresponded to that of her crew. Oviedo (ii. 12) says that Columbus wished to leave enough men to guard against the possi-

fusta, y maestro de la mar en todas artes para fazer otras, y
grande amistad con el rey de aquella tierra, en tanto grado,
que se preciava de me llamar y tener por hermano, é, aunque
le mudase la voluntad á ofender esta gente, él ni los suyos no
saben qué sean armas, y andan desnudos, como ya he dicho,
é son los más temerosos que ay en el mundo; así que solamente la gente que allá queda es para destroir toda aquella
tierra; y es ysla sin peligros de sus personas, sabiéndose regir.

En todas estas islas me parece que todos los hombres sean
contentos con una muger, y á su mayoral ó rey dan fasta
veynte. las mugeres me parece que trabaxan más que los
hombres. ni he podido entender si tienen bienes propios; que
me pareció ver que aquello que uno tenía todos hazían parte,
en especial de las cosas comederas.

En estas islas fasta aquí no he hallado hombres mostrudos,
como muchos pensavan, mas antes es toda gente de muy lindo
acatamiento, ni son negros como en Guinea, salvo con sus
cabellos corredíos, y no se crían adonde ay ímpeto demasiado
de los rayos solares; es verdad qu'el sol tiene allí gran fuerça,
puesto que es distante de la linia equinoccial veinte é seis
grados. en estas islas, adonde ay montañas grandes, aý tenía
fuerça el frio este yvierno; mas ellos lo sufren por la costumbre, y con la ayuda de las viandas que comen con especias
muchas y muy calientes en demasía. así que mostruos no
he hallado, ni noticia, salvo de una ysla 'Quaris', la segunda
á la entrada de las Yndias, que es poblada de una gente que

bility that some might die, and that he was unable to spare more than he
did spare.
    1 Guacanagari, according to Las Casas. The name is given as Goacanagari
(Oviedo), Goachanari (de Cuneo), Guacanari (Bernáldez), and Guaccanarillus or
Guadcanarillus (Peter Martyr).
    2 The nervousness which Columbus betrays concerning the probable fate of
those whom he had left at La Navidad is noteworthy (cp. *The Administration of
the Colons in Española, Proceedings of the Twenty-First International Congress
of Americanists (first part)*, p. 393).
    3 Oviedo (v. 3) says somewhat cynically that an Indian was content with
one woman when he could not afford to keep more.
    4 The lack of any conception of *meum* and *tuum* appeared during the expedi-
tion of Columbus to Cibao; it led to a misunderstanding between the natives and
the Spaniards. (Las Casas, i. 90: Ferdinand Columbus, c. 50.)
    5 Cp. *Imago Mundi*, c. 12, a passage annotated by Columbus (note 48: *Rac.
Col.* I. ii. 380).   6 Either Dominica or Maria Galante (cp. *infra*, p. 32, note 1).

of India and pillage and take as much as they can. They are no more malformed than the others, except that they have the custom of wearing their hair long like women, and they use bows and arrows of the same cane stems, with a small piece of wood at the end, owing to lack of iron which they do not possess. They are ferocious among these other people who are cowardly to an excessive degree, but I make no more account of them than of the rest. These are those who have intercourse with the women of 'Matinino', which is the first island met on the way from Spain to the Indies, in which there is not a man.[1] These women engage in no feminine occupation, but use bows and arrows of cane, like those already mentioned, and they arm and protect themselves with plates of copper, of which they have much.

In another island, which they assure me is larger than Española, the people have no hair. In it, there is gold incalculable, and from it and from the other islands, I bring with me Indians as evidence.

In conclusion, to speak only of that which has been accomplished on this voyage, which was so hasty, their highnesses can see that I will give them as much gold as they may need, if their highnesses will render me very slight assistance; moreover, spice and cotton, as much as their highnesses shall command; and mastic, as much as they shall order to be shipped and which, up to now, has been found only in Greece, in the island of Chios,[2] and the Seignory sells it for what it pleases; and aloe wood, as much as they shall order to be shipped, and slaves, as many as they shall order to be shipped and who will be from the idolaters.[3] And I believe that I have found rhubarb and cinnamon, and I shall find a thousand other things of value, which the people whom I have left there will have discovered, for I have not delayed at any point, so far as the wind allowed me to sail, except in the town of Navidad, in order to leave it secured and well established, and in truth, I should have done much more, if the ships had served me, as reason demanded.

[1] Martinique. For lands entirely inhabited by women, cp. notes of Columbus on *Historia Rerum Ubique Gestarum* (e.g. notes 190 *et seq.*), of Pius II (*Rac. Col.* I. ii. 311 *et seq.*). It may be added that Streicher (*Die Kolumbus-Originale*) holds that none of the notes to Pius II are in the autograph of Columbus.

tienen en todas las yslas por muy ferozes, los quales comen carne humana. estos tienen muchas canoas, con las quales corren todas las yslas de India, y roban y toman quanto pueden; ellos no son más disformes que los otros, salvo que tienen costumbre de traer los cabellos largos como mugeres, y usan arcos y flechas de las mismas armas de cañas, con un palillo al cabo, por defecto de fierro que no tienen. son ferozes entre estos otros pueblos que son en demasiado grado covardes, mas yo no los tengo en nada más que á los otros. estos son aquellos que tratan con las mugeres de 'Matinino', que es la primera ysla, partiendo de España para las Indias, que se falla, en la qual no ay hombre ninguno. ellas no usan exercicio femenil, salvo arcos y flechas, como los sobredichos, de cañas, y se arman y cobigan con launas de arambre, de que tienen mucho.

Otra ysla me aseguran mayor que la Española, en que las personas no tienen ningún cabello. en esta ay oro sin cuento, y d'esta y de las otras traigo comigo Indios para testimonio.

En conclusión, á fablar d'esto solamente que se a fecho este viage, que fué así de corrida, pueden ver Sus Altezas que yo les daré oro quanto ovieren menester, con muy poquita ayuda que Sus Altezas me darán; agora, especiería y algodón quanto Sus Altezas mandarán, y almástiga quanta mandarán cargar, é de la qual fasta oy no se ha fallado salvo en Grecia, en la ysla de Xío, y el Señorío la vende como quiere, y lignáloe quanto mandarán cargar, y esclavos quantos mandarán cargar, é serán de los ydólatras; y creo haver fallado ruybarvo y canela, é otras mill cosas de sustancia fallaré, que havrán fallado la gente que yo allá dexo; porque yo no me he detenido ningún cabo, en quanto el viento me aya dado lugar de navegar; solamente en la villa de Navidad, en quanto dexé asegurado é bien asentado. é, á la verdad, mucho más ficiera, si los navíos me sirvieran como razón demandava.

² Cp. *Journal*, 12 Nov. and 11 Dec. 1492. It is conjectured that Columbus visited Chios in 1474-5. The island had been acquired by the Genoese in 1346; the trade in mastic was in the hands of a company, the 'Albergo degli Justiniani', which had been tributary to the Ottomans since 1453. The island was eventually taken by the Turks in 1566.

³ The idea of securing slaves from the Indies appears to have been constantly present in the mind of Columbus: at a later date, he elaborated a scheme for the development of a slave trade (cp. *infra*, pp. 88, 90, and Las Casas, i. 151).

This is enough . . .[1] and the eternal God, our Lord, Who gives to all those who walk in His way triumph over things which appear to be impossible, and this was notably one; for, although men have talked or have written of these lands, all was conjectural,[2] without suggestion of ocular evidence, but amounted only to this, that those who heard for the most part listened and judged it to be rather a fable than as having any vestige of truth. So that, since Our Redeemer has given this victory to our most illustrious king and queen, and to their renowned kingdoms, in so great a matter, for this all Christendom ought to feel delight and make great feasts and give solemn thanks to the Holy Trinity with many solemn prayers for the great exaltation which they shall have, in the turning of so many peoples to our holy faith, and afterwards for temporal benefits, for not only Spain but all Christians will have hence refreshment and gain.

This, in accordance with that which has been accomplished, thus briefly.

Done in the caravel,[3] off the Canary Islands,[4] on the fifteenth of February, in the year one thousand four hundred and ninety-three.

At your orders.   El Almirante.

After having written this, and being in the sea of Castile, there came on me so great a south-south-west wind, that I was obliged to lighten ship. But I ran here to-day into this port of Lisbon,[5] which was the greatest marvel in the world, whence I decided to write to their highnesses. In all the Indies, I have always found weather like May; where I went in thirty-three days and I had returned in twenty-eight, save for these storms which have detained me for fourteen days, beating about in this sea. Here all the sailors say that never has there been so bad a winter nor so many ships lost.

Done on the fourth day of March.[6]

---

[1] Lacuna in the original.   [2] Cp. *infra*, vol. II, p. 32.

[3] A caravel was a vessel of mobility and was of two types: the 'Portuguese' which had only lateen sails and which could navigate five or six points to the wind, and the 'Castilian' which had sometimes both square and lateen sails, when the foresail was a square sail, and sometimes square sails only. The term 'caravel', however, was used rather loosely, and often less in reference to the type of ship than to the purpose for which she was being used.

Esto es harto . . .y eterno Dios Nuestro Señor, el qual da
á todos aquellos que andan su camino victoria de cosas que
parecen imposibles; y esta señaladamente fué la una; porque,
aunque d'estas tierras ayan fablado ó escripto, todo va por
conjectura sin allegar de vista, salvo comprendiendo atanto,
los oyentes los más escuchavan é juzgavan más por fabla
que por poca c(osa) d'ello. así que, pues Nuestro Redentor
dió esta victoria á nuestros ilustrísimos rey é reyna é á sus
reynos famosos de tan alta cosa, adonde toda la christiandad
deve tomar alegría y fazer grandes fiestas, y dar gracias
solemnes á la Sancta Trinidad con muchas oraciones solemnes
por el tanto enxalçamiento que havrán, en tornándose tantos pueblos á nuestra sancta fe, y después por los bienes temporales; que no solamente la España, mas todos los christianos ternán aquí refrigerio y ganancia.

Esto, según el fecho, así en breve.

Fecha en la caravela, sobre las yslas de Canaria, á .xv. de
febrero, ano mil .cccclxxxxiii.

Fará lo que mandaréys   El almirante.

Después d'esta escripto, y estando en mar de Castilla,
salió tanto viento conmigo sul y sueste, que me ha fecho
descargar los navíos. pero corrí aquí en este puerto de Lis-
bona oy, que fué la mayor maravilla del mundo, adonde
acordé escrivir á Sus Altezas. en todas las Yndias he siempre
hallado los temporales como en mayo; adonde yo fuý en
.xxxiii. días, y volví en .xxviii., salvo qu'estas tormentas me
an detenido .xiiii. días corriendo por este mar. dizen aquá
todos los hombres de la mar que jamás ovo tan mal yvierno
ni tantas pérdidas de naves.

Fecha á .iiii. días de marzo.

---

⁴ Cp. *Journal*, 15–17 Feb. 1493. Columbus was actually off Santa María, one
of the Azores.

⁵ Fernandez Duro (*Pinzón en el Descubrimiento de las Indias*, p. 116) points
out that, as the wind was SSW., Columbus could have made for any port in
northern Spain, as Pinzón actually did, and that he must have gone to Lisbon
by choice. It is clear that his action in doing so caused some suspicion (cp.
infra, vol. II, p. 62).

⁶ For the date of this postscript, and for the endorsement on the cover, cp.
supra, Introduction, p. cxxxv *et seq.*

SECOND VOYAGE OF COLUMBUS

1. Letter of Dr. Chanca, written to the City of Seville.[1]

MOST NOBLE SIR: Since the matters which I write privately to others in other letters cannot be made so generally known as those which go in this communication, I have decided to write the news from here separately from other matters which I have to request of your lordship. And the news is as follows.

The fleet which, by divine permission, the Catholic sovereigns, our lords, sent from Spain to the Indies, under the command of Christopher Columbus, their admiral of the Ocean Sea, left Cádiz on the twenty-fifth of September, in the year . . .,[2] the weather and wind being favourable for our journey.

The weather so continued for two days, during which we were able to make about fifty leagues. Afterwards the weather turned against us for two more days, in which time we made little or no progress. When those days were passed, it pleased God that fair weather set in for us, so that in two days more we reached Grand Canary, where we put into port, which was necessary for us to do in order to repair a ship which had made much water. We remained there all that day and afterwards set out, on the following day, and were somewhat becalmed, so that we were four or five days in reaching Gomera. And at Gomera we were obliged to remain for some while, in order to provide ourselves with as much meat, wood, and water as we could for the long journey which we expected to make without again sighting land.[3]

So with our stay at these ports and owing to our being becalmed for a day after leaving Gomera, which delayed us, we

[1] For the letter, cp. *supra*, Introduction, p. cxliii Diego Alvarez Chanca, a native of Seville, was an eminent doctor and had been physician to the princess. As he wished to go to the Indies and as his services would be of value, Ferdinand and Isabella arranged with Columbus that he should go as physician to the fleet and that he should receive the salary which he had received in Spain (cp. Letter, 23 May 1493: *Navarrete*, ii. p. 54). The contadors were ordered to pay Chanca while he was in the Indies. Bernáldez drew largely upon Chanca for his account of the second voyage of Columbus and mentions his indebtedness to the doctor (*see* c. 119, 120, 123).

SEGUNDO VIAGE DE COLÓN

1. La Carta del Doctor Chanca, que escribió a la Ciudad de Sevilla.

MUY MAGNIFICO SEÑOR: Porque las cosas que yo particularmente escribo á otros en otras cartas no son igualmente comunicables como las que en esta escritura van, acordé de escribir distintamente las nuevas de acá y las otras que á mi conviene suplicar á vuestra Señoría, é las nuevas son las siguientes: Que la flota que los Reyes Católicos, nuestros Señores, enviaron de España para las Indias é gobernacion del su Almirante del mar Océano Cristóbal Colón por la divina permision, parte de Caliz á veinte y cinco de Setiembre del año de ... años con tiempo é viento convenible á nuestro camino, é duró este tiempo dos dias, en los cuales pudimos andar al pie de cincuenta leguas; y luego nos cambió el tiempo otros dos, en los cuales anduvimos muy poco ó no nada; plogó á Dios que pasados los dias nos tornó buen tiempo, en manera que en otros dos llegamos á la Gran Canaria donde tomamos puerto, lo cual nos fue necesario por reparar un navío que hacia mucha agua, y estovímos ende todo aquel dia, é luego otro dia partimos é fizonos algunas calmerías, de manera que estovímos en llegar al Gomera cuatro ó cinco dias, y en la Gomera fue necesario estar algun dia por facer provisiones de carne, leña é agua la que mas pudiesen, por la larga jornada que se esperaba hacer sin ver mas tierra: ansi que en la estada destos puertos y en un dia despues de partidos de la Gomera, que nos fizo calma, que tardamos en

---

[2] 1493. The year is missing in the MS.

[3] According to Michele de Cuneo (*Rac. Col.* III. ii. 96), the delay at Gomera was to some extent due to a love affair between Columbus and 'the lady of the island'. This lady was Beatriz de Bobadilla, widow of Fernan Perraza, and ruler of the island as guardian of her young son, Guillem Perraza. She would appear to have retained her power of attraction to a much later date and to have been a lady of no little character. She was known as 'the huntress' (cp. Millares, *Historia general de las Islas Canarias,* vol. IV, pp. 142 ff.). Columbus had made the acquaintance of the lady on his first voyage (cp. *Journal,* 9 Aug. 1492: where her name is wrongly given as Inés Perraza, who was her mother-in-law).

were nineteen or twenty days in arriving at the island of Ferro. From here, by the goodness of God, we had fair weather, the best which a fleet ever experienced on so long a voyage, so that having left Ferro on the thirteenth of October, within twenty days we sighted land, and we should have sighted it in fourteen or fifteen days if the flagship had been as good a sailer as the other vessels, for on many occasions the other ships shortened sail because they were leaving us so far behind. During all this time we experienced much good fortune, for in it and during the whole voyage we encountered no storm, except on the eve of St. Simon, when there was one which for four hours put us in great peril.

On the first Sunday after All Saints, which was the third day of November, about daybreak, a pilot of the flagship cried, 'Largess! Land in sight!' The delight of the crews was so great that it was extraordinary to hear the cries and exclamations of pleasure which all made, and it was with good reason, for the people were so wearied with bad living and with pumping out water that they all sighed most anxiously for land. On that day some of the pilots of the fleet reckoned about eight hundred leagues from the island of Ferro to the first land which we sighted, others reckoned seven hundred and eighty, so that there was no great difference;[1] and the further three hundred which they reckoned from the island of Ferro to Cádiz made the total one thousand one hundred. So I do not think that anyone had not seen enough water!

On the morning of the Sunday before mentioned, we saw an island lying ahead of the ships,[2] and afterwards another[3] came in sight on the right hand. The first was high and mountainous on the side which we saw; the other was flat and also covered with dense woods. And as soon as it grew lighter, islands began to appear on one side and on the other, so that in the course of that day six islands were seen in different directions and most of them very large.[4] We steered directly to examine the one which we had first sighted and

---

[1] Ferro is 18° W.; Dominica, the first land sighted, is 61° 20′ W. and

[2] Dominica: so named because discovered on a Sunday (Las Casas, i. 84).

[3] María Galante (Marie Galante): so named from the flagship of Columbus (Las Casas, *ibid.*). Castilian ships in this period generally bore three names, of

llegar fasta la isla del Fierro, estovimos diez y nueve ó veinte
dias: desde aqui por la bondad de Dios nos tornó buen tiempo,
el mejor que nunca flota llevó tan largo camino, tal que partidos del Fierro á trece de Octubre dentro de veinte dias hobimos vista de tierra; y vieramosla á catorce ó quince si la nao
Capitana fuera tan buena velera como los otros navíos,
porque muchas veces los otros navíos sacaban velas porque
nos dejaban mucho atras. En todo este tiempo hobimos mucha bonanza, que en él ni en todo el camino no
hobimos fortuna, salvo la víspera de S. Simon que nos vino
una que por cuatro horas nos puso en harto estrecho. El
primero Domingo despues de Todos Santos, que fue á tres
dias de Noviembre, cerca del alba, dijo un piloto de la nao
Capitana: albricias, que tenemos tierra. Fue el alegría tan
grande en la gente que era maravilla oir las gritas y placeres
que todos hacian, y con mucha razon, que la gente venian
ya tan fatigados de mala vida y de pasar agua, que con
muchos deseos sospiraban todos por tierra. Contaron aquel
dia los pilotos del armada desde la isla de Fierro hasta la
primera tierra que vimos unas ochocientas leguas, otros setecientas é ochenta, de manera que la diferencia no ere mucha,
é mas trescientas que ponen de la isla de Fierro fasta Caliz,
que eran por todas mil é ciento; ansí que no siento quien no
fuese satisfecho de ver agua. Vimos el Domingo de mañana
sobredicho, por proa de los navíos, una isla, y luego á la man
derecha pareció otra: la primera era la tierra alta de sierras
por aquella parte que vimos, la otra era tierra llana, tambien
muy llena de árboles muy espesos, y luego que fue mas de dia
comenzó á parecer á una parte é á otra islas; de manera que
aquel dia eran seis islas á diversas partes, y las mas harto
grandes. Fuimos enderezados para ver aquella que primero

which one indicated the place of origin, e.g. 'la Gallega', one was usually the
name of a saint, e.g. 'Santa María', and one a species of nickname, e.g. 'la
Galante', referring very often to some quality in the vessel. The full name of the
flagship of Columbus on this voyage was 'Santa María la Galante'.

⁴ It is impossible that six islands 'most of them very large' should have been
sighted. Probably peaks on one island were taken to be different islands, as they
appeared on the horizon. An instance of such an error occurred during the first
voyage (cp. *Journal*, 14 Oct. 1492, and Cronau, pp. 29–31), and the probability
of a similar mistake being made on this occasion can be gauged from the outline
sketches of the coasts of these islands as given in *The English Pilot*.

reached the coast, going more than a league in search of a harbour where we might anchor, but one was not to be found in all that distance. As much of the island as was in sight was all very mountainous, very beautiful, and very green down to the water, and this was a delight to see, since in our own country at that season there is scarcely any green.

When we found no harbour there, the admiral decided that we should go to the other island [1] which appeared on the right hand, and which was four or five leagues' distance from the first. Meanwhile one ship remained off the first island, seeking for a harbour all that day, in case it should be necessary to return to it, and she found there a good harbour, and houses and people were seen.[2] And later that night she rejoined the fleet which had put into harbour at the other island.

There the admiral, with the royal standard in his hands,[3] landed, and many men with him, and there took possession for their highnesses in form of law. In this island, the trees were so dense that it was marvellous, and there were such varieties of trees, unknown to anyone, as was astonishing. Some of them were with fruit, some were in flower, so that everything was green. There were found a tree, the leaf of which had the finest scent of cloves that I have ever known, and it resembled laurel, except that it was not so large; I think, however, that it was a species of laurel.[4] There were there fruits of different kinds growing wild, which some rather unwisely tasted, and touching them only with their tongues, from the taste their faces became swollen and such great heat and pain came over them that they seemed to be going mad;[5] they cured this with cold things. In this island we found no people, and no sign of any; we believed it to be uninhabited. We were there some two hours, for when we arrived there it was nearly nightfall, and immediately on the next day, in the morning, we left for another island,[6] which appeared beyond this and which was very large, being at a distance of about seven or eight leagues.

We reached it near the side of a great mountain which seemed almost to touch the sky. In the middle of this mountain, there was a peak higher than all the rest of the mountain,

[1] María Galante.

habiamos visto, é llegamos por la costa andando mas de una
legua buscando puerto para sorgir, el cual todo aquel espacio
nunca se pudo hallar. Era en todo aquello que parecia desta
isla todo montaña muy hermosa y muy verde, fasta el agua
que era alegría en mirarla, porque en aquel tiempo no hay
en nuestra tierra apenas cosa verde. Despues que allí no hallamos puerto acordó el Almirante que nos volviesemos á la
otra isla que parescia á la mano derecha, que estaba desta
otra cuatro ó cinco leguas. Quedó por entonces un navío en
esta isla buscando puerto todo aquel dia para cuando fuese
necesario venir á ella, en la cual halló buen puerto é vido
casas é gentes, é luego se tornó aquella noche para donde
estaba la flota que habia tomado puerto en la otra isla, donde
decendió el Almirante é mucha gente con él con la bandera
Real en las manos, adonde tomó posesion por sus Altezas en
forma de derecho. En esta isla habia tanta espesura de arboledas que era maravilla, é tanta diferencia de árboles no
conocidos á nadie que era para espantar, dellos con fruto,
dellos con flor, ansí que todo era verde. Allí hallamos un
arbol, cuya hoja tenia el mas fino olor de clavos que nunca ví,
y era como laurel, salvo que no era ansi grande; yo ansí
pienso que era laurel su especia. Allí habia frutas salvaginas
de diferentes maneras, de las quales algunos no muy sabios
probaban, y del gusto solamente tocándoles con las lenguas
se les hinchaban las caras, y les venia tan grande ardor y
dolor que parecian que rabiaban, los cuales se remediaban
con cosas frias. En esta isla no hallamos gente nin señal della,
creimos que era despoblada, en la cual estovimos bien dos
horas, porque cuando allí llegamos era sobre tarde, é luego
otro dia de mañana partimos para otra isla que parescia en
bajo desta que era muy grande, fasta la cual desta que habria
siete ú ocho leguas, llegamos á ella hácia la parte de una
gran montaña que parecia que queria llegar al cielo, en medio

---

[2] Probably the modern Portsmouth, on St. Rupert's Bay, on the NW. coast
of Dominica.

[3] Cp. *supra*, p. 1 and note 7.

[4] Perhaps the tambixque, described by Oviedo (viii. 32, 34).

[5] Manchineal (*manzanillo*). The Caribs used the fruit of this tree to make the
poison in which they dipped their arrows (Oviedo, ix. 12).

[6] Guadaloupe.

from which many streams flowed in different directions, especially towards the part where we came. At a distance of three leagues, there appeared a waterfall as broad as an ox, which discharged itself from so great a height that it seemed to fall from the sky.[1] It was visible from so great a distance that many wagers were laid on the ships, since some said that it was white rocks and others that it was water. When we came nearer to it, the truth was apparent, and it was the loveliest thing in the world to see from what a height it fell and from how small a space so great a waterfall originated.

As soon as we came near, the admiral ordered a light caravel to proceed along the coast and seek for a harbour. The caravel went in advance and having reached the land, sighted some houses. The captain went to the shore in the boat and made his way to the houses, in which he found their inhabitants. Directly they saw our men, they took to flight. He entered the houses, where he found their possessions, for they had taken nothing away, and there he took two parrots, very large and very different from any that had been seen. He found much cotton, spun and ready for spinning, and articles of food, of all of which he brought away a little. Especially he brought away four or five bones of the arms and legs of men. As soon as we saw this, we suspected that those islands were the Carib islands which are inhabited by people who eat human flesh. For the admiral, in accordance with indications which the Indians of the islands which they had previously discovered had given to him on the former voyage concerning the situation of those islands, had directed his course to discover them, because they were the nearest to Spain and also because from there the route by which to come to the island of Española, where he had left people before, was direct. To those islands, by the goodness of God and by the good judgement of the admiral, we came as directly as if we had been following a known and accustomed route.

This island is very large and on this side it appeared that the coast was twenty-five leagues in length.[2] We coasted along it for more than two leagues, seeking a harbour. In the

---

[1] The fall on the river Carbet, 600 metres high. The river descends from La Soufrière (1,484 metres), and the fall is visible from a considerable distance.

de la cual montaña estaba un pico mas alto que toda la otra
montaña, del cual se vertian á diversas partes muchas aguas,
en especial hácia la parte donde ibamos: de tres leguas
paresció un golpe de agua tan gordo como un buey, que se
despeñaba de tan alto como si cayera del cielo: parescia de
tan lejos, que hobo en los navíos muchas apuestas, que unos
decian que eran peñas blancas y otros que era agua. Desque
llegamos mas á cerca vídose lo cierto, y era la mas hermosa cosa
del mundo de ver cuan alto se despeñaba é de tan poco logar
nacia tan gran golpe de agua. Luego que llegamos cerca
mandó el Almirante á una carabela ligera que fuese costeando
á buscar puerto, la cual se adelantó y llegando á la tierra vido
unas casas, é con la barca saltó el Capitan en tierra é llegó á
las casas, en las cuales halló su gente, y luego que los vieron
fueron huyendo, é entró en ellas, donde halló las cosas que
ellos tienen, que no habian llevado nada, donde tomó dos
papagayos muy grandes y muy diferenciados de cuantos se
habian visto. Halló mucho algodon hilado é por hilar, é cosas
de sus mantenimientos, é de todo trajo un poco, en especial
trajo cuatro ó cinco huesos de brazos é piernas de hombres.
Luego que aquello vimos sospechamos que aquellas islas eran
las de Caribe, que son habitadas de gente que comen carne
humana, porque el Almirante por las señas que le habian dado
del sitio destas islas, el otro camino, los indios de las islas que
antes habian descubierto, habia enderezado el camino por
descubrirlas, porque estaban mas cerca de España, y tambien
porque por allí se hacia el camino derecho para venir á la isla
Española, donde antes habia dejado la gente, á los cuales, por
la bondad de Dios y por el buen saber del Almirante, venimos
tan derechos como si por camino sabido é seguido vinieramos.
Esta isla es muy grande, y por el lado nos pareció que habia
de luengo de costa veinta é cinco leguas: fuimos costeando
por ella buscando puerto mas de dos leguas; por la parte
donde ibamos eran montañas muy altas, á la parte que de-

---

[2] Guadaloupe consists of two islands, Basse Terre and Grand Terre, divided
by la Riviére Salée. Its total area is 716 square miles, of which Basse Terre has
618 square miles. Basse Terre is mountainous; Grande Terre flat. 'Twenty-five
leagues' equals one hundred miles; there is thus some exaggeration, unless, as
elsewhere sometimes seems to be the case, 'leagues' is used to mean miles
(cp. *infra*, p. 124, *note* 2).

direction towards which we were going, there were very
lofty mountains; in the direction which we were leaving, wide
plains appeared. On the seashore there were some small
villages, and as soon as they saw the sails, all the people ran
away. Having gone two leagues, we found a harbour and that
very late. That night the admiral decided that at daybreak
some should go to speak with them and to learn what people
they were, despite the suspicion felt and although those who
had already been seen running away were naked people like
the others whom the admiral had already seen on the previous
voyage.[1]

In the morning certain captains set out. Some returned at
the hour of eating and brought a boy of about fourteen years,
as was afterwards learned, and he said that he was one of
those whom those people held captive. The others went in
different directions. Some took a small boy, whom a man was
leading by the hand and abandoned in order to escape. They
sent him with some of them; others remained and of these
some took certain women, natives of the island, and other
women, who were some of the prisoners, who came of their
own accord. From this party, one captain[2] separated with
six men, not knowing that any information had been gained.
He and those who went with him lost themselves, so that they
never found the way back until at the end of four days they
reached the coast of the sea and following it returned to the
fleet.[3] We had already given them up for lost and eaten by
those people who are called Caribs, for there was not sufficient
reason for thinking that they were lost in any other way,
since there were with them pilots, sailors who by the star
knew how to go and come from Spain, and we believed that
in so small a space they could not lose themselves.

On this first day that we landed there, many men and
women walked along the shore near the water wondering at
the fleet and marvelling at so novel a spectacle. And when
a boat came to land to speak with them, saying to them
tayno, tayno, which means 'good', they waited as long as
our men did not leave the water, remaining near it, in such
a way that when they wished they could escape. The end

---

[1] The suspicion was presumably that the natives were Caribs.

jamos parecian grandes llanos, á la orilla de la mar habia algunos poblados pequeños, é luego que veian las velas huian todos. Andadas dos leguas hallamos puerto y bien tarde.

Esa noche acordó el Almirante que á la madrugada saliesen algunos para tomar lengua é saber que gente era, no embargante la sospecha é los que ya habian visto ir huyendo, que era gente desnuda como la otra que ya el Almirante habia visto el otro viage. Salieron esa madrugada ciertos Capitanes; los unos vinieron á hora de comer é trageron un mozo de fasta catorce años, á lo que despues se sopo, é él dijo que era de los que esta gente tenian cativos. Los otros se dividieron, los unos tomaron un mochacho pequeño, al cual llevaba un hombre por la mano, é por huir lo desamparó. Este enviaron luego con algunos dellos, otros quedaron, é destos unos tomaron ciertas mugeres naturales de la isla, é otras que se vinieron de grado, que eran de las cativas. Desta compañía se apartó un Capitan no sabiendo que se habia habido lengua con seis hombres, el cual se perdió con los que con él iban, que jamas sopieron tornar, fasta que á cabo de cuatro dias toparon con la costa de la mar, é siguiendo por ella tornaron á topar con la flota. Ya los teniamos por perdidos é comidos de aquellas gentes que se dicen los Caribes, porque no bastaba razon para creer que eran perdidos de otra manera, porque iban entre ellos pilotos, marineros que por la estrella saben ir é venir hasta España, creiamos que en tan pequeño espacio no se podian perder. Este dia primero que allí decendimos andaban por la playa junto con el agua muchos hombres é mugeres mirando la flota, é maravillándose de cosa tan nueva, é llegándose alguna barca á tierra á hablar con ellos, diciéndolos *tayno tayno*, que quiere decir *bueno*, esperaban en tanto que no salian del agua, junto con él moran, de manera que cuando ellos querian se podian salvar: en conclusion, que de los hombres ninguno se pudo tomar por fuerza ni por grado, salva dos que se seguraron é despues los trajeron por fuerza

---

[2] Diego Marquez, of Seville (Las Casas, i. 84). He was sent as veedor (Las Casas, i. 82). At a later date, he was treasurer in Castilla del Oro, under Pedrarias (*loc. cit.*).

[3] According to Cuneo (*Rac. Col. loc. cit.*), the lost party were guided to the coast by a native woman and lit a fire to indicate their whereabouts to the fleet.

was that none of the men could be taken by force or persuasion, except two who were over-confident and who were afterwards taken there by force. More than twenty women of the captives were taken and other natives of the island came of their own accord, besides those who were captured and taken by force. Some boys, prisoners, came to our men, flying from the natives of the island who held them captive.

We were in that harbour eight days, on account of the loss of the above-mentioned captain, and there we went on land many times, going about the dwellings and villages which were on the coast. There we found a great quantity of men's bones and skulls hung up about the houses like vessels to hold things. Not many men appeared here; the reason was, as the women told us, that ten canoes had gone with people to raid other islands. This people seemed to us to be more civilized than those who were in the other islands which we have visited, although they all have dwellings of straw, but these have them much better made and better provided with supplies, and in them were more signs of industry, both of men and women. They had much cotton, woven and ready to weave, and many cotton sheets, so well made as to lose nothing by comparison with those of our own country.

We asked the women, who were captive on this island, what these people were; they replied that they were Caribs. After they understood that we abhorred that race for their evil custom of eating human flesh, they rejoiced greatly, and if after that any woman or man of the Caribs were brought in, they said secretly that they were Caribs, for, as a conquered race, they went in terror of them, even here where all were in our power. In this way we knew which of the women were Caribs and which not, for the Caribs wear two bandages, made of cotton, on each leg, one near the knee and the other near the ankles. The result is to make the calves large and the places mentioned very small, and to me it appears that they regard this as an attraction. So, by this difference, we knew the one race from the other.

The customs of this race of Caribs are bestial. There are three islands, this which is called Turuqueira, the other, which we first sighted, called Ceyre, and the third called

allí. Se tomaron mas de veinte mugeres de las cativas, y de su grado se venian otros naturales de la isla, que fueron salteadas é tomadas por fuerza. Ciertos mochachos cabtivos se vinieron á nosotros huyendo de los naturales de la isla que los tenian cabtivos. En este puerto estovimos ocho dias á causa de la pérdida del sobredicho Capitan, donde muchas veces salimos á tierra andando por sus moradas é pueblos, que estaban á la costa, donde hallamos infinitos huesos de hombres, é los cascos de las cabezas colgados por las casas á manera de vasijas para tener cosas. Aquí no parescieron muchos hombres; la causa era, segun nos dijeron las mugeres, que eran idas diez canoas con gentes á saltear á otras islas. Esta gente nos pareció mas pulítica que la que habita en estas otras islas que habemos visto, aunque todos tienen las moradas de paja; pero estos las tienen de mucho mejor hechura, é mas proveidas de mantenimientos, é parece en ellas mas industria ansi veril como femenil. Tenian mucho algodon hilado y por hilar, y muchas mantas de algodon tan bien tejidas que no deben nada á las de nuestra patria. Preguntamos á las mugeres, que eran cativas en esta isla, que qué gente era esta; respondieron que eran Caribes. Despues que entendieron que nosotros aborreciamos tal gente por su mal uso de comer carne de hombres, holgaban mucho, y sí de nuevo traian alguna muger ó hombre de los Caribes, secretamente decian que eran Caribes, que allí donde estaban todos en nuestro poder mostraban temor dellos como gente sojuzgada, y de allí conocimos cuáles eran Caribes de las mugeres é cuáles nó, porque las Caribes traian en las piernas en cada una dos argollas tejidas de algodon, la una junto con la rodilla, la otra junto con los tobillos; de manera que les hacen las pantorrillas grandes, é de los sobredichos logares muy ceñidas, que esto me parece que tienen ellos por cosa gentil, ansi que por esta diferencia conocemos los unos de los otros. La costumbre desta gente de Caribes es bestial: son tres islas, esta se llama Turuqueira, la otra que primero vimos se llama Ceyre, la tercera se llama Ayay; estos todos son conformidad como si fuesen de un linage, los cuales no se hacen mal: unos é otros hacen guerra á todas las otras islas comarcanas, los cuales van por mar ciento é cincuenta leguas á saltear con muchas canoas que tienen, que son unas fustas

Ayay.[1] They are all agreed, as if they were of one family, doing no ill to each other. One and all they make war on all the other neighbouring islands, and they go by sea in the many canoes which they have and which are small *fustas*, made of a single piece of wood, a hundred and fifty leagues to make raids. Their arms are arrows in place of iron weapons. As they do not possess any iron, some of them fix on points made of tortoise-shell, others from another island fix on fish bones which are indented, being so naturally, like very strong saws. For an unarmed people, as they all are, such weapons can kill and do great injury, but for people of our nation they are not arms to be greatly feared.

These people raid the other islands and carry off the women whom they can take, especially the young and handsome. They keep them in service and have them as concubines, and they carry off so many that in fifty houses no males were found, and of the captives more than twenty were girls. These women also say that they are treated with a cruelty which appears to be incredible, for they eat the male children whom they have from them and only rear those whom they have from their own women. As for the men whom they are able to take, they bring such as are alive to their houses to cut up for meat, and those who are dead, they eat at once. They say that the flesh of a man is so good that there is nothing like it in the world, and it certainly seems to be so for, from the bones which we found in their houses, they had gnawed everything that could be gnawed, so that nothing was left on them except what was too tough to be eaten. In one house there a neck of a man was found cooking in a pot. They castrate the boys whom they capture and employ them as servants until they are fully grown, and then when they wish to make a feast, they kill and eat them, for they say that the flesh of boys and of women is not good to eat. Of these boys, three came fleeing to us, and all three had been castrated.

And at the end of four days, the captain who had been lost returned. We were already in despair of his coming, for other bands [2] had already twice gone to search for him and that

---

[1] These islands have been identified as Guadeloupe, Maria Galante, and Santa Cruz. But Turuqueira and Ayay have also been taken to be the two islands

pequeñas de un solo madero. Sus armas son frechas en lugar
de hierros; porque no poseen ningun hierro, ponen unas puntas fechas de huesos de tortugas los unos, otros de otro isla
ponen unas espinas de un pez fechas dentadas, que ansi lo son
naturalmente, á manera de sierras bien recias, que para gente
desarmada, como son todos, es cosa que les puede matar é
hacer harto daño; pero para gente de nuestra nacion no son
armas para mucho temer. Esta gente saltea en las otras islas,
que traen las mugeres que pueden haber, en especial mozas
y hermosas, las cuales tienen para su servicio, é para tener por
mancebas, é traen tantas que en cincuenta casas ellos no
parecieron, y de las cativas se vinieron mas de veinte mozas.
Dicen tambien estas mugeres que estos usan de una crueldad
que parece cosa increible; que los hijos que en ellas han se los
comen, que solamente crian los que han en sus mugeres naturales. Los hombres que pueden haber, los que son vivos lleván-
selos á sus casas para hacer carnicería dellos, y los que han
muertos luego se los comen. Dicen que la carne del hombre
es tan buena que no hay tal cosa en el mundo; y bien parece
porque los huesos que en estas casas hallamos todo lo que se
puede roer todo lo tenian roido, que no habia en ellos sino lo
que por su mucha dureza no se podia comer. Allí se halló en
una casa cociendo en una olla un pezcuezo de un hombre. Los
mochachos que cativan cortanlos el miembro, é sirvense de
ellos fasta que son hombres, y despues cuando quieren facer
fiesta mátanlos é cómenselos, porque dicen que la carne
de los mochachos é de las mogeres no es buena para comer.
Destos mochachos se vinieron para nosotros huyendo tres
todos tres cortados sus miembros. E á cabo de cuatro dias
vino el Capitan que se habia perdido, de cuya venida estabamos ya bien desesperados, porque ya los habian ido á
buscar otras cuadrillas por dos veces, é aquel dia vino la una

which together form Guadeloupe, while Ceyre has been identified with Dominica.
The latter identification would seem to be unsatisfactory, in view of the state-
ment that Dominica was uninhabited. Ceyre is no doubt the same island as the
'Quaris', mentioned in the letter on the first voyage (cp. *supra*, p. 14).

[2] One search party was led by Alonso de Ojeda (cp. *infra*, p. 76 note 3) who
took forty men with him (Las Casas, i. 84). According to Cuneo (*Rac. Col.
loc. cit.*), two hundred men in all were sent to search and it was feared that they
were also lost.

very day one band had returned without learning anything certainly of him. We rejoiced at his coming as if he had been newly found. This captain, besides those who went with him, brought in ten head, boys and women. Neither they nor the others who went to seek for them ever found men, for they had fled or perhaps it was because in that district there were few men, since, as was learned from the women, ten canoes with people had gone to raid the other islands. He and those who were with him came from the mountain so worn out that it was pitiful to see them. When they were asked how they had got lost, they said that the trees were so thick that they could not see the sky, and that some of them, who were sailors, had climbed the trees to look for the star and had never been able to see it, and that if they had not struck the sea, it would have been impossible for them to regain the fleet.

We left this island eight days after we had arrived there.[1] Afterwards, next day at noon, we saw another island, not very large, which was twelve leagues from the first.[2] As on the day immediately after we left we were becalmed for the greater part of the day, we were close to the coast of this island, and the Indian women whom we took with us said that it was not inhabited, for the Caribs had depopulated it, and for this reason we did not stay at it. After that, on this evening, we saw another;[3] this night, near this island, we found many shoals, for fear of which we anchored, as we did not dare to proceed until daylight. Then, in the morning, another very large island appeared.[4] We did not go to any of these in order that we might bring consolation to those who had been left in Española, and it did not please God, as will appear later.

On the next day, at the hour of eating, we reached another island[5] and it appeared to us to be very good, for it seemed to be very populous, judging from the many tracts of cultivated land which were on it. We went there and put into a harbour on the coast. The admiral immediately ordered a boat, well manned, to put to shore in order, if possible, to hold speech to find what people they were, and also because

[1] Sunday, 10 Nov. (Las Casas, i. 85).

cuadrilla sin saber dellos ciertamente. Holgamos con su
venida como si nuevamente se hobieran hallado: trajo este
Capitan con los que fueron con él diez cabezas entre mochachos y mugeres. Estos ni los otros que los fueron á buscar,
nunca hallaron hombres porque se habien huido, ó por ventura que en aquella comarca habia pocos hombres, porque
segun se supo de las mugeres eran idas diez canoas con gentes
á saltear á otras islas. Vino él é los que fueron con él tan
destrozados del monte, que era lástima de los ver: decian,
preguntándoles como se habian perdido, dijeron que era la
espesura de los árboles tanta que el cielo no podian ver, é que
algunos de ellos, que eran marineros, habian subido por los
árboles para mirar el estrella, é que nunca la podieron ver, é
que si no toparan con el mar fuera imposible tornar á la flota.
Partimos desta isla ocho dias despues que allí llegamos.
Luego otro dia á medio dia vimos otra isla, no muy grande,
que estaria desta otra doce leguas ; porque el primero dia que
partimos lo mas del dia nos fizo calma, fuimos junto con la
costa desta isla, é dijeron las Indias que llevabamos que no era
habitada, que los Caribes la habian despoblado, é por esto no
paramos en ella. Luego esa tarde vimos otra: á esa noche,
cerca desta isla, fallamos unos bajos, por cuyo temor sorgimos,
que no osamos andar fasta que fuese de dia. luego á la mañana
paresció otra isla harto grande: á ninguna destas no llegamos
por consolar los que habian dejado en la Española, é no plogó
á Dios segun que abajo parecerá. Otro dia á hora de comer
llegamos á una isla é pareciónos mucho bien, porque parecia
muy poblada, segun las muchas labranzas que en ella habia.
Fuimos allá é tomamos puerto en la costa: luego mandó el
Almirante ir á tierra una barca guarnecida de gente para si
pudiese tomar lengua para saber que gente era, é tambien
porque habiamos menester informarnos del camino, caso quel
Almirante, aunque nunca habia fecho aquel camino, iba muy

---

[2] Montserrat (Las Casas, *ibid.*). It was so named after the mountain near
Barcelona. Its area is 32 sq. miles.
[3] Santa Maria la Redonda (Las Casas, *ibid.*). So named from its shape.
[4] Santa Maria de la Antigua (Las Casas, *ibid.*). According to Ferdinand
Columbus (c. 47), the natives called this island Jamaica. Its area is 108 sq. miles.
[5] San Martin (Las Casas, *loc. cit.*).

we had need to inform ourselves of the route, although the admiral, despite the fact that he had never made that voyage, followed a very direct course, as eventually appeared. But because doubtful matters ought always to be examined with the greatest possible care, he wished to have speech there, for which reason some of the men who went in the boat landed and proceeded by land to a village, from which the people had already gone into hiding. They took there five or six women and some boys, of whom most were of the number of the captives, as in the other island, for the people here also were of the Caribs, as we already knew from the account of the women whom we brought with us.

This boat was already about to return to the ships with the capture which had been made below this place; along the coast came a canoe in which were four men and two women and a boy, and when they saw the fleet, they were so stupefied with amazement that for a full hour they remained there without moving from a place about two lombard shot from the ships. In this time, they were seen by those who were in the boat and even by the whole fleet. Immediately those in the boat went towards them, keeping so close to shore that the others, as a result of the stupefaction which overcame them, wondering and thinking what thing this might be, never noticed them until they were very close to them, so that they could not well escape although they made a great effort to do so, but our men pressed on them so rapidly that they were unable to get away. The Caribs when they saw that flight was useless, with great daring, took up their bows, the women as well as the men. And I say 'with great daring', because they were not more than four men and two women, and our men were more than twenty-five. Of these, they wounded two; one they hit twice with arrows in the breast, and the other once in the side, and if it had not been that our men carried shields of leather and wood, and that they came near them with the boat and upset the canoe, they would have wounded most of them with their arrows. And when their canoe was upset, they remained in the water swimming and occasionally wading, as there were some shallows there, and it was a great trouble to take them, for they still shot as

bien encaminado segun en cabo pareció. Pero porque las cosas
dubdosas se deben siempre buscar con la mayor certinidad que
haberse pueda, quiso haber allí lengua, de la cual gente que
iba en la barca ciertas personas saltaron en tierra, é llegaron
en tierra á un poblado de donde la gente ya se habia escondido.
Tomaron allí cinco ó seis mugeres y ciertos mochachos, de las
cuales las mas eran tambien de las cativas como en la otra
isla, porque tambien estos eran de los Caribes, segun ya
sabiamos por la relacion de las mugeres que traiamos. Ya
que esta barca se queria tornar á los navíos con su presa que
habia fecho por parte debajo; por la costa venia una canoa en
que venian cuatro hombres é dos mugeres é un mochacho, é
desque vieron la flota maravillados se embebecieron tanto que
por una grande hora estovieron que no se movieron de un
lugar casi dos tiros de lombarda de los navíos. En esto fueron
vistos de los que estaban en la barca é aun de toda la flota.
Luego los de la barca fueron para ellos tan junto con la tierra,
que con el embebecimiento que tenian, maravillándose é pensando que cosa seria, nunca los vieron hasta que estovieron
muy cerca dellos, que no les pudieron mucho huir aunque
harto trabajaron por ello; pero los nuestros aguijaron con
tanta priesa que no se les pudieron ir. Los Caribes desque
vieron que el hoir no les aprovechaba, con mucha osadia
pusieron mano á los arcos, tambien las mugeres como los
hombres; é digo con mucha osadia porque ellos no eran mas
de cuatro hombres y dos mugeres, é los nuestros mas de
veinte é cinco, de los cuales firieron dos, al uno dieron dos
frechadas en los pechos é al otro una por el costado, é sino
fuera porque llevaban adargas é tablachutas, é porque los
invistieron presto con la barca é les trastornaron su canoa,
asaetearan con sus frechas los mas dellos. E despues de tras-
tornada su canoa quedaron en el agua nadando, é á las veces
haciendo pie, que allí habia unos bajos, é tovieron harto que
hacer en tomarlos, que todavía cuanto podian tiraban, é con
todo eso el uno no lo pudieron tomar sino mal herido de una
lanzada que murió, el cual trajeron ansi herido fasta los
navíos. La diferencia destos á los otros indios en el hábito, es
que los de Caribe tienen el cabello muy largo, los otros son
tresquilados é fechas cien mil diferencias en las cabezas de

much as they could, and with all this, there was one whom they could not take until he was mortally wounded and whom they brought, so wounded, to the ships.

The difference between these people and the other Indians in appearance is that the Caribs wear their hair very long; the others have it cut irregularly and their heads are decorated with a hundred thousand different devices, such as crosses and other markings of different kinds, which they make with sharpened reeds, each according to his fancy. All, both the Caribs and the others, are a beardless race, so they regard a man who has a beard as a marvel. The Caribs, whom they took there, had their eyes and eyebrows stained, which, I think, they do for show, and from that they appear more terrifying. One of them said that in one of their islands, called Cayre, which is the first that we saw and to which we did not go, there is much gold;[1] that they go there with nails and tools to build their canoes, and that they bring away as much gold as they please.

After this, on that day, we left that island, where we had not stayed more than six or seven hours, and we went towards some other land[2] which came in sight and which was on the route that we had to follow; at night we arrived near it. Next day in the morning we went along its coast; there was very much land, although it was not very continuous, as there were more than forty islands and so many islets.[3] The land was very high and most of it barren, which was not the case with any that we had seen before or which we have since seen. The land seemed to be of a character to have metals in it. We did not go to this land, except that a lateen-rigged caravel went up to one of the islets, on which they found some fishermen's huts. The Indian women whom we had with us said that they were not inhabited.

We went along this coast for the greater part of this day, until on the following day in the evening we came in sight of another island, called Burenquen,[4] along the coast of which we ran for a whole day: it was judged that on that side it extended for thirty leagues. This island is very lovely and appears to be very fertile; thither come the Caribs to conquer

[1] If Cayre be identified with Dominica, the statement that there is much gold

cruces, é de otras pinturas en diversas maneras, cada uno
como se le antoja, lo cual se hacen con cañas agudas. Todos
ansi los de Caribe como los otros es gente sin barbas, que por
maravilla hallarás hombre que las tenga. Estos Caribes que
allí tomaron venian tiznados los ojos é las cejas, lo cual me
parece que hacen por gala, é con aquello parescian mas espantables; el uno destos dice que en una isla dellos, llamada
Cayre, que es la primera que vimos, á la cual no llegamos, hay
mucho oro; que vayan allá con clavos é contezuelas para
hacer sus canoas, é que traerán cuanto oro quisieren. Luego
aquel dia partimos de esta isla, que no estariamos allí mas de
seis ó siete horas, fuemos para otra tierra que pareció á ojo
que estaba en el camino que habiamos de facer: llegamos
noche cerca della. Otro dia de mañana fuimos por la costa
della: era muy gran tierra, aunque no era muy continua,
que eran mas de cuarenta y tantos islones, tierra muy alta, é
la mas della pelada, la cual no era ninguna ni es de las que
antes ni despues habemos visto. Parescia tierra dispuesta
para haber en ella metales: á esta no llegamos para saltar en
tierra, salvo una carabela latina llegó á un islon de estos, en el
cual hallaron ciertas casas de pescadores. Las Indias que
traiamos dijeron que no eran pobladas. Andovimos por esta
costa lo mas deste dia, hasta otro dia en la tarde que llegamos
á vista de otra isla llamada Burenquen, cuya costa corrimos
todo un dia: juzgábase que ternia por aquella banda treinta
leguas. Esta isla es muy hermosa y muy fértil á parecer: á
esta vienon los de Caribe á conquistar, de la cual llevaban

there is inaccurate; nor does gold seem ever to have been found in Maria Galante.
From the context here, it would seem to be possible either that the natives were
misunderstood or that the text is corrupt, and that in place of 'gold', 'wood'
should be read. Both the islands in question are well wooded.

² Santa Cruz, reached on Thursday, 14 Nov. (Las Casas, *loc. cit.*).

³ Columbus called these islands Santa Ursula y las Once Mil Virgines (Las
Casas, *loc. cit.*). It does not appear that any individual island was called Santa
Ursula, which name does not appear in any early maps.

⁴ Puerto Rico. The native name of the island is variously given as Boriquen
(Las Casas), Boluchen (Cuneo), Burenquen or Burenwuen (Chanca). Boriquen
would seem to be the best rendering. Columbus named the island San Juan
Baptista (Las Casas, *loc. cit.*), and in this Ulloa (*La Genèse de la Découverte*,
pp. 28–9) finds a further attempt on the part of the admiral to perpetuate his
own name. It became known as San Juan del Puerto Rico (Las Casas, *ibid.*), and
eventually as Puerto Rico or Porto Rico. The length of Puerto Rico is approximately one hundred miles.

it and thence they carry away many people. These people have no *fustas* and do not know how to go by sea, but, according to that which those Caribs whom we have taken say, they use bows as they do, and if by chance they are able to take those who come to raid them, they also eat them as do the Caribs. We were two days in a harbour of this island, and there many men went ashore, but we were never able to have speech with the people, who all fled as being terrified by the Caribs.

All these above-mentioned islands were discovered on this voyage, for up to then the admiral had seen none of them on the previous voyage. They are all very lovely and have a very fertile soil, but this last seemed to be the best of all. Here almost ended the islands which, on the side lying towards Spain, the admiral had not seen. But we hold it to be certain that there is land more than forty leagues nearer Spain than these first islands, because two days before we sighted land, we saw some birds called *rabihorcados*,[1] which are marine birds of prey and which do not sit or sleep on the water, and about nightfall they were circling upwards in the air and then making their way in search of land on which to sleep. As it was evening, they could not have been going to settle more than twelve or fifteen leagues away and that on our right hand as we were coming, in the direction of Spain. From this all judged that there was more land there, but we did not look for it as it would have taken us round out of our intended course. I hope that in a few voyages it will be found.[2]

From the above-mentioned island we set out one day at dawn and on that day, before nightfall, we came in sight of land, which was also unknown to any of those who had gone on the previous voyage, but which, from the information received from the Indian women whom we had with us, we guessed must be Española, where we are at present. Between it and the other island of Burenwuen, another island[3] appeared at a distance, although it was not large. When we reached Española, at first on that side the land was low and very flat, and on seeing this, all were doubtful as to what land it was, for that part neither the admiral nor those who were with him had seen.[4]

---

[1] *Pelicanus aquilis*, the frigate-bird.

mucha gente; estos no tienen fustas ningunas nin saben andar
por mar; pero, segun dicen estos Caribes que tomamos, usan
arcos como ellos, é si por caso cuando los vienen á saltear los
pueden prender tambien se los comen como los de Caribe á
ellos. En un puerto desta isla estovimos dos dias, donde saltó
mucha gente en tierra; pero jamas podimos haber lengua, que
todos se fuyeron como gente temorizadas de los Caribes.
Todas estas islas dichas fueron descubiertas deste camino, que
fasta aquí ninguna dellas habia visto el Almirante el otro
viage, todas son muy hermosas é de muy buena tierra; pero
esta paresció mejor á todas: aquí casi se acabaron las islas que
fácia la parte de España habia dejado de ver el Almirante,
aunque tenemos por cosa cierta que hay tierra mas de
cuarenta leguas antes de estas primeras hasta España, porque
dos dias antes que viesemos tierra vimos unas aves que
llaman rabihorcados, que son aves de rapiña marinas é no
sientan ni duermen sobre el agua, sobre tarde rodeando sobir
en alto, é despues tiran su via á buscar tierra para dormir,
las cuales no podrian ir á caer segun era tarde de doce ó quince
leguas arriba, y esto era á la man derecha donde veniamos
hasta la parte de España; de donde todos juzgaron allí quedar
tierra, lo cual no se buscó porque se nos hacia rodeo para la via
que traiamos. Espero que á pocos viages se hallará. Desta isla
sobredicha partimos una madrugada, é aquel dia, antes que
fuese noche, hobimos vista de tierra, la cual tampoco era
conocida de ninguno de los que habian venido el otro viage;
pero por las nuevas de las indias que traiamos sospechamos
que era la Española, en la cual agora estamos. Entre esta isla
é la otra de Buriquen parecia de lejos otra, aunque no era
grande. Desque llegamos á esta Española, por el comienzo de
ella era tierra baja y muy llana, del conocimiento de la cual
aun estaban todos dubdosos si fuese la que es, porque aquella
parte nin el Almirante ni los otros que con él vinieron habian
visto, é aquesta isla como es grande es nombrada por provincias, é á esta parte que primero llegamos llaman Hayti, y

² This land was the remaining Leeward Islands.
³ Mona.
⁴ 'Apparently between Point Macao and Point Engaño, which is flat. The
higher land of the north coast commences at Point Macao' (Major, *Select
Letters*, p. 41, note 3).

As this island is large, it has provinces with different names, and the part to which we first came they call Haiti, and the province next after it they call Xamana, and the next in which we now are, Bohio.[1] There are, moreover, many sub-divisions of these provinces,[2] for it is a great land, since, as those who have seen the length of the coast affirm, it extends for two hundred leagues. It appears to me that it is not less than a hundred and fifty leagues in length; as to its breadth, that is not yet known.[3] A caravel went forty days ago to circumnavigate it, and has not yet returned.

The land is very remarkable, and in it there are innumerable great rivers and great mountain ranges and large open valleys and lofty mountains. I imagine that the foliage is green all the year round. I do not believe that there is any winter in this island or in the others, for at Christmas many birds' nests were found, some with young birds in them and some with eggs. Neither in it nor in the other islands has any four-footed animal been seen, except some dogs of various colours, as in our own native land, in appearance like some large *gosques*.[4] There are no savage animals. There is, further, an animal, the colour of a rabbit and with similar fur; it is the size of a young rabbit, has a long tail, and hind and fore feet like those of a rat.[5] These animals climb trees, and many who have eaten them say that the flesh is very good to eat.

There are many small snakes. There are not many lizards, and so the Indians make as great a dainty of them as we make of pheasants at home; they are the same size as those at home, but are of a different shape.[6] In a small islet, however, which lies near a harbour that they call Monte Christi,[7] where we stayed many days, they saw on many occasions a very large lizard, which they say was as great round as a calf, and from tip to tail as long as a lance.[8] They went out many

---

[1] Haiti, 'the land of hills', and Bohio, 'the land of villages', were native names for the whole island. Xamana was part of the Vega Real, lying on the north coast. The district first reached on this voyage was Higuey, the most easterly province of the island, and the 'Bohio' of Chanca was Marien.

[2] Las Casas (*Apologética Historia*, c. 2–7) enumerates and describes some twenty provinces in the island, but in the *Destrucción de las Indias*, he distinguishes five kingdoms—Marien, Magua, Maguana, Xaragua, and Higuey, and these may be regarded as the main divisions of the island (cp. Oviedo, iii. 4).

[3] The extreme breadth of Española is 150 miles.

luego á la otra provincia junta con esta llaman Xamaná, é á
la otra Bohio, en la cual agora estamos; ansi hay en ellas
muchas provincias porque es gran cosa, porque segun afirman
los que la han visto por la costa de largo, dicen que habrá
doscientas leguas: á mi me parece que á lo menos habrá ciento
é cincuenta; del ancho della hasta agora no se sabe. Allá es
ido cuarenta dias ha á rodearla una carebela, la cual no es
venida hasta hoy. Es tierra muy singular, donde hay infinitos
rios grandes é sierras grandes é valles grandes rasos, grandes
montañas: sospecho que nunca se secan las yerbas en todo el
año. Non creo que hay invierno ninguno en esta nin en las
otras, porque por Navidad se fallan muchos nidos de aves,
dellas con pájaros, é dellas con huevos. En ella ni en las otras
nunca se ha visto animal de cuatro pies, salvo algunos perros
de todas colores como en nuestra patria, la hechura como
unos gosques grandes; de animales salvages no hay. Otrosí,
hay un animal de color de conejo é de su pelo, el grandor de
un conejo nuevo, el rabo largo, los pies é manos como de
raton, suben por los árboles, muchos los han comido, dicen
que es muy bueno de comer: hay culebras muchas no grandes;
lagartos aunque no muchos, porque los indios hacen tanta
fiesta dellos como hariamos allá con faisanes, son del tamaño
de los de allá, salvo que en la hechura son diferentes, aunque
en una isleta pequeña, que está junto con un puerto que
llaman Monte Christi, donde estovimos muchos dias, vieron
muchos dias un lagarto muy grande que decian que seria de
gordura de un becerro, é atan complido como una lanza, é
muchas veces salieron por lo matar, é con la mucha espesura

---

⁴ These dogs were of various colours and both rough and smooth haired; their
hair was rather coarser than that of similar dogs in Spain. They had ears like
wolves, and never barked, although, if maltreated, they might yelp or growl.
They were domesticated by the Indians, but were extinct in Española by the
end of the first quarter of the sixteenth century. Owing to the shortage of provisions, after Columbus had reached Española on this voyage, the Spaniards ate
these dogs; to those who became accustomed to it, the taste was not unpleasant,
being rather like that of a kid (cp. Oviedo, xii. 5).

⁵ Aguti (cp. Oviedo, xii. 1).

⁶ For the snakes and lizards of Española, see Oviedo, xii. 7, 8.

⁷ Cabras, of Goat Island, in the bay of Monte Christi, on the north coast of the
island.

⁸ An alligator (cp. Oviedo, xii. 7).

times to kill it, but owing to the thick undergrowth, it escaped from them into the sea, so that they were not able to come face to face with it. In this island and in the others, there are an infinite number of birds like those of our own country and many others which have never been seen there.[1] Of domestic fowl, none have been seen here, except that in Zuruquia[2] there were in the houses some ducks, most of them white as snow and some black, very pretty, with flat crests, and larger than those at home, although smaller than geese.

We ran along the coast of this island about a hundred leagues, for the place where the admiral had left the men, which was at or near the middle of the island, should have been within this distance. Going past the province called Xamana, we cast ashore one of the Indians whom they had carried away on the previous voyage, clothed, and with some trifles which the admiral commanded to be given to him. On that day there died of our men a Biscayan sailor who had been wounded by the Caribs, who, as I have already said, were taken owing to their lack of caution and because we kept near the shore. An opportunity was taken for a boat to go to shore to bury him, and to convoy the boat two caravels went near the land. Many Indians came out to the boat when it reached the shore, and some of them wore gold round their necks and in their ears. They wished to come with the Christians to the ships, and they would not take them, because they had not permission from the admiral. When they saw that our men would not take them, two of them got into a small canoe and went to one of the caravels which had put into shore. They were received on board with kindness and were brought to the admiral's ship. And by an interpreter, they said that a certain king sent them to know what people we were and to ask us to consent to land, for they had much gold and would give of it and of that which they had to eat. The admiral commanded shirts to be given to each of them and caps and other trifles, and told them that as he was on his way to where Guacamari was, he could not wait, but that there would be another time when he would be able to see their king, and with that they went away.

se les metia en la mar, de manera que no se pudo haber dél derecho. Hay en esta isla y en las otras infinitas aves de las de nuestra patria, é otras muchas que allá nunca se vieron: de las aves domésticas nunca se ha visto acá ninguna, salvo en la Zuruquia habia en las casas unas ánades, las mas dellas blancas como la nieve é algunas dellas negras, muy lindas, con crestas rasas, mayores que las de allá, menores que ánsares. Por la costa desta isla corrimos al pie de cien leguas porque hasta donde el Almirante habia dejado la gente, habria en este compás, que será en comedio ó en medio de la isla. Andando por la provincia della llamada Xamana, en derecho echamos en tierra uno de los indios quel otro viage habian llevado vestido, é con algunas cosillas quel Almirante le habia mandado dar. Aquel dia se nos murió un marinero vizcaino que habia seido herido de los Caribes, que ya dije que se tomaron, por su mala guarda, é porque ibamos por costa de tierra, dióse lugar que saliese una barca á enterrarlo, é fueron en reguarda de la barca dos carabelas cerca con tierra. Salieron á la barca en llegando en tierra muchos indios, de los cuales algunos traian oro al cuello, é á las orejas; querian venir con los cristianos á los navíos, é no los quisieron traer, porque no llevaban licencia del Almirante; los cuales desque vieron que no los querian traer se metieron dos dellos en una canoa pequeña, é se vinieron á una carabela de las que se habian acercado á tierra, en la cual los recibieron con su amor, é trajéronlos á la nao del Almirante, é dijeron, mediante un intérprete, que un Rey fulano los enviaba á saber que gente eramos, é á rogar que quisiesemos llegar á tierra, porque tenian mucho oro é le darian dello, é de lo que tenian de comer: el Almirante les mandó dar sendas camisas é bonetes é otras cosillas, é les dijo que porque iba á donde estaba Guacamarí non se podria detener, que otro tiempo habria que le pudiese ver, é con esto se fueron. No cesamos de andar nuestro camino fasta llegar á un puerto llamado Monte Cristi, donde estuvimos dos dias para ver la disposicion de la

---

¹ For the birds of Española, see Oviedo, Bk. xiv (cp. Las Casas, *Apologética Historia*, c. 9).

² This place has not been identified, but should possibly be Xaragua.

We did not cease to follow our course until we arrived at a harbour called Monte Christi, where we remained two days to examine the character of the land, because the place where he had left the men did not seem to the admiral to be suitable for making a settlement. We went on shore to make inspection. Near there was a large river[1] with very good water, but all the land is waterlogged and very unsuitable for habitation. As we went about, looking at the river and the land, some of our men found in one spot near the river two dead men, one with a rope round his neck and the other with his feet bound. This was on the first day. On the next day following, they found two other dead men, farther on than the others, and of these one was in such state that it was possible to know that he had been heavily bearded. Some of our men suspected more evil than good, and with reason, since the Indians are all beardless, as has been said. This harbour is twelve leagues' distance from the place where the Christians were.

After two days, we set sail for the place where the admiral had left the aforesaid people, in company with a king of these Indians, who was called Guacamari[2] and whom I take to be one of the chief men of this island. This day we arrived opposite that place, but it was already evening, and as there are there some shoals, on which had previously been lost the ship in which the admiral had sailed, we did not dare to enter the harbour near the shore until next day in the morning soundings could be taken and they might enter in safety; we remained for that night less than a league from shore.

On this evening, coming in that direction from a distance, a canoe containing five or six Indians came our way and they came rapidly towards us. The admiral, believing it safer for us to keep our sails set, would not allow us to wait for them, and they, persevering, arrived within a lombard shot of us and stopped to watch, and then, when they saw that we did not wait for them, they put back and returned. After we had anchored in that place on the said evening, the admiral commanded two lombards to be fired to see if the Christians, who had remained with the said Guacamari, would answer, for they also had lombards. And they never replied and no fires

tierra, porque no habia parecido bien al Almirante el logar donde habia dejado la gente para hacer asiento. Decendimos en tierra para ver la dispusicion: habia cerca de allí un gran rio de muy buena agua; pero es toda tierra anegada é muy indispuesta para habitar. Andando veyendo el rio é tierra hallaron algunos de los nuestros en una parte dos hombres muertos junto con el rio, el uno con un lazo al pescuezo y el otro con otro al pie, esto fue el primero dia. Otro dia siguiente hallaron otros dos muertos mas adelante de aquellos, el uno destos estaba en disposicion que se le pudo conocer tener muchas barbas. Algunos de los nuestros sospecharon mas mal que bien, é con razon, porque los indios son todos desbarbados, como dicho he. Este puerto está del lugar donde estaba la gente cristiana doce leguas: pasados dos dias alzamos velas para el lugar donde el Almirante habia dejado la sobredicha gente, en compañía de un Rey destos indios, que se llamaba Guacamarí, que pienso ser de los principales desta isla. Este dia llegamos en derecho de aquel lugar; pero era ya tarde, é porque allí habia unos bajos donde el otro dia se habia perdido la nao en que habia ido el Almirante, no osamos tomar el puerto cerca de tierra fasta que otro dia de mañana se desfondase é pudiesen entrar seguramente: quedamos aquella noche no una legua de tierra. Esa tarde, viniendo para allí de lejos, salió una canoa en que parescian cinco ó seis indios, los cuales venian á prisa para nosotros. El Almirante creyendo que nos seguraba hasta alzarnos, no quiso que los esperasemos, é porfiando llegaron hasta un tiro de lombarda de nosotros, é parabanse á mirar, é desde allí desque vieron que no los esperabamos dieron vuelta é tornaron su via. Despues que surgimos en aquel lugar sobredicho tarde, el Almirante mandó tirar dos lombardas á ver si respondian los cristianos que habian quedado con el dicho Guacamarí, porque tambien tenian lombardas, los cuales nunca respondieron ni menos parescian huegos ni señal de casas en aquel lugar, de lo cual se desconsoló mucho la gente é tomaron la sospecha que de tal caso se debia tomar. Estando ansi todos muy tristes,

---

[1] The Yaqui, which formerly flowed into the bay of Monte Christi: it now enters the sea fifteen kilometres to the south.

[2] Guacanagari (cp. *supra*, p. 14, note 1).

were to be seen or sign of houses in that place, and from this the men were much depressed and formed the suspicion to which such a situation naturally gave rise.[1]

All being thus very sad, and when four or five hours of the night had passed, the same canoe which we had seen this evening came, and it came with shouts, asking a captain of the caravel, where they first arrived, for the admiral. They were brought to the admiral's ship and were not willing to board her until the admiral spoke to them; they asked for a light in order to recognize him, and when they knew him, they came on board. One of them was a cousin of Guacamari who had sent them on the previous occasion. After they had turned back that evening, they brought masks of gold which Guacamari sent as a present; one was for the admiral and the other for a captain who had been with him on the previous voyage.

They were on the ship, talking with the admiral in the presence of all, for three hours. Showing much pleasure, he asked them concerning the Christians who had remained there. The relative of Guacamari said that they were all well, although some among them had died of sickness and others in a quarrel which had occurred among them,[2] and that Guacamari was in another place, wounded in his leg, and for this reason had not come, but that he would come another day, for two other kings, one called Caonabo and the other Mayreni,[3] had come to fight with him and had burned his village. And afterwards on that night they went away, saying that they would come next day with the said Guacamari, and with that they left us comforted for that night.

Next day in the morning we waited for the said Guacamari to come, and meanwhile by order of the admiral some landed

---

[1] For the destruction of La Navidad, cp. the varying accounts in Las Casas (i. 86), Ferdinand Columbus (c. 48, 49), Peter Martyr (i. 2), Oveido (ii. 12, 13), Syllacio (in Thacher, *Christopher Columbus*, ii. 253–5), and Cuneo (*Rac. Col.* III. ii. 98).

[2] According to Las Casas (i. 86), Pero Gutierrez and Rodrigo de Escovedo, who had been left at la Navidad as lieutenants to Diego de Arana, killed Jacome el Rico. Gutierrez had been *repostero de estrados del rey* (keeper of the royal hall of ceremony): when Columbus thought that he saw a light, just before land was sighted, he called Gutierrez who agreed that there was a light (*Journal*, 11 Oct.);

pasadas cuatro ó cinco horas de la noche, vino la misma canoa
que esa tarde habiamos visto, é venia dando voces, pregun-
tando por el Almirante un Capitan de una carabela donde
primero llegaron: trajéronlos á la nao del Almirante, los cuales
nunca quisieron entrar hasta que el Almirante los hablase; de-
mandaron lumbre para lo conocer, é despues que lo conocieron
entraron. Era uno dellos primo del Guacamarí, el cual los habia
enviado otra vez. Despues que se habian tornado aquella tarde
traian caratulas de oro que Guacamarí enviaba en presente;
la una para el Almirante é la otra para un Capitan quel otro
viage habia ido con él. Estovieron en la nao hablando con el
Almirante en presencia de todos por tres horas mostrando
mucho placer, preguntándoles por los Cristianos que tales
estaban: aquel pariente dijo que estaban todos buenos,
aunque entre ellos habia algunos muertos de dolencia é otros
de diferencia que habia contecido entre ellos, é que Guacamarí estaba en otro lugar ferido en una pierna é por eso no
habia venido, pero que otro dia vernia; porque otros dos
Reyes, llamado el uno Caonabó y el otro Mayrení, habian
venido á pelear con él é que le habian quemado el logar; é
luego esa noche se tornaron diciendo que otro dia vernian con
el dicho Guacamarí, é con esto nos dejaron por esa noche consolados. Otro dia en la mañana estovimos esperando que
viniese el dicho Guacamarí, é entretanto saltaron en tierra

he was one of those sent to announce the loss of the *Santa Maria* to Guacanagari
(*Journal*, 25 Dec.). Rodrigo de Escovedo, secretary of the fleet, was a native of
Segovia and a nephew of Fray Rodrigo Perez (*Journal*, 2 Jan.), who is to be
identified with Fray Juan Perez, guardian of the monastery of La Rabida (Las
Casas, i. 63). He had been one of those to land with Columbus on Guanahani
(*Journal*, 11 Oct.). Jacome is described as 'el Rico' and as 'genovés' in the
Libro Manual (fol. 29), and as 'Jacome Rico' in the *Cuenta general* (fol. 73). He
is the only known Genoese who was on the first voyage of Columbus, and was
perhaps the first Christian to die in the New World (cp. Gould y Quincy, *B.A.H.*
88, pp. 50–2).

3 Caonabo was 'king' of the district in which lay the mines of Cibao: he showed
consistent hostility to the Spaniards and attacked the fort of St. Thomas (Las
Casas, i. 92). Columbus, before leaving for the voyage of exploration in 1494,
instructed Pedro Margarit to effect the capture of Caonabo (cp. *Rac. Col.* I. i.
284–8), and this capture was afterwards effected by Alonso de Ojeda (Las Casas,
i. 102). Columbus decided to send him to Spain, but either he was drowned in
a storm (Las Casas, *loc. cit.*) or died of grief on the voyage (Peter Martyr, i. 4).
Mayreni is not otherwise known; he may have been one of the brothers of
Caonabo.

and went to the place where they had often been. A certain building, more or less fortified with a palisade,[1] where the Christians had lived, they found burned, and the village itself burned and destroyed, and they found also some rags and clothes which the Indians had brought to throw into the house. Such Indians as did appear there went about very stealthily, and they did not dare to approach our men, but ran away. This did not look well to us, for the admiral had said that on arriving at that place, so many of their canoes would come alongside the ships to see us that we should not be able to keep them off, and that so it had been on the other voyage, and as we saw now that they were suspicious of our men, it did not seem well to us.

Nevertheless, on that day, making advances to them and giving them some presents, such as hawks' bells and beads, we reassured one, the relative of the said Guacamari, and three others, and they entered the boat and were brought to the ship. When they were asked about the Christians, they said that they were all dead. Although an Indian, one of those whom we had brought from Castile, who had been informed of it by the two Indians who had before come to the ship and who had remained alongside the ship with their canoe, had told us this already, we had not believed him. The relative of Guacamari was asked who had killed them; he said that it was the king of Caonabo[2] and king Mayreni, and that they burned the things of the village, and that many of them were wounded, and that the said Guacamari also had been wounded in the thigh, and that he was in another village and that he wished to go there at once to call him. To him some presents were made and he at once went away to the place where Guacamari was.

All that day we were waiting for them, and when we saw that they did not come, many fancied that the Indians who had come the night before had been drowned, for they had been given wine to drink two or three times and they came in a small canoe which might have been upset. Next day in the morning the admiral landed with some of our men, and

[1] According to Peter Martyr (i. 2), the Spaniards had been established in a species of blockhouse, surrounded by an earthwork.

algunos por mandado del Almirante, é fueron al lugar donde
solian estar, é halláronle quemado un cortijo algo fuerte con
una palizada, donde los Cristianos habitaban, é tenian lo
suyo quemado é derribado, é ciertas bernias é ropas que los
indios habian traido á echar en la casa. Los dichos indios que
por allí parecian andaban muy cahareños, que no se osaban
allegar á nosotros, antes huian; lo cual no nos pareció bien
porque el Almirante nos habia dicho que en llegando á aquel
lugar salian tantas canoas dellos á bordo de los navíos á vernos
que no nos podriamos defender dellos, é que en el otro viage
ansí lo facian; é como agora veiamos que estaban sospechosos
de nosotros no nos parecia bien, con todo halagándoles aquel
dia é arrojándolos algunas cosas, ansi como cascabeles é cuentas, hobo de asegurarse un su pariente del dicho Guacamarí
é otros tres, los cuales entraron en la barca é trajéronlos á la
nao. Despues que le preguntaron por los Cristianos dijeron
que todos eran muertos, aunque ya nos lo habia dicho un
indio de los que llevabamos de Castilla que lo habian hablado
los dos indios que antes habian venido á la nao, que se habian
quedado á bordo de la nao con su canoa, pero lo ne habiamos
creido. Fue preguntado á este pariente de Guacamarí quien los
habia muerto: dijo que el Rey de Canoabó y el Rey Mayrení,
é que le quemaron las cosas del lugar, é que estaban dellos
muchos heridos, é tambien el dicho Guacamarí estaba pasado
un muslo, y él que estaba en otro lugar y que él queria ir luego
allá á lo llamar, al cual dieron algunas cosas, é luego se partió
para donde estaba Guacamarí. Todo aquel dia los estobimos
esperando, é desque vimos que no venian, muchos tenian
sospecha que se habian ahogado los indios que antenoche
habian venido, porque los habian dado á beber dos ó tres
veces de vino, é venian en una canoa pequeña que se les
podria trastornar. Otro dia de mañana salió á tierra el
Almirante é algunos de nosotros, é fuemos donde solia estar
la villa, la cual nos vimos toda quemada é los vestidos de los

---

² So in the original. The Spaniards were very often uncertain whether a name
was that of a cacique or that of his territory: this is notably the case in the
various caciques of Castilla del Oro. Examples are to be found in Española, e.g.
Cayacoa is the name of a district to Las Casas (*Apol. Hist.* c. 4) and of a cacique
to Oviedo (iii. 4).

we went to the place where the town had been, and we saw that it was entirely burned and the clothes of the Christians were found in some grass. On that occasion, we did not see any corpses.

Among us there were many different opinions. Some suspected that Guacamari himself was concerned in the betrayal or death of the Christians, and others thought that he was not, since his town was burned; the matter was, indeed, very doubtful. The admiral commanded all the ground where the Christians had fortified themselves to be searched, since he had given orders to them that, when they obtained any quantity of gold, they should bury it. While this was being done, he wished to go to view a place at about a league's distance, where it appeared to us that a site might be found where a town could be built, for it was now time for this. Certain men went there with him, examining the country along the coast, until we arrived at a hamlet where there were seven or eight houses, which the Indians had abandoned as soon as they saw us coming. They carried away what they could and left the rest hidden in the undergrowth near the houses. These people are so degraded that they have not intelligence enough to seek out a suitable place in which to live. As for those who live on the shore, it is marvellous how barbarously they build, for the houses situated there were so covered with green or damp, that it is astonishing how they exist.

In those houses we found many belongings of the Christians, which it could not be believed that they should have bartered, such as a very handsome Moorish mantle, which had not been unfolded since they brought it from Castile, and stockings and pieces of cloth, and an anchor of the ship which the admiral had lost there on the previous voyage, and other things, from which our opinion was the more confirmed. And there, examining the things which they had packed in a wicker basket, carefully sewn up and well concealed, we found the head of a man, well hidden. From this we then concluded that it might be the head of a father or mother, or of some person whom they greatly loved. Since then I have heard that many like this have been found, from which I believe

cristianos se hallaban por aquella yerba. Por aquella hora
no vimos ningun muerto. Habia entre nosotros muchas
razones diferentes, unos sospechando que el mismo Guacamarí fuese en la traicion ó muerte de los Cristianos, otros les
parecia que no, pues estaba quemada su villa, ansí que la
cosa era mucho para dudar. El Almirante mandó catar todo
el sitio donde los Cristianos estaban fortalecidos porquel los
habia mandado que desque toviesen alguna cantidad de oro
que lo enterrasen. Entretanto que esto se hacia quiso llegar
á ver á cerca de una legua do nos parecia que podria haber
asiento para poder edificar una villa porque ya era tiempo,
adonde fuimos ciertos con él mirando la tierra por la costa, fasta
que llegamos á un poblado donde habia siete ú ocho casas,
las quales habian desamparado los indios luego que nos vieron
ir, é llevaron lo que pudieron é lo otro dejaron escondido entre
yerbas junto con las casas, que es gente tan bestial que no
tienen discrecion para buscar lugar para habitar, que los
que viven á la marina es maravilla cuan bestialmente edifican,
que las casas enderedor tienen tan cubiertas de yerba ó de
humidad, que estoy espantado como viven. En aquellas casas
hallamos muchas cosas de los Cristianos, las cuales no se
creian que ellos hobiesen rescatado, ansí como una almalafa
muy gentil, la cual no se habia descogido de como la llevaron
de Castilla, é calzas é pedazos de paños, é una ancla de la nao
quel Almirante habia allí perdido el otro viage, é otras cosas,
de las cuales mas se esforzó nuestra opinion; y de acá hallamos, buscando las cosas que tenian guardadas en una espor-
tilla mucho cosida é mucho á recabdo, una cabeza de hombre
mucho guardada. Allí juzgamos por entonces que seria la
cabeza de padre ó madre, ó de persona que mucho querian.
Despues he oido que hayan hallado muchas desta manera, por
donde creo ser verdad lo que allí juzgamos; desde allí nos
tornamos. Aquel dia venimos por donde estaba la villa, y
cuando llegamos hallamos muchos indios que se habian
asegurado y estaban rescatando oro: tenian rescatado fasta
un marco: hallamos que habian mostrado donde estaban
muertos once cristianos, cubiertos ya de la yerba que habia
crecido sobre ellos, é todos hablaban por una boca que
Caonabó é Mayreni los habian muerto; pero con todo eso

that conclusion which we then reached to be the truth. After that, we returned.

That day we came to the place where the town had been, and when we arrived there, we found many Indians, who were reassured and were bartering gold. They had bartered to the value of a mark. We found that they had shown where eleven dead Christians were, already covered by the grass which had grown over them. All with one voice said that Caonabo and Mayreni had killed them. But with all this they began to complain that the Christians had taken, one three, another four women, from which we came to believe that the evil which had fallen on them was the result of jealousy.

Next day, in the morning, since in all that district there was no place suitable for us to be able to form a settlement, the admiral decided that a caravel should go in one direction to search for a convenient site, and that some of us should go with him in another direction. There we found a very safe harbour and land very suited for habitation. As, however, it was very far from where we wished to be, which was near the mine of gold, the admiral decided not to form a settlement there but in another place which was more certainly near it, if a convenient situation could be found.

When we returned from this place, we found that there had arrived the other caravel which had proceeded in another direction to search for the said place, in which had gone Melchior [1] and four or five other men of worth. And as they went coasting along the land, a canoe had come out to them, in which were two Indians, one of them the brother of Guacamari, who was known to a pilot who went in the said caravel. He asked who went there. The chief men reported that they told the man that Guacamari asked them to come ashore, to the place where he was staying with some fifty houses. The said chief men landed in the boat and went to where he was, and they found him, stretched on his bed, complaining that he was suffering from a wound. They talked with him, asking about the Christians. He answered, in agreement with the statement of the others, that it was Caonabo and Mayreni who had killed them, and that they

---

[1] Melchior Maldonado had been sent by Ferdinand and Isabella to announce

asomaban queja que los Cristianos uno tenia tres mugeres,
otro cuatro, donde creemos quel mal que les vino fue de zelos.
Otro dia de mañana, porque en todo aquello no habia logar
dispuesto para nosotros poder hacer asiento, acordó el Almirante fuese una carabela á una parte para mirar lugar
conveniente, é algunos que fuimos con él fuimos á otra parte,
á do hallamos un puerto muy seguro é muy gentil disposicion
de tierra para habitar, pero porque estaba lejos de donde nos
deseabamos que estaba la mina de oro, no acordó el Almirante
de poblar sino en otra parte que fuese mas cierta si se hallase
conveniente disposicion. Cuando venimos deste lugar hallamos venida la otra carabela que habia ido á la otra parte á
buscar el dicho lugar, en la cual habia ido Melchior é otros
cuatro ó cinco hombres de pro. E yendo costeando por tierra
salió á ellos una canoa en que venian dos indios, el uno era
hermano de Guacamarí, el cual fue conocido por un piloto
que iba en la dicha carabela, é preguntó quien iba allí, al
cual, dijeron los hombres prencipales, dijeron que Guacamarí
les rogaba que se llegasen á tierra, donde él tenia su asiento
con fasta cincuenta casas. Los dichos prencipales saltaron en
tierra con la barca é fueron donde él estaba, el cual fallaron
en su cama echado faciendo del doliente ferido. Fablaron con
él preguntándole por los Cristianos: respondió concertando
con la mesma razon de los otros, que era que Caonabó é
Mayreni los habian muerto, é que á él habian ferido en un
muslo, el cual mostró ligado; los que entonces lo vieron ansí
les pareció que era verdad como él lo dijo: al tiempo del des-
pedirse dió á cada uno dellos una joya de oro, á cada uno como
le pareció que lo merescia. Este oro facian en fojas muy delga-
das, porque lo quieren para facer carátulas é para poderse
asentar en betun que ellos facen, si así no fuese no se asentaria.
Otro facen para traer en la cabeza é para colgar en las orejas
é narices, ansí que todavía es menester que sea delgado, pues

the fall of Malaga to the pope (1487) (Peter Martyr, i. 2). He was engaged on the
preparations for the second voyage (*Doc. Inéd. relativos al descubrimiento* . . .
(1ᵃ serie), 30, p. 158). He was reluctant to go on the voyage, but was ordered to
do so by the sovereigns, the comendador mayor de Leon being instructed to make
provision for his household during his absence (*Doc. Inéd.* (1ᵃ serie), 30, p. 182–3,
Letter, 4 Aug. 1493).

had wounded him in the thigh, which he showed bandaged. When they saw him thus, it appeared to them that what he said was true. At the time of their departure, he gave to each of them a jewel of gold, to each according as each seemed to merit.

This gold they fashion in very thin plates, since they wish to make masks of it, and to be able to do so, they set it in bitumen which they prepare, for if it were not so, it would not be suitable. They fashion other gold to wear on the head and to hang in the ears and nostrils, and for this also it is necessary that it should be thin, since they do not regard this as riches save for its showy appearance.

The said Guacamari said by signs and as well as he could that, as he was so wounded, they should say to the admiral that he wished him to come to see him. As soon as the admiral arrived, the aforesaid men recounted this story to him. Next day, in the morning, he decided to set out for that place, where we could go within three hours, for it was hardly three leagues there from where we were, but as it would be the hour of eating when we arrived there, we ate before going ashore. When we had eaten, the admiral commanded that all the captains should come in their boats to go ashore, for already on this morning, before we set out from where we were, the said brother had come to speak with the admiral, and to urge him to go to the place where the said Guacamari was.

The admiral went ashore there and all the people of importance with him, so richly dressed that they would have made a good show in a capital city. He took some things as presents, because he had already received an appreciable amount of gold from him, and it was right that he should respond to the action and good will which he had shown. The said Guacamari himself was also prepared to make a present to him. When we arrived, we found him stretched on his bed,[1] as they have them, a bed, made of cotton, like a net, hung in the air. He did not get up, but from the bed made as much show of courtesy as he could. He exhibited much feeling, with tears in his eyes for the death of the Christians, and began to talk, showing, as well as he was able, how some had died of disease and how others had gone to Caonabo to search for the mine

que ellos nada desto hacen por riqueza salvo por buen parecer. Dijo el dicho Guacamarí por señas e como mejor pudo, que porque él estaba ansí herido que dijesen al Almirante que quisiese venir á verlo. Luego quel Almirante llegó los sobredichos le contaron este caso. Otro dia de mañana acordó partir para allá, al cual lugar llegariamos dentro de tres horas, porque apenas habria dende donde estábamos allá tres leguas; ansí que cuando allí llegamos era hora de comer: comimos ante de salir en tierra. Luego que hobimos comido mandó el Almirante que todos los Capitanes viniesen con sus barcas para ir en tierra, porque ya esa mañana antes que partiesemos de donde estábamos habia venido el sobredicho su hermano á hablar con el Almirante, é á darle priesa que fuese al lugar donde estaba el dicho Guacamarí. Allí fue el Almirante á tierra é toda la gente de pro con él, tan ataviados que en una cibdad prencipal parecieran bien: llevó algunas cosas para le presentar porque ya habia recibido dél alguna cantidad de oro, é era razon le respondiese con la obra é voluntad quel habia mostrado. El dicho Guacamarí ansí mismo tenia aparejado para hacerle presente. Cuando llegamos hallámosle echado en su cama, como ellos lo usan, colgado en el aire, fecha una cama de algodon como de red; no se levantó, salvo dende la cama hizo el semblante de cortesia como él mejor sopo, mostró mucho sentimiento con lágrimas en los ojos por la muerte de los Cristianos, é comenzó á hablar en ello mostrando, como mejor podia, como unos murieron de dolencia, é como otros se habian ido á Caonabó á buscar la mina del oro é que allí los habian muerto, é los otros que se los habian venido á matar allí en su villa. A lo que parecian los cuerpos de los muertos no habia dos meses que habia acaecido. Esa hora el presentó al Almirante ocho marcos y medio de oro, é cinco ó seiscientos labrados de pedreria de diversos colores, é un bonete de la misma pedrería, lo cual me parece deben tener ellos en mucho. En el bonete estaba un joyel, lo cual le dió en mucha veneracion. Paraceme que tienen en mas el cobre quel oro. Estábamos presentes yo y un zurugiano de

---

[1] Peter Martyr (*Dec.* i. 2) says that his bed was surrounded by those of his seven concubines.

of gold and that there they had been killed, and that as for the
rest they had come to slay them there in his town. From the
appearance of the bodies of the dead, it was not two months
since this had happened.[1]

At this time he presented the admiral with eight and a half
marks of gold, and five or six hundred cut stones of various
colours, and a cap with the same jewellery, which it seems to
me that they must value greatly. On the cap was a jewel,
which he gave to him with much reverence. It appears to
me that they set more store by copper than by gold.

I and a surgeon of the fleet were present. The admiral
therefore told the said Guacamari that we had knowledge of
the ailments of men that he might consent to show us the
wound. He answered that he was willing, upon which I told
him that it would be necessary, if he could, that he should
go out of the house, because from the throng of people, it
was dark and it was impossible to see well. He did so at
once; I believe rather from timidity than from good will.
He went outside leaning on an arm. After he was seated, the
surgeon went to him and began to unbandage him. He then
said to the admiral that the wound had been made with
a *ciba*, which means to say, with a stone. When he was un-
bandaged, we came to examine him. It is certain that he
had no more wound on that leg than on the other, although
he cunningly made out that it pained him greatly.[2]

Certainly the matter could not well be decided, for the
facts were unknown, and there were clearly many things
which pointed to a hostile people having come against him.
The admiral therefore did not know what to do. It appeared
to him and to many others that for the present, until the
truth could be better known, it was right to dissemble, since
after gaining knowledge, it would be possible to secure from
him whatever reparation might be desired.[3]

And that evening he came with the admiral to the ships,
and the horses and what we had there were shown to him.
At this he was very astonished as being something unknown
to him. He took supper on the ship, and this evening returned

---

[1] Cuneo (*loc. cit.*) says that from the appearance of the bodies found, the
disaster must have occurred some fifteen or twenty days earlier.

armada; entonces dijo el Almirante al dicho Guacamarí que
nosotros eramos sabios de las enfermedades de los hombres
que nos quisiese mostrar la herida: él respondió que le placia,
para lo cual yo dije que seria necesario, si pudiese, que saliese
fuera de casa, porque con la mucha gente estaba escura é no
se podria ver bien; lo cual él fizo luego, creo mas de empacho
que de gana; arrimándose á él salió fuera. Despues de asentado, llego el zurugiano á él é comenzó de desligarle: entonces
dijo al Almirante que era ferida fecha con ciba, que quiere
decir con piedra. Despues que fue desatada llegamos á
tentarle. Es cierto que no tenia mas mal en aquella que en
la otra, aunque él hacia del raposo que le dolia mucho.. Ciertamente no se podia bien determinar porque las razones eran
ignotas, que ciertamente muchas cosas habia que mostraban
haber venido á él gente contraria. Ansimesmo el Almirante no
sabia que se hacer: paresció, é á otros muchos, que por
entonces fasta bien saber la verdad que se debia disimular,
porque despues de sabida, cada que quisiesen, se podia dél
recibir enmienda. E aquella tarde se vino con el Almirante á
las naos, é mostráronle caballos é cuanto ahí habia, de lo
cual quedó muy maravillado como de cosa estraña á él;
tomó colacion en la nao, é esa tarde luego se tornó á su casa:
el Almirante dijo que queria ir á habitar allí con él é queria
facer casas, y él respondió que le placia, pero que el lugar era
mal sano porque era muy humido, é tal era él por cierto. Esto
todo pasaba estando por intérpretes dos indios de los que el
otro viage habian ido á Castilla, los cuales habian quedado
vivos de siete que metimos en el puerto, que los cinco se
murieron en el camino, los cuales escaparon á uña de caballo.
Otro dia estuvimos surtos en aquel puerto; é quiso saber

---

[2] Las Casas (i. 86) says that Guacanagari showed his 'wounds', and does not
hint that there was any doubt concerning their genuineness. Peter Martyr
(*Dec.* i. 2) says that Columbus sent Melchior Maldonado to Guacanagari, that
he found the cacique feigning illness, and that he undid the bandages but could
find no trace of a wound. It is possible that Maldonado was acting as a surgeon,
or that Martyr mistook the visit of Melchior to Guacanagari for that which was
paid by Chanca.

[3] Fray Buil and others advocated the immediate arrest of Guacanagari, but
this course of action was considered to be inadvisable by Columbus (Las Casas,
i. 86, and Peter Martyr, i. 2).

to his house. The admiral told him that he wished to settle there with him and wished to build houses, and he answered that it pleased him, but that the place was unhealthy, because it was very damp, and such was in fact the case. All this passed, there acting as interpreters two Indians of those who on the previous voyage had gone to Castile and who had remained alive of the seven whom we embarked in the port, for five of them died on the voyage and the others escaped by a hair's breadth.

The next day we remained anchored in that harbour. And he wished to know when the admiral would depart; he ordered him to be told, on the next day. That day there came to the ship his afore-mentioned brother and others with him and brought with them some gold to barter. So on the day that we left there, a good amount of gold was exchanged.

In the ship there were ten women of those whom we had taken in the islands of the Caribs; most of them were from Boriquen. That brother of Guacamari talked with them; as we believe, he told them to do that which they did immediately on this night. And it was that, in the first watch, they threw themselves very quietly into the water and made their way ashore, so that by the time that they were missed, they had gone such a distance that with the boats they were unable to take more than four, whom they took as they were coming out of the water. They swam more than a full half league. On the morning of the next day, the admiral sent to Guacamari to tell him that he should send to him those women who had fled the night before and that he should command immediate search to be made for them. When they arrived, they found the village abandoned by its inhabitants, so that there was not a soul in it. As a result many were encouraged to declare their suspicion; others said that there might have been a move to another village, for these people are wont to act in this way.[1]

That day we remained there quietly, because the weather was unsuitable for departure. On the next day, in the morning, the admiral decided that, as the weather was unfavourable, it would be well to go in the boats to examine a harbour,

cuando se partiria el Almirante: le mandó decir que otro dia. En aquel dia vinieron á la nao el sobredicho hermano suyo é otros con él, é trajeron algun oro para rescatar. Ansí mesmo el dia que allá salimos se rescató buena cantidad de oro. En la nao habia diez mugeres de las que se habian tomado en las islas de Cariby; eran las mas dellas de Boriquen. Aquel hermano de Guacamarí habló con ellas: creemos que les dijo lo que luego esa noche pusieron por obra, y es que al primer sueño muy mansamente se echaron al agua é se fueron á tierra, de manera que cuando fueron falladas menos iban tanto trecho que con las barcas no pudieron tomar mas de las cuatro, las cuales tomaron al salir del agua; fueron nadando mas de una gran media legua. Otro dia de mañana envió el Almirante á decir á Guacamarí que le enviase aquellas mugeres que la noche antes se habian huido, é que luego las mandase buscar. Cuando fueren hallaron el lugar despoblado, que no estaba persona en el: ahí tornaron muchos fuerte á afirmar su sospecha, otros decian que se habria mudado á otra poblacion quellos ansí lo suelen hacer. Aquel dia estovimos allí quedos por que el tiempo era contrario para salir: otro dia de mañana acordó el Almirante, pues que el tiempo era contrario, que seria bien ir con las barcas á ver un puerto la costa arriba, fasta el cual habria dos leguas, para ver si habria dispusicion de tierra para hacer habitacion; donde fuemos con todas las barcas de los navíos, dejando los navíos en el puerto. Fuimos corriendo toda la costa, é tambien estos no se seguraban bien de nosotros; llegamos á un lugar de donde todos eran huidos. Andando por él fallamos junto con las casas, metido en el monte, un indio ferido de una vara, de una ferida que resollaba por las espaldas, que no habia podido huir mas lejos. Los desta isla pelean con unas varas agudas, las cuales tiran con unas tiranderas como las que tiran los mochachos las varillas en Castilla, con las cuales tiran muy lejos asaz certero. Es cierto que para gente desarmada que pueden

---

[1] One of these women was called Catalina: they are said to have swum about three miles (Peter Martyr, *Dec.* i. 2). According to Martyr, it was Guacanagari who talked to Catalina and was presumed to have suggested her flight.

distant two leagues farther along the coast, to see if the character of the land was suitable for forming a settlement. We went there with all the boats of the fleet, leaving the ships in the harbour. We went running all along the coast, and the natives there also were not reassured about our men; we reached a village from which all had fled. Walking through it, we found near the houses, lying on the mountain, an Indian wounded with a dart, with a wound which gaped between the shoulders, who had not been able to escape farther. The people of this island fight with sharp darts, which they shoot from slings as boys shoot their small darts in Castile, and they shoot them a considerable distance with much accuracy. It is certain that for an unarmed people they can do great damage. This man told us that Caonabo and his men had wounded him and had burned the houses of Guacamari. Thus from the small understanding which we have of them and from the dubious accounts which they have given us, all so confused, up to now it has not been possible to know the truth of the death of our people.

In that harbour also we did not find the character of the land suitable for making a settlement. The admiral decided that we should return up the coast towards where we had come from Castile, because there was news of gold in that direction. The weather was contrary to us, so that it was more labour for us to go back thirty leagues than to come from Castile. As a result of the unfavourable weather and the length of the voyage, three months had already passed when we landed. It pleased our Lord that, owing to the contrary weather which did not allow us to go farther onward, we had to land at the best and most favourable site which we could have found. There is there a very good harbour and much fishing, of which we were in great need owing to the lack of meat.[1]

The fish of this land is very strange and more wholesome than that of Spain.[2] It is true that the climate, being hot and damp, does not allow it to be kept from one day to the next, for animal food quickly becomes putrid. The land is very rich for all purposes.[3] Near by there is one main river, and

---

[1] The site selected was ten leagues east of Monte Christi, on the Puerto de las

hacer harto daño. Este nos dijo que Caonabó é los suyos lo habian ferido, é habian quemado las casas á Guacamarí.

Ansí quel poco entender que los entendemos é las razones equívocas nos han traido á todos tan afuscados que fasta agora no se ha podido saber la verdad de la muerte de nuestra gente, é no hallamos en aquel puerto dispusicion saludable parer hacer habitacion. Acordó el Almirante nos tornásemos por la costa arriba por do habiámos venido de Castilla, porque la nueva del oro era fasta allá. Fuenos el tiempo contrario, que mayor pena nos fue tornar treinta leguas atrás que venir desde Castilla, que con el tiempo contrario é la largueza del camino ya eran tres meses pasados cuando decendimos en tierra. Plugó á nuestro Señor que por la contrariedad del tiempo que no nos dejó ir mas adelante, hobimos de tomar tierra en el mejor sitio y dispusicion que pudieramos escoger, donde hay mucho buen puerto é gran pesquería, de la cual tenemos mucha necesidad por el carecimiento de las carnes. Hay en esta tierra muy singular pescado mas sano quel de España. Verdad sea que la tierra no consiente que se guarde de un dia para otro porque es caliente é humida, é por ende luego las cosas introfatibles ligeramente se corrompen. La tierra es muy gruesa para todas cosas; tiene junto un rio prencipal é otro razonable, asaz cerca de muy singular agua: edificase sobre la ribera dél una cibdad Marta, junto quel lugar se deslinda con el agua, de manera que la metad de la cibdad queda cercada de agua con una barranca de peña tajada, tal que por allí no ha menester defensa ninguna; la otra metad está cercada de una arboleda espesa que apenas podrá un conejo andar por ella; es tan verde que en ningun tiempo del mundo fuego la podrá quemar: hase comenzado á traer un brazo del rio, el cual dicen los maestros que trairán por medio del lugar,

---

Gracias; it was fifty miles west of the modern Puerto Plata. For the report of reconnaissance of the site of Isabella by U.S.S. *Enterprise* in 1891, see Thacher (*op. cit.*, ii. 283, note 1), where will be found a plan of the few remaining ruins. Isabella was abandoned in favour of Santo Domingo two years later, and was left desolate: the site was supposed to be haunted (cp. Las Casas, i. 92).

[2] For the fish of Española, cp. Oviedo, Bk. xii.

[3] On the extreme fertility of the land round Isabella, see Syllacio (Thacher, ii. 257), and *infra*, p. 84 and note 1.

another of reasonable size, not far off, with very remarkable water.[1]

On the bank of one a city, Marta,[2] is being built, one side being bounded by the water with a ravine of cleft rock, so that no defensive work is needed on that side. The other side is protected by a wood, so thick that a rabbit could scarcely pass through it, and so green that never at all will fire be able to burn it. They have begun to canalize a branch of the river, and the foremen say that they will bring this through the centre of the town and that they will place on it mills and water wheels and whatever can be worked with water. They have sown many vegetables, and it is certain that they grow more in eight days than they do in twenty in Spain.

There come here constantly many Indians and with them caciques, who are like commanders among them, and many Indian women. All come laden with ages,[3] which are like turnips, very excellent for food; of these we make here many kinds of food-stuffs in various ways. It is so sustaining to eat that it comforts us all greatly, for in truth the life which has been spent on the sea has been the most straitened that ever men went through, and it was necessarily so because we did not know what weather we should have or how long God would allow that we should be on the voyage. So it was prudent that we should ration ourselves, so that, however long we might be in coming, we should be able to support life. They barter the gold and provisions and all that they bring for ends of straps, for beads, for pins, for fragments of dishes and plates. This age the Caribs call nabi, and the Indians hage.

All these people, as I have said, go about as they were born, except that the women of this island have their privy parts covered, some of them with a cotton cloth which they bind round their hips, others with grass and the leaves of trees. The decoration of men and women among them is to paint themselves, some with black, others with white and red, becoming such sights that to see them is good reason for

---

[1] There seems to have been actually only one river, the Rio Isabella; probably the other was a mere torrent, flowing in rainy weather.

é asentarán en él moliendas é sierras de agua, é cuanto se pudiere hacer con agua. Han sembrado mucha hortaliza, la cual es cierto que crece mas en ocho dias que en España en veinte. Vienen aquí continuamente muchos indios é caciques con ellos, que son como capitanes dellos, é muchas indias: todos víenen cargados de *ages*, que son como nabos, muy excelente manjar, de los cuales facemos acá muchas maneras de manjares en cualquier manera; es tanto cordial manjar que nos tiene á todos muy consolados, porque de verdad la vida que se trajo por la mar ha seido la mas estrecha que nunca hombres pasaron, é fue ansí necesario porque no sabiamos que tiempo nos haria, ó cuanto permitiría Dios que estoviesemos en el camino; ansí que fue cordura estrecharnos, porque cualquier tiempo que viniera pudieramos conservar la vida. Rescatan el oro é mantenimientos é todo lo que traen por cabos de agujetas, por cuentas, por alfileres, por pedazos de escudillas é de plateles. A este *age* llaman los de Caribi *nabi*, é los indios *hage*. Toda esta gente, como dicho tengo, andan como nacieron, salvo las mugeres de esta isla traen cubiertas sus verguenzas, dellas con ropa de algodon que les ciñen las caderas, otras con yerbas é fojas de árboles. sus galas dellos é dellas es pintarse, unos de negro, otros de blanco é colorado, de tantos visajes que en verlos es bien cosa de reir; las cabezas rapadas en logares, é en logares con vedijas de tantas maneras que no se podria escrebir. En conclusion, que todo lo que allá en nuestra España quieren hacer en la cabeza de un loco, acá el mejor dellos vos lo terná en mucha merced. aquí estamos en comarca de muchas minas de ora, que segun lo que ellos dicen no hay cada una dellas de veinte ó veinte é cinco leguas: las unas dicen que son en Niti, en poder de Caonabó, aquel que mató los cristianos; otras hay en otra

---

² There is no evidence that the city was called Marta, and this seems to be an error on the part of Chanca. Syllacio (Thacher, ii, p. 258) fancies that the island was called 'Isola Bella', and that the city was similarly named, on account of the extreme fertility of the soil. The city no doubt received its name in honour of the queen.

³ Yams (cp. Oviedo, vii. 3).

laughter.[1] Their heads are shaved in places and in places
have tufts of tangled hair of such shapes that it cannot be
described. In conclusion, whatever there in our Spain they
might wish to do to the head of a madman, here the best of
them would regard as a great honour.

Here we are in the neighbourhood of many mines of gold,
no one of which, according to what they say, is more than
twenty or twenty-five leagues distant. Some, they say, are
in Niti,[2] in the dominion of Caonabo, he who killed the
Christians; others are in another district which is called
Cibao, which, if it please our Lord, we shall know and see with
our eyes before many days pass. For the journey would be
made now, were it not that there are so many things to
provide that we are not equal to all. In four or five days,
a third of the men have fallen sick. I believe that the chief
cause of this has been the labour and privations of the
voyage; further, the changes of climate.[3] But I hope in our
Lord that all will be restored to health.

That which appears concerning this people is that if we
could talk with them, all would be converted, for whatever
they see us do, they do the same, bending the knees to the
altars and at the Ave Maria, and at other devotions and
crossing themselves. All say that they wish to be Christians,
although actually they are idolaters, because in their houses
they have images of various kinds. I have asked them, 'what
is that?' and they tell me that it is a thing of *Turey*, by which
they mean Heaven. I made as if I wished to throw the objects
into the fire and they took it so ill that they were on the
point of tears. But in the same way they think that whatever
we bring is a thing from Heaven, for they call everything
Turey, which means to say Heaven.

The day on which I went ashore to sleep was the first day
of the Lord. The little time which we have spent on land has
been more spent in making ready the place where we are to
settle and in seeking for necessary things than in finding out
what things there are in the country. But although the time
has been short, things very wonderful have been seen. For
there have been seen trees which bear wool and sufficiently

---

[1] The natives used the fruit of the *jagua* to make a black dye and that of the

parte que se llama Cibao, las cuales, si place á nuestro Señor, sabremos é veremos con los ojos antes que pasen muchos dias, porque agora se ficiera sino porque hay tantas cosas de proveer que no bastamos para todo, porque la gente ha adolecido en cuatro ó cinco dias el tercio della, creo la mayor causa dello ha seido el trabajo é mala pasada del camino, allende de la diversidad de la tierra; pero espero en nuestro Señor que todos se levantarán con salud.

Lo que parece desta gente es que si lengua toviesemos que todos se convertirian, porque cuanto nos veen facer tanto facen, en hincar las rodillas á los altares, é al Ave Maria, é á las otras devociones é santiguarse, todos dicen que quieren ser cristianos, puesto que verdaderamente son idólatras, porque en sus casas hay figuras de muchas maneras; yo les he preguntado que es aquello, dicenme que es cosa de *Turey*, que quiere decir del cielo. Yo acometi á querer echarselos en el fuego é haciaseles de mal que querian llorar, pero ansi piensan que cuanto nosotros traemos que es cosa del cielo, que á todo llaman *Turey*, que quiere decir cielo. El dia que yo salí á dormir en tierra fue el primero dia del Señor: el poco tiempo que habemos gastado en tierra ha seido mas en hacer donde nos metamos, é buscar las cosas necesarias, que en saber las cosas que hay en la tierra, pero aunque ha sido poco se han visto cosas bien de maravillar, que se han visto árboles que llevan lana y harto fina, tal que los que saben del arte dicen que podrán hacer buenos paños dellos. Destos árboles hay tantos que se podrán cargar las carabelas de la lana, aunque es trabajosa de coger, porque los árboles son muy espinosos; pero bien se puede hallar ingenio para la

bixa to make a vermilion dye (Oviedo, viii. 8, 9). By means of the fruit of the *guao*, the native women, after the coming of the Spaniards, endeavoured to make themselves white: Oviedo (ix. 34) says that they were successful, but adds that while they thus secured physical, they did not secure moral whiteness.

² This was the district between the rivers Neiba and Yaqui, where the town of San Juan de la Maguana was afterwards built by order of Nicolas de Ovando (cp. Las Casas, ii. 18: Oviedo, iii. 12: and Herrera, *Descripción de las Indias Occidentales*, c. vi).

³ By the Spaniards themselves, their sickness was partly, if not mainly, attributed to the excessive labour imposed upon them by Columbus in the building of Isabella (cp. Las Casas, i. 88: Herrera, *Historia General*, i. 2. x).

fine, so that those who know the art say that good cloth could be made from them. Of these trees, there are so many that the caravels could be loaded with the wool, although it is laborious to gather, because the trees are very thorny, but it is very possible to find some means for gathering it.[1]

There is an infinite amount of cotton from trees as large as peach trees. There are trees which bear wax, in colour and taste and for burning as good as that of bees, so that there is little difference between the one and the other. There are innumerable trees producing turpentine, very remarkable and of very fine quality. There is much tragacanth, also very good. There are trees which, I think, bear nutmegs, but they were so far without fruit, and I say that I think this because the taste and smell of the bark is like that of nutmegs. I saw a root of ginger which an Indian carried hanging round his neck. There are also aloes, although not of the kind which has hitherto been seen in our parts, but there is no doubt that they are one of the species of aloes which doctors use. There is also found a kind of cinnamon; it is true that it is not so fine as that which is known at home. We do not know whether by chance this is due to lack of knowledge of the time to gather it when it should be gathered, or whether by chance the land does not produce better. Also there have been found yellow mirabolans, but at the moment they were only lying under the tree, and as the land is very damp, they are rotten and have a very bitter taste, as I believe, because of the decay. But in every other respect, except for the taste which is that of rotten fruit, it is the true mirabolan. There is also very good mastic.[2]

None of the people of these islands, as far as they have been seen yet, possess any iron. They have many tools, such as hatchets and axes, made of stone, so handsome and so fashioned, that it is marvellous how they are able to make them without iron. Their food is bread made of the roots of a plant which is between a tree and a vegetable, and the *age*, of which I have already said that it is like turnips and very nourishing. They use, to flavour it, a spice which is called *agi*,[3]

---

[1] Ceiba (cp. Oviedo, ix. 11).

coger. Hay infinito algodon de árboles perpetuos tan grandes como duraznos. Hay árboles que llevan cera en color y en sabor é en arder tan buena como la de abejas, tal que no hay diferencia mucha de la una á la otra. Hay infinitos árboles de trementina muy singular é muy fina. Hay mucho alquitira, tambien muy buena. Hay árboles que pienso que llevan nueces moscadas, salvo que agora estan sin fruto, é digo que lo pienso porque el sabor y olor de la corteza es como de nueces moscadas. Vi una raiz de gengibre que la traía un indio colgada al cuello. Hay tambien linaloe, aunque no es de la manera del que fasta agora se ha visto en nuestras partes; pero no es de dudar que sea una de las especias de linaloes que los dotores ponemos. Tambien se ha hallado una manera de canela, verdad es que no es tan fina como la que allá se ha visto, no sabemos si por ventura lo hace el defeto de saberla coger en sus tiempos como se ha de coger, ó si por ventura la tierra no la lleva mejor. Tambien se ha hallado mirabolanos cetrinos, salvo que agora no estan sino debajo del árbol, como la tierra es muy humida estan podridos, tienen el sabor mucho amargo, yo creo sea del podrimiento; pero todo lo otro, salvo el sabor que está corrompido, es de mirabolanos verdaderos. Hay tambien almástica muy buena. Todas estas gentes destas islas, que fasta agora se han visto, no poseen fierro ninguno. Tienen muchas ferramientas, ansi como hachas é azuelas hechas de piedra tan gentiles é tan labradas que es maravilla

---

[2] For the following notes upon the various trees, I am indebted to Dr. A. B. Rendle, late Keeper of Botany in the Natural History Museum. The trees bearing 'wool' are probably the *Ceiba pentandra* Gaertn. Those producing 'cotton' are probably a species of *Gossypium*; 'wax', probably the 'Candleberry myrtle', *Myrica cerifera* L.; turpentine, 'the Turpentine tree', *Bursera Simaruba* Sarg.; tragacanth, perhaps 'Cashew', *Anacardium occidentale* L. The nutmeg cannot be identified. The 'ginger' is probably a species of *Renealmia: R. antillarum* (Roem. and Schult.) Gagnep., one of the species found in Española, is known to the natives as 'ginembre marron', according to K. Schumann, *Das Pflanzenreich*, iv. 46, p. 206. 'Aloes' is probably *Agave americana* L.; 'cinnamon', 'wild cinnamon', *Canella Winterana* Gaertn. The 'mirabolan' (which is declared by Oviedo (viii. 2) to be the *hobo* and to have been mistaken for mirabolan), is probably the 'Hog Plum', *Spondias Monbin* L. The mastic is probably also *Bursera Simaruba* Sarg.

[3] Agi: Indian pepper (cp. Oviedo, vii. 7). This was the only spice actually occurring in the Indies.

which they also eat with fish, as well as with birds when they can get them; there are an infinite number of many kinds. They have also some grain like hazel nuts, very good to eat.[1] They eat all the snakes and lizards and spiders and all the worms which are found in the ground.[2] So it seems to me that their degradation is greater than that of any beast in the world.

After the admiral had at one time determined to leave the discovery of the mines until he had first dispatched the ships which were to leave for Castile, on account of the great amount of illness that there had been among the people, he resolved to send out two companies under two captains,[3] one to Cibao and the other to Niti, where Caonabo is, of whom I have already spoken. They went and returned, one on the twentieth day of January and the other on the twenty-first. The one who went to Cibao found gold in so many parts that a man hardly dares say it, for in fact they found gold in more than fifty streams and rivers, and out of the rivers on the land, so that in all that province he says that wherever they care to look, they will find it. He brought evidence from many parts, as from the sand of the rivers and from the springs which are in the country. It is believed that by digging, as we know how to dig, it will be found in larger pieces, for the Indians do not know how to dig nor have they anything with which they are able to dig more than a hand's depth. The other, who went to Niti, also brought news of much gold in three or four parts; he also brought evidence of it.

Thus surely the sovereigns, our lords, can henceforth regard themselves as being the most prosperous and richest princes in the world. For such a thing has up to now not been seen

---

[1] Perhaps the nuts described by Oviedo (x. 4), which were not suited to all and which being used medicinally might be expected to have been of special interest to Chanca.

[2] One of the chief delicacies of the Indians was the *iguana*: for the manner in which Anacaona persuaded Bartholomew Columbus to eat it, and for the method of cooking it, see Peter Martyr (i. 5). For the reptiles of Española, see Oviedo (xii. 7, 8); for the insects, see Oviedo (xv). In various passages, Oviedo also comments on the degraded palates of the natives, but Peter Martyr (*loc. cit.*) declares that when once the Spaniards had overcome their repulsion at the smell of cooked *iguana*, they regarded it as the greatest delicacy in the world.

[3] Alonso de Ojeda (cp. *infra*, p. 76, note 2) and Ginés de Gorbalan. The latter returned to Spain with the ships of Antonio de Torres (cp. *infra*, p. 76), and for

como sin fierro se pueden hacer. El mantenimiento suyo es pan hecho de raices de una yerba que es entre árbol é yerba, é el age, de que ya tengo dicho que es como nabos, que es muy buen mantenimiento: tienen por especia, por lo adobar, una especia que se llama *agi*, con la cual comen tambien el pescado, como aves cuando las pueden haber, que hay infinitas de muchas maneras. Tienen otrosí unos granos como avellanas, muy buenos de comer. comen cuantas culebras é lagartos é arañas é cuantos gusanos se hallan por el suelo; ansi que me parece es mayor su bestialidad que de ninguna bestia del mundo. Despues de una vez haber determinado el Almirante de dejar el descobrir las minas fasta primero enviar los navíos que se habian de partir á Castilla, por la mucha enfermedad que habia seido en la gente, acordó de enviar dos cuadrillas con dos Capitanes, el uno á Cibao y el otro á Niti, donde está Caonobó, de que ya he dicho, las cuales fueron é vinieron el uno á veinte dias de Enero, é el otro á veinte é uno: el que fue á Cibao halló oro en tantas partes que no lo osa hombre decir, que de verdad en mas de cincuenta arroyos é rios hallaban oro, é fuera de los rios por tierra; de manera que en toda aquella provincia dice que do quiera que lo quieran buscar lo hallarán. Trajo muestra de muchas partes como en la arena de los rios é en las hontizuelas, que estan sobre tierra, creese que cabando, como sabemos hacer, se hallará en mayores pedazos, porque los indios no saben cabar ni tienen con que puedan cabar de un palmo arriba. El otro que fue á Niti trajo tambien nueva de mucho oro en tres ó cuatro partes; ansi mesmo trajo la muestra dello. Ansi que de cierto los Reyes nuestros Señores desde agora se pueden tener por los mas prósperos é mas ricos Príncipes del mundo, porque tal cosa hasta agora no se ha visto ni leido de ninguno

his services in the Indies and against the Moors was granted lands from the royal demesne in the district of Granada to the value of 200,000 maravedis, to him and his heirs in perpetuity (*Doc. Inéd.* (1ª *serie*), 30, pp. 310–12). For the expedition, see Las Casas (i. 89), Peter Martyr (i. 2), Syllacio (Thacher, ii, p. 259). Oviedo (ii. 12), says that little gold was found, and the disbelief of the Spaniards in the accuracy of the accounts given by Ojeda led Columbus to make his expedition to Cibao (Las Casas, i. 90–1).

or read of anyone in the world, since truly on the next voyage
which the ships make they will be able to carry so great a
quantity of gold, that whoever hears of it will be able to
wonder. Here I think it will be well to stop my account.
I believe that those who do not know me and who hear these
things may find me prolix and a man who has exaggerated
somewhat. But God is witness that I have not gone one iota
beyond the bounds of truth.

en el mundo, porque verdaderamente á otro camino que los navíos vuelvan pueden llevar tanta cantidad de oro que se puedan maravillar cualesquiera que lo supieren. Aquí me parece será bien cesar el cuento: creo los que no me conocen que oyeren estas cosas, me ternán por prolijo é por hombre que ha alargado algo; pero Dios es testigo que yo no he traspasado una jota los términos de la verdad.

2. Memorandum of Christopher Columbus, sent to Ferdinand and Isabella, by Antonio de Torres.[1]

THAT which you, Antonio de Torres, captain of the ship *Mariagalante*,[2] and alcaide of the city of Isabella,[3] are to say and to ask on my behalf of the king and queen, our sovereigns, is the following.

Firstly: Having delivered the letters of credence which you bear from me for their highnesses, you shall kiss for me their royal feet and hands, and you shall commend me to their highnesses, as to the king and queen, my natural sovereigns,[4] in whose service I desire that I may end my days, as you will be able to say more at length to their highnesses, according to that which you have seen and know of me.

Their highnesses receive this service to them.

Item: Although from the letters which I, and also father Fray Buil[5] and the treasurer,[6] write to their highnesses, they will be able to understand all that has been done here since our arrival, and that very minutely and extensively, yet you

[1] For the Memorandum generally, cp. *supra*, Introduction, p. cxlv *et seq.* Antonio de Torres was the brother of Juana de la Torre, the nurse of prince Juan (cp. *infra*, vol. II, p. 48, note 2). Having accompanied Columbus on his second voyage, he returned to Spain with twelve ships, sailing from Isabella, 2 Feb. 1494, and reaching Cádiz, 10 April. He returned to Española with four ships, bringing supplies, and again left for Spain, 24 Feb. 1495, reaching Cádiz, 7 April (cp. Las Casas, i. 89, 102: Navarrete, *Colección de los Viages*, ii, pp. 115, 149, 154, and 158). He conveyed Juan Aguado to Española in 1495. In 1497 it was proposed to entrust to him the control of the affairs of the Indies in Spain, in place of Juan de Fonseca, but de Torres made conditions which proved to be unacceptable and Fonseca was therefore confirmed in his position (Las Casas, i. 126). De Torres commanded the fleet which brought Nicolas de Ovando to Española (Las Casas, ii. 3), and was drowned in the hurricane which destroyed that fleet as it was about to return to Spain in 1502 (Las Casas, ii. 5).

[2] Cp. *supra*, p. 22, note 3.

[3] This is the first appearance of the name of the city in an official document.

[4] This phrase suggests a wish on the part of Columbus to insist on his complete identification with Spain, in answer to the attacks which had been made upon him as an alien (cp. Las Casas, i. 92, and *infra*, p. 94).

[5] Fray Buil (*al.* Boil, Boyl, Buyl, Bruil) was a Catalan, born at Tarragona. He entered the Benedictine monastery of Montserrat, and was high in the favour of the sovereigns, who relied on him to keep them informed of all that occurred (cp. Letter, 4 Aug. 1493: *Doc. Inéd.* (1ª serie), 30, pp. 180–1). Ulloa (*Xristo-*

2. MEMORIAL

Lo que vos Antonio de Torres, capitán de la nao Maria-galante, é alcayde de la çibdad Ysabela, avéys de dezir é suplicar de mi parte al rey é la reyna, nuestros señores, es lo syguiente.

Primeramente, dadas las cartas de crehencia que lleváys de mi para Sus Altezas, besaréys por mi sus reales pies é manos, y me encomendaréys en Sus Altesas, como á rey é reyna, mis señores naturales, en cuyo servicio yo deseo fenecer mis días, como esto más largamente vos podréys dezir á Sus Altezas, segund lo que en mi vistes é supistes.

Sus Altezas se lo tienen en servicio.

Ytem, como quiera que por las cartas que á Sus Altezas escrivo, y aun el padre fray Buil y el thesorero, podrán comprehender todo lo que acá después de nuestra llegada se fizo, y esto harto por menudo y estensamente, con todo,

Ferens Colom, p. 205) suggests that he was sent as a spy on Columbus. He was appointed apostolic vicar, and charged with the duty of superintending the conversion of the Indians, but he found himself to be unfitted for such work and asked to be recalled: the sovereigns urged him to persevere (*Doc. Inéd.* 30, pp. 304–5). He early came into conflict with Columbus, either because he advocated vigorous measures against Guacanagari (cp. *supra*, p. 59, note 2), or because he objected to the severity of the punishments inflicted by Columbus and the short rations on which he kept the Spaniards (cp. Las Casas, i. 92). Oviedo (ii. 13) says that Columbus punished Buil's hostility by cutting down his allowance of food. Buil returned to Spain in 1494, although he had been left as a member of the council to govern Isabella during the absence of Columbus (Las Casas, i. 94, 100). He was called upon by the sovereigns to state his case against Columbus when the latter returned to Spain in 1495 (Oviedo, *loc. cit.*). He became abbot of Cuxá and died in 1520. His character has been vigorously assailed (e.g. by Washington Irving, *Columbus* (ed. 1885), i. 382 ff.), but he has been vindicated by Fidel Fita ý Colomer, who has devoted much industry to the study of all the documents relating to Buil (cp. his monographs in *Boletin de la Real Academia de la Historia*, vols. xix, xx; and *Fray Bernardo Boyl*, in *Boletin Histórico*, 1884).

⁶ Pedro de Villacorta (Las Casas, i. 82). He is mentioned in a letter from Columbus to his son, DiegoColumbus (*Nuevos Autográfos*, p. 11); this letter, which is dated 29 April, with no year given, is assigned by Thacher (iii. 129) to the year 1498, in which case Villacorta had then returned to Spain.

shall say on my behalf to their highnesses that it has pleased God to give me such grace for their service, that up to now I do not find less, nor has less been found, of anything that I have written and said and affirmed to their highnesses in past days. Rather by the grace of God, I hope that from what is done it will appear much more clearly still and that very soon. For in the matter of spices; on the shore of the sea alone, without having penetrated into the interior, such signs and evidence of them have been found, that it is reasonable to expect much better results.[1] And the same in the matter of the mines of gold. For, by two only who went to discover, each in a different direction, without their remaining there because the men were few, there have been found so many rivers, so filled with gold, that all of those who saw it and collected it, merely with their hands as specimens, came back so very delighted and say such great things about its abundance, that I feel diffidence in repeating what they say and in writing it to their highnesses. But as Gorbalan,[2] who was one of the discoverers, is going home, he will say what he saw. The other, however, who is called Ojeda,[3] a client of the duke of Medinaceli, a very discreet young man and one of very great prudence, remains here, and without doubt and without any comparison, he discovered much more, according to the account which he brought back of the rivers, saying that in each one of them there is an amount which is incredible. For this their highnesses may give thanks to God, since He has been so favourable to them in all their affairs.

Their highnesses give great thanks to God, and they regard as a very signal service all that the admiral has done in this matter and is doing, for they appreciate that, under God, they are indebted to him for all which they have had and will have in this matter; and since concerning this, they are writing to him more at length, they refer him to their letter.

[1] Cp. *infra*, p. 69.
[2] Cp. *supra*, p. 70, note 2.
[3] Alonso de Ojeda (or Hojeda) was born at Cuenca, c. 1470: was first cousin to his namesake, a Dominican and one of the first inquisitors, and was a client of Luis de la Cerda, duke of Medinaceli. He attracted the attention of Isabella by a feat of daring on the occasion of a visit which she paid to Seville (cp. Las Casas, i. 82), and was also a favourite of Fonseca (cp. Las Casas, i. 164). He

diréys á Sus Altezas de mi parte que á Dios ha plazido darme
tal gracia para en su servicio, que hasta aquí no hallo yo
menos, ni se ha hallado, en cosa alguna, de lo que yo escriví y
dixe y afirmé á Sus Altezas en los días pasados; antes, por
gracia de Dios, espero que aun muy más claramente y muy
presto por la obra parecerá, porque las cosas d'especería en
solas las orillas de la mar, syn aver entrado dentro en la tierra,
se halla tal rastro é prinçipios d'ella, que es razón que se
esperen muy mejores fines; y esto mismo en las minas del oro,
porque con solos dos que fueron á descobrir, cada uno por su
parte, syn detenerse allá, porque heran poca gente, se han
descubierto tantos ríos, tan poblados de oro, que qualquier
de los que lo vieron é cogieron solamente con las manos por
muestra, vinieron tan alegres, y disen tantas cosas de la
abundancia d'ello, que yo tengo enpacho de las dezir y escrevir á Sus Altezas. pero, porque allá va Gorvalán, que fué uno
de los descubridores, él dirá lo que vió, aunque acá queda otro,
que llaman 'Hojeda', criado del duque de Medinaçeli, muy
discreto moço y de muy grand recabdo, que syn dubda
y aun syn comparaçión descubrió mucho más, segund el
memorial de los ríos qu'él trajo, diziendo que en cada uno
d'ellos ay cosa de non creer, por lo qual Sus Altezas pueden
dar gracias á Dios, pues tan favorablemente se ha en todas
sus cosas.

Sus Altezas dan muchas gracias á Dios por esto, y tienen en
muy señalado servicio al almirante todo lo que en esto ha fecho y
hase, porque conosçen que, después de Dios, á él son en cargo de
todo lo que en esto han avido y ovieren, y, porque çerca d'esto le
escriven más largo, á su carta se remiten.

accompanied Columbus on his second voyage; relieved the fort of St. Thomas
and captured Caonabo (cp. Las Casas, i. 89, 91–93). Having returned to Spain,
he secured a licence to make discoveries, and made three voyages to the New
World; on the third, he had secured a government on the Isthmus, but the
expedition was disastrous (cp. Las Casas, ii. 52, 57–61). He eventually died in
great poverty at Santo Domingo, probably in 1515 or 1516 (cp. Las Casas, ii. 61).
He gave evidence in the action of Diego Columbus against the crown, 7 Dec.
1512, in support of the contention of the Fiscal that the discovery of the mainland was not due to Columbus (*Pleitos de Colón*, i, pp. 203–8). He is to be distinguished from the Alonso de Ojeda, 'a sinner of a man', who raided Cumana
and who was killed by the Indians (Las Casas, iii. 146). (Cp. Pizarro y Orellana,
Varones Ilustres del Nuevo Mundo, pp. 41–64.)

Item: You shall say to their highnesses that which I have already written to them, that I was very desirous to be able to send to them by this fleet a greater quantity of the gold which it is hoped may be collected here, if only the majority of our people here had not fallen suddenly ill.[1] This fleet, however, could not now be detained here longer, both on account of the great cost involved and because this season is suitable for going and such that those will be able to return who are to bring those things of which there is here great need. For, if they were to postpone their departure hence, those who have to come would not be able to come here until May. And besides that, if, with those who are well, who are to be found here, both on the sea and on land in the settlement, I were to wish to undertake to go to the mines or rivers now, there would be many difficulties and even dangers. For to go from here twenty-three or twenty-five leagues, where there are inlets of the sea and rivers to cross,[2] and for so long a journey, and in order to stay there for the time which would be needed for collecting the gold, it would be essential to carry many supplies which could not be borne on our backs. There are here no beasts of burden which could serve for the purpose, and the roads and passes are not sufficiently prepared, although they have begun to make them so that they may be possible to traverse.[3] And it would also be very inconvenient to leave the sick here in an open place and in huts, and with the provisions and supplies which there are in the land. For although these Indians have shown themselves, and do every day show themselves, to the discoverers as being very simple and without malice, yet, as every day they come here among our men, it does not appear that it would be well advised to run any risk and perhaps to lose these people and the supplies, which an Indian with a burning faggot could bring about, setting fire to the huts, for they come and go constantly night and day. On account of them, we have guards in the camp, while the settlement is unwalled and without defence.[4]

He did that well.

---

[1] Cp. *supra*, p. 66.
[2] For the rivers of Cibao, cp. Las Casas, *Apologética Historia*, c. 6. Among them

Ytem, diréys á Sus Altezas, como quier que ya se les escrive, que yo deseava mucho en esta armada poderles enbiar mayor qantidad de oro, d'el que acá se espera poder cojer, sy la gente, que acá está çerca, la mayor parte súbitamente non cahiera doliente. pero, porque ya esta armada non se podía detener acá más, syquiera por la costa grande que haze, syquiera porqu'el tiempo es este propio para yr y poder bolver los que han de traer acá las cosas que aquí hasen mucha mengua, porque sy tardasen de yrse de aquí, non podrían bolverse para mayo los que han de bolver, y, allende d'esto, sy con los sanos que acá se hallan, asý en mar como en tierra, en la población, yo quisiera enprender de yr á las minas ó rríos agora, y avía muchas dificultades y aun peligros, porque de aquí á veynte y tres ó .xxiiii. leguas, en donde ay puertos y ríos para pasar, y para tan luengo camino, y para estar allá al tiempo que sería menester para cojer el oro, avía menester llevar muchos mantenimientos, los quales non podrían llevar á cuestas, ni ay bestias acá, que á esto pudiesen suplir, ni los caminos y pasos non están tan aparejados, como quier que se han començado á adobar, para que se podiesen pasar, y también era grande ynconveniente dexar acá los dolientes en lugar abierto y choças, y las provisiones y mantenimientos que están en tierra, que, como quier que estos Yndios se ayan mostrado á los descubridores y se muestran cada día muy symples y syn maliçia, con todo, porque cada día vienen acá entre nosotros, non paresçió que fuera buen consejo meter á riesgo y á ventura de perderse esta gente y los mantenimientos, lo que un Yndio con un tizón podría haser, poniendo huego á las choças, porque, de noche y de día, syempre van y vienen, á causa d'ellos tenemos guardas en el canpo, mientras la población está abierta y syn defensión.

Que lo hiso bien.

were the Yaqui, or Rio del Oro; a second Rio del Oro, either the Mao or the Nicayagua; the Buenicún or Rio Seco; the Cotteniquin, the Cibú, and the Rio Verde. Most of these were small streams, which cannot be identified. When he went to Cibao, Columbus seems to have proceeded along the coast and then to have struck inland across the Vega.

[3] Cp. Las Casas, i. 90, 91.

[4] The anxiety of Columbus that Isabella should be completed led him to force the Spaniards to work at the building and roused opposition to him (cp. Las Casas, i. 88).

Further: As we have seen that of those who went inland to explore, the majority have fallen ill after their return, and that some were even forced to turn back on the way, there was also ground for fearing that the same might happen to such of the healthy as were to be found, if they were to go now. And it followed that there were there two dangers; the one, that they might fall ill there, while engaged on the work itself, where there is not a house or any protection from that cacique whom they call Caonabo,[1] who is a man, according to all accounts, very evil and much more daring, and who, seeing us there, discouraged and ill, might be able to undertake something which he would not dare if we were well. And with this, another difficulty may be urged, that of bringing here the gold which we might collect, for either we should have to bring a little and go and come every day, and expose ourselves to the risk of illness, or it would have to be sent with some part of the people with the same danger of loss.

He has done well.

So that: You shall say to their highnesses that these are the reasons why the armada has not been kept back at present, and why no more gold than specimens has been sent to them. But, trusting in the mercy of God, Who in all and through all has guided us until now, this people will speedily be restored to health, as is already coming to pass, for the country only tries them for some space of time and after that they recover. And it is certain that if they had some fresh meat to restore their health more rapidly, they would all, with the help of God, be on their feet, and the majority even would by this time be already convalescent; however, they are regaining their health. With these few healthy who remain here, every day is employed in enclosing the settlement and putting it in some posture of defence and the supplies in a secure position.[2] This will be done in a few days, as there need be nothing but dry walls.[3] For these Indians are not a people, unless they were to find us sleeping, to undertake anything, even if they had the thought. So they did to the others, who remained

---

[1] Cp. *supra*, p. 49 and note 4.

[2] Owing to the dissatisfaction of the Spaniards with the rations allowed to them by Columbus, it was probably necessary to protect the food supplies from

Otrosý, como avemos visto en los que fueron por tierra á descobrir, que los más cayeron dolientes, después de bueltos, y aun algunos se ovieron de bolver del camino, hera tanbién razón de temer que otrotal contesçiese á los que agora yrían d'estos sanos, que se allan, y seguirse hían dos peligros de allí, el uno, de adoleser allá en la misma obra, do non ay casa ni reparo alguno de aquel caçique que llaman 'Caonabó', que es onbre, segund relaçión de todos, muy malo y muy más atrevido, el qual, viéndonos allá asý desbaratados y dolientes, podría emprender lo que non osaría, sy fuésemos sanos. y con esto mismo se allega otra dificultad, de traer acá lo que llegásenos de oro, porque, ó avíamos de traer poco, y yr y venir cada día, y meterse en el riesgo de las dolençias, ó se avía de enbiar con alguna parte de la gente, con el mismo peligro de perderlo.

Que lo hiso bien.

Asý que diréys á Sus Altesas que estas son las cabsas porque de presente non se ha detenido el armada, ni se les enbía oro más de las muestras. pero, confiando en la misericordia de Dios, que en todo y por todo nos ha guiado hasta aquí, esta gente convalesçerá presto, como ya lo hasen, porque solamente les prueva la tierra de algunas çeçiones, y luego se levantan ; y es çierto que sy tuviesen algunas carnes frescas para convalesçer, muy presto serían todos en pie, con ayuda de Dios, é aun los más estarían ya convalesçidos en este tiempo, enpero que ellos convalesçen. con estos pocos sanos, que acá quedan, cada día se entiende en çerrar la poblaçión y meterla en alguna defensa, y los mantenimientos en seguro, que será fecho en breves días, porque no ha de ser syno albarradas ; que non son gente los Yndios, que, sy dormiendo no nos fallasen, para enprender cosa ninguna, aunque la toviesen pensada ; que asý hizieron á los otros que acá quedaron por su mal recabdo, los quales, por pocos que

---

their depredations, as well as from the natives and the weather (cp. Las Casas, i. 92). He was also carrying out the explicit orders of the sovereigns [cp. Navarrete, ii. 70].

3 *Albarradas*: an Arabic word, meaning stone walls put up without mortar (from *al* and *parata*).

here, owing to their lack of care, for few as they were and for all the occasions which they gave to the Indians to have and to do that which they did do, they would never have dared to attempt to injure them if they had seen that they were watchful.[1] And when this work has been done, I will undertake to go to the said rivers,[2] either taking the route there from here and seeking the best means possible, or by sea, rounding the island to that part from which it is said that it cannot be more than six or seven leagues to the said rivers. I will act in such a way that the gold may be able to be collected in safety and placed in security in some fort or tower which may be immediately made there, to hold it collected for the time when the two caravels go there, so that, immediately at the first time which may be fit for making this journey, it may be sent with good security.

This is well and so he should do.

Item: You shall say to their highnesses, as has been said, that the cause of the illness, so general among all, is the change of water and air, for we see that it spreads to all one after another, and few are in danger. It follows that, under God, the preservation of health depends upon this people being provided with the food to which they are accustomed in Spain, for none of them, or others who may newly arrive, can serve their highnesses unless they are in health. And this provision should continue until here a supply can be secured from that which is here sown and planted, I mean from wheat and barley and grapes, towards which little has been done this year, since it was not possible earlier to select a site for a settlement.[3] And directly after it was selected, those few labourers who were here fell ill, and even if they had been well, they had so few beasts and those so lean and weak, that it is little that they would have been able to do. Nevertheless, they have sown something, mainly in order to test the soil, which appears to be very wonderful, so that from this some relief in our necessities may be expected. We are very sure, as what has been done shows, that in this country wheat as

---

[1] Columbus would here seem to be defending himself against the charge that he had not taken sufficient precautions to ensure the safety of those whom he

fuesen y por mayores ocasiones que dieran á los Yndios
de aver é de hazer lo que hizieron, nunca ellos osaran
enprender de dañarles, sy los vieran á buen recabdo. y,
esto fecho, luego se entenderá en yr á los dichos ríos, ó desde
aquí tomado el camino, y buscando los mejores espedientes
que se puedan, ó por la mar, rodeando la ysla fasta
aquella parte, de donde se dize que non deve aver más de
seys ó syete leguas hasta los dichos ríos, por forma que con
seguridad se pueda cojer el oro y ponerlo en recabdo de alguna
fortaleza ó torre, que allí se haga luego, para tenerlo cogido
al tiempo que las dos caravelas bolverán acá, é para que
luego con el primer tiempo que sea para navegar este camino,
se envíe á buen recabdo.

Que está bien y así lo deve haser.

Ytem, dirés á Sus Altezas, como dicho es, que las cabsas de la
dolençia tan general de todos es de mudamiento de aguas y
ayres, porque vemos que á todos arreo se estiende, y peligran
pocos. por consyguiente, la conservaçión de la sanidad, después de Dios, está que esta gente sea proveýda de los mantenimientos, que en España acostunbravan, porque d'ellos, ni
de otros que viniesen de nuevo, Sus Altezas se podrían servir,
sy no están sanos. y esta provisyón ha de durar hasta que
acá se aya fecho cimiento de lo que acá se sembrare y plan-
tare, digo de trigos y cevadas y viñas, de lo qual para este año
se ha fecho poco, porque no se pudo de antes tomar asyento,
y liego que se tomó, adolescieron aquellos poquitos labradores,
que acá estavan; los quales, aunque estovieran sanos,
tenían tan pocas bestias, y tan magras y flacas, que poco es lo
que podieran hazer. con todo, alguna cosa han senbrado,
mas para provar la tierra, que paresçe muy maravillosa, para
que de allí se puede esperar remedio alguno en nuestras
necesidades. somos bien çiertos, como la obra lo muestra,
que en esta tierra asý el trigo, como el vino, naçerá muy bien ;

had left at La Navidad and that he had trusted too much to the apparent
friendliness of the natives.
² The rivers were the Yaqui, or Rio del Oro, and the Neiba.
³ Cp. *supra*, p. 60 *et seq.*, and Las Casas (i. 88). Cuneo (*loc. cit.*) seems to have
underestimated the length of time which was occupied in finding a suitable place
for a settlement: his account differs in some material respects from that given by
Las Casas and Chanca.

well as vines will grow very well. But it is necessary to wait for the fruit, and if it be such as the rapid growing of the wheat, and of some few vines which have been planted, suggests, it is certain that here there will be no need of Andalucia or of Sicily, and the same applies to sugar canes, judging from the way in which some few that have been planted have taken root.[1] For it is certain that the beauty of the land of these islands, as well of the mountains and sierras and rivers, as of the plains, where there are broad rivers, is such to behold that no other land on which the sun shines can be better to see or more lovely.

Since the land is of such character, it should be arranged that as much as possible be sown with all things, and Don Juan de Fonseca [2] *is instructed to send at once all that may be needed for this purpose.*

Item: You shall say that, on account of much of the wine of that which the fleet carried having run away on this voyage, and this, as the majority say, being the fault of the bad work which the coopers did in Seville, the greatest need which we now have, or which we expect to have for the present, is of wine. And though we have enough biscuit, as well as corn, for some while, yet it is necessary that some reasonable amount should also be sent, for the voyage is long and provision cannot be made every day, and likewise some salt meat, I mean bacon, and other salt flesh, which should be better than that which we have brought on this voyage.[3]

---

[1] Columbus had taken supplies of various seeds with him (cp. Las Casas, i. 83: Peter Martyr, i. 1). Wheat, sown in January, was cut in March; fruit stones, if sown, sprouted in seven days; sugar canes grew with equal rapidity (Ferdinand Columbus, c. 53).

[2] Juan Rodriguez de Fonseca, son of Dr. Juan Alonso de Fonseca, by Beatriz Rodriguez. He was a nephew of Alonso de Fonseca, archbishop of Seville, while his brothers were Alonso de Fonseca, señor de Coca y Alaejos, and Antonio de Fonseca, contador mayor of Castile. He was a pupil of Antonio de Lebrija, who dedicated to him his *Vafre dictis Philosophorum carminibus Latinis reddita.* Fonseca became archdeacon of Seville and gained the favour of Ferdinand and Isabella, who commissioned him to escort the widowed Margaret of Austria through France (1499), when she returned to her father after the death of prince Juan. Fonseca was successively bishop of Badajoz, Córdoba, Palencia, and Búrgos, and was created conde de Pernia. He was entrusted with the duty of directing the preparations for the second voyage of Columbus, and from that time exercised a preponderating influence on the affairs of the Indies; he was the

pero, háse de esperar el fruto, el qual, sy tal será como muestra la presteza del nasçer del trigo é de algunos poquitos de sarmientos, que se pusyeron es cierto que non fará mengua el Andalusía ni Seçilia aquí, ni en las cañas de açucar segund unas poquitas, que se pusyeron, han prendido. porqu'es çierto que la fermosura de la tierra d'estas yslas, asý de montes é syerras y aguas, como de vegas, donde ay ríos cabdales, es tal la vista, que ninguna otra tierra que sol escaliente puede ser mejor, al paresçer, ni tan fermosa.

Pues la tierra es tal, que deve procurar que se sienbre lo más que ser pudiere de todas cosas, y á don Juan de Fonseca se escrive que enbíe de contino todo lo que fuere menester para esto.

Ytem, dirés que á cabsa de averse derramado mucho vino en este camino d'el que la flota traýa, y esto, segund disen los más, á culpa de la mala obra que los toneleros hizieron en Sevylla, la mayor mengua que agora tenemos aquí, ó esperamos para esto tener, es de vinos ; y, como quier que tengamos para más tiempo asý vizcocho como trigo, con todo, es neçesario que también se enbíe alguna quantidad razonable, porqu'el camino es luengo, é cada día no se puede proveer, é asymismo algunas carnes, digo toçinos y otra çeçina, que sea mejor que la que avemos traýdo este camino. de carneros

first president of the Council of the Indies, which, however, was not really organized during his lifetime. He was the patron of Alonso de Ojeda, of Magellan, and of other early explorers, but was very hostile to Cortés. Peter Martyr [i. 1 and elsewhere] and Bernaldez (c. 118) speak in the highest terms of his work in connexion with Indian affairs, but Las Casas, who had quarrelled with him on the question of the treatment of the Indians, accuses him of inveterate hostility towards Columbus (cp. Las Casas, i. 167 ; iii. 130 *et seq.*). He declares that 'the lord bishop knew far more about fitting out fleets than about saying mass in an episcopal manner', and that he engaged in forms of employment 'better suited to a Biscayan than a bishop' (Las Casas, i. 78). The unfavourable verdict of Las Casas has been generally accepted by later writers (e.g. Washington Irving, i. 281 ; iii. 420, and Appendix 34). There would seem to be little direct evidence that Fonseca had any particular antipathy to Columbus. His capacity would seem to be beyond question. He died in 1524.

[3] Supplies of provisions for the fleet on the second voyage were drawn partly from royal stores at Seville and Cádiz, but as the supplies there were inadequate, additional amounts were drawn from elsewhere: Jacinto Berardi was accorded a contract for the supply of biscuit (cp. *Doc. Inéd.* (1ª serie), 38, pp. 140–2; 30, pp. 108–9, 159–60, 161). There does not appear to be any document dealing directly with the supply of wine, and it is not possible to fix the responsibility for the fraud, if fraud there were.

As to livestock, sheep and lambs above all, more females than males, and some calves and young heifers are necessary, so that they should come always in every caravel which may be sent here, and some he- and she-asses, and mares for labour and tillage, for there are here none of those animals which can be put to use or which are of value.[1] And since I fear that their highnesses may not be found in Seville, and that their officials or ministers, without their express command, may not make provision for that which now, in this next voyage, it is necessary should come, and since in consulting and answering the season for the departure of the ships, as it is necessary that they should be here in May in any case, will pass, you shall say to their highnesses how I have already given you charge and command that, pledging the gold which you are taking home, or placing it in the power of some merchant in Seville, he will defray and supply the money which may be needed to load two caravels with wine and corn and with the other things of which you carry a memorandum. And this merchant shall carry or send the said gold to their highnesses that they may see it, receive it and cause to be paid from it that which has been expended and employed for the despatch and lading of the said two caravels, which are to console and revive this people who remain here. It is well that everything should be done that is possible in order that they may come here in any case in the month of May, so that the people, before the beginning of summer, may see and have some refreshment from these things, especially the sick. Of these things we have already great need, such as of raisins, sugar, almonds, honey and rice, of which a great quantity should have come and very little arrived, and that which did come has been expended and consumed, as well as the greater part of the medicines, which we brought from there, owing to the number of the many sick. Of these things, as has been said, both for the healthy and for the sick, you carry memoranda, signed by my hand. These things, completely if the money be sufficient, or at least the most necessary, shall be despatched immediately, so that they may be able to be

---

[1] A certain amount of livestock was taken by Columbus on his second voyage (cp. Ferdinand Columbus, c. 45: Peter Martyr, i. 1). More was shipped at

bivos, y aun antes corderos y cordericas, más fembras que
machos, y algunos bezerros y bezerras pequeños, son menester
que cada vez venga en qualquier caravela, que acá se enbiare, y algunas asnas y asnos, y yeguas, para trabajo y
symiente; que acá ninguna d'estas animalias ay, de que onbre
se pueda ayudar ni valer. y porque reçelo que Sus Altezas no
se fallarán en Sevilla, ni los oficiales ó ministros suyos, syn
espreso mandamiento, non proveerán en lo que agora con este
primero camino es neçesario que venga, porque en la consulta
y en la respuesta se pasaría la sazón del partir los navíos, que
acá por todo mayo es neçesario que sean, dirés á Sus Altezas
como yo vos dí cargo y mandé que del oro, que allá lleváys,
enpeñándolo ó poniéndolo en poder de algund mercader en
Sevilla, el qual distraya y ponga los maravedís que serán
menester para cargar dos caravelas de vino, y de trigo, y de
las otras cosas que lleváys por memorial. el qual mercader lleve
ó enbíe el dicho oro para Sus Altezas, que le vean, resçiban,
é hagan pagar lo que oviere distraýdo é puesto para el despacho y cargazón de las dichas dos caravelas, las quales, por
consolar y esforçar esta gente, que acá queda, cumple que
hagan más de poder de ser acá bueltas por todo el mes de
mayo; porque la gente, antes de entrar en el verano, vean
é tengan algún refrescamiento d'estas cosas, en espeçial para
las dolençias, de las quales cosas acá ya tenemos gran
mengua, como son pasas, açúcar, almendras, miel é arroz, que
deviera venir en grand quantidad, y vino muy poca, é aquello
que vino es ya consumido é gastado, y aun la mayor parte de
las medeçinas, que de allá troxieron, por la muchedumbre de
los muchos dolientes; de las quales cosas, como dicho es,
vos lleváys memoriales, asý para sanos como para dolientes,
firmados de mi mano. los quales complidamente, sy el dinero
bastare, ó á lo menos lo que más neçesario sea para agora,

Gomera (Las Casas, i. 83), including eight pigs, 'from whom all the swine of
the Indies, which are innumerable, are descended'. For further provision in
this matter, cp. *Cédula*, 9 April 1495 (Navarrete, ii. 162–4), when six mares,
four male and two female asses, four calves and two heifers, a hundred head of
small livestock, two hundred hens, eighty sows and twenty hogs, live rabbits,
'as many as it seems right to send', some sheep and cows, as well as 'a priest of
conscience and learning', were to be dispatched to Española. If these swine
were actually sent, the statement of Las Casas on the pedigree of the swine of
the Indies would seem to be inaccurate.

brought at once by the said two ships. And as to what remains, you shall procure from their highnesses that it shall come with other ships as speedily as may be possible.

Their highnesses will send orders to Don Juan de Fonseca that he shall immediately make inquiry concerning those who committed this fraud in the matter of the casks, and from their own goods there shall be taken enough to cover all the loss of the wine which occurred, with the costs; and in the matter of the sugar canes, that those which are sent shall be good, and as to the other things which he mentions here, that they be provided forthwith.[1]
It is already provided with the two caravels which go first.

Item: You shall say to their highnesses that, owing to the fact that there is here no interpreter,[2] by means of whom it is possible to give to these people understanding of our holy Faith, as their highnesses desire and also those of us who are here, although every possible effort has been made, there are now sent with these ships some of the cannibals, men and women and boys and girls. These their highnesses can order to be placed in charge of persons so that they may be able better to learn the language, employing them in forms of service, and ordering that gradually greater care be given to them than to other slaves, so that some may learn from others. If they do not speak to each other or see each other until much later, they will learn more quickly there than here, and they will be better interpreters, although here there has been no failure to do what could be done. It is the truth that, as among these people those of one island have little intercourse with those of another,[3] in languages there is some difference between them, according to whether they are nearer to or farther from each other. And since of all the islands, those of the cannibals are much the largest and much more fully populated, it is thought here that to take some of the men and women and to send them home to Castile would not be anything but well, for they may one day be led to abandon that inhuman custom which they have of eating men, and there in Castile, learning the language, they will much more readily receive baptism and secure the welfare of their souls. Further,

---

[1] In a letter from the sovereigns, 4 July 1494, Fonseca is instructed to send

despacharés, para que lo puedan luego traer los dichos dos navíos; y lo que quedare procurarés con Sus Altezas que con otros navíos venga lo más presto que ser pudiere.

Sus Altezas enbiaron á mandar á don Juan de Fonseca que luego aya ynformación de los que hisieron ese engaño en los toneles, y de sus bienes haga que se cobre todo el daño que vino en el vino, con las costas; y en lo de las çeçinas vea como las que se enbiaren sean buenas, y en las otras cosas que aquí dise, que las provea luego.

Ya se proveyó con las dos caravelas que fueron primero.

Ytem, dirés á Sus Altesas que á cabsa que acá no ay lengua, por medio de la qual á esta gente se pueda dar á entender nuestra sancta fee, como Sus Altezas desean y aun los que acá estamos, como quier que se trabajará quanto pudieren, se enbían de presente con estos navíos asý de los Caníbales, honbres y mugeres, y niños y niñas, los quales Sus Altezas pueden mandar poner en poder de personas, con quien puedan mejor aprender la lengua, exerçitándolos en cosas de serviçio, y poco á poco mandando poner en ellos algún más cuidado que en otros esclavos, para que deprendan unos de otros, que non se hablen ni se vean syno muy tarde, que más presto deprenderán allá que non acá, y serán mejores yntérpetres, como quier que acá no se dexará de haser lo que se pueda. es verdad que como esta gente plática poco los de la una ysla con los de la otra, en las lenguas ay alguna diferençia entre ellos, segund como están más cerca ó más lexos, y porque entre las otras yslas las de los Caníbales son mucho grandes y mucho bien pobladas, paresçerá acá que tomar d'ellos y d'ellas, y enbiarlos allá á Castilla, no será syno bien; porque quitarse ẏan una vez de aquella ynhumana costunbre, que tienen, de comer hombres, y allá en Castilla, entendiendo la lengua, muy más presto resçibirian el baptismo, y farían el provecho de sus ánimas. aun entre estos pueblos, que non son de esas costum-

---

four caravels at once; they were to carry various things, of which a list is given, for the personal use of Columbus (Navarrete, ii. 149–52).

² Fray Buil complained that his ignorance of the language hampered the work of conversion (cp. *Doc. Inéd.* (1ª *serie*), 30, pp. 304–5).

³ Cp. *supra*, p. 12, and note 1.

among those peoples who have not these habits, great credit will be gained by us when they see that we take and make captive those men, from whom they are accustomed to suffer injury, and of whom they go in such fear that they are terrified at their very name. Assure their highnesses that here, in this land, our arrival and the sight of the fleet, so under control and beautiful, has given us very great authority for the present and very great security for our affairs in the future. For all the people of this great island, and of the other islands, when they see the good treatment which is meted out to well-doers and the punishment which is inflicted upon those who do evil, will quickly come to obedience so that it will be possible to command them as vassals of their highnesses. And as already here, wherever a man of them is to be found, they not only do willingly all that they are wished to do, but of their own accord set themselves to everything which they understand may please us, their highnesses may also be certain that on that side equally, among Christian princes, the coming of this fleet has given them great reputation in many respects, both now and hereafter, which their highnesses will be better able to understand and know than I have power to say.

Let him be informed of that which has occurred in the case of the cannibals who came here.[1]

That is very well, and so it should be done, but let him endeavour, as it may be possible, that they there be converted to our holy Faith, and so let him endeavour in those islands where he may be.

Item: You shall say to their highnesses that the welfare of the souls of the said cannibals, and also of those here, has induced the idea that the more that may be sent over, the better it will be, and in this their highnesses may be served in the following way. That, having seen how necessary cattle and beasts of burden are here, for the support of the people who have to be here, and indeed for all these islands, their highnesses might give licence and a permit for a sufficient number of caravels to come here every year and to carry the said cattle and other supplies and things for the colonization

bres, se ganaría grand crédito por nosotros, viendo que aquellos prendiésemos y cativásemos, de quien ellos suelen
resçibir daños, y tienen tamaño miedo, que del nombre solo
se espantan; çertificando á Sus Altezas que la venida é vista
d'esta flota acá en esta tierra, asý junta y fermosa, ha dado
muy grande abtoridad á esto, y muy grand seguridad para las
cosas venideras, para que toda esta gente d'esta tan grande
ysla y de las otras, viendo el buen tratamiento, que á los
buenos se hará y el castigo que á los malos se dará, verná á
obediencia prestamente, para poderlos mandar como vasallos
de Sus Altezas, como quier que ellos agora, donde quier que
onbre se halle, non solo hazen de grado lo que honbre quiere
que fagan, mas ellos de su voluntad se ponen á todo lo que
entienden que nos puede plazer. y también pueden ser çiertos
Sus Altezas que non menos allá entre los christianos príncipes
aver dado gran reputaçión la venida d'esta armada, por
muchos respectos, asý presentes como venideros, los quales Sus
Altesas podrán mejor pensar y entender, que non sabría dezir.

*Desirle éys lo que acá ha avido de lo de los Caníbales, que acá
vinieron.*

*Que está muy bien, y así lo deve haser; pero que procure
allá como, sy ser pudiere, se redugan á nuestra santa fe católica,
y asimismo lo procure con los de las yslas donde está.*

Ytem, diréis á Sus Altezas qu'el provecho de las almas de los
dichos Caníbales, y aun d'estos de acá, ha traýdo en pensa-
miento que quantos más allá se llevasen sería mejor, y en
ellos podrían Sus Altezas ser servidos d'esta manera: que
visto quanto son acá menester los ganados y bestias de trabajo para el sostenimiento de la gente que acá ha de estar y
bien de todas estas yslas, Sus Altesas podrán dar liçençia é
permiso á un número de caravelas suficiente, que vengan acá
cada año, y trayan de los dichos ganados, y otros mantenimientos y cosas, para poblar el canpo, y aprovechar la tierra; y esto
en precios razonables, á sus costas de los que las truxieren;
las quales cosas se les podrían pagar en esclavos d'estos Caní-

---

¹ The cannibals were distributed as slaves.

of the country and the development of the land, and this at reasonable prices at the cost of those who transport them. Payment for these things could be made to them in slaves, from among these cannibals, a people very savage and suitable for the purpose, and well made and of very good intelligence. We believe that they, having abandoned that inhumanity, will be better than any other slaves, and their inhumanity they will immediately lose when they are out of their own land. And of these they will be able to take many with the oared *fustas* which it is proposed to build here. It is, however, to be presupposed that each one of the caravels which come from their highnesses will have on board a reliable person, who will prevent the said caravels from stopping at any other place or island except here, where the lading and unlading of all the merchandise must be. And further, on these slaves which they carry, their highnesses could levy a duty there. And on this matter you shall bring or send an answer, in order that here the preparations which are necessary may be made with more confidence, if it seems well to their highnesses.

As to this, the matter has been postponed for the present, until another voyage has been made from there, and let the admiral write that which occurs to him concerning this matter.[1]

Item: You shall also say to their highnesses that it is more profitable, and less cost, to freight ships as the merchants of Flanders do by the tonnage than in another way. Therefore I give it in charge to you to freight in this manner the two caravels which you are to despatch at once. And so it should be done in the case of the other vessels which their highnesses despatch, if they approve of this method. But I do not mean to say this in the case of the vessels which are to come with their licence for the merchandise of slaves.

Their highnesses command Don Juan de Fonseca that in the freighting of the caravels, he is to employ this method if it be possible.

Item: You shall say to their highnesses that, in order to avoid some greater expense, I have bought these caravels, of

bales, gente tan fiera, y dispuesta, y bien proporcionada, y de muy buen entendimiento; los quales, quitados de aquella ynhumanidad, creemos que serán mejores que otros ningunos esclavos; la qual luego perderán que sean fuera de su tierra, y d'estos podrán aver muchos con las fustas de remos, que acá se entienden de haser, fecho enpero presupuesto que cada una de las caravelas que viniesen de Sus Altesas pusyesen una persona fiable, la qual defendiese las dichas caravelas, que no descendiesen á ninguna otra parte ni ysla salvo aquí, donde ha de estar la carga y descarga de toda la mercaduría; y aun d'estos esclavos que se llevaren á Sus Altesas podrían aver sus derechos allá, y d'esto traeréis ó enbiaréis respuesta, porque acá se hagan los aparejos que son menester con más confiança, sy á Sus Altesas paresçiere bien.

En esto se ha suspendido por agora, hasta que venga otro camino de allá, y escriva el almirante lo que en esto le paresçe.

Ytem, también diréys á Sus Altezas que más provechoso es y menos costa fletar los navíos, como los fletan los mercaderes para Flandes, por toneladas, que non de otra manera, por ende que yo vos dí cargo de fletar á este respecto las dos caravelas que avéys luego de enbiar, y así se podrá hazer de todas las otras que Sus Altesas enbiaren, sy de aquella forma se ternán por servidos. pero no entiendo dezir esto de las que han de venir con su licencia por la mercaduría de los esclavos.

Sus Altezas mandan á don Juan de Fonseca que en el fletar de las caravelas tengan esta forma, sy ser pudiere.

Ytem, dirés á Sus Altesas que á cabsa de escusar alguna más costa, yo merqué estas caravelas que lleváys por memorial, para retenerlas acá con estas dos naos, conviene á saber la Gallega y esa otra capitana, de la qual merqué, por semejante,

---

[1] Ferdinand and Isabella did not accept this suggestion of Columbus, although he afterwards elaborated it considerably. The fact that, in anticipation of royal approval, he sent some slaves to Spain was perhaps one of the causes of his eventual removal of his government of Española (cp. Las Casas, i. 106, 122, 151).

which you carry a memorandum, in order to retain them here with these two ships, that is to say, *la Gallega*, and the other, the flagship.[1] And in her, in the same way, I have bought a three-eighths share from her master, for the price which appears in the memorandum of these documents, which you carry, signed by my hand. And these ships will not only give authority and great security to the people who have to be on shore and to treat with the Indians for the collection of gold, but further they will be a protection against any kind of danger which might be experienced from a strange people. Further the caravels are needed for the discovery of Tierra Firme and other islands which lie between here and there. And you shall beg their highnesses that they will command the money which these ships have cost to be paid at the times at which it has been promised, for without doubt they will fully make good the expense, as I believe and hope in the mercy of God.

The admiral has done well, and you shall tell him that here payment has been made to him who sold the ship, and that they have commanded Don Juan de Fonseca that the cost of the caravels, which the admiral has bought, be paid.

Item: You shall say to their highnesses, and pray them on my behalf in the most humble manner possible, that it may please them to consider carefully that which they will see more at length in the letters and other writings, touching the peace and safety and concord of those who are here. And that their highnesses will select for employment in their service such persons, that there be no suspicion of them and that they consider rather the purpose for which they have been sent than their personal interests. And on this point, as you have seen and know all these matters, you shall speak and tell their highnesses the truth of all affairs as you understand them. And you shall see that the decision which their highnesses shall command to be taken in this matter shall come with the first ships, if it be possible, in order that there may not be scandals in a matter which so nearly concerns the service of their highnesses.[2]

---

[1] Cp. *supra*, p. 22, note 3. The flagship was *Santa María la Galante*.

del maestre d'ella los tres ochavos, por el presçio que en el
dicho memorial d'estas copias lleváys firmado de mi mano.
los quales navíos non solo darán abtoridad y grand seguridad
á la gente, que ha de estar dentro, y conversar con los Yndios
para coger el oro, mas aun para otra qualquier cosa de peligro
que de gente estraña pudiese acontesçer; allende que las
caravelas son necesarias para el descubrir de la tierra firme y
otras yslas que entre aquí é allá están. y suplicarés á Sus
Altezas que los maravedís que estos navíos cuestan manden
pagar en los tiempos que se les ha prometido, porque syn
dubda ellos ganarán bien su costa, segund yo creo y espero en
la misericordia de Dios.

*El almirante lo hiso bien, y desirle éys como acá se pagó al que
vendió la nao, y mandaron á don Juan de Fonseca que pague lo
de las caravelas qu'el almirante conpró.*

Ytem, dirés á Sus Altezas y suplicarés de mi parte, quanto
más húmillmente pueda, que les plega mucho mirar en lo que
por las cartas y otras escripturas verán más largamente
tocante á la paz é sosiego é concordia de los que acá están, y
que para las cosas del servicio de Sus Altezas escojan tales
personas que non se tenga reçelo d'ellas, y que miren más á
lo por que se enbían, que non á sus propios yntereses; y en
esto, pues que todas las cosas vistes é supistes, hablarés é
diréis á Sus Altezas la verdad de todas las cosas como la
comprehendistes, y que la provisyón de Sus Altezas, que sobre
ello mandaren faser, venga con los primeros navíos, sy posible
fuere, á fin que acá no se hagan escándalos en cosa que tanto
va en el servicio de Sus Altezas.

---

² The allusion is to that growing hostility to Columbus at Isabella which was
illustrated by the case of Firmin Zedo (Bernáldez, c. 120). It seems to be clear
that the contador, Bernal de Pisa, had already quarrelled with Columbus,
although his plot did not come to a head until a later date: in their letter,
acknowledging the receipt of this Memorandum, the sovereigns instruct Columbus
to send Bernal de Pisa home and to appoint a successor to him, with the approval
of Fray Buil (Letter, 13 April 1494: Navarrete, ii. 113–16). Las Casas (i. 92)
finds in the opposition to Columbus a judgement of God on the Admiral.

Their highnesses are well informed concerning this, and for all provision will be made as is fitting.

Item: You shall tell their highnesses of the situation of this city and the beauty of the surrounding district, as you have seen and know it, and how I have made you alcaide of it, in virtue of the powers which I hold from their highnesses for this, and that I pray them humbly that as some part recompense for your services, they will receive the said appointment favourably, as I hope from their highnesses.

It pleases their highnesses that you shall be alcaide.

Item: As Mosen Pedro Margarite,[1] a servant of their highnesses, has done good service, and I hope that he will so do in the future in the matters which may be entrusted to him, I have had pleasure at his remaining here, and also concerning Gaspar and Beltrán,[2] as being known servants of their highnesses, to have them to employ in confidentia' matters. You shall pray their highnesses that they will especially provide for the said Mosen Pedro, who is married and has children, some appointment in the order of Santiago, of which he wears the habit, in order that his wife and children may have wherewith to live. Likewise you shall give account of Juan Aguado,[3] servant of their highnesses, how well and diligently he has served in all that has been entrusted to him, and so I supplicate their highnesses for him and for the above-mentioned, that they will advance and reward them.

---

[1] Pedro Margarite (more accurately, Margarit) was a Catalan of noble family, son of Bernardo Margarit. He became a member of the royal household and a knight of the order of Santiago; was aguacil of the Inquisition in the diocese of Zaragoza (1478). Accompanied Columbus on his second voyage (Las Casas, i. 82); was left in command of the fort of St. Thomas in Cibao and was there besieged by Caonabo, being relieved by Ojeda (Las Casas, i. 91, 92, 93; Oviedo, ii. 13). When Columbus left Española on his voyage of discovery, Margarit was given command of a force with which he was to traverse and subdue the island, and to effect the capture of Caonabo (Las Casas, i. 94: and *Instructions to Margarite, Rac. Col.* I. i. 284–88). He did not carry out these instructions, quarrelled with the council left by Columbus to govern Isabella, threw up his command and returned to Spain with Fray Buil (cp. Las Casas, i. 100; Peter Martyr, i. 4; Oviedo, ii. 14). The reason for his action has not been elucidated; the suggestion that he was the victim of his excesses (cp. Washington Irving, ii. 16 ff. and Asensio

*Sus Altezas están bien ynformados d'esto, y en todo se pro-
veerá como conviene.*

Ytem, dirés á Sus Altezas el asyento d'esta cibdad é la fermosura de la provinçia al derredor, como lo vistes y comprehendistes, y como yo vos hize alcayde d'ella, por los poderes
que de Sus Altesas tengo para ello, á las quales omillmente
suplico que en alguna parte de satisfación de vuestros servicios tengan por bien la dicha provisión, como de Sus Altesas
yo espero.

A Sus Altezas plase que vos seáys alcayde.

Ytem, porque mosén Pedro Margarite, criado de Sus Altezas,
ha bien servido, y espero que asý lo hará adelante en las cosas
que le fueren encomendadas, he avido plaser de su quedada
aquí, y también de Gáspar, y de Beltrán, por ser coñosçidos
criados de Sus Altezas, para los poner en cosas de confiança.
suplicarés á Sus Altezas, que especial al dicho mosén Pedro,
que es casado y tiene hijos, le provean de alguna encomienda
en la horden de Santiago, de la qual él tiene el hábito, porque
su muger é hijos tengan en que bivir. asymismo harés
relaçión de Juan Aguado, criado de Sus Altesas, quan bien é
deligentemente ha servido en todo lo que le ha sydo mandado,
que suplico á Sus Altesas á él é á los sobredichos los ayan por
encomendados é por presentes.

y Toledo, *Cristóbal Colón*, i. 273) rests only on an indefinite statement in Oviedo
(*loc. cit.*), nor is there any evidence for the suggestion of Ulloa (*Xristo-Ferens
Colom*, p. 195) that Margarit, like Buil, had been sent to spy upon Columbus.
On his return to Spain, Margarit vigorously attacked the conduct of Columbus
in Española (cp. Las Casas, i. 107; Oviedo, *loc. cit.*). Margarit was married to
María de Carrillo. He is not to be confused with the 'converso' of the same name.
(Cp. Serrano y Sanz, *Origines de la Dominación Española en América*, p. 132
et seq.)

² Nothing appears to be known of these two men.

³ Juan Aguado was a member of the household of Isabella, by whom he was
specially recommended to Columbus (Letter, 30 June 1493: Navarrete, ii. 77).
He accompanied Columbus on his second voyage, but seems to have returned
to Spain with Antonio de Torres in 1494. In 1495, he was sent to Española to
investigate the charges brought against Columbus (Letter, 12 April 1495:
Navarrete, ii. 169, and Letter, 19 April 1495, *Doc. Inéd.* (1ª *serie*), 30, p. 347:
cp. *Nuevos Autografos*, pp. 25, 29). On reaching the island, he seems to have
shown extreme hostility towards Columbus and to have behaved very intempe-
rately. As a result of his mission Columbus decided to return to Spain, where the
report of Aguado was rejected (Las Casas, i. 107–9, 112).

Their highnesses command to grant to Mosen Pedro thirty thousand maravedis every year, and to Gaspar and Beltran every year fifteen thousand maravedis, from to-day, 15 August 1494, henceforth, and so the admiral shall cause them to be paid in respect of that which has to be paid there, and Don Juan de Fonseca in respect of that which has to be paid here; and as to the matter of Juan Aguado, their highnesses will have it in mind.

Item: You shall tell their highnesses of the work imposed upon doctor Chanca owing to there being so many sick and further from the scarcity of supplies, and that despite all this he still shows the greatest diligence and charity in all that concerns his duty. And since their highnesses left to me the question of the salary which should be given to him here, although it is certain that, being here, he does not take and cannot receive anything from anyone, or earn through his profession that which he earned in Castile, or that which he would be able to earn, being at his ease and living in a different manner from that in which he lives here, and although he swears that what he earned at home was more, I do not wish to pay more than fifty thousand maravedis a year, beyond the salary which their highnesses give him, for the work which he does while he remains here. This sum I ask their highnesses to command to be paid with the salary here, and that although he says and affirms that all the physicians of your highnesses, who go to camps or who are employed in such matters as these, are accustomed to have of right a day's pay a year from all the people. Nevertheless I have been informed and they tell me that, however this may be, the custom is to give them a certain sum, estimated at will and by command of their highnesses, in lieu of that day's pay. You shall pray their highnesses to command provision to be made in this matter, as well concerning the question of the salary as concerning that of this customary payment, in such manner that the said doctor may have reason to be satisfied.

Their highnesses are pleased in this matter of doctor Chanca, and that there shall be paid to him that which the admiral has allowed to him, and that it be paid to him in addition to his salary.[1]

*Sus Altezas mandan asentar á mosén Pedro treynta mill
maravedís cada año y á Gáspar y Béltrán á cada uno quinse
mill maravedís cada año, desde oy quinse de agosto de
.lxxxxiiii. en adelante, y así les haga pagar el almirante en lo
que allá se oviere de pagar, y don Juan de Fonseca en lo que acá
se oviere de pagar; y en lo de Juan Aguado Sus Altezas avrán
memoria d'él á su cuesta.*

Ytem, dirés á Sus Altezas el trabajo qu'el doctor Chanca
tiene con el afruenta de tantos dolientes, y aun la estrechura de
los mantenimientos, é aun con todo ello se dispone con grand
deligencia y caridad en todo lo que cunple á su oficio, y porque
Sus Altesas remitieron á mi el salario que acá se le avía de
dar, porque, estando acá, es cierto qu'él non toma ni puede
aver nada de ninguno, ni ganar de su oficio como en Castilla
ganava ó podría ganar, estando á su reposo é biviendo de
otra manera que acá non bive, y así que como quiera qu'él
jura que es más lo que allá ganava allende el salario que
Sus Altezas le dan, y non me quise estender más de cinquenta
mill maravedís por el trabajo que acá pasa cada un año,
mientra acá estoviere, los quales suplico á Sus Altezas le
manden librar con el sueldo de acá, y eso mismo porqu'él
dise y afirma que todos los físicos de Vuestras Altezas, que
andan en reales ó semejantes cosas que estas, suelen aver de
derecho un día de sueldo en todo el año de toda la gente, con
todo, he seýdo ynformado, y dísenme que como quier que
esto sea la costumbre, es de darles çierta suma tassada á
voluntad y mandamiento de Sus Altezas, en compensa de
aquel día de sueldo. suplicarés á Sus Altesas que en ello manden proveer asý en lo del salario como d'esta costumbre, por
forma qu'el dicho doctor tenga rasón de ser contento.

*A Sus Altezas plase d'esto del dotor Chanca, y que se le
pague esto desde qu'el almirante ge lo asentó y que ge lo pague
con lo del sueldo.*

---

[1] For Chanca, cp. *supra*, p. 20, note 1. Ferdinand and Isabella wrote to
thank him for his services (Letter, 11 Sept. 1494: *Doc. Inéd.* (1ª *serie*), 30,
pp. 207-8).

In the matter of the day's pay of the physicians, they are not accustomed to have it except where the king, our lord, is in person.

Item: You shall speak to their highnesses of Coronel,[1] how he is a man to serve their highnesses in many ways, and how he has served up to now in all that is most essential, and how we feel his loss now that he is ill, and that having so served, it is reasonable that he should receive the fruit of his service, not only in rewards in the future, but in the matter of his salary at present, in such a way that he and those who are here may realize how service profits them. For, having regard to the labour which has to be performed here in collecting the gold, the persons in whom there is such diligence are not to be held in small consideration. And since for his capacity he has been granted by me the office of *aguacil mayor* of the Indies, and in the record of the appointment the salary is left blank, I pray their highnesses that they will command that it be filled up as may be best for their service, confirming the provision which I have here given to him, and granting it to him legally.

Their highnesses command that fifteen thousand maravedis be assigned to him above his salary annually, and that the sum be paid to him when his salary is paid.

In the same way you shall say to their highnesses that the bachiller Gil Garcia [2] came here as alcalde mayor, and that no salary has been assigned to him or fixed, and that he is a good man and learned and diligent, and is here very necessary. So that I pray their highnesses that they command to appoint and assign to him a salary, in such a way that he may be able to support himself, and that it may be paid to him with the money of his pay here.

Their highnesses command that there be assigned to him every year twenty thousand maravedis as long as he is there and beyond his salary, and that this be paid to him when his salary is paid.

[1] Pero Hernandez Coronel, who was one of the members of the council left

En esto del día del sueldo de los físicos non lo acostunbran aver syno donde el rey nuestro señor sea en persona.

Ytem, dirés á Sus Altezas de Coronel, quanto es hombre para servir á Sus Altezas en muchas cosas, y quanto ha servido hasta aquí en todo lo más neçesario, y la mengua que d'él sentimos agora que está doliente, y que, sirviendo de tal manera, es rasón qu'él sienta el fruto de su servicio, non solo en las mercedes para después, mas en lo de su salario en lo presente, en manera qu'él é los que acá están syentan que los aprovecha el servicio; porque, segund el exerçiçio que acá se ha de tener en cojer este oro, non son de tener en poco las personas en quien tanta diligençia ay; y porque por su abilidad se proveyó acá por mi del ofiçio de alguazil mayor d'estas Yndias, y en la provisyón va el salario en blanco, que suplico á Sus Altesas gelo manden henchir como más sea su servicio, mirando sus servicios, confirmándole la provisión que acá se le dió, é proveyéndole d'el de juro.

Sus Altezas mandan que le asyenten quinse mill maravedís cada año más su sueldo, é que se le paguen quando le pagaren su sueldo.

Asymismo dirés á Sus Altesas como aquí vino el bachiller Gil García por alcayde mayor, é non se le ha consignado ni nombrado salario, y es persona de bien, y de buenas letras, y diligente, é se acá bien neçesario, que suplico á Sus Altezas le manden nombrar é consignar su salario, por manera qu'él se pueda sostener é le sea librado con el dinero del sueldo de acá.

Sus Altezas le mandan asentar cada año veyntemill maravedís, en tanto que allá estoviere, y más su sueldo, y que gelo paguen quando pagaren el sueldo.

by Columbus to administer Isabella when he went on his voyage of discovery (cp. Las Casas, 82, 94). He commanded the caravels sent in advance by Columbus on his third voyage (Las Casas, i. 119), and was sent by Bartholomew Columbus to negotiate with Roldán, in which mission he was unsuccessful (Las Casas, *ibid.*).

² Nothing seems to be known of him.

Item: You shall say to their highnesses, although I have already written it in letters, that I do not consider that it will be possible during this year to go exploring, until the matter of these rivers, in which gold has been found, be settled in the manner proper for their highnesses' service. For afterwards it can be much better done, since it is not a matter which can be settled without my presence, according to my wish and the service of their highnesses, since, well as it might be done, yet it would be less certain than that which a man personally superintends.

Let him endeavour that the . . .[1] of this gold may be known as exactly as possible.

Item: You shall say to their highnesses that the *escuderos* [2] who came from Granada, at the inspection which was held in Seville, showed good horses, and that afterwards at the time of embarcation, I did not see to it, because I was a little indisposed, and they substituted such animals that the best of them does not seem to be worth two thousand maravedis. For they sold the others and bought these, and I see very well that this is the kind of thing which has been done to many people in the shows at Seville. It seems that Juan de Soria,[3] after he had been given the money for the payment, for some personal interest, substituted others in place of those which I thought to find here, and I find people whom I had never seen. In this very bad faith has been shown, so I do not know whether to complain of him alone. For, although expenses have been paid to these attendants up to the present, in addition to their wages and the hire of their horses, and are now being paid, yet they are men who, when they are ill or it does not happen to suit them, will not allow their horses to be used except by themselves. In the same way, these men do not think that they should serve in any way except on horseback, and now at present that is not much needed. And consequently it seems that it would be better to buy the horses from them, though they are worth little, and not every

---

[1] Lacuna in the original.

[2] *Lanzas* of the Santa Hermandad. Ferdinand de Zafra was instructed to find twenty lanzas from among those of the Santa Hermandad in the kingdom of Granada, who were to be men of good character and willing to go to the Indies;

Ytem, dirés á Sus Altesas, como quier que ya se le escrivió
por las cartas, que para este año no entiendo que sea posible
yr á descobrir hasta que esto d'estos ríos, que se hallaron,
de oro, sea puesto en el asyento devido á servicio de Sus
Altesas; que después mucho mejor se podrá faser, porque no
es cosa que nadie la podiese faser syn mi presençia á mi
grado ni á servicio de Sus Altesas, por muy bien que lo fiziesen,
como es en dubda, segund lo que honbre vee por su presençia.

Trabaje como, lo más presto que ser pueda, se sepa lo ... d'este
oro.

Ytem, dirés á Sus Altezas como los escuderos de cavallo,
que vinieron de Granada, en el alarde que fizieron en Sevilla
mostraron buenos cavallos, é después, al enbarcar, yo no lo
vý, porque estava un poco doliente, y metiéronlos tales qu'el
mejor d'ellos non paresçe que vale .ii. mil maravedís; porque
vendieron los otros y compraron estos, y esto fué de la suerte
que se hiso lo de mucha gente, que allá en los alardes de
Sevilla yo vý muy buena paresçía, que Juan de Soria, después
de dado el dinero del sueldo por algund ynterese suyo, puso
otros en lugar de aquellos que yo acá pensava fallar, y fallo
gente que yo nunca avía visto. en esto ha avido grand maldad,
de tal manera que yo no sé sy me quexe d'él solo; por esto,
visto que á estos escuderos, allende de su sueldo, se a fecho la
costa hasta aquí, y también á sus cavallos, y se haze de presente, y son personas que, quando ellos están dolientes, ó non
se les antoja, non quieren que sus cavallos sirvan syn
ellos mismos, y esto mismo non les paresçe que devan
servir en cosa ninguna syno á cavallo, lo que agora de presente non fase mucho al caso, é por esto paresçe que sería

five of them were to bring led mares; their pay and maintenance for themselves
and their horses were provided, and they were to appear at Seville, 20 June 1493,
to be inspected by Fonseca and Columbus: Villalva, veedor of the Hermandad
at Seville, was to command them, pending embarcation (*Cédula to Zafra*,
23 May 1493; *Doc. Inéd.* (1ª *serie*), 19, pp. 501–3).

³ Juan de Soria, secretary to prince Juan, was appointed to countersign and
pass all orders for payment on account of the preparations for the second voyage,
and to receive all goods coming from the Indies. Columbus quarrelled with him
and complained of his lack of respect: Fonseca was ordered to reprimand Soria,
who was also personally reprimanded by the sovereigns (cp. Navarrete, ii,
pp. 44, 46, 48,71, 89–90, 92, 93, 94, 95).

day to have these petty disputes with them. Therefore you shall ask that their highnesses determine this matter as may be for their service.

Their highnesses order Don Juan de Fonseca to make inquiries concerning the matter of the horses, and if it be found that such a deception has been practised, to send word to their highnesses that they may order it to be punished; and also that he secure information concerning that which is said of the other people, and send the result of the inquiry to their highnesses; and in the matter of these attendants, their highnesses command that they remain there and give service, since they are from the guards and servants of their highnesses; and their highnesses order the attendants that they shall hand over their horses whenever it be necessary and the admiral commands it, and if the horses receive any damage while ridden by others than them, by the medium of the admiral their highnesses order that payment shall be made to them.

Their highnesses do not wish these horses to be bought from them, but that they should serve as is said in the article on this matter.

Item: You shall say to their highnesses that there have come here more than two hundred persons without pay, and there are some of them who do good service, and moreover the others have similarly been ordered to do likewise. And since for these first three years it would be a great advantage that there should be here a thousand men to set in order and to place in a state of very great security this island and the rivers of gold, and though if there were a hundred mounted men, it would be no disadvantage but rather it is necessary, yet in the matter of these mounted men, until gold has been sent, their highnesses may leave the matter over ; nevertheless, as to these two hundred persons who came without pay, their highnesses should send to say if wages should be paid to them as to others who are doing good service, for it is certain that they are needed as I have said at the beginning of this.

Of these two hundred persons who, he here says, went without pay, their highnesses command that they shall take the place of

mejor comprarles los cavallos, pues que tan poco valen, y non
estar cada día con ellos en estas pendençias ; por ende que Sus
Altesas determinen esto como fuere su servicio.

*Sus Altezas mandan á don Juan de Fonseca que se ynforme
d'esto d'estos cavallos, y, si se hallare que es verdad que hisieron
ese engaño, lo enbíen á Sus Altezas, porque lo mandarán casti-
gar; y tanbién se ynforme d'eso que dise de la otra gente, y enbíe
la pesquisa á Sus Altesas. y en lo d'estos escuderos Sus
Altesas mandan qu'estén allá y sirvan, pues son de las guardas
y criados de Sus Altezas, y á los escuderos mandan Sus Altezas
que den los cavallos cada vez que fuere menester y el almirante
lo mandare; y si algund daño reçibieren los cavallos, yendo otros
en ellos, por medio del almirante mandan Sus Altezas que gelo
paguen.*

*Sus Altezas no quieren que se les conpren estos cavallos, syno
que sirvan así como en el capítulo d'esto dise.*

Ytem, dirés á Sus Altezas como aquí han venido más de
dozientas personas syn sueldo, y ay algunos d'ellos que sirven
bien, y aun los otros por semejante se mandan que lo hagan
asý. y porque para estos primeros tres años será grand bien
que aquí estén mill onbres para asentar y poner en muy
grand seguridad esta ysla y ríos de oro, y aunque oviese çiento
de cavallo non se perdería nada, antes paresçe neçesario,
aunque en estos de cavallo, fasta que oro se enbíe, Sus Altesas
podrán sobreseer, con todo, á estas dozientas personas, que
vienen syn sueldo, Sus Altesas deven enbiar á dezir sy se les
pagará sueldo como á los otros, syrviendo bien, porque çierto
son neçesarios, como dicho tengo, para este comienço.

*D'estas dozientas personas que aquí dise que fueron syn
sueldo, mandan Sus Altezas que entren en lugar de los que han*

those who have failed or shall fail among those who went for wages, they being capable and it being satisfactory to the admiral, and their highnesses command the contador that he enrol them in place of those who shall be at fault as the admiral may direct.[1]

Item: In order that to some extent the expense of these people may be reduced by care, and by the methods which other princes are accustomed to employ in other cases, the greater part of the expenditure here may be avoided, it seems that it would be well to give orders that in the ships which come there be brought in addition to the other things, which are for the maintenance of the community, and to medicine, shoes and skins from which they can be ordered to be made, coarse shirts, and for other things, doublets, linen, sacking, breeches, cloth for making clothes, at a reasonable price; and other things, such as conserves, which are outside the rations and which are for the preservation of health. All these things the people here would receive with pleasure on account of their pay, and if this supply were bought there by honest agents and such as consider the service of their highnesses, there would be some economy. Accordingly you shall learn the will of their highnesses in this matter, and if it appear to them to be for their service, the matter should at once be put in train.

For this voyage it may be postponed, until the admiral writes more fully, and they will send orders already to Don Juan de Fonseca and Jimeno de Bribiesca that provision be made in this matter.[2]

Item: You shall also say to their highnesses that inasmuch as yesterday in the inspection which was held, the people were found to be very deficient in arms, which I think resulted in some degree from the exchange which was made there in Seville or in the port, when those who appeared armed were left, and others taken who gave something to those who exchanged with them, it seems that it would be well that two hundred cuirasses, and a hundred arquebuses and a hundred crossbows, and much ammunition should be

---

[1] Columbus had laid down, in a memorial on the needs of Española (assigned

faltado y faltaren de los que yvan á sueldo, seyendo ábiles y á contentamiento del almirante, y Sus Altezas mandan al contador que los asiente en lugar de los que faltaren, como el almirante lo dixere, &c.

Ytem, porque en algo la costa d'esta gente se puede aliviar con yndustria y formas que otros príncipes suelen tener en otras, lo gastado mejor que acá se podría escusar. paresçe que sería bien mandar traer en los navíos que vinieren, allende de las otras cosas que son para los mantenimientos comunes y de la botica, çapatos y cueros para los mandar fazer, camisas comunes y de otras, jabones, lienço, sayos, calças, paños para vestir, en razonables preçios, y otras cosas, como son conservas, que son fuera de ración y para conservaçión de la salud ; las quales cosas todas la gente de acá resçibiría de grado en descuento de su sueldo, y sy allá esto se mercase por ministros leales y que mirasen el provecho de Sus Altesas, se ahorrarian algo. por ende sabréis la voluntad de Sus Altesas çerca d'esto, y, sy les paresciere ser su servicio, luego se deve poner en obra.

Por este camino se sobreser, fasta que más escriva el almirante, y ya enbiarán mandar á don Juan de Fonseca con Ximeno de Briviesca que provea esto.

Ytem, tanbién dirés á Sus Altesas que, por quanto ayer en el alarde que se tomó se halló la gente muy desarmada, lo qual pienso que en parte contesçio por aquel trocar que allá se hizo en Sevilla ó en el puerto, quando se dexaron los que se mostraron armados y tomaron otros que davan algo á quien los trocava, paresçe que sería bien que se mandase traer dozientas coraças, y cien espingardas, y cien ballestas, y

by De Lollis to the eve of the second voyage), that two thousand settlers were needed (*Rac. Col.* I. i. p. 136). From motives of economy, the sovereigns were unwilling to pay for more than two hundred, although others were allowed to go at their own expense and actually fifteen hundred men embarked on the second voyage (Las Casas, i. 82). The difficulty of reconciling the needs of the colony with the royal desire for economy was recurrent, and led at a later date to the idea of converting Española into a penal settlement (cp. Navarrete, ii. 212–18 ; and Las Casas, i. 112).

² Cp. Navarrete, ii. 162–4.

ordered to be sent, for it is material of which we have much need and from all these arms, those who are unarmed could be supplied.[1]

It has been already written to Don Juan de Fonseca that he make provision in this matter.

Item: Inasmuch as some artisans who have come here, such as masons and men of other trades, are married and have wives at home, and wish that what is due to them for wages should be given to their wives at home or to the persons to whom they may send their requirements, in order that they may buy for them the things of which they have need here, I ask their highnesses that they order payment to be made to them, for their service is that provision be made for these men here.

Their highnesses have already sent to command Don Juan de Fonseca that he provide for this.

Item: Besides the other things which have been sent for according to the request in the memorials which you bear, signed by my hand, for the maintenance of the healthy as well as for the sick, it would be very well that there should be obtained from the island of Madeira fifty pipes of molasses, for it is the best nourishment in the world and very healthy. And each pipe does not generally cost more than two ducats, excluding the casks, and if their highnesses command that on the return voyage some caravel goes that way, it would be possible to buy them and also ten cases of sugar, which is very necessary. For this is the best season of the year, I mean between now and the month of April, for getting it and for having it at a reasonable rate, and, by command of their highnesses, it would be possible to give the order and that they should not know there for what destination it is required.

Don Juan de Fonseca is to provide for this.

Item: You shall say to their highnesses that, although the rivers contain the amount of gold which is reported by

---

[1] For the supply of arms to those going on the second voyage, Garcia Fernandez

mucho almaçén, que es la cosa que más menester avemos, y de
todas estas armas se podrán dar á los desarmados.

Ya se escrive á don Juan de Fonseca que provea esto.

Ytem, por quanto algunos ofiçiales que acá vinieron, como
son albañies y de otros ofiçios, que son casados y tienen sus
mugeres allá, y querrían que allá lo que se les deve de su
sueldo se diese á sus mugeres ó á las personas á quien ellos
enbiaren sus recabdos para que les compren las cosas que
acá han menester, que á Sus Altezas suplico los manden
librar, porque su servicio es que estos estén proveýdos acá.

*Ya enbiaron mandar Sus Altezas á don Juan de Fonseca que
provea en esto.*

Ytem, porque, allende las otras cosas que allá se enbían á
pedir por los memoriales que lleváys de mi mano firmados
asý para mantenimientos de los sanos como para los dolientes,
sería muy bien que se oviesen de la ysla de la Madera çinquenta pipas de miel de açúcar, porqu'es el mejor mantenimiento del mundo y más sano, y non suele costar cada pipa
syno á dos ducados syn el casco, y, sy Sus Altezas mandan que
á la buelta pase por allí alguna caravela, las podrá mercar,
y también diez caxas de açúcar, que es mucho menester, que
esta es la mejor sazón del año, digo entre aquí é el mes de
abril, para hallarlo é aver d'ello buena rasón ; y podríase dar
horden, mandándolo Sus Altesas, é que non supiesen allá para
donde lo quieren.

Don Juan de Fonseca que provea en esto.

Ytem, dirés á Sus Altezas, por quanto aunque los ríos tengan
en la quantidad que se dise por los que lo han visto, pero que
lo çierto d'ello es qu'el oro non se engendra en los ríos, mas en
la tierra, qu'el agua, topando con las minas, lo trae enbuelto

Manrique, alcaide of Malaga, and Rodrigo de Narvaez were responsible (cp.
Navarrete, ii. pp. 45, 46).

those who have seen them, yet it is certain that the gold is produced not in the rivers, but on land, and that the water, penetrating the mines, carries it away mingled with sand. And among as many rivers as have been discovered, although there are some which are large, there are others so small that they are rather brooks than rivers, for they have only two fingers' depth of water, and the source from which they come may be speedily found. Accordingly not only will labourers to collect it from the sand be useful, but further others to dig it from the earth, where it will be of the best quality and in the greatest abundance. And for this reason it will be well that their highnesses should send labourers and from among those who work in the mines there in Almaden,[1] so that the work may be carried on in the one way and the other. We shall not here wait for them, however, for with the labourers whom we have here, we hope, with the help of God, if once the people be restored to health, to send a good quantity of gold by the first caravels that go.

For the next voyage, provision shall be made for this completely; meanwhile their highnesses command Don Juan de Fonseca that he sends at once as many miners as he can get, and they write to Almaden that from there they take as many as they can and send them.

Item: You shall pray their highnesses very humbly on my behalf that they will be pleased to regard Villacorta[2] as strongly recommended. As their highnesses know, he has done much service in this matter, and with very good will, and, as I know him, he is a person, diligent and devoted to their service. I shall regard it as a favour if some position of trust be given to him, for which he may be suited, and be able to show his desire to serve and his diligence. And this you shall procure in such a way that Villacorta may know from the event that what he has done for me when I had need of him, has been of profit to himself.

So it shall be done.

Item: That the said Mosen Pedro and Gaspar and Beltran and others who have remained here came as captains of caravels, which have gone back, and they do not enjoy the

en las arenas ; y porque en estos tantos ríos se han descubierto,
como quiera que ay algunos grandecitos, ay otros tan pequeños, que son más fuentes que no ríos, que non llevan de dos
dedos de agua, y se halla luego el cabo donde nasçe, para lo
qual non solo serán provechosos los labadores para cojerlo
en l'arena, mas los otros para cavarlo en la tierra, que será lo
más especial é de mayor quantidad, é por esto será bien que
Sus Altesas enbíen labadores é de los que andan en las minas
allá en almadenes, porque en la una manera y en la otra se
haga el exerçiçio, como quier que acá non esperaremos á ellos,
que con los labadores que aquí tenemos esperamos, con la
ayuda de Dios, sy una vez la gente está sana, allegar un buen
golpe de oro para las primeras caravelas que fueren.

*Otro camino se proveerá esto complidamente. en tanto mandan
Sus Altezas á don Juan de Fonseca que enbíe luego los más
minadores que pudiere aver, y escriven al almadén que de allí
tomen los que más pudieren, y los enbíen.*

Ytem, suplicarés á Sus Altezas de mi parte muy húmilmente
que quieran tener por muy encomendado á Villacorta, el qual,
como Sus Altezas saben, ha mucho servido en esta negoçiación
y con muy buena voluntad ; y, segund le conosco persona
diligente y afeçionada á su servicio, resçibiré merced que
se le dé algund cargo de confiança, para lo qual él sea sufiçiente
y pueda mostrar su deseo de servir, y diligençia ; y esto pro-
curaréis por forma qu'el Villacorta conosca por la obra que lo
que ha trabajado por mi en lo que yo le ove menester le
aprovecha en esto.

Asy se hará.

Ytem, que los dichos mosén Pedro, y Gáspar, y Beltrán, y
otros, que han quedado acá, traxieron capitanías de caravelas
que son agora bueltas, y non gozan del sueldo ; pero, porque

---

[1] Almadén de Azoque, in Estremadura, one of the richest quicksilver mines
in the world, which has been worked since Roman times.

[2] Cp. *supra*, p. 74, note 6.

pay, but as they are such persons as should be employed in important and confidential matters, their pay has not been settled but should be such as may be different from that of the others. You shall pray their highnesses on my behalf to determine that which should be given to them annually or monthly, as may be best for their service.

Done in the city of Isabella, on the thirtieth day of January of the year one thousand four hundred and ninety-five.[1]

This has been already answered above, but as in the said clause he says that they should receive their salary, it is now the command of their highnesses that their salaries shall be paid to them from the time when they gave up their commands.

[1] The sovereigns acknowledged the receipt of the letters of Columbus, 13 April 1494 (Navarrete, ii. 115). De Torres did not immediately go to the court on arrival, but forwarded some of the documents entrusted to him.

son tales personas que se han de poner en cosas prinçipales y de confiança, no se les ha determinado el sueldo, que sea diferençiado de los otros. suplicarés de mi parte á Sus Altesas determinen lo que se les da de dar en cada un año ó por meses, como más fueren servidos. Fecho en la cibdad Ysabela, á .xxx. días de henero de .lxxxxiiii. años.

Ya está respondido arriba; pero, porque en el dicho capítulo que en esto habla dise que gosan del salario, desde agora mandan Sus Altezas que se les cuenten á todos sus salarios desde que dexaron las capitanías.

3. Andrés Bernáldez, History of the Catholic Sovereigns, Don Ferdinand and Doña Isabella.[1] Chapters 123-131.

THE admiral set out to discover the mainland of the Indies on the twenty-fourth day of the month of April of the said year 1494. He left in the city as presidents his brother[2] and a friar, who was called Fray Benil, and he ordained that which each one was to do.[3] And he set out with three square rigged caravels[4] and in a few days arrived at the very famous harbour of San Nicolas,[5] which is in the same island of Española and opposite cape Alfaeto,[6] which is in Juana, which he judged to be an island and which is mainland, the end and extremity of the Indies to the east. And he directed his course to that cape and reached it and did not follow the line of the coast to the north, in which direction he had gone on his first voyage, and steered to the west, following the other coast on the southern side. Both these shores trend westwards, the one pointing away from the arctic pole and the other approaching towards it owing to the narrowness of the land, which begins in a point and broadens to the northward. He navigated for the southern part, leaving the land of Juana on his right hand, expecting to round it and to run, after leaving the cape, towards that which he desired, which was to seek the province and city of Catayo, which is under the

[1] For Andrés Bernáldez, cp. *supra*, Introduction, pp. cxlvi *et seq.*

[2] The brother was Diego Columbus. The date of his birth is usually given as *c.* 1466, but Ulloa (*Xristo-Ferens Colom*, pp. 119–123) has argued that he was really the eldest of the three brothers. He accompanied Columbus on his second voyage, but after acting as president of the council for governing Isabella in the absence of the admiral, he returned to Spain, probably in 1495, and received permission to reside where he pleased in that country (Navarrete, ii. 175). Having returned to Española, he was arrested by Bobadilla (Las Casas, i. 181 and *infra*, vol. II, p. 56), and sent back to Castile. Diego was anxious to enter the church; Las Casas (i. 82) says that he seems to have aspired to a bishopric, and this suggestion is borne out by the fact that Diego secured letters of naturalization (8 Feb. 1504: Navarrete, ii. 300), which were not required for mere ordination as a priest, but which were essential if high preferment were desired, since in the case of the bishop of Cuenca, Ferdinand and Isabella had insisted that such preferment should be confined to their own subjects. Diego returned to Española with his nephew, the second admiral, and eventually died at Seville in 1515. He held a repartimiento of Indians in Española and seems to have amassed a small

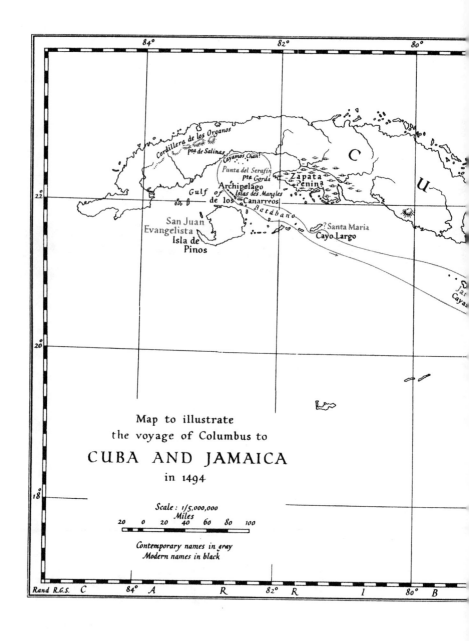

Map to illustrate
the voyage of Columbus to

CUBA AND JAMAICA

in 1494

Scale : 1/5,000,000
Miles
20   0   20   40   60   80   100

Contemporary names in gray
Modern names in black

Rand R.G.S.   C   84°   A   R   82°   R   I   80°   B

ORNOFAY
CAMAGUEY
A

M
O
R
I
E
N
T
E
A
C
A

a Reina
Leguas

Rio de las Misas
Rio Cauto

SIERRA MAESTRA

C. Alfaeto
C. Maysi

Cabo Cruz

Santiago Bay

Puerto Grande
Guantanamo Bay

C. San Nicolas

ESPAÑOLA

Buen Tiempo
Montego Bay

Rio Bueno
Santa Gloria St. Ann's Bay

Galina Pt

C. San Miguel

JAMAICA

? Punta del Farol
Morant Pt
Morant Bay
Punta del Farol
Yallah Pt
Portland Bight
Monte Cristalino
Portland Cristalino

E   78°   A   N   76°   S   E   74°   A

3. Andrés Bernáldez, Historia de los Reyes Católicos, Don Fernando y Doña Isabel, Capítulos 123–131.

PARTIÓ el almirante á descubrir la tierra firme de las Indias á .24. días del mes de abril del dicho año de .1494. dexó en la ciudad por presidentes á su hermano é á un fraile, que se decía fray Benil, y, ordenado lo que cada uno avía de hazer; é partió con tres carabelas de bela redonda, y en pocos días llegado a(1) muy señalado puerto de San Nicolao, el qual está en la mesma isla Española, frontero del cavo de Alfaeto, que es en la Juana, que él juzgava por isla y es tierra firme, fin y cavo de las Indias por el oriente, y endereçó al dicho cavo, é llegó á él é dexó de seguir la tierra de la costa del setentrión, por donde el biaje primero avía andado, y navegó al poniente corriendo la otra costa de la parte del austro, las quales costas ban ansí anbas al poniente, desbiándose la una del polo ártico y la otra acercándose á él por la anchura de la tierra, que comienza por angosto y ba subiendo al setentrión. y por la parte del austro, dexando la tierra de la Juana sobre la mano derecha, navegó, pensando dar la buelta al rrededor,

fortune, since in his will he left a considerable sum to the son of Barbola, a negress and a former domestic servant in the household of his nephew. Las Casas (i. 82) describes Diego as virtuous, peace-loving and simple-minded; he appears to have been wholly unfitted for the position assigned to him by Columbus on this occasion.

³ The friar was Fray Buil. The government of Isabella was actually entrusted to a commission of five, consisting of Diego Columbus, as president; Buil; Pero Hernandez Coronel, the *alguacil mayor*; Alonso Sanchez de Carvajal, and Juan de Lujan. Pedro Margarit was left in command of the military forces. The appointment of Diego Columbus seems to have aroused much jealousy, and was certainly an error (cp. Las Casas, i. 94, 100, 101).

⁴ Las Casas (i. 94) says that Columbus took a *nao*, large ship, and two caravels, but it is more probable that all three were small vessels, judging from their apparent draught. They were the *Santa Clara Niña*, the *San Juan*, and the *Cardera*.

⁵ In the extreme west of Española. It figures on the sketch-map of the coast of the island probably drawn by Columbus himself (cp. *Nuevos Autografos*; and Streicher, *Die Kolumbus-Originale*).

⁶ Alpha et Omega, so named by Columbus because he supposed it to be the end of the East (Peter Martyr, i. 3). As Oviedo (xvii. 1) says that it was within sight from Cape San Nicolas, the point must be the modern Cape Maysi, the extreme easterly point of Cuba. Las Casas (i. 94) says that the cape was called in the native language, Bayatiquiri.

dominion of the Grand Khan, saying that he could reach it by this route. Of it is read, as John Mandeville says and others who have seen it, that it is the richest province in the world and the most abounding in gold and silver, in all metals and silks. But the people are all idolaters and subtle; they are necromancers and are learned in all arts and noble, and of them many marvels are written, as the noble English knight, John Mandeville relates, who went there and saw and lived with the Grand Khan for some while. Any one who wishes to know the truth of this may read in his book in the eighty-fifth and eighty-seventh and eighty-eighth chapters, and there he will see that the city of Catayo is very noble and rich, and that its district has the name of the city.[1] This province and city lie in the parts of Asia, near the lands of Prester John of the Indies,[2] in the district which dominates and looks towards the north, and in that direction in which the admiral sought it. I say that it must needs take a great space of time to reach it, for the Grand Khan was anciently lord of the Tartars, and Grand Tartary is on the borders of Ruxia[3] and Bahia,[4] and we may say that Grand Tartary begins from Hungary, which are lands that, looking from this Andalucia, are on the right where the sun rises in the month of the longest days in the year, and in that direction the merchants were accustomed to go into that country. Accordingly it is my belief that in the direction in which the admiral sought for Catayo, traversing the firmament of sea and land for a further thousand two hundred leagues, he would not arrive there, and so I told him and gave him to understand in the year 1496,[5] when he came the first time into Castile after he had gone to discover and was my guest and left with me some of his writings,[6] in the presence of the lord Don Juan de Fonseca,[7] whence I have drawn and have compared them with other writings which the honoured lord, doctor Anca

---

[1] Cp. Mandeville, ed. Pollard, cc. 23–8.
[2] Mandeville, c. 30.
[3] Russia (cp. Mandeville, cc. 1, 27).
[4] Not identified with any certainty.
[5] The visit of Columbus to Bernáldez must have occurred when the admiral returned to Spain after the mission of Aguado. Bernáldez is strictly accurate in

y correr después de ber el cavo la vía de su deseo, que hera
buscar la provincia y ciudad del Catayo, diciendo que la
podría allar por allí, que es en el señorío del gran can, la cual
se lee, según dice Juan de Mandavilla y otros que la bieron,
que es la más rica provincia del mundo, é la más abundosa de
oro é plata, é de todos metales é sedas; pero son todos
idólatras y jente muy agudísima, y nigromántica, y savia en
todas artes y cavallerosa, y de ella se escriven muchas
maravillas, según quenta el noble cavallero inglés Juan de
Mandavilla, que lo andubo y vido y bivió con el gran can
algún tiempo. quien d'esto quisiere saver lo cierto lea en su
libro en el ochenta y cinco, é ochenta y siete, é ochenta é ocho
capítulos, y allí berá como la ciudad del Catayo es muy
noble é rica, é como la provincia suya tiene el nombre de la
ciudad. la qual provincia é ciudad es en las partidas de Asia
cerca de las tierras del preste Juan de las Indias, en la parte
que señorea y mira el norte, y por donde el almirante lo
buscava. yo digo que avía menester grande distançia de
tienpo para lo hallar, porque el gran can fué antiguamente
señor de los Tártaros; é desde la Gran Tartaria, que es en los
fines de Ruxía é Bahía, é podemos decir que se comiença la
Gran Tartaria desde Ungría, que son tierras que están
mirando desde esta Andalucía por el derecho de donde sale el
sol en el mes de los mayores días del año, y por aquel derecho
solían yr los mercadeles en aquella tierra, que por la banda
que el almirante buscava el Catayo, es mi creer que con otras
mill é ducientas leguas, andando el firmamento de la mar
é tierra en derredor no llegase allá, y así se lo dixe y hice
entender yo el año de .1496., quando bino en Castilla la
primera bez después de aver ido á descubrir, que fué mi
guésped é me dejó algunas de sus escrituras, en presencia del
señor don Juan de Fonseca, de donde yo saqué y cotejélas

saying that this was the first visit of the 'admiral' to Castile, after he had gone
to discover, since it was only after his return from his first voyage that Columbus
was formally created 'Almirante del Mar Océano'.
    ⁶ The account which follows of the voyage of Columbus supplies many indica-
tions that it was directly derived from the admiral (cp. *supra*, Introduction,
pp. cxlix–cl). It is possible that Bernáldez had in his possession the 'book'
which he says that Columbus made about his voyage (cp. *infra*, p. 158).
    ⁷ Cp. *supra*, p. 84, note 2.

or Ochanca,[1] has written and other noble gentlemen who were with him on the voyages already mentioned and who wrote that which they saw, by which I was informed. And I have written this of the Indies, as being a thing marvellous and unparalleled, which Our Lord willed to be made manifest in the time of the good fortune and reign of king Don Ferdinand and of queen Doña Isabella, his first wife.

So the admiral, thinking that Juana was an island, went for a great distance along its coast and asked the Indians whether it was an island or Tierra Firme. And as they are a brutish race and think that the whole world is an island and knew not what thing Tierra Firme might be, and have neither letters nor ancient memorials, and take no pleasure in anything save eating and women, they said that it was an island, although some said that it was an island but that it was not to be traversed in forty moons.[2] And as they followed the coast farther, so the land continued to stretch on farther towards the south. Accordingly he thought well to leave Juana and to go to the west and then to the north, where he thought to find the noble city and most rich province of Catayo. And he had of necessity to follow this course which led him farther from the land, and in this way he discovered the island of Jamaica, and he returned to follow the coast of Tierra Firme,[3] proceeding along it for seventy days, until he had reached a point very near the Golden Chersonese,[4] where he turned back from fear of the weather and on account of the very great length of the voyage and the scarcity of supplies. And there he formed the opinion that, if he were fortunate, he would be able to return to Spain by the East, coming to the Ganges and thence to the Arabian Gulf, and afterwards by way of Ethiopia, and afterwards he would be able to come by land to Jerusalem, and thence to Jaffa, and to embark and enter upon the Mediterranean Sea and thence come to Cadiz. The voyage could certainly be made in this way, but it would be very dangerous by land, since they are all Moors from Ethiopia to Jerusalem. But he could nevertheless have gone by sea and have gone from there to Calicut which is the city that the Portuguese have

---

[1] Dr. Chanca. The account which Bernáldez gives of the first part of the

con las otras que escrivieron el onrrado señor el doctor Anca
ó Ochanca, é otros nobles cavalleros que con él fueron en los
biajes ya dichos, que escribieron lo que bieron, de donde yo
fuí informado, y escriví esto de las Indias, por cosa muy
maravillosa y açañosa, que Nuestro Señor quiso demostrar
en la buena bentura y tienpo del rey don Fernando y de la
reyna doña Isabel, su primera mujer.

Ansí que el almirante, pensando que la Juana hera isla,
andubo mucho por la costa de ella, y preguntaba á los Indios
si era ysla ó tierra firme, y como ellos son jente bestial y
piensan que todo el mundo es isla y no saben qué cosa sea
tierra firme, ni tienen letras ni memorias antiguas, ni se
deleitan en otra cosa sino en comer é en mujeres, decían que
hera ysla, enpero algunos le dijeron que hera isla, mas que
no la andaría en quarenta lunas, é mientras más seguían la
costa, más los echava la tierra al austro; que él bien pensó
dar buelta á la Juana y bolver al poniente, y dende al
setentrión, donde pensava allar la noble probincia y ciudad
riquísima del Catayo, y ubo por fuerça de seguir aquella
banda, por donde la tierra lo desbiava de sí, y descubrió por
aquella bía la isla de Jamaica, y bolvió á seguir la costa de
la tierra firme setenta días andando por ella, hasta aver
pasado á estar muy cerca al Aurea Chersoneso, donde tomó
la buelta por el temor de los tienpos y por la grandísima
navegazión y mengua de mantenimientos, é allí le bino en
miente que, si próspero se hallara, que probara el bolver á
España por oriente, biniendo al Ganjes, y dende al sino
arábico, y después por Etiopía, é después pudiera benir por
la tierra á Jerusalem, y dende á Japha, y enbarcar y entrar
en el mar mediteráneo, é dende á Cális. el biaje bien se
pudiera hazer d'esta manera, enpero hera muy peligroso de
la tierra, porque son todos Moros dende Etiopía á Jerusalem,
enpero él pudiera yr por la mar todavía, y ir desde allá fasta
Calicud, que es la ciudad que descubrieron los Portugueses, y
para no salir por tierra sino todavía por agua, él avía de

second voyage, down to the foundation of Isabella, is drawn almost entirely
from Chanca.
  ² Cp. *infra*, pp. 134, 136, 138.
  ³ Cuba (cp. *infra*, p. 128).
  ⁴ The Malay Peninsula.

discovered, and in order not to go by land but by water always, he would have had to return by the same Ocean Sea circumnavigating all Libya, which is the country of the negroes, and to go by the route by which the Portuguese come with the spice of Calicut.

Let it suffice to say that after the admiral had on this voyage gone three hundred and twenty-two leagues,[1] at the rate of four miles to the league, as they are wont to reckon at sea, from cape Alfaeto, he returned but not by the route by which he had gone. And when he passed by that cape Alfaeto, which is at the beginning of the lands of Juana, he set up there columns, crosses, taking possession for their highnesses. And it was very well done, since it was the extreme cape and harbour, for you must know that this is the extreme headland point of Tierra Firme: to the west, the extreme point is Cape St. Vincent which is in Portugal. Between these two capes is contained all the population of the world, so that one who should set out by land from Cape St. Vincent could go always eastwards without crossing any part of the Ocean Sea until he arrived at Cape Alfaeto and from Alfaeto in the opposite direction he whom God should aid on the journey could come to Cape St. Vincent by dry land.

Turning to continue the account and to record more in detail the islands and lands and seas which the said admiral discovered on that voyage, he proceeded by sea, as has been said, leaving Tierra Firme on the right hand, as far as a very remarkable harbour, which he named *Puerto Grande*.[2] In that land the trees and plants bear fruit twice a year; this is known and proved to be true. From them came a very sweet scent which was wafted out to sea in many places. In that harbour there was no settlement, and as they entered it, they saw to the right hand many fires close to the sea and a dog and two beds, but no people. They went on shore and found more than four *quintals*[3] of fish cooking over the fire, and rabbits,[4] and two serpents, and very near there in many places they were laid at the foot of the trees. In

---

[1] It was upon this occasion that Columbus caused Fernand Perez de Luna, notary public, to take the sworn depositions of the crews of the three vessels on the question whether Cuba was in their opinion an island or the mainland. It

bolver por el mismo mar Oçéano rodeando toda Libia, que es
la tierra de los negros, y bolver por donde bienen los Portugueses con la espeçiería de Calaud. abasta que después de
aver andado el almirante en este biaje trecientas é veinte y
dos leguas, á quatro millas cada una, ansí como acostumbran
en la mar, desde el cavo de Alfaeto, se bolvió sino por el
camino por donde avía ido, y quando pasó por aquel cavo de
Alfaeto, que está al comienço de la tierra Juana, puso allí
colunas de cruces, tomando la posesión por Sus Alteças, y
fué muy bien fecho, pues remaneció ser el estremo cavo é
puerto, que devéis saver que aquel es estremo cavero cavo
de la tierra firme; del poniente, el cavo de San Vicente que
está en Portugal, en medio de los quales cavos ambos se
contiene todo el poblado del mundo, que quien partiese por
tierra desde el cavo de San Vicente podrá ir sienpre al lebante
sin pasar ninguna cosa del mar Océano hasta llegar al cavo
de Alfaeto é desde Alfaeto por la contra benir hasta el cavo
de San Vicente por tierra firme á quien Dios ayudase en el
viaje.

Tornando á proseguir é recontar más á menudo las islas
é tierras é mares que el dicho almirante descubrió de aquel
biaje, siguió por la mar, como dicho es, dejando la tierra
firme á la mano derecha, hasta un puerto muy singularísimo,
al qual llamó 'puerto Grande'. en aquella tierra los árboles
y las yervas lleban dos beces en el año frutos; esto se supo y
experimentó por verdad, de los quales muy suabísimo olor
salía, que alcançaba en gran parte á la mar. en aquel puerto
no abía población, y como entraron en él, bieron á mano
derecha muchos fuegos juntos con el agua, y un perro y dos
camas sin personas. decindieron en tierra y hallaron más de
quatro quintales de peces en asadores al fuego, y conejos,
y dos serpientes, y allí en muy cerca estaban en muchos
lugares puestas al pie de los árboles. ay en muchos lugares

was on the supposition that they had coasted along it for three hundred and
twenty-two leagues that the crews declared that Cuba could not be an island
(cp. Navarrete, ii. 143–9, and *Geographical Journal*, March 1929). It is from
this document that the names of the three caravels can be drawn.

² The bay of Guantananamo.

³ A quintal is equivalent to forty-six kilogrammes.

⁴ Oviedo (xvii. 4) mentions the 'guabiniquinax' and the 'ayre' as being
animals in Cuba which were similar to rabbits.

many places there were many serpents, the most disgusting
and nauseating things which men ever saw, all with their
mouths sewn up.[1] And they were the colour of dry wood,
and the skin of the whole body was very wrinkled, especially
that of their heads, and it fell down over their eyes. And
they were venomous and terrifying, and were all covered
with very hard shells, as a fish is covered with scales. From
the head to the tip of the tail, down the middle of the
back, they had long projections, disgusting, and sharp as
the points of diamonds. The admiral ordered the fish to be
taken, and with it refreshed his men.

And afterwards, while exploring the harbour in the boat,
they saw on the crest of a hill many people, naked according
to the custom there, and making signs to them that they
should come near, one did so. There was an Indian, one of
those who had come to Castile, whom the admiral carried
with him as an interpreter, and who now knew Castilian well
and also understood the Indians.[2] He spoke to this man and
the strange Indian answered from the top of a rock, and as
he understood the other, he gained confidence and called the
rest, who were some seventy men in all. They said that they
were going hunting by command of their cacique, in preparation for a feast which they were going to make. And the
admiral commanded that hawks' bells and other trifling things
should be given to them, and ordered them to be told that
they must pardon him, that he had taken the fish and nothing
else. And they were greatly rejoiced when they knew that
they had not taken their serpents, and replied that all was
well, since they would fish again at night.

Next day he left that place before sunrise and followed the
coast of the country westward. They saw that it was a very
populous and very lovely land. When they saw such great
ships, many people and children, small and great, came down
to the shore, bringing to them bread and things to eat, running
along, showing the bread and calabashes full of water, and
crying, 'Eat! Take! Men from heaven!' and asking them to
land and to come to their houses, and others came out in their
canoes for the same purpose. So they navigated to a gulf where

[1] Cp. *supra*, p. 10.

muchas serpientes, las más asquerosas y feas cosas que los
hombres bieron, é todas cosidas las bocas, y eran de color de
madera seca, y el cuero de todo el cuerpo muy arugado, en
especial en la caveça, que le decendía sobre los ojos, los quales
tenían benenosos y espantables, y todas heran cubiertas de
sus conchas muy fuertes, como un pece, de escama; y desde
la caveça hasta la punta de la cola por medio del cuerpo
tenían unas conchas altas, feas y agudas como puntas de
diamantes; é mandó el almirante tomar el pescado, con que
ubo refresco la jente, y después andando buscando puerto
con la barca, vieron del cavo de un cerro mucha jente desnuda
á la costumbre de allá, y, haciéndoles señal que se allegasen,
allegó uno y falló un Indio que el almirante llebava por intérprete de los que avían benido á Castilla, que entendía ya bien
castellano, y entendía tanbién á los Indios, y el Indio estraño
fablava desde encima de una piedra, y como entendió al otro,
aseguróse y llamó á la otra jente, que heran obra de setenta
honbres, los quales dixeron que andaban caçando por
mandado de su cacique para una fiesta que querían facer,
y el almirante les mandó dar cascaveles y otras cosillas, y
mandóles decir que perdonasen, que él avía tomado el pescado,
y no otra cosa, y olgaron mucho quando supieron que no les
avían tomado las serpientes, y respondieron que fuese todo
en buena hora, que ellos pescarían más á la noche.

salió de allí otro día, antes que saliese el sol, siguió al
poniente la costa de la tierra, la qual bían ser muy poblada
y muy fermosa tierra, y como bían tales navíos, benían á las
playas á ber muchas jentes y niños chicos y grandes, trayén-
doles pan y cosas de comer, corriendo mostrando el pan y las
calabaças llenas de agua, llamando 'comed, tomad, jente del
cielo', y rogávanles que decindiesen y fuesen á sus casas, y
otros benían en canoas á lo mesmo, y ansí navegaron hasta un
golfo donde avía infinitas poblaciones, y las tierras y canpos
heran tales, que todas parecían guertas las más fermosas del
mundo y todas tierras altas y montañas. surjieron allí y la
gente de la comarca luego vinieron allí y traíanles pan y agua

---

[2] According to Las Casas (i. 96), this interpreter was the Indian who had been
baptized in Castile as Diego Colón.

there was an infinite number of dwellings, and the lands and fields were such that they appeared to be the loveliest gardens in the world, and the whole district was lofty and mountainous.[1] There they anchored and the people of the neighbourhood at once came thither and brought to them bread and water and fish. And afterwards, on the following day, at dawn, they left that place, and having gone as far as a cape,[2] the admiral then resolved to abandon that course and that land. And they navigated in search of the island of Jamaica, to the southward, and at the end of two days and two nights, with a fair wind, they reached it, striking a central point in it.[3]

And the island is the most lovely that eyes have seen. It is not mountainous, and the country seems to rise towards the sky. It is very large, greater than Sicily, having a circumference of eight hundred leagues—I mean, miles—and all full of valleys and fields and plains.[4] It is a very mighty land, and beyond measure populous, so that even on the sea-shore as well as inland, every part is filled with villages and those very large and very near one another, at four leagues' distance. They have more canoes than in any other part of those regions, and the largest that have yet been seen, all, as has been said, made each from a single tree trunk. In all those parts, every cacique has a great canoe, of which he is proud and which is for his service, as here a caballero prides himself on possessing a great and beautiful ship. So they have them decorated at the bow and stern with metal bands and with paintings, so that their beauty is wonderful. One of these large canoes which the admiral measured was ninety-six feet long and eight feet broad.

As soon as the admiral arrived off the coast of Jamaica, there immediately came out against him quite seventy canoes, all full of people with darts as weapons. They advanced a league out to sea, with warlike shouts and in battle array. And the admiral with his three caravels and his people paid no attention to them and continued to steer towards the shore, and when they saw this, they became alarmed and turned in flight. The admiral made use of his interpreter,[5] so that one of those canoes was reassured and came to him

[1] The bay of Santiago de Cuba, behind which lies the Sierra Maestra.

y pescado; y luego otro día siguiente, en amaneciendo,
partieron de allí, y andando hacia un cavo, después determinó
el almirante de dejar aquel camino y aquella tierra, y navegaron en busca de la isla Jamaica al austro, y en cavo de dos
días y dos noches allegaron á ella con buen biento, y fueron
á dar en el medio d'ella, la qual es la más fermosa que los ojos
bieron. ella no es montañosa, y parece que llega la tierra al
cielo, es muy grande, mayor que Sicilia, tiene en cerco
ochocientas leguas, digo millas, é toda llena de balles é
campos é planos; es fortísima y populentísima ultramodo,
que ansí á la lengua del mar como en la tierra adentro toda
es llena de poblaciones y muy grandes y muy cerca unos de
otros á quatro leguas; tienen canoas más que en ninguna otra
parte de por allí, y las más grandes que fasta entonces se
avían visto, todas de un tronco, como dicho es, enteras de un
árbol, y cada cacique de todas aquellas partes tiene una
canoa grande, de que se precia y sirve como acá un cavallero
que se precia de tener una nao grande y fermosa. ellos ansí
traen labradas aquellas canoas en proa y popa á laços y
pinturas, que es maravilla la fermosura de ellas; en una de
aquellas grandes midió el almirante nobenta y seis pies de
luengo, y ocho pies de ancho.

Ansí como el almirante llegó acerca de la tierra de Jamayca,
luego salieron contra él bien setenta canoas, todas cargadas de
jente y baras, por armas, una legua en la mar, en son y forma
de pelear, y el almirante con sus tres caravelas é jente no dió
por ellos nada, é siguió todavía el camino de la tierra, é,
desque esto bieron, ubieron miedo é bolvieron huyendo, é
el almirante tubo forma con su faraute, como una de aquellas

---

² Some point between Santiago de Cuba and Cabo Cruz.

³ The exact point at which Columbus reached Jamaica cannot be determined,
but it was probably somewhere near Galina Point.

⁴ The estimated area of Jamaica is 4,200 square miles: that of Sicily, 9,700
square miles. This passage of Bernáldez suggests that the persistent exaggeration of distances, found in the letters of Columbus, may to some extent be explained by the casual use of the word 'legua', and that 'millas' is actually meant,
and that the distances given should be divided by four, or by three. In the
latter case, the estimate given in the letter to Santangel, for example, of the
coastline of Española would be approximately accurate.

⁵ Clearly the 'herald' is the Indian already mentioned.

with its crew. He gave them clothes and many other things which they held in great regard, and accorded them permission to depart. He then anchored at a place which he named *Santa Gloria*,[1] on account of the extreme beauty of its glorious country, in comparison with which the gardens of Valencia are nothing, nor is there anything to compare with it elsewhere, and so it is in all the island. And they slept there that night. Next day, at dawn, they went to seek for a sheltered harbour, where they might be able to careen and repair the ships. And having gone four leagues to the westward, they found a very remarkable harbour and the admiral sent the boat to examine its entrance.[2] And two canoes with many people came out to it and shot many darts at it, but they fled as soon as they found opposition and that not so quickly that they suffered no punishment. The admiral entered the harbour and anchored, and so many Indians came down to it that they covered the land, and all were painted a thousand colours, but the majority black, and all were naked as is their custom. They wore feathers of various kinds on the head and had the breast and stomach covered with palm leaves. They made the greatest howling in the world and shot darts, although they were out of range. And in the ships, there was need of water and wood, and it was further necessary to repair the vessels. The admiral saw that it was not reasonable to allow them to be so daring without chastisement, in order that on another occasion they might not be so bold. He assembled all three boats, since the caravels could not proceed and reach the place where they were owing to the shallows, and that they might become acquainted with the arms of Castile, they approached close to them in the boats and fired at them with crossbows and thus pricked them well, so that they became frightened. They landed, continuing to shoot at them, and as the Indians saw that the Castilians were speaking with them, they all took to flight, men and women, so that not one was to be found in all that neighbourhood. And a dog which they let loose from a ship chased them and bit them, and did them great damage, for a dog is the equal of ten men against the Indians.[3] Next day, before

[1] St. Ann's Bay.

canoas se aseguró y bino á él con la jente, é dióles vestidos é
otras muchas cosas que ellos tubieron en gran precio, é dióles
lizencia que se fuesen, y él fué á surjir á un lugar que puso
nombre 'Santa Gloria', por la estrema hermosura de su
gloriosa tierra, porque ninguna conparazión tienen á ella las
guertas de Balencia, ni de otra parte, y esto es en toda la
isla. y durmieron allí aquella noche. otro dia, en amaneciendo,
fueron á buscar puerto cerrado para despalmar y adovar los
navíos, y, andando al poniente quatro leguas, hallaron un
singularísimo puerto, y el almirante enbió la barca á ber
la entrada, y salieron á ella dos canoas con mucha jente y le
tiraron muchas baras, enpero luego uieron desque bieron
resistençia, y no tan presto que no recivieron castigo, y el
almirante entró en el puerto y surjió, y binieron tantos Indios
sobre él que cubrían la tierra, y todos teñidos de mill colores
y la mayor parte de negro, y todos desnudos, á su uso, y
traían plumajes en la caveça, de diversas maneras, y traían el
pecho y el bientre cubierto con ojas de palma, dando la
mayor grita del mundo, y tirando baṛas, aunque no alcança-
ban; y en los navios tenían necesidad de agua y de leña,
allende de adobar los navíos; y el almirante bió que no hera
rraçón dejarlos en aquella osadía sin pena, porque otra bez no
se atrebiesen ansí. arrimó todas tres barcas, por(que) las
carabelas no podían andar y llegar adonde ellos estaban por
el poco ondo, y porque conociesen las armas de Castilla
allegaron cerca d'ellos con las varcas, y tiráronles con las
ballestas, y desque los picaron bien, y començaron de cojer
miedo, saltaron en tierra ellos despeldando tiros, y, como los
Indios bieron que los Castellanos decían á ellos, dieron todos
buelta á huir, honbres y mujeres, que no pararon ninguno en
toda la comarca, é un perro que soltaron de un navio los
seguía é mordía, é los fiço gran daño, que un perro bale para
contra los Indios como diez hombres. el día siguiente, antes

[2] The mouth of the Rio Bueno.

[3] This is the first mention of the use of dogs to chase Indians; afterwards,
they were generally employed by the Spaniards and trained for the purpose.
For the story of Becerrillo, the most famous of these dogs, see Las Casas, ii. 55.
For his hardly less famous son, Leonzico, see Oviedo, xxix. 3; he belonged to
Balboa.

sunrise, six men of those Indians came to the shore, calling and saying to the admiral that all those caciques asked him not to go away, because they desired to see him and to bring him bread and fish and fruits. And the admiral was much pleased with this embassy, and they protested their friendship and assured him of his safety, and the caciques and many Indians came to him, and they brought to them many provisions with which the people were much refreshed, and they were very abundant all the days that they were there, and the Indians were very content with the things which the admiral gave to them. And, having repaired the ships and rested the people, they departed thence.

The admiral with his three caravels left Jamaica, and navigated thirty-four leagues westward, as far as the Golfo de Buen Tiempo.[1] And there they met with contrary winds as they proceeded farther along the coast of the said island of Jamaica. Of that island, the general character was well-known and observed, that there was in it no gold nor any metal, although for the rest it was a very paradise and to be regarded as more than gold.[2]

They turned the contrary wind to their favour and proceeded to the mainland of Juana, with the intention of following its coast, where they had left it, in order to know certainly whether it was Tierra Firme. And they arrived at a province which they call 'Macaca',[3] which is very beautiful, and they came to anchor at a very large village, the cacique of which already knew of the admiral, and of the caravels, before they came on this voyage. For on the first occasion when the admiral went to discover, they had arrived off that coast, so that all the caciques of that land knew of it, and all that land and the islands were amazed at so new a thing and at the ships, and all said that they were people from the sky, despite the fact that he had not sailed along that coast, but the other coast to the north. And having arrived there, the admiral sent presents to the said cacique of the things which they there held to be of great price. And the cacique sent

---

[1] Montego Bay.

[2] During his first voyage, Columbus heard much of a somewhat mysterious island, 'Bebeque' or 'Beneque', which was said by the natives to lie to the south

del sol salido, bolvieron seis hombres de aquellos Indios á la
playa, llamando y diziendo al almirante que aquellos caciques
todos le rogavan que no se fuese, que los querían ber é traer
pan é pescado, é frutas, é el almirante le plugo mucho de la
enbajada, é ficieron su amistançia é seguro, é binieron los
caciques é muchos Indios á él, é truxéronles muchos mantenimientos con que refrescó mucho la jente, é estubieron muy
abundosos de todo todos los días que allí estubieron, y los
Indios quedaron muy contentos con las cosas que el alamirante
les dió ; é, adobados los navíos é descansada la jente, partieron
de allí.

Partió el almirante con sus tres caravelas de Jamaica, é
navegó .34. leguas al poniente, fasta el golfo de Buen Tiempo,
é allí obieron los bientos contrarios para seguir la costa
adelante de la dicha isla de Jamaica, de la qual su calidad
hera bien conocida y bista, que no avía en ella oro ni metal
ninguno, aunque de lo otro era como un paraíso, y por más
que oro tenida, ficieron de biento contrario bueno y bolvieron
á la tierra firme de la Juana con propósito de seguir la costa
de ella que avían dejado por saver cierto si era tierra firme ;
é fueron á parar á una provincia que llaman 'Macaca', que
es muy fermosa, y fueron á surjir á una población muy
grande, el cacique de la qual ya conocía á el almirante y las
caravelas de antes que fuesen á esta jornada, que allegaron
por aquella costa las idas de la primera bez que el almirante
fué á descubrir, que todos los caciques de aquella tierra lo
supieron, y fué toda aquella tierra y islas alborotadas de tan
nueva cosa é navios, é todos decían que heran jente del cielo,
no enbargante que él no avía navegado aquella costa, salvo
la otra del setentrión ; y, llegados allí, el almirante enbió presentes al dicho cacique de las cosas que ellos tenían allá en
mucho precio ; y el cacique les enbió buen refresco, y á decir

and to be very rich in gold. Pinzón claimed to have visited it, and to have found
that there was no gold in it (cp. *Journal*, 13, 14 Nov., 5, 11, 14, 16 Dec. 1492,
and 6 Jan. 1493).   Las Casas (i. 94) says that this island was Jamaica, and it is
possible that the visit of Columbus to the island at this time was made with the
intention of discovering whether or no Jamaica was such an island as that of
which the Indians had told him.

³ On the south coast of Cuba, part of the later province of Oriente. Columbus
arrived at Cabo de Cruz (Ferdinand Columbus, c. 55; Las Casas, i. 95).

them good refreshment, and sent to say how they knew of them and of the admiral by hearsay, and knew the father of Simon, an Indian whom the admiral had taken to Castile and had given to prince Don Juan.[1] And the admiral landed and asked the said cacique and the Indians of that place whether this was Tierra Firme or an island. And he like all the rest replied to him that there was an infinity of land of which no one had seen the end, although it was an island.

Although the people were very gentle and devoid of evil thoughts, there is a very great difference between these people of this land of Juana and the others of all the neighbouring islands. And the same is true of the birds and of all other things, for all are of better appearance and more gentle.[2]

Next day they left that place and navigated to the northward, bearing north-east, following the coast of the land. At the hour of vespers,[3] they saw in the distance that the coast turned westward and steered that course in order to take the shortest way, leaving the land on the right hand. Next day, at sunrise, they looked from the top of the mainmast and saw the sea full of islands to all the four winds, and all green and full of trees, the loveliest sight that eyes have seen. And the admiral wished to go to the south and to leave these islands on the right hand, but, remembering that he had read that all that sea is so entirely filled with islands, and that John Mandeville says that in the Indies there are more than five thousand islands,[4] he resolved to go forward, and to follow and not to lose sight of the mainland of Juana and to see certainly whether it was an island or no. And the farther he went, the more islands they discovered, and on one day he caused to be noted a hundred and sixty-four islands.[5] And for navigating among them, God constantly gave him fair weather, so that the ships so ran through those seas that they seemed to be flying. And on Whitsunday, 1494, they arrived off the coast of the mainland at a place which was uninhabited, and that not on account of an intemperate climate nor on account of the barrenness of the land, and at a great grove of palms which seemed to touch the sky, there on the sea-

---

[1] The six Indians whom Columbus brought back with him after his first voyage were baptized, the king, queen, and prince acting as sponsors. One

como lo(s) conocían, y al almirante por oídas, y conocían á
su padre de Simón, un Indio que el almirante avía traído á
Castilla é dado al príncipe don Juan; y el almirante decindió
en tierra, y preguntó al dicho cacique y á los Indios de aquel
lugar, si aquella hera tierra firme ó isla; y él con todos los
otros le respondieron que hera tierra infinita de que nadie
avía bisto el cavo, aunque era isla. aunque hera jente muy
mansa, y desbiada de malos pensamientos, ay diferençia en
gran manera de esta jente d'esta tierra Juana á las otras de
todas las islas comarcanas, y eso mesmo ay en las aves, y en
las otras cosas todas, que todas son de mejor condición
y más mansas. otro día partieron de allí é navegaron al
setentrión, declinando al norueste, siguiendo la costa de la
tierra. á oras de vísperas bieron de lejos que aquella costa
bolvía al poniente y tomaron aquel camino por atajar, dejando la tierra á mano derecha. otro día, de salir del sol,
miraron de encima del mástel, y vieron la mar llena de islas
á todos quatro bientos; y todas berdes y llenas de árboles,
la cosa más fermosa que ojos bieron, y el almirante quesiera
pasar al austro y dejar estas yslas á la mano derecha, mas,
acordándose aver leído que toda aquella mar es ansí toda
llena de yslas, y Juan de Mandavilla dize que en las Indias ay
más de cinco mill yslas, determinó de andar adelante, é
seguir é no dexar la vista de la tierra firme de la Juana y ber
lo cierto si era isla ó no, y quanto más andava más islas
descubrían, y día se fizo á notar ciento y sesenta y quatro islas,
y el tienpo para navegar entre ellas sienpre se le dió Dios
bueno, que corrían los navios por aquellos mares que parecían
que bolavan, y allegaron el dia de Pasque del Espíritu Santo
de .1494. á parar à la costa de la tierra firme á un lugar

Indian was given to prince Juan as a servant, but did not long survive. 'Piety,'
adds Las Casas (i. 81), 'compels us to believe that he was the first of all his race
to enter Heaven.'

² Oviedo (xvii. 4) denies that there was any essential difference between the
natives of Cuba and those of Española; except that the former had certain
marriage customs not found among the latter. He notes certain differences in
the fauna (*ibid.*, and xvii. 5); the reptiles were larger. Las Casas (iii. 22–3) is
enthusiastic about the natural productions of the island; according to him, the
inhabitants were worthy of their land.

³ At sundown.   ⁴ 'In and about Ind' (Mandeville, c. 18).

⁵ Ferdinand Columbus (c. 55) and Las Casas (i. 95) both give one hundred
and sixty as the number.

shore. And there in the ground beneath it, there sprang forth two fountains of water, so abundant that at the outlet each was the size of a very large orange, and this water spouted up with force. When the tide was coming in, it was so cold and such and so sweet, that no better could be found in the world, and this cold is not harsh, as that of other waters, so as to injure the stomach, but very healthy. And all rested there on the grass by those fountains, and amid the scent of the flowers, which there was marvellous, and to the sweet singing of the birds, which were very many and very tuneful, and under the shade of those palms, so tall and so lovely, that it was a wonder to see it all. There no people appeared, but there was some indication that people had been there, since the branches of the palms had been cut.

From that place, the admiral entered a boat and went in it and with the other boats to see a river, a league to the east of that spot. And they found the water in it so hot that a man could scarcely bear his hand in it. And they went up it for two leagues without finding people or houses, and always the land was of the same beauty and the fields very green and full of an infinity of fruits, as red as scarlet, and everywhere there was the perfume of flowers and the singing of birds, very sweet. All this they saw and experienced in as many islands as they reached there. And as there were so many islands that they could not give a separate name to each one, he gave to them all generally as a name, *el Jardín de la Reina*.[1]

And on the following day, when the admiral was very anxious to have speech, there came a canoe to hunt fish. And so they call it, hunting, because they hunt some fish with others. For they have certain fish, fastened at the tail with cords, and these fish are the shape of congers and have a large mouth, all full of suckers just like the cuttlefish, and they are very daring, as ferrets are here. And when they are thrown into the water, they go to fasten themselves on some fish; of these they do not leave hold in the water, but only when they are pulled out, which is before their prey is dead. And

[1] A collection of islets and rocks off the south coast of Cuba, the Cayas de las Leguas.

despoblado, y no por destenperança del cielo ni esterilidad de
la tierra, y en un grande palmar de palmas que parecian que
llegavan al cielo, allí en orilla de la mar, y salían en la tierra dos
ojos de agua debajo d'ella, tan gordos que en el ahujero cupiera
una muy gorda naranja, y benia esta agua en alto con ínpetu.
quando la marea era del creciente, hera tan fría y tal y tan
dulce, que en el mundo (no) se podía aver mejor, y este frior
no es salvaje, como otros, que daña el estómago, salvo
sanísimo; y descansaron todos allí en las yervas de aquellas
fuentes, y al olor de las flores, que allí se sentia maravilloso, y
al dulçor del cantar de los pajaritos, tantos heran y tan suaves,
y á las sonbras de aquellas palmas tan grandes y tan fermosas,
que hera maravilla ber lo uno y lo otro. allí no parecía jente
ninguna, enpero señal avía de andar jente por allí que avía
ramas de palmas cortadas. de allí el almirante entró en una
barca y fué con ella y con las otras á ver un río al lebante de
allí una legua, y hallaron el agua d'él tan caliente que escasa-
mente se sufría la mano en ella; é andubieron por él ariva dos
leguas sin hallar gente ni casas, y sienpre la tierra hera en
aquella hermosura y los canpos muy berdes y llenos de
infinitas ubas y tan coloradas como escarlatas, y en toda
parte por allí avía el olor de las flores y el cantar de los
pájaros muy suave, lo qual todo bieron y sintieron en quantas
islas por allí llegaron, y porque heran tantas que no se podían
en singular nombrar cada una, púsoles en todas en general
por nombre 'el Jardín de la reina'. y el día siguiente,
estando el almirante en mucho deseo de aver lengua, bino una
canoa á caça de pezes, que ansí le llamaban ellos caza, que
cazan con unos pezes otros, que traen atados unos peces por
la cola con unos cordeles, y aquellos peces son de hechura de
congrios y tienen la boca larga, toda llena de sosas, ansí como
de pulpo, y son muy osados, como acá los urones, é, lançán-
dolos en el agua, ellos ban á pegarse á qualquier peçe; d'estos
en el agua non los desapegarán fasta que lo saquen fuera, antés
morirá, y es peçe muy ligero, y desque se apegan tian por el
cordel muy luengo en que lo traen atado, y sacan cada vez
uno, é tómanlo en llegando á la cunbre del agua, ansí que
aquellos caçadores andavan muy desviados de las caravelas,
y el almirante inbió las barcas armadas y con arte que no les

these fish are very active, and as soon as they have fixed on anything, the Indians draw them in by a very long cord to which they are fastened, securing one at a time and taking it by bringing the hunting fish to the surface of the water.[1]

So, as those hunters passed at some distance from the caravels, the admiral sent out armed boats and with care that they should not flee to land, and when they came up with them, all those hunters talked to them like gentle lambs without guile, as if they had seen them every day of their lives. They came alongside the boats, for they had one of these fish fastened at the bottom on a large turtle, and they waited to get it into the canoe, which they did. And they took the canoe and the men, with four turtles, and each one of them three *cordos* long, and brought them to the ships to the admiral. And there those men gave him information concerning all that land and the islands, and concerning their cacique, who was staying very near there and who had sent them to hunt. And they asked the admiral to go there and said that they would make a great feast for him and they gave him all four turtles. And he gave them many things of those which he carried with him, with which they were very content.[2]

And he asked them how it was, whether that land was very great, and they answered that towards the west it had no end, and they said that to the south and west all that sea was full of islands. He gave them leave to depart; and they asked him how he was called, and they said the name of their cacique, and they returned to their employment of fishing.

The admiral departed from that place, making his way among those islands by the most navigable channels, steering a westerly course, not keeping very far from the mainland. And after having gone many leagues with a fair wind, he found a great island, and at the end of it there was a large village.[3] And although the caravels were sailing well, they anchored there and they landed, but they found not a single person, for all had fled and abandoned the place. It was

---

[1] This method of fishing, which is said to have been general on the coasts of Cuba, Jamaica and Española, is also described by Peter Martyr (i. 3), and in much greater detail by Oviedo (xiii. 9). The hunting fish, a kind of lamprey,

fuyesen á tierra, y, llegados á ellos, los hablaron todos aquellos
caçadores como corderos mansos sin malicia, como si toda su
bida los ubiera visto, que se detubiesen con las varcas, porque
tenían uno d'estos peçes pegado en fondo á una grande
tortuga, fasta que lo ubiesen recojido adentro en la canoa,
y ansí lo ficieron, y después tomaron la canoa, y á ellos con
quatro tortugas, y cada uno tenía tres cordos en luengo, é los
truxeron á los navíos al almirante; y allí aquellos le dieron
nueva de toda aquella tierra y yslas, y de su cacique, que
estava allí muy cerca, que los avía enviado á caçar, y rogaron
al almirante que se fuese allá, y que le harían gran fiesta, y
diéronle todas quatro tortugas, y él les dió muchas cosas de
las que llevava, con que fueron muy contentos.

y preguntóles que si aquella tierra hera muy grande, y
respondieron que al poniente no tenía cavo, y dijeron que
toda aquella mar al austro é poniente hera llena de islas.
dióles licencia; y ellos le preguntaron cómo se llama, y ellos
dijeron el nombre de su cacique, y bolviéronse á su exercicio
de pescar.

Partió el almirante de allí por entre aquellas islas por los
canales más navegables, siguiendo al poniente, no se desbiando
de tierra firme, y después de con buen tiempo aver andado
muchas leguas, falló una isla grande, y al cavo d'ella una
gran población; y aunque las carabelas llevavan buen tienpo,
surjieron allí, y fueron á tierra; mas no hallaron persona
alguna, que todos fuyeron y dejaron el lugar. creyóse ser

was called 'guacicomo' by the natives and 'reverso' by the Spaniards. It was
used to catch manatis, as well as turtles and various large fish. Turtles, caught
in this way, were drawn ashore or into a canoe; manatis were harpooned. The
hunting fish had a buoy attached to the cord by which it was held, in order that
the moment when it had fixed on its prey might be known. The reversos were
taken when young and kept in salt water, being fed until they were large enough
to go hunting. Before putting them in the water, the Indians talked encourag-
ingly to them and when the reversos had caught anything, they were in the
same way induced to leave hold of their prey by persuasive words and effusive
thanks; Oviedo remarks that the natives were so frivolous as to believe that
the fish understood all that they said to them.

    [2] This incident is also described by Las Casas (i. 95) and by Ferdinand
Columbus (c. 55).

    [3] Columbus called this island 'Santa María' (cp. Ferd. Columbus, c. 56; Las
Casas, i. 95). The island was, perhaps, one of the islands of the Jardín de la
Reina, but more probably Cayo Largo, farther to the west.

believed that they were a people supporting themselves by fishing; they found there traces of innumerable turtles which were on that shore. There they found forty dogs all together, which were not large or very ugly. They did not bark; it seemed that they were reared and fattened on fish. They learned that the Indians ate them, and that they are as tasty as kids are here in Castile, for some Castilians tried them.[1] There those Indians had many tame herons, and many other birds.[2] The admiral ordered that they should take nothing from them, and left that place with his ships.

And immediately they found another island, larger than that,[3] and they did not examine it, but shaped their course directly for some very lofty mountains which they saw on the mainland and which were fourteen leagues from there.[4] And they found there a large village, and the cacique and all the inhabitants were very friendly and very courteous, and there they gave very good refreshment to the admiral and to his people, of bread and fruits and water. And the admiral asked them if that land extended much farther to the west, and the cacique answered, as did other old men, his contemporaries, for he was an aged man, that the land was very great and that he had never heard that it had an end, but that farther on he might learn more from the people of Magón,[5] with which province they marched.

On the following day, they steered westwards, always following the coast of the land, and they went many leagues continually among larger islands and not so close to one another as at first. And they arrived at a very extensive and lofty sierra, which stretched very far inland, so much so that it was impossible to see the end of it.[6] And on the side of the sea, there were innumerable villages, from which there came immediately to the ships innumerable people with fruit, bread and water, and spun cotton, and rabbits, and pigeons, and a thousand other marvels and birds of other kinds which are not found here. They came singing with joy, believing that the people and the ships came from the heavens; and although the Indian interpreter, whom the

---

[1] Cp. *supra*, p. 42, and note 4.

gente que se governava de pescados; allí hallaron infinitas
cosas de tortugas que tenían por aquella plaia; allí allaron
todos juntos quarenta perros, no grandes ni muy feos, no
ladravan, parecía estar criados á pescado y cevados. supieron
como los Indios los comían, y que tienen tan buen sabor
como acá cabritos en Castilla, proque algunos Castellanos los
probaron. tenían allí aquellos Indios muchas garçotas man-
ças, é otras muchas aves. el almirante mandó que no les toma-
sen ninguna cosa, y partióse de allí con sus navíos, y luego
hallaron otra isla mayor que aquella, y no curaron d'ella, mas
endereçaron á unas montañas que bieron, muy altas, de la
tierra firme, que estaban de allí catorce leguas, y allí hallaron
una gran población, y el cacique y todos los avitadores de
muy buena conversación, y de muy buen trato, y allí dieron
muy buen refresco al almirante y á su jente de pan, y frutas
y agua; y preguntóles el almirante si aquella tierra se andava
mucho adelante al poniente, y respondió el cacique que con
otros biejos de su tienpo, ca era honbre viejo, que aquella
tierra que era grandísima y jamás oió decir que tubiese cavo,
mas que adelante sabría más de la jente de Magón, de la qual
provincia ellos estaban comarcanos.

Navegaron el día siguiente al poniente, siguiendo sienpre
la costa de la tierra, y andubieron muchas leguas sienpre por
islas más grandes, y no tan espesas como primero; y llegaron
á una sierra muy grande y muy alta, que andava mucho
adentro en la tierra, tanto que no se pudo ber el fin de ella;
y de la parte de la mar avía poblaciones infinitas, de las quales
luego binieron á los navíos jente infinita con fruta, pan y
agua, y algodón hilado, y conejos, y palomas, y de otras mill
maravillas, y de aves de otras maneras que no ay acá, can-
tando por fiesta, creyendo que aquella jente y navíos benían
del cielo; y aunque el Indio intérprete que llebava el almirante
les decía que heran jente de Castilla, creían que Castilla hera

---

[2] For the tame herons, see Oviedo (xiv. 8) and Las Casas (iii. 22): for the birds
of Cuba and the neighbouring islands generally, see Las Casas (*loc. cit.*).

[3] If the former island be identified with Cayo Largo, this 'larger island' will
be the Isla de Pinos (for which, cp. *infra*, p. 150).

[4] The Cordilleras de los Organos.   [5] Cp. *infra*, p. 138.

[6] The mountain system of Cuba which, in the east, is near the coast on the
south, trends in a north-westerly direction.

admiral carried with him, told them that they were men of Castile, they believed that Castile was Heaven, and that the king and queen, sovereigns of those ships, whose these men were, dwelt in the sky.

That province is called Ornofay.[1] They arrived there one evening and had passed through shallows and there could not find bottom, and the breeze from the land drove them out to sea. And they were there all one night lying to with sails furled, and it seemed to them to be no more than one hour of toil, owing to the most delicious perfume wafted from the land and the singing of the birds and of the Indians, which was very wonderful and comforting.

There they told the admiral that beyond there lay Magón, where all the people had tails, like beasts or small animals, and that for this reason they would find them clothed.[2] This was not so, but it seems that among them it is believed from hearsay and the foolish among them think that it is so in their simplicity, and I believe that the intelligent did not credit it, since it seems that it was first told as a jest, in mockery of those who went clothed. So John Mandeville, in the seventy-fourth chapter of his book,[3] says that in the Indies, in the province of Moré, all go naked as when they were born, and that they make a jest of those who go clothed. And he says that they are a people who do not believe in God, that He made Adam and Eve our parents, Who made them naked, and they say that none should feel shame of that which is natural. And so those of this province of Ornofay, as they all go naked, men and women, make a mock of those of whom they have heard say that they go clothed, and the admiral knew it to be a jest, so that if, where they said it to be so, some go clothed, yet they have not tails, as they declared.

There they also told the admiral that farther on there were innumerable islands and little depth of water, and that the end of that land was very far away, and so much so that in forty moons it would not be possible for him to reach the end. And they spoke according to the speed of their canoes, which is very small, for a caravel will go farther in one day than they in seven.

---

[1] The modern district of Camaguey, on the south coast of the island.

el cielo, y que el rey y la reyna señores de aquellos navíos, cuya hera aquella jente, estaban en el cielo. llámase aquella provincia 'Ornophay'; llegaron allí una tarde, y avia(n) andado en poca agua, y allá no pudieron allar ondo, y el biento de la tierra los echava fuera, y estuvieron allí toda una noche á la cuerda pairando, que no les pareció una ora de mano por el suavísimo olor que de la tierra benía, y el cantar de los pájaros y de los Indios, que hera muy maravilloso y contentable; allí dixeron al almirante que adelante de allí hera Magón, donde todas las jentes tenían rabo, como las bestias ó alimañas, y que á esta causa los hallarían bestidos, lo qual no hera ansí, mas parece que entre ellos (a)y este crédito de oídas, y los sinples d'ellos lo creen ser ansí con su sinpleça, y los discretos creo yo que no lo creerán, porque parece que ello fué dicho primeramente por burla, faciendo escarnio de los que andan bestidos, como dice Juan de Mandavilla en el .74. capítulo de su libro, que en las Indias en la provincia de la Moré todos andan desnudos como nacieron, y que hacen burla de los que andan bestidos; y dice que es jente que no creen en Dios, que hiço á Adán y á Eba nuestros padres, el qual los hiço desnudos, y dicen que de lo que es natural ninguno deve aber bergüenza; é ansí lo(s) d'esta provincia de Ornofay, como ellos todos andan desnudos, honbres y mujeres, facen escarnio de los que oyen decir que andan bestidos, y el almirante supo ser burla, que si algunos donde ellos decían andan bestidos, tampoco tienen ravos, como ellos dixeron. (dixeron) también allí al almirante que adelante avía islas inumerables y poco hondo, y que el fin de aquella tierra hera muy lejos, é tanto que en quarenta lunas no le podría llegar al cavo, y ellos fablavan según el andar de sus canoas, que es muy poco, que una caravela andará más en un día, que ellos en siete.

Partió el almirante de Ornofay el día siguiente con buen biento con sus caravelas, é cargó de belas y andubo muy grande camino fasta que entró en una mar blanca todo de un golpe, é pasó muchos bajos antes de llegar á ella, la qual mar hera blanca como leche y espesa como el agua en que los çurradores adovan los cueros; y luego les faltó el agua, y quedaron

<hr />

² Cp. *supra*, p. 12, end note 3. ³ Mandeville, c. 74.

The admiral with his caravels set out from Ornofay on the following day with a fair wind. And he set all sail and made very good progress, until he suddenly entered a white sea, having passed through many shallows before he reached it. This sea was white as milk and as thick as the water in which tanners treat their skins. And afterwards water failed them and they found themselves in two fathoms' depth.[1] The wind was strongly abaft and they were in a channel, where it would have been very dangerous to turn back, nor was it possible for the ships to anchor, since they could not lie anchored to the wind and there was no depth for them, since the anchor always dragged on the bottom. And so they went through these channels behind these islands for ten leagues, as far as an island where they found two fathoms and a half of water and space for the caravels.[2] There they anchored and they were in a state of extreme distress, considering the abandonment of the undertaking and how they were little able to return to that place from which they had set out. But Our Lord, Who ever succours men of good will when they are afflicted, gave them courage and put it into the heart of the admiral to proceed farther. And on the following day he sent a small caravel to the shore of that sea near there, to discover whether on the mainland there was to be found fresh water of which all the ships had great need. She returned with the report that on the shore of the land there was very deep mud[3] and in the seas beyond it such thick vegetation that a cat could not pass through it. There were in that place very many islands[4] which were more crowded together than in the Jardín already mentioned and which were so thickly wooded everywhere down to the seashore that they seemed to be walls. And beyond these woods there was very high land, and many and very green mountains, and on them there seemed to be much smoke and great fires. The admiral resolved to go forward and navigated through those channels among those islands, which, as has been said, were more crowded together than in the Jardín de la Reina, and he made his way onwards until they arrived at a very low headland, to which the admiral gave the name *Punta del Serafín*.[5]

---

[1] Columbus was in the Golfo de Batábano. All the sea between Cuba and the

en dos braças de fondo, y el biento les acudió mucho, é estando
en una canal muy peligrosa para bolver atrás, ni para surjir
con los navíos, porque no podrían birar sobre el ancla la
proa al biento, ni avía ondo para ellos porque sienpre andavan
rastreando la ancla por el suelo, é andubieron ansí por estas
canales de dentro d'estas islas diez leguas hasta una isla donde
hallaron dos brazas é un codo de agua, y largura para estar las
caravelas. allí surjieron y estuvieron con muy grande pena,
pensando dexar la enpresa, y que no harían poco en poder
bolver adonde avían partido; mas Nuestro Señor, que sienpre
socorre á los honbres humillados de buena boluntad, les puso
esfuerço y puso en coraçón al almirante que siguiese adelante,
y el día siguiente enbío una caravela pequeña al fondo de
aquella mar allí cerca, á ver sí fallaría agua dulce en la tierra
firme, de que tenían todos los navíos mucha necesidad.
bolvió con la respuesta que á la orilla de la tierra hera el lodo
muy ondo y estava dentro en la mar el arboleda tan espesa,
que no entraría por ella un gatto; avía por allí tantas islas que
heran más espesas que en el Jardín ya dicho, y tantas arboledas en derredor á la orilla de la mar, que parecían muros,
y juntos con aquellas arboledas avía tierra alta, y muchas
montañas y muy berdes, y en ellas parecían muchas umadas
y grandes fuegos. el almirante determinó ir adelante, y
navegó por aquellas canales entre aquellas islas, las quales,
como dicho es, heran más espesas que en la Jardín de la
reyna, y navegó fasta llegaron á una punta muy baja de la
tierra, á la qual el almirante puso nombre la 'punta del
Serafín'; allí obieron muchos travajos, que muchas bezes se
hallaron con los navíos en secos; y dentro d'esta punta la
tierra bajava al oriente, y se descubrían al septentrión
montañas muy altas lejos d'esta punta y entremedias limpio
de islas, que todas quedavan al austro y al poniente. obieron

Isla de Pinos is very shallow. Las Casas (i. 96) says that the sea was first green
and white and then white, and finally black as ink, and that it was sometimes
very shallow and at other times very deep, and that the sailors were terrified at
the changes in its character.
² The islands constitute the Archipelago de los Canarreos.
³ The coast of the Zapata peninsula: the Gran cienega occidental de Zapata.
⁴ These islands were the Islas de Mangles.
⁵ Punta Gorda, the western point of the Zapata Peninsula.

There they met with great difficulties, for many times they found the ships aground. Beyond this point, the land to the eastward was low and to the north, at a distance from that point, very high mountains appeared and in the interval it was clear of islands, since they all lay to the south and west.[1] There they had a fair wind and found three fathoms' depth of water, and the admiral determined to steer a course towards those mountains, at which he arrived on the following day. And they proceeded to anchor at a very lovely and very large palm grove, where they found springs of water, very sweet and very good, and evidence that people had been there.

While they were there, furnishing the ships with wood and water, a crossbowman from the caravels happened to go ashore with his crossbow to hunt, and when he had gone a short distance, he came upon a band of thirty Indians, one of whom was dressed in a white tunic down to his feet. He came upon them so suddenly that he thought that the one so dressed was a friar of La Trinidad who was walking there in the field. And afterwards there came towards him two others with white tunics which they wore down to the knees, and in colour they were as fair as men of Castile. Then he took fright and shouted and made off, fleeing to the sea. And he saw that, while the others remained where they were, the one in the full tunic came after him, calling to him, and he never dared to wait. So he came to the ships in flight and when the admiral learned it, he sent there to discover who those people were, and those who went found no one, and they believed that the one with the full tunic must have been the cacique of the others.[2]

On the following day the admiral sent twenty-five men, well armed, who were to go eight or ten leagues into the interior of the land, until they should find people. And when they had gone a quarter of a league, they found a plain which extended from west to east and away from the coast, and as they did not know the route, they proposed to cross the plain, and they were quite unable to do so owing to the abundant and tangled vegetation, on account of which they

[1] The Cordillera de los Organos lie to the north of the Golfo de Batábano,

allí el biento bueno y allí hallaron tres braças de agua de ondo, y el almirante determinó de tomar el camino de aquellas montañas, á las quales llegó otro día siguiente, y fueron á surjir á un palmar muy fermoso y muy grande, adonde hallaron fuentes de agua dulçe y muy buena, y señal que allí avía estado jente.

Acaeçió allí que estando forneciendo los navíos de leña é agua, salió un ballestero de las caravelas á caza por la tierra con su ballesta, é, alejado un poco, se halló con obra de treinta Indíos, y el uno d'ellos era bestido de una túnica blanca hasta los pies; y se halló tan súpito sobre ellos, que pensó por aquel bestido que hera un fraile de la Trinidad que iva allí en la campaña, y después vinieron á él otros dos con túnicas blancas, que les llegaban abajo de las rodillas, los quales heran tan blancos como honbres de Castilla en color; entonces obo miedo, é dió boçes, é bolvió, huyendo, á la mar, y vido que los otros se estavan quedos y el de la túnica cumplida benía tras d'el llamándolo, y él nunca osó esperar; y ansí fuyendo se vino á los navíos, y el almirante, desque lo supo, enbió allá por saver qué jente hera, é quando fueron, no hallaron á ninguno, y creyeron que aquel de la túnica cumplida sería el cacique d'ellos.

El día siguiente envió el almirante .25. honbres bien armados, que aduviesen ocho ó diez leguas por la tierra adentro, hasta allar jente, y, andando un quarto de legua, hallaron una bega que andaba de poniente á lebante é luengo de la costa, y por no saver el camino, quisieron travesar la vega, y nunca pudieron con yerva tanta y tan entretejida, que nunca pudieron andar, y bolviéronse cansados como si ubieran andado veinte leguas, y dixeron que por allí hera inposible poder andar la tierra, que no avía camino ni bereda.

where a large expanse of open water, free from islands, is to be found. As Bernáldez reports, the islands lie south and west.

² Las Casas (i. 95) and Ferdinand Columbus (c. 56), who place this incident in the island of Santa María, relate it somewhat differently, but they agree in essentials with the description of the country given by Bernáldez in the following passage. As that description accords with the character of the mainland of Cuba in that district, it seems to be probable that the incident occurred on the mainland.

could make no progress. And they came back as exhausted as if they had gone twenty leagues, and they said that it was impossible to traverse the land, as there was neither a road nor a path.

Next day others went along the shore and they found tracks of very large wild animals with five claws, an alarming thing, and they supposed them to be griffons, and tracks of other animals which they judged to be lions.[1] So they returned. There they found many vines and very large, laden with unripe fruit which covered all those trees and it was a wonderful sight. The admiral took a basket full of that fruit and of cuttings of the vines and of the white sand of the sea to exhibit and to send to the king and queen. There were also in that place many aromatic fruits, as in the other places already mentioned. There were also there cranes, twice as large as those of Castile.

The admiral, seeing that he had left Punta del Serafín, where the land was low to the eastward, and that he had crossed to the mountains in the north, navigated from there to the east along the same coast, until he saw that the one shore and the other joined and made continuous dry land. They went back again towards the west, and although the ships laboured and the people were very weary, the admiral thought to navigate to the west to some mountains which he had seen thirty-five leagues distant from the place where they had taken in water, and when they had gone nine leagues, they reached shore and took the cacique of that place. And he, being ignorant and as one who had never stirred from those mountains, told them that the sea was very deep and clear[2] to the north and for many days' journey. They weighed anchor and went on their journey very joyful, thinking that it would be as he had said to them, and having gone a certain number of leagues, they found themselves involved among many islands and in very shallow water, so that they found no channel which would allow them to proceed farther. And at the end of a day and a half, they had to drag the ships overland in scarcely a fathom of water through a very narrow

---

[1] Griffons were to be expected (cp. Mandeville, c. 29). The 'lions' were not less imaginary.

otra día fueron otros á el luengo de la playa y hallaron rastro de bestias grandísimas de cinco uñas, cosa espantable, é juzgaban que fuesen grifos, é de ótras bestias, que juzgaban fuesen leones. tanbién se bolvieron atrás. allí hallaron muchas parras y muy grandes, cargadas de agraz, que cubrían todos aquellos árboles, que hera maravilla de ber. tomó el almirante de aquel agraz una espuerta llena, é de los troços de las parras, é de la tierra blanca de la mar para mostrar, é para enbiar al rey é la reyna; tanbién allí avía muchas aromáticas frutas, como en los otros lugares suso-dichos; tanbién avía allí grullas mayores dos beces que las de acá de Castilla.

Bisto el almirante que avía dejado la punta del Serafín, donde la tierra bajava al oriente y avía travesado á las mon-tañas al setentrión, navegó de allí al orientte por la mesma costa, hasta que bido que la una costa é la otra se juntavan y hacían seco; bolvieron atrás otra vez al poniente, y aunque andavan los navíos y jente muy cansada, pensó el almirante navegar al poniente á unas montañas que avía bisto lejos treinta y cinco leguas de donde avían tomado el agua, y andando las nueve leguas, hallaron una playa é tomaron el cacique d'ella, el qual como inorante y persona que no avía salido de aquellas montañas, que les dixo que hera la mar muy onda y baja al setentrión é muy gran número de hornadas, levantaron las áncoras, é siguieron su camino muy alegres, pensando que sería como él les avía dicho, y andando ciertas leguas, se hallaron embaracados entre muchas islas, y en muy poco ondo, de manera ques no hallavan canal que los consin-tiese pasar adelante, é á cavo de un día y medio por una canal muy angosta é baja por fuerças de anclas.é cavestral ovieron de pasar los navíos por la tierra en seco casi una braça, hasta aver andado bien dos leguas, adonde hallaron dos bracas y media de agúa, en que navegaban dos navíos, y andando más adelante hallaron tres brazas. allí binieron muchas canoas á los navíos, y las jentes de ellas decían que las jentes de aquellas montañas dezían tenían (un rey de grande estado;

---

² The translation is conjectural, but from the context it would appear that the Indian said that the sea was deep and free from islands.

and shallow channel by means of anchors and capstan, until they had gone a good two leagues. There they found two and a half fathoms of water, in which two ships floated, and when they had gone farther on, they found three fathoms.[1]

Many canoes came to the ships there, and the people in them said that the people of those mountains had a king of great estate, and it seemed that they held in wonder the character and the magnificence of his land and great estate, saying that it contained innumerable provinces and that they called him 'holy' and that he wore a white tunic which trailed upon the ground.

And so they followed that course continually along the shore of that sea, always with three fathoms' depth of water, and when they had sailed four days and when the mountains, which stretched away far to the east, had been passed, they always found the seashore marshy as before and such dense vegetation along it, as has been said, that it was impossible to pass through it. And having with the ships reached a bay,[2] where the land again trended eastward, they saw some very high mountains there where that coast formed a headland, twenty leagues distant from them. The admiral determined to go there, as the sea was not open towards the north, and here it was of the very greatest depth as the cacique had said. He said also that in the direction in which the admiral proposed to go, no end of the land would be found in fifty moons, and that so he had heard it said. They navigated within many islands and at the end of two days and nights they reached the mountains which they had seen, and they found that they were as serrated a range as that of la Aurea, as the island of Corsica.

They rounded it completely and they could never find an entry by which to go to the land behind, for the shore was as full of mud and of thickly growing trees as was the other which has been mentioned, and the dwellings of the natives on the land behind were very large and numerous. They were there on that coast for seven days, seeking fresh water, of which they had need, and they found it on land on the eastern side among some very fine palm groves. And there they

---

[1] The channel, through which the caravels were dragged, was perhaps the

é ellos parecía lo tenían) en maravilla el modo é summa
de su rejión é grande estado, diciendo que tenía infinitas
provincias, y que le llamaban santo, y que traía túnica
blanca que le arastrava por el suelo, y ansí siguieron
aquel camino siempre por la costa de aquella mar, sienpre
con tres brazas de agua de hondo, y después de navegado
quatro días y pasadas las montañas, que quedavan mucho
al oriente, y sienpre allaron la costa de la mar ansí anegada,
y arboledas espesas, cerca d'ella, como dicho es, que hera
imposible entrar por ellas; y, estando metidos con los
navíos en un seno por donde otra bez la tierra bolvía al
oriente, bieron unas montañas muy altas allí adonde aquella
tierra hacía cavo, lejos de ellos veinte leguas. determinó el
almirante ir á ella, pues la mar no coxía al setentrión, y hera
de muy grandísimo ondo, como el cacique avía dicho y dixo
que por allí por donde el almirante quería ir que en cinquenta
lunas no hallaría cavo, y que ansí lo avía él oýdo decir.
navegaron por de dentro de muchas islas, y al cavo de dos
días con sus noches llegaron á las montañas que avían visto,
y hallaron que hera un c!
chererojo tan grande como el de la
Aurea, como la isla de Córcega. cercáronla toda, y nunca
pudieron hallar entrada para ir á la tierra adentro, porque
hera ansí la tierra llena de lodo é de árboles espesos, como
lo otro que dicho es, y las aumadas de jente heran en la tierra
adentro muy grandes é muchas. estubieron allí por aquella
costa siete días buscando agua dulce, de que tenían neçesidad,
la qual hallaron en la tierra de parte de oriente en unos pal-
mares muy lindos, y allí allaron nácares y grandísimas perlas;
bieron que allí abría buenas pesquerías si las continuasen.
después que tomaron agua y leña, navegaron al austro
siguiendo la costa de la tierra, y después al poniente, siguiendo
siempre la costa de la tierra firme fasta que los llevava al

Cayamos Channel, where the average depth of water is about one and a half
fathoms. A little farther west, the channels between the islands are still shallower.
The mean draught of a caravel has been estimated at about nine feet, with a
maximum draught of ten feet and a minimum of six feet.

² Probably near Punta de Salinas.

found mother of pearl and very large pearls; they saw that there would be good fisheries if they persevered.[1]

After they had taken in water and wood, they navigated to the south following the coast of the land, and then to the west, always following the coast of the mainland until it bore them to the south-west and it seemed that they had to follow that course for a great number of days' journey. And to the south they saw all the sea full of islands after having proceeded with great difficulty from the point from which they had set out.

And here the ships were very distressed owing to having grounded many times in the shallows, and the ropes and tackle were wasted, and the greater part of the provisions was much injured, especially the biscuit, on account of the quantity of water which the vessels had shipped. And all the people were very exhausted and troubled about supplies of food and doubtful whether the prevailing winds would not be against them on their return journey. They had gone up to that point from cape Alfaeto a thousand two hundred and eighty-eight miles, which are three hundred and twenty-two leagues, in the course of which they had discovered very many islands, as has been said, and Tierra Firme.[2]

The admiral then resolved to make the return voyage by another route and not by that by which he had gone, and to return by way of Jaime,[3] to which the admiral had given the name of Santiago, and to end by circumnavigating all the southern part which was left for them to go round. And so they set out on their return, expecting to pass within those islands which were there, among which they never found a channel. And they were compelled to go back by an arm of the sea by which they had navigated as far as Punta del Serafín to the islands where they had first anchored in the white sea.

Having set out on their return voyage, after they had gone a day's journey beyond the houses of the above-mentioned cacique, one day before the sun was up, they saw rising from the sea in the opposite direction from that of the land more than a million and a half cormorants, all together, and they

[1] This hope was not well founded, and although there were pearl-fisheries off

sorueste y parecía que avían de llebar por aquella via grande
número de jornadas, y al austro bieron toda la mar llena de
yslas después de aver andado gran pieza de donde avían
partido. y aquí los navíos estavan muy desconcertados por las
muchas dadas en lo bajo, y las cuerdas y aparejos gastados, y
la mayor parte de los mantenimientos muy perdidos, en
especial el bizcocho, por la mucha agua que haçían los navíos,
y toda la jente estava muy cansada y temerosos de mantenimientos, y dudando que la saçón de los bientos á la buelta les
podrían ser adbersos. avían andado hasta allí desde el cavo
de Alfaeto mill é ducientas é ochenta é ocho millas, que son
.322. leguas, en que avían descubierto muy muchas islas,
según dicho es, y la tierra firme.

Entonces accordó el almirante dar la buelta por otro camino,
y no por donde avían ydo, y bolver por Jaime, el qual nombre
de Santiago el almirante le avía puesto, y acabar de redondear
toda la parte del austro que les avía quedado por andar, y
así dieron la buelta pensando pasar dentro d'estas islas que
allí estavan, en las quales nunca hallaron canal, y les fué
forçado bolver atrás por un braço de mar por donde avían
navegado hasta la punta del Serafín á las islas donde primero
avían surjido en la mar blanca.

Biniendo de buelta, después que obieron pasado las casas
del cacique susodicho una hornada, un día antes que el sol
saliese, bieron benir de mar en fuera al camino de la tierra
más de quento y medio de cuerbos marinos todos juntos, é lo
obieron por maravilla de tanta multitud de cuerbos; y el día
siguiente binieron á los navíos tantas mariposas, que escure-
cían el ayre del çielo, y duraron ansí hasta la noche, que las
destruyó una grande agua que llovió, y truenos con ella.
tanvién desde donde dejaron la tierra donde decían que

---

the Cuban coast, they never attained the importance of those of Cubagua and
Margarite.

[2] Although the greatest length of Cuba is only 750 miles, the extreme in-
dentation of the shore gives the island a total coast line of nearly six thousand
miles.

[3] Jamaica. The island is not elsewhere so named, and it would seem to be more
probable that the appearance of the name here is due to an error in writing, than
that it is some unconscious revelation, on the part of Columbus, of his Catalan
origin (cp. Ulloa, *Xristo-Ferens Colom*, p. 98).

were amazed at so great a multitude of cormorants. And on the following day, there came to the ships so many butterflies that they darkened the face of the sky, and so they remained until night, with the result that a great rain which fell, and thunder with it, destroyed them. Moreover, from the point where they left the land, in which they said that the holy king was, in order to go to el Teroneso, to which they gave the name *San Juan Evangelista*,[1] certainly throughout that voyage they saw that there were many turtles and very large. But in those twenty leagues, they saw very many more, for the sea was all thick with them, and they were of the very largest, so numerous that it seemed that the ships would run aground on them and were as if bathing in them. The Indians value them highly and regard them as very good to eat and as very healthy and savoury.[2]

They departed from there and navigated through an arm of the sea, white, as is all the rest there, and of little depth, and when they had gone a few leagues, they arrived at the end of the many islands, where they had anchored for the first time in the white sea. And it was a marvel of Our Lord to bring it to pass that they came there and a miracle, beyond the knowledge and wit of man. And thence they came as far as the province of Ornofay, with no less peril than before, and there they anchored in a river [3] and supplied the ships with water and wood, preparatory to steering to the south and not to return by the way by which they had come, and to leave the Jardín de la Reina on the left hand. And so they proceeded, and they were not able to omit visiting many islands which they had not hitherto seen. Here, as has been said, the land is mountainous and very fertile, and the people are notably gentle, and there is great abundance of fruits and of animal food, of all of which they gave them a very great part. The fruits were very sweet and aromatic. There they brought them innumerable birds, parrots and other birds, and the majority of them were pigeons and very large, and as savoury as partridges here in Castile. And they had their crops full of flowers which smelt sweeter than orange blossom.

There the admiral had mass said, and he caused a very large

[1] Isla de Pinos (cp. Las Casas, i. 96).

estava el rey santo para ir al Teroneso á quien de 'San Juan Ebanjelista' pusieron el nombre, bien que en todo el biaje bieron que avía muchas tortugas é muy grandes, enpero muy muchas más bieron en estas veinte leguas, ca la mar hera toda quajada de ellas, é muy grandísimas, atantas, que pareçían que los navíos se querían encallar en ellas, y así ruiján entre ellas. tiénenlas los Indios en gran precio y por muy buen manjar, y por muy sanas y sabrosas.

Partieron de allí y navegaron por un braço de mar blanco, como es todo lo otro de por allí, y poco ondo, y, andadas pocas leguas, llegaron al cavo de las muchas islas donde avían surjido la primera bez en la mar blanca, que fué maravilla de Nuestro Señor aportar á benir allí y milagro, más que no por saver (ni) injenio de honbre; y dende binieron fasta la provinçia de Ornofay con no menos peligro del pasado, y allí surjeron en un río, é fornecieron los navíos de agua é leña para navegar al austro é no bolver por donde avían ido, y dejar el Jardín de la reina á la mano izquierda, y ansí binieron, é no se pudieron escusar de comunicar con muchas islas que hasta entonces no avían visto. aquí, como es dicho, es la tierra montañosa y fertilísima, y jente mansa en gran manera, y muy abundosa de frutas, y de biandas, que de todo les dieron muy gran parte. heran frutas suavísimas y aromáticas; allí les trujeron infinitas aves, papagayos, y de otras aves, é las más d'ellas heran palomas y muy grandes, y tan sabrosas como perdiçes de acá de Castilla, y tenían el papo lleno de flores, que olían más que açahar de los naranjos.

allí hiço el almirante decir misa, y hiço plantar una cruz de un gran madero, así como acostumbrava fazer en todos los otros cavos donde llegavan y le parecía que convenía. hera domingo quando al almirante dijeron misa, y él decendió en tierra, y el cacique de allí hera honbre muy onrrado, y señor de mucha jente é familia. quando vido al almirante decendido de la barca en tierra, le tomó de la mano, y otro Indio de más de ochenta años que benía con él le tomó de la otra mano,

---

² Las Casas (i. 95) also declares that the ships had difficulty in navigating among the turtles.
³ Perhaps the Rio Cauto.

wooden cross to be set up, as he was accustomed to do on all
the other headlands where they came and as appeared to him
to be right.¹ It was Sunday when they said mass for the
admiral, and he landed. And the cacique of that place was
a man very honoured and lord of a great people and household. When he saw the admiral come on shore from the boat,
he took him by the hand, and another Indian, of more than
eighty years of age, who came with him, took him by the
other hand, making great festivity for him. And that old
man wore round his neck a string of beads, made from a stone
like marble, which they greatly value there, and he carried a
small basket of apples in his hand and these he gave at once
to the admiral as a present directly he landed from the boat.
The cacique and the old man and all the others, without any
embarrassment, went naked as when they were born, as they
go in all parts of the land discovered by the admiral Columbus.

And so they went hand in hand, and all the other Indians
behind them, until the admiral came to the place where he
was to offer up prayer and to hear mass, and where he had
ordered preparation for that purpose to be made. And when
the admiral had ended his prayer, the old Indian, in a very
pleasing and confident manner, made a speech there and said
that he had heard how the admiral was going about and seeking out all the islands and the mainland of those parts, and
that they knew that he had been on the mainland there. And
he told the admiral that he should not become vainglorious,
because it chanced that all the people feared him, since he was
mortal like other men. And he began by words and signs,
illustrating from his own person how all men were born
naked and had an immortal soul, and how for the ill of each
member, it was the soul that suffered pain, and how at the
moment of death men felt very great anguish at parting from
the body, and how they went to the king of the sky or to the
depth of the earth, according to the good or evil which they
had done or wrought in the world. And since he learned
from the admiral that he was pleased to hear him, he ex-
panded his speech more, using such signs that the admiral
understood all.

And the admiral answered him by the medium of the Indian

haciéndole mucha fiesta, y traía aquel biejo un ramal de
quentas de piedra mármol al pescuezo, las quales ellos tienen allá en gran precio, un cestillo de mançanas en la mano,
las quales luego dió al almirante, ansí como decindió de la
barca en presente; y el cacique, y el biejo y todos los otros
andavan desnudos como nacieron, sin ningún enpacho, ansí
como andan en todas aquellas partes de la tierra descubierta
por el almirante Colón; é ansí por las manos fueron y todos
los otros Indios en pos de ellos fasta donde el almirante fué
á facer su oración é oir misa, donde avía mandado aparejar
para ello. é después que el almirante acavó su oración, el
biejo Indio con muy buen semblante y osadía hiço allí racona-
miento y dixo que él avía savido como el almirante corría y
buscava todas las islas y tierra firme de aquellas partes, y que
supiesen que allí estava en la tierra firme de allá, y dixo al
almirante que no tomase banagloria, puesto caso que toda la
jente le obiese miedo, porque él hera mortal como los otros
honbres, y començó por palabras y señas figurando en su
persona como todos los hombres nacieron desnudos y tenían
el ánima ynmortal, y que del mal de cada miembro el ánima
hera la que se dolía y como al tienpo de la muerte del despe-
dimiento del cuerpo sentían muy gran pena, y que iban al rey
del çielo, ó al abismo de la tierra, según el bien ó mal que
avían fecho ó obrado en el mundo; y porque él conoció del
almirante que avía placer de lo oir, él se alargava más en el
raçonamiento con tales señas que todo lo entendía el almirante; y el almirante le respondió por intercesión del Indio
intérprete que traía, que avía venido á Castilla, el qual entendía bien la lengua castellana y la pronunciava, y hera muy
buen honbre y de muy buen injenio, y respondió que él
no avía fecho mal á nunguna persona ni hera benido por
facer mal á los buenos, salvo á los malos, y que antes bienes y
merçedes á los buenos u mucha onrra, y que esto hera lo que
los señores suyos el rey don Fernando y la reyna doña Isabel,
muy grandes reyes de España, le avían mandado, y el Yndio
respondió, muy maravillado, al intérprete, diciendo: ' ¿cómo,

---

[1] If the river be the Rio Cauto, the headland would be the promontory at
its mouth.

interpreter whom he carried with him and who had come to Castile and who understood the Castilian language well and talked it, and who was a very good man and of very good intelligence. And he replied that he had not done ill of any person nor had he come to do ill to the good, but only to the evil, and rather to give presents and rewards to the well doers and much honour, and that this was that which his sovereigns, the king Don Ferdinand and the queen Doña Isabella, the very great rulers of Spain, had commanded him.

And the Indian, greatly marvelling, replied to the interpreter, saying: 'How? Has this admiral another lord, and does he yield obedience?' And the Indian interpreter said: 'To the king and to the queen of Castile, who are the greatest sovereigns in the world.' And forthwith he recounted to the cacique and to the old man and to all the other Indians the things which he had seen in Castile and the marvels of Spain, and told them of the great cities and fortresses and churches, and of the people and horses and animals, and of the great nobility and wealth of the sovereigns and great lords, and of the kinds of food, and of the festivals and tournaments which he had seen, and of bull-fighting, and of that which he had learned of the wars. And all this he told very well and in such a way that the old man and the others were satisfied and greatly rejoiced to know it, and they passed it on, the one to the other.

And the old man said that he desired to go to see such great things and he was himself determined to go with the admiral, had not his wife and sons opposed it and wept, and for this cause, from his sense of duty towards them, with much sorrow he refrained. And from there the admiral took another, a young man, whom he carried off from the land without any question being raised. This man, with the other cacique whom he had with him and whom he had seized, he sent to the king and queen, after he had come to Española from this voyage.[1]

All those peoples of the islands and of the mainland there, although they appear to be savages and go naked, yet, according to the admiral and to those who were with him on this voyage, appear to be quite rational and of acute intelli-

[1] This incident is recorded very shortly by Ferdinand Columbus (c. 57); at

este almirante otro señor tiene y obedece ?' y el intérprete
indio dijo: 'al rey y á la reyna de Castilla, que son los mayores
señores del mundo'; y de aquí les contó al cacique y al biejo,
y á todos los otros Indios las cosas que él avía visto en Castilla
y las maravillas de España, y de las grandes çiudades y forta-
leças, y iglesias, y jentes, y cavallos, y alimañas, y de la
grande nobleça y riqueça de los reyes y grandes señores, y de
los mantenimientos, y de las fiestas y justas que avía bisto,
y del correr de los toros, y de las guerras lo que avía savido, y
todo se lo rrecontó muy bien y en forma que el biejo y los
demás se sosegaron y olgaron mucho por saber; é lo
comunicaban los unos á los otros, y el biejo dixo que él
quería benir á ber tales cosas, é determinaba de se benir con
el almirante, salvo por el inpedimiento de su mujer y hijos
que lloravan, y por esto por piedad de ellos lo dexó con mucha
pena, y el almirante tomó otro mancebo de allí, que truxo sin
escándalo de la tierra, el qual con el otro cacique que traía,
que avía tomado, envió al rey y á la reina, después d'él
benido del biaje en la Española.

Todas aquellas jentes isleñas y de la tierra firme de allá,
aunque parecen bestiales y andan desnudos, según el almirante y los que con él fueron este biaje, les pareció ser bien
raçonables y de agudos injenios, los quales todos olgaban y
guelgan mucho de saver cosas de nuebas, como hacen acá los
honbres que desean saver todas las cosas, que aquello no
nace sino de vibez y agudo injenio, y son aquellas jentes muy
obedientes y muy leales á sus caciques, que son sus reyes é
señores, é los tienen en muy gran quenta é honrra; y luego
dondequiera que las caravelas llegavan hacían saver quales-
quier Indios que allí estubiesen ó llegasen el nombre de su
cacique, y preguntavan por el nombre del cacique de las
caravelas para replicarlo entre ellos, y el uno con el otro lo
replicaban porque no se les olvidase, y después preguntavan
cómo llamaban á los navíos, y sí benían del çielo, ó de dónde
benían, y aunque les decían que hera jente de Castilla, ellos

more length by Las Casas (i. 96), and at still greater length by Peter Martyr (i. 3).
Martyr professes to report the *ipsissima verba* of the cacique and of Columbus,
and adds one or two typical touches of his own, thereby winning the approval
of Las Casas (*loc. cit.*).

gence. And they all are pleased and are greatly delighted to learn new things, as here those men are who wish to know about everything, and that can only arise from a lively and active mind. And those peoples are very obedient and very loyal to their caciques,[1] who are their kings and lords, and hold them in very great account and honour. And immediately, at whatever point the caravels arrived, the Indians, who were there or who came there, made known the name of their cacique, and they asked for the name of the cacique of the caravels in order to repeat it among themselves, and the one told it to the other that they might not forget it. And afterwards they asked what the ships were called and whether they came from the heavens, and whence they did come. And although they told them that they were people of Castile, they thought that Castile was in the heavens, for they have no letters, and they know nothing of law or of history, nor do they know what it means to read, nor have they reading or writing, and for this cause they are so ignorant. And they said that the people of Magón went clothed because they had tails, in order to conceal that disgrace, and among themselves they regard it as a shame to go clothed, as has been said.

The land is so fertile that it may be renowned for this among all those islands and lands of those seas, since, even if there were many more people and even if they were a hundred times more numerous, the supplies of food would suffice for them. It may well be that in the interior of the land there are other forms of government and other differences and manners and peoples, and things which may be no less strange, which on this voyage they could not see or know. The admiral bade farewell to that cacique of Ornofay and to that honoured old man, his favourite or relative, with much friendship and with many protestations.

The admiral departed from the province of Ornofay and from the *Rio de las Misas*, which name he gave, and they navigated to the south in order to leave on the left hand the Jardín de la Reina, which consists of many green and lovely islands, on account of the perilous voyage which they had experienced before on the outward journey. They arrived at

---

[1] To the Spaniards, it appeared that the caciques tyrannized over the natives,

pensaban que Castilla hera en el cielo, porque ellos no tienen
ningunas letras, ni saven de ley, ni de historias, ni saben qué
cosa es leer, ni leyenda, ni escriptura, y por esto están tan
inorantes; é ellos dizen que los de Magón andan bestidos
porque tienen ravo, por cobijar aquella fealdad, é tienen por
injuria entre ellos andar bestidos, como dicho es. la tierra es
tan fértil en lo que se puede conocer por todas aquellas islas y
tierras de aquellas mares, que, aunque fuesen muchas más
jentes y fuesen cien beçes otros tantos, les sobrarían los mantenimientos. bien puede aver en la tierra adentro otros reji-
mientos é otras diferençias é modos é jentes é cosas estrañas,
que no puede ser menos, las quales d'este biaje no se pudieron
ver ni saver. despidióse el almirante de aquel cacique, y de
aquel biejo onrrado, su privado ó pariente, de Ornofay, con
mucha amistanza é con muchas obligaciones.

Partió el almirante de la provincia de Ornafay del 'Río de
las misas', que puso nombre, navegaron al austro por dejar el
Jardín de la reyna, que heran muchas yslas berdes y hermosas,
á la mano yzquierda, por el peligro de navegar que primero
á la ida avían pasado, binieron á tener á la provincia de
Macaca por causa de los bientos que le resistieron, y allí
en toda la provinçia los recivieron muy bien, y allí en un
golfo muy grande adonde puso el almirante 'Buen tiempo'
por nombre, allí navegaron al poniente, hasta que llegaron
al cavo de la isla, y dende al austro, hasta que llegaron á la
tierra bojía al oriente, y así al cavo de ciertos días binieron al
monte Cristalino y de alli á la punta del Farol y á la baía que
es más al lebante once leguas, donde hace fin la isla sobredicha.
allí obieron ciertos días de bientos contrarios. los marineros
tienen que el común navegar de una caravela en un día
son docientos millas de quatro en legua, que son en un día
natural çinquenta leguas, en un día grande setenta é dos
leguas. d'estas les acaecieron al almirante y á su jente en
este biaje hartas hornadas, según ellos contaban y escrivió
el almirante en el libro que d'ello hiço, y no parezca á mara-

and at a comparatively early date, Ferdinand and Isabella gave instructions
that measures should be taken to prevent the oppression of the Indians by their
own chiefs (cp. *Doc. Inéd.* (1ª *serie*), 31, p. 161).

the province of Macaca, owing to the winds which were contrary, and there in the whole province they were very well received.[1]

And there, across a very wide bay, to which the admiral gave the name *Buen Tiempo*, they navigated westward until they reached the end of the island,[2] and thence to the south, until they came to a point where the land jutted out to the east. And so at the end of some days they came to Monte Cristalino[3] and thence to Punta del Farol,[4] and to the bay which is eleven leagues more to the east, where is the end of the above-mentioned island. There, for some days, they had contrary winds.

Sailors hold that the ordinary going of a caravel in a day is two hundred miles, so that, at the rate of four miles to a league, in a normal day they make fifty, in a long day seventy-two leagues. This was achieved on many days by the admiral and his men during this voyage, as they reckoned and as the admiral wrote in the book which he made concerning it.[5] And it is not a thing beyond belief that in navigating it is possible to lay the course exactly; on the contary, it is proved to be very true. For on many occasions a ship returns to an island from which she has set out and that not with the same, but with contrary and adverse wind and weather. Herein lies the skill of the master and salvation in time of tempest. No one is regarded as a good pilot and master who, although he has to pass from one land to another far distant without seeing any sign of other land, makes an error of ten leagues, even if the crossing be one of a thousand leagues, unless it be that the violence of the storm overpowers him and deprives him of the use of his skill.

So, navigating in a southerly direction, they came to anchor in a bay, in the neighbourhood of which there were many villages.[6] And a cacique of a very large village, which was on a height, came to the ships and brought to them very good supplies of food. And the admiral gave to him and to his men of the things which he had, and they were pleased with them. And the cacique asked whence they came and what the

---

[1] Columbus proceeded eastwards along the coast of Cuba as far as Cabo de Santa Cruz (Las Casas, i. 97), where he found that owing to contrary winds, he

villa que navegando se pueda arbitriar el camino en cierto;
mas antes se prueva por muy berdadero, porque por muchas
veces se buelve el navío á la isla otra de donde partió, y no
con el mesmo tiempo y biento, salvo con lo contrario y adberso.
aquí consiste el saber del maestro y el remediarse al tiempo de
la tormenta. nin se tiene por buen piloto é maestro aquel que,
aunque aya de pasar de una tierra en otra muy lejos, sin ber
señal de otra tierra alguna, que yerre diez leguas, aunque en
tránsito sea de mil leguas, salvo si la fuerça de la tormenta
le fuerça é priva el usar del injenio. ansí que, navegando ellos
á la partida del austro, fueron á surjir una tarde á una baia,
adonde allí en aquella comarca avía muchas poblaciones, y
bino un cacique de una muy grande población, que está en un
alto, á los navíos, y trújoles muy buen refresco, y el almirante
les dió á él y á los suyos de las cosas que él tenía é les agrada-
van, y el cacique preguntó de dónde benían y cómo llamaban
al almirante, y el almirante respondió que él era basallo de los
grandes y muy onrrados reyes el rey y reyna de Castilla, sus
señores, los quales lo avían enviado en aquellas partes á saver
é descubrir aquellas tierras y honrrar mucho á los buenos
y obedientes y destruir los malos; y esto fué por intercesión

could not sail towards Española. He therefore stood across to Jamaica, which he
reached near Montego Bay.

² Bernáldez does not make it clear that Columbus had left the coast of
Cuba and crossed to Jamaica; 'Buen Tiempo' is Montego Bay in the latter
island.

³ Probably Portland Point, where the land is high.

⁴ Las Casas (i. 97) says that this point was the most easterly of the island,
which identifies it with the modern Morant Point. But if the account in
Bernáldez be accurate, it was not the extreme east of the island and should be
identified rather with Yallah Point, the bay mentioned immediately afterwards
being then probably Port Morant.

⁵ This 'book' was presumably one of the 'writings' which Columbus left with
Bernáldez, and was possibly an account of this voyage, since there is evidence
that the story of the exploration of Cuba and Jamaica at this time is not drawn
from the log-book of which Ferdinand Columbus and Las Casas made use.

⁶ This may be any one of the bays on the southern coast of Jamaica, but may,
perhaps, be most probably identified with Portland Bight. Las Casas (i. 97)
mentions that Columbus was especially impressed by one bay in which were
seven islets, and near which there was very high land. This bay can be almost
certainly identified with Portland Bight, and since Las Casas says further that
the country near was very populous, it seems to be likely that it is the bay
mentioned by Bernáldez.

admiral was called, and the admiral replied that he was a vassal of the great and most honoured sovereigns, the king and queen of Castile, his lords, who had sent him into those parts to learn about and to discover those lands and to do great honour to the good and obedient and to destroy the evil doers. This reply was made through the medium of the Indian interpreter who spoke. At it, the said cacique was much pleased and inquired of the said Indian at very great length concerning things here. And he described many things in detail at which the cacique and the other Indians were greatly amazed and were very delighted. They remained there until nightfall and then took leave of the admiral.

And next day the admiral departed from there. He was already under sail with a light wind when the cacique came with three canoes and overtook the admiral. He came with so much ceremony that some description of his pomp must not be omitted. One of the canoes was as large as a large *fusta* and brightly painted. In her, he came in person, with his wife and two daughters, of whom one was a very lovely girl of some eighteen years, entirely nude, as they are wont to be there, and very modest; the other was younger. He had with him also two sons, callow youths,[1] and five brothers, and other dependants, and all the others must undoubtedly have been his vassals. In his canoe he carried as a herald a man who stood alone at the bow, wearing a loose cloak of red feathers, shaped like a coat of arms, and on his head a large plume, which looked very well. And in his hand he carried a white banner with no design on it. Two or three men had their faces painted in colours in the same way, and each one of them wore on his head a large plume, in the shape of a helmet, and on his forehead a round tablet as large as a plate. And each one of them was painted in the same manner and colours, so that there was no more difference there than in their plumes. Each held in his hand a *juguete*,[2] upon which they played. There were two other men also painted, but in a different way, and these carried two wooden trumpets, with elaborate carvings of birds and other conceits; they were of very black wood of excellent quality. Each one of them

---

[1] The absence of any further reference to the sons, while the appearance of

del Indio intérprete que fablava. de lo qual el dicho cacique se olgó mucho y preguntó muy por estenso al dicho Indio de las cosas de acá, y él se las recontó mucho por estenso, de lo qual el cacique y los otros Indios muy maravillados se olgaron mucho y estubieron allí hasta la noche é se dispidieron del almirante. y otro día partió el almirante de allí. ya que iba á la bela con poco biento, bino el cacique con tres canoas, y alcançó al almirante, el qual benía tan concertado, que no es de dejar de escribir la forma de su estado. la una de las canoas hera muy grande como una grande fusta y muy pintada. allí benía su persona, y la muger é dos fijas, la una de hasta diez y ocho años, muy hermosa, desnuda del todo, como allá acostumbran, muy onesta; la otra hera menor; y dos hijos machos, y cinco hermanos, y otros criados; y los otros todos devían de ser sus basallos. traýa él en su canoa un hombre como alférez. este sólo benía en pie á la proa de la canoa con un sayo de plumas coloradas de echura de cota de armas, y en la caveça traía un grande plumaje. que parecía muy bien, y traýa en la mano una bandera blanca sin señal alguna. dos ó tres honbres benían con las caras pintadas de colores de una mesma manera y cada uno traýa en la caveca un gran plumaje de echura de zelada, y en la frente una tableta redonda tan grande como un platto y pintadas así la una como la otra de una mesma obra y color, que no avía diferencia ansí como en los plumajes. traýan estos en la mano un juguete con que tañían. avía otros dos honbres ansí pintados en otra forma, é estos traían dos tronpetas de palo, muy labradas de pájaros é otras sutileças; el leño de que heran era muy negro, fino. cada uno d'estos traía un muy lindo sombrero de plumas berdes muy espesas y de muy sutil obra. otros seis traían sombreros de plumas blancas y benían todos juntos en guarda de las cosas del cacique. el cacique traía al pescueço unas joias de alanbre de una ysla que es en aquella comarca, que se llama 'guaní', que es muy fino é tanto que parece oro de ocho quilates. hera de echura

the father, mother and elder daughter is described, suggests that the word 'machos' is here used in an uncomplimentary sense. But it may mean merely that they were robust.

2 Some kind of small or childish musical instrument.

wore a very handsome hat of green feathers, very close together and very ingeniously worked. Six others wore hats of white feathers, and these were all together on guard over the belongings of the cacique. The cacique wore round his neck some ornaments of *alanbre*,[1] which is called '*guaní*', from an island which is in that neighbourhood, and which is very fine and of such a character that it seems to be gold of eight carats. It was the shape of a fleur de lis, as large as a plate. He wore it round his neck with a string of large beads of marble, which they also value highly, and on his head he wore a garland of small stones, green and red, arranged in order, and intermingled with some larger white stones, producing a pleasing effect. And he also wore a large ornament hung over his forehead, and from his ears two large disks of gold were suspended by some little strings of very small green stones. Although he was naked, he wore a girdle, of the same workmanship as the garland, and all the rest of his body was exposed. His wife was likewise adorned, naked and exposed, except that she had one single part of her person covered with a little piece of cotton, no bigger than an orange leaf. On her arms, about the armpits, she wore a roll of cotton, made like the upper part of the sleeves of old-fashioned French doublets. She wore two others, also made of cotton, like these and larger, on each leg below the knee, as *ajorcas*.[2] The elder and more lovely daughter was completely nude. She only wore round her waist a single string of stones, very black and small, from which hung something shaped like an ivy leaf, made of green and red stones fastened on woven cotton. The large canoes came between the other two and further, slightly in advance of them.

And as soon as this cacique came alongside the ship, he began to give things from his store to the masters and to each one of the crew. It was morning, and the admiral was praying, so that he did not so soon know of the presents or the determination with which this cacique had come. Presently the cacique came on board the caravel with all his people, and when the admiral appeared, he had already sent away his

[1] Perhaps copper, the ordinary meaning of the word 'alanbre'. But Oviedo

de una flor de lis, tamaña como un platto. traíala al pescueço con un sartal de cuentas gordas de piedra mármol, que tanbién tienen en gran precio, y en la caveça traýa una guirnalda de piedras menudas, verdes y coloradas, puestas en orden, y entremedias algunas blancas, mayores, adonde bien parecían, y traía más una joia grande colgada sobre la frente, y á las orejas le colgavan dos grandes tabletas de oro con unas sartitas de quentas berdes, más menudas. traýa un cinto, aunque andava desnudo, ceñido de la misma obra de la guirnalda, y todo lo otro del cuerpo descubierto; y asimismo su mujer benía adornada, desnuda, descubierta, salvo un solo lugar de su miembro, que de una cosilla no mayor que una oja de naranjo de algodón traía tapado. traía en los braços junto con el sobaco un bulto de algodón echo en semejança de los baraones de los jubones antiguos de los Franceses. traía otros dos como aquellos y más grandes, en cada pierna el suyo, como ajorcas, también de algodón, abajo de las rodillas. la hija mayor y más ermosa toda andava desnuda. un solo cordón de piedras muy negras y menudas solamente traía ceñido; del qual colgava una (cosa de) echura de oja de yedra, de piedras verdes y coloradas pegadas sobre algodón texido. la canoa grande benía entre las otras dos, é más, con una poca de bentaja adelante; y luego como llegó este cacique al bordo de navío, començó de dar á los maestres é jente cosas de su cámara á cada uno. era de mañana, y el almirante estava reçando y no bido tan aýna las dádibas ni la determinación de la benida d'este cacique, el qual luego entró en la caravela con toda su jente, y quando el almirante salió ya tenía enbiado los basallos que bolviesen las canoas á tierra, y iban ya lejos, y luego que bido al almirante se fué á él con cara muy alegre, diciendo: 'amigo, io tengo determinado dejar la tierra y irme contigo y ber el rey é la reyna y el príncipe su hijo, los mayores señores del mundo, los quales tienen tanto poder, que an sojuz-

---

says that the natives of the Amazon district used 'guaní' for purposes of personal decoration, and explains guaní as being gold of inferior quality.

[2] The large rings worn by Moorish women round their arms or ankles.

servants, so that the canoes were on their way back to land and had already gone a considerable distance.

And directly he saw the admiral, he went up to him with a very joyous expression, saying: 'Friend, I have resolved to leave the land and to go myself with you and to behold the king and the queen and their son, the prince, the greatest sovereigns in the world, who have so much power that they have brought under their sway so many lands through you who obey them and by their command go about subduing all this world, as I have learned from these Indians whom you carry with you. For, in every quarter, the nations so greatly fear you that it is marvellous, and as for the Caribs, who are a people without number and very fierce, you have destroyed their canoes and houses and have taken their women and sons, and those who did not flee, you have slain. I know how in all the islands round about, which is a vast world of innumerable people, they tremble before you and are in great fear, and that you are able to do to them great injury and ill, if they do not obey the king of Castile, your lord, for already you know the peoples of these islands and their weakness, and you are acquainted with the land. Accordingly, before you take from me my land and dominion, I desire to go with my household in your ships with you to see the great king and queen, your sovereigns, and to see the richest and most opulent land in the world, wherein they dwell, and to behold the wonders of Castile, which are many, as your Indian has told me.'

And the admiral, having compassion on him and on his daughter and his sons and his wife, seeing his innocence and good will, withstood him and told him that he received him as a vassal of the king of Spain and of the queen, and that for the present he should remain where he was, since much was still left for him to discover, and that when he returned there would be time to fulfil his desire. And they plighted friendship and so he was obliged to remain with his people and household.[1]

The admiral sailed thence to the south and to the east through those seas, among other islands, a multitude of islands, inhabited by those same naked people, according to the admiral's account of the matter.[2] Of these, that I may

---

[1] This incident is not found in Las Casas or in Ferdinand Columbus.

gado acá tantas tierras por ti que les obedeces y bas por su mandado todo este mundo sojuzgando, como e savido d'estos Indios que contigo traes, que en todo cavo están las jentes de ti tan temerosos que es maravilla, y á los Caribes que es jente ynumerable y muy brava les as destruído las canoas é casas é tomado las mujeres é fijos é muertos d'ellos los que no huían. yo sé que en todas las yslas d'esta comarca, que es infinito mundo de gente inumerable, te temen y an gran miedo, y los puedes hacer mucho daño y mal, si no obedecen al rey de Castilla, tu señor, pues ya conoces las jentes d'estas yslas y su flaqueça y saves la tierra. pues, antes que me tomes mi tierra é señorío, yo me quiero yr contigo con mi casa en tus navíos á ver á los grandes rey é reyna tus señores y á ver la tierra más rica y abundosa del mundo, de donde ellos están, y á ver las maravillas de Castilla, que son muchas, según tu Indio me a dicho.' y el almirante, aviendo compasión d'él y de su fija y de sus fijos y de su muger, se lo estorbó, biendo su inocencia y sana boluntad, y le dixo que él lo rrecivía por basallo del rey de España y de la reyna, y que por entonces que se quedase, que aun le quedava mucho por descubrir, y que tiempo abía de otra buelta para cumplir su deseo; y ficieron su amistad, y ansí se obo de quedar con su jente é casa.

El almirante navegó dende al austro é al oriente por aquellas mares entre otras islas, muchas islas pobladas de aquellas mesmas jentes desnudas, según escrivió d'ello el almirante, de las quales, por no hacer tan larga escriptura, dexo de escrivir, y basta esto, porque toda la jente hera como la susodicha.

---

[2] From Jamaica Columbus sailed directly to cape San Miguel in Española, proceeded along the south coast of that island, and then, by way of the island of Mona (which Las Casas says was so named by Columbus after Anglesey) to Isabella, which he reached 29 Sept. 1494 (Las Casas, i. 97–9). Bernáldez is not accurate in saying that at this time Columbus sailed among many other islands.

not make my book too long, I abstain from writing, and that
which has been written is enough, for all the people were as
those who have been already mentioned. And when he had
returned to Española, whence he had set out, he went forth
among the islands of the Caribs, near the part where he had
gone on his second voyage.[1]

[1] It would seem that Bernáldez here misunderstands some expression of

é quando bolvió para la Española, de donde avía partido, bino
á salir por entre las yslas de los Carives facia por donde había
ido el segundo viaje.

Columbus; he perhaps mistook an intention for an act. Las Casas (i. 99) says
that in a letter to the sovereigns, Columbus declared that he had wished to
proceed to 'destroy'—or, as Las Casas suggests, to 'discover'—the islands of
the cannibals, but 'so great had been his labours and watchings, night and day,
and so continuous, with no hour of rest', and so severe was his own illness at
the time, that he could not carry out his wish.

INDEX

VOLUME II

The Third and Fourth Voyages

PREFATORY NOTE

MR. CECIL JANE died on February 15, 1932, after a very brief illness, leaving the Introduction to the present volume, upon which he was working to within two days of his death, unfinished. His early death was a heavy loss both to learning and to the many friends who had followed his career with keen interest. He was already known as a lecturer on history in the Universities of Oxford and Aberystwith when, in 1929, the Hakluyt Society published the first volume of the present work, edited by him. The critical knowledge and judgement which he displayed in his introduction and notes to that volume quickly gained for him a high reputation as an authority on Columbus and on the early history of Spanish America. In appreciation of his work, the municipal authorities of Genoa presented him with facsimiles of all the Columbian documents belonging to that city, while he was frequently consulted by historians in France and Spain as well as in England.

Although Mr. Jane had only written about one-third of his projected Introduction to the present volume, the President and Council of this Society felt that no other person could complete it in a manner which would do justice to its author, and therefore decided to publish the fragment just as he left it. The text which he used was that established by De Lollis (*Scritti di Cristoforo Colombo*), except in the case of the *Relación* of Diego Méndez, where he followed Fernández de Navarrete. Professor E. G. R. Taylor was good enough to write a supplementary introduction, 'Columbus and the World-Map', to supply notes on the documents and to fill in the routes on the two maps. Mrs. Peter Cornish has kindly read the proofs and compiled the Index, while the present writer has arranged the material, supplied some notes, and seen the work through the press. But most of the labour and all the inspiration were Cecil Jane's.

EDWARD LYNAM.

September, 1932.

CONTENTS OF VOLUME II

LIST OF MAPS AND ILLUSTRATIONS

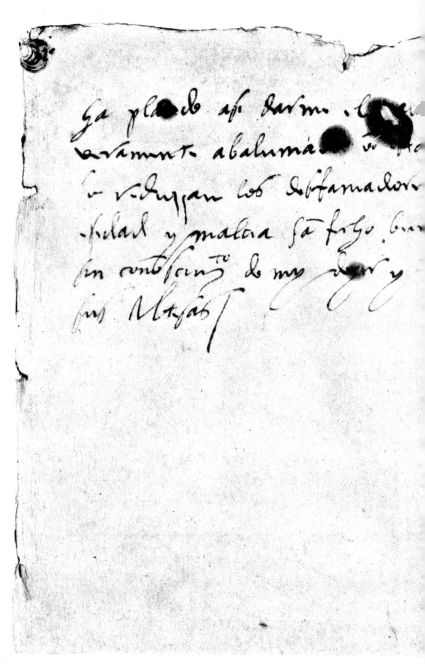

EXTRACT FROM COLUMBUS'

Written during the first voyage. From the original i

on d-ttos a fanes y p. l. gggs
rando vitoria. plos a dios
d my fonrra g con tanta dssho
d-my - dsfamado my ēpr̄sa
l briros - asycamiamunto d.

MARGARITA I.

11°

Cubagua I.

Cordil

Rio de Paria

Boca Aj.

G

R

P

A

R

I

A

10°

M   O   N   A   G   A   S

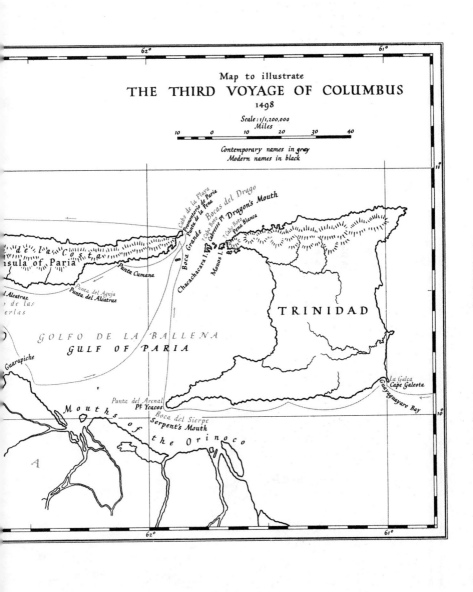

Map to illustrate
THE THIRD VOYAGE OF COLUMBUS
1498

Scale : 1/1,200,000
Miles

10 0 10 20 30 40

Contemporary names in grey
Modern names in black

62° 61°

11°

Cabo de la Playa
Promontorio de Paria
Punta de la Peña
Bocas del Drago
Pt Dragon's Mouth
Boca Grande
Cabeza Peña Blanca
Chacachacare I.
Monos I.
Cabo Boto

d e l a C o s t a
sula of Paria
Punta Cumana
Punta del Aguja
Punta del Alcatraz

Alcatraz
de las
erlas

TRINIDAD

GOLFO DE LA BALLENA
GULF OF PARIA

Guarapiche

La Galea
Cape Galeota
Guayaguayare Bay

Punta del Arenal
Pt Ycacos
Boca del Sierpe
Serpent's Mouth

M o u t h s
o f   t h e   O r i n o c o

10°

62° 61°

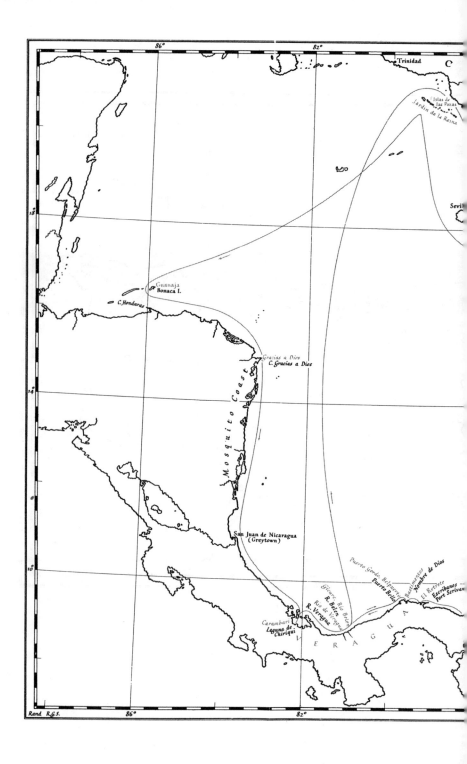

86°   82°   Trinidad C

Islas de
las Fozas
Jardin de la Reina

Sevi

18°

Guanaja
Bonaca I.

C. Honduras

Gracias a Dios
C. Gracias a Dios

14°

Mosquito Coast

San Juan de Nicaragua
(Greytown)

10°

Puerto Gordo. Belpuerto
Bastimentos
Nombre de Dios
Gigante Rio Belen
Puerto Bello
R. Belen
El Retrete
Rio de Veraguas
Escribanos
R. Veragua
Port Scrivan

Carambari
Laguna de
Chiriqui

V E R A G U A

Rand R.G.S.   86°   82°

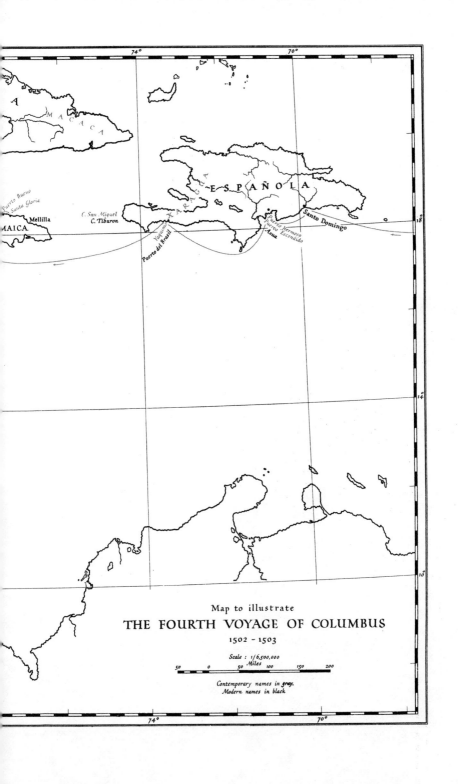

Map to illustrate
THE FOURTH VOYAGE OF COLUMBUS
1502 - 1503

Scale : 1/6,500,000
Miles

Contemporary names in grey.
Modern names in black.

INTRODUCTION
THE NEGOTIATIONS OF COLUMBUS WITH FERDINAND AND ISABELLA

1

AMONG the factors which determined the conduct of Columbus during his four voyages and throughout his whole later career, a foremost place must be assigned to the character of the reception with which he met at the Castilian court when he sought to obtain material assistance to enable him to execute the design which he had formed. Such assistance was absolutely necessary for him; whatever may have been the nature of the objective which he set before himself, unaided he could not hope even to attempt its attainment. Had he designed no more than to sail across the Atlantic, he would still have required help; 'a poor foreigner', he would have been unable to procure a ship, nor, had a ship been at his disposal, would he have been able to find a crew to man her. His need was the greater, since he assuredly aspired to win for himself something more substantial than that barren reputation which might be the portion of a successful navigator. If he desired fame, he still more desired wealth, position, and power, deliverance from that obscurity and poverty in which he had been born, from that subjection against which his very soul revolted. He was thus compelled to seek assistance, but when he did so, modest as were the means for which he asked, he encountered very considerable difficulties. The King of Portugal, to whom he first applied, was deeply committed to African adventure and wedded to the attempt to open the easterly route to India; he listened, indeed, to the proposals which were laid before him, but he listened only in the end to reject them. Disappointed at Lisbon, Columbus turned to Castile, to meet there with a reception which was little more encouraging. He was obliged to consume some seven or eight years in urging his case upon the sovereigns and their council, or in awaiting some definite answer from them, and it was, perhaps, only at the eleventh hour, when his patience was almost exhausted and his hope almost dead, that he obtained that for which he pleaded.

So much is attested by all who have borne witness on the matter. Columbus himself refers more than once to the painful character of his experiences at the Castilian court; he complains of the delays which he endured and of the reluctance of those whom he approached even seriously to consider his proposals. His statements are elaborated and emphasized in the *Historie* and the *Historia de las Indias*, where this period of his life is depicted as having been a time when he was constantly baulked of his hopes and when he was forced to taste the bitter cup of repeated disappointment. Peter Martyr Angleria declares that it was 'with difficulty' that Columbus obtained three small vessels for his voyage, and this testimony carries the greater weight since the letter, in which it is contained, probably bears a semi-official character. That there were difficulties and delays is, indeed, the one indubitable fact which emerges from that dark obscurity in which the early history of Columbus is enveloped. It is the one fact for which there is, perhaps, something in the nature of independent and documentary evidence. The existence of records of payments made to him from the Castilian Treasury some years before the date of the first voyage may not unreasonably be regarded as showing that he was then already negotiating with Ferdinand and Isabella and urging them to embrace 'the enterprise of the Indies'.

While, however, it is certain that Columbus found it no easy matter to obtain the assistance which he sought, the origin and the nature of the difficulties which he encountered are by no means clearly revealed. It has been very generally assumed, and it has often been asserted as a fact, that the root cause of his troubles was the character of those to whom consideration of his offers was entrusted by the sovereigns. It is, indeed, admitted that some part in creating delays was, or at least may have been, played by the fact that the attention of Ferdinand and Isabella was absorbed by the war of Granada. It is admitted that this war taxed the resources of Castile to the uttermost and that the exiguous revenues of the Crown were possibly unable to bear any additional strain, however slight. But it is contended that any such causes of difficulty were of secondary importance and that they cannot be regarded as having determined the attitude adopted by the sovereigns and their advisers. That attitude is declared to have been the result of the mentality of those who examined the proposals of Columbus. It is alleged that they were unwilling to hear and that they were even intellectually incapable of understanding the case which he presented and the arguments upon which that case rested. It is at least suggested that the advisers of Ferdinand and Isabella were the victims of their own preconceived ideas, that they were both ignorant and obstinate, that they were carried away by prejudice, all the stronger and all the more insurmountable because it was in accord with orthodox religious opinion and reinforced by all the weight of ecclesiastical authority. Betrayed by those upon whose counsel they relied, the sovereigns were led to play the part of the Man with the Muck Rake, as they concentrated their attention upon the Moorish war and refused to lift their eyes to behold that dazzling crown of glory which was held out towards them. They were offered dominion over a New World; they seemed to be reluctant to accept the offer, and the curious spectacle was presented of aspiring rulers hesitating to grasp a prize, than which none could be more calculated to satisfy even the most vaulting ambition.

This view of the origin of the difficulties of Columbus, and of the nature of the opposition with which he met, is embodied in the classical version of the story of the discovery and has been accepted with little or no hesitation by the majority of writers. It is primarily derived from the pages of the *Historie* and the *Historia de las Indias*, in which the advisers of Ferdinand and Isabella are charged with having failed to make any impartial examination of the case presented to them. It is there asserted that to the arguments which were adduced in support of the project, some were content to return a simple negative, disdaining even to discuss the matter. Some argued that, if the Antipodes existed, they would long since have been discovered; some that their discovery would be an achievement of no value, since they would be found to be entirely, or almost entirely, covered by water. Some held that any land which might exist in the other hemisphere was certainly both uninhabited and uninhabitable by man. Some denied that a voyage of such prolonged duration as that which was projected could be made, since sufficient supplies of food could not be carried. Some insisted that, were the Antipodes to be reached, return from them would be impossible, since, owing to the sphericity of the globe, the ascent to Spain would be so arduous that it could not be accomplished by any ship even were that ship favoured by the mightiest wind. Some rested their objection upon theological grounds, and to the assertions of Columbus opposed the supreme authority of St. Augustine of Hippo. Las Casas insists that the greatest ignorance of cosmography then prevailed in Castile, and in this ignorance he is disposed to find the chief source of opposition to the project. His piety, however, compels him to admit that the truest explanation of all that occurred must be sought in the mysterious workings of the Divine Providence.

The impression thus conveyed by the *Historie* and the *Historia de las Indias* is conveyed also by Columbus himself. In his references to this period of his life he declares that he then received encouragement from no one, with the honourable exception of Antonio de Marchena or of 'two friars'.[1] He alleges that it was in vain that he employed every argument. Those who should have been moved remained placidly indifferent, shrinking from embarking upon a course of action the issue of which might even appear to be uncertain. He complains that he was ridiculed and exposed to contempt, and that his ideas were regarded as the product of an untutored or disordered mind, as being fantasies such as might be expected to be born in the fevered brain of a wild visionary. He suggests that to the very end he failed to carry conviction to those who were resolved not to be convinced; if Ferdinand and Isabella did at last accede to his requests, it was because they were divinely led to do so, because where man could not instruct or persuade, the Holy Trinity inspired.

In favour of the generally accepted view, there is thus some considerable body of evidence, nor is there available any

[1] ii. 244, Cebreus; ii. 232, Deza.

direct evidence to support a contrary opinion. It would, however, be unwise therefore to conclude that this view must be regarded as being established beyond all dispute or to suppose that the case as it has been presented has been presented with entire justice. There is, on the contrary, some reason for doubting whether the story of this period in the life of Columbus has been accurately told, whether the opposition to him was really so irrational as has been contended. It may be questioned whether the advisers of Ferdinand and Isabella were so unenlightened, whether they were either ignorant or prejudiced; it may be questioned whether, in the circumstances in which they were placed, they would have been justified in recommending an immediate acceptance of the proposals or in tendering any other advice than that which they did in fact tender.

2

To unravel the true story of the negotiations between Columbus and the Castilian court would certainly be a less difficult task if he had left any connected account of this period of his life. No such account, however, exists; on the contrary, the references which he does make to the events which preceded the first voyage are both fragmentary and somewhat obscure; they are scattered through letters written long afterwards and appear in documents which are primarily concerned with other matters; they are, as it were, rather incidental than formal. He does not describe the precise character of the case which he presented, nor does he detail the arguments which he advanced in its support. He no more than asserts that he pointed out the spiritual and temporal advantages which would ensue upon prosecution of 'the enterprise of the Indies', and that he insisted upon the obligation, laid upon great princes and upon their subjects, to engage in magnanimous undertakings, justifying this contention by citing the examples of Alexander and Nero in the past and of the Portuguese kings in more recent times. To the objections urged by those who were disinclined or who were wholly unwilling to accept his proposals, he makes no more than a passing allusion, alleging that his opponents were steeped in a dull conservatism and that they were therefore reluctant to follow any adventurous course. He creates the impression that, being themselves blind, they charged him with being ignorant or insane, and that they returned no reasoned answer to him because they were unable to do so, taking refuge, since they had no other recourse, in abuse or ridicule of his project and of himself. But he does nothing to establish the justice of this impression. His assertions are no more than assertions; it is as legitimate to deny as it is to affirm their accuracy. The contribution which he makes to the elucidation of the story of his negotiations is thus less valuable than might, perhaps, have been expected or hoped; upon the dark places in that story he throws no very certain light.

That light may well seem to be less certain, and rather to emphasize than to diminish the darkness, since it is easy to show that Columbus was guilty both of inconsistency and of inaccuracy. When his various statements are compared with one another, they are found to be sometimes mutually destructive and at other times at least difficult to reconcile; he makes some assertions which are demonstrably, and others which are probably, untrue. If he pleaded his cause in vain for fourteen years at the court of Lisbon, he cannot have also been from the first so resolved to enter the service of Ferdinand and Isabella as to have been unwilling to listen to the overtures which he received from Portugal, from France, and from England. If he was constantly encouraged by the unswerving faith of 'two friars', it cannot have been from Antonio de Marchena alone that he received encouragement. He cannot have spent fourteen years in endeavours to persuade 'the King of Portugal', since during that period John II succeeded his father, Affonso V, nor can the Portuguese king have been at once altogether blind and distinguished for his far-sightedness and intelligence. His statement that he left wife and children in order to enter the service of Ferdinand and Isabella must, perhaps, be regarded as inexact; he does not otherwise suggest that he had any children by his wife except his son, Diego, who accompanied him to Castile. Nor is it in fact true that he experienced so little sympathy as he asserts; it was not only by Antonio de Marchena, it was not only by 'two friars', that he was encouraged; he secured the support of at least one powerful grandee, of at least one mighty ecclesiastic, and of at least one influential lady of the court, while there is every reason to believe that several other personages of importance heard his proposals with favour and strongly urged their acceptance. It may thus appear that a witness, in whose evidence such manifest defects are to be found, deserves no credence at all.

To these defects, however, it is easy to attach an undue significance. It must be remembered that it is not entirely just to expect to find in the references which Columbus makes to this period that scrupulous accuracy of statement which might be desired and which in other circumstances might be legitimately demanded. Those references are, after all, somewhat incidental; they should not be treated as if they formed part of a considered report upon his negotiations with Ferdinand and Isabella and still less as if they had been made upon oath in a court of justice. They were made, moreover, long after the event, and it is no more than reasonable to allow, therefore, a certain latitude to their maker; quite apart from the fact that in matters of detail his memory may have played him false, it is perhaps only natural that the sorrows of that time should have made a more acute impression upon him than its joys, and that, looking back years afterwards, he should have entertained a more lively recollection of the bitterness, than of any sweetness, in his experiences.

Nor must the intellectual character of the man be forgotten. Columbus was not highly educated; he had not been carefully trained in habits of systematic thought, nor had he ever learned the value of exact expression. He had all that inclination towards exaggeration which marks the untutored mind; he was even unconsciously prone to make emphatic statements when qualified statements would have been more appropriate. So much is abundantly clear from the descriptions which he has left of the lands which he discovered. When he overestimated the area, when he exaggerated the perfection of the climate, the fertility, the mineral wealth, and the populousness of Española, he was perhaps hardly aware that he had in any wise deviated from the truth, nor did he perhaps appreciate the fact that upon many occasions he found to be altogether extraordinary that which, had his practical or intellectual experience been wider, he would have found to be altogether commonplace. But those who are inclined to form extravagant estimates of the material are even more inclined to form such estimates of the moral; a man to whom a small nugget of gold appears to be enormous, a collection of rude huts to be a great city, is likely enough to find intense hostility in a mere difference of opinion and to convert a trivial obstacle into a very mountain of difficulty. He is the more likely to do so with the passage of time when salient features, instead of assuming in his mind their due proportions, stand out clearly to the obscuring of all features which are less prominent.

In the case of some of his apparent mis-statements, it is perhaps a little hypercritical to regard them as mis-statements. It is strictly true that he cannot have negotiated for fourteen years with 'the King of Portugal'; his negotiations, if they extended over such a period, must have been actually conducted not with one king, but with two kings. Men of far greater education than Columbus, however, and men far more habituated to the exact use of words, have been guilty of such venial inaccuracies; they have thought rather of the office than of the individual holder of that office, and that in such laxity of thought the origin of the error committed here by Columbus is to be found is sufficiently probable. His mistake is the more venial, the less significant, since in actual fact the greater part of his negotiations must have been conducted with one individual monarch, and since it is at least possible that, even while Affonso V was still king, it was to his son and heir that Columbus more especially addressed himself and from whom he expected to secure that which he sought. John II was interested, as his father had not been interested, in exploration and in discovery; it is to his lively intelligence that Columbus bears witness and to his will to adventure, while, even before he ascended the throne, he undoubtedly exerted no inconsiderable influence upon the conduct of affairs.

In the same tendency towards unconscious, rather than towards deliberate, exaggeration may perhaps be found the cause of the inaccuracy and inconsistency which marks his references to the degree of sympathy and support which he received. As he looked back upon the period of his negotiations, as the bitter memory of the repulses which he had suffered returned to him, it was hardly more than natural that he should almost forget that he met also with encouragement. That at one moment he should have been able only to recall the moral assistance which was rendered to him by 'two friars', that at another he should even forget that he had received such assistance from more than one single individual, is not surprising. Most men who have endured disappointment, who have met with coldness where they hoped to find warmth, with indifference or hostility where they hoped to find enthusiasm and friendliness, are disposed to such forgetfulness. Nor is it by any means improbable that it was from no more than one or two individuals that Columbus received that degree of understanding for which his sensitively poetical nature must have craved; it is not improbable that if at one moment he felt that he had received such understanding from two men, at another he should have recalled some real or imagined lack in one of the two and in all sincerity have believed that one man alone had been faithful to him from first to last. It is, moreover, more than possible that when he so wrote, he was thinking less of material than of moral aid and that he legitimately ignored the help which he had received from such men as Luis de la Cerda, Duke of Medinaceli, because that help had not been of the type of which a man of his temperament stood so desperately in need. His references would appear to be to the whole period of his negotiations, or if they were to a part of that period only, then to the earlier rather than to the later. It is permissible to argue that it was only in the last stages of his struggle that he enjoyed the countenance of the Cardinal of Spain, of Juana de la Torre, and of the others who are known or who are supposed to have shown him favour. It may well be true that, when all was darkest and when he was most in need of sympathy, he was in fact as friendless as he represents himself to have been. His technical inaccuracy thus becomes one of slight importance; it may, perhaps, have been hardly an inaccuracy at all.

Nor should much weight be attached to the inconsistency which exists between his assertion of constant devotion to the service of Ferdinand and Isabella and his admission that, before he approached them, he had vainly endeavoured to persuade the King of Portugal to embrace his project. His enemies had accused him of actual, or of meditated, disloyalty, and it was natural that he should protest his unfaltering allegiance; they had, at least in his opinion, belittled the service which he had rendered, and it was natural that he should insist upon the steadfastness with which he had served. It is true that, in so doing, he was guilty of some exaggeration, but this exaggeration may have been more apparent than real. If he would appear to have ignored his earlier overtures to John II, he was perhaps intending no more than to assert that, from the moment when he entered the service of the sovereigns, he had lent no ear to offers from any other quarter. In making such an assertion, he was probably asserting no more than the truth. There is no reason to believe that he ever entertained the idea, attributed to him, of handing over Española to some foreign power. Any attempt to realize such an idea would have been, as he himself says, foredoomed to failure; it would have indicated a complete inability to recognize the facts of the situation, and despite his mysticism, despite his tendency to dream dreams, he was not without appreciation of realities.

Upon two occasions only, indeed, would he appear to have supplied any ground for questioning his absolute loyalty to the Castilian Crown. On his return from his first voyage, he put into the Tagus, proceeded to Lisbon and was received by John II. As he himself admits, his action gave rise to some suspicion, nor is his explanation of his conduct entirely convincing. He declares that stress of weather forced him to shelter in the river, but while there is no doubt that he had passed through a storm and while it is probable enough that the condition of the *Niña* rendered it imperative that he should seek some harbour of refuge, his selection of the Tagus was as unreasonable as it was impolitic. The entrance to that river was difficult to negotiate; the distance to some Galician port was not so much greater as sensibly to increase the danger of shipwreck, and it would have been possible for him, as it was for Martin Alonso Pinzón, to have made for a Castilian harbour. That he did not do so may be explained upon various grounds. It is conceivable that he was unmanned by the storm, as he was generally unmanned by rough seas, and that he therefore allowed his fear to overcome his discretion; finding himself outside the mouth of the Tagus, he entered it under the influence of terror, of dread lest at the eleventh hour he should be drowned within sight of land and be deprived of the fruits of all his labours. It may be that he suspected Pinzón of some desire to usurp the credit of the discovery, and that he resolved to reach shore at the earliest possible moment, in order that the news might first reach Ferdinand and Isabella from himself. It may be that he was actuated by a desire to parade his triumph before the king who had refused to listen to him. No one of these motives, however, appears to be entirely adequate, since it was so obviously unwise of him to seek refuge in a harbour belonging to a monarch who was almost openly hostile to Castile, and since it was still more unwise of him to seem to be on friendly terms with that monarch. It is thus at least arguable that his motive is to be found in his uncertainty concerning the manner in which he would be received by the sovereigns, an uncertainty which is revealed in the *Letter* describing the first voyage. By preparing a way in which he might, if need arose, renew his interrupted relations with the Portuguese court, he might safeguard his own future; he might, as it were, address a warning to Ferdinand and Isabella that it was not upon them alone that he relied for the means which would enable him to pursue his enterprise, that it was within his power to transfer to another the gift which he had made to them. That such was his motive was undoubtedly alleged at the time; the allegation is not inconsistent with the businesslike side to the character of Columbus, and it is by no means entirely improbable that, to this extent, he then wavered in his loyalty to the sovereigns.

Upon a second occasion, he would, perhaps, seem to have wavered more decidedly. When Bobadilla arrived at Santo Domingo, Columbus at first refused to recognize the validity of the powers with which the royal envoy was invested, denying that the sovereigns could vary the terms of the *Capitulations* or affect his own status as viceroy. It was alleged that he went farther and that for a moment at least he entertained some idea of offering armed resistance. It is, however, hard to believe that, even in the hour of such intense distress, he should have been so far blind to facts as to imagine that the Spaniards in the island would rally to his side or that the natives, even had they been eager to do so, could have successfully defended him against the settlers. On the other hand, his mere refusal immediately to acknowledge Bobadilla, however understandable, however capable of plausible justification, however strictly defensible, was yet an indication that he fell short in some measure of that height or depth of unquestioning obedience which monarchs of that age expected from their servants and which contemporary conceptions of loyalty recognized as being obligatory upon subjects.

When, however, so much has been admitted, the steady allegiance of Columbus to those whose commission he bore cannot be seriously doubted. His letters to Ferdinand and Isabella are instinct with a spirit of submissive loyalty, which, when every allowance has been made for the formalities of correspondence in that age between a subject and his sovereigns, can still only be regarded as being no less genuine than it was entire. His references to the monarchs in his other letters are of the same character; if fault is to be found with his expressions, it is that they are too humble, that they border upon the abject. Even when he had been removed from his governorship, even when in his heart he felt that Ferdinand and Isabella had broken the solemn undertaking which they had given to him, so that, as he says, 'in this neither justice nor mercy has been regarded', it is only in one or two chance phrases that some complaint of royal ingratitude can be detected. In protesting, therefore, that he desired only to serve the Castilian Crown, he was, perhaps, no more than expressing a truth so far as his period of service was concerned, nor does that truth become more than a technical falsity because earlier in his life he had wished to assume another allegiance. It is not a falsity such as would serve to discredit him as a witness.

Nor is this the effect of the inaccuracy, if inaccuracy it be, of his declaration that, in order to enter the service of Ferdinand and Isabella, he 'left wife and children'. Even if it were proved that his wife was already dead when he came to Castile, and that by her he had no other child than Diego, his statement would be no more than a somewhat pardonable exhibition of over-emphasis, of over-emphasis such as might be expected from a man of poetic temperament writing under the influence of intense depression and eager to display both the greatness of his past devotion and the magnitude of the wrongs which had been inflicted on him. It is, however, at least possible that his statement is accurate. It must be remembered that, concerning his married life, nothing can really be said to be known, since the account which is given in the *Historie* and the *Historia de las Indias* will not bear critical examination. The very identity of his wife is uncertain; it is no more than an assumption, based upon the statement of Las Casas, that 'he had been delivered from his wife in order that he might devote himself to his enterprise', that he was a widower when he arrived in Castile; it is no more than an assumption that Diego was the only issue of his marriage. It follows that when he asserted that he 'left wife and children, whom I never saw again', he may have been stating a fact.

That he was stating a fact is, perhaps, suggested by a passage which appears in a letter addressed by him to his son, Diego. During his residence in Castile, and probably when he was at Córdoba, he formed a liaison with Beatrix Enriquez, who bore him a son, Ferdinand. Of the details of this intrigue or romance, of the manner in which it began, of the time for which it lasted, of the manner in which it ended, no more is known than that it was broken while both parties to it were still alive. That in his treatment of Beatrix, Columbus found some cause for self-reproach is, however, clear; he instructed Diego to pay to her a small sum of money annually, because on her account his conscience was burdened. He adds that he is unable to explain this statement more fully, and hence the reason for his sense of guilt can only be conjectured, and of the conjectures which have been advanced some are manifestly absurd. It has been suggested that he was troubled because his union with her had not received the blessing of the Church, but this suggestion cannot be seriously entertained. To suppose that his conscience was so tender would be to suppose that his moral standards were radically different from those of the most respectable among his contemporaries. That age was as tolerant as is the present towards such voluntary alliances. Ferdinand the Catholic set, in this respect, an example which his subjects were not slow to follow, or which, perhaps, they had rather anticipated. The biographer of the Cardinal of Spain, 'the glory of the house of Mendoza', regards the amorous adventures of his hero as being very far from discreditable to him, and Rodrigo Ponce de León, in the eyes of Andrés Bernáldez the very pattern of chivalry and upright conduct, was certainly not a model of chastity. There is no reason for supposing that Columbus held more rigid ideas on the subject of sexual morality than those which were current in his day; on the contrary, if Michele de Cuneo may be credited, he was extremely sympathetic towards those who were subject to temptation, and that the Italian was not here guilty of misrepresentation is suggested, if it be not proved, by a passage in a letter written by Columbus himself.

Nor can it be legitimately argued that his conscience was troubled because a child was the fruit of this illicit union. It is true that a legal distinction was drawn between those who were born in, and those who were born out of, wedlock, but this distinction was in practice often almost obliterated, and in no case did any stigma really attach to the illegitimate. Ferdinand the Catholic was ever solicitous for the welfare of his natural children, even to the extent of quarreling with the Holy See on account of one of his sons; Isabella herself attended the wedding of a daughter of the Cardinal of Spain, nor would the public conscience appear to have been greatly outraged when Archbishop Alonso Carrillo caused Troilus to be buried before the high altar of the cathedral of Toledo. The attitude of the age is, indeed, somewhat forcibly illustrated by the remark of one chronicler that a certain bishop must have been a very saint, since, 'so far as is known', he had no bastards, and by the contempt which was poured upon the half-brother and predecessor of Isabella on the ground that he had not proved the consummation of his union with his mistresses. It can thus have hardly been a cause of self-reproach to Columbus that his son Ferdinand had been born, a son whom he frankly acknowledged and to whom he was very tenderly attached.

It is equally improbable that the cause of that self-reproach is to be found in the fact that his liaison with Beatrix was no more than temporary in character. In that age fidelity to a mistress would seem to have been determined solely by her retention of the power of physical attraction, nor was a transference of male affection regarded as being in any way reprehensible. So wayward was the love of Ferdinand that Isabella was constantly troubled and was careful to select as her personal attendants those ladies whose beauty was rather of the soul than of the body. The Cardinal of Spain was hardly less catholic in his appreciation of feminine charms than he was in his religious opinions, while the genealogical notes of Galindez Carvajal reveal clearly enough that the affections of the grandees and notables of the period were rarely fixed steadfastly upon a single individual. If it be true that Columbus not merely broke off his relations with Beatrix, but also, as Michele de Cuneo suggests, replaced her by another, he acted as, in the opinion of that period, he was assuredly entitled to act. He did nothing which his contemporaries would have regarded as unbecoming to a man of honour, or which would have incurred even the mildest ecclesiastical censure, and he can hardly have suffered pangs of conscience on this account.

It cannot even be supposed that he would have been so afflicted even if he had been guilty of seduction. Isabella is recorded to have regarded with marked concern the appearance at her court of any attractive maiden, and to have hastened to remove such temptation from the path of her husband by arranging a speedy marriage for each possible victim of his amorous attentions. The Cardinal of Spain is said to have prided himself on his success in assaulting the citadels of feminine chastity, and an anecdote related of one of the Enriquez family suggests that maidenly modesty was held to be almost unbecoming, maidenly innocence to be hardly meritorious. It is only at a somewhat later date that a change of opinion on this matter is to be traced, under the influence of that puritan revolution which was sponsored by Isabella and Cardinal Ximenes.

If, however, there were such laxity in the contemporary attitude towards sexual morality, there was much rigidity of attitude towards questions of manly honour. When the French general in southern Italy endeavoured to secure a military advantage by attacking the Spaniards at an hour earlier than that at which he had arranged with Gonsalvo de Córdoba that he would attack, his conduct was emphatically condemned, and the defeat which he sustained was regarded as being a just punishment for his breach of faith. According to Peter Martyr Angleria, Pedro Margarit resigned his command in Española because he felt 'certain scruples of honour', and these scruples were not improbably aroused by the orders which he received from Columbus, the execution of which would have involved the betrayal of a man to whom he was to profess friendship. If it be true that the Spaniards of that age were sometimes, and even always, ready to meet treachery with treachery, it is also true that they held treachery in contempt and that they placed a very definite limit upon the use of deception even in war; the story of the final struggle with the Moors abounds with illustrations of the manner in which an obligation of honour was regarded as absolutely binding, as being, perhaps, more binding than any other form of obligation. But as it was held to be imperative that a man should behave honourably towards other men, so it was held to be even more imperative that he should so behave towards women. Their virtue might be openly assaulted, but it ought not to be betrayed, and a promise to a lady should be kept even to death. A distinction was drawn between seduction, for which no abhorrence was felt, and seduction achieved as a result of some breach of faith, which was regarded as an offence against that code of honour which was so much more important and so much more binding than the moral code. If, therefore, Columbus achieved his conquest of Beatrix by inducing her to believe that he was unmarried, and still more if he did so by inducing her to believe that marriage would follow upon her surrender, he would have so acted as to incur the condemnation of his contemporaries and hence the later reproaches of his own conscience. The supposition that this is the explanation of the passage in his instruction to Diego is by no means unreasonable. It is in accord with the sentiment of the age, and it can hardly be regarded as being in disaccord with that which is known of the character of Columbus. Such an action as that of which he would in this case have been guilty cannot be held to have been impossible for a man who took for himself a reward which, save for a technicality, was certainly due to one of his sailors, or to a man who could devise that scheme for the capture of Caonabo which Alonso de Ojeda afterwards executed. This explanation of the passage is consistent also with his statement that he could not be more explicit concerning the reason for his sense of guilt; a father might well be unwilling to confess to his son that he had once acted in a manner which that son could not be expected to excuse or pardon, and such a confession would have been almost impossible for a man, such as Columbus, who was ever eager that others should think well of him and who reveals himself as pining for that affection, the danger of forfeiting which he would thus incur. But if this be the cause of those pangs of conscience, if he did induce Beatrix to believe that he was in a position to marry her when in fact he was not in that position, it follows that his wife must have been still alive when he was in Castile, and that so far from his statement that he left wife and children when he came to the court of Ferdinand and Isabella being untrue or inaccurate, it is an example of the revelation of a fact which he had otherwise been almost at pains to conceal.

The actual or apparent errors and inconsistencies in the

references which he makes to his negotiations with the sovereigns are thus, perhaps, less important than has been sometimes supposed, and are not of such moment as to detract from the value of his evidence as a whole. Nor is that value really diminished by the fact that the references date from a period long subsequent to the event. Columbus must at the moment have been aware of the manner in which he was received at the Castilian court, and he must then also have formed an opinion concerning the mental attitude of those with whom he came into contact, of their feeling towards himself. It can hardly be doubted that the events of this most critical period of his life were almost indelibly imprinted on his mind; it can hardly be supposed that he subsequently forgot that which then occurred, or that at some later date he came to believe that he had then formed any other impression concerning the circumstances in which and the reasons for which his proposals were not at once accepted, than that which he did in fact form at the time. His evidence, therefore, despite its late date, must be regarded as decisive in establishing that he did experience difficulties and delays; so much it would in reality do, even if it were wholly unsupported by other testimony.

It is, perhaps, hardly less decisive in revealing the opinion which he formed concerning the opposition which he encountered; it may, perhaps, be taken as proving him to have regarded that opposition as having been irrational and the product of ignorance and prejudice. His references to this period of his life are contained in letters addressed to the sovereigns, to Juana de la Torre, and to 'certain personages of the court'. They were thus made to persons who either knew or who were in a position to discover the facts and whose favour he was anxious to retain or to conciliate. Ferdinand and Isabella held his destiny in their hands; denied their countenance, he could not hope to continue the prosecution of 'the enterprise of the Indies', to defeat those who were, or whom he thought to be, eager to overthrow him, or even to escape a return to that poverty and obscurity from which he had so painfully emerged. And if he must therefore have been concerned not to offend the sovereigns, he was perhaps only a degree less concerned to secure the favour of the others to whom his letters were addressed. Juana de la Torre had been the nurse of Prince Juan; she exercised considerable influence, and when Columbus expatiated to her on the wrongs which he had suffered, or which he supposed himself to have suffered, at the hands of Bobadilla, he was clearly seeking her intervention on his behalf and was inviting her to assist him to secure the redress of his grievances. His letter to 'the personages of the court' is a frank appeal for sympathy and help; he exposes to them the injustice of which he felt that he had been the victim, and he implores them to consider his devotion to the Castilian Crown and the services which he had rendered. In such circumstances, for him to have lied would have been for him to commit a fatal blunder. It would have been for him to have done the very thing most calculated to alienate those whom he wished to conciliate; it would have been an act of supreme folly.

It would be idle to pretend that Columbus was never guilty of errors of judgement; he was so guilty on more than one occasion. But whatever else he was, he was not devoid of astuteness, and it is hardly credible that he should have been so blind to his own interest as to forget that Ferdinand and Isabella, and those who were in their court, could easily detect a gross misrepresentation of facts which were more or less within their own knowledge. It follows necessarily that he must have sincerely believed that the opposition, with which he met in the period before his first voyage, had been an unreasonable opposition, and that the hostility which he then encountered had been personal and even malicious. He must be supposed accurately to represent the impression which he had received at the moment, although it may be admitted that he may somewhat have emphasized the unhappy character of that impression, an emphasis naturally produced by lapse of time.

3

If, however, it must be admitted that Columbus can hardly have failed to retain a vivid memory of the events of this period of his life, and that he faithfully records the impression which was then made upon him, it does not therefore necessarily follow that his impression was just or that the opposition to him actually bore that character which he ascribes to it. It is, on the contrary, possible that the opinion which he formed, and which he expresses, was at least in some measure mistaken and that he misjudged those who refused or who were unwilling to countenance his enterprise. It must be remembered that, while he was assuredly in a position to reach an opinion, there is no proof that he was also in a position to verify that opinion, and that, however distinct may have been the impression made upon him, it can still have been no more than an impression. It would appear to have been sometimes forgotten that the obscurity, which so completely envelops the early life of Columbus, envelops also his negotiations with Ferdinand and Isabella, and that, however plausible may be the accounts which have been written of those negotiations, these accounts are still no more than conjectural, based not upon actual evidence but upon a conception of that which is regarded as probable. It is true that the sovereigns are known to have appointed a commission or commissions to investigate the offers made by Columbus and that the names of two of the commissioners have been preserved. But nothing more is definitely known concerning the manner in which the offers were treated, except the bare fact that they were not immediately but were ultimately embraced. There is no record of the proceedings of the commission; there is no proof that any formal meeting was held, and the graphic descriptions which have been written of the appearance of Columbus before his judges and of his facile triumph over his critics or opponents are mere products of the imagination. It is, perhaps, more probable than not that he was invited to state his case and that he was questioned concerning it; it is at least possible that objections were urged and that he was afforded some opportunity to answer those objections. Of so much, the presence of Talavera among the commissioners may be almost regarded as a guarantee; the first Archbishop of Granada was a man of vision and of rare tolerance, and it is only the personal animosity of Las Casas towards him which has created the belief that he was hostile to Columbus, the evidence of Peter Martyr Angleria showing that he was, as might be expected from such a man, rather favourably disposed towards him. But there is no definite proof that Columbus was so examined; there is no documentary account of the case which was submitted to the commission, and there is accordingly nothing to show conclusively that his opponents were so deaf to reason, so unwilling to listen to him, as he alleges them to have been.

Even if he were summoned before those especially appointed to report upon his offers, even if he then heard the objections which were urged against those offers, he was still in no position to know definitely either the terms of the report which was presented to the sovereigns, or the grounds upon which that report was actually based, or, indeed, whether any report at all was rendered. Talavera and his colleagues constituted no more than a special committee for the investigation of a particular matter; they did not form the Royal Council, by which body alone a decision could be reached and submitted to the sovereigns, and to which body alone, or to the sovereigns personally, the opinion of the commissioners could be frankly communicated. It cannot be seriously supposed that Columbus was present at any meeting of the Council of Castile; it is to the last degree improbable that he received any official information concerning that which passed at the council. It is, indeed, unlikely that more was conveyed to him than that his proposals could not be accepted, or that they could not be accepted immediately, with, perhaps, the addition of some ostensible reasons for this decision, reasons which may or may not have borne some relation to those upon which the decision was actually based. Even in the most modern and democratic states, those who are responsible for the conduct of affairs are rarely willing frankly to reveal the grounds upon which they act; the grounds which they allege publicly are not infrequently designed rather to obscure than to make known the truth. Under a despotic system of government this is even more often the case, if only because there is under such a system less need for the conciliation or consideration of public

opinion. Merely upon general grounds, then, it is improbable
that Columbus was informed of the tenor of any discussion
which took place in the Council or in the presence of the
sovereigns, or of the arguments which led to the decision
reached. It becomes more improbable when the special circumstances of the case are considered. It is obvious that in
any discussion which occurred some reference must have been
made to the relations between Castile and Portugal and to
the possible effect upon those relations of prosecution of the
scheme suggested by Columbus ; that such reference was made
is, indeed, shown by the terms of the royal *cedula* forbidding
the expedition to proceed along the African coast. But the
relations between the two States were somewhat delicate,
and to improve them was a cardinal point in the policy of
Ferdinand and Isabella, one to which they attached so much
weight as to force their favourite daughter to contract a
marriage against which her conscience revolted. To have
canvassed the diplomatic situation publicly would in the
circumstances have been unwise and even dangerous ; to
have revealed the influence which that situation must have
exercized in determining the attitude of the Royal Council in
this case to Columbus, would have been tantamount to can-
vassing it publicly, since he was as loquacious as he was
reticent. It may be added that any such frankness would
have been antipathetic to the sovereigns. In that age the
value of secrecy in all proceedings of State was exaggerated
into an article of faith ; the most skilled ruler was held to be
the ruler who could most completely hide his thoughts and
motives, who was the most convincing liar and the most
unscrupulous deceiver. To this conception of statesmanship,
Ferdinand the Catholic certainly subscribed. To pursue a
course of action, the springs of which were kept secret, was
almost habitual to him, nor is there any ground for supposing
that in this respect he was at variance with the ideas of
Isabella. It would thus have been indeed surprising if Columbus had been informed of the actual process by which the
Royal Council, or the sovereigns, reached a decision ; it is
probable enough that he was not even informed whether a
decision had been reached and that he was rather allowed to

await an answer indefinitely. In any case, he could do no more than arrive at a conjectural explanation of the attitude adopted towards him. Something, it is true, he may have gathered from the gossip of the court, from half-heard remarks, from looks, from the accidental and partial revelations of some who knew the facts, but there is little likelihood that he had any clearly conveyed information or direct personal knowledge, and it may be regarded as certain that he had no detailed information and no complete knowledge. The impression which he formed was essentially an impression; while he was sincerely convinced that it was just, he had no proof that it was so, no proof that it was not far less favourable to his opponents than the facts warranted.

He was, perhaps, so placed that he was more likely than not to form an unduly unfavourable impression of all that occurred and of the conduct of those who considered his proposals. It may be admitted that, during a large part of the time during which negotiations were in progress, he was only a passive spectator, that he was awaiting a reply and that while he so waited, he could do little or nothing, since to press too frequently for a decision might have the effect of producing a verdict adverse to him. Even so, however, he was still in a sense a principal actor in those events of which he records his opinion. The outcome of the deliberations was obviously of vital importance to him, and the very intensity of his consequent anxiety may well have obscured his vision and warped his judgement. He would have been more or less than human if he had been able to preserve an attitude of detachment at a time when his whole future was at stake. Deep feeling is rarely compatible with entire sobriety of judgement. As those who love and those who hate alike tend to be prejudiced, so those who enthusiastically embrace some cause are in danger of becoming bigoted; only the intellectual giant can view with absolute fairness a question upon which he holds strong views. To his depth of feeling on the subject of 'the enterprise of the Indies' the extant letters of Columbus bear eloquent testimony, nor can it be doubted that all through his life he was eager to fulfil that which he conceived to be his destiny. For this reason, if for no other, it is little likely that, during the period of his negotiations with Ferdinand and Isabella, he was capable of reaching a calm judgement. He must then have been the prey of hopes and fears so lively that they may well have disturbed his mental balance, that his mind must at least have been in a state of constant turmoil. But in view of the difficulties and delays which he encountered, it may be reasonably supposed that he was more often fearful than hopeful concerning the answer which he would receive, and it thus becomes probable that the impression left upon him was darkly coloured by his anxiety, that he was led to be less than just towards those who seemed to him to be labouring to prevent the realization of his dearest hopes.

And if anxiety may so have betrayed him into injustice, the circumstances of his previous career were such as also to lead him to form an unduly dark impression of the events of this time and of the actors in those events. Poverty, and that frustration of hope which is so constantly attendant upon poverty, may sometimes serve to refine and to exalt, but it is assuredly only in very rare instances that they do so, in the case of a chosen few whose souls are something purer, something nobler, than those of their fellows. A very contrary effect is produced upon the generality of mankind. Those who have tasted little or nothing of the sweetness of life, and who have been tortured by repeated blows of fortune, are thereby more often debased than refined, degraded than exalted. They lose all generosity of judgement; they become embittered and soured; they grow suspicious of all who seem to be more happily circumstanced than themselves, and they tend to regard them as being for that single reason almost their natural enemies. This effect is most surely and most strongly produced by material anxiety and want in the case of a man who is convinced that he is possessed of abilities beyond the ordinary, that he is fitted for something better and higher than a life of sordid struggling. Such a man becomes resentful that those whom he feels to be far less capable than himself, far less worthy of recognition, are yet successful and honoured. He revolts against the position of subordination which is his lot, against the fact that he is compelled oftentimes to obey where he is assured that it should be his to command, to humble himself before those whom he feels to be in truth his inferiors. He rails against fortune whose favours are so blindly distributed and so wrongly; he accuses the world of injustice. As his bitterness becomes more intense, as he suffers each fresh blow, he becomes the more convinced that he is wronged, that he is persecuted, that the human race is conspiring against him, denying him that which is his due, and that every man is hostile to him.

There is every reason for believing that Columbus was so influenced by the experiences through which he passed in the years which preceded his first voyage. He was born and bred in poverty; in childhood and in boyhood he endured to the full all those anxieties and sorrows which fall upon such as are condemned to battle for the bare necessities of life. Nor is there any very good reason for supposing that he had escaped at all from such distress when he appeared at the court of Ferdinand and Isabella. It is true that Oviedo declares that, during his residence at Lisbon, he contributed to the support of his father, a statement which might be taken to imply that he was then free from personal need. But this assertion is not confirmed by any other writer, and the account of Columbus in the *Historia Natural y General de las Indias* is so confused and so inaccurate that the testimony of this author cannot be given great weight and should perhaps be entirely rejected. It is also true that, if the story of his marriage as told in the *Historie* and in the pages of Las Casas were accepted as being substantially in accord with fact, it might be supposed that Columbus then attained some measure of material prosperity. Here again, however, doubt is far more legitimate than credence, and it would be altogether unwise to assume that when he married, he was at least momentarily relieved from financial distress. It may, indeed, be asserted with some assurance that, down to the eve of his first voyage, he was never free from anxiety, never released from the cramping fetters of poverty. In any case, he was certainly poor when he arrived in Castile, nor were the grants made to him from the royal Treasury so lavish in amount or so long continued as to do much more than preserve him for a time from actual want.

With more assurance it may be assumed that he was from the first convinced that he was capable of great deeds, and that he needed no more than an opportunity in order to attain both fame and fortune. The mere fact that he early abandoned the country of his birth and that way of living to which he had been accustomed, in order to embark upon a more adventurous career, argues that he was fired by a longing to improve his lot and that he believed himself to be able to do so. The very terms upon which he offered his services to Ferdinand and Isabella, terms which were seemingly more than exorbitant and of which he would not abate one iota, even when his prospects were at their darkest, are indicative of his almost sublime self-confidence, a quality which he displayed also in his manner of speaking of the lands which he proposed to discover, 'as if he had them in his chamber under lock and key'. His conviction of his own merit is evident in his extant letters; he had rendered to the sovereigns services such as no other man could have rendered, and if he might seem to be 'unlettered, a mere sailor', yet, 'out of the mouths of babes and sucklings, hath He ordained strength'. If he were despised by men, he was chosen of God, chosen to be His ambassador and to reveal the new Heaven and the new Earth.

Endowed with such a temperament and fired by such a conviction, Columbus could not but feel acutely the restraints imposed upon him by material circumstances. He could not but resent the denial of that opportunity, for which he longed, of which he was assured in his own mind that he could make so full a use, which was all that he needed in order that he might prove his worth and be enabled to reduce to shame and silence those who now regarded him with contempt or indifference. And he undoubtedly felt this the more acutely because he was blessed or cursed with the instincts of a poet. His extant writings, and the précis of his *Journal*, exhibit him as deeply sensible of the beauty of nature. He was entranced by the wonder of colour, by the scent of flowers, by the song of birds; he was profoundly alive to the fact that 'the Heavens declare the glory of God, and the firmament sheweth His handywork'. But as he was poetical in temper, so he was the prey of all that sensitiveness, or of all that hypersensitiveness, which would appear to be inseparable from the soul of an artist. During his first voyage, if the précis of the *Journal* may be trusted, he was deeply wounded by the treatment which he received from Martin Alonso Pinzón, as he was moved to tears of happiness by the kindness shown to him by Guacanagari when the *Santa Maria* was wrecked. While he was preparing for his second voyage, he was tortured by the slights, or by the imagined slights, which he suffered at the hands of those who were appointed to assist him; more than once he was driven to implore the sovereigns to intervene that he might be protected from insult. To the very end of his life he was the victim of this side of his nature; to the very end of his life he suffered that mental distress which falls to the lot of such as are cast in a softer mould than are the majority of their fellows.

His sensitiveness seemed to develop in him another quality of which he was possessed. It cannot be seriously doubted that he was by nature reticent. Had he not been, it would have been impossible for him to draw so dark a veil over his early life; some reference to his father, to his mother, would surely have escaped him, and he would perhaps have made more than one brief allusion to his wife or to his mistress. Had he not been reticent by nature, he would assuredly have revealed more clearly the hopes and dreams by which he was so inspired; he would, perhaps, have been unable to abstain from announcing the nature of the objective which he sought. As it was, he was self-condemned to mental isolation; he was unable to win that friendship or that love for which his sensitive nature craved; he was unable to confide in others the sorrows which he endured until at last they had become unendurable, and he was driven to burst forth into bitter lamentation over his own sufferings, driven to expose his wounds like some Neapolitan beggar. But the almost repellent frankness with which he revealed those wounds to the sovereigns, to Juana de la Torre, to 'certain personages of the court', may be legitimately regarded as the measure of his earlier abstinence from such frankness. It was the final blow inflicted upon him, when he was arrested by Bobadilla, that tore from his heart such confessions and which served to betray him into an exhibition of weakness, as pathetic as it was vain. In his earlier days, although he more than once foreshadowed that which was to come, although he more than once half revealed that yearning for sympathy which was at last to master him, he still endured in silence and in loneliness of soul. He brooded upon his undeserved misfortunes, upon his condition of poverty, to which he was led to ascribe all the difficulties which he encountered, all the frustration of hope. 'Gold is a thing most excellent,' he once cried, 'for he who possesses it may have what he will in this world', and thereby declared that it was to lack of material wealth that he attributed all the sorrows from which he suffered.

If upon such a man, convinced of his own capacity, ambitious, sensitive, and mentally isolated, poverty and all the ills which poverty implies had not exercised some adverse moral effect, it would have been indeed remarkable. Columbus would then be revealed as a man of exceptional moral fibre, of exceptional nobility of soul, of exceptional magnanimity; he would stand out as a superman, as having been more than deserving of the most enthusiastic panegyrics that could be showered upon him. But with all his greatness, and he was undoubtedly a great man, he was yet morally imperfect, and those very human imperfections, to which he was heir, were intensified by the material anxieties which he was condemned by fate to suffer. He became embittered and in his bitterness of soul he lost all readiness to credit others with sincerity or with a desire to be just. He felt that he was ill-used by the world and that he was persistently misjudged; 'should I build churches,' he was brought to cry at last, 'I should be accused of building lairs for robbers'. The hand of every man seemed to be against him; all who differed from him were moved by personal hostility; all who were not enthusiastically on his side were his enemies and malicious. He became convinced that he was persecuted; he ceased to be able to recognize that the fault might conceivably lie with himself, that his troubles might even conceivably be in some measure due to his own defects, that he could in anywise be the architect of his own sorrows. In his bitterness he was almost tempted to utter the prayer of the Psalmist, to call down curses upon those who seemed so to oppose him; 'may my enemies be confounded,' he wrote, 'and those who would not believe the message which I bore to them'.

In any event, perhaps, poverty would have produced some such effect upon him; it could but do so the more surely if, as is probable, he was from the first convinced that it was his destiny to perform some divinely ordained mission. Those who were, or whom he considered to be, hostile to him were not merely his enemies; they were the enemies of God. As he was the servant of Heaven, employed to carry out the work entrusted to him by the Almighty, so they were the servants of Satan, endeavouring to thwart the designs of Providence. It was impossible that they should be anything but malicious; to credit them with honesty of purpose, with sincerity, with any good qualities, would be to assert that the Wicked One himself had some redeeming virtues. His opponents were, in fact, sinning against the light. They knew in their hearts that the cause which he proclaimed was that of God, but they stifled the voice of conscience and denied the truth of that which they were well aware was true. To stand in the path of Columbus, to impede him or to attempt to impede him, to do anything but aid him actively, was to be guilty of the one unpardonable sin.

It was thus rather inevitable than merely natural that he should place the most unfavourable construction upon the attitude adopted by those whom he approached and that he should be more pessimistic than the facts warranted; the more so, since, as he himself admits, he was subject to fits of extreme depression. It was difficult for him or impossible for him to recognize that criticism did not necessarily imply hostility, or that a difference of opinion was not necessarily an expression of personal animosity. It is at least possible that he both underestimated the degree of sympathy, and over-estimated the degree of contempt, with which his proposals were regarded, and that, misled by his own feelings, he misinterpreted words or looks. And it is certain that he had a more acute memory for that which was unpleasant than for that which was pleasant; had it not been so, he would not so emphatically have declared that he met with no encouragement save from Antonio de Marchena, a statement which illustrates the pessimism which coloured his recollection of the facts. While, therefore, it may, and indeed must, be admitted that in his references to this period he was sincerely endeavouring to record the truth, it must be also admitted that his evidence is open to suspicion, and that the true story of the negotiations is not beyond all doubt that which he relates or suggests.

4

While some caution must thus be exercised in using the material supplied by Columbus himself, at least equal caution must be observed in dealing with that derived from other sources. Accounts of this period of his life are found both in the *Historie* and in the *Historia de las Indias*, and are in all essentials identical, alike in their record of events and in their estimate of the motives actuating those who were unfavourable to the prosecution of the enterprise. The two accounts, however, cannot be regarded as being entitled to the same degree of credit. The authenticity of the work ascribed to the son of the admiral is by no means established beyond dispute. It is true that on this point the testimony of Las Casas is sufficiently explicit; it does not, however, follow that it is therefore also decisive, nor, perhaps, would it ever have been so regarded, had it not been that the integrity and veracity of the witness have been somewhat hastily and somewhat unjustifiably assumed to be unimpeachable. And even if it be admitted that Ferdinand Columbus did write a life of his father in Spanish, and that of this life Alfonso Ulloa did produce an Italian version which had been preserved, the *Historie* would none the less be open to all the suspicion necessarily attaching to a translation, the character and the accuracy of which cannot be tested by reference to the original from which it was prepared. Its precise value must in any case remain somewhat dubious; so far as the negotiations between Columbus and the sovereigns are concerned, that value may be regarded as practically negligible. The *Historie* adds nothing to the information contained in the *Historia de las Indias*; at best, it does no more than reveal the principal source upon which Las Casas drew and indicate that he may be presumed to have accepted and to have repeated the tradition which passed current in the family of the admiral, as he might have been expected to do in view of the friendship which subsisted between him and the sons of Columbus. The work may thus be here dismissed from consideration; it is neither an independent source of information nor really confirmatory of the story told in the *Historia de las Indias*.

To that story, however, full consideration must be given. If Columbus supplied any verbal account of the period of the negotiations to his sons, it may be presumed that with this account Las Casas was fully conversant. He himself claims to have had access to 'the papers of the admiral' and to have made the fullest use of the materials thus placed at his disposal. He was, moreover, personally acquainted with some òf the chief actors in the events which culminated in the signing of the *Capitulations* and was thus in a position to check by means of independent inquiry any report of those events which he had received from the family of Columbus. His deep interest in all that concerned the Indies is beyond dispute, nor would it be legitimate to question his anxiety to obtain information regarding the discovery. A special value thus attaches to his testimony, which is, perhaps, the most important direct evidence which has been preserved.

Its value and its importance may none the less be very easily exaggerated. It would seem that the *Historia de las Indias* has been sometimes misjudged. It has been regarded as serious history, whereas it is no more than necessary to read a few chapters of the work in order to realize that it is a piece of special pleading; despite its length, its turgid style, and its assumption of sobriety, it is after all nothing but a party pamphlet. Las Casas was not concerned to discover the truth, nor did he make any effort to do so; his purpose was to secure evidence which would support the particular thesis which he was advancing, and, as he himself admits, he had no hesitation in ignoring any evidence which might have tended to controvert that thesis. Nor have the circumstances in which the work was written been always remembered. Las Casas was compelled, as he remarks, to rely very largely upon his memory, some part of the written materials which he had prepared having been destroyed, and nothing is more certain than that his memory was not invariably to be trusted. It would appear, indeed, to have been less defective than peculiar. He would seem to have been able to recall without difficulty even the minutest details which served to illustrate or to support his contentions regarding the affairs of the Indies. He would seem also to have been wholly unable to remember, or to have been well able to forget, even important facts which weighed against that thesis which lay so near his heart and which he was so concerned to maintain. This mental characteristic serves somewhat to discount the value of his testimony concerning the negotiations between Columbus and the sovereigns, since on the subject of those negotiations he was undoubtedly anxious to establish a certain conclusion.

It was his firm belief, or it was at least his reiterated opinion, that the Indies were the gift of God to Castile, a sacred trust committed to the Catholic sovereigns, and that Columbus was divinely chosen to reveal the existence of the New World and to be the means by which a rich harvest of souls should be garnered for Christ. It followed that those who assisted the discovery were true labourers in the vineyard and that those who opposed, and even those who did not actively assist, were in fact endeavouring to thwart the purposes of Heaven. Charity might, indeed, allow that they erred through ignorance, but they none the less erred, and were, wittingly or unwittingly, acting as servants of Satan, whose dominion over the New World was threatened and who was consequently eager to prevent the sovereigns from listening to the missioner of God. Holding such an opinion, however, Las Casas was no better able than was Columbus himself to believe that those who would not sustain 'the enterprise of

the Indies' could have been actuated by respectable motives
or that they could have honestly doubted the validity of the
case presented to them. He was bound to suppose them to
have been at best blind; it was difficult for him not to suppose
that they were malicious and that their failure to recognize
the truth was wilful. It was natural for him to feel concerning
them as the Spaniards in the New World felt concerning the
Indians who were not at once convinced of the truth of the
cardinal doctrines of the Christian faith and of the legitimacy
of the rule imposed upon them; it was natural for him to feel
that they were sinning against the light and that, if they were
not persuaded, it was because they had hardened their hearts
against the voice of persuasion.

Few men find it difficult to discover evidence in support
of an opinion which they have ardently embraced, and Las
Casas experienced no such difficulty at any period of his
career. It is, indeed, probable enough that in actual fact the
evidence which he desired to find did exist. It would be somewhat extraordinary if among those who were hostile to
Columbus there were not some who were dominated by their
own preconceived ideas and who were prejudiced judges.
Even in the most enlightened age, prejudice does not entirely
disappear, and the close of the fifteenth century was a period
when Europe was perhaps no more than emerging out of
darkness into light and when the very light was somewhat
fitful. It is reasonable to assume that, of the objections urged
against the project of Columbus, some were sufficiently
puerile and some indicative of ignorance. It is no less reasonable to assume that, were any such objections urged, they
would have been known to the family of the discoverer and
hence to Las Casas, and it is certain that he would have
recalled them when he was writing the *Historia de las Indias*,
since the fact that they were advanced seemed to justify his
point of view and to illustrate his contention. But it cannot
be therefore regarded as certain that no arguments of a
different character were produced. Had they been, Las Casas
might well not have heard of them, since Columbus would not
have been anxious to insist upon their existence when
describing this period of his life. Nor if he had learned from

other sources that rational objections to the enterprise were urged, would Las Casas have been likely to remember that he had done so. His faculty for forgetting that which he wished to forget would have served him; they would have escaped his memory as all escaped his memory which might have possibly cast a doubt upon his assertion that the Indians were wholly blameless in their conduct towards the Spaniards and that they were so free from all vice that they appeared not to have incurred the consequences of the Fall.

Even, however, if his memory had been as accurate as it was in some respects retentive, even if he had not held a particular view concerning 'the enterprise of the Indies', Las Casas might still have failed to believe that any valid objections could have been urged against the proposals of Columbus or that those who were hostile to him could have been anything but ignorant or prejudiced. It must be remembered that the *Historia de las Indias* was written at a much later date than that of these events and at a time when there had been a very great development in knowledge. It was by then obvious that many, if not all, of the assertions made by Columbus, or supposed to have been made by him, were fully justified. It was by then certain that vast and populous lands could be reached by sailing westwards across the Atlantic and that the circumnavigation of the globe was as practically as it was theoretically possible. The discovery and conquest of Mexico and Peru had proved that 'the Indies' were rich in gold and silver, and it was not less proved that the New World abounded in other commodities of value. Ideas which, at the close of the fifteenth century, had appeared to be fantastic, were, when Las Casas wrote, recognized as being entirely rational and had been adopted even by the most conservatively minded. But there are few who find it easy, and many who find it to be impossible, to realize that what to them is commonplace and obviously true may to those of any earlier generation have appeared strange and incredible. It is therefore not unreasonable to suggest that Las Casas may have been intellectually incapable of putting himself in the place of those who lived more than half a century before the date at which he was writing. It is probable enough that even if he heard that some of those who opposed Columbus did so upon grounds such as appealed to the most enlightened of their contemporaries, he was unable to believe that this had actually been the case and that he was thus led to reject the statement as being palpably untrue. It is possible enough that he was unintentionally less than just to those who did not favour 'the enterprise of the Indies'.

The possibility that he was so is the greater since he could not correct his memory or test the accuracy of any impression which he formed by reference to documentary material. Perhaps because he claims to have made use of 'the papers of the admiral', it would appear to have been sometimes assumed that his account of the negotiations was drawn from materials which have now been lost. Any such assumption, however, is unjustified and must be regarded as altogether erroneous. It may be asserted with complete confidence that no such materials ever existed, that Columbus never wrote, and never caused to be written, any account of this period of his life. Had he done so, it can hardly be doubted that the fact would have been known to his sons and that it would by them have been communicated to Las Casas. It can hardly be questioned that Las Casas would not merely have used but would also have referred to this account, since, as the *Historia de las Indias* abundantly proves, he was always eager to mention the sources of his information and indeed to quote those sources, especially when by so doing he could apparently strengthen the case which he was propounding. As, moreover, he was certainly an admirer of the admiral and was as certainly predisposed to accept his statements and his estimates of those with whom he came into contact, it is reasonable to suggest that he would have regarded as authoritative, and even as absolutely decisive, an account of the negotiations for which Columbus was himself responsible. This suggestion is the more reasonable since any such account would have been in conformity with his own ideas. The admiral would hardly have failed to insist upon the folly or malice of his opponents; he would have readily admitted that the eventual acceptance of his proposals was due to the Divine Providence. But had Las Casas been able to draw upon a source, in his eyes so satisfactory, the account in the *Historia de las Indias* would have acquired a definition and a certainty which it is very far from possessing. Its author would have been aware, or would at least have imagined himself to be aware, of the actual course of events and in all probability of the exact arguments used. He would have known, or would have supposed himself to know, whether the story of the mysterious pilot, of whose deathbed confidences Columbus was alleged to have availed himself, was true or false.

But while Las Casas does certainly enumerate both the reasons which led Columbus, or which may have led Columbus, to conceive of his project and to be convinced of its practicability, and while he does supply a list of the objections urged against that project, he yet reveals the fact that he was not himself confident that he was accurately informed. He is careful to qualify his statements concerning the grounds upon which the scheme was rested by the use of the subjunctive; he admits that he is unaware of the precise course of events. If he appears to be somewhat more definite in the case of the arguments used by the opponents of Columbus, the very diversity of those grounds creates a suspicion that he was not doing more than giving a list of such objections as he felt might have been urged. Even so, he is driven in the end to adopt a facile way of escape and to explain everything by a reference to the mysterious working of Providence, rather in the manner of the Oxford undergraduate who described as 'an act of God', 'plague, pestilence, or famine, or anything else, so abominable that it cannot be attributed to human agency'.

In the case of some writers, such economy of explicit assertion might be ascribed to a legitimate hesitation, to a certain reluctance to be dogmatic concerning the course of a discussion at which the writer was not present, and concerning the workings of a mind, of which the operations were somewhat tortuous and obscure and perhaps also somewhat confused. To urge any such explanation in the case of Las Casas, however, would be to betray a misunderstanding of his literary character. He was very far from exhibiting that cautious reserve which may be considered as becoming to an historian. He was rarely unable to supply the exact number of the natives whom the Spaniards did to death; he was rarely unable to describe the precise tortures to which the Indians were subjected; he was frequently able to record, even upon occasions when he was not personally present, the actual words in which the victims were taunted as they writhed in the agonies of death. When contradictory accounts of an event, of which he was not an eyewitness, were preserved, he was never embarrassed by such conflict of evidence, if that event occurred in the New World; he has, indeed, no hesitation in often rejecting the testimony of those who might have been supposed to be best informed. If, then, in his discussion of the negotiations between Columbus and the sovereigns, he displays a lack of assurance, if he hesitates to venture on clear assertion, such lack of assurance and such hesitancy can hardly be ascribed to his burning passion for historical truth, accuracy, and justice.

There is, indeed, a less creditable but more probable explanation of the appearance in the *Historia de las Indias* of characteristics so generally alien from that work. An assertion concerning the conduct of Spaniards in the New World was most unlikely to be refuted or even to be seriously questioned. Of the majority of those events, upon which Las Casas dwelt, it was reasonably certain that no indubitably authentic account was in existence, and it could be assumed that any eyewitnesses would be no longer alive at the date to which the publication of the *Historia de las Indias* was so carefully postponed. To be equally definite concerning events in Castile, or even concerning the opinions of the advisers of Ferdinand and Isabella, would have been to risk a damaging contradiction. Las Casas could not be certain that no account of these events was preserved in the royal archives; he could not be certain that those advisers had left no written record of their views or that, although dead, they might not yet bear witness against him. His work, however, was essentially a piece of special pleading, and to introduce into it an appearance of scrupulous fairness, of readiness to confess ignorance, was obviously calculated to render the pleading

more convincing; no advocate is so effective as he who creates
the impression that he is anxious to do the fullest justice to
the case which he is endeavouring to destroy. A natural desire
to avoid conviction of error, and an equally natural desire to
seem to be incapable of making unfounded assertions, will
suffice to explain that admission, or tacit admission, of
ignorance which marks the account of the negotiations in the
Historia de las Indias, and it is safe to assume that here Las
Casas had no sure foundation of knowledge. It may, indeed,
be suggested that his account was at best based upon somewhat shadowy information and in some measure at least
upon nothing more substantial than his own conjectures.

5

Some colour is lent to this suggestion by a consideration of
the description which Las Casas gives of the objections
advanced by the opponents of Columbus, objections which,
according to him, so far prevailed as to delay the adoption
of 'the enterprise of the Indies'. At first sight, they may seem
to be precisely such as would have been put forward by the
ignorant or the prejudiced, since they reveal either an almost
gross misconception of cosmography or a reluctance to consider unfamiliar ideas. They thus seem to be also in accord
with the thesis which Las Casas was concerned to establish
and to be such as he would naturally have supposed to have
been urged. But while it may be admitted that opinions of
this nature may have been entertained by some individuals,
that they should have been seriously advanced is unlikely,
and that they should in any way have influenced the decisions
of the commission, of the Council or of the sovereigns is so
improbable that it can hardly be regarded as being even
barely credible. If they did exercise any such influence, it
must be assumed that the task of examining the proposals
of Columbus was entrusted to men who were out of harmony
with the spirit of the age in which they lived and who were
also the least qualified to deliver an opinion. It must be
assumed that 'the learned men', upon whom Ferdinand and
Isabella called, were less well informed than the fathers of
La Rábida, less intelligent than the cura of Los Palacios, less

interested in the novel and the strange than were the many
who so eagerly devoured the tales of Sir John Mandeville.
It must further be assumed that the report which they presented, if they presented any report at all, was, at least for a
moment, accepted without criticism by the Council of Castile
and by the sovereigns, or that the arguments upon which
such a report was based were, after consideration, regarded
as valid. It must in reality be assumed that Ferdinand and
Isabella, and their most immediate advisers, were guilty
either of stupidity or of dereliction of duty, that they lacked
either the wit to detect the futility or the energy to examine
the details of an opinion for which they had asked and which
was rendered to them.

Any such assumptions, however, would be altogether
illegitimate. It is obvious that Las Casas puts forward in
effect two propositions. He implies, and he even goes so far
as to assert, that the members of the commission, or at least
some of the members, were ignorant. He also suggests that
they were so influenced by that prejudice to which ignorance
gives birth as to have been no less unwilling than they were
intellectually unable to consider intelligently the proposals
submitted to them. But it would appear that these two propositions are incompatible with one another and that acceptance of the one compels rejection of the other. It may be
admitted that in all ages ignorance has been allied with prejudice; it must also be admitted that it has been allied with
credulity. In the age of Columbus this latter alliance was
peculiarly strong, and was the stronger because even those
who were reputed to be wise were also credulous. During the
later fifteenth century western Europe was dominated by a
spirit of inquiry or of curiosity which was often rather active
than discriminating, causing men to be avid of all that was
new. The immense popularity enjoyed by all travellers' tales
is sufficient evidence that this spirit exercised itself to a
notable degree upon accounts of recently discovered lands
and upon speculations concerning lands which were still
undiscovered. It is hardly too much to say that the geographical advance of the period would have been impossible
had not men been ready to dare much in order that they

might gratify their desire to know more of the hitherto un-known parts of the globe. But it was of that 'other hemi-sphere', 'concerning which there was no certain knowledge', that Columbus talked as confidently as if he had personally visited it, and to which he professed, or was thought to profess, to be able to proceed. It was across the Atlantic, that mysterious ocean, shrouded in mists, the abode of Kraken and of other horrors, that he designed to sail. It was to the fabled Indies that he was at least believed to design to penetrate by some hitherto unknown route, to all those riches of which Marco Polo had written, to all those things of wonder of which Mandeville had given such marvellous accounts. If, then, his auditors were men of their own age, if they shared in the common sentiments and in the general mentality of their fellows, it is hardly credible that they should have been unwilling to listen to stories such as Colum-bus told. In exact proportion to their ignorance, they would rather have been eager to hear and eager also to believe, nor would those who could accept without criticism the most extravagant absurdities have been disposed to entertain philosophic doubts concerning the existence of the antipodes or even concerning the practicability of a voyage such as had not hitherto been accomplished. If the members of the com-mission were, as Las Casas argues, steeped in ignorance, they would in that age have been steeped also in credulity; if, on the contrary, they were free from credulity, they might indeed have questioned the feasibility of the undertaking projected, but they would hardly have advanced against that undertaking objections such as they are alleged to have advanced. It can hardly be supposed that they were so inconsistent with their own character.

Las Casas would, indeed, appear to have fallen into a very common error. Fifty years later, when he was writing, it is possible enough that the effects of ignorance would have been such as he represents them to have been in the time of Colum-bus. The spirit of inquiry had by then been in some measure satisfied and had certainly diminished in intensity; men were no longer fired by that burning curiosity which had marked the last years of the previous century. So much that had been unknown had by then become known that there was less room for vagrant speculation, less readiness to accord credence to unsupported assertions. If men were still ready to seek for El Dorado, they were now so ready because sources of wealth so vast had been discovered that it seemed to be credible enough that sources still vaster were to be found; their desire to find the new was now less the result of mere curiosity than of actual accomplishment. They were more sober in their mental outlook; if oceanic voyaging were still a great adventure, there was no longer room for any expectation that the other hemisphere might be found to be elongated like the stalk-end of a pear. Men felt that they knew, not indeed exactly but in general, that which they might expect to find; they had attained an approximately accurate conception of the area and of the shape of the globe, not by conjecture but by experiment; they had attained also a similar conception of the races or beings by which the globe was inhabited and no longer hoped or feared that they might encounter the awful progeny of the lust of abandoned women for the devils of Hell, or even that milder race whose venial peculiarity it was to wear their head beneath their shoulders. In such an age, there might indeed have been unwillingness to listen to tales which were not founded upon experience, and to offer objections such as ignorance might suggest to ideas which were unfamiliar. Past achievement, after having for a while produced a belief that anything, however amazing, might be achieved, had proceeded to cause the inevitable reaction, to lead men once more to feel that the limit of knowledge had been reached. Columbus lived in one of those periods in the history of human thought when mankind is disposed to believe that marvellous discoveries may presently be made; Las Casas was writing in one of those periods when a contrary belief prevailed and when mankind was rather disposed to hold that 'since the fathers fell asleep, all things have continued as they were'. In his anxiety to establish his thesis, he was really guilty of a mental anachronism, such as is not infrequently committed by those who lack that degree of imaginative power which would enable them to put themselves intellectually in the place of those who lived long before their day. He was led to picture the ignorant of the time of Columbus as being akin to the ignorant of the second half of the sixteenth century and hence to ascribe to them an attitude of mind such as they were assuredly incapable of adopting.

It is, however, very far from probable that the 'wise men and lettered and sailors', to whom consideration of the proposals of Columbus was entrusted, were in fact ignorant or disposed to allow prejudice to obscure their judgement. The exact contrary, indeed, is suggested by that which is known concerning the two members of the commission whose names have been preserved. Hernando de Talavera was a man of learning, no less than of piety: his gentleness and reasonableness of temper are displayed in the correspondence which passed between him and the queen, whose confessor he was, nor did he lack tolerance, even if he did display a Pauline readiness to magnify his own office. He was, indeed, notably free from that narrowness of outlook which characterized and disgraced so many of the higher ecclesiastics of his age. When he became Archbishop of Granada, after the capture of that city, the enlightened attitude which he adopted won for him the affectionate regard and confidence of the Moors and incurred the censure of the more rigid Cardinal Ximenes. Such a man was little likely either to refuse a hearing to Columbus or to reject ideas presented to him, merely because they were unfamiliar or because they were in disaccord with his personal opinion; he was, perhaps, as little likely to be influenced by a somewhat servile reverence for the writings of St. Augustine or by misconceptions of cosmography, even supposing that he was incapable of appreciating the fact that they were misconceptions. Of his only known colleague, Dr. Rodrigo Maldonado de Talavera, little enough can be predicated. His title, however, argues that he was possessed at least of formal learning and his position as regidor of Salamanca and as a member of the Council of Castile suggests that he was credited with capacity. There is some indirect evidence that he was intellectually honest and fair-minded. Many years later, he frankly admitted that he and his colleagues were unanimously of opinion that Columbus could not accomplish that which he proposed to accomplish, and that the event proved them to have been entirely mistaken. A man so ready to acknowledge that he had committed an error, to his commission of which there was no other testimony, may well be supposed to have been sufficiently liberal to be prepared to listen to argument. It would thus seem to be a fact that the only two members of the commission concerning whom anything is known were qualified to discharge the duty laid upon them. It is still possible that they were in this respect exceptional and that their colleagues, or a number of their colleagues, were not so qualified, but while this is possible, it can hardly be regarded as probable. In the absence of any definite evidence to the contrary, it is more rational to assume that Las Casas was mistaken in his estimate of the intellectual capacity of those who examined the proposals of Columbus.

That he was so mistaken is somewhat forcibly suggested by another consideration. It must be presumed that Ferdinand and Isabella made some effort to select suitable persons to be members of the commission of inquiry, since throughout their reign there is nothing to suggest that they were careless in choosing their servants and agents. If, then, those selected were in general ignorant, the sovereigns must be supposed to have committed a serious error of judgement. Unless it be contended that their realm was so enveloped in intellectual darkness that in it there was neither wisdom nor learning, it must be supposed that they regarded as wise and learned those who were actually the reverse. While, however, it cannot be proved that they were not so mistaken, that they were so is most improbable. The suggestion that they selected wholly unsuitable persons to perform a particular task is entirely inconsistent with that which is known of the character of the sovereigns. In the opinion of her contemporaries, Isabella was a remarkably shrewd judge of men. She displayed a peculiar talent in her choice of those who should occupy the most varied positions; she surprised those around her by the accuracy with which she summed up those with whom she had scarcely come into personal contact. Her appointment of Hernando de Talavera to the archbishopric of Granada and her selection of Ximenes to conduct the moral regeneration of the Castilian Church are illustrations of her ability to find suitable instruments to carry out her policy. Her handling of the turbulent Andalusian grandees, of the riotous mob of Segovia, and of the hotheaded Fadrique Enriquez show how well fitted she was to analyse the temperament of her subjects, and to this quality, indeed, she undoubtedly owed much of the success which she achieved. Nor was Ferdinand a poor judge of his fellow men; his European reputation for astuteness was not undeserved. When, at the beginning of his reign, he was obliged to contend against Castilian hatred for a prince of Aragon, he showed no little skill in playing upon the vanity of the nobles whose hostility he disarmed and whose obedience he conciliated. After the death of Isabella, his position was one of extreme delicacy, but he dealt successfully alike with the dangerous popularity of Gonsalvo de Córdoba, with the mutinous nobles, and with the somewhat intractable Archbishop of Toledo. It can hardly be supposed that two rulers, who thus exhibited capacity for the estimation of character and a knowledge of human nature, failed in the relatively simple task of selecting the men best fitted to deliver an opinion upon the proposals of Columbus. It may, indeed, be taken for granted that those who were chosen were well chosen, and that of any men then to be found in Castile they were the most competent to pronounce upon the questions submitted to them.

Their competence may, however, still have been defective; while they were the best judges who could be found, they may still have been unable to judge rationally. Such is, in effect, the suggestion of Las Casas, who contends that the members of the commission were ignorant of cosmography and that some at least among them were carried away by theological prejudice. But he would here seem to have taken refuge in conjecture and to have conjectured somewhat unhappily. There is little or no warrant for his reiterated insistence upon the lack of cosmographical knowledge in Castile. It may be admitted that in Spain, as elsewhere, erroneous ideas concerning geography were current; in the period antecedent to the great discoveries it was perhaps inevitable that there should be no accurate appreciation of the true relationship between east and west, or of the true distribution of land and water. It was, perhaps, equally inevitable that some should question the possibility of accomplishing voyages which had never been accomplished and of navigating seas which had never been navigated. It is probable enough that there is no justification for the boast of Columbus that he was the first to discover that the world was really shaped like a pear, the stalk-end being the other hemisphere. It is also probable that in Castile there was less general interest in, and hence less general knowledge of, geographical matters than there was in Portugal or in Cataluña. The centres of intellectual were divorced from those of maritime activity; the seafaring inhabitants of Galicia and Vizcaya were distinguished rather for their physical than for their spiritual virtues, and were rather turbulent and daring than mentally agile.

But it must be remembered that the Catalans had early displayed considerable skill in the construction of maps, that after the accession of Ferdinand and Isabella there was a considerable increase of intercourse between Castile and Aragon, and that natives of both kingdoms were included in the Royal Council. It may be true that the queen somewhat jealously guarded the rights of her own immediate subjects, but she was not so parochial in outlook as to refuse help from any quarter whence it might be profitably drawn, and, except in such matters as concerned the Church and morality, she placed great trust in the judgement of her husband. In the particular case of 'the enterprise of the Indies', there is evidence that an important part was played by Aragonese. Nor was the work of the Arabian geographers entirely unknown in Castile, in which kingdom there was also a lively interest in such books as those of Marco Polo and of Sir John Mandeville.

There is, indeed, little reason for supposing that contemporary Castilian opinion was as ill-informed as Las Casas asserts. Even a simple country curate, such as was Andrés Bernáldez, could conceive a judicious scepticism concerning the marvellous stories of the east, greedily as he devoured those stories, but could be fully persuaded that, as he expresses it, a man could 'go and pass by the westward, to the right of St. Vincent, and proceed by way of Jerusalem to Rome and to Seville'. All the educated of the period accepted the sphericity of the globe as a fact, even if they questioned the practical possibility of its circumnavigation; Columbus, indeed, credits them with believing that the world was a perfect sphere and uses this fact to illustrate the greatness and originality of his own contribution to the sum total of human knowledge. Peter Martyr Angleria, in his letters, refers in glowing terms to the intellectual activity of Castile, and if his enthusiasm may be supposed to have been in some measure due to his gratification at the success of his own public lectures, there is no doubt that the Renaissance in Spain was both vigorous and fruitful. The development of learning was fostered by such patrons as Cardinal Mendoza and his relative, the Conde de Tendilla; it was notably encouraged by the queen, herself a humble student of Latin, whose influence was steadily employed to lead the maidens of her court to worship rather at the shrine of Athene than at that of Aphrodite.

Nor can more justification be discovered for the further contention of Las Casas that acceptance of the proposals of Columbus was delayed because the ideas, upon which those proposals were based, were regarded as conflicting with the teaching of St. Augustine. The obvious suggestion here is that there was in Castile a considerable, or at least an influential, body of opinion which held that belief in the existence of the Antipodes was heretical and that this body of opinion was represented on the commission of inquiry and was treated with some deference by the sovereigns and their Council. It may, perhaps, be admitted that there were not improbably some, among the less enlightened, who were disposed to follow blindly so mighty a father of the Church as the great Bishop of Hippo, and to consider any criticism of his views as being at least on the borderline of heresy. But it can hardly be supposed that these narrow-minded, or rigidly orthodox, theologians were numerous or that they carried sufficient weight as to be able to sway the decisions of Ferdinand and Isabella; had they been so numerous or so powerful, it may be questioned whether the *Capitulations* would have ever been signed. Whatever else she may have been, the queen was both by temperament and policy anxious that all her actions should be in the fullest accord with ecclesiastical sentiment. A deeply religious woman, she was disposed to pay rather too much than too little attention to her spiritual advisers, to whom she even condescended to defend her personal expenditure and to explain that if in the matter of dress she appeared to be extravagant, it was really that she had positively nothing to wear. For those who were even vaguely tainted with heresy she never displayed any sympathy. She was the less prepared to do so, since it was her considered opinion that the political unity of her dominions, the attainment of which was a primary object of all her endeavours, could be best secured, and could perhaps only be secured, by insistence upon the most absolute religious conformity and by the enforcement of the most rigid orthodoxy. The reform of the Sacred Office, the expulsion of the Jews, and the persecution of the conquered Moors may testify to her reverence for the Catholic Church; they testify not less to her devotion to her political ideals; despite her womanly tenderness of heart, she approved the severity of Ximenes, even if she loved better the mildness of Talavera, nor did she endeavour to curb the energy of Torquemada, even if she regretted the necessity for that energy. For her to have embraced a project, upon the strict orthodoxy of which any breath of suspicion had fallen, would hardly have been possible; it would have involved the denial of the whole tenor of her private and of her public life. Rather than disregard a body of religious opinion, sufficiently numerous or influential to make its voice heard in her councils, she would in all probability have been prepared to sacrifice even assured dominion over a new world with all its opportunities for winning souls for Christ; she would certainly have rejected without hesitation proposals for an expedition, the objective of which was no more than obscurely defined, the success of which was uncertain, and the profit from which in event of success was at best somewhat problematical. It may with some assurance be concluded that Isabella was never informed that the ideas of Columbus conflicted with those of St. Augustine.

With perhaps almost equal assurance it may also be concluded that no such suggestion had come to the ears of Columbus himself. There is abundant evidence that he was a religious man and that he was extremely superstitious; he was, further, in all probability as uneducated as others in his position in life in that period of history. Such a man could hardly have possessed the intellectual daring which enables a man to flout authority and to become a heretic; such a man would almost necessarily have accepted without question the judgement of the professional exponents of that wisdom which is not of this world. Innate respect for the teaching of the Church may well have been reinforced in his case by that lively fear of eternal damnation which was so general in that age, impelling men to endeavour to excuse the imperfection of their works by the perfect orthodoxy of their faith. But when the circumstances of his life are considered, the humility of his birth, the exigency of his material resources, the nature of the occupations in which he engaged, it is clear enough that his boasted intercourse with the learned of various nations and creeds can have occurred only in his dreams, and that those ecclesiastics with whom he came into contact were in all probability the most ignorant and the most narrow of their profession. If to such men he had propounded ideas which savoured of the heretical, he would assuredly have been rebuked for his presumption, and to him the rebuke would have been an imperative warning, filling him with panic dread of the wrath of an outraged Deity. It may be admitted that when he dreamed of reaching that which lay at 'the stalk end of the pear', when he conceived of himself as the envoy of the Holy Trinity and as being destined to reveal 'the New Heaven and the New Earth', he did wander somewhat from the narrow path of orthodoxy and did stray dangerously near the seductive fields of heterodox speculation. It may, however, be safely presumed that he kept the secret of such mental adventures securely hidden in his own heart, and that he was no more communicative concerning his hopes for his future than he was concerning the experiences of his past. The ideas which he propounded publicly were doubtless such as could cause no qualms of conscience even to the most ignorantly orthodox ecclesiastic and such as could not suggest that he was disposed to call in question the authority of even the humblest among the fathers of the Church.

There is, indeed, no evidence at all to suggest that Columbus aroused clerical opposition. It is true that with three ecclesiastics he did come into more or less acute conflict, but in no one of these cases was the cause of conflict theological. Juan de Forseca is alleged to have pursued him with rancorous hostility, but even if it be admitted that this allegation is justified, it is impossible to attribute the hostility to some difference of religious opinion. The future Bishop of Burgos was, as Las Casas sarcastically remarks, 'better skilled in equipping fleets than in saying mass in an episcopal manner', and was constantly engaged in occupations 'better suited to a Biscayan than to a bishop'. He is little likely to have interested himself in the possible doctrinal vagaries of the admiral. Nor was the quarrel between Columbus and Fray Buil the outcome of some dispute upon speculative questions, unless, indeed, it be supposed that the friar felt that it was heretical on the part of a mere layman to set an example of Christian charity to an apostolic vicar. The case of the Abbot of Luxerna is somewhat more obscure. That enterprising ecclesiastic would appear to have proceeded upon the second voyage in the capacity of a tourist and to have been refused permission to return home until Ferdinand and Isabella intervened on his behalf. But the cause of the admiral's displeasure seems to have been fear that the visitor might spread unfavourable reports concerning Española; there is nothing to suggest anything in the nature of theological controversy. And, save in these three instances, Columbus was, as far as is known, on excellent terms with the clergy, among whom were numbered some of his most steadfast and most valuable supporters. Of the higher ecclesiastics, the Cardinal of Spain, the Archbishop of Granada, and Diego de Deza favoured his enterprise. Among seculars, Peter Martyr Angleria was his personal friend, at least from the moment when his friendship appeared to be of some value or of some interest, while Andrés Bernáldez would seem to have shown him kindness in the days of his obscurity and poverty. The Fathers of La Rábida were advocates of his cause ; Antonio de Marchena is especially mentioned for his consistent loyalty, and Juan Pérez was employed to act for Columbus at the critical moment when the agreement with the sovereigns was to be concluded. At a later date, Fray Gaspar Gorricio appeared to have been as intimate with the admiral as any man ever was intimate. There is some reason for thinking that Columbus found less difficulty in harmonizing with the ecclesiastics than with the laymen with whom he came into contact, and this suggests that his orthodoxy was regarded as being beyond question.

It would thus appear to be improbable that any such arguments as Las Casas describes were actually advanced by the opponents of Columbus, or that any such reasons were used to justify any report delivered by the commission. It would appear to be still more improbable that, had a report been based upon such grounds, it could have produced the effect ascribed to it in the *Historia de las Indias*. According to Las Casas, those who were appointed to examine the proposals of Columbus acted only in an advisory capacity and this statement may be accepted as accurate. Ferdinand and Isabella were little inclined to delegate executive authority : they were disposed to allow too little rather than too much latitude to their advisers and ministers. It was the normal practice that all matters, even the most seemingly trivial, should be referred to, and should be decided by, the sovereigns, either with or without the assistance of the Council of Castile, and there is no reason for supposing that an exception was made in the case of 'the enterprise of the Indies'. It may really be taken for granted that the opinion of the commission was reported directly or indirectly to Ferdinand and Isabella, and that it was by them accepted either with or without examination of the basis upon which it rested.

But it is hardly credible that there should have been no examination of that basis. Throughout the reign Ferdinand

and Isabella were well served by their advisers, who discharged their functions zealously and conscientiously. The laborious arguments on the question of the treatment to be accorded to the natives of the New World illustrates the manner in which a case was weighed in the Council, or by those who were charged with the duty of delivering an opinion. The very delay which so often occurred before any decision was reached is the measure of the careful deliberation which marked the conduct of all affairs of State. Nor were the sovereigns temperamentally inclined to hasty action or to blind acceptance of advice. The story of the creation of the Santa Hermandad supplies an example of the caution with which they proceeded: the same caution was displayed in those negotiations which culminated in the Treaty of Tordesillas or in that of Medina del Campo. Ferdinand would seem to have taken a keen pleasure in the work of government; if his panegyrist gently censures him for his love of games, that censure was perhaps called forth less by a feeling that he was disposed to neglect business for pleasure than by a fear on the part of the queen that when he was at play, he was insufficiently solicitous of his royal dignity. Isabella was notably conscientious. She refused to allow consideration for her own health or the most acute personal grief to distract her from the discharge of her public duties; where those duties were concerned, she was ready even to disregard the fatherly admonitions of her confessor. Neither the king nor the queen can be regarded as having been likely to have accepted a report from any commission, however trusted and however distinguished, without examining its basis.

If, then, Las Casas is to be believed, it must be supposed that the arguments advanced by the opponents of Columbus exerted sufficient influence upon the Council and the sovereigns to cause at least delay in accepting 'the enterprise of the Indies'. But if these arguments were such as they are described as having been, it is little probable that they could have produced such an effect. It may be admitted that Ferdinand and Isabella were not essentially students of cosmography or of navigation, but they were also not unenlightened; they were gifted with natural intelligence and they were by disposition receptive. The king proved to be well able to profit from, and to correct, his mistakes; during the War of Granada he certainly developed his military capacity as a result of his appreciation of his initial errors. The queen was interested in all intellectual activities ; she was a patroness of education and of learning. The grasp of the art of war which she acquired, her realization of the imperative need for improved communications in her dominions, and her creation of the first military field-hospital in western Europe, indicate that she was very far from being mentally sterile. The presence of Cardinal Mendoza in the Council was almost in itself a guarantee against the prevalence of narrow views or of petty considerations; that of Quintanilla was a security that new ideas should be carefully considered. There is no reason for thinking that the majority of the advisers of the sovereigns were ignorant or prejudiced or devoid of the spirit of initiative. It is most unlikely that either upon the members of the Royal Council or upon the King and Queen would arguments such as Las Casas enumerates have produced such an effect as he assigns to them. In such circumstances it would be unsafe to regard the account of the negotiations given in the *Historia de las Indias* as being altogether trustworthy; it is at least probable that in some important respects it is inaccurate and misleading.

6

Although there is thus reason enough for thinking that, in his account of the commission of inquiry, Las Casas was guilty of inaccuracy, it is improbable that his guilt was conscious. It must, indeed, be admitted that he was by no means incapable of deliberate distortion of facts. There is, on the contrary, abundant evidence that he was never unwilling to give currency to a falsehood, of the salutary character of which he was convinced: no undue tenderness of conscience, no exaggerated regard for the truth, ever deterred him from doing that which he conceived to be calculated to advance the cause to which he had devoted his life and of which he was so passionate a champion. It must also be admitted that, in this instance, the inaccuracy, if there be inaccuracy, is of such a nature as to lend support to that thesis which he was concerned to establish. His thesis required belief in the contention that the Indies were the gift of God to Castile, and it was a corollary of this belief that those who were reluctant to receive this gift were in effect attempting to thwart the divine will, that they were assuredly ignorant and blind. It was not, however, necessary to suppose that they were culpably ignorant or wilfully blind. They might be supposed to be in the position of those who 'erred, not knowing the scriptures'; they might have been honestly mistaken or have been misled, as Las Casas declares that Ferdinand the Catholic was afterwards misled when he sanctioned the Laws of Burgos. It was not essential for the establishment of his thesis that they should be declared, as they are declared, to have been prejudiced or to have sinned against the light.

In such circumstances it is little likely that Las Casas knowingly represented their attitude as having been other than that which he sincerely believed it to have been. He had no inducement to do so, and he had the very strongest inducement to be truthful. He was nothing if not astute. When every allowance has been made for the apparently inevitable defects of autobiography, the story of his experiences at the court of Charles V, of his conflicts with the Bishops of Burgos and of Darien, shows that he was not unmindful of the injunction, 'Be ye therefore wise as serpents', even if the latter part of that injunction had escaped his memory. It cannot be doubted that he was fully aware of the importance of establishing his own reputation for veracity, in order that his description of the crimes and violences of the Spaniards in the New World might not be questioned; it was almost essential that he should be regarded as an impartial judge in order that his panegyric on the natives might win credence. The very fact that the *Historia de las Indias* is not a history, but a piece of special pleading, is really a guarantee that its author would not willingly endanger his own credit and that he would not willingly incur the risk of being found guilty of misrepresentation, unless to do so was absolutely necessary, as it appeared to him to be in the case of the relations between Oviedo and Pedrarias.

So far as the proceedings of the commission of inquiry are concerned, veracity was obviously dictated by prudence. It is true that Las Casas had every reason to believe that no account of these proceedings had been preserved in the royal archives and that the death of the last surviving commissioner precluded the possibility of some personal narrative being produced. But it is equally true that some official report might conceivably exist and that some member of the inquiring body might have left a record of the part which he had himself played, of the arguments advanced and of the answers given. To have deliberately invented a story, to have suppressed the truth, or to have suggested the false would thus have been to risk at least possible detection and to have endangered his own credit without adequate reason for doing so. It would have been to expose his thesis to the danger of being overthrown by an attempt to establish it too surely. Common prudence would have suggested that it was here wise to sacrifice a certain possible strengthening of his case, such as a distortion of the facts might have supplied, and Las Casas was imprudent only when imprudence was politic.

The probability that he was, as far as he knew, both accurate and truthful on this occasion is the greater since the source whence he derived his account appears to be ascertainable and the nature of that source to explain the inaccuracy of which he was guilty. It has been generally assumed, and the justice of this assumption can hardly be questioned, that Las Casas based his narrative upon those 'papers of the admiral' to which he claims to have had access. So far, indeed, as his description of the arguments which led Columbus to form his project and which confirmed him in his belief in its practicability is concerned, Las Casas professes to have followed Ferdinand Columbus, but even so, it may be presumed that the son of the admiral, if he did compose a life of his father, did so from the same 'papers', and the debt of Las Casas to them thus becomes merely indirect instead of direct. But it is certain that among those 'papers' he found no detailed account of the negotiations, since had he done so he would probably have mentioned the fact, would probably have quoted the document, and would undoubtedly have been positive and not hesitant in his own account of this period. Nor is it probable that he was even acquainted with some fugitive references to these transactions, contained in documents emanating from Columbus, to which he had access and which are no longer extant. It is true that some 'papers of the admiral' have undoubtedly been lost. The famous chest at La Mejorada in all probability contained a number of documents which have been mislaid or destroyed. The originals of the journals of the voyages have not been preserved; there is no trace of that 'book' to which Andrés Bernáldez alludes, or of those letters which Peter Martyr Angleria claims to have received. It is obviously possible that in some of these lost documents there may have been allusions to this period. Columbus was always somewhat inclined to stray from the subject immediately under discussion, and in actual fact the references which he does make to the negotiations with the sovereigns are scattered through letters and papers ostensibly dealing with entirely different matters. While, however, there is no evidence that any such further allusions occurred, it is certain that, if they did occur, they were either unknown to Las Casas or added nothing to his information. For he assuredly made no use of them. Every statement which he makes concerning the arguments employed by Columbus and by his opponents, and concerning the attitude of the commission of inquiry, can be shown to be based upon the extant 'papers of the admiral', even when they are alleged by Las Casas to have been drawn from the *Historie*.

So much appears clearly enough when the account given in the *Historia de las Indias* is subjected to critical analysis. It may be legitimately presumed that, at least in the opinion of Las Casas, the arguments which he enumerates as having served to influence Columbus are those which Columbus urged upon the commission and which failed to carry conviction. Those arguments were that the world was spherical; that its size had been exaggerated and that the eastward extension of Asia had been underestimated, and that hence the extreme east was nearer to the extreme west than had been supposed, the voyage from Europe to the Indies across the Atlantic being proportionately shorter. Las Casas adds that Columbus was probably influenced by such further considerations as that of the well-known passage in the *Medea* of Seneca, and that he was encouraged to hold to his opinion by his study of the *Imago Mundi*, by the letters which he received from Pablo Toscanelli, and by the stories which he heard in the Azores, in Madeira, and at Lisbon—stories of strange objects thrown up by the sea, of islands seen dimly through the western mists, and of the experiences of those who had dared to voyage far out into the Atlantic or who had been driven from their intended course by storms.

With the exception of the letters of Toscanelli, to which Columbus makes no allusion, the operation of each of these arguments might be fairly deduced from his extant writings. In the *Journal* he alludes to his experiences in the Atlantic islands and to his conversation with Pedro Correa, revealing the fact that he was thus assured that between Europe and the Indies there lay some islands, presumably those concerning which traditions were current. His elaborate annotations of the tracts of Cardinal Pierre d'Ailly would seem to justify the contention that his study of those works strengthened his conviction of the practicability of his projected undertaking; his interest in the passage from Seneca might be presumed from the fact that he transcribed it. Both in his letter describing the third voyage, and in the notes which he wrote on the margins of books, he insisted upon all those cosmographical arguments which Las Casas declares to have influenced him. The very letters from Toscanelli are found copied on the fly-leaf of a volume which was in his possession. It is thus entirely unnecessary to suppose that Las Casas had any further information concerning the arguments used by Columbus than that which is contained in, or which may be readily deduced from, the extant 'papers of the admiral'.

Nor would the possession of additional information concerning the arguments of the opponents of the undertaking seem to be probable. Of those arguments, Columbus says no more than that they were dictated by conservatism, by a lack of the spirit of adventure, and perhaps by ignorance and prejudice. But his notes, and more especially those on the *Imago Mundi*, may appear to reveal the objections which he was required to meet. Las Casas declares that those objections were the great duration of the voyage proposed, the non-existence of the Antipodes, the absence of land, the uninhabitable character of any land which might exist, the impossibility of the return journey, and the heterodoxy of the project generally. Each one of these arguments might well be supposed to have been urged by the opponents of the admiral, if the notes written by him are considered. In those notes he insists in effect that the proposed voyage would be of no great duration, since he argues that the estimate of the size of the world given by Marinus of Tyre was more accurate than that given by Ptolemy and that the eastward extension of Asia had never been accurately determined. He underlines, as it were, all references to the Antipodes and by transcribing the relevant passage from St. Augustine may seem to have attempted to answer the objection that his own views conflicted with those of that eminent Father of the Church. He notes with obvious satisfaction all references to the excellence of the other hemisphere: he draws attention to arguments in favour of the habitability of all zones and the navigability of all seas, and he quotes the prophet Esdras in support of his contention that the proportion of land to water has been underestimated. In his letter on the third voyage he summarizes the very points upon which Las Casas dwells, and thus while it is true that he does not positively assert that such arguments were used by his opponents, he may fairly be considered to have implied that they were. It would seem that Las Casas did no more than recognize this implication, and transform a suggestion into a statement of fact; his materials were the extant writings of Columbus and his method was to interpret them, no doubt accurately in his own opinion.

That Las Casas made use of no materials which are not still extant is further suggested by the fact that the source of his remarks concerning the attitude of individuals towards the enterprise is equally ascertainable. For the most part, here also he relied upon the extant 'papers of the admiral', and where he did not do so, he would appear to have drawn from the *Letters* of Peter Martyr Angleria, which was printed long before the date of the writing of the *Historia de las Indias*. Columbus himself mentions the assistance which he received from Antonio de Marchena, from 'two friars', from Juan Cabrero, and from Diego de Deza. That he was supported by Santangel, whose supposed speech is obviously a *jeu d'esprit* on the part of Las Casas, might be fairly deduced from the fact that one printed version of the letter describing the first voyage is so endorsed as to suggest that he hastened to announce the discovery in a private letter to the *escribano de ración*.

The classical version of the commission of inquiry thus appears to rest upon a somewhat insecure basis. Such evidence as is supplied by Columbus himself is inconclusive and indefinite; it is fragmentary and is in all probability darkly coloured by the personal feelings of its author. Only at first sight is the testimony of Las Casas more satisfactory. There is no reason for supposing that it is based upon anything more substantial than his conjectural elaboration of the fugitive references found in the 'papers of the admiral' and his equally conjectural deductions from the notes written by Columbus in books which were at one time in his possession.

7

While the basis upon which the clerical view of the commission of inquiry rests is thus somewhat insecure, it must be admitted that it would appear to receive a certain measure of support from the testimony of Dr. Rodrigo Maldonado and that for any contrary view there is nothing in the nature of direct evidence. It must, therefore, be also admitted that it is possible that the clerical view is just and that it supplies an accurate explanation of the undoubted fact that it was only after much hesitation and delay that Ferdinand and Isabella entered 'the enterprise of the Indies'. At the same time, however, there are legitimate grounds for regarding this explanation as erroneous and for thinking that the hesitation and delay, so far from having been due to ignorance, to prejudice, or to a dull conservatism, was the outcome of a rational caution and of due consideration for the interests of Castile. It is certainly possible, and it is perhaps more probable than not, that the attitude adopted towards Columbus and towards his proposals was statesmanlike, and that it was dictated by a clear appreciation both of the character of the man and of the potentialities contained in his offers. It is possible, and it is perhaps more probable than not, that the clerical version of the story does not do justice to those to whom the project was submitted for examination, and that it conveys an impression of the negotiations which is almost entirely erroneous.

That in some measure this impression is inaccurate may appear at first sight to be suggested by the fact that Las Casas, from whom it is so largely derived, makes two assumptions, both of which would seem to be of dubious validity. He assumes that the ultimate, no less than the immediate, objective of Columbus was to reach Asia by sailing westwards, and that the lands, of which he spoke so confidently and which he was to 'discover and gain', were Cipangu, Cathay, and the Indies. It is certainly true that Columbus proposed to cross the Atlantic, nor can it be seriously questioned that he believed that by so doing he would reach the regions of which Marco Polo had written and concerning which Sir John Mandeville had related such marvellous things. But that the accomplishment of such a voyage was his whole purpose is improbable ; to reach the eastern coast of Asia was for him almost certainly less an end in itself than a means to an end, nor was it there that he expected to find the seat of his future vice-royalty and governor-generalship. The assumption made by Las Casas, therefore, would appear to indicate a lack of any special knowledge and an imperfect acquaintance with the ideas entertained by Columbus. It may seem to follow that the representation of the arguments employed during the negotiations must be more or less fallacious, and that his whole account of these negotiations is vitiated by his misapprehension of the point at issue.

Even, however, if it be true, and it is probably true, that

such a misapprehension existed in the mind of Las Casas, it was perhaps not of such a nature as seriously to prejudice his account. Whatever may have been the actual purpose of Columbus, it would appear to be morally certain that his proposals were regarded by those to whom they were submitted as amounting to no more than a suggestion for the opening of a new, and presumably shorter, route to those regions which the Portuguese were endeavouring to reach by doubling the southernmost point of Africa. That such was the impression conveyed to Ferdinand and Isabella is in reality proved by the terms of the letters of credence which they issued, even if their *cédula*, forbidding the expedition to proceed along the African shore, may betray a certain doubt concerning the course which that expedition proposed to follow. But this being so, it cannot be questioned that the same impression existed in the minds of the members of the commission of inquiry; they cannot be supposed to have been more fully or more accurately informed than were the sovereigns. It follows that any arguments urged in support of the proposals must have been at least consistent with the supposition that the objective of the projected voyage was the eastern shore of Africa and that, even if the existence of some further design on the part of Columbus were vaguely suspected by those who examined his scheme, no such design was clearly revealed in any discussion which occurred. The assumption made in the *Historia de las Indias*, therefore, does not necessarily vitiate the account of the negotiations there given; the same assumption was made by the members of the commission, as a result of the cautious or suspicious reticence of Columbus, and Las Casas was no more ill-informed than were those whose proceedings he described.

Nor is his account, perhaps, vitiated by the second assumption which he makes. Las Casas assumes that, at the time of the negotiations, Columbus was literate and that he was somewhat highly educated. He accepts the statement of João de Barros that the future admiral was an expert Latinist and declares him to have been well acquainted with those branches of knowledge which were necessary for his purpose. By asserting that Columbus owed much to his

study of the tracts of the *Imago Mundi* and other works, he
in effect dates these annotations as having been written
before the time of the first voyage. There is, however, little
reason for thinking that this estimate of the intellectual
equipment of Columbus has any relation to the truth. It is
only necessary to read a few of his notes to discover that he
was assuredly not 'learned in the Latin tongue', and it is
morally certain that he was not versed in those sciences, to
knowledge of which he himself lays somewhat ambiguous
claim and with proficiency in which he has been credited.
It may be at least questioned whether, at the time of his
discovery, he was even able to read and write. His position
as the representative abroad of a Genoese mercantile house
may, indeed, at first sight appear to argue his literacy; it may
appear that it must have been necessary for him to communicate by letter with his principals. But such an argument
is somewhat fallacious. Illiteracy was not then incompatible
with the occupancy of the most responsible positions; with
the exception of ecclesiastics, few even of the more highly
placed were educated, and Isabella the Catholic herself, after
her accession to the throne, began the painful attempt to
acquire a knowledge of Latin. In general, the ignorance of a
Francisco Pizarro was far more normal than the relative
erudition of an Hernando Cortés. Nor would it appear that
the duties of Columbus were such as to demand that he
should be literate. He seems to have been employed to
purchase and to superintend the shipment of cargoes, and
capacity for successful bartering, ability to make a profitable
bargain, which he assuredly possessed, was far more important than epistolary skill; he was not a clerk but a trader.
Upon all other grounds the presumption of his illiteracy is
most reasonable. Having regard to his circumstances as a
boy, it is difficult to believe that he was vouchsafed any
educational opportunities; to those of his class such opportunities did not normally occur, nor does Domenico Columbus
seem to have been in a position to afford the necessary
expenditure. Even more significant is the fact that he made
no record of the demands which he presented, of the answers
which he received, or of the promises which were ultimately

made to him. Had such a record existed, it is hardly credible that it should have been lost. In the *Libro de los Privilegios* Columbus collected with most meticulous care all that touched upon his rights, and this is in itself a sufficient guarantee that he would have preserved a document so precious to him as would have been the account of the attainment of his desires. Nor is it credible that a man, so temperamentally suspicious and so assured of his own diplomatic capacity, should have permitted the actual concluding of the agreement to pass into the hands of an agent, even of an agent so responsible as Fray Juan Pérez, unless it had been that the task of reducing verbal agreements to writing and of reading that which was written had been beyond his power. It is further a significant fact that the earliest extant autograph of Columbus dates only some years after the discovery; having regard to his notorious passion for writing in his later life, it is hardly probable that all earlier autographs should have been lost. While indeed it is obviously impossible to prove that he was unable to write at the time of the negotiations, it is thus highly probable that he was so unable, and that the assumption of Las Casas that the notes on the *Imago Mundi* and other works antedate the first voyage is devoid of foundation in fact.

Balance of Introduction

8. Proposals of Columbus were vague as to his offers: definite as to his demands: he invited co-operation in a scheme which he would not explain: he demanded extravagant rewards: in these circumstances, caution was legitimate.

9. Legitimate to ask for certain qualifications: these not possessed so far as Columbus was concerned.

10. Absence of any evidence that he possessed these qualifications.

11. Objections to accepting his proposals: diplomatic and internal.

12. Attitude adopted by Ferdinand and Isabella: postponement.

COLUMBUS AND THE WORLD-MAP

By E. G. R. TAYLOR

WHO can read, without being moved to wonder and pity, the tragedy of Columbus, the man, as he unconsciously reveals himself in his later letters ? Since to the majority of mankind a paradox is abhorrent, it is generally claimed that the discoverer of so vast a continent as America must himself have been proportionately great. Columbus, we are therefore told, was a powerful thinker, a supreme navigator, a born leader, a hero, almost a saint. But the truth is more wonderful than this. The discovery was made by a self-educated, emotional, unpopular man, prone to self-pity, who clung tenaciously and fervently to a quite mistaken cosmographical theory. Blind chance determined that his error should prove the key that unlocked the New World. Where he declared the hithermost coasts of Asia to lie, there as a matter of fact lay a quite unsuspected America!

So vast has the Columbian literature become, and so intricate are many of the debatable points raised, that to the general reader some of the controversies must now appear almost as futile as the famous medieval puzzle regarding the number of angels who can dance on the point of a needle, Only a Columbian scholar of the calibre of Mr. Jane himself, steeped in the documents, could contribute anything of value to these discussions, but since the views put forward by Columbus with regard to the interpretation of the discoveries made during his third and fourth voyages arose from his study of scholastic cosmography, a brief amplification of Mr. Jane's sketch[1] of current trends of thought will be attempted.

In the fifteenth century, as in the twentieth, there were men who followed keenly the most recent advances of philosophy, side by side with men who passionately rejected anything new, and with men who were neither advanced nor reactionary, but merely indifferent to scholarship, or 'practical', as they would term themselves to-day. Then, as now,

[1] Vol. i, p. xxi.

there was also a fourth class, men who, attracted by learning, read bravely but stumblingly in books which their defective education allowed them only very partially to comprehend. The very ignorance of such men allows them to make dogmatic statements, to come to unorthodox conclusions, from which scholars would shrink. If we dare to place Columbus in this class, and view him as a man, courageously self-educated, whose intellectual reach exceeded his grasp, much that was formerly dark becomes clear.

What were the accepted cosmographical ideas of his day? As Mr. Jane has pointed out, to all but the most ignorant or reactionary, it was axiomatic that the earth was a globe, poised motionless in the centre of the empyrean. Round about it the heavens wheeled, carrying the fixed stars, and the moon, the planets, and the sun circled in their several courses. The arctic and antarctic poles were the poles of the wheeling sky, not of the earth, while the equinoctial line and the tropics and circles were likewise traced out upon the sky. Hence, the phrase 'under' or 'beneath the equinoctial line' meant *on* the terrestrial equator, while the lands termed 'beneath the arctic pole' embraced the whole hemisphere from which that pole of the heavens was visible, and so, too, with the antarctic. It was usually assumed that the known habitable lands—Europe, western Asia, and north Africa—lay on the upper surface of the stationary earth, and that unknown lands and waters lay on the lower surface, or loosely, 'beneath' the earth. The zenith of those who lived 'under the equinoctial' was the highest point of the heavens, and the island or city of Aryn,[1] placed midway between north and south, east and west, of the upper hemisphere, was at the cupola or highest point of the earth. The use of such an expression as 'highest point' indicates that, although the terms 'above' and 'beneath' were admitted by philosophers only to have meaning relative to the centre of the universe, then supposed coincident with the centre of the earth, yet even among scholars this fact was scarcely kept in mind. It was therefore understandable that, to the uneducated, just as the sun to all appearance climbed the heavens, so a ship returning from

[1] Cf. p. 30 and note 4.

the margin of the known world below the horizon might have to climb back towards the land.

Views as to the distribution of land and water on the globe were diverse and confused, since no very clear distinction was maintained between the theoretical distribution, as deduced from first principles, and the distribution actually observed. Theoretically the two polar regions were uninhabitable because of the cold, and the region under the equinoctial was uninhabitable because of the heat. Hence the world was divisible into two habitable sections, and the observation that the known habitable land was everywhere environed by sea resulted in a 'schematic' globe whereon each quadrant included a land area isolated by sea from the other three. Actually it was known that Africa stretched across the equator, but the sudden popularizing of Ptolemy's Geography and maps in the fifteenth century gave very widespread currency to the belief that the known habitable land area, like the theoretical quadrant, had a width of 180° under the equinoctial.

Ptolemy considered the remaining 180° of the earth's surface to be water, and against the possibility of there being other unknown land quadrants beyond the seas, or at least against such lands being inhabited, the scriptures offered an insuperable difficulty. 'We have no description of them', wrote Roger Bacon, 'because no man has come from thence, and no man has gone thither.' But if the lands existed, this total absence of intercourse was in contradiction to the accepted belief in the descent of all mankind from Noah, and to the universality of the drowning of all mankind by the Flood. If no man had gone thither, whence came any race of men ? And since the preaching of the Gospel and offer of salvation had been promised to all mankind, how could there therefore be sections of humanity cut off from that message ? It was from this standpoint, not from any disbelief in a globular earth, that St. Augustine and others of the Fathers held it heretical to believe in the Antipodes, or people foot to foot with ourselves. The writings of Lactantius, who mocked at the idea of people hanging head downwards, while rain fell upwards, were recognized, except by the vulgar, as coming from a man more to be revered for his piety than for his learning. 'And that might right well be,' wrote Sir John Mandeville of a fabled circumnavigation, 'for all it be that simple men of cunning trow not that men may go under the earth, but if they fall into the firmament.' Nevertheless, no direct evidence could be offered to disprove the belief of some that the underside of the globe was waste and void, ruled still by Chaos, or alternatively that it bred non-human monsters; and the view that there was but a single limited tripartite land area, inhabited by men, surrounded by the ocean, and interpenetrated by five seas, remained the orthodox opinion of Columbus's day. The term 'continent' or *tierra firme* was used of countries forming part of this single land mass, as opposed to the islands that were adjacent to it: France, for example, was *tierra firme*, or continent with Europe, as opposed to Sicily which was an island, or Italy which was a peninsula. The modern use of 'continent' as a separate large land area only arose after the true nature of the new discoveries was realized. Columbus, an intensely religious man, held to his death the belief that he had discovered a hitherto unknown extremity of the tripartite 'firme'.

Within the circle of orthodox belief there was room for much diversity of opinion as to the dimensions of the single land area, with its adjacent islands. The famous Cardinal Pierre d'Ailly, writing before he had fully studied Ptolemy, offered to what proved to be an ever-widening circle of readers (for long after his death his works were printed) the views of Roger Bacon, which in their turn were based on a study of Aristotle and the Arab philosophers, side by side with the Almagest of Ptolemy, and the narratives of contemporary travellers such as William of Rubruck. Columbus's seeming wide knowledge of medieval and classical authors is due to the fact that he quoted them from d'Ailly, who in his turn has taken long passages verbatim from Roger Bacon. It is Bacon who develops at length,[1] relying upon a remark of Aristotle and a passage from St. Jerome, the thesis that Ptolemy's limit of 180° for the width of the land area was much too low, and that the distance between the extremity, or most westerly

[1] S. Jebb, *Opus Majus Rogeri Baconis*, 1733, pp. 192–5.

point, of Africa and the most easterly point of Asia across the intervening ocean could only be relatively small, although he could suggest no actual longitude for this space. Bacon, too, went thoroughly into the question of the extension of India across the equator, and accepted the existence of the well-populated kingdom of Patalis under the Tropic of Capricorn, taking care to point out where the Fathers, St. Basil and St. Ambrose, seemed in their writings to concur with such a possibility. So far as Bacon makes himself clear, he appears to indicate this southern India as an extension of modern peninsular India across the equator, having Taprobane (Ceylon) to the east of it, but both lying far east of their true position. Bacon wrote, however, before Marco Polo had described his voyage home from China, and fifteenth-century map-makers, so far as they took account of this view, drew on the eastern side of the Sinus Magnus a peninsula which ran southwards to Capricorn and then westwards, and afforded a location for Ptolemy's Cattigara, for Marco Polo's Lochac, and, if need be, for Patalis. In some instances authentic names belonging to the extreme south of the Indian peninsula, e.g. Moabar, and the Church of St. Thomas, were transferred to this peninsula in the attempt to reconcile conflicting authorities. There can be little doubt, and the view has recently been emphasized also by Mr. George Nunn,[1] that Columbus thought he was exploring this tropical peninsula of Eastern Asia on his third and fourth voyages, and believed that it was very much more extensive than had hitherto been supposed. As it appears on Behaim's Globe, we probably have this peninsula in a form which is typical of late fifteenth-century maps.

Roger Bacon has a further significant passage, which was adopted and reproduced by d'Ailly, and which probably influenced Columbus's interpretation of what he found. It was to the effect that Aristotle, and with him Averroes, had held that south of the equinoctial lay the more elevated and therefore the more noble part of the earth, and that above this part shone, too, the more noble stars. It has therefore been

---

[1] G. E. Nunn, *The Columbus and Magellan Concepts of South American Geography.*

conjectured by some, he adds, that here is the Earthly Paradise.[1] A comparison of Columbus's letters on the Third and Fourth Voyages[2] with the relevant sections of the *Opus Majus* makes it clear that, unknown to himself, the Admiral was relying on this cosmographical theory formulated in the thirteenth century, and it is permissible to believe that, if not on his first, yet on his later voyages, he had these equatorial and southern parts of Asia in view as rich in possibilities. That he sought a *far* southern continent, in the zone deemed 'uninhabitable because of the cold', or indeed that he sought at all a continent detached from the tripartite world,[3] the present writer deems inadmissible, alike in the light of current concepts, in the light of Columbus's religious orthodoxy, and in the light of the many statements in his letters that show his belief that he had reached the far side of the Sinus Magnus.

The gravest difficulty he had to face in impressing his belief upon his contemporaries was the fact that the lands of his discovery lay so short a distance from the Old World—a mere fortnight's sail, under favourable conditions, from the Canaries. Even when his cosmographical reading enabled him to substitute, to his own satisfaction, the estimate of Marinus of Tyre of the longitude of eastern Asia for that of Ptolemy, there were still 135 degrees, or nine hours of fifteen degrees, to be accounted for between the two seaward extremities of the tripartite main or firm. This space he shortened in linear measure by declaring for Alfragan's degree of $56\frac{2}{3}$ miles, in lieu of what was becoming more and more widely accepted, Ptolemy's degree of $62\frac{1}{2}$ miles. That he made the remeasurement which he claims, and independently arrived at this figure cannot seriously be maintained: Roger Bacon, who took it from Alfragan, pointed out that these miles were of 4,000 cubits, or 6,000 ft., i.e. $56\frac{2}{3}$ equalled 68 Italian miles. The equivalent, however, of $56\frac{2}{3}$ Italian miles (as Columbus assumed them to be) in sea leagues was just over 14, and so by dividing the day's run by the appropriate derivative figure, Columbus was able to calculate a very rapid longitudinal progress westward. But the pilots and shipmasters could not

[1] Cf. vol. i, p. cxv.   [2] pp. 2–111.   [3] vol. i, p. cxxi.

have been deceived; their stereotyped rules for fixing the ship's position were based on a degree of 17½ leagues, or 70 Italian miles, and it is confirmatory evidence that Columbus was never brought up to the sea that he could ignore this value, the least faulty of his day. According to the pilots' reckoning of the length of the second voyage (vol. i, p. 22) it was 780 leagues from Ferro to Dominica, which works out at about 48° of longitude, the correct figure being 43½°. Yet even his shortening of the degree fails to explain in its entirety Columbus's faulty reckoning. 'That which I know', he suddenly exclaims, in narrating his fourth voyage, 'is that in the year '94, I navigated westwards in 24° (N.) to the term of nine hours', i.e. to 135° W. longitude.[1] Actually he had reached only 65° west of Ferro, and conscious of what others will say, he continues obstinately, 'I cannot be in error, because there was an eclipse'. It is more probable that the admiral was self-deceived than deliberately deceiving, and if indeed he made so faulty an observation of, or calculation from, a lunar eclipse, it is only additional evidence that he was not trained as seamen were in the use of the *balestilha*, astrolabe, and quadrant. This enormous over-estimate of his longitude enabled him to recognize in Cuba the Province of Mangi, which marched with Cathay, and he proposed to seek the latter. But 'it is my belief', wrote Bernaldez (vol. i, p. 116), 'that traversing the firmament of sea and land for a further 1200 leagues, he would not arrive there, and so I told him'.

If further proof be needed that Columbus was not a professional seaman, it may be found in his handling of the *Rule for the North Star*, which formed another stereotyped section of a pilot's training.[2] According to the Rule, when the Guards (two stars of the Lesser Bear) were between the feet and the west arm (of the observer supposed with arms outstretched), the Tramontane or North Star was 3½° above the Arctic Pole, while when they had moved round to a position between the head and the east arm, the Star was 3½° beneath the Pole. Thus the North Star was considered to describe a

[1] pp. 82 and 83 n.
[2] See E. G. R. Taylor, *A Brief Summe of Geographie*, App. I (Hak. Soc. pub., ser. ii, vol. 69).

circle of diameter 7° about the Pole, but Columbus[1] puts the figure at 5°. Moreover, in order to support his contention that on his third voyage he had, like a divine messenger, discovered 'a new heaven and a new earth', he was able to observe a quite impossible series of altitudes for the tramontane between sunset and sunrise.[2] He told his story to Peter Martyr, who dismissed it as incredible, not only from the astronomical standpoint, but because as a rationalistic thinker, he regarded as legendary the high-perched Earthly Paradise whose neighbourhood Columbus believed to be heralded by this change of the heavens.

It is interesting to notice that it was along the line of longitude 100 leagues west of the Azores, the original line of demarcation of the Spanish sphere by the Papal Bull, and the line beyond which Columbus was to be viceroy, admiral, and governor-general, that he noted all the changes which he associated with his entry into the 'new heaven and new earth'. Not only did the motions of the stars change, but the variation (or declination) of the compass altered by a quarter of the wind ($11\frac{1}{4}°$), the scorching heat of the 'burning zone' gave place to a temperate air, and the people of that zone were no longer black, ill-formed, and woolly haired, but with fair, handsome countenances and silky locks. Among these remarkable changes, that of the magnetic declination was certainly true. That the needle did not, in Europe, point to the exact geographical north had long been known, and was allowed for by compass-makers, but everywhere it pointed a greater or smaller number of degrees east of north. After passing mid-Atlantic the declination was west of north, a phenomenon which had never been observed before Columbus's first voyage, and which well deserved emphasis. It is worth remark, however, that long after Columbus's death there were highly trained pilots who denied that what was called the 'easting and westing of the needle' had any other origin than a fault in the instrument. Certainly it could afford no proof that the underside of the earth had upon it a protuberance like the stalk-end of a pear, nor was a single globe-maker or cartographer influenced by such a view.

[1] pp. 10, 28 with note 1, and 32.   [2] pp. 30–34.

Unhappy Columbus! Obstinate to the last in his medie-
valism. Even while he strove to prove that Veragua was in
Asia within nineteen days of Ganges, the Portuguese were revealing the true longitude and contour of peninsular India,
Ludovic Varthema was voyaging in a Moorish vessel to the
Spice Islands, and the English were passing to and from
New Found Land. All the world was bent on discovery, and
well might the Admiral of the Ocean Sea, seeing so many and
so rich prizes fall into the hands of every one but himself,
cry out in the anguish of his disillusionment: 'Weep for me,
whoever has charity, truth and justice'.

NOTES ON THE DOCUMENTS

1. *Letter of Columbus on the Third Voyage*

(pp. 2–47.)

THE original letter of Columbus describing his third voyage is not known, but a copy in the autograph of Las Casas is preserved in the National Library of Madrid, and is printed by de Lollis.[1] The letter was dispatched from Española on 18 October 1498, and describes the discovery of Trinidad. From the Cape Verde Islands Columbus ran south-west for 480 miles until, as he says, the Pole Star was elevated 5° at nightfall, giving a latitude of about $8\frac{1}{2}°$ according to the current method of calculation. This is confirmed by his remark that he was in the latitude of Sierra Leone, approximately 8° 19′ N. This was within the traditional 'burning zone' (although constantly passed and repassed by the Portuguese), and Columbus paints an exaggerated picture of the sufferings of himself and his crew in order to enhance the supposed advantages of the hemisphere that lay beyond the Pope's Line. He proposed on reaching this bounding meridian to take advantage of the cooler climate and turn towards the equinoctial, but altered his plans and turned north-west, thus reaching Trinidad in 10° N. Here he found, he says, a climate like that of Valencia in April, although the sun's noontide rays were vertical. This confirmed his view that the original east point, where after the Creation the first sunrise occurred, was at the point where the meridian of demarcation cut the equator: this then was the true beginning of the East, or end of the West, i.e. the farthest bound of the tripartite world. The whole letter is written to support the thesis of Columbus's discovery of a 'new heaven and a new earth', a thesis which was born, perhaps unconsciously, of the disappointments that the Admiral had suffered with respect to any material gains from the first and second voyages.

[1] De Lollis, *Scritti*, vol. i, pt. 2, p. 26, Document XVI.

2. *The Letter to the Nurse*
(pp. 48–71.)

The letter to Donna Juana de la Torre, the gentlewoman who had been nurse to the young Prince of Castile and his sister, is known in four copies, which are discussed by de Lollis, who prints the text as Document XXXI.[1] Donna Juana was the sister of Antonio de Torres, who had accompanied Columbus on the second voyage, and it is witness to her gentle, sympathetic nature that the admiral turns to her to pour out his grief after the disasters of misgovernment and mismanagement in the young colony had ended in a revolt against his brother and himself, and when both found themselves prisoners and in chains. His announcement of the 'new heaven and new earth' had made no impression in Española, nor had he been able to carry out, what appears from an obscure passage in this letter to have been his intention (p. 68), a journey round the world westward to settle the further line of division of sea and land with Portugal.

3. *Letter of Columbus on the Fourth Voyage*
(pp. 72–111.)

Columbus's letter to their Highnesses of Spain describing his fourth voyage was written from Jamaica on 7 July 1503. It is printed as Document XXXXI by de Lollis,[2] from the copy preserved in the Royal Library of Madrid, which was first published by Navarrete. This is the only writing of Columbus which concerns his fourth voyage, and an Italian translation of the letter was printed at Venice during his lifetime (in 1505), under the title of *Lettera Rarissima*. The letter describes Columbus's westward journey in search of *tierra firme*, and sets forth the arguments by which he sought to prove that he had reached the south-eastern peninsula of Asia on the eastern side of the Sinus Magnus. On his return by western Cuba he reasserted that this was Mangi, the southern province of Cathay, while he was fully convinced that he had by his

---

[1] *De Lollis, Scritti*, vol. i, pt. 2, p. 66.
[2] *Ibid.*, p. 175.

discovery of Veragua placed King Solomon's Mines in the possession of the Crown of Spain. The picture which the Admiral draws of himself, trembling and weeping, but consoled by a heavenly vision, shows that disappointment and hardship had gone far to transform his religious fervour into fanaticism, and his belief in his destiny into an *idée fixe* from which he could not escape.

4. The Testament of Diego Mendez

(pp. 112–143.)

The last will and testament of Diego Mendez contains an account of his heroic voyage from Jamaica to obtain succour for the Admiral, who was marooned there after the conclusion of the westward voyage. The original document is in the archives of the Duke of Veragua in Madrid, and has been printed by Navarrete.[1] It was drawn up on 26 June 1536, long after the events which it records, but de Lollis suggests that while Columbus himself kept no log of his fourth voyage he entrusted the task to the faithful Mendez who here makes use of it.

[1] *Ibid.*, Appendices to Document **XXXXI**.

NOTES ON THE ILLUSTRATIONS AND MAPS

THROUGH the kindness of the Duque de Bérwick y de Alba, a drawing by the hand of Columbus, and what is probably a passage from a letter by him, are here reproduced. They are part of the contents of a very damaged and fragmentary note-book, evidently kept by Columbus during his first voyage, which the Duquesa de Bérwick y de Alba purchased from a private owner some thirty years ago. The vendor could give no information about the provenance or history of the note-book, but there is no doubt about its authenticity. The extract, as far as it can be deciphered, reads as follows: 'Ha placido asi darme el galardon destos afanes y peligros veramente abalumado con esta grande vitoria pleje a dios se redusgan los disfamadores de my honrra q con tanta deshoesidad y malcia ha fecho burla de my e disfamado my empresa sin conoscimiento de my dezir y del servicio e acrescentamiento de sus Altesas'. This may be translated: 'He has been pleased therefore to give me the reward of my toils and perils, [and I am] truly elated by this great victory. May it please God that the detractors of my honour may be abased, who with so much dishonesty and malice have made a mockery of me and defamed my enterprise without knowing either my statements or what advantages and increase of dominions would accrue to Their Majesties'.

The pages immediately following have been torn out of the note-book.

The map recently discovered at Constantinople and associated with Columbus is not reproduced in this volume, as it has not been possible to provide a critical commentary on it written by a cartographer well versed in Turkish. This map, which was found in 1929, was drawn by the Turkish geographer Piri Re'ìs in 1517. Piri Re'ìs states that he copied the islands and coasts of Central America from a map made by the Genoese Columbus which had come into his hands,— probably carried off by the Turks from a Spanish ship. From internal evidence it is thought that Columbus probably drew the original map, now lost, between 1494 and 1496; but he drew it to accord with his conviction that he had discovered a part of Asia, and there is no reason to think that it contained anything important or new. Piri Re'īs's map shows the town of Isabella, but only the name of San Domingo, which had not yet been built in 1496. *See* Kahle (Paul) in *Forschungen und Fortschritte*, Jhrg. 8, Nr. 19, Juli 1932, p. 248; Oberhummer (Eugen) in *Anzeiger der Akademie der Wissenschaften in Wien*, 1931, Nr. xviii–xxvii, pp. 99–112.

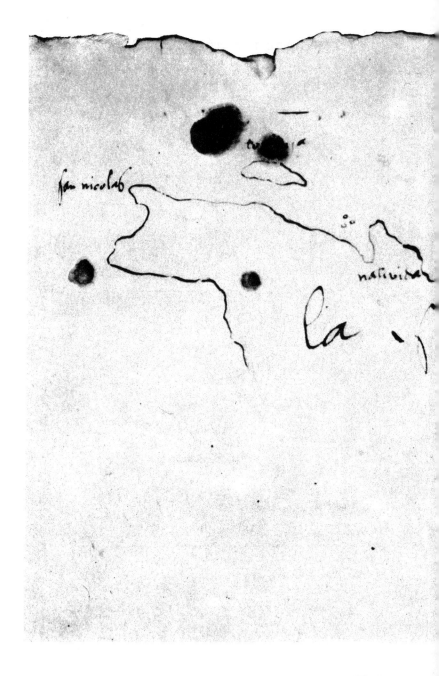

SKETCH OF TH

Drawn by Columbus on the first voyage. From the origin

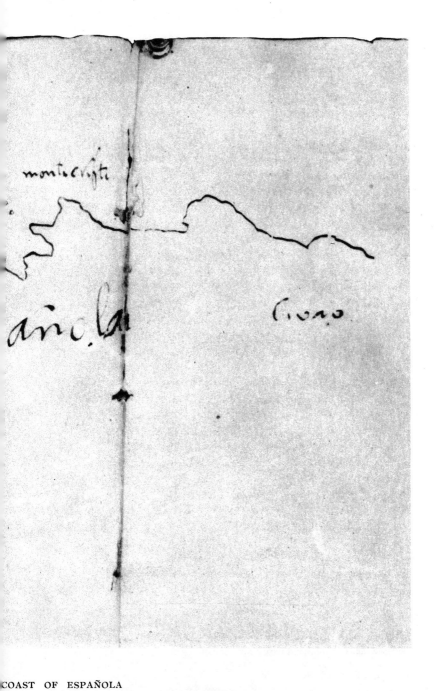

COAST OF ESPAÑOLA

in the possession of the Duque de Bérwick y de Alba.

THIRD VOYAGE OF COLUMBUS

1. *Narrative of the voyage which the admiral, Don Christopher Columbus, made the third time that he came to the Indies, when he discovered Tierra Firme, as he sent it to the sovereigns from the island of Española.*[1]

MOST serene and most high and most powerful princes, the king and queen, our sovereigns: The Holy Trinity moved Your Highnesses to this enterprise of the Indies, and of His infinite goodness, He made me the messenger thereof, so that, being moved thereunto, I came with the mission to your royal presence, as being the most exalted of Christian princes and so ardently devoted to the Faith and to its increase.[2] The persons who should have occupied themselves with the matter held it to be impossible, for they made of gifts of chance their riches and on them placed their trust.

On this matter I spent six or seven years[3] of deep anxiety, expounding, as well as I could, how great service might in this be rendered to the Lord, by proclaiming abroad His holy name and His faith to so many peoples, which was all a thing of so great excellence and for the fair fame of great princes and for a notable memorial for them. It was needful also to speak of the temporal gain therein, foreshadowed in the writings of so many wise men, worthy of credence, who wrote histories and related how in these parts there are great riches.[4] And it was likewise necessary to bring forward in this matter that which had been said and thought by those who have written of the world and who have described it.[5] Finally, Your Highnesses determined that this enterprise should be undertaken.

Here you displayed that lofty spirit which you have always shown in every great affair, for all those who had been engaged on the matter and who had heard the proposal, one and all

---

[1] For this letter, cp. *supra*, Introduction, p. lxxxv.

[2] Although too much stress has, perhaps, been laid upon this passage (e.g. by André, *La Véridique Aventure de Christophe Colomb*, p. 268), there is abundant evidence that Columbus did regard himself as being an instrument in the hands of Providence and as being under the special protection of the Almighty (cp. *supra*, vol. I, Introduction, p. lii).

TERCER VIAGE DE COLÓN

1. *La ystoria del viaje qu'el almirante don Christóval Colón hizo la tercera vez que vino á las Yndias, quando descubrió la tierra firme, como lo enbió á los reyes desde la isla Española.*

SERENÍSSIMOS é muy altos e muy poderosos príncipes, rey é reyna nuestros señores.

La Sancta Trinidad movió á Vuestras Altezas á esta empresa de las Yndias, y, por su infinita bondad, hizo á mi mensajero d'ello, al qual vine con el embaxada á su real conspetu, movido como á los más altos prínçipes de christianos y que tanto se exerçitavan en la fe y acreçentamiento d'ella. las personas que entendieron en ello lo tuvieron por impossible, y el caudal hazían sobre bienes de fortuna, y allí echaron el clavo. puse en esto seys ó siete años de grave pena, amostrando, lo mejor que yo sabía, quánto serviçio se podía hazer á Nuestro Señor en esto, en divulgar su sancto nombre y fe á tantos pueblos; lo qual todo era cosa de tanta exçelençia y buena fama y gran memoria para grandes prínçipes. fué también necessario de hablar del temporal, adonde se les amostró el escrevir de tantos sabios dignos de fe, los quales escrivieron hystorias, los quales contavan que en estas partes avía muchas riquezas. y asimismo fué neçessario traer á esto el dezir y opinión de aquellos qu'escrivieron y situaron el mundo. en fin, Vuestras Altezas determinaron qu'esto se pusiese en obra. aquí mostraron el grande coraçón que siempre fiçieron en toda cosa grande; porque todos los que avían entendido en ello y oýdo esta plática, todos á una mano lo tenían á burla, salvo dos frayles que siempre fueron con-

---

[3] Cp. *supra*, Introduction, p. xiii.

[4] Cp. the notes, perhaps written by Columbus himself, to the *Historia Rerum Ubique Gestarum* of Pius II (*Rac. Col.* I. ii. 291 *et seq.*). Streicher (*op. cit.*) holds that these notes are not in the autograph of Columbus, but there is little doubt that Columbus had in any case read the work of Pope Pius.

[5] Columbus was here certainly thinking primarily of Pierre d'Ailly and Marco Polo, whose writings he had studied and annotated. It is uncertain whether he had actually read the *Imago Mundi* before his first voyage (cp. *supra*, vol. I, Introduction, p. lxviii). From Bernáldez (cp. *supra*, vol. I, p. cxlvii), it would seem that Columbus had also read John Mandeville.

laughed it to scorn, save two friars who were ever constant.[1]

I, although I suffered weariness, was very sure that this
would not come to nothing, and I am still, for it is true that all
will pass away,[2] save the Word of God, and all that He has
said will be fulfilled. And He spake so clearly of these lands by
the mouth of Isaiah, in many places of his Book, affirming
that from Spain His holy name should be proclaimed to them.[3]

And I set forth in the name of the Holy Trinity, and I
returned very speedily, with evidence of all, as much as I had
said, in my hand. Your highnesses undertook to send me
again, and in a little while I say that, not by . . . ,[4] but by the
grace of God, I discovered three hundred and thirty-three
leagues of Tierra Firme,[5] the end of the East,[6] and seven
hundred islands of importance,[7] over and above that which I
discovered on the first voyage, and I circumnavigated the
island of Española, which in circumference is greater than all
Spain, wherein are people innumerable,[8] all of whom should
pay tribute.[9]

Then was born the defaming and disparagement of the
undertaking which had been begun there, because I had not
immediately sent caravels laden with gold, no thought being
taken of the brevity of the time and the other many obstacles
which I mentioned. And on this account, for my sins or, as I
believe that it will be, for my salvation, I was held in abhorrence and was opposed in whatever I said and asked.[10]

For this cause, I decided to come to Your Highnesses,[11] and
to cause you to wonder at everything, and to show you the

---

[1] The allusion is, of course, to the initial rejection of the propositions of
Columbus by the committee appointed to investigate them (cp. *supra*, Introduction, p. xvi). The two friars were probably Juan Pérez, guardian of the friary
of La Rábida, and Antonio de Marchena, a member of the same community,
who have been wrongly regarded as one and the same person. But the friars may
be Juan Perez and Diego de Deza. The latter, a native of Toro, was a Dominican
and a master in theology. He was tutor to Prince Juan and was afterwards
successively bishop of Salamanca, Jaen, and Palencia, archbishop of Seville, and
archbishop of Toledo. He was also confessor to Ferdinand and succeeded
Torquemada as grand inquisitor. His position in the Church made his support of
Columbus peculiarly valuable. Deza died in 1523.   [2] Matt. xxiv. 35.
[3] Columbus was probably alluding to Isaiah lv. 5 and lx. 9. Acosta (*Historia
Natural y Moral de las Indias*, i. 42) finds a prophecy of the discovery of the
New World in Isaiah xviii. 1. Las Casas (i. 127), commenting on this letter of

stantes. yo, bien que llevase fatiga, estava bien seguro qu'esto
no vernía á menos, y estoy de contino, porqu'es verdad que
todo pasará, y no la palabra de Dios, y se complirá todo lo
que dixo, el qual tan claro habló d'estas tierras por la boca
de Isaýas en tantos lugares de su escriptura, afirmando que
de España les sería divulgado su sancto nombre.
E partí en nombre de la Sancta Trinidad, y bolví muy
presto con la experiençia de todo quanto yo avía dicho en la
mano. tornáronme á enbiar Vuestras Altezas ; y en poco espaçio
digo no de ... le descubrí por virtud divinal trezientas y treinta
y tres leguas de la tierra firme, fin de oriente, y setecientas yslas
de nombre, allende de lo descubierto en el primero viaje, y le
allané la ysla Española, que boja más qu'España, en que la
gente d'ella es sin cuento, y que todos le pagasen tributo.
naçió allí maldezir y menospreçio de la ympresa començada
en ello ; porque no avía yo enbiado luego los navíos cargados
de oro, sin considerar la brevedad del tiempo y lo otro que
yo dixe de tantos inconvenientes. y, en esto, por mis pecados
ó por mi salvaçión creo que será, fué puesto en abhorreçi-
miento y dado impedimento á quanto yo dezía y demandava.
por lo qual acordé de venir á Vuestras Altezas, y maravi-
llarme de todo, y mostrarles la razón que en todo avía. y les

Columbus, remarks that since Isaiah was a prophet, he no doubt foretold the
discovery of the Indies, but adds that it would be presumptuous to specify any
particular passage in which the prophecy is to be found.
    [4] Lacuna in the original: obviously some such phrase as 'my own might'
should be inserted. (Cp. Zechariah, iv. 6.)
    [5] Cp. *supra*, p. 2.   [6] Cp. *infra*, p. 30.
    [7] Las Casas (i. 127) says that the islands in the Jardín de la Reina numbered
seven hundred, but they can hardly be called 'islands of importance'.
    [8] Cp. *supra*, vol. I, pp. 6–12.
    [9] For the imposition of tribute on the native population of Española, see Las
Casas, i. 105, and Peter Martyr, i. 4. There is some ground for thinking that the
tribute was never generally exacted, and it may have been some doubt in the
mind of Columbus as to whether it would be paid, that suggested the phrase used
in this passage (cp. *The Government of the Colonies in Española*, in *Twenty-First
International Congress of Americanists* (first part), p. 381 *et seq.*).
    [10] The allusion is to the attacks made upon him by Firmin Zedo, Buil, Margarit,
and others, and perhaps also to the opposition experienced from Juan de Soria (cp.
supra, vol. I, p. xlv, note 1), and possibly from Fonseca. Personal antipathy to Columbus is said to have been illustrated by the treatment accorded by the hangers-
on of the court to his sons, Diego and Ferdinand (cp. Ferdinand Columbus, c. 85).
    [11] The reference is to the return of Columbus to Spain after the mission of Juan
Aguado.

reason that I had for all. And I told you of the peoples whom I had seen, among whom or from whom many souls may be saved. And I brought to you the service of the people of the island of Española, how they were bound to pay tribute and how they held you as their sovereigns and lords. And I brought to you abundant evidence of gold, and that there are mines and very great nuggets, and likewise of copper. And I brought to you many kinds of spices,[1] of which it would be wearisome to write, and I told you of the great amount of brazil and of other things, innumerable.[2]

All this was of no avail with certain persons who were determined, and who had begun, to malign the enterprise. Nor did it avail to speak of the service of Our Lord in the salvation of so many souls, nor to say that from this the greatness of Your Highnesses had reached a higher point than any prince had attained hitherto, because the labour and expense was for both spiritual and temporal ends, and that it could only be that in process of time Spain would derive thence great benefits. Of this very manifest proofs appear in that which has been written concerning these parts, so that the fulfilment of all else will also be seen hereafter.[3]

And it did not avail to speak of the things which great princes throughout the world have done to increase their fame, as of Solomon who sent from Jerusalem to the end of the East to visit Mount Sopora,[4] in which the ships were engaged for three years, which mountain Your Highnesses to-day possess in the island of Española, or of Alexander who sent to examine the government of the island of Taprobana in India,[5] or of Nero Caesar who sent to explore the sources of the Nile and the reason why they increased in the summer, when the rivers are low,[6] or of many other great things which

[1] Cp. *supra*, vol. 1, p. 76, note 1.

[2] Commenting on this passage, Las Casas (i. 127) says that the only spice in the island was pepper (axi, or agi); that there was much mastic, but that it was neglected for the sake of gold hunting, and that as to brazil, Columbus brought some to Spain, but that its collection was afterwards neglected. Oviedo (ix. 15) says that brazil wood was found in Española near the lake of Xaragua, the modern Lake Enriquillo.

[3] The allusion is probably to such accounts as had been already written concerning the New World, e.g. to his own letters, to that of Dr. Chanca, and, perhaps, to the letters which Peter Martyr was writing to various correspondents in Italy: nineteen of these letters had been written before Columbus set out on his

dixe de los pueblos que yo avía visto, en qué ó de qué se
podrían salvar muchas ánimas, y les truxe las obligaçiones de
la gente de la ysla Española, de como se obligavan á pagar
tributo, é les tenían por sus reyes y señores, y les truxe abas-
tante muestra de oro, y que ay mineros y granos muy grandes,
y asimismo de cobre, y les truxe de muchas maneras de espe-
çerías, de que sería largo de escrevir. y les dixe de la grande
cantidad de brasil y otras infinitas cosas. todo no aprovechó
para con algunos personas que tenían gana y dado comienço á
maldezir del negoçio, ni entrar con fabla del servicio de
Nuestro Señor con se salvar tantas ánimas, ni á dezir qu'esto
era grandeza de Vuestras Altezas, de la mejor calidad que
hasta oy aya usado príncipe, porqu'el exerçiçio y gasto era
para el espiritual y temporal, y que no podía ser que, andando
el tiempo, no oviese la España de aquí grandes provechos, pues
que se veýan las señales que escrivieron de lo d'estas partidas
tan manifiestas, que también se llegaría á ver todo el otro
complimiento, ni á dezir cosas que usaron grandes prínçipes
en el mundo, para creçer su fama, así como Salamón que
embió desde Hierusalem en fin de oriente á ver el monte
Sopora, en que detovieron los navíos tres años, el qual tienen
Vuestras Altezas agora en la isla Española: ni de Alexandre
que enbió á ver el regimiento de la isla de Trapobana en Yndia,
y Nero Çésar á ver las fuentes del Nilo y la razón porque

third voyage, if the dating of the letters in the *Opus Epistolarum* can be trusted.
  ⁴ Mount Sophora (not Sopora) is the name given to Ophir by Pierre d'Ailly
(*Imago Mundi*, c. 38: *Rac. Col.* I. ii. 394). This passage is annotated by Columbus
(notes 303–4: *Rac. Col. ibid.*), and is no doubt the source from which he derived
the name. The voyage of the ships of Solomon to Ophir, and the situation of that
land, were clearly of special interest to Columbus (cp. his notes 166 and 374, to the
Imago Mundi, and 500, to the *Epilogus Mappe Mundi*: *Rac. Col.* I. ii. 394, 399,
408). At the end of the *Historia Rerum Ubique Gestarum*, of Pius II, the passage
from Josephus (*Antiquities of the Jews*, viii. 3) dealing with the voyage to Ophir,
is transcribed, but Streicher (*op. cit.*) holds that this note is not in the autograph
of Columbus. Las Casas (i. 128), commenting on this passage, remarks that no
Christian or pagan writer mentions 'Sophora' and that no one can say where it
is; he adds that it is certainly not in Española and that it was never owned by
Ferdinand and Isabella.
  ⁵ The expedition of Onesicritus (Pliny, vi. 22 &c.), which is mentioned by
Pierre d'Ailly (*Imago Mundi*, c. 42) in a passage which is annotated by Columbus
(note 324; *Rac. Col.* I. ii. 396).
  ⁶ Cp. Seneca, *Naturales Questiones*, vi. 8. The exploration is mentioned by
Pius II (*Hist. Rerum*, c. 5), and this passage was possibly annotated by Columbus
(cp. note 27, to Pius II; *Rac. Col.* I. ii. 294).

princes have done, and to say that these things are given to princes to do.

Nor did it avail to say that I have never read that princes of Castile had ever gained lands beyond their own borders[1] and that this land here is another world from that in which the Romans and Alexander and the Greeks laboured to gain dominion with great toils, nor to speak of the present, of the kings of Portugal who have had courage to penetrate to Guinea and for the discovery of that land, and who have spent gold and people to such an extent that, if the whole population of the realm were numbered, it would be found that as many more as the half have died in Guinea, and still they persevered until there came to them from it that which is known, and this they began long ago and there is very little which brings them revenue. They have also dared to make conquests in Africa and to maintain their undertaking at Ceuta, Tangier and Arcilla, and Alcazar, and continually to give battle to the Moors, and all this at great expense, only to do something princely, for the service of God and for the increase of His dominion.[2]

The more I said, the more was redoubled the effort to bring this into reproach, abhorrence for it being displayed, without considering how well it appeared throughout the world, and how well Your Highnesses are regarded among all Christians for having undertaken this enterprise, so that there was no one, great or small, who did not desire news of it. Your Highnesses answered me, encouraging me and saying that I should feel no concern, since you gave no weight or credit to any who maligned this enterprise to you.[3]

I departed, in the name of the Most Holy Trinity, on Wednesday, 30 May, from the town of San Lucar,[4] very wearied from my journey, for I had hoped for rest there when I left these Indies, and my pain had been doubled.[5] And I navi-

---

[1] This would seem to ignore the acquisition of the Canary Islands. Although the conquest of the first islands was undertaken by private adventurers, Alonso de Lugo received a commission for the conquest of Palma from Ferdinand and Isabella (1493) and for that of Tenerife (1495).

[2] Ceuta was taken by the Portuguese in 1415, lost and regained in 1471; Tangier was taken in 1437, lost and regained in 1471; Arcilla was taken in 1471

creçían en el verano quando las aguas son pocas, y otras
muchas grandezas que hizieron prínçipes, y que á prínçipes
son estas cosas dadas de hazer. ni valía dezir que yo nunca
avía leýdo que prínçipes de Castilla jamás oviesen ganado
tierra fuera d'ella, y que esta de acá es otro mundo en que se
trabajaron Romanos y Alexandre y Griegos, para la aver, con
grandes exerçiçios, ni dezir del presente de los reyes de Portugal que tovieron coraçón para sostener á Guinea y del descobrir d'ella, y que gastaron oro y gente atanta que quien con-
tase toda la del reyno, se hallaría que otra tanta como la
mitad son muertos en Guinea; y todavía la continuaron hasta
que les salió d'ello lo que pareçe. lo qual todo començaron
de largo tiempo, y a muy poco que les da renta. los quales
también osaron conquistar en Africa y sostener la empresa
á Cepta, Tánjar y Arcilla y Alcáçar, y de contino dar guerra á
los Moros. y todo esto con grande gasto, sólo por hazer
cosa de prínçipes, servir á Dios, y acreçentar su señorio.
quanto yo más dezía, tanto más se doblava á poner esto á
vituperio, amostrando en ello aborreçimiento, sin considerar
quánto bien pareçió en todo el mundo y quánto bien se dixo
en todos los christianos de Vuestras Altezas, por aver tomado
esta empresa, que no ovo grande ni pequeño que no quisiese
d'ello carta. respondiéronme Vuestras Altezas riéndose y
diziendo que yo no curase de nada, porque no davan auctoridad ni creençia á quien les maldezía de esta empresa.

Partí, en nombre de la Sanctíssima Trinidad, miércoles,
treynta de mayo, de la villa de San Lúcar, bien fatigado de

and Alcazar in 1458. Las Casas (i. 127), copying this letter of Columbus, gives
Arguin and Angola, for Arcilla and Alcazar.

³ The allusion is to the favourable reception of Columbus by the sovereigns
on his return to Spain in 1496 and to the rejection of the unfavourable report
made by Juan Aguado.

⁴ Columbus sailed, 30 May 1498, from San Lucar de Barrameda, at the mouth
of the Guadalquivir. It was from this port that Magellan sailed on his voyage
round the world.

⁵ In his account of this voyage of Columbus, Las Casas, who may have been
using the admiral's diary, elaborates this passage, with a curious confusion of
personal pronouns. He says that Columbus complained of the annoyance which
he had experienced from the officials of the king and of the opposition with which
he met from those who were most influential with the sovereigns, and that his
past service counted for nothing, so that it was necessary to undertake fresh
labours (cp. Las Casas, i. 130).

gated to the island of Madeira by an unaccustomed route, to avoid trouble which I might have had with a fleet from France, which waited for me at Cape Saint Vincent.[1] And from there I navigated to the Canary Islands,[2] whence I departed with one ship and two caravels, and I sent the other ships on the direct course to the Indies to the island of Española.[3] And I sailed southwards, with the intention of reaching the equinoctial line, and from there following it westwards so that the island of Española would be left to the north of me.

And having reached the islands of Cape Verde, a false name,[4] since they are so barren that I saw no green thing in them and all the people were infirm, so that I did not dare to remain in them, I sailed to the south-westward, four hundred and eighty miles, which is a hundred and twenty leagues, where, when it grew dark, I found the north star to be in the fifth degree[5]. There the wind failed me and I came into so great heat and so intense that I believed that the ships and people would be burned, so that all suddenly fell into such confusion that there was no one who dared to go below deck to attend to the water cask and provisions. This heat lasted for eight days. On the first day, it was fine, and on the seven days following it rained and was cloudy, and yet we found no relief.[6] I believe certainly that if it had been sunny as it was on the first day, it would have been in no wise possible to escape.

I recalled that, in navigating to the Indies, whenever I passed to the westward of the islands of the Azores a hundred leagues, there I found the temperature change, and that everywhere from north to south. And I determined that, if it pleased Our Lord to give me a wind and fair weather so that I could get away from where I was, I would cease to go more to the south and would not go back either, but navigate westward, following that course in the hope of finding the same

[1] The League of Venice had been formed and war had begun between Spain and France early in the year.

[2] At Gomera he encountered a French corsair, who had captured two Castilian vessels; on the approach of Columbus, the corsair cut his cables and fled with one of the two captured vessels, abandoning the other. Columbus sent a ship in pursuit, whereupon the Spaniards on board the captured vessel overpowered their French guards and brought her back to Gomera (Las Casas, i. 130).

[3] Columbus sailed with six ships, but at Gomera he decided to send three vessels forward to Española with supplies. They were placed under the com-

mi viaje, que, adonde esperaba descanso quando yo partí
d'estas Yndias, se me dobló la pena. y navegué á la ysla de la
Madera por camino no acostumbrado, por evitar escándalo
que pudiera naçer con un'armada de Françia, que me aguar-
dava al cabo de San Viçeynte, y de allí á las yslas de Canaria,
de adonde me partí con una nao y dos caravelas; y enbié
los otros navíos á derecho camino á las Yndias á la isla
Española, y yo navegué al austro, con propósito de llegar á
la línea equinoçial y de allí seguir al poniente hasta que la
ysla Española me quedase al setentrión. y, llegado á las yslas
de Cabo Verde, falso nombre, porque son atán secas que no ví
cosa verde en ellas, y toda la gente enferma, que no osé
detenerme en ellas, y navegué al sudueste quatroçientas y
ochenta millas, que son çiento y veynte leguas, adonde, en
anocheçiendo, tenía la estrella del norte en çinco grados.
allí me desamparó el viento, y entré en tanto ardor y tan
grande, que creý que se me quemasen los navíos y gente;
que, todo de un golpe, vino atán desordenado, que no avía
persona que osase desçendir debaxo de cubierta á remediar la
vasija y mantenimientos. duró este ardor ocho días; al
primer día fué claro, y los siete días siguientes llovió y hizo
ñublado; y, con todo, no fallamos remedio, que, çierto, si
así fuera de sol como el primero, yo creo que no pudiera
escapar en ninguna manera. acórdome que, navegando á
las Yndias, siempre que yo passo al poniente de las islas de los
Açores çient leguas, allí fallo mudar la temperança, y esto
es todo de septentrión en austro. y determiné que, si á Nuestro Señor le pluguiese de me dar viento y buen tiempo que
pudiese salir de adonde estava, de dexar de yr más al austro

mand of Pedro de Arana, the brother of Beatriz Enriquez, Alonso Sanchez
de Carvajal, and 'Juan Antonio Colombo, a Genoese, a relative of the
Admiral, a man of great capacity and discretion, and of weight, with whom
I have often talked' (Las Casas, *loc. cit.*). According to the account of this voyage
given by Las Casas, the six vessels did not actually part company until the Cape
Verde Islands had been reached. He says that Columbus gave the commanders
of the ships that he sent forward careful instructions concerning the course which
they were to steer to Española.

⁴ The islands were named from the cape on the mainland of Africa, not from
any characteristics of their own.

⁵ Cp. *supra*, Introduction, p. lxxxiii.

⁶ Las Casas (i. 131) says that the rain and cloudy weather brought some relief
to the crews, although they still had no hope of escape.

temperature as I had found when I navigated in the parallel of the Canaries. And then, if it were so, I should still be able to proceed more to the south.

And it pleased Our Lord at the end of these eight days to give me a favourable east wind, and I steered westward, but I did not dare to go lower down to the south, because I found a very great change in the sky and in the stars, but I did not find change in the temperature. So I decided to proceed further always directly westward, in a straight line from Sierra Leone, with the intention of not changing my course up to the point where I had thought that land would be found, and there to repair the vessels and, if possible, to renew our supplies and to take in the water which was needed.

And at the end of seventeen days, during which Our Lord gave me a favouring wind, on Tuesday 31 July, at midday, land appeared to us, and I had expected to sight it on the previous Monday and held to this course up to then. But as the strength of the sun grew, and on account of deficiency of water, of which we were short, I determined to go to the islands of the Caribs and took that route. And as the divine Majesty has always shown mercy towards me, a sailor went up to the main-top to look out and to the westward saw three mountains near one another.[1] We repeated the *Salve Regina*[2] and other prayers, and we all gave many thanks to Our Lord.

And after this I abandoned the northerly course and made for the land, and I arrived there at the hour of compline at a cape which I called *la Galea*,[3] having already named the island *Trinidad*.[4] There is there a very good harbour if bottom could be reached, and there were houses and very fair lands, as lovely and as green as the orchards of Valencia in March. It weighed upon me that I could not enter the harbour, and I ran along the coast of this land to the westward, and having gone five leagues I found a very good bottom and anchored.[5]

---

[1] Land was first sighted by Alonso Pérez, a sailor from Huelva and a servant of Columbus. It was the island of Trinidad (Las Casas, i. 132).

[2] The opening words of one of the breviary anthems to the Virgin.

[3] Las Casas (i. 133) says that the cape was called 'la Galera' because a rock there had the appearance of a galley. It is now known as Cape Galeota, and is the south-easterly point of Trinidad.

ni bolver tampoco atrás, salvo de navegar al poniente, atanto que yo llegase á estar con esta raya, con esperança que yo fallaría allí así temperamiento, como avía fallado quando yo navegava en el pararelo de Canaria, y que, si así fuese, que estonçes yo podría yr más al austro. y plugo á Nuestro Señor que, al cabo de estos ocho días, de me dar buen viento levante, y yo seguí al poniente, mas no osé declinar abaxo al austro, porque fallé grandíssimo mudamiento en el çielo y en las estrellas; mas no fallé mudamiento en la temperançia. así, acordé de proseguir adelante, siempre justo al poniente, en aquel derecho de la sierra Lioa, con propósito de no mudar derrota fasta adonde yo avía pensado que fallaría tierra, y allí adobar los navíos, y remediar, si pudiese, los mantenimientos, y tomar agua que no tenía.

Y al cabo de .17. días, los quales Nuestro Señor me dió de próspero viento, martes, treynta y uno de julio, á medio día, nos amostró tierra; y yo la esperava al lunes antes, y tuve aquel camino fasta entonçes, que, en saliendo el sol, por defecto del agua, que no tenía, determiné de andar á las islas de los Caníbales, y tomé esa buelta. y como Su Alta Majestad aya siempre usado de misericordia comigo, por açertamiento subió un marinero á la gavia, y vido al poniente tres montañas juntas. diximos la Salve Regina y otras prosas, y dimos todos muchas gracias á Nuestro Señor. y después dexé el camino del septentión, y bolví hazia la tierra, adon de yo llegué, á ora de completas, á una cabo á que dixe 'de la Galea', después de aver nombrado á la isla 'de la Trinidad'; y allí oviera muy buen puerto, si fuera fondo, y avía casas y gente y muy lindas tierras, atán fermosas y verdes como las

---

⁴ The devotion of Columbus to the Trinity constantly appears and Las Casas (i. 132) says that on this occasion the admiral had resolved that the first land sighted should be named in honour of the Trinity. He adds, quoting Columbus, 'It pleased Our Lord, by His exalted majesty, that there were first seen three mountains, I say three mountains, all at one time and at one view. Of His goodness, His exalted power guides me, and in such manner that He receives much service and your highnesses much pleasure, since it is certain that the discovery of this land in this place was as great a miracle as the discovery of land on the first voyage.'

⁵ Columbus had entered Guayaguayare Bay. Off Cape Galeota, the sea has sixteen fathoms depth, and there is deep water to the east and south. To the west it becomes shallower, and there good anchorage could be found in the bay, which has a clean sandy bottom.

And the next day I set sail on this course, seeking a harbour in order to repair the ships and take in water, and to add to the corn and the only provisions which I had brought. There I took in a pipe of water, and then went on so until we arrived at the cape. There I found shelter from the east wind and a good bottom, and so I commanded to anchor and to repair the water cask and to take in water and wood. And I ordered the people to land to rest themselves on account of having suffered fatigue for so long a time during which they were voyaging. To this point I gave the name *del Arenal.*[1] And there all the ground was trodden by some animals[2] which had footprints like those of a goat, and although, as it appeared, there were many there, I saw none except one that was dead.

On the following day there came from towards the east a large canoe with twenty-four men, all in the prime of life and very well provided with arms, bows and arrows and wooden shields, and they, as I have said, were all in the prime of life, well-proportioned and not negroes, but whiter than the others who have been seen in the Indies, and very graceful and with handsome bodies, and hair long and smooth, cut in the manner of Castile. They had their heads wrapped in scarves of cotton, worked elaborately and in colours, which, I believed, were *almaizares.*[3] They wore another of these scarves round the body and covered themselves with them in place of drawers.

When this canoe arrived, it hailed us from a great distance, and neither I nor anyone else could understand them. However, I ordered signs to be made to them that they should approach, and in this way more than two hours passed, and if they came a little nearer, they at once sheered off again. I caused pans and other things which shone to be shown to them in order to attract them to come, and after a good while they came nearer than they had hitherto done. And I greatly desired to have speech with them and it seemed to me that I had nothing that could be shown to them now which would induce them to come nearer. But I caused to be brought up to the castle of the poop a tambourine, that they might play

---

[1] Columbus sailed along the south coast of Trinidad from Cape Galeota to the extreme south-westerly point of the island, which he named Punta del

huertas de Valençia en março. pesóme quando no pude
entrar en el puerto, y corrí la costa d'esta tierra, del luengo,
fasta el poniente; y, andadas çinco leguas, fallé muy buen
fondo y surgí. y en el otro día dí la vela á este camino, buscando puerto para adobar los navíos y tomar agua y remediar
el trigo y los bastimentos que llevava, solamente. allí tomé
una pipa de agua, y con ella anduve ansí hasta llegar al cabo;
y allí fallé abrigo de levante y buen fondo. y así mandé
surgir y adobar la vasija y tomar agua y leña y desçendir la
gente á descansar de tanto tiempo que andavan penando.
á esta punta llamé 'del Arenal'. y allí se falló toda la tierra
follada de unas animalias que tenían la pata como de cabra; y
bien que, según pareçe ser, allí aya muchas, no se vido sino
una muerta.

El día siguiente vino de hazia oriente una grande canoa
con veynte y quatro hombres, todos mançebos y muy ataviados de armas, arcos y flechas y tablachinas; y ellos, como
dixe, todos mançebos de buena disposiçión, y no negros, salvo
más blancos que otros que aya visto en las Yndias, y de muy
lindo gesto y fermosos cuerpos; y los cabellos largos y llanos,
cortados á la guisa de Castilla, y trayan la cabeça atada con
un pañuelo de algodón, texido á labores y colores, el qual
creya yo que era almayzar. otro d'estos pañuelos trayan
çeñido, y se cobijavan con él en lugar de pañetes. quando
llegó esta canoa, habló de muy lexos; y yo ni otro ninguno no
los entendíamos, salvo que yo les mandava hazer señas que
se allegasen. y en esto se passó más de dos oras. y si se
llegavan un poco, luego se desviavan. yo les hazía mostrar
baçines y otras cosas que luzían, por enamorarlos porque
viniesen, y á cabo de buen rato allegaron más que hasta
estonçes no avían. y yo deseava mucho aver lengua y no
tenía ya cosa que me pareciese que era de mostrarles para que
viniesen, salvo que hize sobir un tanborín en el castillo de

Arenal, and which is now known as Point Ycacos. His course, as is pointed out
by Thacher (ii. 384, note 3), can be gathered quite clearly from the account given
by Las Casas (i. 133).

² Probably one of the species of deer existing in this district (cp. Oviedo, xii.
19).

³ A gauze veil or scarf, worn by the Moors in Spain, generally as a head
covering. The reason for the interest shown by Columbus in this is obvious.

it, and some young men to dance, believing that they would draw near to see the festivity. And as soon as they observed the playing and dancing, they all dropped their oars and laid hand on their bows and strung them, and each one of them took up his shield, and they began to shoot arrows. I immediately stopped the playing and dancing, and then ordered some crossbows to be discharged. They left me and went quickly to another caravel and in haste got under its stern. And the pilot accosted them and gave a coat and a hat to a man who seemed to be one of the chief among them, and it was arranged that he should go to speak with them there on the shore, where they went at once in the canoe to wait for him. And he would not go without my permission, and when they saw him come to my ship in the boat, they entered their canoe again and went away, and I never saw any more of them or of the other inhabitants of this island.

When I reached this Punta del Arenal, I found that the island of Trinidad formed with the land of Gracia[1] a strait, two leagues broad from west to east, and that it was necessary to enter it in order to pass to the north. There were some signs of currents which crossed that strait and which made a very great roaring, and I believed that there must be a reef with shallows and rocks, owing to which it would not be possible to enter it. And behind this current, there was another and another which all made a great roaring like that of the sea when it breaks and dashes against rocks. I anchored there at the said Punta del Arenal, outside the said strait, and I found that the water came from the east towards the west with as much fury as that of the Guadalquivir when it is in flood. This was continuous, night and day, so that I believed that it would not be possible to go against the current, or to go forward owing to the shallows.[2]

And in the night, when it was already very late, being on the deck of the ship, I heard a very terrible roaring which came from the direction of the south towards the ship. And I stayed to watch, and I saw the sea from west to east rising, like a hill as high as the ship, and still it came towards me

---

[1] The strait here mentioned is the Boca de la Sierpe, and the coast opposite is not the modern peninsula of Paria, but the delta of the Orinoco, part of the

popa, que tañesen, y unos mançebos que dançasen, creyendo que se allegarían á ver la fiesta. y luego que vieron tañer y dançar, todos dexaron los remos y echaron mano á los arcos y los encordaron, y enbraçó cada uno su tablachina, y començaron á tyrarnos flechas. çessó luego el tañer y dançar, y mandé luego sacar unas ballestas; y ellos dexáronme, y fueron, á más andar, á otra caravela, y de golpe se fueron debaxo la popa d'ella. y el piloto entró con ellos, y dió un sayo y un bonete á un hombre prinçipal, que le pareçio, d'ellos y quedó conçertado que le yría á hablar allí en la playa, adonde ellos luego fueron, con le canoa, esperándole; y él, como no quiso yr sin mi liçençia, como ellos le vieron venir á la nao con la barca, tornaron á entrar en la canoa y se fueron, y nunca más los vide, ni á otros d'esta isla.

Quando yo llegué á esta punta del Arenal, allí se haze una boca grande de dos leguas de poniente á levante, la isla de la Trinidad con la tierra de Graçia, y que, para aver de entrar dentro para passar al septentrión, avía unos hyleros de corriente que atravesavan aquella boca, y trayan un rugir muy grande; y creý yo que sería un arraçife de baxos y peñas, por el qual no se podría entrar dentro en ella. y detrás d'este hilero avía otro y otro, que todos trayan un rugir grande como ola de la mar que va á romper y dar en peñas. surgí allí á la dicha punta del Arenal, fuera de la dicha bocha, y fallé que venía el agua del oriente fasta el poniente con tanta furia como haze Gualdalquivir en tiempo de avenida, y esto de contino, noche y día, que creý que no podría bolver atrás, por la corriente, ni yr adelante, por los baxos. y en la noche, ya muy tarde, estando al bordo de la nao, oý un rugir terrible que venía de la parte del austro hazia la nao, y me paré á mirar, y ví levantando la mar de poniente á levante, en manera de una loma tan alta como la nao; y todavía venía hazia mi poco á poco. y ençima d'ella venía un filero de corriente, que venía rugiendo con muy grande estrépito con aquella furia de aquel

State of Monagas of the modern republic of Venezuela. Columbus, however (cp. *infra*, p. 18), gave the name 'Gracia' to all the land opposite Trinidad and hence it was all called Paria, which was said to be the native name of the country (cp. *infra*, p. 20).

² The current and roaring were the result of the entrance of the Orinoco into the sea.

little by little. And above it, there came a wave which advanced, roaring with a very great noise with the same fury of roaring as that of the other currents, which, I have said, appeared to me as the waves of the sea breaking on rocks. To this very day, I remember the fear that I had lest the wave should overwhelm the ship when it came upon her, and it passed by and reached the strait where it continued for a great while.

And the next day following I sent the boats to take soundings and I found that in the shallowest part of the strait there were six or seven fathoms of water, and there were constantly those currents flowing, some into and others out of the strait. And it pleased Our Lord to give me a fair wind, and I passed into this strait and soon found calm water. And by chance I drew some water from the sea and I found it to be fresh.

I navigated northwards as far as a very lofty mountain range,[1] twenty-six leagues or so[2] from this Punta del Arenal, and there were there two headlands of very high ground, one on the eastern side, which belonged to the same island of Trinidad,[3] and the other on the west, belonging to the land which I called *Gracia*.[4] And there a strait was formed,[5] much narrower than that by Punta del Arenal, and there were there the same currents and that great roaring of the water as there was at Punta del Arenal, and there also the sea was fresh water.

Up to then I had not had speech with any people of these lands and I greatly desired to do so. For this reason, I navigated along the coast of this land towards the west, and the further I went, the fresher and more wholesome I found the water of the sea. Having gone a great distance, I arrived at a place where the land appeared to me to be cultivated. I anchored and sent the boats ashore. They found that there had recently been people there, and they found the whole mountain covered with monkeys.[6] They returned and, as the country here was mountainous, it appeared to me that

---

[1] The Cordillera de la Costa, in the peninsula of Paria.

[2] This would at the rate of four leagues to the mile be one hundred and four miles, more than twice the actual distance from Punta del Arenal to the Bocas del Drago.

rugir, que de los otros hileros tengo el miedo en el cuerpo que
no me trabucasen la nao quando llegasen debaxo d'ella. y
passó y llegó fasta la boca, adonde allí se detuvo grande
espaçio.

Y el otro día siguiente enbié las barcas á sondar, y fallé
en el más baxo de la boca que avía seys ó siete braços de
fondo, y de contino andavan aquellos hileros, unos por entrar
y otros por salir. y plugo á Nuestro Señor de me dar buen
viento; y atravesé por esa boca adentro, y luego hallé tran-
quilidad; y por açertamiento se sacó del agua de la mar, y la
hallé dulçe. navegué al septentrión fasta una sierra muy alta,
adonde serían veynte y seys leguas d'esta punta del Arenal,
y allí avía dos cabos de tierra muy alta: el uno de la parte
del oriente, y era de la misma isla de la Trinidad, y el otro del
ocçidente de la tierra que dixe 'de Gracia'; y allí hazía una
boca muy angosta, más que aquella de la punta del Arenal, y
allí avía los mismos hileros y aquel rugir fuerte del agua, como
era la punta del Arenal; y asimismo allí la mar era agua dulçe.
y fasta entonçes yo no avía avido lengua con ninguna gente
d'estas tierras, y io deseava en gran manera. y por esto
navegué al luengo de la costa d'esta tierra hazia el poniente;
y quanto más andava, hallava el agua de la mar más dulçe y
más sabrosa. y, andando una gran parte, llegué á un lugar
donde me parecían las tierras labradas, y surgí, y enbié las
barcas á tierra, y fallaron que de fresco se avía ydo de allí
gente, y fallaron todo el monte cubierto de gatos paules.
bolviéronse. y como esta fuese sierra, me pareçió que más

---

[3] Las Casas (i. 134, 138) says that Columbus called the cape on the mainland
Cabo de la Playa, and that in Trinidad Cabo Boto. Navarrete (i. 250) identified
the cape on the mainland with Punta de la Peña, the modern Promontorio de
Paria, and that in Trinidad with Peña Blanca (cp. *infra*, note 5).

[4] The peninsula of Paria.

[5] The statement that the strait here was much narrower than that at Punta
del Arenal suggests that Columbus was speaking not of the whole Bocas del
Drago, but only of the Boca Grande, the strait between Paria and the island of
Chacachacara. This view is further suggested by the fact that on this island
Cabresse Point rises to a height of 787 feet, and although lower than Monos
Island (942 feet) is higher than the nearest point on the actual mainland of
Trinidad. In this case the 'two headlands' would be the Promontorio de Paria
and Cabresse Point.

[6] The 'macacos', the great foes of cocoa growers.

further to the west, there would be flatter land, and that, for that reason, it would be inhabited.

I ordered the anchors to be weighed and I ran along this coast to the end of this mountainous part, and there I anchored in a river.[1] And immediately many people came, and they told me that they called this land *Paria* and that further westward from there it was more populated. I took four of them and afterwards I navigated to the west, and having gone eight leagues further westward, beyond a point which I named *Punta del Aguja*,[2] I found there some lands, the most lovely in the world and very populous. I arrived there one morning at the hour of tierce, and on seeing this verdure and this beauty, I decided to anchor and to see these people.

Of them, some came at once in canoes to the ship to ask me, on behalf of their king, that I should land. And when they saw that I was not concerned at them, they came in infinite numbers to the ship in canoes, and many wore pieces of gold on their breasts, and some had some pearls round their arms. I rejoiced greatly when I saw these things and made great efforts to know where they procured them, and they told me, in that place and to the northward of that land.[3] I could have wished to remain there, but these supplies, which I was carrying, corn and wine and flesh for these people who are here, were on the verge of being lost, when I had brought them so far with such great labour. And accordingly I sought to do nothing else than to go on to be able to place them in security, and not to wait for anything.

I endeavoured to obtain some of those pearls, and I sent the boats ashore. These people are very numerous, and all are of very good appearance, of the same colour as the others before, and very tractable. Our people who went ashore found them very well disposed, and they received them very courteously. They say that as soon as the boats reached land, two principal persons came with all the people; they believe that one was the father and the other his son. And they led them to a very large house, built with two *aguas*[4] and not round,

---

[1] This would seem to mean that Columbus navigated along the coast of the peninsula of Paria until he reached a point where the mountains were no longer

allá, al poniente, las tierras eran más llanas, y que allí sería poblado, y por esto sería poblado. y mandé levantar las anclas, y corrí esta costa fasta el cabo d'esta sierra, y allí á un río surgí; y luego vino mucha gente, y me dixeron como llamavan á esta tierra 'Paria', y que de allí, más al poniente, era más poblado. tomé d'ellos quatro, y después navegué al poniente. y, andadas ocho leguas más al poniente, allende una punta, á que yo llamé 'de l'Aguja', hallé unas tierras las más hermosas del mundo y muy pobladas. legué allí una mañana, á ora de terçia, y, por ver esta verdura y esta hermosura, acordé surgir y ver esta gente, de los quales luego vinieron en canoas á la nao á rogarme, de partes de su rey, que descendiese en tierra. y quando vieron que no curé d'ellos, vinieron á la nao infinitíssimos en canoas, y muchos traýan pieças de oro al pescueço, y algunos atados á los bracos algunas perlas. holgué mucho, quando las ví, y procuré mucho de saber dónde las hallavan: y me dixeron que allí, y de la parte del norte de aquella tierra.

Quisiera detenerme, mas estos bastimentos que yo traýa, trigo y vino y carne, para esta gente que acá está, se me acabavan de perder, los quales ove allá con tanta fatiga, y por esto yo no buscava sino, á más andar, á venir á poner en ellos cobro, y no me detener para cosa alguna. procuré de aver de aquellas perlas, y enbié las barcas á tierra. esta gente es muy mucha, y toda de muy buen pareçer, de la misma color que los otros de antes y muy tratables. la gente nuestra, que fué á tierra, los hallaron tan convenibles, y los reçibieron muy honrradamente. dizen que, luego que llegaron las barcas á tierra, que vinieron dos personas prinçipales con todo el pueblo: creen qu'el uno el padre, y el otro era su hijo, y los llevaron á una casa muy grande, hecha á dos aguas, y no redonda como tienda del campo, como son estas otras; y

close to the sea. The river was identified by Navarrete (*Coleccion de los Viages y Descubrimientos que hicieron por mar los Españoles desde fines del siglo XV*, tom. 1.) as being just west of Punta Cumaná.

² Punta del Alcatraz, 10° 27' N. 56° 13' W. (Navarrete, *loc. cit.*).

³ Las Casas (i. 136) makes the natives say that the pearls are found 'to the north'; they obviously came from the islands of Margarita and Cubagua. No pearls have been found in the Gulf of Paria.

⁴ This probably means that the roof sloped in two directions and not merely in one direction.

like field tents, as are the others. They had there many seats on which they caused them to sit, and others on which they seated themselves. They caused bread to be brought and fruit of many kinds and wine of many kinds, white and red,[1] but not made from grapes; the wine must be made from fruits of different kinds, some from one fruit and some from another, and also some of it may be made from maize,[2] which is a plant bearing an ear like an ear of wheat, some of which I brought home and there is now much in Castile. It seems that the best is regarded as most excellent and has great value. All these men were together at one end of the house, and the women at the other. Both parties were grieved that they did not understand one another, they in order to ask the others of our country, and our men in order to learn about their land. And after they had been given a meal there in the house of the elder, the younger took them to his own house, and made them another equal meal, and after that they got into the boats and came back to the ship.

And at once I weighed anchor, for I went in great haste to save the supplies, which were being ruined and which I had brought with so great toil, and also to restore my own health. For, as a result of lack of sleep, I was suffering in my eyes, and although on that voyage, when I went to discover Tierra Firme, I was thirty-three days without tasting sleep and was for so great a time blind, my eyes were not so injured, nor did they run with blood and cause so much pain as now.[3]

These people, as I have already said, are all of very fine stature, tall and very graceful in their movements; their hair is very long and smooth, and they have their heads bound with certain worked scarves, as I have said, handsome, which from a distance appear to be of silk and *almaizares*. They wear another scarf, very large, girded round them, with which they cover themselves in place of drawers, as well men as women. The colour of these people is whiter than that of any other race that has been seen in the Indies. They all wear something on the breast and on the arms, as is the custom in these lands, and many wear pieces

---

[1] The wine was perhaps the *cocuiza*, made from the leaves of the agave.

allí tenían muchas sillas, adonde los fiçieron assentar, y otras,
donde ellos se assentaron, y hizieron traer pan y de muchas
maneras frutas, y vino de muchas maneras, blanco y tinto, mas
no de uvas, deve el de sen de diversas maneras, uno de una
fruta y otro de otra; y asimismo deve de ser d'ello de mahíz,
que es una simiente que haze una espiga como una maçorca,
de que llevé yo allá, y ay ya mucho en Castilla; y pareçe que
aquel que lo tenía mejor, lo traýa por mayor exçelençia y lo
dava en gran preçio. los hombres todos estavan juntos á un
cabo de la casa, y las mugeres en otro. recibieron ambas las
partes gran pena porque no se entendían, ellos para preguntar
á los otros de nuestra patria, y los nuestros por saber de la
suya. y después que ovieron resçebido colaçión allí en casa
del más viejo, los llevó el moço á la suya, y fizo otro tanto;
y después se pusieron en las barcas, y se vinieron á la nao, y
yo luego levanté las anclas, porque andava mucho de priesa
por remediar los mantenimientos que se me perdían, que yo
avía avido con tanta fatiga, y también por remediarme á mi,
que avía adolesçido por el desvelar de los ojos; que, bien qu'el
viaje que yo fuí á descubrir la tierra firme, estoviese treynta
y tres días sin conçebir sueño, y estoviese tanto tiempo sin
vista, no se me dañaron los ojos ni se me rompieron de sangre
y con tantos dolores como agora.

Esta gente, como ya dixe, son todos de muy linda estatura,
altos de cuerpos y de muy lindos gestos, los cabellos muy
largos, y llanos, y traen las cabeças atadas con unos pañuelos
labrados, como ya dixe, hermosos, que pareçen de lexos de
seda y almayzares. otro traen çeñido, más largo, que se
cobijan con él en lugar de pañetes, ansí hombres como
mugeres. la color d'esta gente es más blanca que otra que
aya visto en las Yndias. todos traýan al pescueço y á los
braços algo, á la guisa d'estas tierras. y muchos traýan pieças
de oro baxo colgado al pescueço. las canoas d'ellos son muy
grandes y de mejor hechura que non son estas otras, y más
livianas; y en el medio de cada una tienen un apartamiento

---

² *Chicha*, a heavy, white drink, much sweetened, is made from maize in
modern Venezuela. Las Casas (ii. 26) mentions red and white wine made from
maize in Tierra Firme, and expresses his approval of it.

³ The reference is to the voyage of discovery of 1494: for the illness of Columbus at that time cp. Las Casas, i. 99.

of gold, hanging below the breast.[1] Their canoes are very large and better built than are those of the others, and lighter, and in the middle of each they have a separate division, like a room, in which I saw that the chief men went with their women. I called this place there *Jardines*, for it corresponded to that name.

I made great endeavours to know where they collected that gold and they all indicated to me a land bordering on them to the west, which was very lofty but not at a distance. But all told me that I should not go there, for there they ate men, and I understood then that they said that there were cannibals there, and that they were like the other cannibals. And since I have thought that it may be that they said this because there are there wild animals. Also I asked them where they gathered the pearls, and they also indicated that it was to the westward and to the north, beyond this land, where they were. I omitted to prove this, on account of the supplies and of the bad state of my eyes, and because a large ship which I had was not suited for such an undertaking. And as the time was short, it was all spent in questioning, and they returned to the ships which was at the hour of vespers, as I have said.

And at once I weighed anchor and navigated to the westward, and so on the following day, in the belief that this was certainly an island and that I should be able to come out to the northward, until I found that there were hardly three fathoms of water. Having seen this, I sent a light caravel in advance to see if there was a way out or if it was closed. And so it went a great distance as far as a very large gulf, where it appeared that there were four other gulfs of moderate size and into one a very great river flowed.[2] They always found five fathoms depth and the water very fresh, in very great quantity, and such that I never drank its like. I was very discomforted at that, when I saw that it was not possible to come out to the north and that it was already impossible to go to the south or to the west, because I was shut in by the land on all sides. So I weighed anchor and turned back to go out to the northward by the passage which I have mentioned above, and I was not able to go by the village

[1] Oviedo (xxv. 10, 22) describes the customs of the natives of Venezuela.

como cámara, en que ví que andavan los prinçipales con sus mugeres.

Llamé allí á este lugar 'Jardines', porque así conforman por el nombre. procuré mucho de saber dónde cogían aquel oro, y todos me aseñalavan una tierra frontera d'ellos, al poniente, que era muy alta, mas no lexos. mas todos me dezían que no fuese allá, porque allí comían los hombres, y entendí entonçes que dezían que eran hombres caníbales y que serían como los otros. y después e pensado que podría ser que lo dezían porque allí avría animalias. también les pregunté adónde cogían las perlas, y me señalaron también que al poniente y al norte, detrás d'esta tierra donde estavan. dexélo de probar por esto de los mantenimientos y del mal de mis ojos, y por una nao grande que traygo, que no es para semejante hecho. y como el tiempo fué breve, se passó todo en preguntas, y se bolvieron a los navíos que sería ora de bísperas, como ya dixe. y luego levanté las anclas, y navegué al poniente.

Y asimesmo el día siguiente, fasta que me fallé que no avía sinon tres braços de fondo, con creencia que todavía esta sería isla y que yo podría salir al norte. y, así visto, enbié una caravela sotíl adelante á ver si avía salida ó si estava çerrado; y ansí anduvo mucho camino fasta un golfo muy grande, en el qual pareçía que avía otros quatro medianos, y del uno salía un río grandíssimo. fallaron siempre cinço braços de fondo, y el agua muy dulçe, en tanta cantidad, que yo jamás beví la pareja d'ella. fuý yo muy descontento d'ella, quando ví que no podía salir al norte ni podía ya andar al austro ni al poniente, porque yo estava cercado por todas partes de la tierra. y así levanté las anclas y torné atrás para salir al norte por la boca que yo arriba dixe, y no pude bolver por la poblaçión adonde yo avía estado, por causa de las corrientes que me avían desviado d'ella. y siempre en todo cabo hallava el agua dulçe y clara, y que me llevava al oriente muy rezio fazia las dos bocas que arriba dixe. y entonçes conjeturé que los hilos de

---

² Columbus may here mean either the Boca Ajes and the Rio de Paria, at the extreme western end of the peninsula, or the Rio Guarapiche, which also enters the western part of the Gulf of Paria, but further to the south. The latter identification would seem to be, on the whole, the more probable, since the river was obviously of considerable size.

where I had been, on account of the currents which bore me away from it.[1] And always, at every cape, I found the water fresh and clear, and that it carried me very swiftly to the eastward towards the two straits which I have mentioned above.

Then I surmised, concerning the streaks of current and the rolling waves, which went out of and entered into these straits, with that great and violent roaring, that there was a battle between the fresh water and the salt. The fresh struggled with the other to prevent its entrance, and the salt with the other that it might not come out. And I conjectured that there where are these two straits there may at one time have been continuous land between the island of Trinidad and the land of Gracia, as Your Highnesses will be able to see from the drawing of it which I send to you with this.[2] I went out by this strait to the north and I found that the fresh water was always victorious, and when I passed through, which was by the force of the wind, being on one of these waves, I found in those waves, on the inner side fresh water, and on the outer side salt.

When I navigated from Spain to the Indies, I found that, immediately after passing a hundred leagues to the west of the Azores, there was a very great change in the sky and in the stars and in the temperature of the air and in the waters of the sea.[3] I have used much care in verifying this. I found that from north to south, passing there the said hundred leagues from the said islands, immediately the needle of the compass, which up to then had turned to the north-east, turned a full quarter of the wind to the north-west. And on reaching that line there it is as if a hill had been carried there. And also I found all the sea full of vegetation of a kind which resembles pine branches and very full of fruit like that of the mastic tree.[4] And it is so dense that, on the first voyage, I thought that it was a shallow and that the ships would run aground, and until this line was reached not a single branch was found. I found also on arriving there, the sea very gentle and smooth, and that though the wind was strong, it never became rough. Also I found within this line, towards the west, the temperature of the sky very mild, and that there was no

---

[1] For the strength of the currents, cp. the *West India Pilot*.

la corriente, y aquellas lomas que salían y entravan en estas
bocas con aquel rugir tan fuerte, que era pelea del agua dulçe
con la salada. la dulçe empuxava á la otra porque no
entrasse, y la salada porque la otra no saliese. y conjeturé
que allí donde son estas dos bocas que algún tiempo sería
tierra contina á la isla de la Trinidad con la tierra de Graçia,
como podrán ver Vuestras Altezas por la pintura de lo que
con esta les embío. salí yo por esta boca del norte, y hallé
qu'el agua dulçe siempre vençía; y quando passé, que fué con
fuerça de viento, estando en una de aquellas lomas, hallé en
aquellos hylos, de la parte de dentro, el agua dulçe, y, de
fuera, salada.

Quando yo navegué d'España á las Yndias, fallo luego,
en passando çient leguas á poniente de los Açores, grandíssimo
mudamiento en el çielo y en las estrellas y en la temperancia
del ayre y en las aguas de la mar; y en esto e tenido mucha diligençia en la experiençia. fallo que de septentrión en austro,
passando las dichas çient leguas de las dichas islas, que,
luego, en las agujas de marear que fasta entonçes nordesteavan,
noruestean una quarta de viento todo entero. y esto es en
allegando allí á aquella línea, como quien traspone una cuesta.
y asimesmo fallo la mar toda llena de yerva de una calidad que
pareçe ramitos de pino, y muy cargada de fruta como de
lentisco. y es tan espessa que al primer viaje pensé que era
baxo, y que daría en seco con los navíos; y hasta llegar con
esta raya no se falla un solo ramito. fallo también, en
llegando allí, la mar muy suave y llana, y bien que vente
rezio, nunca se levanta. asimesmo, hallo dentro de la dicha
raya, hazia poniente, la temperançia del çielo muy suave, y
no discrepa de la cantidad, quier sea invierno, quier sea en
verano. quando allí estoy, hallo que la estrella del norte
escrive un çírculo, el qual en el diámetro çinco grados, y,
estando las guardas en el braço derecho, estonçes está la

---

² This drawing was seen by Alonso de Ojeda and led him to undertake a voyage
of discovery in that direction (cp. evidence of Ojeda, *Pleitos*, i. 204).

³ Cp. *supra*, p. 10, where Columbus has made almost exactly the same
statements.

⁴ The Sargasso Sea, which lies between 16° and 38° N. and 35° and 80° W. The
vegetation is most abundant about 45° W. (cp. Gaffarel, 'La Mer des Sargasses',
Bul. de Société de Géographie, Dec. 1872: and Humboldt, *Examen Critique*).

change in its character whether it was winter or whether it was summer. When I was there, I found that the north star described a circle which was five degrees in diameter, and when the guards are in the right arm, the star is at its lowest point, and it continues to rise until they are in the left arm, and then it is five degrees, and from that point it sinks until they reach again the right arm.[1]

On this occasion I went from Spain to the island of Madeira, and thence to the Canaries, and thence to the Cape Verde islands. From that point, I steered a course to navigate southwards to below the equinoctial line, as I have already said. Arriving at a point directly on the parallel which passed through Sierra Leone in Guinea, I found so great heat, and the rays of the sun were so intense, that I thought that I should be burned, and although it rained and the sky was very overcast, I was always in that state of exhaustion, until Our Lord gave me a fair wind and put into my heart the wish to navigate to the west, with the encouragement that on reaching the line of which I have already spoken, I should find there a change in temperature.[2] As soon as I came to be directly on this line, immediately I found the temperature very mild, and as I went further forward, so it became more mild, but I did not find the stars corresponding with this. I found there that when night came on the pole star was five degrees high, and then the guards were overhead, and afterwards at midnight the star had risen to ten degrees, and at daybreak to fifteen, when the guards were below. I found the same smoothness of the sea, but not the same vegetation. In the matter of the pole star, I felt great wonder, and accordingly with great care I spent many nights in examining it carefully with the quadrant, and always I found that the lead and line fell to the same point. I regard this as something new, and it may be that it will be held that the sky undergoes a great change in a brief space.

I have always read that the world, land and water, was spherical, and authoritative accounts and the experiments which Ptolemy and all the others have recorded concerning this matter,[3] so describe it and hold it to be, by the eclipses of

[1] According to the conventional sailing manuals, the Pole Star described a

estrella en el más baxo, y se va alçando, fasta que llega al
braço izquierdo; y estonçes está çinco grados, y de allí se va
abaxando, fasta llegar á bolver otra vez al braço derecho.

Yo allegué agora d'España á la ysla de la Madera, y de
allí á Canaria, y dende á las islas de Cabo Verde, de adonde
cometí el viaje para navegar al austro fasta debaxo la línea
equinoçial, como yo dixe. allegado á estar en derecho con el
paralelo que passa por la sierra Leoa en Guinea, fallo tan
grande ardor, y los rayos del sol tan calientes, que pensava
de quemar, y, bien que lloviese y el çielo fuese muy turbado,
siempre yo estava en esta fatiga, fasta que Nuestro Señor
proveyó de buen viento, y á mi puso en voluntad que yo
navegase al occidente, con este esfuerco, que en llegando á
la raya, de que yo dixe, que allí fallaría mudamiento en la
temperançia. después que yo emparejé á estar en derecho
d'esta raya, luego fallé la temperançia del çielo muy
suave, y, quanto más andava adelante, más multiplicava;
mas no hallé conforme á esto las estrellas. fallé allí que, en
anocheçiendo, tenía yo la estrella del norte alta çinco grados,
y estonçes las guardas estavan ençima de la cabeça, y después,
á la media noche, fallava la estrella alta diez grados, y, en
amaneçiendo, que las guardas estavan en los pies quinze.
la suavelidad de la mar fallé conforme, mas no en la yerva.
en esto de la estrella del norte tomé grande admiración; y por
esto muchas noches con mucha diligençia tornava yo á
repricar la vista d'ella con el quadrante; y siempre fallé que
caýa el plomo y hilo á un punto.

Por cosa nueva tengo yo esto, y podrá ser que será tenida,
que en poco espaçio haga tanta differençia el çielo.

Yo siempre leý qu'el mundo, tierra y agua, era espérico, y
las auctoridades y esperiençias que Ptolomeo y todos los
otros qu'escrivieron d'este sitio davan y amostraban para ello,
así por ecclipses de la luna y otras demonstraçiones que
hazen de oriente fasta occidente, como de la elevaçión del

circle of 7° diameter, and was lowest when the guards stood between the right
arm and the head. Cp. *supra*, Introduction, pp. lxxxii–lxxxiii.
² Cp. *supra*, p. 12. This is another duplicated passage.
³ Cp. the notes of Columbus on the *Imago Mundi* (note 5) and on the *Epilogus
Mappe Mundi* (note 480: *Rac. Col.* I. ii. 374, 406). The reference to Ptolemy
would seem to be to the *Almagestum*, i. 4.

the moon and by other demonstrations made from east to west, as well as from the elevation of the pole star from north to south. Now, as I have already said, I have seen so great irregularity that, as a result, I have been led to hold this concerning the world, and I find that it is not round as they describe it, but that it is the shape of a pear which is everywhere very round except where the stalk is, for there it is very prominent, or that it is like a very round ball, and on one part of it is placed something like a woman's nipple, and that this part, where this protuberance is found, is the highest and nearest to the sky, and it is beneath the equinoctial line and in this Ocean sea at the end of the East.[1] I call that 'the end of the East', where end all the land and islands.[2]

And in support of this, I urge all the arguments given above, concerning the line which passes from north to south a hundred leagues west of the Azores.[3] For in passing thence to the westward, the ships went rising gently towards the sky, and then the mildest weather was enjoyed, and the needle shifted a quarter of the wind on account of this mildness, and the further we went, the more the needle shifted towards the north-west, and this elevation causes the variation of the circle which the north star describes with the guards, and the nearer I approached to the equinoctial line, the more they rose and the greater difference there was in the said stars and in their orbits.

And Ptolemy and the other wise men who have written of this world believed that it was spherical and that this hemisphere was round as that in which they lived and which had its centre in the island of Arin,[4] which is under the equinoctial line between the Arabian gulf and that of Persia; and the circle passes over Cape St. Vincent in Portugal westward and eastward by Cangara[5] and the Seres.[6] In that hemisphere, I do not question at all that it is spherical, rounded, as they say, but I declare that this other hemisphere is as the half of a very round pear, which has a raised stalk, as I have said, or like a woman's nipple on a round ball. Of this half, neither Ptolemy nor the others who wrote of the

---

[1] Cp. *infra*, pp. 32–34, and notes of Columbus to the *Imago Mundi* (note 16: *Rac. Col.* I. ii. 375).

polo de septentrión en austro. agora ví tanta disformidad,
como ya dixe; y por esto me puse á tener esto del mundo, y
fallé que no era redondo en la forma qu'escriven, salvo que
es de la forma de una pera que sea toda muy redonda, salvo
allí donde tiene el peçón, que allí tiene más alto, ó como quien
tiene una pelota muy redonda, y en un lugar d'ella fuesse
como una teta de muger allí puesta, y qu'esta parte d'este
peçón sea la más alta y más propinca al çielo, y sea debaxo
la línea equinoçial, y en esta mar Ocçéana, en fin del oriente,
(llamo yo fin de oriente adonde acaba toda la tierra y islas).

y para esto allego todas las razones sobre escriptas de la raya
que passa al ocçidente de las islas de los Açores çient leguas
de septentrión en austro, que, en passando de allí al poniente,
ya van los navíos alçándose hazia el çielo suavamente, y
entonçes se goza de más suave temperançia, y se muda el
aguja del marear, por causa de la suavidad, d'esa quarta de
viento, y quanto más va adelante y alçándose, más norvestea,
y esta altura causa el desvariar del çírculo que escrive la
estrella del norte con las guardas. y quanto más passare junto
con la línea equinoçial, más se subirán en alto y más differençia avrá en las dichas estrellas y en los çírculos d'ellas. y
Ptolomeo y los otros sabios, qu'escrivieron d'este mundo,
creyeron que era espérico, creyendo qu'este hemisperio que
fuese redondo como aquel de allá donde ellos estavan, el qual
tiene el çentro en la isla de Arín, qu'es debaxo la línea equinoçial, entre el sino Arábico y aquel de Persia; y el çírculo passa
sobre el cabo de San Viçeynte en Portogal por el poniente; y
passa en oriente por Cangara y por las Seras. en el qual hemisperio no hago yo que ay ninguna dificultad, salvo que sea
espérico redondo, como ellos dizen. mas este otro digo que es
como sería la mitad de la pera bien redonda, la qual toviese
el peçón alto, como yo dixe, ó como una teta de muger en una
pelota redonda. así que d'esta media parte non ovo notiçia

<hr>

2 Cp. note of Columbus to *Imago Mundi* (note 166: *Rac. Col.* I. ii. 386–7).
3 Cp. *supra*, pp. 10–11.
4 The sacred city of Odjein or Ougein in Malwa. Cp. the notes of Columbus
on the *Epilogus Mappe Mundi* (notes 483, 484: *Rac. Col.* I. ii. 406), and *supra*,
Introduction, p. lxxvii.
5 China.
6 Cp. *Imago Mundi* (c. xxiii. and note 142 of Columbus: *Rac. Col.* I. ii. 384).

world had knowledge, as it was then utterly unknown, and they based their arguments on the hemisphere where they were, which is a round sphere, as I said above.

And now that Your Highnesses have commanded navigation and search and discovery, it is very evidently revealed, for I, being on this voyage twenty degrees north of the equinoctial line, was there in the latitude of Hargin[1] and of those lands, and there the people are black and the land very burned; and afterwards I went to the Cape Verde Islands, and there in those lands the people are much blacker, and the more they are to the south, the more they approach the extreme, so that on the line on which I was, which is that of Sierra Leone, where when night came on the north star rose five degrees, there the people are black to an extreme degree, and after that, as I sailed westward, there were the same excessive heats. And when I had passed the line of which I have spoken, I found that the temperature became milder, becoming so to such an extent that when I reached the island of Trinidad, where the north star as night came on also rose five degrees, both there and in the land of Gracia I found a very mild climate and the land and the trees very green and as lovely as the orchards of Valencia in April. And the people there I found to be of very fair stature and whiter than the others who have been seen in the Indies, and their hair long and smooth, and they are shrewder and have greater intelligence and are not cowards. The sun was then in Virgo, above our heads and theirs. Thus all this must proceed from the very mild climate that is there, and this in turn from the fact that the land is the highest in the world, nearest to the sky, as I conceive.[2] And so I affirm that the world is not spherical, but that it has this different form which I have already described, which is in this hemisphere where end the Indies and the Ocean sea, and its extremity is under the equinoctial line.

And it argues much that this is so, that the sun, when Our Lord made it, was at the first point of the east, or the first light was here in the East, there where is the extreme height of the world. And although the opinion of Aristotle[3] was that

---

[1] The island of Arguin, twenty-five miles S.E. of Cape Blanco, on the west coast of Africa, and eight miles from the shore.

Ptolomeo, ni los otros que escrivieron del mundo, por ser muy
ignoto. solamente hizieron raýz sobre el hemisperio adonde
ellos estavan, qu'es redondo espérico, como arriba dixe. y
agora que Vuestras Altezas lo an mandado navegar y buscar
y descobrir, se amuestra evidentíssimo; porque, estando yo
en este viaje al septentrión veynte grados de la línea equinoçial, allí era en derecho de Hargín y de aquellas tierras, y
allí es la gente negra y la tierra muy quemada. y después que
fuí á las islas de Cabo Verde, allí en aquellas tierras es la gente
mucho más negra, y quanto más baxo se van al austro, tanto
más llegan al estremo. en manera que allí en derecho, donde
yo estava, qu'es la sierra Leoa, adonde se me alçava la estrella
del norte, en anocheçiendo, çinco grados, allí es la gente negra
en estrema cantidad, y, después que de allí navegué al ocçidente, tan estremos calores. y passada la raya, de que yo dixe,
fallé multiplicar la temperançia, andando en tanta cantidad
que quando yo llegué á la isla de la Trinidad, adonde la estrella
del norte, en anocheçiendo, también se me alçava çinco grados,
allí y en la tierra de Graçia hallé temperançia suavíssima, y las
tierras y árboles muy verdes y tan hermosos como en abril
en las guertas de Valençia, y la gente de allí de muy linda
estatura, y blancos que más otros que aya visto en las Yndias,
y los cabellos muy largos y llanos, y gente más astuta y de
mayor ingenio, y no cobrades. estonçes era el sol en Virgen
encima de nuestras cabeças y suyas. ansí que todo esto proçede por la suavíssima temperançia que allí es, la qual pro·
çede por estar más alto en el mundo, más çerca del ayre que
cuento. y así me afirmo qu'el mundo no es esférico, salvo
que tiene esta differençia, que ya dixe, la qual es en este hemisperio adonde caen las Yndias y la mar Occéana, y el estremo
d'ello es debaxo la línea equinoçial. y ayuda mucho á esto que
sea ansí, porqu'el sol, quando Nuestro Señor lo hizo, fué en
el primer punto de oriente, ó la primera luz fué aquí en oriente,
allí donde es el estremo de la altura d'este mundo. y bien
qu'el pareçer de Aristótel fuese que el polo antártico, ó la

<hr />

² Cp. Pierre d'Ailly, *De concordia Discordantium Astronomorum*, and the notes
of Columbus (notes 866, 868, 869, 880: *Rac. Col.* I. ii. 443-4).

³ Cp. Aristotle, *Meteorologia*, ii. 2, and *Imago Mundi* (c. 6), with the notes of
Columbus (notes 16, 17: *Rac. Col.* I. ii. 375).

the antarctic pole or the land which is beneath it, is the highest part of the world and nearest the sky, other wise men impugn this, saying that it is that which is beneath the arctic pole, from which reasoning it appears that they understood that one part of this world must be loftier and nearer to the sky than the other. And they did not consider in this matter that it might be beneath the equinoctial in the way that I have said, and it is not surprising that they did not, for of this hemisphere there was no certain knowledge, but only very vague information and that supposititious, because no one had ever gone or sent to seek it out, until now when Your Highnesses commanded me to explore and to discover sea and land.

I found that there between these two straits, which, as I have said, face each other in a line from north to south, it is twenty-six leagues from the one to the other, and I cannot be wrong in this because the calculation was made with a quadrant. And from these two straits westward to the gulf which I have mentioned and which I called *de las Perlas*,[1] it is sixty-eight leagues, of four miles each, as we are accustomed to reckon at sea, and from this gulf the water runs constantly with great force towards the east, and for this reason these two straits have that conflict with the salt water. In that on the south, which I named *la Boca de la Sierpe*, I found that at nightfall I had the pole star at nearly five degrees' elevation, and in the other on the north, which I named *la Boca del Drago*, it was at almost seven. And I find that the said Golfo de las Perlas is westward of the . . .[2] of Ptolemy almost three thousand nine hundred miles, which is nearly seventy equinoctial degrees, counting for each degree fifty-six and two thirds miles.

Holy Scripture testifies that Our Lord made the earthly paradise and in it placed the tree of life,[3] and from it issues a fountain from which flow four of the chief rivers of this world, the Ganges in India, the Tigris and Euphrates in . . . ,[4] which cut through a mountain range and form Mesopotamia and flow into Persia, and the Nile which rises in Ethiopia and enters the sea at Alexandria.[5]

[1] The gulf at the extreme western end of the Gulf of Paria, which Columbus had named the Golfo de la Ballena (Las Casas, i. 138). No pearls are actually

tierra qu'es debaxo d'él, sea la más alta parte en el mundo y
más propinqua al çielo, otros sabios le impungan, diziendo
que es esta qu'es debaxo del ártico. por las quales razones
pareçe que entendían que una parte d'este mundo devía de
ser más propinqua y noble al çielo que otra, y no cayeron en
esto que sea debaxo del equinoçial, por la forma que yo dixe.
y no es maravilla, porque d'este hemisperio no se oviese notiçia çierta, salvo muy liviana y por argumento; porque nadie
nunca lo a andado ni embiado á buscar, hasta agora, que
Vuestras Altezas le mandaron explorar y descubrir, la mar y
la tierra.

Fallo que de allí d'estas dos bocas, las quales, como dixe,
están frontero, por línea de septentrión en austro, que aya
de la una á la otra veynte y seys leguas; y no pudo aver en
ello yerro, porque se midieron con quadrante. y d'estas dos
bocas del occidente fasta el golpho, que yo dixe, al qual llamé
'de las Perlas', que son sesenta y ocho leguas, de quatro
millas cada una, como acostumbramos en la mar, y que de
allá d'este golfo corre de contino el agua muy fuerte hazia el
oriente y que por esto tienen aquel combate estas dos bocas
con la salada. en esta boca del austro, á que yo llamé 'de la
Sierpe', fallé, en anocheçiendo, que yo tenía la estrella del
norte alta quasi çinco grados, y en aquella otra del septentrión,
á que yo llamé 'del Drago', eran quasi siete; y fallo qu'el
dicho golpho de las Perlas está occidental al occidente de
elan ... de Ptolomeo quasi tres mill é noveçientas millas, que
son quasi septenta grados equinoçiales, contando por cada
uno çinquenta y seys millas y dos terçios.

La Sacra Escriptura testifica que Nuestro Señor hizo al
paraíso terrenal, y en él puso el árbol de la vida, y d'él sale
una fuente de donde resultan en este mundo quatro ríos
prinçipales: Ganges en Yndia, Tygris y Eufrates en . . . , los
found in the 'Golfo de las Perlas' or in the Golfo de la Ballena (Gulf of Paria).
² Lacuna in the text. The passage probably means that it was this distance
west of the first meridian of Ptolemy.
³ Genesis ii. 8–10.   ⁴ Lacuna in the original.
⁵ Pison, Gihon, Hiddekel, and Euphrates, the rivers of Eden, were generally
identified in the Middle Ages with the Ganges, Nile, Tigris, and Euphrates. The
identification of the Gihon with the Nile rested upon Jeremiah ii. 18. Columbus
annotates the passage in the *Imago Mundi* (c. 55), dealing with the rivers of
Eden and the sources of the Nile (notes 401–5: *Rac. Col.* I. ii. 401).

I do not find and I have never found any writing of the
Romans or of the Greeks which gives definitely the position
in the world of the earthly paradise, nor have I seen it in any
world map, placed with authority based upon proof.[1] Some
placed it there where are the sources of the Nile in Ethiopia,
but others traversed all these lands and found no similarity
to it in the climate or in elevation towards the sky, to
make it comprehensible that it was there, nor that the rising
waters of the deluge had reached that place, &c.[2] Some
Gentiles wished to show by arguments that it was in the
Fortunate islands, which are the Canaries, &c.[3] St. Isidore[4]
and Bede[5] and Strabo[6] and the Master of Scholastic History[7]
and St. Ambrose[8] and Scotus[9] and all the learned theologians
agree that the earthly paradise is in the East, &c.[10]

I have already said that which I hold concerning this
hemisphere and its shape, and I believe that if I were to pass
beneath the equinoctial line, then, arriving there at the highest
point,[11] I should find an even more temperate climate and
difference in the stars and waters.[12] Not that I believe that to
the summit of the extreme point is navigable, or water, or that
it is possible to ascend there, for I believe that the earthly
paradise is there and to it, save by the will of God, no man
can come.[13] And I believe that this land which Your High-

---

[1] For a discussion of the various views concerning the situation of the Earthly
Paradise, cp. Las Casas (i. 142-6). There is an interesting note on the different
opinions held on this question during the Middle Ages, in Humboldt (*Examen
Critique*, iii. 119 *et seq.*), and there is an appendix on the question in Washington
Irving (*Columbus*, iii. Appendix No. xxxv).

[2] Cp. *Imago Mundi*, c. 55, a passage annotated by Columbus (notes 397-405:
Rac. Col. I. ii. 401). The idea that the Earthly Paradise might be at the sources
of the Nile was the outcome of the identification of the Gihon with the Nile
(cp. Las Casas, i. 144).

[3] Cp. *Imago Mundi*, c. 12, 31: both of which are annotated by Columbus
(notes 47, 313: *Rac. Col.* I. ii. 379, 395). Pierre d'Ailly rejected the idea that the
Fortunate Islands were the Earthly Paradise. The Fortunate Islands were
generally identified with the Canaries. (Cp. Las Casas, i. 143.)

[4] St. Isidore of Seville. The reference is to his *Etymologiae*, 14. iii. 2: *De Asia*.

[5] Bede, *Hexameron*, i (*ad verba*, 'Plantaverat autem Dominus Deus', &c.).

[6] Walafridus Strabo, abbot of Reichenau: ob. c. 849. The reference is to the
Glosae ordinarie, on Genesis ii. 8.

[7] Petrus Comestor, canon and dean of St. Martin at Troyes: ob. c. 1178. He
was surnamed 'Comestor' because he was an inveterate bookworm. The
reference is to the *Historia Scholastica*: *Historia Libri Genesis*, c. 13: *De Paradiso
et lignis ejus*.

quales apartan la sierra y hazen la Mesopotamía y van á
tener en Persia, y el Nilo, que naçe en Ethiopía y va en la
mar en Alexandría. yo no hallo ni jamás e hallado escriptura
de Latinos ni de Griegos que çertificadamente diga ál, sino en
este mundo, del paraýso terrenal; ni e visto en ningún mapa-
mundo, salvo situado con autoridad de argumento. algunos
le ponían allí donde son las fuentes del Nilo en Ethiopía;
mas otros anduvieron todas estas tierras y no hallaron conformidad d'ello en la temperançia del çielo, en la altura hazia
el çielo, porque se pudiese comprehender que él era allí, ni que
las aguas del diluvio oviesen llegado allí, las quales subieron
ençima &c. algunos gentiles quisieron dezir por argumentos,
que él era en las islas Fortunate, que son las Canarias, &c. sant
Isidro, y Beda, y Strabo, y el maestro de la Hystoria scolástica,
y sant Ambrosio, y Scoto, y todos los sanos theólogios con-
çiertan qu'el paraýso terrenal es en el oriente &c.

Ya dixe lo que yo hallava d'este hemisperio, y de la hechura:
y creo que, si yo passara por debaxo de la línea equinoçial,
que, en llegando allí en esto más alto, que fallara muy mayor
temperançia y diversidad en las estrellas y en las aguas. no
porque yo crea que allí, donde es el altura del estremo, sea
navegable, ni agua, ni que se pueda subir allá; porque creo
que allí es el paraýso terrenal, adonde no puede llegar nadie,
salvo por voluntad divina. y creo qu'esta tierra, que agora

---

[8] St. Ambrose of Milan. The reference is to his *De Paradiso*, c. 1.

[9] John Scotus Erigena (Duns Scotus). The reference is to his *Questiones* on the *Sententiae* of Peter Lombard, Questio 2, Distinctio 17.

[10] Cp. *Imago Mundi*, c. 7, a passage noted by Columbus (note 19: *Rac. Col.* I. ii. 376). The idea that the Earthly Paradise was in the East was due to the fact that the words in the Vulgate 'a principio' (Genesis ii. 8) were taken to mean, not 'in the beginning', but 'in the east'; this meaning was more readily accepted because Aristotle was supposed to have declared that the east was superior to the west, an opinion with which St. Thomas Aquinas agreed. (Cp. Las Casas, i. 143.)

[11] Cp. *Imago Mundi*, c. 7 and 11, and the notes of Columbus (notes 19 and 40: *Rac. Col.* I. ii. 376, 379).

[12] Cp. *Imago Mundi*, c. 7 and 11, and the notes of Columbus (notes 18, 20, 33–35, 40: *Rac. Col.* I. ii. 375, 378, 379), and *Compendium Cosmographie*, c. 16: and the note of Columbus (note 673: *Rac. Col.* I. ii. 425–6).

[13] It was generally held that God had placed an impassable sea between the Earthly Paradise and the inhabited world, in order that men should not rediscover it. Columbus, however, believed that all this sea was navigable (cp. note 23, to *Imago Mundi* (*Rac. Col.* I. ii. 377).

nesses have now sent to discover is very extensive and that
there are many other lands in the south, of which there has
never been any report.[1]

I do not hold that the earthly paradise is in the form of a
rugged mountain, as its description declares to us,[2] but that
it is at the summit, there where I have said that the shape of
the stalk of the pear is, and that, going towards it from a distance, there is a gradual ascent to it. And I believe that no
one could reach the summit as I have said, and I believe that
this water may originate from there, though it be far away
and may come to collect there where I came and may form
this lake. These are great indications of the earthly paradise,
for the situation agrees with the opinion of those holy and
wise theologians, and also the signs are very much in accord
with this idea, for I have never read or heard of so great a
quantity of fresh water so coming into and near the salt. And
the very mild climate also supports this view, and if it does
not come from there, from paradise, it seems to be a still
greater marvel, for I do not believe that there is known in the
world a river so great and so deep.[3]

After that I had issued forth from la Boca del Drago, which
is the one of the two straits which is towards the north and
to which I so gave a name, on the following day, which was
the day of Our Lady in August, I found that the sea ran so
strongly to the westward, that from the hour of mass when I
began the voyage, to the hour of compline, I travelled sixty-
five leagues of four miles each. And the wind was not violent,
but very gentle, and this confirmed the view that, going
thence to the south, there is a continuous ascent, and going
thence to the north, as we then did, there is a continuous
descent.

I hold it to be very certain that the waters of the sea take their
course from east to west with the heavens, and that there in
this region, when they pass, they go more rapidly and accordingly have eaten away so great a part of the land, for which
cause there are here so many islands. And the very islands
themselves supply evidence of this, for on the one hand all

---

[1] Columbus was firmly convinced of the existence of inhabited lands of great
extent south of the equator (cp. the notes cited above, p. 37, note 12).

mandaron descubrir Vuestras Altezas, sea grandíssima, y aya otras muchas en el austro, de que jamás se ovo notiçia.

Yo no tomo qu'el paraýso terrenal sea en forma de montaña áspera, como el escrevir d'ello nos amuestra, salvo qu'él sea en el colmo, allí donde dixe la figura del peçón de la pera, y que, poco á poco, andando hazia allí, desde muy lexos se va subiendo á él. y creo que nadie no podría llegar al colmo, como yo dixe, y creo que pueda salir de allí esa agua, bien que sea lexos y venga á parar allí donde yo vengo, y faga este lago. grandes indiçios son estos del paraýso terrenal, porqu'el sitio es conforme á la opinión d'estos sanctos y sanos theólogos. y asimismo las señales son muy conformes, que yo jamás leý ni oý que tanta cantidad de agua dulçe fuese así adentro y vezina con la salada. y en ello ayuda asimismo la suavíssima temperancia. y si de allí del paraýso no sale, pareçe aun mayor maravilla, porque no creo que se sepa en el mundo de río tan grande y tan fondo.

Después que yo salí de la 'boca del Dragón', qu'es la una de las dos, aquella del septentrión, á la qual así puse nombre, el día siguiente, que fué día de Nuestra Señora de agosto, fallé que corría tanto la mar al poniente, que después de ora de missa, que entré en camino, anduve fasta ora de completas sesenta y çinco leguas, de quatro millas cada una, y el viento no era demasiado, salvo muy suave. y esto ayuda el cognoscimiento que, de allí yendo al austro, se va más alto, y, andando hazia el septentrión, como entonçes, se va descendiendo.

Muy cognosçido tengo que las aguas de la mar llevan su curso de oriente á occidente con los çielos, y que allí en esta comarca, quando passan, lievan más veloce camino: y por esto an comido tanta parte de la tierra; porque por eso son acá tantas islas, y ellas mismas hazen d'esto testimonio, porque todas á una mano son largas de poniente á levante, y norueste y sueste, que son poco más alto y baxo, y angostas de norte á sur y nordeste y sudueste, que son en contrario de

---

² Cp. *Imago Mundi*, c. 7 and 33, and the notes of Columbus (notes 19, 399: *Rac. Col.* I. ii. 276, 401).

³ For the impression which the character of the gulf made upon Columbus, cp. the account in Las Casas (i. 141). Abundance of fresh water was to be expected to come from the Earthly Paradise, in accordance with Genesis (ii. 9, 10).

those which lie west and east, or a little more obliquely north-west and south-east, are broad, and those lying north and south, and north-east and south-west, are narrow, for they are opposed to the said winds. And here, in all the islands, precious things are produced, owing to the mild climate, which comes to them from heaven as they lie towards the loftiest part of the world. It is true that in some parts the waters do not appear to take this course, but this is only so in some particular places, where there is some land which meets them, and causes it to seem that they flow in different directions.

Pliny[1] writes that the sea and the land together form a sphere, and he lays down that this Ocean sea is the greatest mass of water and that it lies towards the sky, and that the land is beneath it and supports it, and that the two are related, the one to the other, as the kernel of a nut to a thick shell which contains it. The Master of Scholastic History, on Genesis,[2] says that the waters are very small, although when they were created they covered all the land, since they were then gaseous like a cloud, and afterwards they became condensed and consolidated so that they occupied much less space, and in this Nicolaus de Lyra agrees.[3] Aristotle says that the world is small and that the water is limited in extent, and that it is easily possible to pass from Spain to the Indies,[4] and this is confirmed by Avenruyz,[5] and by cardinal Pedro de Aliaco,[6] who alleges the same. He supports this opinion and that of Seneca, agreeing with them and saying that Aristotle was able to learn many secrets of the world through Alexander the Great, and Seneca through Caesar Nero, and Pliny by means of the Romans, who all spent money and men and employed great diligence in learning the secrets of the world and in making them known to mankind. And this cardinal accords to them greater authority than to Ptolemy and to others, Greeks and Arabs, and in confirmation of the opinion that the waters are few and that they cover a small part of the world, in comparison with that which they were believed to cover on the authority of Ptolemy[7] and of his followers, he

[1] Pliny, ii. 66, 67.
[2] Petrus Comestor, *Historia Scholastica: Historia Libri Genesis: De opere*

los otros dichos vientos. y aquí en ellas todas nasçen cosas preçiosas por la suave temperançia que les proçede del çielo, por
estar hazia el más alto del mundo. verdad es que pareçe en
algunos lugares que las aguas no hagan este curso; mas esto
no es salvo particularmente en algunos lugares donde alguna
tierra le está al encuentro, y hace pareçer que andan diversos
caminos.

Plinio escrive que la mar y la tierra haze todo una espera,
y pone qu'esta mar Ocçéana sea la mayor cantidad del agua y
está hazia el çielo, y que la tierra sea debaxo, y que le sos-
tenga; y mezclado es uno con otro como el ámago de la nuez
con una tela gorda que va abraçado en ello. el maestro de la
Hystoria scolástica, sobre el Genesis, dize que las aguas son
muy pocas, que bien que quando fueron criadas que cobijasen
toda la tierra, que entonçes eran vaporables en manera de
niebla, y que después que fueron sólidas y juntadas, que
ocuparon muy poco lugar. y en esto conçierta Nicolao de
Lira. el Aristótel dize que este mundo es pequeño, y es el
agua muy poca, y que fácilmente se puede passar d'España
á las Yndias. y esto confirma el Avenruýz, y le alega el
cardenal Pedro de Aliaco, autorizando este dezir, y aquel
de Séneca, el qual conforma con estos, diziendo que el
Aristóteles pudo saber muchos secretos del mundo á causa
de Alexandre Magno, y Séneca á causa de Çésar Nero, y
Plinio por respecto de los Romanos, los quales todos gastaron
dineros y gente, y pusieron mucha diligençia en saber los
secretos del mundo y darlos á entender á los pueblos. el qual
cardenal da á estos grande auctoridad, más que á Ptolomeo ni á

tertii diei. (Cp. the notes of Columbus to the Imago Mundi, note 23: Rac. Col.
I. ii. 377.)
   3 Nicolaus de Lyra: Glosae ordinarie, on Genesis i. 2.
   4 Aristotle, De Coelo et Mundo.
   5 'Avenruyz' is Averroes of Córdoba (1126–98), the Moorish philosopher, who
commented on Plato and Aristotle and who was very largely responsible for such
knowledge of the writings of these philosophers as there was in western Europe
after his time until the Renaissance.
   6 Imago Mundi, c. 7 and 11 (cp. notes of Columbus, 23 and 43: Rac. Col. I. ii.
376, 379): Epilogus Mappe Mundi; De figura terre and De Mari (cp. notes of
Columbus, 486, 487, 489, 494, and 495: Rac. Col. I. ii. 406, 408): and Compendium
Cosmographie, c. 19 (cp. note of Columbus, 677: Rac. Col. I. ii. 426).
   7 Cp. Ptolemy, Almagestum, ii.; and Imago Mundi, c. 8.

brings forward a passage in the third book of Esdras, where he says that of the seven parts of the world, six are uncovered and the one remaining is covered by water.[1] This authority is confirmed by saints, who give weight to the third and fourth books of Esdras, as do St. Augustine[2] and St. Ambrose in his *Exameron*,[3] where he says, 'Here My son Jesus shall come and My son Christ shall die,'[4] and they say that Esdras was a prophet and also Zacharias, the father of St. John, and the blessed Simon;[5] and these authorities Francisco de Maironis also urges.[6] With respect to the dryness of the land, it has been shown by experience that it is much greater than the vulgar believe, and this is no wonder, for the further one goes, the more one learns.[7]

I turn to my subject, the land of Gracia and the river and lake which I found there, the latter so great that it is possible to call it a sea rather than a lake, since a 'lake' is a small expanse of water, and if the expanse be great it is called a 'sea', as we talk of the *Sea* of Galilee and the Dead *Sea*. And I say that if it be not from the earthly paradise that this river comes, it originates from a vast land, lying to the south, of which hitherto no knowledge has been obtained. But I am much more convinced in my own mind that there where I have said is the earthly paradise, and I rely upon the arguments and authorities given above. May it please Our Lord to grant long life and health and leisure to Your Highnesses that you may be able to persevere in this most noble undertaking, from which in my opinion our Lord will receive much service and Spain greatly increase her grandeur and all Christians receive much consolation and pleasure, since there will be spread abroad the name of Our Lord.

And in all the lands to which the ships of Your Highnesses go, and on every cape, I command a lofty cross to be set up, and I inform all the people whom I find of the estate of Your Highnesses and how your seat is in Spain, and I tell them of our holy Faith, as far as I am able, and of the creed of Holy

---

[1] 2 Esdras (4 Esdras, in the Vulgate) vi. 42.

[2] *De Civitate Dei*, xvii. 24. The passage is transcribed at the end of the *Historia* of Pius II, perhaps by Columbus himself (*Rac. Col.* I. ii. 366). (Cp. the notes of Columbus to the *Imago Mundi*, note 23: *Rac. Col.* I. ii. 376-7.)

otros Griegos ni Arabes. y á confirmaçión de dezir qu'el agua
sea poca, y qu'el cubierto del mundo d'ella sea poco, al respecto de lo que se dezía por auctoridad de Ptolomeo y de
sus sequaçes, á esto trae una auctoridad de Esdras, del .3°.
libro suyo, adonde dize que de siete partes del mundo las
seys son descubiertas, y la una es cubierta de agua. la qual
auctoridad es aprovada por sanctos, los quales dan auctoridad al .3°. y .4°. libro de Esdras, ansí como es sant Augustín,
y sant Ambrosio en su Exameron, adonde alega: 'Allí vendrá
mi hijo Jesú y morirá mi hijo Christo.' y dizen que Esdras fué
propheta, y asimismo Zacharías padre de san Juan y el beato
Symón: las quales auctoridades también alega Francisco de
Mayrones. en quanto en esto de enxuto de la tierra, mucho se
a experimentado qu'es mucho más de lo qu'el vulgo crea. y
no es maravilla, porque, andando más, más se sabe.

Torno á mi propósito de la tierra de Graçia y río y lago que
allí fallé, atán grande, que más se le puede llamar mar que
lago, porqu'el lago es lugar de agua, y en seyendo grande, se
dize mar, como se dixo á la mar de Galilea y al mar Muerto. y
digo que si no procede del paraýso terrenal, que viene este río
y proçede de tierra infinita, pues al austro, de la qual fasta
agora no se a avido notiçia. mas yo muy assentado tengo
en el ánima que allí, adonde dixe, es el paraýso terrenal, y
descanso sobre las razones y auctoridades sobre escriptas.

Plega á Nuestro Señor de dar mucha vida y salud y descanso á Vuestras Altezas para que puedan proseguir esta tan
noble empresa, en la qual me pareçe que resçibe Nuestro
Señor mucho serviçio, y la España creçe de mucha grandeza,
y todos los christianos mucha consolaçión y plazer, porque

---

[3] The passage to which reference is made is not to be found in the *Exameron*
of St. Ambrose, but in his *Bono mortis*, c. 10.

[4] 2 (4) Esdras vii. 28, 29.

[5] Simeon (Luke ii. 25–35).

[6] The reference is to Francisco de Maironis, *Flores Beati Augustini extractae per
veritates ex libris de Civitate Dei* (Liber XVII, veritas xii). It is inaccurate to say
that Francisco de Maironis actually urges the arguments put forward by
Augustine; he only notes the passage in the *De Civitate Dei* (xvii. 24) with
approval. The passage from Maironis is quoted in full by Columbus in a note to
the *Imago Mundi* (note 23: *Rac. Col.* I. ii. 377).

[7] Cp. *Epilogus Mappe Mundi*, and the notes of Columbus (notes 486, 487,
494, 495: *Rac. Col.* I. ii. 406–8).

Mother Church, which has her members in all the world, and I speak to them of the civilization and nobility of all Christians, and of the faith which they have in the Holy Trinity.

May it please Our Lord to forgive the persons who have calumniated and who do calumniate so excellent an undertaking, and who have opposed and do oppose it so that it may not go forward, without considering how much honour and glory it is for your royal estate throughout the world. They do not know what to urge in order to malign it, save that there is in it expense and that there have not been immediately sent back ships laden with gold, without regarding the brevity of the time and the many difficulties which there have been here. And they do not consider that in Castile, in the household of Your Highnesses, there are every year persons who by their merit earn, each one of them, more there than it is necessary should be expended on this undertaking. Nor do they consider that no princes of Spain ever won lands beyond their own borders, except now that Your Highnesses have here another world, where our holy Faith may be so greatly increased, and whence so great benefits can be derived, for although ships, laden with gold, have not been sent back, sufficient evidence of it and of other things of value has been sent back, whence it is possible to judge that in a little while much profit may be gained. And they do not regard the great courage of the princes of Portugal who have for so much time prosecuted the enterprise of Guinea, and who prosecute that of Africa, where they have expended half the population of their realm, and to-day the king is more determined on the undertaking than ever. Our Lord provide in this matter as I have said, and lead them to consider all this which I have written, which is not the thousandth part of that which I might write of the deeds of princes who have occupied themselves in gaining knowledge and with conquests and their maintenance.

All this I have said, and not because I believe that Your Highnesses have any wish save to persevere in this as long as you live, and I regard as very sure that which Your Highnesses once answered me concerning this by word of mouth, and not because I have seen any change in Your Highnesses, but from

aquí se divulgará el nombre de Nuestro Señor. y en todas las tierras adonde los navíos de Vuestras Altezas van, y en todo cabo, mando plantar una alta cruz; y á toda la gente que hallo notifico el estado de Vuestras Altezas y como su asiento es en España; y les digo de nuestra sancta fe todo lo que yo puedo, y de la creençia de la sancta madre Iglesia, la qual tiene sus mienbros en todo el mundo; y les digo la poliçía y nobleza de todos los christianos, y la fe que en la Sancta Trinidad tienen. y plega á Nuestro Señor de tyrar de memoria á las personas que an impugnado y impugnan tan exçelente empresa, y impiden y impidieron porque no vaya adelante, sin considerar quánta honrra y grandeza es del real estado de Vuestras Altezas en todo el mundo. no saben qué entreponer á maldezir d'esto, salvo que se haze gasto en ello, y porque luego no enbiaron los navíos cargados de oro, sin considerar la brevedad del tiempo y tantos inconvinientes, como acá se an avido, y no considerar que en Castilla, en casa de Vuestras Altezas, salen cada año personas que por su mereçimiento ganaron en ella más de renta cada uno d'ellos, más de lo qu'es neçessario que se gaste en esto; ansimesmo sin considerar que ningunos prínçipes de España jamás ganaron tierra alguna fuera d'ella, salvo agora, que Vuestras Altezas tienen acá otro mundo, de adonde puede ser tan acreçentada nuestra sancta fe, y de donde se podrán sacar tantos provechos, que, bien que no se ayan enbiado suffiçientes muestras d'ello y de otras cosas de valor, por donde se puede juzgar que en breve tiempo se podrá aver mucho provecho, y sin mirar el gran coraçón de los prínçipes de Portugal, que a tanto tiempo que prosiguen la impresa de Guinea y prosiguen aquella de Africa, adonde an gastado la mitad de la gente de su reyno, y agora está el rey más determinado á ello que nunca. Nuestro Señor provea en esto, como yo dixe, y les ponga en memoria de considerar de todo esto que va escripto, que no es de mill partes la una de lo que yo podriá escrevir de cosas de prínçipes que se ocuparon á saber y conquistar y sostener.

Todo esto dixe, y no porque crea que la voluntad de Vuestras Altezas sea salvo proseguir en ello en quanto bivan, y tengo por muy firme lo que me respondió Vuestras Altezas una

fear of that which I have heard of those whom I have mentioned, for so a drop of water falling on a stone will make a hole. And Your Highnesses answered me with that magnanimity which you are known throughout the world to possess, and told me to feel no concern at all this, since it was your will to prosecute this undertaking and to support it, although there should be from it nothing but stones and sand, and that you took no account of the expense which was incurred in it, since on other affairs, not so great, you were spending much more, and that you held that which had been expended in the past, and that which might be expended in the future, as having been very well spent, since you believed that our holy Faith would be increased and your royal dignity enhanced, and that they were not friends of your royal estate who spoke evil of this enterprise.

And now, while you receive information concerning the matter of these lands which I have newly discovered, in which I am assured in my heart that the earthly paradise is, the adelantado[1] will go with three ships, well equipped, to that place to examine it further, and they will discover all that they can in those parts. Meanwhile, I will send to Your Highnesses this writing and the drawing of the land,[2] and you will determine that which is to be done in the matter and will send to me your orders, and with the help of the Holy Trinity it shall be fulfilled with all diligence, so that Your Highnesses be served and have pleasure. Thanks be to God.

---

[1] Bartholomew Columbus. When Columbus returned to Isabella from the exploration of Cuba and Jamaica in 1495, he found that Bartholomew had just arrived in the island, and he created him adelantado. Ferdinand and Isabella held that he had no right to make any such appointment on his sole authority,

vez que por palabra le dezía d'esto, no porque yo oviese visto
mudamiento ninguno en Vuestras Altezas, salvo por temor
de lo que yo oyá d'estos que yo digo; y tanto da una
gotera de agua en una piedra, que le haze un agujero. y
Vuestras Altezas me respondió con aquel coraçón que se sabe
en todo el mundo que tienen, y me dixo que no curase de
nada d'eso, porque su voluntad era de proseguir esta empresa
y sostenerla, aunque no fuese sino piedras y peñas, y qu'el
gasto que en ello se hazía, que lo tenía en nada; que en otras
cosas no tan grandes gastavan mucho más, y que lo tenían
todo por muy bien gastado, lo del pasado y lo que se gastase
en adelante, porque creýan que nuestra santa fe sería acreçentada y su real señorío ensanchado, y que no eran amigos
de su real estado aquellos que les maldezían d'esta empresa.
y agora entretanto que vengan á notiçia d'esto d'estas tierras
que hagora nuevamente e descubierto, en que tengo assentado
en el ánima que allí es el paraýso terrenal, yrá el adelantado
con tres navíos, bien ataviados para ello, á ver más adelante,
y descubrirán todo lo que pudieren hazia aquellas partes.
entretanto yo enbiaré á Vuestras Altezas esta escriptura y la
pintura de la tierra, y acordarán lo que en ello se deva fazer,
y me enbiarán á mandar, y se cumplirá con ayuda de la Santa
Trinidad con toda diligençia, en manera que Vuestras Altezas
sean servidos y ayan plazer.

Deo graçias.

but they eventually confirmed it (cp. Las Casas, i. 101: and Grant of the title
by the sovereigns, 22 July 1497: Navarrete, ii. 122). The expedition here proposed was not undertaken, probably owing to the disturbed state of Española
when Columbus reached that island.

[2] Cp. *supra*, p. 26, and note 2.

THIRD VOYAGE OF COLUMBUS *(cont.)*

CARTA

2. Letter[1] which the admiral of the Indies, coming from the Indies as a prisoner, sent to the nurse[2] of prince Don Juan of Castile,[3] in the year 1500.

MOST VIRTUOUS LADY: If it be something new for me to complain of the world, its custom of maltreating me is of very old standing. A thousand battles have I fought with it, and I have withstood all until now when neither arms nor wit avail me. With cruelty, it has cast me down to the depth. Hope in Him Who created all men sustains me; His succour has been always very near. On one occasion, and that not long ago, when I was deeply distressed, He raised me with His divine arm, saying: 'O man of little faith, arise, it is I, be not afraid!'[4]

I came with such earnest love to serve these princes, and I have served with a service that has never been heard or seen. Of the new heaven and of the new earth, which Our Lord made, as St. John writes in the Apocalypse,[5] after He had spoken of it by the mouth of Isaiah,[6] He made me the messenger and He showed me where to go. In all there was incredulity, and to the queen my lady He gave the spirit of understanding and great courage, and He made her the heiress of all, as His dear and very loved daughter. I went to take possession of all this in her royal name. All wished to cover the ignorance in which they were sunk, hiding their little knowledge by speaking of difficulties and expense. Her highness on the contrary approved and supported the enterprise as far as she was able. Seven years were spent in discussion and nine in performance. Remarkable and memorable events[7] took place in that time. Of all this, there had been no conception.

I came to be, and I am, such that there is none so vile as not to dare to insult me. Throughout the world, it will be

---

[1] For the letter in general, cp. *supra*, Introduction, p. lxxxvi.
[2] Juana de la Torre, sister of Antonio de Torres (cp. *supra*, vol. I, p. 74, note 1).

TERCER VIAGE DE COLÓN

2. *Treslado de una carta qu'el almirante de las Yndias embió al ama del prínçipe don Juan de Castilla el año de .MD., viniendo preso de las Yndias.*

MUY VIRTUOSA SEÑORA: Si mi quexa del mundo es nueva, su uso de maltratar es de muy antiguo. mill combates me ha dado, y á todos resistí fasta agora que no me aprovechó armas ni avisos. con crueldad me tiene echado al fundo. la esperança de aquél que crió á todos me sostiene: su socorro fué siempre muy presto. otra vez, y no de lexos, estando yo más baxo, me levantó con su braço derecho, disiendo: 'o ombre de poca fe, levántate, que yo soy, no ayáys miedo.' yo vine con amor tan entrañable á servir á estos prínçipes, y he servido de servicio de que jamás se oyó ni vido. del nuevo çielo é tierra que hasía Nuestro Señor, escriviendo sant Juan el Apocalis, después de dicho por boca de Ysaýa, me hiso d'ello mensagero, y amostró á qual parte. en todos ovo yncredulidad, y á la reyna mi señora dió d'ello el spíritu de ynteligencia y esfuerço grande, y le fiso de todo heredera como á cara y muy amada fija. la posesión de todo esto fué yo á tomar en su real nombre. la ygnorançia en que avían estado todos, quisieron emendalle, traspasando el poco saber á fablar en ynconvenientes y gastos. Su Alteza lo aprovava, al contrario, y lo sostuvo fasta que pudo. siete años se pasaron en la plática, y nueve executando. cosas muy señaladas y dignas de memoria se pasaron en este tiempo; de todo no se fiso concepto. llegué yo, y estoy, que no ha nadie

It would seem that she succeeded María de Guzman as nurse to Prince Juan. She was high in the favour of Isabella, by whom a pension was assigned to her. Juana de la Torre died *c.* 1503.

[3] Only son of Ferdinand and Isabella. He was born at Seville, 28 June 1478; married Margaret, daughter of the emperor-elect, Maximilian of Austria, 3 April 1497; and died at Salamanca, 4 Oct. 1497. All contemporary writers are unanimous in describing him as having been a boy of remarkable promise.

[4] Mark vi. 50; John vi. 20; and cp. *infra*, pp. 68 and 92.

[5] Revelation xxi. 1.

[6] Isaiah lxv. 17; lxvi. 22.

[7] Cp. *supra*, p. 2, and Introduction, p. xv.

counted virtue in any that he is not able to consent to this reviling. If I had violently seized the Indies or the land made holy because in it there is to-day the fame of the altar of St. Peter, and had given them to the Moors,[1] they could not have shown greater enmity towards me in Spain. Who would believe such a thing of a land where there has always been so great nobility ?

I would very gladly rid myself of the whole business if it were honourable towards my Queen for me to do so. The support of Our Lord and Her Highness has caused me to persevere in it, and in order somewhat to mitigate the grief that death has brought upon her,[2] I entered upon a new voyage to a new heaven and a new earth, which up to then had lain hidden, and if this, like the other voyages of the Indies, be not regarded there, it is no wonder, for through my exertions it has come to knowledge. The Holy Spirit inspired St. Peter and the other Twelve with him, and they all wrestled here below, and many were their labours and great their weariness; in the end, they were victorious in all. I believed that this voyage to Paria would be some appeasement on account of the pearls and the finding of gold in Española. I ordered the people to gather and to fish for the pearls, and with them an agreement was made concerning my return for them, and as I understood it, they should amount to the measure of a *fanega*.[3] If I have not written this to Their Highnesses, it was because I wished first to have the matter of the gold settled.

This issued for me as many other things have issued. I should not have lost them or my honour, if I had sought my own advantage and if I had allowed Española to be ruined, or if my privileges and the agreements made with me had been respected. And I say also as much concerning the gold, which I had by then collected and which with so great loss of life and with so many labours, I have brought in perfectly.

When I went on the voyage to Paria, I found almost half the people in Española in revolt,[4] and they have made war on me to this day, as if I had been a Moor, and at the same

---

[1] This appears to be the meaning of a passage which is certainly corrupt in the original.

tan vil que no piense de ultrajarme. por virtud se contará en el mundo á quien puede, no consintillo. sy yo robara las Yndias ó tierra que jaz fase ellas, de que agora es la fabla del altar de sant Pedro, y las diera á los Moros, no pudieran en España amostrarme mayor enemiga. ¿quién creyera tal, adonde ovo siempre tanta nobleza? yo mucho me quisyera despedir del negoçio, si fuera onesto para con me reyna. el esfuerço de Nuestro Señor y de Su Alteza fiso que continuase, y, por aliviarle algo de los enojos en que á cabsa de la muerte estava, cometí viage nuevo al nuevo çielo y mundo, que fasta entonçes estava oculto; y, sy non es tenido allí en estima, asý como los otros de las Indias, no es maravilla, porque salió á pareçer de mi yndustria.

A sant Pedro abrasó el Spíritu Santo, y, con él, otros dose; y todos conbatieron acá, y los trabajos y fatigas fueron muchas: en fin, de todo llevaron la vitoria.

Este viage de Paria creý que apaziguaría algo por las perlas y la fallada del oro en la Española. las perlas mandé yo ayuntar é pescar á la gente con quien quedó en conçierto de my buelta por ellas, y, á mi comprehender, á medida de fanega: sy yo non lo escriví á Sus Altezas, fué porque asý quisiera aver fecho del oro antes. esto me salió como otras cosas muchas; non las perdiera, ni mi honrra, sy buscara yo mi bien propio, y dexara perder la Española, ó se guardaran mis privilegios y asientos. é otro tanto digo del oro que yo tenía agora junto, que, con tantas muertes y trabajos, por virtud divinal he llegado á perfecto.

Quando yo fué de Paria, fallé casi la mitad de la gente en la Española alçados, y me han guerreado fasta agora como á Moro, y los Yndios, por otro cabo, gravemente. en esto, vino Fojeda, y provó á echar el sello: dixo que Sus Altezas le

---

² The reference is to the death of Prince Juan.

³ A measure of capacity of varying value; most often, equivalent to fifty-five litres. There is no other evidence of this agreement between Columbus and the pearl fishers.

⁴ On reaching Española from Paria (31 Aug. 1498), Columbus found the revolt of Roldán in progress and although he came to terms with the rebels, unrest was not subdued and further conspiracies occurred (cp. Las Casas, i. 117–20, 148, 150–61).

time there has been a serious conflict with the Indians.[1] It was then that Ojeda[2] came and he endeavoured to put the seal on this state of affairs, saying that Their Highnesses had sent him with promises of gifts and franchises and wages. He gathered a great following, for in all Española there are few who are not vagabonds,[3] and there is no one with a wife and children. This Ojeda troubled me greatly and it was necessary that he should be sent away; and he went, declaring that he would speedily return with more ships and men, and that he had left the royal person of the queen at the point of death.

At this time there arrived Vicente Yañez;[4] he caused tumult and suspicions, but no damage. The Indians spoke of many other caravels at the cannibal islands and in Paria,[5] and afterwards there was a report of six other caravels which a brother of the alcalde[6] commanded, but this was due to malice. And this was already at a time when there was now very little hope that Their Highnesses would ever send ships to the Indies, and when we did not expect them, and when they said generally that Her Highness was dead.

At this time one Adrian[7] attempted to revolt again as before, but Our Lord would not permit his evil purpose to be carried into effect. I had resolved in my own mind not to touch a hair of anyone's head, and owing to his ingratitude, I was not able to save him, as I had intended to do. I would not have done less to my own brother, if he had desired to

---

[1] The allusion is probably to the revolt of Guarionex and Mayobanex, which presented considerable difficulty to Bartholomew Columbus, governor of the island in the absence of his brother (cp. Las Casas, i. 113, 120–1).

[2] Alonso de Ojeda (cp. *supra*, vol. I, p. 76, note 3). He arrived in Española in Feb. 1500, and landing in Xaragua, attempted to stir up the former partisans of Roldán (cp. Las Casas, i. 160, 164, 168–9). At the moment when he left Spain, Isabella was not dangerously ill, but she had recently suffered the loss of prince Juan and of her favourite daughter, the infanta Isabel, while Margaret of Austria had only given birth to a still-born child.

[3] Columbus is referring partly to the criminals who had been transported to Española in accordance with his own suggestion (cp. *Cédula*, 22 Jan. 1497; Navarrete, ii. 212–15), and partly to the labourers who had been sent out, but who had largely joined Roldán (cp. Las Casas, i. 112, 119, 148). Las Casas had a better opinion of the criminals, one of whom at least 'was a good enough fellow, although he had lost an ear', than of the labourers, who 'having been born to serve, to do manual labour and to be ordered about', would insist on walking upright.

embiavan con promesas de dádivas y franquezas y paga:
allegó grand quadrilla, que en toda la Española muy pocos
ay, salvo vagamundos, y ninguno con muger y fijos. este
Fojeda me trabajó harto. fuéle neçessario de se yr, y dexó
dicho que luego sería de buelta con más navíos y gente, y que
dexava la real presona de la reyna, nuestra señora, á la
muerte. en esto, llegó Viçentiánes con quatro caravelas: ovo
alboroto y sospecha, mas no daño. los Yndios dixeron de
otras muchas á los Caníbales y en Paria, y después una nueva
de seys otras caravelas que traýa un hermano del alcalde;
mas fué con maliçia. esto fué ya á la postre, quando ya
estava muy rota la esperança que Sus Altezas oviesen jamás
de enbiar navío á las Yndias, ni nos esperarlos, y que vulgar-
mente dezían que Su Alteza era muerta.

Un Adrián en este tiempo provó á alçarse otra vez, como
de antes, mas Nuestro Señor no quiso que llegase á efecto su
mal propósito. yo tenía propuesto en mi de no tocar el cabello
á nadie: y á este, por su yngratitud, con lágrimas no se pudo
guardar, asý como yo lo tenía pensado. á mi hermano no
hisiera menos, sy me quisyera matar y robar el señorio que

---

⁴ Vicente Yañez Pinzón, brother of Martin Alonso Pinzón, and captain of the
Niña on the first voyage of Columbus. Having made an agreement with
Fonseca (Dec. 1495: Navarrete, iii. 75–6), he went on a voyage of discovery with
four caravels, sailing from Palos (Dec. 1499). He reached the coast of Brazil,
which he called the land of Santa María de la Consolación, and was the first
Spaniard to sight the Amazon (1500). Having sailed along the coast of Paria,
and having collected pearls, he reached Española (23 June 1500), where he lost
two of his caravels in a storm. Thence he returned to Spain (cp. Las Casas, i.
173).

⁵ Licences to make voyages of discovery had been granted by the sovereigns to
Peralonso Niño and Cristobal Guerra, and it is probably to their appearance on
the coast of Venezuela that Columbus is referring (cp. Las Casas, i. 171).

⁶ Francisco Roldán, who had been appointed alcalde by Columbus and who
had been restored to that position when the rebellion was settled (cp. Las Casas,
i. 160).

⁷ Adrian de Moxica, a young man of good family, who had been one of the
partisans of Roldán. He seems to have been roused by the treatment of his
cousin, Hernando de Guevara (cp. *infra*), to plot against Columbus. His
treason was revealed to the admiral by one of the plotters and he was arrested.
Columbus ordered Moxica to be hanged, but when the condemned man seemed
to attempt to evade punishment by refusing to be confessed, Columbus caused
him to be thrown from the walls of Concepción, the fort in which he had been
arrested and confined (Las Casas, i. 170; Ferdinand Columbus, c. 84).

kill me and to deprive me of the lordship which my king and queen had given into my keeping. This Adrian, as is now demonstrated, had sent Don Fernando[1] to Xaragua[2] to assemble some of his followers, and there was there a dispute with the alcalde, whence arose a deadly quarrel, but the purpose was not attained. The alcalde arrested him and some of his band, and the fact was that he punished them without my having ordered it. They were prisoners, awaiting a caravel in which they were to go; the news of Ojeda, whom I have mentioned, caused hope to be lost that it would come any more.

For six months I had been ready to leave to come to Their Highnesses with the good news of the gold and to escape from having to govern a dissolute people, who have no fear of God or of their king and queen, and who are full of folly and malice. I should have been able to pay the people with six hundred thousand maravedis, and for this purpose, I had four *contos* from the tithes and something over, besides the third from the gold.[3]

Before my departure I many times prayed Their Highnesses that they would send there at my cost someone who might have charge of the administration of justice, and after I had found the alcalde in revolt, I asked this again, or for some men or at least for some servant, bearing their letters, since my reputation is such that although I were to build churches and hospitals, they would always be called lairs for robbers.[4] They have now at last made provision, and it has been very different from that which the business demanded; let that be, since it is their pleasure. I was there for two years without being able to secure any provision in my favour or in

---

[1] Fernando (or Hernando) de Guevara. For the story of the loves of Guevara and Higueymota, daughter of Anacaona, see Las Casas (i. 170) and Ferdinand Columbus (c. 84). It was the attempt of Roldán to put an end to this love affair which produced the 'deadly quarrel', mentioned by Columbus: Las Casas suggests that the lady had been Roldán's mistress and that she had abandoned him in favour of his younger rival. Roldán arrested Guevara and sent him a prisoner to Santo Domingo, to await the judgement of Columbus. Bobadilla found Guevara imprisoned in the castle there and was told that he was under sentence of death; he released him. The version given by Columbus in this letter is not entirely clear, but he perhaps means that the prisoners were awaiting

mi rey é reyna me tenían dado en guarda. este Adrián,
segund se muestra, tenía enbiado á don Fernando á Xoraguá
á allegar algunos sus sequaces, y allá ovo debate con el
alcalde, adonde nació discordia de muerte; mas no llegó
á efecto. el alcalde le prendió, y á parte de su quadrilla, y el
caso era qu'él los justiçiara, sy yo no lo proveyera. estovieron
presos, esperando caravela en que se fuesen: las nuevas de
Fojeda, que yo dixe, fisieron perder la esperança que ya no
vernía.

Seys meses avía que yo estava despachado por venir á Sus
Altezas con las buenas nuevas del oro y fuyr de governar
gente disoluta que no teme á Dios ni á su rey ni reyna, llena
de achaques y de maliçias.

A la gente acabara yo de pagar con seysçientas mill, y para
ello avía quatro cuentos de diezmos, é alguno syn el terçio del
oro. antes de mi partida, supliqué tantas vezes á Sus Altezas
que enbiasen allá á mi costa á quien toviese cargo de la
justiçia; y, después que fallé alçado el alcalde, se lo supliqué
de nuevo ó por alguna gente, ó al menos algund criado, con
cartas: porque mi fama es tal, que, aunque yo faga yglesias
y ospitales, siempre serán dichas espeluncas para ladrones.
proveyeron ya al fin, y fué muy al contrario de lo que la
negoçiación demandava: vaya en buen ora, pues que fué á su
grado.

a caravel to convey them back to Castile. Las Casas (*loc. cit.*) comments on the
extreme severity of Columbus and his brother at this time.

² Xaragua, the district ruled by Anacaona, was the most westerly part of
Española, and was very fertile. When he came to terms with Columbus, Roldán
fixed his residence there (Las Casas, i. 161).

³ A *conto* is one million. The financial system which prevailed in Española
while Columbus governed the island was originally determined by the terms of
the Capitulations concluded between him and the sovereigns at Santa Fé
(17 April 1492), and confirmed at Barcelona after his return from his first
voyage (28 May 1493). Columbus was entitled to receive a tithe of all produce,
and further, if he wished, to contribute one-eighth of the cost of any expedition
and to receive one-eighth of the profit made (Navarrete, ii. 7–8, 57–62). One
third of the product of all mines had been the customary due of the crown in
Spain before the discovery of the New World, and this third was at first exacted
also in Española.

⁴ Cp. Las Casas (i. 160), who remarks that Columbus realized that since he
was an alien, he could not secure respect from the Spaniards, 'that being the
peculiar temper or pride of Spain'. Columbus stipulated in writing to the
sovereigns that his own privileges should be maintained.

favour of those who were there, and he[1] brings a purseful; whether all will be employed for their service, God knows. Already there are franchises for twenty years, which is the age of a man, and gold is collected, so that a man has the value of five marks in four hours, of which I will speak more at length hereafter.[2]

It would be a charity if it were to please Their Highnesses to put to shame a mob of those who know my weariness, for their evil speaking has done me the greater injury, so that my great service has not profited me, and my preservation of their property and dominion. So I should regain my honour and I should be renowned throughout the world, for the matter is of the kind that every day is more famous and in higher esteem.

At this time the comendador Bobadilla came to Santo Domingo. I was in the Vega and the adelantado was in Xaragua where this Adrian had made his attempt, but already all was settled and the land prosperous and in all peace.[3] On the day after his arrival, he created himself governor and appointed officials and performed executive acts, and he proclaimed franchises for the collection of gold and remitted tithes, and granted a general indulgence for everything else for twenty years, which as I say is the age of a man.[4] And he declared that he was come to pay everyone, although they have not served duly up to this day. And he published abroad that he was to send me back in fetters and my brothers, as he has done, and that I was never to go there more, nor any other of my family, saying a thousand unjust and insulting things of me.

All this was on the day after he arrived, as I have said, I being absent at a distance and knowing nothing of it or of his coming. Some letters of Their Highnesses, signed in blank, of which he brought a quantity, he filled up and sent to the alcalde and to his company with compliments and flattery.[5] To me he never sent a letter or a messenger, nor has he done so down to this day.[6]

---

[1] Francisco de Bobadilla, comendador in the order of Alcantara and a member of the royal household. His commission was issued 21 May 1499 and confirmed 30 May 1499, but he did not reach Santo Domingo until 23 Aug. 1500. His

Yo estuve allá doss años, syn poder ganar una provisón de
favor por mi ni por los que allá fuesen, y éste llevó un arca
llena: sy pararán todas á su serviçio, Dios lo sabe. ya, por
comienço, ay franquezas de .xx. años, que es la hedad de un
ombre, y se coje el oro, que ovo presona de çinco marcas en
quatro oras; de que diré después más largo.

Sy pluguiesse á Sus Altezas de desfaser un vulgo de los que
saben mis fatigas, que mayor daño me ha fecho el maldesyr
de las gentes que no me ha aprovechado el mucho servir
y guardar su fazienda y señorío, sería limosna, é yo restituýdo
en mi honrra, y se fablaría d'ello en todo el mundo, porque
el negoçio es de calidad que cada día ha de ser más sonado
y en alta estima.

En esto vino el comendador Bovadilla á Santo Domingo.
yo estava en la Vega, y el adelantado en Xoraguá, adonde
este Adrián avía fecho cabeça, mas ya todo era llano, y la
tierra rica, y todos en paz. el segundo día que llegó, se crió
governador, y fiso ofiçiales y exsecutiones, y apregonó franquezas del oro y diezmos, y generalmente de toda otra cosa
por veynte años, que, como digo, es la hedad de un ombre,
y que venía para pagar á todos, bien que no avían servido
llenamente fasta ese día, y publicó que á mi me avía de enbiar
en fierros, y á mis hermanos, ansí como ha fecho, y que nunca
más bolvería yo allí, ni otrie de mi linaje, disiendo de mi mill
desonestas y descorteses cosas. esto todo fué el segundo día
que él llegó, como dixe, y estando yo lexos, absente, syn saber
d'él ni de su venida. unas cartas de Sus Altezas, firmadas en
blanco, de que él llevava una cantidad, enchió y enbió al

character has been bitterly attacked by Ferdinand Columbus (c. 84–5), and this
view has been adopted by most later writers. New light was thrown on the
relations between Columbus and Bobadilla by the publication of the *Autógrafos
de Cristóbal Colón*, and the character of Bobadilla has been energetically
defended by Luis Vidart (*Colón y Bobadilla*, and *Colón y la Ingratitud de España*).

² Cp. *infra*, p. 70. ³ Cp. Las Casas, i. 178.
⁴ For the actions of Bobadilla, cp. Las Casas (i. 179–81) and Ferdinand
Columbus (*loc. cit.*). ⁵ Cp. Las Casas (i. 180).
⁶ According to Las Casas (*loc. cit.*), Bobadilla did not write to Columbus, but
sent him notice of his arrival by an alcalde. Columbus had already received an
account from his brother, Diego, who had been left in command at Santo
Domingo. Afterwards Bobadilla sent a royal letter, addressed to Columbus, to
the admiral by a Franciscan, Juan de Traslerra, and Juan Velazquez, the
treasurer.

Consider what a man who held my position was to think! Honour and favour to one who proved to be robbing Their Highnesses of their lordship and who had done so much evil and damage! And disgrace for one who had supported it through so great perils! When I learned this, I believed that this would be as the affair of Ojeda, or of one of the others. I refrained myself when I knew of a certainty from the friars that Their Highnesses had sent him.[1] I wrote that his coming was welcome, and that I was prepared to go to the court,[2] and that I had put up for sale all that I possessed, and that in the matter of the franchises, there should be no haste, for I would immediately give him this and the government absolutely, and so I wrote to the religious. Neither he nor they gave me an answer, but he adopted a hostile attitude, and he compelled as many as went there to swear to him as governor; they told me, for twenty years.[3]

As soon as I knew of these franchises, I thought to repair so great an error and that he would be content. Without necessity and reason, he had given so great a thing and to a vagabond people, that which would have been an excessive grant to a man who had brought out a wife and children. I proclaimed by word of mouth and by letters that he was not empowered to make use of his provisions, since mine were of greater authority,[4] and I showed the grants brought by Juan Aguado.[5] All this that I did was in order to gain time, that Their Highnesses might be informed of the state of the country and that they might have occasion to order that in the matter which might be for their service.

It is not advantageous to them that such franchises should be proclaimed in the Indies. It is a favour to the inhabitants who have acquired residence, for to them are given the best lands and at a low estimate they will be worth two hundred thousand maravedis at the end of the four years, when the time of residence is completed, without a single sod being turned in them. I would not so speak if the settlers were married men, but there are not six among them all whose aim is not to amass as much as they can and to return home speedily. It would be well that people should come from

---

[1] Only one friar is mentioned by Las Casas (loc. cit.).

alcalde y á su compaña, con favores y encomiendas. á mi
nunca me enbió carta ni mensagero, ni me ha dado fasta oy.
¡piense Vuestra Merçed qué pensaría quien toviera mi cargo!
¡honrrar y favorecer á quien provó á robar á Sus Altezas el
señorio y ha fecho tanto mal y daño! ¡y arastrar á quien con
tantos peligros se lo sostuvo! quando yo supe esto, creý que
este sería como lo de Hojeda, ó uno de los otros: templóme
que supe de los grayles de cierto que Sus Altezas le embiavan.
escrivíle yo que su venida fuese en buen ora, y que yo estava
despachado para yr á la corte y fecho almoneda de quanto yo
tenía, y que en esto de las franquesas que no se açelerase, que
esto y el govierno que yo se lo daría luego tan llano como la
palma; y ansý lo escriví á los religiosos. ni él ni ellos me
dieron respuesta, antes, se puso él en son de guerra, y
apremiava á quantos allí yvan que le jurasen por governador,
dixéronme que por .xx. años.

Luego que yo supe d'estas franquesas, pensé de adobar un
yerro tan grande, y qu'él sería contento, las quales dió syn
neçesidad ni cabsa de cosa tan gruessa, y á gente vagamunda,
que fuera demasiado para quien troxiera muger y fijos.
publiqué por palabra y por cartas que él no podía usar de sus
provisiones, porque las mías eran las fuertes; y les mostré las
franquesas que llevó Juan Aguado.

Todo esto que yo hise era por dilatar, porque Sus Altezas
fuesen sabidores del estado de la tierra, y que oviesen lugar de
tornar á mandar en ello lo que fuese su servicio.

Tales franquesas escusado es de las apregonar en las Yndias.
los vezinos que han tomado vezindad, es logro, porque se les
dan las mejores tierras, y, á poco valer, valerán dosientas mill
al cabo de los quatro años que la vezindad se acaba, syn que
den un'açadonada en ellas. no diría yo asý, sy los vezinos
fuesen casados; mas no ay seys entre todos que no estén

---

[2] According to Las Casas (*loc. cit.*), this answer was sent to the message
received through the alcalde.   [3] Cp. Las Casas (*loc. cit.*).

[4] This contention had already been urged by Diego Columbus, but was met
by Bobadilla by the production of fuller royal letters (Las Casas, i. 179).

[5] Columbus appears to have contended that Bobadilla had come only to
administer justice, in answer to the request which he had himself already made
to the sovereigns, and that it was usurpation on his part to assume the government of the island (Las Casas, i. 180).

Castile, and only such as are well known, and that the country should be peopled with honest men.[1]

I had agreed with these settlers that they should pay a third of the gold and the tithes, and this at their request, and they received it as a great favour from Their Highnesses.[2] I blamed them when I heard that they were departing from it, and they expected that he would make another such as I had done, but the contrary was the case. He irritated them against me, saying that I wished to deprive them of that which Their Highnesses had given to them, and he laboured that they should hurl accusations at me, and he achieved this and that they should write to Their Highnesses that they should not send me again as governor, and so I pray for myself and for all who belong to me, while there is not another people, and he ordered an inquiry to be made into my misdeeds, which were such as were never known in hell.

Our Lord is there, Who saved Daniel and the Three Children with so much wisdom and power, and with such a manifestation, as was pleasing to Him, for His honour. I should have known how to remedy all this and the rest that is said and that has passed since I have been in the Indies, if I had admitted a wish to procure my own good for myself, and it had been honourable for me to do so. But the maintenance of justice and the extension of the lordship of Their Highnesses up to now has brought me to the depth.

Now at the time when so much gold is found, there is a dispute whether there is more to be gained by going about robbing or by going to the mines. For one woman moreover a hundred castellanos are given, as if for a farm, and this is very common, and there are now many merchants who go seeking for girls; nine or ten are now for sale; for women of all ages, there is a good price to be had.[3]

I declare that the violence of the evil speaking of disaffected persons has done me more injury than my service has profited me; it is an evil example for the present and for the future. I make oath that a number of men have gone to the Indies who did not deserve baptism in the eyes of God

[1] For the complaints of the settlers made by Columbus, in his letters to Ferdinand and Isabella, cp. Las Casas (i. 155, 156, 159, 160). Las Casas declares that

sobre el aviso de ayuntar lo que pudieren, y se yr en buen ora. de Castilla sería bien que fuesen, y aun saber quién y cómo, y se poblase de gente honrrada.

Yo tenía asentado con estos vesinos que pagarían el terçio del oro, y los diezmos, y esto á su ruego, y lo reçibieron en grand merced de Sus Altezas. repregendílos, quando yo oý que se dexavan d'ello, y esperava qu'el comendador faría otro tanto; mas fué al contrario. yndignólos contra mi, disiendo que yo les quería quitar lo que Sus Altezas les davan, y trabajó de me los echar á cuestas, y lo hiso, y que escriviesen á Sus Altezas que no me enbiasen más al cargo (y ansý se lo suplico yo por mi y por toda cosa mía, en quanto no aya otro pueblo), y me ordenó él con ellos pesquisas de maldades, que al ynfierno nunca se supo de las semejantes. allí está Nuestro Señor que escapó á Daniel y á los tres muchachos, con tanto saber y fuerça como tenía, y con tanto aparejo, si le pluguiere, como con su gana.

Supiera yo remediar todo esto, y lo otro que está dicho y ha pasado después que estoy en las Yndias, sy me consyntiera la voluntad á procurar por mi bien propio, y me fuera onesto; mas el sostener de la justiçia y acreçentar el señorío de Su Altesa fasta agora, me tiene al fondo oy en día que se falla tanto oro. ay división en que aya más ganançia: ó yr robando ó yr á las minas. por una muger tanbién se falla çient castellanos como por una labrança; y es mucho en uso, y ay fartos mercaderes que andan buscando muchachas: de nueve á diez son agora en preçio: de todas hedades ha de tener un bueno.

Digo que la fuerça del maldesyr de desconçertados me ha más dañado que mis serviçios [han] fecho provecho. mal exemplo es por el presente y por lo futuro. fago juramento que cantidad de ombres han ydo á las Yndias que no meresçian el agua para con Dios y con el mundo, y agora buelven allá y se les consiente.

Digo que en dezir yo qu'el comendador no podía dar

especially after the coming of Ojeda to the island, the settlers were unsatisfactory (i. 170).

² Cp. *supra*, p. 54 and note 3.

³ On this, cp. Las Casas (ii. 3). Judging from the relative temper with which Las Casas describes the situation, Columbus was here somewhat exaggerating.

and man, and now they are returning thither, and he con-
nives at it.

I declare that in saying that the comendador could not
grant franchises, I did that which he wished, although I told
him that it was to gain time until Their Highnesses should
have an account of the land and come to see and to command
that which would be to their service.

He has made all hostile to me, and it appears, from that
which he has done and from his methods, that he came
already very inflamed against me, and it is said that he has
spent much to come on this business; I know of this no more
than I have heard. I never heard that a *pesquisidor*[1] should
gather rebels and bring them as witnesses against one who
was governing them, and others without faith and unworthy
of it. If Their Highnesses would command a general inquiry
to be made there, I declare to you that they would find it
a great marvel that the island has not been swallowed up.

I believe that you will remember that when the storm
drove me without sails into Lisbon, I was falsely accused as
having gone there to the king in order to give the Indies to
him.[2] Afterwards Their Highnesses knew the contrary and
that it was all malice. Although I have little knowledge, I do
not know who regards me as so dull that I do not know that
even if the Indies were mine, I should not be able to maintain myself without the aid of a prince.[3] If this be so, where
could I have better support and security against being driven
out from them entirely than in the king and queen, our
sovereigns, who from nothing have set me in such honour
and who are the most exalted princes in the world by sea and
land? And they know how I have served them and they
preserve my privileges and rewards for me, and if any infringe them, Their Highnesses increase them to my advantage,
as was seen in the case of Juan Aguado,[4] and they command
much honour to be done me, and as I have said, Their Highnesses have received services from me and have taken my
sons to be their servants,[5] which could in nowise have

---

[1] A special judge, appointed to hold an inquiry into acts of administration.

[2] Cp. *supra*, vol. I, p. 18 and note 5.

franquesas, que hise yo lo qu'él deseava, bien que yo á el
dixese que era para dilatar fasta que Sus Altesas toviessen
el aviso de la tierra y tornasen á ver y mandar lo que fuesse
su servicio.

Enemistólos á ellos todos comigo, y él pareçe, segund se
ovo y segund sus formas, que ya lo venía, y bien ençendido,
ó es que se dise que ha gastado mucho por venir á este
negoçio: no sé d'ello más de lo que oyo. yo nunca oý qu'el
pesquisidor allegase los rebeldes y los tomase por testigos
contra aquel que govierna á ellos, ni á otros, syn fe, ni dignos
d'ella.

Si Sus Altesas mandasen faser una pesquisa general allí,
vos digo yo que verían por grand maravilla como la ysla no
se funde.

Yo creo que se acordará Vuestra Merçed quando la tormenta syn velas me echó en Lisboa, que fuý acusado falsa-
mente que avía yo ydo allá al rey, para darle las Yndias.
después supieron Sus Altezas el contrario, y que todo fué con
maliçia.

Bien que yo sepa poco, no sé quien me tenga por tan turpe
que yo no conozca que, aunque las Yndias fuesen mías, que
yo no me pudiera sustener syn ayuda de prínçipe. sy esto es
asý, ¿ adónde pudiera yo tener mejor ánimo y seguridad de
no ser echado d'ellas del todo que en el rey y reyna, nuestros
señores, que de nada me han puesto en tanta honrra y son los
más altos prínçipes, por la mar y por la tierra, del mundo ?
y los quales tienen que yo les aya servido, y me guardan mis
privilegios y merçedes, y, sy alguién me los quebranta, Sus
Altezas me los acreçientan con avantaja, como se vido en lo
de Juan Aguado, y me mandan faser mucha honrra, y, como
dixe ya, Sus Altezas reçibieron de mi serviçio, y tienen á mis
fijos sus criados, lo que en ninguna manera pudiera esto
llegar con otro prínçipe, porque adonde no ay amor todo lo
otro çesa.

³ Las Casas notes that it was alleged that Columbus wished to hand over
Española to the Genoese.
⁴ Cp. *supra*, p. 8, note 3.
⁵ Diego and Ferdinand Columbus had become pages in the court after the
first voyage of Columbus.

happened with another prince, for where there is no love, all else is lacking.

I have now spoken so against a malicious calumny severely and against my wish, for it is a matter which I would not recall even in my dreams. The comendador Bobadilla has with malice wished openly to exhibit his methods and actions in this matter, but with the utmost ease I will make it appear that his small understanding and his great cowardice, united with his inordinate greed, have caused him to fail in this. I have already said how I wrote to him and to the friars, and immediately, as I said to him, I set out utterly alone, because all the people were with the adelantado, and also in order to disarm his suspicion.[1] When he knew this, he threw Don Diego, as a prisoner, loaded with fetters, into a caravel, and to me when I arrived he did the same, and to the adelantado when he came.[2] I have not spoken more to him, nor, up to this day, has he allowed anyone to speak with me, and I make oath that I could not think why I was a prisoner.[3]

His first care was to take the gold, which he had without measuring or weighing it, and, I being absent, he said that he wished to pay the people from it, and, as I have heard, he took the first part for himself, and that he would appoint new persons to superintend the exchange. Of this gold I had put aside certain specimens, grains as large as a goose's egg, and a hen's egg, and a pullet's egg, and of many shapes, which some persons had collected in a little while and with which Their Highnesses would have been pleased, and in order that they might realize the nature of the business from a number of great stones, full of gold. This was the first that he maliciously took for himself, that Their Highnesses might not consider this business as anything until he had feathered his own nest, which he hastened to do. The gold, which was to be melted, diminished in the fire; a chain which weighed up to twenty marks has never been seen. I have been more aggrieved in the matter of the gold than even in that of the pearls, because I have not brought it to Your Highnesses.[4]

---

[1] Columbus was suspected of an intention of arming the natives against Bobadilla (cp. Las Casas, i. 180).

[2] Diego Columbus, after handing over the castle of Santo Domingo to

Dixe yo agora ansí esto contra un maldezir con maliçia
y contra mi voluntad, porque es cosa que ni en sueños deviera
llegar á memoria; porque las formas y fechos del comendador
Bovadilla, con maliçia las quiere alumbrar en esto: mas yo le
faré ver con el braço ysquierdo que so poco saber y grand
covardía, con desordenada codiçia, le ha fecho caer en ello.
Ya dixe como yo le escriví, y á los frayles; y luego partí,
asý como le dixe, muy solo, porque toda la gente estava con
el adelantado, y tanbién por le quitar de sospecha. él, quando
lo supo, echó á don Diego preso en una caravela, cargado de
fierros, y á mi, en llegando, hiso otro tanto, y después al
adelantado, quando vino. ni le fablé más á él, ni consintió que
fasta oy nadie me aya fablado. y fago juramento que no
puedo pensar por qué sea yo preso.

La primera diligençia qu'él fiso, fué á tomar el oro, el qual
ovo sin medida ni peso, é, yo absente, dixo que quería él pagar
d'ello á la gente, y, segund oý, para sý hiso la primera parte,
y enbía por resgate resgatadores nuevos. d'este oro tenía yo
apartado ciertas muestras, granos muy gruessos, como huevos
de ánsara y de gallina y de pollas, y de otras muchas fechuras,
que algunas personas tenían cogido en breve espaçio, con que
se alegrasen Sus Altezas, y por ello comprehendiesen el
negoçio con una cantidad de piedras grandes llenas de oro.
este fué el primero á se dar con maliçia, porque Sus Altezas no
toviesen este negoçio en algo, fasta que él tenga fecho el nido;
de que se da buena priesa. el oro que está por fundir mengua
al fuego: unas cadenas que pesarían fasta veynte marcos,
nunca se han visto.

Yo he seýdo muy agraviado en esto del oro, más aun que
de las perlas, porque no lo he traýdo á Sus Altezas.

Bobadilla, was arrested before his brother had arrived. Bartholomew Columbus
was arrested later (cp. Las Casas, i. 181).

³ For the arrest of Columbus, cp. Las Casas (i. 181) and Ferdinand Columbus
(c. 84). Peter Martyr (i. 7) says that the sovereigns were weary of the continual
dissensions in Española, but that he does not know what exact charges were
brought against the admiral. It is curious that Bernáldez (c. 131, 196) passes
over the arrest of Columbus very casually and speaks in complimentary terms
of Bobadilla.

⁴ According to Las Casas (i. 177), Columbus was meditating the establishment
of a fort in Paria and the development of the pearl fisheries there, at the moment
when Bobadilla arrived.

The comendador showed energy always in everything that he thought would injure me. I have already said that with six hundred thousand maravedis I should have paid everyone without defrauding anyone, and I had more than four *contos* from the tithes and from police dues, without touching the gold.[1] He made some gifts which are laughable, although I believe that he rewarded himself first; there Their Highnesses will know the truth when they command him to render an account, especially if I may be present at it. He says continually that a great sum is due, and it is that amount which I have stated and even less.

I have been very much aggrieved in that there has been sent to inquire into my conduct a man who knew that, if the report which he sent back were very damaging, he would remain in charge of the government.[2] Would that it had pleased Our Lord that Their Highnesses had sent him or another two years ago, for I know that then I should have been free from scandalous abuse and infamy, and I should not have been deprived of my honour or have lost it.[3] God is just, and He will cause it to be known by whom and how it was done.

At home they judge me as a governor sent to Sicily or to a city or two under settled government, and where the laws can be fully maintained, without fear of all being lost; and at this I am greatly aggrieved. I ought to be judged as a captain who went from Spain to the Indies to conquer a people, warlike and numerous, and with customs and beliefs very different from ours, a people, living in highlands and mountains, having no settled dwellings, and apart from us; and where, by the will of God, I have brought under the dominion of the king and queen, our sovereigns, another world, whereby Spain, which was called poor, is now most rich. I ought to be judged as a captain, who, for so long a time, down to this day, has borne arms, never laying them down for an hour, and by knights of the sword and by men of action, and not by men of letters, unless they had been as the Greeks or Romans, or as others of the present day of whom there are so many and so noble in Spain, for in any other way

---

[1] Cp. *supra*, p. 54 and note 3.

El comendador, en todo lo que le pareçió que me dañaría, luego fué puesto en obra. ya dixe con .DCM. pagara á todos, syn robar á nadie, y que avía más de .IIII. quentos de diesmos y alguaziladgo, syn tocar en el oro. hiso unas larguezas, que son de risa, bien que creo que encomençó en sí la primera parte: allá lo sabrán Sus Altezas, quando le mandaren tomar cuenta, en espeçial si yo estoviese á ella. él no fase syno desyr que se deve grand summa, y es la que yo dixe, y no tanto.

Yo he sido muy mucho agraviado en que se aya enbiado pesquisidor sobre mi, que sepa que, sy la pesquisa qu'él enbiare fuera muy grave, qu'él quedará en el govierno.

Pluguiera á Nuestro Señor que Sus Altezas le enbiaran á él ó á otro doss años ha, porque sé que yo fuera ya libre d'escándalo y de disfamia, y no se me quitara mi honrra, ni la perdiera. Dios es justo, y ha de haser que se sepa por qué y cómo.

Allí me juzgan como á governador que fué á Çiçilia ó çibdad ó villa puesta en regimento, y adonde las leyes se pueden guardar por entero, syn temor que se pierda todo: y reçibo grande agravio. yo devo de ser juzgado como capitán que fué d'España á conquistar fasta las Yndias á gente belicosa y mucha, y de costumbres y seta á nos muy contraria, los quales biven por sierras y montes, syn pueblo asentado, ni nosotros; y adonde, por voluntad divina, he puesto so el señorio del rey y de la reyna, nuestros señores, otro mundo; y por donde la España, que hera dicha pobre, es la más rica.

Yo devo de ser judgado como capitán que de tanto tiempo fasta oy trae las armas á cuestas, sin las dexar una ora, y de cavalleros de conquistas y del uso, y no de letras, salvo si fuesen de Griegos ó de Romanos, ó otros modernos, de que ay tantos y tan nobles en España, ó, de otra guisa, reçibo grande agravio, porque en las Yndias no ay pueblo, ni asiento.

² There is no evidence that Bobadilla had any such knowledge, although the vague powers given to him by Ferdinand and Isabella may well have suggested to him that his appointment would be permanent if once Columbus were out of the island.

³ Columbus is probably alluding to the increased antipathy towards him which resulted from the severity shown after the rebellion of Roldán.

I am greatly aggrieved, because in the Indies there is neither a town nor any settled dwelling.[1]

To the gold and pearls the gate is already opened, and they may surely expect a quantity of all, precious stones and spices and a thousand other things. And would that never more ill might come to me, so that I might undertake the great voyage, and so make the negotiation for Arabia Felix as far as Mecca, as I wrote to Their Highnesses by Antonio de Torres, in my answer concerning the division of the sea and land with the Portuguese,[2] and afterwards I would go to Colucuti, as I have said and laid down in writing in the monastery of la Mejorada.[3]

The news of the gold which I said that I would give is that, on the day of the Nativity, being greatly afflicted owing to my struggles with evil Christians and with the Indians, and being on the verge of leaving all and escaping with my life, if possible, Our Lord miraculously consoled me and said: 'Take courage, be not dismayed nor fear; I will provide for all; the seven years, the term of the gold, are not passed, and in this and in the rest I will give thee redress.'[4] On that day I learned that there were eighty leagues of land and in every part of them mines; it now appears that they are all one. Some have collected a hundred and twenty castellanos in a day, others ninety, and it has risen to two hundred and fifty. To collect from fifty to seventy, and many others from fifteen to fifty, is held to be a good day's work, and many continue to collect it; the average is from six to twelve, and any who falls below this is not content. The opinion of all is that, were all Castile to go there, however inexpert a man might be, he would not get less than a castellano or two a day, and so it is up to the present time. It is true that he who has an Indian collects this amount, but the matter depends on the Christian.

Observe the discretion of Bobadilla! He gave all for nothing and four *contos* of tithes without reason and without being asked, and without first giving notice to Their Highnesses! And this is not the only damage that has been done.

<hr/>

[1] Cp. with this whole passage the Letter of Columbus to certain personages of the court, dated by de Lollis at the end of 1500 (*Rac. Col.* I. ii, pp. li–liii, 64–5).

Del oro y perlas ya está abierta la puerta, y cantidad de todo, piedras preçiosas y espeçiería, y de otras mill cosas se pueden esperar firmemente; y, nunca más mal me viniese, como, con el nombre de Nuestro Señor, que le daría el primer viage, asý como diera la negoçiaçión del Arabia Felis fasta la Meca, como yo escriví á Sus Altezas con Antoño de Torres, en la respuesta de la repartiçión del mar y tierra con los Portugueses, y después viniera á lo de Colucuti, asý como le dixe y dí por escripto en el monasterio de la Mejorada.

Las nuevas del oro que yo dixe que daría, son que día de Nabidad, estando yo muy aflegido, guerreado de los malos christianos y de Yndios, en término de dexar todo y escapar, sy pudiese, la vida, me consoló Nuestro Señor milagrosamente, y dixo: 'esfuerça, no desmaytes ni temas; yo proveeré en todo; los siete años del término del oro no son pasados, y en ello y en lo otro te daré remedio.' ese día supe que avía .lxxx. leguas de tierra, y, en todo cabo d'ellas, minas. el pareçer agora es que sea toda una: algunos han cogido .cxx. castellanos en un día, y otros .xc., y se ha llegado fasta .ccl. de .l. fasta .lxx., otros muchos de .xv. fasta .l. y es tenido buen jornal, y muchos lo continuan: el común es de .vi. fasta .xii., y, quien de aquí abaxa, no va contento. pareçe tanbién que estas minas son como las otras, que responden en los días no ygualmente: las minas son nuevas, y los cogedores. al pareçer de todos es que, aunque vaya allá toda Castilla, que, por torpe que sea la presona, que no abaxará de un castellano ó doss cada día: y agora, es esto ansý en fresco. es verdad que tienen algund Indio; mas el negoçio todo consiste en el christiano. ¡ved qué discriçión fué de Bovadilla dar todo por ninguno y quatro quentos de diezmos syn cabsa, ni ser requerido, syn primero lo notificar á Sus Altezas! y el daño no es este solo.

Yo sé que mis hierros no han seýdo con fin de faser mal, y creo que Sus Altezas lo tienen asý como yo lo digo, y sé y veo que usan de misericordia con quien maliçiosamente les

---

[2] This answer is not preserved, but the opinion of Columbus concerning the line of demarcation is to be found in his *Book of Privileges* (*Rac. Col.* II. ii. 30).

[3] Near Olmedo. Columbus deposited various papers there but they do not appear to be now extant.

[4] Cp. *supra*, p. 48, and *infra*, p. 92.

I know that my errors have not been committed with intention to do ill, and I believe that Their Highnesses will credit me when I say so. And I know and see that they are merciful to one who maliciously does them disservice. I believe and regard as very certain that they will treat me much better and with more kindness, for I have fallen into error innocently and under compulsion, as they will hereafter know fully, and that I am their humble servant, and they will regard my services and will every day know better that they have been greatly to their advantage. They will weigh all in the balance, as Holy Scripture tells us the good will be weighed with the evil on the day of judgement. If still they command that another judge me, which I do not expect, and that there be an inquiry concerning the Indies, I pray them humbly that they send there two persons, conscientious and honourable, at my expense, and they will easily find that now gold is won at the rate of five marks in four hours. Be this as it may, it is very necessary that they should make provision in the matter.

The comendador, on arriving at Santo Domingo, took up his residence in my house. All that he found there, he appropriated for himself; well and good, perhaps he had need of it; a pirate never treated a merchant so. Concerning my papers I complain most, that they have been taken from me by him, and that I have never been able to recover one, and those which would have been most useful to me in my defence, he has most carefully concealed. Observe the just and honest pesquisidor. Whatever he may have done, they tell me that he has ceased to regard justice and is acting as a despot. Our Lord God lives, with His power and wisdom, as in the past, and above all things, He punishes ingratitude and wrongs.

diserve. yo creo y tengo por muy çierto que muy mejor y más
piedad avrán comigo, que caý en ello con ygnorancia y
forçosamente, como sabrán después por entero, y el qual soy
su fechura, y mirarán á mis servicios, y conoçerán de cada
día que son muy avantajados. todo pornán en una balança,
ansý como nos cuenta la sacra Escriptura que será el bien
con el mal el día del juysio. sy todavía mandan que otrie me
judgue, lo qual no espero, y que sea por pesquisa de las
Yndias, muy humillmente les suplico que enbién allá doss
personas de conçiençia, y honrrados, á mi costa, los quales
creo que fallarán de ligero agora que se falla el oro .v. marcos
en quatro oras. con esto, y syn ello, es muy neçesario que
lo provean.

El comendador, en llegando á Santo Domingo, se aposentó
en mi casa, é ansý como lo falló, asý dió todo por suyo. vaya
en buen ora, que, quiçá, lo avía menester. corsario nunca tal
usó con mercader. de mis escripturas tengo yo mayor quexa,
que asý me las aya tomado, que jamás se le pudo sacar una,
y aquellas de más mi desculpa, esas tenía más ocultas. ¡ved
qué justo y onesto pesquisidor! cosa de quantas él aya fecho,
me disen que aya seýdo con término de justiçia, salvo abso-
lutamente. Dios Nuestro Señor está con sus fuerças y saber,
como solía, y castiga en todo cabo, en espeçial la yngratitud
de injurias.

FOURTH VOYAGE OF COLUMBUS

1. *A letter which Don Christopher Columbus, viceroy and admiral of the Indies, wrote to the most Christian and most mighty king and queen of Spain, our sovereigns, in which he notified them of that which had occurred on his voyage, and of the lands, provinces, cities and rivers, and other marvellous things, and where there are mines of gold in great abundance, and other things of great richness and value.*[1]

MOST serene and very high and mighty princes, the king and queen, our sovereigns: From Cadiz I passed to the Canaries in four days and thence, in sixteen, to the Indies,[2] whence I wrote that my intention was to hasten my voyage, while I had ships, crews, and supplies in good condition, and that my course lay to the island of Jamaica,[3] and I wrote this in the island of Dominica.[4] Until I arrived there, I had most excellent weather. On the night that I came there, a great storm burst, and ever since bad weather has pursued me.

When I arrived off Española, I sent away a budget of letters,[5] and asked as a favour that I might be supplied with

---

[1] For this letter, cp. *supra*, Introduction, p. lxxxvi.

[2] Columbus sailed from Cadiz, 9 May 1502 (Ferdinand Columbus, c. 87; Las Casas, ii. 5) or 11 May (Diego de Porras, Navarrete, i. 282). He had with him four ships: the flagship, known only by the descriptive epithet, *la capitana*, in which Columbus sailed and of which the captain was Diego Tristan; the *Santiago de Palos*, captain, Francisco de Porras; the *Gallega*, captain, Pedro de Terreros; and the *Vizcaina*, captain, Bartolomé de Fresco (Fieschi), a Genoese (cp. Diego de Porras, Navarrete, i. 289–96, or in *Rac. Col.* I. ii. 211–17). The fleet reached Santa Caterina, 11 May, and Arzilla, 13 May, where it halted to assist the Portuguese, besieged there by the Moors. It reached Grand Canary, 20 May, Palma, 24 May, and the Indies, 15 June (cp. Ferdinand Columbus, c. 87; Las Casas, ii. 5; Diego de Porras, Navarrete, i. 282).

[3] Columbus calls the island 'Janahica' in this letter. Pedro de Ledesma, who described himself as having been 'captain and pilot of the ship *Vizcaina*' on this voyage, stated that Columbus directed his course for 'San Juan' (Puerto Rico), but this may be only a careless way of saying that this island was passed on the way to Española (cp. *Pleitos*, i. 263). In the list of the crews of the four ships, given by Diego de Porras (Navarrete, i. 289–94, and *Rac. Col.* I. ii. 211–17), Ledesma appears as an ordinary seaman in the *Vizcaina*, her master being Juan Pérez and her mate Martin de Fuenterabia. Since Martin de Fuenterabia died, 17 Sept. 1502, and Pérez, 7 Oct. 1503, Ledesma may have succeeded one or other of them, but the *Vizcaina* was abandoned 15 Feb. 1503 (cp. *infra*, p. 86, note 3).

QUARTA VIAGE DE COLÓN

1. *Copia de la carta que escrivió don Cristóval Colón, virrey y almirante de las Indias, á los cristianíssimos i mui poderosos rei i reina de España, nuestros señores, en que les notifica quanto le ha acontecido en su viaje, i las tierras, provinçias, çiudades, ríos, i otras cosas maravillosas, i donde ai minas de oro en mucha cantidad, i otras cosas de gran riqueça i valor.*

SERENÍSIMOS i mui altos i poderosos prínçipes, rei i reina, nuestros señores. De Cádiz pasé á Canaria en quatro días, i dende á las Indias en diez i seis, donde escriví que mi intención era dar prisa á mi viaje, en quanto io tenía los navíos buenos, la gente i los bastimentos, i que mi derrota era en la isla de Janahica: i en la isla Domínica escriví esto. fasta allí truxe el tiempo á pedir por la boca; esa noche que allí entré, fué con tormenta, i grande, i me persiguió después siempre. quando llegué sobre la Española, invié el emboltorio

⁴ Presumably a report on his progress so far, prepared to send off on reaching Española; in a letter to Oderigo (cp. *Rac. Col.* I. ii. 246–7), Columbus says that on this voyage he wrote three or four times to the sovereigns. It seems to be doubtful whether he actually called at Dominica. Peter Martyr (iii. 4), who was not present, says that he did. On the other hand, Ferdinand Columbus (*loc. cit.*), Diego de Porras (Navarrete, i. 282), Diego Martin Barranco (*Pleitos*, i. 254), and probably Juan de Quexo (or Quijo) (*Pleitos*, i. 274), all of whom were present, do not mention Dominica and agree in bringing Columbus from the Canaries to Martinique, where, according to Ferdinand Columbus, he allowed the crews to land and rest after the voyage, and where, according to Porras, he explained the course which he was intending to follow and asked the advice of the masters of the four ships. They are supported by Las Casas (*loc. cit.*), who had seen the log-book of the admiral, but they are apparently, although not explicitly, contradicted by Juan de Noya (*Pleitos*, i. 257), Francisco de Porras (*ibid.* i. 282), and Pedro de Toledo (*ibid.* i. 371), all eyewitnesses, who seem to bring Columbus directly from the Canaries to Guadeloupe; they also do not mention Dominica. Columbus may mean that he wrote to the sovereigns on board ship while off the island of Dominica.

⁵ The context shows that the letters were for the sovereigns. Before leaving Spain, Columbus had written to Ferdinand and Isabella, asking to be allowed to go to Española; his request was refused and Ovando was instructed not to allow him to land, no doubt on the ground that in the existing state of feeling in the island, his presence there would lead to renewed disorder (cp. Las Casas, ii. 4, 5). Pedro de Terreros was sent ashore by Columbus at Santo Domingo (cp. Ferdinand Columbus, c. 87).

a ship at my own cost, since one which I had with me was unseaworthy and could not carry sail.[1] They took the letters and Your Highnesses will know if they delivered them to you. So far as I was concerned, the answer was that I was ordered from here not to come or go on shore. The hearts of the people who were with me failed them, for fear that I should take them further,[2] and they said that were any danger to come upon them, they would not be aided there, but would rather have some great ill done to them. Moreover, any who pleased could say that the comendador[3] would have control of the lands which I might gain.

The storm was terrible and on that night the ships were parted from me.[4] Each one of them was reduced to an extremity, expecting nothing save death; each one of them was certain that the others were lost. What man has been born, not excepting Job, who would not have been ready to die of despair? For, in such weather, when it was for my safety and for that of my son, my brother,[5] and my friends, I was forbidden the land and harbours which, by the will of God, I, sweating blood, gained for Spain.

I return to the ships, which the storm had so carried away from me as to leave me alone. Our Lord restored them to

---

[1] Bartholomew Columbus was in this 'unseaworthy' vessel. Ferdinand Columbus (c. 87), in his account of the storm off Santo Domingo, calls her the *Bermuda*, a name which does not appear as that of one of the four ships in Diego de Porras (Navarrete, i. 289–96). But Ferdinand Columbus was with his father in the flagship (cp. *infra*, p. 78); he mentions the *Vizcaina* (c. 88), and a vessel which he calls the *Santo*, and which can certainly be identified with the *Gallega*, since she was commanded by Pedro de Terreros (Ferdinand Columbus, c. 87), and lost a boat in the storm (*ibid.*), which the *Gallega* is stated by Columbus to have done (cp. *infra*, p. 76). The *Bermuda* can thus be identified with the *Santiago de Palos*. (For an explanation of the variation in the names of the ships as given by Porras and Ferdinand Columbus, cp. *supra*, p. 72, note 2.) It may be added that the *Santiago de Palos* was one of the two ships which survived to reach Jamaica, the *Gallega* and the *Vizcaina* having been abandoned at an earlier date (cp. *infra*, p. 86, note 3). It would thus appear that Columbus somewhat exaggerated her unseaworthiness at the time of his arrival off Santo Domingo, and it is not impossible that Ovando was advised of this exaggeration by Antonio de Torres, who was in command of his fleet, and was thus led to regard the request of Columbus for leave to exchange her for another ship as being merely an attempt to find an excuse for entering the harbour of Santo Domingo and perhaps for landing in the island despite the royal prohibition.

de cartas, i á pedir por merçed un navío por mis dineros,
porque otro que io llevava era innavegable, i no sufría velas.
las cartas tomaron, i sabrán si se las dieron. la respuesta para
mi fué mandarme de parte de aí, que io no pasase, ni llegase
á la tierra. caió el coraçón á la gente que iva conmigo, por
temor de los llevar io lexos, diçiendo que, si algún caso de
peligro les viniese, que no serían remediados allí; antes les
sería fecha alguna grande afrenta. tanbién, á quien plugo,
dixo que el comendador avía de proveer las tierras, que io
ganase. la tormenta era terrible, i en aquella noche me
desmembró los navíos: á cada uno llevó por su cabo, sin
esperanças, salvo de muerte; cada uno d'ellos tenía por çierto
que los otros eran perdidos. ¿ quién nasçió, sin quitar á Job,
que no muriera desesperado, que por mi salvaçión, i de mi
fijo, hermano, i amigos, me fuese en tal tiempo defendido la
tierra, i los puertos, que io por voluntad de Dios gané á
España, sudando sangre? é tornó á los navíos, que assí me
avía llevado la tormenta, i dexado á mi solo. deparómelos
Nuestro Señor, quando le plugo. el navío sospechoso avía
echado á la mar por escapar; fasta la isla, la Gallega perdió
la barca, i todos gran parte de los bastimentos: el en que io

---

² Diego de Porras (*loc. cit.*) says that three members of the crew of the
Gallega, Francisco de Medina, Gonzalo Gallego, and Francisco de Córdoba,
deserted in Española. It was perhaps at this time that they did so and from
fear of coming disaster.

³ Nicolas de Ovando, comendador de Lares in the order of Alcántara, and
afterwards comendador mayor of that order. He was sent out to replace Bobadilla as governor of Española and landed in the island, 15 April 1502. He held
this position until 1509, when Diego Columbus was given the government of the
island. For the character of Ovando, cp. Las Casas (ii. 3) and Oviedo (iii. 12).
He has been described as the 'sworn enemy' of Columbus (e.g. by Harrisse,
Christophe Colomb, ii. 233, and other writers), but this description is perhaps
unjust.

⁴ The storm was that in which the fleet of Antonio de Torres was destroyed;
Bobadilla, Roldán, and others who had been hostile to Columbus were drowned,
and, according to Ferdinand Columbus (c. 87), only a ship which was carrying
the property of the admiral escaped. Columbus warned Ovando of the coming
storm, but his opinion was ignored by the seamen of the fleet of de Torres; he
asked to be allowed to shelter in the harbour of Santo Domingo, but was refused
permission by Ovando. Actually, he sheltered in a harbour called Puerto
Hermoso, fifteen leagues west.

⁵ Columbus was accompanied on this voyage by his son Ferdinand and his
brother Bartholomew.

me, when it pleased Him. The unseaworthy vessel[1] had put out to sea in order to escape ; near the island the *Gallega* lost her boat,[2] and all lost a great part of their provisions ; that in which I was, although amazingly tossed about, Our Lord saved, so that she suffered no damage at all. My brother was in the unseaworthy vessel, and he, after God, was her salvation.[3]

With this storm I made my way painfully and slowly to Jamaica. There the sea changed from rough to calm and there was a strong current which carried me as far as the Jardín de la Reina, without land being sighted. Thence, when I was able, I steered for Tierra Firme. On the way the wind and a terrible current were against me ; I struggled with them for sixty days and in the end had not been able to make more than seventy leagues. During all this time, I did not put into harbour, nor could I, nor did the storm from heaven cease ; there was rain and thunder and lightning continuously, so that it seemed as if it were the end of the world.[4]

[1] In the Spanish text, as printed by Navarrete (i. 297), the word 'sospechoso' is written 'Sospechoso', as if it were the name of the ship. But in the Italian version (cp. Thacher, ii. 671), the word is 'inavicabile', while in his account of the storm, Ferdinand Columbus says that the *Bermuda*, i.e. the *Santiago de Palos*, ran out to sea (c. 87). There is thus no doubt that 'sospechoso' is merely an adjective, describing the vessel mentioned earlier in the letter as being in a bad condition.

[2] In the Spanish text, as printed by Navarrete (*loc. cit.*), this passage reads: 'El navio Sospechoso habia echado á la mar, por escapar, fasta la isola la Gallega; perdió la barca . . .,' which Major (*Select Letters*, p. 177) translated: 'The ship which we had the greatest fear for, had put out to sea for safety, and reached the island of Gallega, having lost her boat . . .' In the Italian version (cp. Thacher, *loc. cit.*), 'Gallega' also appears as the name of an island. But there is no island of that name off the coast of Española, while Ferdinand Columbus (*loc. cit.*) says that the vessel commanded by Terreros, i.e. the *Gallega* (cp. *supra*, p. 74, note 1), lost her boat in the storm. It is thus apparently clear that 'Gallega' is the ship and not an island. 'La Gallega' is taken to be the ship of that name by de Lollis, who makes the passage read: 'el navío sospechoso avía echado á la mar, por escapar fasta la isla; la Gallega perdió la barca . . .' (cp. *Rac. Col.* I. ii. 177 and note 2), 'the unseaworthy vessel put out to sea, to escape to the island; the *Gallega* lost her boat . . .' But this reading is not entirely satisfactory, since it makes the seamanship of the navigating officer of 'el navío sospechoso' somewhat unintelligible. He 'puts out to sea to escape', obviously fearing that his ship would be driven ashore, but makes for an 'island', thus apparently running into the very danger which he was anxious to avoid. He may certainly have been at the mercy of the storm, but there is a further difficulty that there is no island off the coast of Española to fit the case. The wind must have been NE. to

iva, avalumado á maravilla, Nuestro Señor le salvó, que no
uvo daño de una paja. en el sospechoso iva mi hermano, i él,
después de Dios, fué su remedio. é con esta tormenta, assí
á gatas, me llegué á Janahica. allí se mudó de mar alta en
calmería, i grande corriente, i me llevó fasta el Jardín de la
reina, sin ver tierra. de allí, quando pude, navegué á la tierra

E., since Columbus was able to make Puerto Hermoso, fifteen leagues west of
Santo Domingo (cp. Ferdinand Columbus, *loc. cit.*, and Las Casas, ii. 5), which
he could not have accomplished in the teeth of the storm. If, then, 'el navio
sospechoso' reached an island, it must have been one lying either directly out
to sea or to the west. There is no such island in the first of these positions; in
the second, the nearest is the island of Beata, and the configuration of the south
coast of Española makes it practically impossible that this island should have
been reached by a ship which, *ex hypothesi*, was at the mercy of the storm.
It would thus seem to be probable that the semicolon should be placed after
'escapar', 'fasta la isla' being taken to indicate the place where the *Gallega* lost
her boat. This involves giving to the word 'fasta', 'as far as', the sense of 'near',
which it does not really possess, but Columbus did not invariably write exact
Castilian. If this reading be accepted, the account of the storm in the letter is
in accord with that given by Ferdinand Columbus (*loc. cit.*), who says that the
Gallega only saved herself by abandoning the boat in which her captain, Terreros,
had gone ashore, and that the *Bermuda*, 'el navio sospechoso' (cp. *supra*, p. 74,
note 1), ran out to sea. The whole story further thus becomes clear. Columbus,
in the flagship, succeeded in making Puerto Hermoso and, sheltering there,
suffered no damage; the *Gallega*, which was waiting inshore to pick up Terreros,
was in considerable danger and was obliged to abandon her attempt to save her
boat; the *Santiago de Palos* ran before the storm out to sea.

³ This passage suggests that Bartholomew Columbus was in command, or was
at least the navigating officer, of the *Santiago de Palos*. Neither his name, nor
that of his nephew, Ferdinand, appears in the list of the crews given by Diego
de Porras (Navarrete, i. 289–96), a list which may be regarded as official since
Porras was the 'escribano' of the fleet. It is thus clear that Bartholomew was
a supercargo, and there is no reason to suppose that he had anything to do with
the navigation of the ship in which he was. Columbus seems to have been led
to exaggerate by his fraternal affection.

⁴ After the storm off Santo Domingo (29 June), Columbus collected his fleet
at Puerto Hermoso, or Puerto Escondido (Azua, on the south coast of Española,
fifteen leagues west of Santo Domingo). Thence he sailed along the coast to
Yaquimo (Puerto del Brasil, eighty leagues west of Santo Domingo), whence he
crossed to Jamaica (14 July), sighting that island two days later (16 July). Here
he was becalmed and a current carried him north-west to the Jardín de la Reina
(24 July), which he left three days later for Tierra Firme (27 July). He reached
the island of Guanaja (Bonaca, thirty miles north of Cape Honduras), where the
fleet anchored and Bartholomew Columbus landed (30 July) (cp. Diego de
Porras, Navarrete, i. 283; Ferdinand Columbus, c. 88; Las Casas, ii. 20). As
only thirty-one days had elapsed since the storm off Santo Domingo when
Guanaja was reached, and as during that time some calm weather had been
experienced, it is hardly possible to fit in the 'sixty days' of storm, mentioned
in the text.

I reached cape Gracias á Dios,[1] and from that point our
Lord gave me a favouring wind and current. This was on the
twelfth of September. Eighty-eight days had there been
during which the awe-inspiring tempest did not cease, so
that for so long I saw neither sun nor stars for the sea.[2] My
ships were stripped, and anchors, rigging and cables were lost,
with the boats and many stores; the crews were weak and all
were contrite and many turned to religion, nor was there one
who did not make vows and promise pilgrimages. Many
times they came to the point of confessing one another.
Other storms have been seen, but none has ever endured so
long or been so terrible.

Many whom we regarded as men of courage were in a state
of great terror and that many times. The distress of my son,
whom I had there, racked my soul, and the more since I saw
him, at the tender age of thirteen years,[3] so exhausted and
for so long a time. Our Lord gave him such courage that he
revived the spirit of the others, and he acted as if he had been
a sailor for eighty years and he consoled me. I had fallen ill
and had many times come to the point of death. From a little
shelter, which I ordered to be fixed up on deck, I directed
the course.

My brother was in the worst ship and that which was in
the greatest danger. My grief was great, and was the greater
because I had brought him with me against his will. Speaking
of myself, little profit had I won from twenty years of service,
during which I have served with so great labours and perils,
for to-day I have no roof over my head in Castile; if I wish
to sleep or eat, I have no place to which to go, save to an inn
or tavern, and most often I lack the wherewithal to pay
the score.[4]

Another sorrow tore my very heartstrings, and that was
for Diego,[5] my son, whom I had left in Spain an orphan and
dispossessed of my honour and estate. Yet I was assured

---

[1] The frontier point between the modern republics of Honduras and
Nicaragua.

[2] Cape Gracias á Dios was reached seventy-six days after the storm off Santo
Domingo (29 June to 12 September). At the end of eighty-eight days Columbus

firme, adonde me salió el viento í corriente terrible al opósito:
combatí con ellos sesenta días, i en fin no le pude ganar más
de setenta leguas. en todo este tiempo no entré en puerto, ni
pude: ni me dexó tormenta del çielo, agua, i trombones,
i relámpagos de continuo, que pareçía el fin del mundo.
llegué al cabo de 'Graçias á Dios', i de allí me dió Nuestro
Señor próspero el viento i corriente. esto fué á doçe de
septiembre. ochenta i ocho días avía que no me avía dexado
espantable tormenta, atanto que no vide el sol ni estrellas por
mar; que á los navíos tenía io abiertos, á las velas rotas,
i perdidas anclas i xarcias, cables, con las barcas, i muchos
vastimentos, la gente mui enferma, i todos contritos, i muchos
con promesa de religión, i no ninguno sin otros votos i
romerías. muchas vezes avían llegado á se confessar los unos
á los otros. otras tormentas se an visto, mas no durar tanto,
ni con tanto espanto. muchos esmoreçieron harto, i hartas
vezes, que teníamos por esforzados. el dolor del fijo, que io
tenía allí, me arrancava el ánima, i más por verle, de tan
nueva edad de treçe años, en tanta fatiga, i durar en ello
tanto. Nuestro Señor le dió tal esfuerzo, que él avivava á los
otros, i en las obras hacía él como si uviera navegado ochenta
años. i el me consolava. io avía adolesçido, i llegado fartas
vezes á la muerte. de una camarilla, que io mandé fazer sobre
cubierta, mandava la vía. mi hermano estava en el peor
navío, i más peligroso. gran dolor era el mío, i maior, porque
lo truxe contra su grado; porque, por mi dicha, poco me an
aprovechado veinte años de serviçio, que io he servido con
tantos trabaxos i peligros, que oi día no tengo en Castilla una
teja; si quiero comer ó dormir, no tengo salvo al mesón
ó taverna, i las más de las vezes falta para pagar el escote.
otra lástima me arrancava el coraçón por las espaldas, i era
de don Diego, mi hijo, que io dexé en España, tan huérfano

had reached Cariay (cp. *infra*, p. 80 and note 1). There is thus an obvious
exaggeration in the text.
    [3] Ferdinand Columbus was born 15 Aug. 1488 (cp. Harrisse, *Don Fernando
Colón*).
    [4] For the supposed poverty of Columbus, cp. Vidart, *Colón y la Ingratitud de
España*, and Fernandez Duro, *Colón y la Historia póstuma*.
    [5] Diego Columbus was at this time a page at the court (cp. *supra*, p. 62 and
note 5).

that there, as just and grateful princes, you would make restitution to him of all, with increase.

I reached the land of Cariay,[1] where I halted to repair the ships and to replenish the stores, and to give relaxation to the people who were very weak.[2] There I, who, as I have said, had many times come to the point of death, heard of the mines of gold of the provinces of Ciamba, which I was seeking.[3] Two Indians brought me to Carambaru,[4] where the people go naked and have a golden mirror hanging at the neck, but are unwilling to sell it or to give it in exchange.[5]

They named to me many places on the sea-coast, where they said that there was gold and mines; the last was Veragua,[6] distant from there a matter of twenty-five leagues. I departed with the intention of examining these places fully, and having gone half way, I learned that there were mines at two days' journey. I decided to send to visit them. The vigil of SS. Simon and Jude was fixed for our departure; on that night there arose so great a sea and wind that it was necessary to run before it where it drove us; and the Indian who was the guide to the mines was always with me.

In all these places where I have been, I found all that I had heard to be true. This convinced me that it is so in the case of the province of Ciguare, which, according to them, lies in-

[1] Oviedo (xxi. 7) and Diego de Porras (Navarrete, i. 284) agree with Columbus in making Cariay the name of a district, but Ferdinand Columbus (c. 90) and Las Casas (ii. 21), who calls it, wrongly, 'Cariarí', agree in describing it as an Indian village on a river, near an island, Quirivi, which Columbus called 'la Huerta', on account of its great fertility. Peter Martyr (iii. 4) also makes Cariay a village, near an island which he calls 'Quicuri'. Columbus was at the time on the modern Mosquito Coast.

[2] Columbus halted from 25 Sept. to 5 Oct. (cp. Ferdinand Columbus, *loc. cit.*; Las Casas, *loc. cit.*). This halting place was perhaps the modern San Juan de Nicaragua (Greytown).

[3] Peter Martyr (*loc. cit.*) says that Columbus gave the name 'Ciamba' to the native province of Quiriquetana, and adds that this province was of wide extent and was divided into two parts, Taia and Maia—the first appearance of the word 'Maya'. Columbus, however, only says that he 'heard' of the mines of Ciamba, not that he had reached that land. In the geography of the period, Ciamba was the east Asiatic province, lying to the west of Cipango. Columbus perhaps wished to say that in this part of Tierra Firme he found natives who knew of Ciamba, and hence to suggest that he was near that part of Asia.

i despossessionado de mi honrra é hazienda, bien que tenía
por çierto que como justos i agradesçidos príncipes le resti-
tuirían con acrescentamiento en todo. llegué á tierra de
'Cariai', adonde me detuve á remediar los navíos i bastimentos, i dar aliento á la gente que venía mui enferma. yo
que, como dixe, avía llegado muchas vezes á la muerte, allí
supe de las minas del oro de la provinçia de Çiamba, que io
buscava. dos Indios me llevaron á 'Carambarú', adonde la
gente anda desnuda, i al cuello un espejo de oro, mas no le
querían bender ni dar á trueque. nombráronme muchos
lugares en la costa de la mar, adonde deçían que avía oro
i minas; el postrero era 'Beragna', i lexos de allí obra de
veinte i cinco leguas. partí con intençión de los tentar á todos;
i llegado ia el medio, supe que avía minas á dos jornadas de
andadura. acordé de inviarles á ver. víspera de sanct Simón
i Judas, que avía de ser la partida, en esa noche se lebantó
tanta mar i viento, que fué necessario de correr açia adonde
él quiso, i el Indio, adalid de las minas, siempre conmigo.
en todos estos lugares adonde ío avía estado, fallé verdad
todo lo que io avía oído: esto me çertificó que es assí de la provinçia de 'Ciguare', que, según ellos, es descrita nueve jornadas
de andadura por tierra al poniente. allí dicen que ai infinito
oro, i que traen corales en las cabeças, manillas, á los pies
i á los braços, d'ello, i bien gordas; i d'él sillas, arcas, i mesas,
las guarnecen i enforran. tanbién dixeron que las mugeres de

---

⁴ Carambaru (or Cerabarún) only appears in this letter. Ferdinand Columbus
(c. 91) writes 'Cerabora', Las Casas (ii. 22) writes 'Cerevaro', Oviedo (*loc. cit.*)
and Diego de Porras (*loc. cit.*) 'Cerebaro'. The last variant of the name is also
given in various 'preguntas', and appears to be the most probable form (cp. de
Lollis, *Rac. Col.* I. ii, p. 181, note 5). From the description in Ferdinand Columbus and Las Casas, the district can be identified as the Laguna de Chiriquí.
⁵ Cp. Ferdinand Columbus (*loc. cit.*) and Las Casas (*loc. cit.*).
⁶ The eastern part of the modern republic of Costa Rica and the western part
of that of Panama; the exact limits of the district were matter of dispute (cp.
Las Casas, ii. 52; and *Pleitos, passim*). The district took its name from the river,
although there were larger rivers in the country, because the cacique had his
residence on the banks of the Rio Veragua (cp. Peter Martyr, *loc. cit.*). In this
letter Columbus always calls the district 'Veragna' or 'Beragna', and it was this
form of the name which he adopted. But the form 'Veragua' is that which is
sanctioned by tradition and which appears in the oldest maps. It has been
pointed out by Humboldt (*Examen Critique*, iii. 380) that most of these native
names have doubtless been hopelessly corrupted in transmission.

land to the west nine days' journey.[1] They say that there is in
that land an infinite amount of gold, and that the people wear
corals on their heads and very large bracelets of coral on their
feet and arms, and that with coral they adorn and inlay chairs
and chests and tables. They said also that the women there
have necklaces hanging down from the head to the shoulders.
All the people of these places agree in this that I have related,
and they say so much that I should be content with the tenth
of it. They also know of pepper.

In Ciguare they are accustomed to trade in fairs and
markets; so these people related, and they showed me the
way and manner in which they carry on barter.[2] Further
they said that the ships carry cannon, bows and arrows,
swords and shields, and that the people go clothed, and that
in the land there are horses, and that the people are warlike
and wear rich clothing and have good houses. Also they say
that the sea surrounds[3] Ciguare, and that from there it is
ten days' journey to the river Ganges. It appears that these
lands lie in respect of Veragua as Tortosa does in respect of
Fuenterabia, or Pisa in respect of Venice.[4] When I left Carambaru and arrived at these places which I have mentioned,
I found the same customs among the people, except that
any who had the mirrors of gold bartered them at the rate
of one for three hawks' bells, although they were ten or fifteen
ducats in weight. In all their customs they are as those of Española. They collect gold by different methods, although these are
all nothing in comparison with those of the Christians.

This which I have said is that which I have heard. That
which I know is that in the year ninety-four I navigated in
twenty-four degrees to the westward to the end of nine hours,
and I cannot be in error because there was an eclipse; the sun
was in Libra and the moon in Aries.[5] That also which I heard
by word of mouth, I knew in detail from the written word.

Ptolemy believed that he had well corrected Marinus,[6]
who is now found to have been very near the truth. Ptolemy
places Catigara twelve lines from his west,[7] which he fixed

---

[1] For the name 'Ciguare', cp. de Lollis (*Rac. Col.* I. ii, p. 183, note 2).
Columbus was certainly hearing accounts of Maya civilization.

allí traían collares colgados de la cabeça á las espaldas. en
esto que io digo, la gente toda d'estos lugares conciertan en
ello, i dicen tanto, que io sería contento con el diezmo.
tanbién todos conocieron la pimienta. en Çiguare usan tratar
en ferias, i mercaderías: esta gente assí lo cuentan, i me
amostravan el modo i forma, que tienen en la barata. otrosí
diçen que las naos traen bombardas, arcos i flechas, espadas
i coraças, i andan vestidos; i en la tierra ai cavallos, i usan la
guerra, i traen ricas vestiduras, i tienen buenas casas. tanbién
dicen que la mar boxa á Çiguare, i de allí á diez jornadas es el
río de Gangues. pareçe que estas tierras están con Veragua
como Tortosa con Fuenterravía, ó Pisa con Veneçia. quando
io partí de Cerabarún, i llegué á esos lugares que dixe, fallé
la gente en aquel mismo uso, salvo que los espejos del oro,
quien los tenía los dava por tres cascaveles de gavilán por
el uno, bien que pesasen diez ó quince ducados de peso. en
todos sus usos son como los de la Española: el oro cojen con
otras artes, bien que todas son nada con las de los cristianos.
esto que io dicho es lo que oio. lo que io sé es que el año de
.94. navegué en .24. grados al poniente en término de .9.
horas; i no pudo aver ierro, porque uvo eclipses; el sol estava
en Libra, i la luna en Ariete. tanbién esto que io supe por
palabra, avíalo io sabido largo por escrito. Ptolomeo creió
de aver bien remedado á Marino, i ahora se falla su escritura
bien propinqua al cierto. Ptolomeo assienta Catigara á doçe
líneas lejos de su ocçidente, que él assentó sobre el cabo de
S. Vicente, en Portugal, dos grados i un terçio. Marino en
.15. líneas constituió la tierra, é términos. Marino en Ethiopía

---

² Cp. Ferdinand Columbus (c. 88) and Las Casas (ii. 20) for an account of
a canoe obviously going to one of these fairs.

³ In the Italian version of the letter (cp. Thacher, ii. 673) the word 'boglie',
'boils', appears, but the word 'bojaba', 'surrounds', is a far more rational
reading and is generally accepted.

⁴ From this passage it has been argued that Columbus heard a report of the
Pacific and realized its existence. Thacher (ii. 589–93) gives three sketch maps,
showing the relative positions of Veragua and the Pacific, of Fuenterabia and
Tortosa, and of Pisa and Venice.

⁵ The sense of this passage is that being in 24°, Columbus reached long. 135°
W., equivalent to 9 hours of the sun's course. Cp. *supra*, Introduction, p. lxxxii.

⁶ *Geographia*, i. 6–9.

⁷ *op. cit.* viii. 3.

at two and one third degrees above Cape St. Vincent in Portugal. Marinus comprised the earth and its limits in fifteen lines.[1] In Ethiopia Marinus draws beyond the equinoctial line more than twenty-four degrees,[2] and now that the Portuguese have sailed there, they find that this is true. Ptolemy says that the most southern land is the first place and that it does not lie more than fifteen and one third degrees south. The world is small. The dry land is six parts of it; the seventh only is covered with water. Experience has already shown this, and I have written it in other letters and with illustration from Holy Scripture concerning the situation of the earthly paradise, as Holy Church approves. I say that the world is not so great as the vulgar believe, and that a degree from the equinoctial line is fifty-six and two-thirds miles; easily this may be proved exactly.[3] I leave this subject, inasmuch as it is not my intention to speak of this matter, but only to give an account of my voyage, hard and toilsome, although it is the most noble and profitable.

I have said that on the vigil of SS. Simon and Jude I ran where the wind bore me, without being able to resist it. In a harbour I sheltered for ten days from the great violence of sea and wind; there I decided not to go back to the mines and I left them as gained already. I departed, to continue my voyage, in rain. I reached the harbour of Bastimentos,[4] where I entered and not of my free will; the storm and a great current kept me in it for fourteen days. And afterwards I departed and that not with fair weather. When I had gone fifteen leagues with difficulty, the wind and current with fury drove me back. Returning to the harbour whence I had set out, I found on the way el Retrete,[5] where I put in with great danger and distress and being myself, and the ships and the people, very worn out. There I stayed for fifteen days, compelled to do so by the cruel weather, and when I believed that it was ended, I found that it was beginning.

---

[1] 'The "line" of Columbus implies fifteen degrees, or one hour of longitude; and the twelve lines which describe the distance of Catigara from the meridian of Ptolemy, equal one hundred and eighty degrees. Marinus of Tyre reckoned two hundred and twenty-five degrees to the same space, which is equivalent to the fifteen lines stated by Columbus' (Major, *Select Letters*, p. 183, note 1).

escrive aliende la línea equinoçial más de .24. grados; i ahora
que los Portugueses la navegan, le fallan çierto. Ptolomeo
diz que la tierra más austral es el plazo primero, i que no
abaxa más de quince grados i un terçio. el mundo es poco; el
injuto d'ello es seis partes, la séptima sólamente cubierta de
agua. la experiençia ia está vista, i la escriví por otras letras,
i con adornamiento de la Sacra Escritura, con el sitio del
Paraíso terrenal que la sancta Iglesia aprueva. digo que el
mundo no es tan grande como diçe el vulgo, i que un grado
de la equinoçial está .56. millas i dos terçios: presto se tocará
con el dedo. dexo esto, por quanto no es mi propósito de
fablar en aquella materia, salvo de dar cuenta de mi duro
i trabaxoso viaje, bien que él sea el más noble i provechoso.
digo que víspera de sanct Simón i Judas, corrí donde el viento
me llevava, sin poder resistirle. en un puerto escusé diez días
de gran fortuna de la mar i del çielo: allí acordé de no volver
atrás á las minas, i dexélas ia por ganadas. partí por seguir
mi viaje, lloviendo; llegué á 'puerto de Vastimientos', adonde
entré, i no de grado: la tormenta i gran corriente me cerró
allí catorce días, i después partí, i no con buen tiempo.
quando io uve andado quinçe leguas, forzosamente me reposó
atrás el viento i corriente con furia. volviendo io al puerto
donde avía salido, fallé en el camino al 'Retrete', adonde me
retruxe con harto peligro, i enojo, i bien fatigado, io, i los
navíos, i la gente. detúveme allí quince días, que assí lo quiso
el cruel tiempo; i quando creí de aver acabado, me fallé de
comienço. allí mudé de sentençia de volver á las minas,
i hazer algo, fasta que me viniese con ella para mi viaje

---

2 In the Spanish text, as printed by Navarrete (i. 301), this passage reads:
'Marino in Ethiopia escribe al Indo la linea equinocial mas de veinte y cuatro
grados,' which Major (*loc. cit.*) translated, '. . . and the same author describes the
Indus in Ethiopia as being more than twenty-four degrees from the equinoctial
line . . .' This reading, however, is certainly wrong, and the restoration of the
true reading is suggested by the Italian version (cp. Thacher, ii. 673), 'Questo
medemo Marino in Ethiopia scrive la linea ecquinoctiale piu de 24 gradi,' 'this
same Marinus in Ethiopia draws above the equinoctial line more than twenty-
four degrees', i.e. of S. lat.

3 For the whole of this passage, cp. *supra*, pp. 28–34, and notes.

4 Nombre de Dios (Las Casas, ii. 23).

5 Escribanos, or Port Scrivan. Columbus called it 'el Retrete' on account of
its narrowness (Las Casas, *loc. cit.*).

There I changed my intention of going to the mines and of doing anything until the weather should be favourable for my voyage and for putting to sea.

When I had gone four leagues, the storm returned and so wearied me that I knew not what to do. There my wound reopened.[1] For nine days I was lost, without hope of life; eyes never saw the sea so high, so rough, so covered with foam. The wind did not allow us to go forward, nor did it permit us to run under any headland. There was I held, in a sea turned to blood, boiling as a cauldron on a mighty fire. Never did the heavens appear more terrible. For a day and a night they blazed like a furnace, and the lightning darted forth in such flashes that I wondered every moment whether it had destroyed my masts and sails; the flashes came with such terrifying fury that we all believed that the ships must be consumed. All this while the water from heaven never ceased, and it cannot be said that it rained, but rather that there was a second universal deluge.[2] The crews were already so broken in spirit that they longed for death as a release from such martyrdom. The ships had already twice lost their boats, anchors, and rigging, and were stripped bare, without sails.

When it pleased Our Lord, I returned to Puerto Gordo,[3] where I repaired things as well as I could. Once more I turned back towards Veragua; for my voyage, although I was set upon it, the winds and currents were still contrary.[4] I arrived almost where I had been before, and there again the wind and currents opposed me, and once more I put into port, since I did not dare to await the opposition of Saturn with Mars,[5] so tossed about on a dangerous coast, since that generally

---

[1] Las Casas (ii. 24) says that Columbus was suffering from gout, but knows nothing of a wound, the reference to which has been taken to show that Columbus had been wounded in the Moorish war and as evidence in favour of the genuineness of the 'restos de Colón' found at Santo Domingo (cp. Thacher, iii. 603 *et seq.*). The absence of any mention of a wound in Las Casas, who had this letter before him (cp. Las Casas, *loc. cit.*), suggests that Columbus was possibly using the word in a figurative sense.

[2] During the height of the storm a waterspout appeared, but the sailors delivered themselves from the threatened danger by reciting the Last Gospel according to St. John (Las Casas, *loc. cit.*).

[3] In reply to one of the questions of the interrogatories in the *Probanzas del*

i marear. i, llegado con quatro leguas, revino la tormenta, i me fatigó tanto á tanto, que ia no sabía de mi parte. allí se me refrescó del mal la llaga: nueve días anduve perdido, sin esperança de vida: ojos nunca vieron la mar tan alta, fea, i hecha espuma. el viento no era para ir adelante, ni dava lugar para correr hacia algún cabo. allí me detenía en aquella mar fecha sangre, herviendo como caldera por gran fuego. el cielo jamás fué visto tan espantoso: un día con la noche ardió como forno, i assí echava la llama con los raios, que cada vez mirava io si me avía llevado los másteles i velas: venían con tanta furia i espantables, que todos creíamos que me avían de fundir los navíos. en todo esto tiempo jamás cessó agua del çielo, i no para dezir que llovía, salvo que resegundava otro diluvio. la gente estava ia tan molida, que desseavan la muerte, para salir de tantos martirios. los navíos ia avían perdido dos vezes la barcas, anclas, cuerdas, i estavan aviertos, sin velas.

Quando plugo á Nuestro Señor, volví á 'puerto Gordo', adonde reparé lo mejor que pude. volví otra vez açia Veragna; para mi viaje, aunque io estuviera para ello, todavía era el viento i corrientes contrarios. llegué casi adonde antes, i allí me salió otra vez el viento i corrientes al encuentro, i volví otra vez al puerto, que no osé esperar la oposiçión de Saturno con Martes, tan desvaratado en costa

Almirante, the following witnesses, who were on the fourth voyage of Columbus, testified that the *Gallega* was wrecked at Puerto Gordo: Alonso Zea (or de Zea), of the *Santiago de Palos* (*Pleitos*, i. 408), Juan Moreno, of the *Vizcaina* (*ibid.*, ii. 77), Diego Rodriguez Ximon, of the *Santiago de Palos* (*ibid.*, ii. 92), Rui Hernandez, of the *Gallega* (*ibid.*, ii. 93), Pedro Fernandez Coronel, of the flagship (*ibid.*, ii. 95), and Gonzalo Diaz, of the *Vizcaina* (*ibid.*, ii. 86). From Diego de Porras (Navarrete, ii. 295) it is known that it was at Belem that the *Gallega* was abandoned, and this is confirmed by Ferdinand Columbus (c. 99), who states that the *Vizcaina* was abandoned at Puerto Bello and hence implies that it was the *Gallega* which was abandoned at Belem (cp. *infra*, p. 88, note 1), and by the story told by Bartolomé de Caso (cp. *Pleitos*, i. 425, and *infra*, p. 94, note 1). Puerto Gordo, which is not named by Ferdinand Columbus or by Las Casas, must therefore be the harbour at the mouth of the Rio Belen.

⁴ By 'my voyage' Columbus means his search for a strait, which he hoped to find towards the east. Contrary winds drove him back westward, and he therefore proposed to shelter in or near the Rio de Veragua, until the wind changed.

⁵ In the text as printed by Navarrete (i. 301) this passage runs, 'la oposición de Saturno con mares tan desbaratados . . .' The Italian version (cp. Thacher, ii. 674) gives 'Marte'.

brings storms or heavy weather. This was on the day of the Nativity, at the hour of mass. I came again to the point whence I had so laboriously set forth, and when the new year had come in, I resumed my struggling. But even if I had found good weather for my voyage, the ships were un-seaworthy, and the crews dead or sick.

On the day of the Epiphany I reached Veragua, being now without spirit. There Our Lord gave me a river and a safe harbour, although at the entrance there were only ten spans of water.[1] I made an entry with difficulty, and on the following day the storm began again; if it had found me outside, I should not have been able to enter, on account of the bar. It rained without ceasing until the fourteenth of February, so that there was no opportunity to penetrate into the interior or to repair my situation in any way. And on the twenty-fourth of January, when I was already safely within, suddenly the river rose to a great height and violence. The cables were broken and the post to which they were fastened, and it almost tore away my ships, and certainly I saw them in greater danger than ever. Our Lord gave me a remedy, as He has always done. I do not know of anyone who has suffered greater martyrdom.

On the sixth of February, while the rain continued, I sent seventy men ashore into the interior. At five leagues' distance, they found many mines. The Indians, who went with them, led them to a very lofty hill and from it showed them the country all round as far as the eye could reach, saying that there was gold everywhere and that towards the west the mines extended for twenty days' journey, and they named the towns and villages, saying where there were more or less of them. Afterwards I learned that the Quibian who had given these Indians, had commanded them to show distant mines which belonged to one who was his enemy, and that within his own territory, a man might collect in ten days as much gold as a child could carry, whenever he wished. I bear with me the Indians, his servants, and witnesses to this.[2]

---

[1] Ferdinand Columbus (c. 93) gives the native name of this river as 'Gicure', Las Casas (i. 24) as 'Yebra', Diego de Porras (Navarrete, i. 286) as 'Yrebra'.

brava; porque las más de las vezes trae tempestad ó fuerte tiempo. esto fué día de Navidad, en horas de missa. volví otra vez adonde io avía salido con harta fatiga, i, pasado año nuevo, torné á la porfía; que, aunque me hiçiera buen tiempo para mi viaje, ia tenía los navíos innavegables, i la gente muerta, i enferma. día de la Epiphanía, llegué á Veragna ia sin aliento; allí me deparó Nuestro Señor un rio, i seguro puerto, bien que á la entrada no tenía salvo diez palmos de fondo; metíme en él con pena, i el día siguiente retornó la fortuna. si me falla fuera, no pudiera entrar á causa del vanco. llovió sin cessar fasta catorçe de febrero, que nunca uvo lugar de entrar en la tierra, ni de me remediar en nada; i, estando ia seguro, á veinte i quatro de enero, de improviso vino el río mui alto i fuerte; quebróme las amarras, i proeses, i uvo de llevar los navíos, i cierto los ví en maior peligro que nunca. remedió Nuestro Señor, como siempre hizo; no sé si uvo otro con más martirios. á seis de febrero, lloviendo, invié setenta hombres la tierra adentro, i á las çinco leguas fallaron muchas minas. los Indios, que ivan con ellos, los llevaron á un cerro mui alto, i de allí les mostraron açia toda parte quanto los ojos alcançavan, diciendo que en toda parte avía oro, i que açia el poniente llegavan las minas veinte jornadas, i nombravan las villas i lugares, i adonde avía d'ellos más ó menos. después supe io que el 'Quibián', que avía dado estos Indios, les avía mandado que fuesen á mostrar las minas lexos, i de otro su contrario, i que adentro de su pueblo cogían, quando él quería, un hombre, en diez días, una mozada de oro. los Indios, sus criados, i testigos d'esto, traigo conmigo. adonde él tiene el pueblo llegan las barcas. volvió mi hermano con esa gente, i todos con oro que avían cogido en quatro horas que fué allá á la estada. la cantidad es grande,

---

It was a league east of the Rio Veragua (cp. Oviedo xxi. 7). Columbus called it the Rio Belén (Betlén in Ferdinand Columbus, Santa María de Belén in Porras), because he entered it on the day of the Epiphany. During the period in which the river was in flood, the flagship collided heavily with the *Gallega*, which may account for the abandonment of the latter vessel at Belén. The river is known to-day as the Rio Belem.

² For this expedition cp. Ferdinand Columbus (c. 95) and Las Casas (ii. 25). 'Quibian' appears to be a title, and not the name of an individual.

The boats went to the place where he had his village.
My brother returned with these people, and all came back
with the gold that they had collected in the four hours for
which they stayed there. The quantity is great, for none of
these men had ever seen mines and most of them had never
seen gold; the majority of them were sailors and most of
them grummets. I had much building material and stores in
abundance. I formed a settlement and I gave many gifts to
the Quibian, as they call the lord of the country. And I knew
that harmony would not long continue; they were very
barbarous and our people were very importunate, and I had
assumed possession within his territory. When he saw the
houses built and trading so active, he decided to burn the
buildings and to put all to death. But his scheme had just
the contrary result. He was taken prisoner, with his women,
sons and servants. It is true that his captivity did not last
long; the Quibian escaped from a trustworthy man who had
him under his charge with a guard of men, and his sons
escaped from the master of a ship, into whose special care
they had been given.[1]

In the month of January, the mouth of the river silted up.
In April, the ships were all worm-eaten, and it was impossible
to keep them above water. At this time, the river made
a channel, by which with difficulty I brought out three empty.
The boats went back into the river for salt and water. The
sea became high and rough and did not allow them to come
out. The Indians were many and gathered together and
attacked them, and in the end they slew them. My brother
and all the rest of the people were in a ship which remained
inside. I was outside on so dangerous a coast, utterly alone,
in a high fever and in a state of great exhaustion. Hope of
escape was dead.

I toiled up to the highest point of the ship, calling in a
trembling voice, with fast-falling tears, to the war captains
of your highnesses, at every point of the compass, for succour,
but never did they answer me. Exhausted, I fell asleep,
groaning. I heard a very compassionate voice, saying: 'O fool
and slow to believe and to serve thy God, the God of all!

[1] In the Italian version of the letter the Quibian is made to escape 'to'

porque ninguno d'estos jamás avía visto minas, i los más oro; los más eran gente de la mar, i casi todos grumetes. io tenía mucho aparejo para edificar, i muchos vastimentos; assenté pueblo, i dí muchas dádivas al 'Quibián' (que assí llaman al señor de la tierra); i bien sabía que no avía de durar la concordia; ellos mui rústicos, i nuestra gente mui inportunos, i me aposesionava en su término. después que él vido las casas fechas i el tráfago tan vivo, acordó de las quemar, i matarnos á todos. mui al revés salió su propósito: quedó preso él, mugeres, i fijos, i criados, bien que su prisión duró poco; el Quibián se fuió á un hombre honrrado, á quien se avía entregado con guarda de hombres, é los hijos se fueron á un maestre de navío, á quien se dieron en él á buen recaudo. en enero se avía cerrado la boca del río. en abril los navíos estavan todos comidos de broma, i no los podia sostener sobre agua. en este tiempo hizo el rio una canal, por donde saqué tres d'ellos, vaçíos, con gran pena. las barcas volvieron adentro por la sal i agua. la mar se puso alta, i fea, i no les dexó salir fuera: los Indios fueron muchos, i juntos, i las combatieron, i en fin los mataron. mi hermano i la otra gente toda estavan en un navío, que quedó adentro, io mui solo de fuera, en tan brava costa, con fuerte fiebre, en tanta fatiga. la esperança de escapar era muerta: subí assí, trabaxando, lo más alto, llamando á voz temerosa, llorando, i mui á prisa, los maestros de la guerra de Vuestras Altezas, á todos quatro los vientos, por socorro: mas nunca me respondieron. cansado, me dormeçí, gimiendo: una voz mui piadosa oí, diçiendo: 'o estulto i tardo á creer, i á servir á tu Dios, Dios de todos, ¿qué hizo él más por Moisés, ó por David, su siervo? desque nasciste, siempre él tuvo de ti mui grande cargo. quando te vido en edad, de que él fué contento, maravillosamente hizo sonar tu nombre en la tierra. las Indias, que son parte del mundo tan ricas, te las dió por tuias; tu las repartiste adonde

a trustworthy man, and his sons 'to' the master of a ship (cp. Thacher, ii. 675), but the story in the text agrees with the version given by Diego Mendez (cp. *infra*, p. 118), who was an eyewitness, and with that given by Ferdinand Columbus (c. 96) and Las Casas (ii. 27). Diego de Porras (Navarrete, i. 286–7) regards the arrest of the chief as unnecessary and blames Columbus.

What more did He for Moses or for His servant David?
Since thou wast born, ever has He had thee in His most
watchful care. When He saw thee of an age with which He
was content, He caused thy name to sound marvellously in
the land. The Indies, which are so rich a part of the world,
He gave thee for thine own; thou hast divided them as it
pleased thee, and He enabled thee to do this. Of the barriers
of the Ocean sea, which were closed with such mighty chains,
He gave thee the keys;[1] and thou wast obeyed in many lands
and among Christians thou hast gained an honourable
fame. What did He more for the people of Israel when He
brought them out of Egypt? Or for David, whom from
a shepherd He made to be king in Judaea? Turn thyself to
Him, and know now thine error; His mercy is infinite; thine
old age shall not prevent thee from achieving all great things;
He has many heritages very great. Abraham had passed
a hundred years when he begat Isaac, and Sarah was no girl.
Thou criest for help, doubting. Answer, who has afflicted thee
so greatly and so often, God or the world? The rewards and
promises which He gives, He does not bring to nothing, nor
does He say after He has received service, that His intention
was not such and that it is to be differently regarded, nor
does He inflict suffering in order to display His power. Not
one jot of His word fails; all that He promises, He per-
forms with interest; is this the manner of men? I have said
that which thy Creator has done for thee and does for all
men. Now in part He shows thee the reward for the anguish
and danger which thou hast endured in the service of others.'

I heard all this as if I were in a trance, but I had no answer
to give to words so true, but could only weep for my errors.
He, whoever he was, who spoke to me, ended saying: 'Fear
not; have trust; all these tribulations are written upon
marble and are not without cause.'[2]

I arose when I was able, and at the end of nine days came
fine weather, but not such as allowed the ships to be brought
out of the river.[3] I gathered together the people who were on
land, and all the rest that I could, because they were not

---

[1] Paraphrased from Seneca, *Medea* (cp. *Libro de las Profecias, Rac. Col.* I.
ii. 141).

te plugo, i te dió poder para ello. de los atamientos de la mar Occéana, que estavan çerrados con cadenas tan fuertes, te dió las llaves, i fuiste ovedesçido en tantas tierras, i de los cristianos cobraste tan honrrada fama. ¿ qué hizo él más al pueblo de Isrrael, quando le sacó de Egipto, ni por David, que de pastor hizo rei en Judea? tórnate á él, i conoçe ia tu ierro; su missericordia es infinita, tu begez no impedirá á toda cosa grande; muchas heredades tiene él grandíssimas. Abraan pasava de çien años quando engendró á Isaac, ni Sarra era moça: tu llamas por socorro, inçierto. responde: ¿ quién te ha afligido tanto i tantas vezes, Dios ó el mundo? los privilegios i promesas que da Dios, no las quebranta; ni diçe, después de aver reçibido el serviçio, que su intençión no era esta, i que se entiende de otra manera; ni da martirios por dar color á la fuerza. él va al pie de la letra; todo lo que él promete, cumple con acrescentamiento: esto es su uso. dicho tengo lo que tu Criador ha fecho por ti, i haçe con todos. ahora me dió muestra del galardón d'estos afanes i peligros, que as pasado, sirviendo á otros.' io, assí amortecido, oí todo, mas no tuve io respuesta á palabras tan çiertas, salvo llorar por mis ierros. acabó él de fablar, quienquiera que fuese, diciendo: 'no temas, confía: todas estas tribulaciones están escritas en piedra mármol, i no sin causa.' levantéme quando pude, i al cabo de nueve días hizo bonança, mas no para sacar navíos del rio. recogí la gente que estava en tierra, i todo el resto que pude, porque no bastavan para quedar i para navegar los navíos. quedara io á sostener el pueblo con todos, si Vuestras Altezas supieran de ello: el temor que nunca aportarían allí navíos me determinó á esto, i la cuenta que, quando se aia de proveer de socorro, se proveerá de todo. partí en nombre de la Sancta Trinidad la noche de Pasqua, con los navíos podridos, abrumados, todos fechos agujeros. allí en 'Beleen' dexé uno, i hartas cosas; en 'Belpuerto' hice otrotanto: no me quedaron salvo dos, en el estado de los otros, i sin barcas i vastimentos, por aver de pasar siete mil millas de mar i de aguas, ó morir en la vía con fijo i hermano

---

[2] Cp. *supra*, pp. 48 and 68, for a similar message of encouragement.
[3] Cp. *infra*, Diego Mendez, p. 118.

sufficiently numerous for some to remain on shore and others to navigate the ships. I would have remained with all of them to maintain the settlement, if Your Highnesses had known of it. The fear that ships might never come there determined me, and the consideration that, when there was a question of providing succour, provision might be made for all.

I departed in the name of the Holy Trinity on Easter night, with ships rotten, worm-eaten, all full of holes. There in Belén I left one and many things; in Belpuerto I did the same with another.[1] There remained for me two only, in the condition of the others, and without boats and stores, with which to traverse seven thousand miles of sea and waves, or to die on the way with my son and brother and so many people. Let those, who are accustomed to find fault and to censure, asking there, where they are in safety, 'Why was not so and so done in that case?', make answer now. I could wish them on this voyage; I verily believe that another voyage of another kind is in store for them, or our Faith is vain.

On the thirteenth of May, I reached the province of Mago,[2] which marches with that of Cathay, and thence I departed for Española. For two days I navigated with good weather, and after that it was unfavourable. I followed a route which would avoid the very numerous islands, in order that I might not be in difficulties in the shallows near them. The stormy sea assailed me, and I was driven backwards without sails. I anchored at an island where I suddenly lost three anchors, and at midnight, when it seemed that the world was dissolving, the cables of the other ship broke and it bore down on me, so that it was a wonder that we were not dashed to pieces. The anchor, such as remained to me, was that which, after Our Lord, saved me.

At the end of six days, when fair weather came, having thus already lost all my tackle, I proceeded on my voyage. My ships were more riddled with holes than a honeycomb, and the crews were spiritless and despairing. I passed somewhat beyond the point at which I had previously arrived, where

[1] The *Gallega* was abandoned at Belem (cp. Diego de Porras; Navarrete, i. 295, and *supra*, p. 88, note 1). The *Vizcaina* was abandoned at Puerto Bello

i tanta gente. respondan ahora los que suelen tachar i reprehender, diçiendo allí de en salvo: '¿porqué no haçiades esto allí?' los quisiera io en esta jornada; io bien creo que otra de otro saber los aguarda, ó nuestra fe es ninguna. llegué á treçe de maio en la provinçia de 'Mago', que parte con aquella del Cataio, i de allí partí para la Española. navegué dos días con buen tiempo, i después fué contrario. el camino, que io llevava, era para desechar tanto número de islas, por no me embaraçar en los baxos de ellas. la mar brava me hizo fuerça, i uve de volver atrás sin velas: surgí á una isla adonde de golpe perdí tres anclas, i á la media noche, que pareçía que el mundo se ensolvía, se rompieron las amarras al otro navío, i vino sobre mi, que fué maravilla como no nos acabamos de se hazer rajas: el ancla, de forma que me quedó, fué ella, después de Nuestro Señor, pues me sostuvo. al cabo de seis días, que ia era bonança, volví á mi camino assí ia perdido del todo de aparejos, i con los navíos horadados de gusanos más que un panal de avejas, i la gente tan acobardada i perdida. passé algo adelante de donde io avía llegado denantes: allí me tornó á reposar atrás la fortuna; paré en la mesma isla en más seguro puerto. al cabo de ocho días torné á la via, i llegué á Janahica en fin de junio, siempre con vientos punteros, i los navíos en peor estado. con tres bombas, tinas, i calderas, no podia con toda la gente bençer el agua, que entrava en el navío; ni para este mal de broma ai otra cura. cometí el camino para me acercar á lo más cerca de la Española, que son veinte i ocho leguas, i no quisiera aver començado. el otro navío corrío á buscar puerto casi anegado; io porfié la buelta de la mar con tormenta. el navío se me anegó, que milagrosamente me truxo Nuestro Señor á tierra.

(cp. Ferdinand Columbus, c. 99). Bartolomé de Caso told a story of the finding of an anchor at Puerto Bello during the expedition of Nicuesa, which was identified as having belonged to one of these ships by Diego Martin de la Cabrera, who had sailed in the *Gallega* on this voyage (cp. *Pleitos*, i. 425).

² The district of Macaca in Cuba (cp. Las Casas, ii. 29; Ferdinand Columbus, c. 99; and *infra*, p. 122 and note 2). Las Casas and Ferdinand Columbus say that contrary winds and currents prevented Columbus from proceeding to Jamaica. The explanation of the somewhat curious course which Columbus followed from the Rio Belén in order to reach Española is perhaps to be found in the statement of Ferdinand Columbus (*loc. cit.*), that his father and uncle knew that it was impossible to sail directly to Española from Veragua owing to the currents.

the storm had driven me back, and I put into a much safer harbour in the same island.

At the end of eight days I resumed my voyage and at the end of June reached Jamaica, having always contrary winds and the ships in a worse state.[1] With three pumps, pots and kettles, and with all hands working, they could not keep down the water which came into the ship, and there was no other remedy for the havoc which the worm had wrought. I steered a course which should bring me as near as possible to the coast of Española, from which we were twenty-eight leagues distant, and I wished that I had not begun to do so. The other ship, half under water, was obliged to run for port. I struggled to keep the sea against the storm. My ship was sinking under me, when Our Lord miraculously brought me to land. Who will believe that which I write here ? I declare that in this letter I have not told the hundredth part. Those who were with the admiral can testify to this.

If it please Your Highnesses graciously to accord me the help of a ship of above sixty-four tons, with two hundred quintals of biscuit and some other provision, that would suffice to bring me and these people to Spain from Española. I have already said that it is only twenty-eight leagues from Jamaica to Española. I would not have gone to Española, even if the ships had been fit to do so ;[2] I have already said that orders were given me on behalf of Your Highnesses that I should not come there. If this command has profited, God knows. This letter I send by means and by the hand of Indians ; it will be a great wonder if it reach its destination.[3]

I say this of my voyage, that there were with me a hundred and fifty persons, among whom there were some very capable pilots and great sailors. No one of them can give any certain account of where I went or where I came. The reason is not far to seek. I set out from a point above Puerto del Brasil ; off Española, the storm prevented me from following the course which I desired ; owing to its violence I had to run where the wind drove me. At that time, I fell very sick ; no one had navigated in that direction. Then the wind and sea

---

[1] Columbus first reached the coast of Jamaica at a point which he called

¿ quién creiera lo que io aquí escrivo ? digo que de çien partes no he dicho la una en esta letra. los que fueron con el almirante lo testigüen. si place á Vuestras Altezas de me hazer merçed de socorro, un navío que pase de sesenta i quatro, con duçientos quintales de vizcocho, i algún otro vastimento, abastará para me llevar á mi i á esta gente á España. de la Española en Janahica ia dixe que no ai veinte i ocho leguas. á la Española no fuera io, bien que los navíos estuvieran para ello: ya dixe que me fué mandado de parte de Vuestras Altezas que no llegase á ella. si este mandar a aprovechado, Dios lo sabe. esta carta invío por vía i mano de Indios: grande maravilla será, si allá llega. de mi viaje digo que fueron ciento i cinquenta personas conmigo, en que ai hartos suficientes para pilotos, i grande marineros: ninguno puede dar razón çierta por dónde fuí io, ni vine. la razón es mui presta. io partí de sobre el puerto del Brasil, en la Española; no me dexó la tormenta ir al camino que io quería: fué por fuerza correr adonde el viento quiso; en ese día caí io mui enfermo; ninguno avía navegado açia aquella parte; cessó el viento i mar, dende á çiertos días, i se mudó la tormenta en calmería, i grandes corrientes. fuí á aportar á una isla, que se dixo 'de las Pozas', i de allí á la tierra firme. ninguno puede dar cuenta verdadera d'esto; porque no ai razón que abaste; porque fué ir con corriente, sin ver tierra, tanto número de días. seguí la costa de la tierra firme: esta se assentó con compás i arte. ninguno ai que diga debaxo quál parte del çielo sea, é quando io partí de ella para venir á la Española, los pilotos cerían venir á parar á la isla de Sanct

Puerto Bueno; he then sailed on to Santa Gloria, where he entered harbour (cp. Ferdinand Columbus, c. 99; Las Casas, ii. 29). There is no other record of his effort to reach Española at this time, although both Ferdinand Columbus and Las Casas credit him with the desire to do so.

² This appears to contradict the statement made a little earlier, and does not agree with Las Casas (*loc. cit.*) and Ferdinand Columbus (*loc. cit.*), both of whom state that the aim of Columbus was to reach Española. Ferdinand Columbus says that the sailors were afraid that Columbus intended to try to sail directly for Spain, an impossible voyage for ships in such a condition, but is quite clear that there was no such idea in his father's mind.

³ This letter was presumably sent to Española by Diego Mendez, and by him transmitted to Spain. It is hardly accurate to describe it as having been confided to the hands of Indians.

abated for some days, and in place of the storm there were calms and strong currents. I put into harbour at an island which is called *de las Pozas*,[1] and thence steered for Tierra Firme. None can give a true account of this, for there was no sufficient reckoning, for I was obliged to go with the current, without seeing land, for so very many days. I followed the coast of Tierra Firme; this I ascertained by the compass and my skill. There was no one who could say under what part of the heavens we were, and when I set out thence to come to Española, the pilots believed that we were going to reach the island of San Juan, and it was the land of Mango, four hundred leagues more to the west than they said. Let them answer, if they know how, where Veragua is situated.[2] I declare that they can give no other explanation or account, save that they went to lands where there is much gold, and this they are able to certify. But to return to it, they would have to follow an unknown route; it would be necessary for them to go to discover it as if for the first time. There is a method and means derived from astrology and certain, which is enough for one who understands it. This resembles a prophetic vision.

In the Indies, if ships do not sail except with the wind abaft, it is not because they are ill built or because they are clumsy. The strong currents that are there, together with the wind, bring it about that none can sail with the bowline, for in one day they would lose as much way as they might have made in seven, nor does a caravel serve, even if it be a Portuguese lateen rigged vessel.[3] This is the reason why they do not sail except with a regular breeze, and they sometimes remain in harbour waiting for it for seven or eight months, nor is this strange, since the same thing often occurs in Spain.

The people of whom Pope Pius II writes, the country and its characteristics,[4] have been found, but not the horses with saddles, poitrels, and bridles of gold. Nor is this strange, for there the coast lands require only fisherfolk, nor did I stay there, since I went in haste. In Cariay and in these lands near, there are great enchanters and very awe-inspiring.

---

[1] Ferdinand Columbus (c. 88) places these islands off the coast of Jamaica. In the Spanish text, as printed by Navarrete (i. 306), the island is called 'las

Joan, i fué en tierra de 'Mango', quatrocientas leguas más al
poniente de adonde deçían. respondan, si saben, adónde es
el sitio de Veragna. digo que no pueden dar otra razón ni
cuenta, salvo que fueron á unas tierras adonde ai mucho oro,
i certificarle; mas para volver á ella, el camino tienen ignoto;
sería necessario, para ir á ella, descubrirla como de primero.
una cuenta ai, i razón de astrología, i çierta: quien la entiende,
esto le abasta; á visión profética se asemeja esto. las naos de
las Indias si no navegan salvo á popa, no es por la mala
fechura ni por ser fuertes; las grandes corrientes, que allí
vienen, juntamente con el viento, hacen que nadie porfíe con
bolina; porque en un día perderían lo que uviesen ganado en
siete; ni saco caravela, aunque sea latina portuguesa. esta
razón hace que no naveguen salvo con colla, y, por esperarle,
se detienen á las vezes seis i ocho meses en puerto: ni es
maravilla; pues que en España muchas veces acaeçe otrotanto. la gente de que escrive papa Pio segundo el sitio y
señas, se a hallado, más no los cavallos, pretales, i frenos de
oro. ni es maravilla; porque allí las tierras de la costa de la
mar no requieren salvo pescadores, ni io me detuve, porque
andava á prisa. en Cariay y en esas tierras de su comarca son
grandes fechiceros i mui medrosos: dieran el mundo, porque
no me detuviera allí una hora. quando llegué allí, luego me
inviaron dos muchachas, mui ataviadas; la más vieja no

Bocas', but in the Italian version it appears as 'de las Pozzas' (cp. Thacher, ii.
677). Juan de Noya, in his evidence on the fourth voyage, said that on the way
to Tierra Firme, the fleet called at 'unas islas anegadas' (cp. *Pleitos*, i. 257):
and in a question in a later interrogatory, the island receives the name 'Isla
Anegada' (cp. *Pleitos*, i. 397): this name appears in early maps as that of an
island off the coast of Puerto Rico. Probably the island meant by Columbus
was one of those of el Jardin de la Reina (cp. Las Casas, ii. 20).

² Diego de Porras (Navarrete, i. 287) asserts that Columbus had taken from
the sailors all their charts, which, if true, might account for their disorienta-
tion.

³ Cp. *Rac. Col.* IV. i. 66–7, and *infra*, p. 106, note 1.

⁴ In the Spanish text, as printed by Navarrete (i. 307), this passage reads:
'... escribe Papa Pio, segun el sitio ...' The Italian version (cp. Thacher, ii. 677)
has: '... scrive papa Pio secondo el sitio ...' De Lollis (*Rac. Col.* I. ii. 198 and
note 3) takes '... escrive Papa Pio segundo el sitio ...' to be the true reading of
the Spanish. The allusion is to a passage in the *Cosmographia Pape Pii* (cp.
Major, *op. cit.*, p. 198, note 2), and not to the *Historia*, as Navarrete (*loc. cit.*,
note) suggests.

They would have given the world that I should not have remained there an hour. When I arrived there, they sent to me at once two girls, very showily dressed; the elder was not more than eleven years old and the other seven; they were both so abandoned that they were not better than prostitutes. They carried magic powder concealed about them. When they came, I commanded that they should be decorated with some of our things and sent them back to land at once.[1]

There on a mountain I saw a tomb, as large as a house and carved, and the corpse was lying in it exposed and embalmed.[2] They told me of other works of art and very excellent. There are many animals, small and large, and very different from ours. I had at the time two hogs, and an Irish dog did not dare to face them. A crossbowman had wounded an animal, which appeared to be an ape, except that it was much larger and had the face of a man.[3] The arrow had pierced it from the neck to the tail, and as a result it was so fierce that it was necessary to cut off an arm and a leg. When the hog saw it, it bristled up and fled. When I saw this, I ordered the *begare*, as it is called there, to be thrown where the hog was; coming within reach, although it was on the point of death and although the arrow was still in its body, it twisted its tail round the hog's snout and holding it very firmly, seized it by the nape of the neck and with its remaining hand struck it on the head, as if it were an enemy. This action was so novel and such fine hunting that I have described it. They have many kinds of animals, but they all die of *barra*.[4] I saw many very large fowls, with feathers like wool; lions, stags, besides fallow-deer, and also birds.

While I wearily traversed that sea, a delusion came to some that we were bewitched and they still persist in that idea.[5] I found another people who eat men; their brutal appearance showed this. They say that there are there great mines of copper; of it they make hatchets, other worked articles, cast and soldered, and forges with all the tools of a goldsmith, and crucibles. There they go clothed. And in

---

[1] Ferdinand Columbus (c. 90) and Las Casas (ii. 21) place this incident at Cariay, and describe it as the outcome of the refusal of Columbus (hypocritical, according to Las Casas) to receive the presents offered by the natives. Ferdinand

sería de once años, i la otra de siete, ambas con tanta desemboltura, que no serían más unas putas. traían polvos de hechizos, escondidos. en llegando, las mandé adornar de nuestras cosas, i las invié luego á tierra. allí vide una sepultura en el monte, grande como una casa, i labrada, i el cuerpo descuvierto, i mirrado, en ella. de otras artes me dixeron y más excelentes. animalias, menudas i grandes, ai hartas, i mui diversas de las nuestras. dos puercos uve io en presente, i un perro de Irlanda no osava esperarlos. un ballestero avía herido una animalia que se parece á gato paul, salvo que es mucho más grande, i el rostro de hombre; teníale atravesado con una saeta desde los pechos á la cola, i, porque era feroz, le uvo de cortar un braço i una pierna: el puerco, en viéndole, se le encrespó, y se fué huiendo. io, quando esto ví, mandé echarle el 'begare', que assí se llama, adonde estava; en llegando á él, assí estando á la muerte, y la saeta siempre en el cuerpo, le echó la cola por el hocico, y se la amarró muy fuerte, y, con la mano que le quedava, le arrebató por el copete, como á enemigo. el auto tan nuevo y hermosa montería me hizo escrivir esto. de muchas maneras de animalias se uvo, mas todas mueren de barra. gallinas mui grandes, i la pluma como lana, vide hartas. leones, cierbos, corços otrotanto, y assí aves. quando io andava por aquella mar en fatiga, en algunos se puso heregía que estávamos enfechizados, que oi día están en ello. otra gente fallé que comían hombres. la desformidad de su gesto lo dice. allí dicen que ai grandes mineros de cobre: hachas de ello, otras cosas, labradas, fundidas, soldadas uve, i fraguas con todo su aparejo de platero, i los crisoles. allí van vestidos; i en

Columbus and Las Casas know nothing of the immodesty of the girls, whose ages they give as fourteen and eight, or of the magic powder.

² This passage would seem to suggest that Columbus had landed himself; the accounts given by Las Casas and Ferdinand Columbus imply that he did not personally go on shore.

³ In the Italian version (cp. Thacher, ii. 678) the wound is inflicted by Columbus himself, which would again argue that he had landed. The animal was a peccary.

⁴ The nature of this disease cannot be determined, since its name appears to be unknown, but the word would seem to suggest a skin disease.

⁵ Cp. Las Casas, ii. 22. The sailors perhaps believed that the incantations had produced some effect, when they experienced so many misfortunes afterwards.

this province I saw large cotton sheets, very cleverly worked; others were very cleverly painted in colours with pencils. They say that in the country inland towards Cathay, they have them worked with gold. Of all these lands and of that which there is in them, owing to lack of an interpreter, they could not learn very much. The villages, although they are very close together, have each a different language, and it is so much so that they do not understand one another any more than we understand the Arabs. I believe that this is the case with the uncivilized people of the coast, but not inland.

When I discovered the Indies, I said that they were the richest dominion that there is in the world. I was speaking of the gold, pearls, precious stones, and spices, with the trade and markets in them, and because everything did not appear immediately, I was held up to abuse. This punishment leads me now to say only that which I have heard from the natives of the land. Of one thing I dare to speak, because there are so many witnesses, and this is that in this land of Veragua I saw greater evidence of gold on the first two days than in Española in four years, and that the lands in this district could not be more lovely or better cultivated, nor could the people be more timid, and there is a good harbour and a beautiful river and it is defensible against the world. All this makes for the security of the Christians and the assurance of their dominion, and gives great hope for the honour and increase of the Christian religion. And the voyage thither will be as short as to Española, since it will be with the wind. Your Highnesses are as much sovereigns of this land as at Jerez or Toledo; your ships may go there as if they were going home. Thence they will obtain gold: in other lands, in order to become masters of that which is in them, it requires that they should seize it or return empty, and inland it is necessary for them to trust their persons to a savage.

Concerning the rest, of which I refrain from speaking, I have said why I put a guard on myself. Accordingly, I do not mention the sixth part in all that I have ever said and written, nor do I assert it as true, nor do I declare that I am at the fountain head. Genoese, Venetians, and all who have pearls, precious stones, and other things of value, all carry

aquella provinçia vide sábanas grandes de algodón, labradas
de mui sotiles labores, otras pintadas mui sotilmente á colores
con pinceles. dicen que en la tierra adentro haçia el Cataio
las ai texidas de oro. de todas estas tierras, i de lo que ai en
ellas, falta de lengua, no se sabe tan presto. los pueblos, bien
que sean espesos, cada uno tiene diferençiada lengua, i es en
tanto, que no se entienden los unos con los otros, más que nos
con los de Aravía. io creo que esto sea en esta gente salvaje
de la costa de la mar, mas no en la tierra dentro. quando io
descubrí las Indias, dixe que eran el maior señorio rico que ai
en el mundo. io dixe de oro, perlas, piedras preciosas,
especerías, con los tratos i ferias; i, porque no pareçio todo
tan presto, fuí escandaliçado. este castigo me hace agora que
no diga salvo lo que io oigo de los naturales de la tierra. de
uno oso dezir, porque ai tantos testigos, i es que io vide en
esta tierra de Beragna maior señal de oro en dos días primeros,
que en la Española en quatro años, i que las tierras de la
comarca no pueden ser más fermosas, ni más labradas, ni la
gente más cobarde, i buen puerto, i fermoso rio, i defensible
al mundo. todo esto es seguridad de los cristianos, i certeça
de señorío, con grande esperança de la honrra i acresecenta-
miento de la religión cristiana; i el camino allí será tan breve
como á la Española, porque a de ser con viento. tan señores
son Vuestras Altezas d'esto, como de Gerez ó Toledo; sus
navíos, que fueren allí, van á su casa. de allí sacarán oro;
en otras tierras, para aver de lo que ai en ellas, conviene que
se lo lleven, ó se volverán baçíos, i en la tierra es necessario que
fien sus personas de un salvaje. del otro que io dexo de dezir,
ia dixe por qué me encerré: no digo assí, ni que io me afirme
en el tresdoble en todo lo que io aia jamás dicho i escrito, i que
io estó á la fuente. Genoveses, Veneçianos, i toda gente que
tenga perlas, piedras preçiosas i otras cosas de valor, todos las
llevan hasta el cabo del mundo, para las trocar, convertir en
oro : el oro es exçelentíssimo; de oro se hace tesoro, i con él,
quien lo tiene, hace quanto quiere en el mundo, i llega á que
echa las ánimas al Paraíso. los señores de aquellas tierras de
la comarca de Beragna, quando mueren, entierran el oro que
tienen con el cuerpo: assí lo dicen. á Salomón llevaron de un
camino seiscientos i sesenta i seis quintales de oro, allende lo

them to the end of the world in order to exchange them, to turn them into gold. Gold is most excellent. Gold constitutes treasure, and he who possesses it may do what he will in the world, and may so attain as to bring souls to Paradise. When the lords of those lands which are in the district of Veragua die, they bury the gold which they have with the body; so they say.

To Solomon on one journey they brought six hundred and sixty-six *quintals* of gold, besides that which the merchants and sailors brought, and besides that which was paid in Arabia. From this gold, he made two hundred lances and three hundred shields, and he made the covering that was at the back [of his throne] of massive gold and adorned with precious stones. Josephus writes this in his chronicle of the *Antiquities*;[1] in the book of Chronicles,[2] and in the book of Kings,[3] there is an account of this. Josephus holds that this gold was obtained in the Aurea. If it were so, I declare that those mines of the Aurea are one and the same as these of Veragua, which, as I have said above, extend westward twenty days' journey, and are everywhere at the same distance from the pole and from the equator. Solomon bought all that gold, precious stones, and silver, and you may command it to be collected there, if you wish. David, in his will, left three thousand *quintals* of gold[4] of the Indies to Solomon to aid in building the Temple, and according to Josephus, it was from these same lands.[5]

Jerusalem and Mount Sion are to be rebuilt by the hand of a Christian; who this is to be, God declares by the mouth of His prophet in the fourteenth psalm.[6] Abbot Joachin said that he was to come from Spain.[7] St. Jerome showed the way of it to the holy lady. The emperor of Cathay, some time since, sent for wise men to instruct him in the faith of Christ.[8] Who will offer himself for this work? If Our Lord bring me back to Spain, I pledge myself, in the name of God, to bring him there in safety.

The people who came with me have suffered incredible toils and dangers. I pray Your Highnesses, since they are poor, that you will command that they be paid immediately, and

---

[1] Bk. VIII, c. 7.   [2] 2 Chronicles ix. 13–17.

que llevaron los mercaderes i marineros, i allende lo que se
pagó en Aravía. d'este oro fiço doçientos lanças i treçientos
escudos, i fizo el tablado, que avía de estar derriba, de pellas
de oro, i adornado de piedras preciosas, i fizo otras muchas
cosas de oro, i vasos muchos i mui grandes, i ricos de piedras
preciosas. Josepho en su corónica De antiquitatibus lo
escrive; e nel Paralipómenon i en el libro de los Reies se cuenta
d'esto. Josepho quiere que este oro se oviese en la Áurea:
si assí fuese, digo que aquellas minas de la Áurea son unas,
i se contienen con estas de Beragna, que, como io dixe arriba,
se alarga al poniente veinte jornadas, i son en una distançia,
lexos del polo, i de la linea. Salomón compró todo aquello
oro, piedras, i plata, é á él le pueden mandar á cojer, si le
aplacen. David en su testamento dexó tres mil quintales de
oro de las Indias á Salomón para aiuda de edificar el templo,
i, según Josepho, era el d'estas mismas tierras. Hierusalem
i el monte Sion ha de ser reedificado por mano de cristiano:
quien a de ser, Dios por boca del Propheta en el déçimo quarto
Psalmo lo diçe. el abbad Joachín dixo que este avía de salir
de España. sanct Gerónimo á la sancta muger le mostró el
camino para ello. el emperador del Cataio ha días que mandó
sabios que le enseñen en la fe de Cristo; ¿quién será que se
ofrezca á esto? si Nuestro Señor me lleva á España, io me
obligo de llevar[les] con el nombre de Dios en salvo. esta gente,
que vino conmigo, an pasado increibles peligros i trabaxos:
supplico á Vuestras Altezas, porque son pobres, que les
manden pagar luego i les hagan mercedes á cada uno, según
la calidad de la persona, que les certifico que, á mi creer, les
traen las mejores nuevas que nunca fueron á España. el oro

³ 1 Kings x. 14–18.
⁴ 1 Chronicles xxix. 2–7.
⁵ Bk. VIII, c. 14.
⁶ Psalms xiv. 7.
⁷ Joachin, abbot of Flores, in Calabria. The reference is to his *Oraculum
Turcicum* (cp. *Vaticiniae sive Prophetiae Abbatis Joachimi et Anselmi Episcopi
Marsicani*). The same interpretation of the prophecy appears in the *Libro de
las Profecías (Rac. Col.* I. ii. 83). There is no reference to Spain in the original
of Joachin.
⁸ The allusion is to the embassy sent by the Grand Khan to Pope Eugenius IV.
Reference to this mission appears in the letter of Toscanelli to Martims (cp. *Rac.
Col.* I. ii. 364–5), and in the prologue to the *Journal* (cp. *Rac. Col.* I. i. 2).

that you will grant rewards to each one of them according to their quality, for I certify that to my belief they bear the best news that ever there came to Spain.

Although the gold which the Quibian has in Veragua and which others in that neighbourhood have, is, according to accounts, very abundant, it does not appear to me to be well or for the service of Your Highnesses that it should be seized violently. Fair dealing will avoid scandal and ill report, and it will be that all will come to the treasury, so that not a grain is left.

With a month of fair weather, I shall complete all my voyage. I did not persist in delaying to enter on it, because there was a lack of ships, and for all that concerns your service, I hope in Him Who made me, that I shall be of use. I believe that Your Highness will remember that I wished to order the construction of ships in a new manner;[1] the brevity of the time did not give room for this, and I foresaw certainly that which has come to pass. I hold that in this trade and mines of such extent and such dominion there is more than there is in all else that has been done in the Indies. This is not a child to be left to the care of a step-mother.

Of Española, Paria, and the other lands, I never think without weeping. I believed that their example would have been to the profit of others; on the contrary, they are in an exhausted state; although they are not dead, the infirmity is incurable or very extensive; let him who brought them to this state come now with the remedy if he can or if he knows it; in destruction, everyone is an adept. It was always the custom to give thanks and promotion to him who imperilled his person. It is not just that he who has been so hostile to this undertaking should enjoy its fruits or that his children should. Those who left the Indies, flying from toils and speaking evil of the matter and of me, have returned with official employment.[2] So it has now been ordained in the case of Veragua. It is an ill example and without profit for the business and for justice in the world.

The fear of this, with other sufficient reasons, which I saw

[1] There appears to be no other record of this idea of Columbus, but his experiences in the West Indies may well have led him to wish to have ships

que tiene el Quibián de Beragna i los otros de la comarca, bien que, según informaçión, él sea mucho, no me paresçió bien, ni servicio de Vuestras Altezas, de se le tomar por vía de robo; la buena orden ebitará escándalo i mala fama, i hará que todo ello venga al tesoro, que no quede un grano. con un mes de buen tiempo io acabara todo mi viaje: por falta de los navíos no porfié á esperarle para tornar á ello, i para toda cosa de su servicio espero en aquél que me hizo, si estaré bueno. io creo que Vuestra Alteza se acordará que io quería mandar hazer los navíos de nueva manera: la brevidad del tiempo no dió lugar á ello, i cierto io avía caído en lo que cumplía. io tengo en más esta negociaçión i minas, con esta escala i señorio, que todo lo otro que está hecho en las Indias. no est este hijo para dar á criar á madrasta. de la Española, de Paria, i de las otras tierras, no me acuerdo d'ellas que io no llore; creía io que el exemplo d'ellas oviese de ser por estotras: al contrario, ellas están boca á iuso; bien que no mueren, la enfermedad es incurable ó mui larga: quien las llegó á esto venga agora con el remedio, si puede ó sabe: al descomponer cadauno es maestro. las graçias i acrescentamiento siempre fué uso de las dar á quien puso su cuerpo á peligro. no es razón que quien ha sido tan contrario á esta negoçiación le goçe, ni sus fijos. los que se fueron de las Indias, fuiendo los trabaxos, i diçiendo mal d'ellas i de mi, volvieron con cargos; así se ordenará agora en Beragna: malo exemplo, i sin provecho del negoçio i para la justicia del mundo. este temor, con otros casos hartos que io veía claro, me hizo supplicar á Vuestras Altezas, antes que io viniese á descubrir esas islas i tierra firme, que me las dexasen governar en su real nombre. plúgoles: fué por privilegio i asiento, i con sello i juramento, i me

---

built on the lines of the 'Portuguese caravels', perhaps with their special characteristics further developed (cp. *supra*, p. 98).

² It is not clear whether Columbus was here alluding to special individuals or merely making a general statement. The man who had been so hostile might appear to be Fonseca, were it not for the reference to 'children'; the bishop's moral character has not been assailed. Alonso de Ojeda may be suggested as one of those who had returned, with official sanction, if not with official employment. It is, of course, possible that some who had left the island returned in the service of Nicolas de Ovando.

clearly, led me to pray your highnesses before I went to discover these islands and Tierra Firme, that you would leave them to me to govern in your royal name. It pleased you; it was a privilege and agreement, and under seal and oath, and you granted me the title of viceroy and admiral and governor general of all. And you fixed the boundary, a hundred leagues beyond the Azores and the Cape Verde Islands, by a line passing from pole to pole, and you gave me wide power over this and over all that I might further discover. The document states this very fully.

The other most important matter, which calls aloud for redress, remains inexplicable to this moment. Seven years I was at your royal court,[1] where all to whom this undertaking was mentioned, unanimously declared it to be a delusion. Now all, down to the very tailors,[2] seek permission to make discoveries. It can be believed that they go forth to plunder, and it is granted to them to do so, so that they greatly prejudice my honour and do very great damage to the enterprise. It is well to give to God that which is His due and to Caesar that which belongs to him. This is a just sentiment and based on justice.

The lands which here obey Your Highnesses are more extensive and richer than all other Christian lands. After that I, by the divine will, had placed them under your royal and exalted lordship, and was on the point of securing a very great revenue, suddenly, while I was waiting for ships to come to your high presence with victory and with great news of gold, being very secure and joyful, I was made a prisoner and with my two brothers was thrown into a ship, laden with fetters, stripped to the skin, very ill-treated, and without being tried or condemned. Who will believe that a poor foreigner could in such a place rise against Your Highnesses, without cause, and without the support of some other prince, and being alone among your vassals and natural subjects, and having all my children at your royal court ?[3]

I came to serve at the age of twenty-eight years, and now I have not a hair on my body that is not grey, and my body is

---

[1] Cp. *supra*, Introduction, p. xiii.

intitularon de visorei i almirante i governador general de todo, i aseñalaron el término sobre las islas de los Azores cien leguas, i aquellas del Cabo Verde, por línea que pasa de polo á polo, i esto de todo que jamás se descubriese, i me dieron poder largo; la escritura á más largamente lo dice. el otro negocio famosíssimo está con los braços abiertos llamando: estrangero ha sido fasta agora. siete años estuve io en su real corte, que á quantos se fabló de esta empresa, todos á una dixeron que era burla; agora fasta los sastres suplican por descubrir. es de creer que van á saltear, i se les otorga, que cobran con mucho perjuicio de mi honrra i tanto daño del negoçio. bueno es de dar á Dios lo suio, i á Çésar lo que le perteneçe. esta es justa sentençia i de justo. las tierras, que acá obedecen á Vuestras Altezas, son más que todas las otras de cristianos, i ricas. después que io por voluntad divina las uve puestas debaxo de su real i alto señorio, i en filo para aver grandísima renta, de inproviso, esperando navíos para venir á su alto conspecto, con vitoria i grandes nuevas del oro, mui seguro i alegre, fué preso i echado con dos hermanos en un navío, cargados de fierros, desnudo en cuerpo, con mui mal tratamiento, sin ser llamado, ni bençido por justiçia: ¿ quien creerá que un pobre estrangero se oviese de alçar en tal lugar contra Vuestras Altezas, sin causa ni sin braço de otro príncipe, i estando solo entre sus basallos i naturales, i teniendo todos mis fijos en su real corte? io vine á servir de veinte i ocho años, i agora no tengo cavello en mi persona que no sea cano, i el cuerpo enfermo i gastado. quanto me quedó, de aquellos me fué tomado i bendido, i á mi i á mis hermanos, fasta el saio, sin ser oido ni visto, con gran deshonor mío. es de creer que esto no se hizo por su real mandado. la restituçión de mi honrra, i daños, i el castigo en quien lo fizo fará sonar su real nobleça: i otrotanto en quien me robó las perlas i de quien ha fecho daño en ese almirantado. grandíssima virtud, fama con exemplo será, si haçen esto, i quedará á la España gloriosa memoria con . . . de Vuestras Altezas de

---

² Cp. *supra*, p. 52, note 5. The allusion here is probably to Baltasar Calvo, who was actually a tailor (cp. *Pleitos*, i. 347).

³ Cp. *supra*, p. 78, note 5.

infirm, and whatever remained to me from those years of service has been spent and taken away from me and sold, and from my brothers, down to my very coat, without my being heard or seen, to my great dishonour. It must be believed that this was not done by your royal command. The restitution of my honour, the reparation of my losses, and the punishment of him who did this, will spread abroad the fame of your royal nobility. The same punishment is due to him who robbed me of the pearls, and to him who infringed my rights as admiral.[1] Very great will be your merit, fame without parallel will be yours, if you do this, and there will remain in Spain a glorious memory[2] of Your Highnesses, as grateful and just princes.

The pure devotion which I have ever borne to the service of Your Highnesses, and the unmerited wrong that I have suffered, will not permit me to remain silent, although I would fain do so; I pray Your Highnesses to pardon me. I am so ruined as I have said; hitherto I have wept for others; now, Heaven have mercy upon me, and may the earth weep for me. Of worldly goods, I have not even a blanca for an offering in spiritual things. Here in the Indies I have become careless of the prescribed forms of religion. Alone in my trouble, sick, in daily expectation of death, and encompassed about by a million savages, full of cruelty and our foes, and so separated from the holy Sacraments of Holy Church, my soul will be forgotten if it here leaves my body. Weep for me, whoever has charity, truth, and justice.

I did not sail upon this voyage to gain honour or wealth; this is certain, for already all hope of that was dead. I came to Your Highnesses with true devotion and with ready zeal, and I do not lie. I humbly pray Your Highnesses that if it please God to bring me forth from this place, that you will be pleased to permit me to go to Rome and to other places of pilgrimage. May the Holy Trinity preserve your life and high estate, and grant you increase of prosperity.

Done in the Indies in the island of Jamaica, on the seventh of July, in the year one thousand five hundred and three.

---

[1] The allusion is to Alonso de Ojeda, who brought back pearls from Paria to

agradesçidos i justos prínçipes. la intençión tan sana, que io
siempre tuve al serviçio á Vuestras Altezas i á la afrenta tan
desigual, no da lugar al ánima que calle, bien que io quiera.
suplico á Vuestras Altezas me perdonen. io estoi tan perdido,
como dixe; io he llorado fasta aquí á otros; aia missericordia
agora el çielo, i llore por mi la tierra. en el temporal no tengo
solamente una blanca para el oferta en el espiritual. he
parado aquí en las Indias de la forma que está dicho; aislado,
en esta pena, enfermo, aguardando cada día por la muerte,
i cercado de un cuento de salvajes, i llenos de crueldad i
enemigos nuestros, i tan apartado de los sanctos sacramentos
de la sancta Iglesia, que se olvidará d'esta ánima, si se aparta
acá del cuerpo. llore por me quien tiene caridad, verdad
i justiçia. io non vine este viaje á navegar por ganar honrra
ni hazienda; esto es çierto, porque estava ia la esperança de
todo en ello muerta. io vine á Vuestras Altezas con sana
intençión i buen celo, i no miento. suplico úmilmente á
Vuestras Altezas que, si á Dios plaçe de me sacar de aquí, que
aia por bien mi ida á Roma i otras romerías. cuia vida i alto
estado la Sancta Trinidad guarde i acresciente.

Fecha en las Indias en la isla de Janahica, á siete de julio
de mil i quinientos i tres años.

Spain and whose expedition was held by Columbus to have infringed his
privileges.
² Lacuna in the original.

FOURTH VOYAGE OF COLUMBUS (cont.)

2. An account, given by Diego Mendez, of certain things that occurred on the last voyage of the admiral, Don Christopher Columbus.[1]

DIEGO MENDEZ,[2] inhabitant of the city of Santo Domingo, in the island of Española, being in the town of Valladolid, where at the time was the court of their majesties, made his testament on the sixth day of the month of June in the year one thousand five hundred and thirty-six, before Fernan Perez, clerk of their majesties and their notary public in their court and in all their kingdoms and lordships, there being witness, Diego de Arana, Juan Diez Miranda de la Cuadra, Martin de Orduña, Lucas Fernandez, Alonso de Angulo, Francisco de Hinojosa, and Diego de Aguilar, all servants of the lady Vicereine of the Indies.[3] And among other clauses of the said will, there is one which runs literally as follows.

Clause of the will. Item: The very illustrious lords, the admiral Don Christopher Columbus, of glorious memory, and his son, the admiral Don Diego Columbus, and his grandson, the admiral Don Luis,[4] whom may God long preserve, and through them, the Vicereine, my lady, as his

---

[1] For this document, cp. *supra*, Introduction, p. lxxxvii.

[2] Diego Mendez de Segura sailed on the fourth voyage of Columbus as a squire in the caravel *Santiago de Palos*, whose captain was Francisco de Porras. Little seems to be known of him beyond the information contained in his will. He is described as a mayordomo of Columbus (*Pleitos*, ii. 31), and actively interested himself in the vindication of the claims of Diego Columbus (cp. his letter to Diego Columbus, *Autógrafos de Cristóbal Colón*, p. 59). He was one of the sources of information used by Oviedo, who speaks in complimentary terms of him (iii. 9).

[3] María de Toledo y Rojas, widow of Diego Columbus, the second admiral. She was the daughter of Hernando de Toledo, señor de Villoria and comendador mayor de León, by María de Rojas; was grand-daughter of García Alvarez de Toledo, duke of Alba, and niece of Fadrique de Toledo, duke of Alba. She was related to Ferdinand the Catholic, her grandmother being the king's aunt. María de Toledo married Diego Columbus (1508) and went with him to Española (1509), establishing a brilliant vice-regal court at Santo Domingo. After the death of her husband (1526) she acted as guardian for her son, Luis, whose interests she energetically defended, visiting Spain in order to urge his rights upon Charles V. She died at Santo Domingo (1549). She seems always to have been styled 'Vireina'. (Cp. Harrisse, *Christophe Colomb*, ii. 246 *et seq*.)

QUARTA VIAGE DE COLÓN

RELACION

2. Hecha por Diego Mendez, de algunos aconteci-mientos del último viage del Almirante Don Cristóbal Colon.

DIEGO MENDEZ, vecino de la ciudad de Santo Domingo de la Isla Española, hallándose en la villa de Valladolid, donde á la sazon estaba la Corte de SS. MM., otorgó testamento en seis dias del mes de Junio del año de mil quinientos treinta y seis, por testimonio de Fernan Perez, escribano de SS. MM., y su notario público en la su Corte y en todos los sus Reinos y Señoríos; siendo testigos al otorgamiento Diego de Arana, Juan Diez Miranda de la Cuadra, Martin de Orduña, Lucas Fernandez, Alonso de Angulo, Francísco de Hinojosa y Diego de Aguilar, todos criados de la Señora Vireina de las Indias. y entre otros capítulos del mencionado testamento hay uno que á la letra dice así.

Cláusula del testamento. Item: Los muy ilustres Señores, el Almirante D. Cristobal Colon, de gloriosa memoria, y su hijo el Almirante D. Diego Colon, y su nieto el Almirante D. Luis, á quien Dios dé largos dias de vida, y por ellos la Vireina

---

[4] Luis Columbus, third admiral and first duke of Veragua, was the son of Diego Columbus by María de Toledo. He was born in 1521 or 1522, and succeeded his father at the age of four or five, his mother acting as his guardian. The original grants made by Ferdinand and Isabella were commuted (1536), in accordance with the judgement of Cardinal Garcia de Loaysa, for an annual pension, an estate in Veragua, and the titles of admiral of the Indies and duke of Veragua: this arrangement was modified at a later date. Luis Columbus married (1542) María de Orozco; while she was still alive, he married María de Mosquera (1547). From 1540 to 1551 he was captain general of Española, where he showed complete incompetence. Returning to Spain, he became betrothed, during the lifetime of his other two wives, to Ana de Castro Osorio, with whom he went through a form of marriage (c. 1556), and was for this sentenced to detention in various fortresses for five years. He was condemned for polygamy and sentenced to ten years' exile, but having appealed, used his liberty to marry first Ana de Castro (1563) and then his mistress, Luisa de Carvajal (1565). His appeal failing, he was sent into exile at Oran (1565), where he died in 1572. He left two daughters by María de Mosquera, the elder of whom became a nun and the younger of whom, Felipa, married her cousin, Diego Columbus, duke of Veragua. (Cp. Harrisse, op. cit., ii. 251 et seq.)

tutor and guardian, are in debt to me on the ground of the many and great services which I have rendered to them, in which I have consumed and spent the greater part of my life, even to its close, in their service.

Especially did I serve the great admiral, Don Christopher, going with his lordship to the discovery of islands and Tierra Firme, in which service I many times put myself in danger of death in order to save his life and the lives of those who went and were with him. More particularly did I so, when we were shut up in the harbour of the Rio Belén or Yebra,[1] where we were owing to the force of the violent seas and winds which drove up and raised the sand in such quantities that they closed the entrance of the harbour.

His lordship being there in great affliction, there assembled a vast multitude of the Indians of the country, in order to come to burn our ships and to kill us all, under pretence, as they said, that they were going to attack other Indians, of the provinces of Cobrava and Aurira, with whom they were at war.[2] And although many of them passed by that harbour in which our ships were, no one in the fleet took notice of the matter, but I only. And I went to the admiral and said to him: ' My lord, these people who had passed by here say that they are going to join with those of Veragua to make war on those of Cobrava and Aurira. I do not believe it, but, on the contrary, I think that it is in order to burn the ships and to kill us all that they are joined together.' And such was the fact.

And when the admiral asked me how the danger might be prevented, I told his lordship that I would go with a boat and proceed along the coast towards Veragua, in order to see where they pitched their camp. I had not gone half a league when I found a thousand men of war with many provisions and stores, and I landed alone among them, leaving my boat afloat. And I spoke to them as well as I knew how, and offered to do battle with them with that armed boat. But they strongly refused this offer, saying that they had no need of it. And so I returned to the boat and was there all night in view of them, so that they saw that they could not go to the

---

[1] Cp. *supra*, p. 88 and note 1.
[2] Ferdinand Columbus (c. 95) and Las Casas (ii. 24) say that Bartholomew

QUARTA VIAGE DE COLÓN

mi Señora, como su tutriz y curadora, me son en cargo de
muchos y grandes servicios que yo les hice, en que consumí y
gasté todo lo mejor de mi vida hasta acaballa en su servicio ;
especialmente serví al gran Almirante D. Cristóbal andando
con su Señoria descubriendo Islas y Tierra firme, en que puse
muchas veces mi persona á péligro de muerte por salvar su
vida y de los que con él iban y estaban ; mayormente cuando
se nos cerró el puerto del rio de Belen ó Yebra donde estábamos con la fuerza de las tempestades de la mar y de los
vientos que acarrearon y amontonaron la arena en cantidad
con que cegaron la entrada del puerto. y estando su Señoria
allí muy congojado, juntóse gran multitud de Indios de la
tierra para venir á quemarnos los navíos y matarnos á todos,
con color que decian que iban á hacer guerra a otros Indios de
las provincias de Cobrava Aurira con quien tenian guerra : y
como pasaron muchos dellos por aquel puerto en que teniamos nosotros las naos, ninguno de la armada caia en el negocio
sino yo, que fuí al Almirante y le dije: 'Señor, estas gentes
que por aquí han pasado en orden de guerra dicen que se
han de juntar con los de Veragoa para ir contra los de Cobrava
Aurira: yo no lo creo sino el contrario, y es que se juntan para
quemarnos los navíos y matarnos á todos,' como de hecho lo
era. y diciéndome el Almirante cómo se remediaria, yo dije á
su Señoría que saldria con una barca é iría por la costa hácia
Veragoa, para ver donde asentaban el real. Y no hube andado
media legua cuando hallé al pie de mil hombres de guerra con
muchas vituallas y brevages, y salté en tierra solo entre ellos,
dejando mi barca puesta en flota : y hablé con ellos segun pude
entender, y ofrecíme que queria ir con ellos á la guerra con
aquella barca armada, y ellos se escusaron reciamente diciendo
que no le habian menester : y como yo me volviese á la barca
y estuviese allí á vista dellos toda la noche, vieron que no
podian ir á las naos para quemallas y destruillas, segun tenian
acordado, sin que yo lo viese, y mudaron propósito : y aquella

Columbus, on the second expedition on which he was sent out from Belén,
reached a river called Aurira and a district which was called Cobraba (Zobraba,
in Ferdinand Columbus). It seems to be obvious that it is of this river and
district that Diego Mendez is speaking, and the appearance of the plural
'provincias' suggests that a 'y' has slipped out in the text. 'And' has therefore
been inserted twice in the translation.

ships to burn and destroy them, as they had intended, without my seeing them. And they changed their purpose and that night they all went to Veragua, and I returned to the ships and gave an account of all to his lordship, and he did not think it a small matter.

And when he talked over this matter with me and discussed how the intention of these people might be more clearly known, I offered to go there with a single companion, and I undertook this task, being more certain of death than of life. And having journeyed along the beach as far as the river of Veragua, I found two canoes of strange Indians who related to me in great detail how those people were gone to burn the ships and to kill us all, and that they had abandoned their intention owing to a boat which came upon them there, and that they still designed to return to do this after two days. And I asked them to take me in their canoes up the river and offered payment to them for this, and they refused, warning me that on no account should I go, since it was certain that if we went, they would kill both me and the companion whom I had with me.

And despite their advice, I brought it about that they should take me in their canoes up the river as far as the villages of the Indians, who were all drawn up in battle array and who did not wish me to go to the chief residence of their cacique. I pretended that I was going to him as a surgeon to cure him of a wound which he had in one leg, and in return for the gifts which I made to them, they allowed me to go to the royal residence. It was on the top of a level hill, with a large open space about it, surrounded by the heads of three hundred dead whom they had killed in a battle.

As I crossed the whole open space and approached the royal house, there was a great uproar among the women and children who were at the gate, and they went screaming into the palace. Out of it came a son of the chief, very enraged, uttering angry words in his own language, and laying hands on me, he sent me with one push far from him. When, in order to appease him, I said that I was come to cure his father's leg and showed an ointment which I carried for this purpose, he replied that on no account was I to go in where his

noche se volvieron todos á Veragoa, y yo me volví á las naos y hice relacion de todo á su Señoría, é no lo tuvo en poco. y platicando conmigo sobrello sobre que manera se ternia para saber claramente el intento de aquella gente, yo me ofrecí de ir allá con un solo compañero, y lo puse por obra, yendo mas cierto de la muerte que de la vida: y habiendo caminado por la playa hasta el rio de Veragoa hallé dos canoas de Indios extrangeros que me contaron muy á la clara como aquellas gentes iban para quemar las naos y matarnos á todos, y que lo dejaron de hacer por la barca que allí sobrevino, y questaban todavia de propósito de volver á hacello dende á dos dias, é yo les rogué que me llevasen en sus canoas el rio arriba, y que gelo pagaria; y ellos se escusaban aconsejándome que en ninguna manera fuese, porque fuese cierto que en llegando me matarian á mí y al compañero que llevaba. e sin embargo de sus consejos hice que me llevasen en sus canoas el rio arriba hasta llegar á los pueblos de los Indios, los cuales hallé todos puestos en orden de guerra, que no me querian dejar ir al asiento principal del Cacique; y yo fingiendo que le iba á curar como cirujano de una llaga que tenia en una pierna, y con dádivas que les dí me dejaron ir hasta el asiento Real, que estaba encima de un cerro llano con una plaza grande, rodeada de trescientas cabezas de muertos que habian ellos muerto en una batalla; y como yo hubiese pasado toda la plaza y llegado á la Casa Real hubo grande alboroto de mugeres y muchachos que estaban á la puerta, que entraron gritando dentro en el palacio. y salió de él un hijo del Señor muy enojado diciendo palabras recias en su lenguage, é puso las manos en mí y de un empellon me desvió muy lejos de sí: diciéndole yo por amansarle como iba á curar á su padre de la pierna, y mostrándole cierto unguento que para ello llevaba, dijo que en ninguna manera habia de entrar donde estaba su padre. y visto por mí que por aquella via no podia amansarle, saqué un peine y unas tijeras y un espejo, y hice que Escobar mi compañero me peinase y cortase el cabello. lo cual visto por él y por los que allí estaban quedaban espantados; y yo entonces hice que Escobar le peinase á él y le cortase el cabello con las tijeras, y díselas y el peine y el espejo, y con esto se amansó; y yo pedí que trajesen algo de comer, y

father was. And seeing that in that way I could not soothe him, I brought out a comb and a pair of scissors and a mirror, and caused my companion, Escobar,[1] to comb my hair and cut it. When he and those who were there saw this, they were amazed, and then I caused Escobar to comb his hair and cut it with the scissors, and I gave him the scissors and the comb and the mirror, and at that he was appeased. And I asked them to bring something to eat, and they brought it at once, and we ate and drank in love and good-fellowship, and became friends. I took my leave of him and came to the ships, and gave an account of all this to my lord admiral, who was no little pleased to learn all these facts and to know what had befallen me. And he commanded strict watch to be kept in the ships and in certain straw huts which we had built there on the shore with the intention that I should remain there with some people to examine and discover the secrets of the country.

On the morning of the next day, his lordship called me to take counsel with him as to what had best be done, and my opinion was that we should take that lord and all his captains, since when they were made prisoner, the common people would be subdued. And his lordship was of the same opinion, and I suggested the stratagem and plan by which this might be achieved, and his lordship ordered that the lord adelantado, his brother, and I with him should go with eighty men to carry the said plan into effect. And we went and the Lord gave us such good fortune that we took the cacique and most of his captains and wives and sons and grandsons, with all the chief men of his family. We sent them prisoners to the ships, but the cacique escaped from the man to whom he had been entrusted owing to his careless watch, a circumstance which afterwards did us much damage.[2]

At that moment, it pleased God that it should rain heavily, and owing to the flood which followed, the harbour was opened for us, and the admiral brought the ships out to sea in order to go to Castile, I remaining on land in order to stay there as contador of his highness, with seventy men, and there

---

[1] Rodrigo de Escobar, a sailor belonging to the *Vizcaya* (cp. Diego de Porras, Navarrete, i. 295).

luego lo trajeron, y comimos y bebimos en amor y compaña,
y quedamos amigos; y despedime dél y vine á las naos, y hice
relacion de todo esto al Almirante mi Señor, el cual no poco
holgó en saber todas estas circumstancias y cosas acaecidas
por mí; y mandó poner gran recabdo en las naos y en ciertas
casas de paja, que teniamos hechas allí en la playa con intencion que habia yo de quedar allí con cierta gente para calar
y saber los secretos de la tierra.

Otro dia de mañana su Señoría me llamó para tomar parecer conmigo de lo que sobre ello se debia hacer, y fue mi parecer que debiamos prender aquel Señor y todos sus Capitanes,
porque presos aquellos se sojuzgaria la gente menuda; y su
Señoria fue del mismo parecer: é yo di el ardid y la manera
con que se debia hacer, y su Señoría mandó que el Señor
Adelantado, su hermano, y yo con él fuesemos á poner en
efecto lo sobredicho con ochenta hombres. y fuimos, y dió-
nos Nuestro Señor tan buena dicha que prendimos el Cacique y los mas de sus Capitanes y mugeres y hijos y nietos con
todos los principales de su generacion; y enviándolos á las
naos ansí presos, soltóse el Cacique al que le llevaba por su
mal recabdo, el cual despues nos hizo mucho daño. en este
instante plugó á Dios que llovió mucho, y con la gran avenida
abriósenos el puerto, y el Almirante sacó los navíos á la mar
para venirse á Castilla, quedando yo en tierra para haber de
quedar en ella por Contador de su Alteza con setenta hombres,
y quedábame allí la mayor parte de los mantenimientos de
bizcocho y vino y aceite y vinagre.

Acabado de salir el Almirante á la mar, y quedando yo en
tierra con obra de veinte hombres porque los otros se habian
salido con el Almirante á despedir, subitamente sobrevino
sobre mi mucha gente de la tierra, que serian mas de cuatro-
cientos hombres armados con sus varas y flechas y tiraderos,

---

² For another version of this incident, cp. Ferdinand Columbus (c. 96) and
Las Casas (ii. 27). The cacique was Quibian. He was entrusted to Juan Sanchez
de Cádiz, chief pilot of the fleet and one of the crew of the flagship (cp. Diego de
Porras, Navarrete, i. 289). He joined in the conspiracy of Francisco de Porras
and Diego de Porras and was killed in a fight with Bartholomew Columbus and
his men (17 May 1504). (Cp. Ferdinand Columbus, c. 101; Las Casas, ii. 35.)

was left with me there the greater part of the supplies of biscuit and wine and oil and vinegar. Just as the admiral had got out to sea, and while I remained on land with some twenty men, for the rest had gone with the admiral to take leave of him, suddenly there came upon me many natives, so that there were more than four hundred men armed with bows and arrows and slings. They spread across the mountain opposite, and they gave a shriek and then another and again another, and, thanks be to God, they thus gave me time to prepare for the battle and to make ready a defence against them. While I was on shore among the huts which had been built, and they were on the mountain at an arrow's flight's distance, they began to shoot their arrows and to hurl their darts as if they were attacking a bull, and the arrows and missiles were as thick as hailstones and continuous. Some of them separated from the rest to come to attack us with clubs, but none of them got back, for they were left there, with their arms and legs cut off with swords and dead. At this the rest took such fright that they fled, we having lost in the fight seven out of the twenty that we were, and of them there fell ten or nine of those who came most boldly against us. This fight lasted three full hours, and Our Lord gave us a miraculous victory, we being so few and they so very numerous.[1]

When this fight was over, there came from the ships captain Diego Tristan with the boats to go up the river in order to fetch water for their voyage. And although I advised him and warned him that he should not go up the river, he would not believe me, and against my will, he went up it with the two boats and twelve men. There those people came upon him and fought with him and slew him and all whom he had with him, so that one alone escaped by swimming and brought the news.[2] And they took the boats and broke them to pieces, as a result of which we were left in a great difficulty, for the admiral was at sea with his ships without boats while we were on land without means by which we could go to him. In addition to all this, the Indians did not cease to come to attack us, every moment sounding trumpets and small drums and making loud cries, believing that they had us at their

---

[1] For this fight, cp. Ferdinand Columbus (c. 97) and Las Casas (ii. 27).

y tendierónse por el monte en haz y dieron una grita y otra y
luego otra, con las cuales plugo á Dios me apercibieron á la pelea
y defensa de ellos: y estando yo en la playa entre los bohios que
tenia hechos, y ellos en el monte á trecho de tiro de dardo,
comenzaron á flechar y á garrochar como quien agarrocha
toro, y eran las flechas y tiraderas tantas y tan continuas
como granizo; y algunos dellos se desmandaban para venirnos á dar con las machadasnas; pero ninguno dellos volvian
porque quedaban allí cortados brazos y piernas y muertos á
espada: de lo cual cobraron tanto miedo que se retiraron atras,
habiéndonos muerto siete hombres en la pelea de veinte que
eramos, y de ellos murieron diez ó nueve de los que se venian
á nosotros mas arriscados. duró esta pelea tres horas grandes,
y Nuestro Señor nos dio la vitoria milagrosamente, siendo
nosotros tan poquitos y ellos tanta muchedumbre.

Acabada esta pelea vino de las naos el Capitan Diego
Tristan con las barcas para subir el rio arriba á tomar agua
para su viage; y no embargante que yo le aconsejé y amonesté
que no subiese el rio arriba no me quiso creer, y contra mi grado
subió con las dos barcas y doce hombres el rio arriba, donde le
toparon aquella gente y pelearon con él, y le mataron á él y
todos los que llavaba, que no escapó sino uno á nado que trujo la
nueva; y tomaron las barcas y hiciéronlas pedazos, de que quedamos en gran fatiga, ansí el Almirante en la mar con sus naos
sin barcas como nosotros en tierra sin tener con que poder ir á él.
y á todo esto no cesaban los Indios de venirnos á cometer cada
rato tañiendo bocinas y atabales, y dando alaridos pensando
que nos tenian vencidos. el remedio contra esta gente que
teniamos eran dos tiros falconetes de fruslera, muy buenos,
y mucha pólvora y pelotas con que los ojeábamos que no
osaban llegar á nosotros. y esto duró por espacio de cuatro

---

[2] For this incident, which occurred 6 April 1503, cp. Ferdinand Columbus
(*loc. cit.*) and Las Casas (*loc. cit.*). Diego Tristan was captain of the flagship.
The names of his companions may be gathered from Diego de Porras (cp.
Navarrete, i. 289–95). They were Alonso Ramón, mate of the *Gallega*; Pedro
Rodriguez and Pedro de Maya, sailors, Domingo Vizcaino, caulker, Mateo,
gunner, and Alonso, a servant, from the flagship; Juan Rodriguez and Juan
Reyanltes, sailors, Domingo Danara, caulker, and Juan de Noya, of Seville,
cooper, from the *Santiago*; and Julian Martín and Bartolomé Ramirez, sailors,
from the *Gallega*. The one to escape was Juan de Noya.

mercy. The defence which we had against these people con-
sisted in two very good brass falconets and much powder and
ball, with which we so terrified them that they did not dare to
come up to us.

This lasted for the space of four days, during which time I
caused many bags to be made from the sails of the one ship
which remained to us, and in them I placed all the biscuit
which we had. I then took two canoes and secured the one to
the other with sticks fastened across the tops, and in these I
loaded all the biscuit and the pipes of wine and oil and vinegar fastened with a rope, and towing them over the sea, when
it was calm, in seven journeys which they made, they brought
all to the ships, and the people who were with me they also
carried little by little. I remained with five men to the last,
when it was night, and in the last boatful I embarked. The
admiral thought highly of this, and was not content with
embracing me and kissing me on the cheeks, for having performed so great a service as I had done, but also asked that I
would take the command of the flagship and the control of all
the people and of the voyage, and this I accepted in order to
do service to him, it being, as it was, a matter of great labour.[1]

On the last day of April, in the year one thousand five
hundred and three, we left Veragua with three ships, intending to make our way back to Castile. And as the ships were
all pierced and eaten by worms, we could not keep them above
water. Having gone twenty leagues, we abandoned one, the
other two remaining to us being in a worse state than she was,
so that all the crews with the pumps and kettles and vessels
were not sufficient to draw off the water which came through
the worm holes. In this way, not without very great toil
and danger, intending to come to Castile, we navigated for
thirty-five days, and at the end of that time we reached the
island of Cuba at its lowest point, in the province of Homo,[2]
there where now is the town of la Trinidad.[3] Thus we were
three hundred leagues further from Castile than when we
left Veragua to go there, and, as I have said, the ships were
in a bad state, and could not be sailed, and our provisions

---

[1] This incident is described by Ferdinand Columbus (c. 99) and by Las Casas
(ii. 29).

dias, en los cuales yo hice cosar muchos costales de las velas
de una nao que nos quedaba, y en aquellos puse todo el bizcocho que teniamos, y tomé dos canoas y até la una con la
otra parejas, con unos palos atravesados por encima, y en
estos cargué el bizcocho todo en viages, y las pipas de vino y
azeite y vinagre atadas en una guindaleja y á jorno [*sic*,
jorro] por la mar, tirando por ellas las canoas, abonanzando
la mar, en siete caminos que hicieron lo llevaron todo á las
naos, y la gente que conmigo estaba poco á poco la llevaron, é
yo quedé con cinco hombres á la postre siendo de noche, y en
la postrera barcada me embarqué: lo cual el Almirante tuvo
á mucho, y no se hartaba de me abrazar y besar en los carrillos
por tan gran servicio como allí le hice, y me rogó tomase la
capitanía de la nao Capitana y el regimiento de toda la gente
y del viage, lo cual yo acepté por le hacer servicio en ello por
ser, como era, cosa de gran trabajo.

Postrero de Abril de mil quinientos y tres partimos de Veragoa con tres navíos, pensando venir la vuelta de Castilla: y
como los navíos estaban todos abujerados y comidos de gusanos no los podiamos tener sobre agua ; y andadas treinta
leguas dejamos el uno, quedándonos otros dos peor acondicio-
nados que aquel, que toda la gente no bastaba con las bombas
y calderas y vasijas á sacar el agua que se nos entraba por los
abujeros de la broma: y de esta manera, no sin grandísimo
trabajo y peligro, pensando venir á Castilla navegamos
treinta y cinco dias, y en cabo dellos llegamos á la isla de
Cuba á lo mas bajo della, á la provincia de Homo, allá donde
agora está el pueblo de la Trinidad ; de manera que estábamos
mas lejos de Castilla trescientas leguas que cuando partimos
de Veragoa para ir á ella ; y como digo los navíos mal acon-
dicionados, innavegables, y las vituallas que se nos acababan.
plugo á Dios Nuestro Señor que pudimos llegar á la isla de
Jamaica, donde zabordamos los dos navíos en tierra, y hicimos
de ellos dos casas pajizas, en que estabamos no sin gran peligro
de la gente de aquella isla, que no estaba domada ni con-

---

² Macaca (cp. *supra*, p. 94 and note 2).
³ On the south coast of Cuba, Trinidad was founded by Diego Velazquez (1514
or 1515), 'on a harbour, but a poor one' (cp. Las Casas, iii. 32).

almost exhausted. It pleased our Lord God that we should be able to reach the island of Jamaica, where we ran the two ships aground,[1] and made of them two houses, roofed with straw, in which we remained, not without great danger from the people of that island, who were not subdued or conquered, and who might set fire to our dwellings in the night, which they would have been easily able to do despite our greatest watchfulness.

There I had to give out the last ration of biscuit and wine. I took a sword in my hand and three men with me, and went inland into this island, because no one dared to go to seek food for the admiral and those who were with him. And it pleased God that I found people so gentle that they did me no ill, but were friendly to me and gave me food with good will. And in a village which is called Aguacadiba, I agreed with the Indians and their cacique that they should make cassava bread, and that they should hunt and fish and that of all the provisions they should give to the admiral a certain amount every day and that they should bring it to the ships, where there should be someone who would pay them in blue beads and combs and knives and hawks' bells and fish-hooks and other articles which we had brought for this purpose. And with this understanding, I sent one of the Christians whom I had with me to the admiral, in order that he might send some one who should have the charge of paying for those provisions and of seeing that they were supplied.[2]

And thence I went to another village which was three leagues from the first and I made the same agreement with the cacique and the Indians of that village, and I sent another Christian to the admiral in order that he might send there another person on the same mission. And from there I went on further and reached a great cacique who was called Huareo, in the place that is now called Melilla,[3] which was thirteen leagues from the ships. By him I was very well received, for he gave me abundance to eat, and commanded that all his vassals should in three days bring many provisions, which they laid before him, and I paid him for them in such manner that they were content. And I agreed with him

---

[1] The two ships were the flagship and the *Santiago de Palos*.

quistada, nos pusiesen fuego de noche, que fácilmente lo podian hacer por mas que nosotros velabamos.

Aquí acabé de dar la postrera racion de bizcocho y vino, y tomé una espada en la mano y tres hombres conmigo, y fuíme por esa isla adelante, porque ninguno osaba ir á buscar de comer para el Almirante y los que con él estaban: y plugo á Dios que hallaba la gente tan mansa que no me hacian mal, antes se holgaban conmigo y me daban de comer de buena voluntad. y en un pueblo que se llama Aguacadiba, concerté con los Indios y Cacique que harian pan cazabe, y que cazarian y pescarian, y que darian de todas las vituallas al Almirante cierta cuantía cada dia, y lo llevarian á las naos, con que estuviese allí persona que ge lo pagase en cuentas azules y peines y cuchillos y cascabeles y anzuelos y otros rescates que para ello llevabamos: y con esto concierto despaché uno de los dos cristianos que conmigo traía al Almirante, para que enviase persona que tuviese cargo de pagar aquellas vituallas y enviarlas.

Y de allí fuí á otro pueblo que estaba tres leguas de este y hice el mismo concierto con el Cacique y Indios, de él, y envié otro cristiano al Almirante para que enviase allí otra persona al mismo cargo.

Y de allí pasé adelante y llegué á un gran Cacique que se llamaba Huareo, donde agora dicen Melilla, que es trece leguas de las naos, del cual fuí muy bien recebido, que me dió muy bien de comer, y mandó que todos sus vasallos trajiesen dende á tres dias muchas vituallas, que le presentaron, é yo ge las pagué de manera que fueron contentos: y concerté que ordinariamente las traerian, habiendo allí persona que ge las pagase, y con este concierto envié el otro cristiano con los mantenimientos que allá me dieron al Almirante, y pedí al Cacique que me diese dos Indios que fuesen conmigo fasta el cabo de la isla, que el uno me llevaba la hamaca en que

---

[2] The negotiations with the native chiefs for supplies of food, described in the text, are unknown to Ferdinand Columbus (cp. c. 99) and to Las Casas (cp. ii. 30), who make the Indians give food of their natural goodness of heart and without being asked to do so.

[3] On the north coast of the island, fourteen leagues east of Sevilla (Herrera, *Descripción de las Indias Occidentales*, c. 7).

that they should bring them regularly, and that there should be someone who would there pay for them, and with this agreement I sent another Christian to the admiral. And I asked the cacique to give me two Indians who should go with me to the end of the island, in order that one might carry the hammock in which I slept and the other the food.

In this manner I journeyed as far as the eastern end of the island and I came to a cacique who was called Ameyro, with whom I entered into close friendship, giving him my name and taking his, which among them is regarded as a sign of great brotherhood. From him I bought a very good canoe which he had, and for it I gave him a very good brass helmet which I carried in a bag and a cloak and one of the two shirts which I had. In that canoe, with six Indians whom the cacique had given to me to aid in navigating, I embarked and went by sea, looking for the place which I had left.

When I reached the places whence I had sent the provisions, I found in them the Christians whom the admiral had sent, and I gave them charge of all the provisions which I had found for them, and I went myself to the admiral. By him I was very well received. He was not content with seeing me and embracing me, but asked concerning all that had occurred on the expedition, giving thanks to God Who had brought me back and Who had delivered me in safety from so savage a people. And as at the time when I reached the ships, there was not in them a crust to eat, all were very glad with my coming, for hunger was killing them in a time of so great need. And after that time henceforth every day came the Indians, laden with provisions, to the ships, from those places where I had made agreement, and there was enough for the two hundred and thirty persons who were with the admiral.

Ten days after this, the admiral called me aside and declared to me the great danger in which he was, speaking thus to me: 'Diego Mendez, my son; no one of all those whom I have here realizes the great peril in which we are, save only I and you. For we are very few and these savage Indians are many and very fickle and capricious, and at the moment when they have the fancy to come and burn us here where we are in these two ships, converted into houses with straw roofs,

dormia é el otro la comida. y desta manera caminé hasta el
cabo de la isla, á la parte del Oriente, y llegué á un Cacique
que se llamaba Ameyro, é hice con él amistades de hermandad,
y díle mi nombre y tomé el suyo, que entre ellos se tiene por
grande hermandad. y compréle una canoa muy buena que él
tenia, y díle por ella una bacineta de laton muy buena que
llevaba en la manga y el sayo y una camisa de dos que
llevaba, y embarquéme en aquella canoa, y vine por la mar
requiriendo las estancias que habia dejado con seis Indios que
el Cacique me dió para que me la ayudasen á navegar, y
venido á los lugares donde yo habia proveido, hallé en ellos los
cristianos que el Almirante habia enviado, y cargué de todas
las vituallas que les hallé, y fuime al Almirante, del cual fuí
muy bien recebido, que no se hartaba de verme y abrazarme,
y preguntarlo que me habia sucedido en el viage, dando gracias
á Dios que me habia llevado y traido á salvamiento libre de
tanta gente salvage. y como el tiempo que yo llegué á las naos
no habia en ellas un pan que comer, fueron todos muy alegres
con mi venida, porque les maté la hambre en tiempo de tanta
necesidad, y de allí adelante cada dia venian los Indios cargados de vituallas á las naos de aquellos lugares que yo
habia concertado, que bastaban para doscientas y treinta
personas que estaban con el Almirante. dende á diez dias
el Almirante me llamó á parte y me dijo el gran peligro en
que estaba, diciéndome ansi: 'Diego Mendez, hijo: ninguno
de cuantos aquí yo tengo siente el gran peligro en que estamos
sino yo y vos, porque somos muy poquitos, y estos indios
salvages son muchos y muy mudables y antojadizos, y en la
hora que se les antojare de venir y quemarnos aquí donde
estamos en estos dos navios hechos casas pajizas fácilmente
pueden echar fuego dende tierra y abrasarnos aquí á todos:
y el concierto que vos habeis hecho con ellos del traer los
mantenimientos que traen de tan buena gana, mañana se les
antojará otra cosa y no nos traerán nada, y nosotros no somos
parte para tomargelo per fuerza si no estar á lo que ellos
quisieren. yo he pensado un remedio si á vos os parece: que
en esta canoa que comprastes se aventurase alguno á pasar á
la Isla Española á comprar una nao en que pudiesen salir de
tan gran peligro como este en que estamos. decidme vuestro

they will easily be able to set fire to them from the land and consume us all here. And the agreement which you have made with them for bringing provisions, which they bring with such good will, may appear to-morrow to them to be disagreeable, and they may bring us nothing, and we are not in a position to take it from them by force, if it be not that which they wish. I have devised a remedy if you think it fitting, that in this canoe which you have bought, some one adventure to cross to the island of Española, to buy a ship in which it may be possible to escape from the very great danger in which we are. Tell me your opinion.'

I answered him: 'My Lord, I well see the danger in which we are, which is much greater than that which might be thought. The passage from this island to the island of Española in so small a vessel as the canoe, I regard not only as dangerous, but as impossible, for I know of no one who would dare to venture into so very obvious a danger as to attempt to cross a gulf of forty leagues of sea and among islands where the sea is very rough and rarely calm.'

His lordship did not agree with me, earnestly persuading me that I was the one who should do this, and to this I replied: 'My lord, I have many times put my life in danger to save yours and the lives of all those who are here, and Our Lord has miraculously preserved my life. Nevertheless there have not been wanting murmurers who have said that your lordship entrusts to me all honourable undertakings, there being in the company others who would perform them as well as I. And accordingly it seems to me that your lordship should call them all together and propound this business to them, in order to see if among them all there is any one who is willing to undertake it, which I doubt. And when they all hold back, I will expose my life to death for your service, as I have many times done.'

Immediately on the following day his lordship caused all to assemble before him and proposed the matter to them as he had done to me. And when they heard it, they were all silent, and some said that it was out of the question to discuss such a thing, since it was impossible in so small a vessel to cross so

parecer.' yo le respondí: 'Señor: el peligro en que estamos
bien lo veo, que es muy mayor de lo que se puede pensar.
el pasar desta Isla á la Isla Española en tan poca vasija como
es la canoa, no solamente lo tengo por dificultoso, sino por
imposible: porque haber de atravesar un golfo de cuarenta
leguas de mar y entre islas donde la mar es mas impetuosa
y de menos reposo, no sé quien se ose aventurar á peligro tan
notorio.' Su Señoría no me replicó, persuadiendome reciamente que yo era el que lo habia de hacer, á lo cual yo respondí: 'Señor: muchas veces he puesto mi vida á peligro de
muerte por salvar la vuestra y de todos estos que aqui estan,
y nuestro Señor milagrosamente me ha guardado y la vida;
y con todo no han faltado murmuradores que dicen que
vuestra Señoría me acomete á mí todas las cosas de honra,
habiendo en la compañía otros que las harian tan bien como
yo: y por tanto paréceme á mí que vuestra Señoría los haga
llamar á todos y los proponga este negocio, para ver si entre
todos ellos habrá alguno que lo quiera emprender, lo cual yo
dudo; y cuando todos se echen de fuera, yo pondré mi vida
á muerte por vuestro servicio, como muchas veces lo he hecho.
    Luego el dia siguiente su Señoría los hizo juntar á todos
delante sí, y les propuso el negocio de la manera que á mí: é
oido, todos enmudecieron, y algunos dijeron que era por demas
platicarse en semejante cosa, porque era imposible en tan
pequeña vasija pasar tan impetuoso y peligroso golfo de
cuarenta leguas como este, entre estas dos islas donde muy
recias naos se habian perdido andando á descubrir, sin poder
romper ni forzar el ímpetu y furia de las corrientes. entonces
yo me levanté y dije: 'Señor: una vida tengo no mas, yo la
quiero aventurar por servicio de vuestra Señoría y por el bien
de todos los que aquí estan, porque tengo esperanza en Dios
nuestro Señor que vista la intencion con que yo lo hago me
librará, como otras muchas veces lo ha hecho.' oida por el
Almirante mi determinacion levantóse y abrazóme y besóme
en el carrillo, diciendo: 'Bien sabia yo que no habia aquí
ninguno que osase tomar esta empresa sino vos: esperanza
tengo en Dios nuestro Señor saldreis della con vitoria como
de las otras que habeis emprendido.'
    El dia siguiente yo puse mi canoa á monte, y le eché una

rough and dangerous a gulf of forty leagues, such as this, between two islands where very strong ships had been lost in
going to make discoveries, without being able to break or to
resist the force and fury of the currents.[1]

Then I rose and said: 'My lord, I have no more than one
life. I am ready to adventure it for the service of your lordship and for the good of all those who are here, since I have
hope in our Lord God that, being witness of the motive from
which I act, He will deliver me, as He has many times delivered me.' When the admiral heard my resolution, he rose
and embraced me and kissed me on the cheek, saying: 'Well
did I know that there was here no one save yourself who
would dare to undertake this enterprise. I have hope in our
Lord God that you will issue from it victoriously, as you
have issued from the other enterprises which you have undertaken.'

On the following day I drew my canoe on shore, and fixed
a false keel to it, and pitched and greased it, and I nailed
some boards on the stern and bow as a defence against the
sea that it might not come in as it might come owing to the
low freeboard. And I put up a mast and sail, and laid in the
supplies necessary for me and for one Christian and for six
Indians, for we were eight persons, and the canoe would not
carry more. And I took my leave of his lordship and of them
all, and went up the coast of the island of Jamaica where we
were, there being from the place where the ships were to the
end of the island thirty-five leagues. This distance I navigated with great danger and toil, for on the journey I was
made prisoner by Indians, sea raiders, from whom God
miraculously delivered me.

Having reached the end of the island, while waiting there
for the sea to grow calm in order to continue my voyage,
many Indians gathered together and resolved to kill me and
to take the canoe and that which was in it, and being so
gathered together, they cast lots for my life, to see to which of
them would fall the execution of their design. When I became
aware of this, I went secretly to my canoe which I had three
leagues from there, and set sail and came to where the admiral
was, it being fifteen days since I had left there. I told him all

quilla postiza, y le dí su brea y sebo, y en la popa y proa cla-
véle algunas tablas para defensa de la mar que no se me entrase como hiciera siendo rasa; y púsele un mástil y su vela,
y metí los mantenimientos que pude para mí y para un cristiano y para seis indios, que éramos ocho personas, y no
cabian mas en la canoa: y despedíme de su Señoría y de todos,
y fuime la costa arriba de la Isla de Jamaica, donde estábamos, que hay dende las naos hasta el cabo della treinta y
cinco leguas, las cuales yo navegué con gran peligro y
trabajo, porque fuí preso en el camino de Indios salteadores
en la mar, de que Dios me libró milagrosamente. y llegado
al cabo de la isla, estando esperando que la mar se amansase
para acometer mi viage, juntáronse muchos Indios y determinaron de matarme y tomar la canoa y lo que en ella llevaba;
y así juntos jugaron mi vida á la pelota para ver á cual dellos
cabria la ejecucion del negocio. lo cual sentido por mí víneme
ascondidamente á mi canoa, que tenia tres leguas de allí, y
hícime á la vela y víneme donde estaba el Almirante, habiendo quince dias que de allí habia partido: y contele todo lo
sucedido, cómo Dios milagrosamente me habia librado de las
manos de aquellos salvages. su Señoría fue muy alegre de mi
venida, y preguntóme si volveria al viage. yo dije que sí,
llevando gente que estuviese conmigo en el cabo de la isla
hasta que yo entrase en la mar á proseguir mi viage. su
Señoría me dió setenta hombres y con ellos á su hermano el
Adelantado, que fuesen y estuviesen conmigo hasta embar-
carme, y tres dias despues. y desta manera volví al cabo de
la isla donde estuve cuatro dias. viendo que la mar se aman-
saba me despedí dellos y ellos de mí, con hartas lágrimas;
y encomendéme á Dios y á nuestra Señora del Antigua, y
navegué cinco dias y cuatro noches que jamas perdí el remo
de la mano gobernando la canoa y los compañeros remando.
plugo á Dios nuestro Señor que en cabo de cinco dias yo
arribé á la Isla Española, al Cabo de S. Miguel, habiendo dos
dias que no comiamos ni bebiamos por no tenello; y entré

---

[1] For the perils of navigation in the seas round Española, cp. Oviedo (I.,
especially c. 27).

that had happened, how God had miraculously delivered me out of the hands of those savages.[1]

His lordship was very joyful at my arrival and asked me if I would again set out on my voyage. I said that I would if I might take some men who should remain with me at the end of the island until I put out to sea to prosecute my voyage. His lordship gave me seventy men and with them his brother, the adelantado, who were to go and to remain with me until I embarked and to wait for three days afterwards. And in this way I went back to the end of the island where I remained four days.[2]

Finding that the sea became calm, I took my leave of them and they of me, with many tears, and I commended myself to God and to Our Lady of Antigua, and I navigated for five days and four nights without leaving hold of the oar, steering the canoe, while my companions rowed. It pleased Our Lord God that at the end of five days, I should reach the island of Española at cape San Miguel,[3] there having been two days during which we had neither eaten nor drunk, our provisions being exhausted.

I beached my canoe on a very beautiful part of the coast, where there came at once many people of the land and they brought with them many eatables, and there I remained for two days resting. I took six Indians from there, leaving those whom I had brought, and began to navigate along the coast of the island of Española. It was a hundred and thirty leagues from there to the city of Santo Domingo, to which place I had to go, since the governor who was the comendador de Lares was there.

Having gone for eighty leagues along the coast of the island, not without great dangers and labour, because the island was not conquered or pacified, I reached the province of Azoa,[4] which is twenty-four leagues from Santo Domingo. There I learned from the comendador Gallego[5] that the governor had gone to the province of Xaragua to pacify it; that province was fifty leagues from there. When I heard this, I left my canoe and made my way by land to Xaragua, where I found the governor.

[1] Ferdinand Columbus (c. 100) and Las Casas (ii. 30) know nothing of this initial attempt of Diego Mendez.

con mi canoa en una ribera muy hermosa, donde luego vino mucha gente de la tierra y trajeron muchas cosas de comer, y estuve allí dos dias descansando. yo tomé seis Indios de allí, dejados los que llevaba, y comencé á navegar por la costa de la Isla Española, que hay dende allí hasta la Cibdad de Santo Domingo ciento y treinta leguas que yo habia de andar, porque estaba allí el Gobernador, que era el Comendador de Lares; y habiendo andado por la costa de la isla ochenta leguas, no sin grandes peligros y trabajos, porque la isla no estaba conquistada ni allanada, llegué á la Provincia de Azoa, que es veinte y cuatro leguas antes de Santo Domingo, y allí supe del Comendador Gallego como el Gobernador era partido á la Provincia de Xuragoa á allanarla; la cual estaba cincuenta leguas de allí. y esto sabido dejé mi canoa y tomé el camino por tierra de Xuragoa, donde hallé el Gobernador, el cual me detuvo allí siete meses hasta que hizo quemar y ahorcar ochenta y cuatro Caciques, señores de vasallos, y con ellos á Nacaona la mayor señora de la isla, á quien todos ellos obedecian y servian. y esto acabado vine de pie á tíerra de Santo Domingo, que era setenta leguas de allí, y estuve esperando viniesen naos de Castilla, que habia mas de un año que no habian venido. y en este comedio plugo á Dios que vinieron tres naos, de las cuales yo compré la una y la cargué de vituallas, de pan y vino y carne y puercos y carneros y

---

² The account of the voyage of Diego Mendez, given by Ferdinand Columbus (c. 100, 103, 108) and Las Casas (ii. 30, 31, 33, 34, 36), who are in agreement, differs in some material respects from that given by Mendez himself. According to their version, Diego Mendez was accompanied by the Genoese gentleman, Bartolomé Fresco (q.v. *supra*, p. 72, note 2); each had a canoe, with six Spaniards and ten Indian rowers. Mendez was to go to Santo Domingo, inform Ovando of the situation of Columbus, and then to proceed to Spain. Fresco, having seen the safe arrival of Mendez in Española, was to return with the news to Jamaica. Nothing is known of the history of Fresco and of the twelve Spaniards after their arrival in Española; it does not appear that they attempted the return journey to Jamaica.

³ Cape Tiburon, the south-west point of the island.

⁴ Azua la Compostella, founded by order of Ovando; it was on the south coast of the island. Azua was the name of the native village; the epithet 'la Compostella' was doubtless due to the fact that its actual founder was a comendador who was a Gallego (cp. Las Casas, ii. 18; Oviedo, iii. 12; Herrera, *Historia General*, I. 6. iv.).

⁵ This man was the founder of Azua.

He detained me there for seven months, until he had burned and hanged eighty-four caciques, lords of vassals, and with them Nacaona, the greatest lady of the island, whom all those obeyed and served.[1] And when this had been accomplished, I went on foot to the district of Santo Domingo, which was seventy leagues from there, and I remained there expecting ships to come from Castile, since it was more than a year since any had come. And in this interval, it pleased God that three ships should come, of which I bought one and loaded her with provisions, with bread and wine and flesh and pigs and sheep and fruits, and sent her to where the admiral was in order that he might come in her with all the people, so that they might reach Santo Domingo from there and thence go to Castile. And I myself went forward in the other two ships to give an account to the king and queen of all that had occurred on that voyage.

It appears to me that it will be well that I should say something of that which befel the admiral and his company during the year that they remained lost in that island. A few days after I had departed, the Indians became disaffected and would not bring food as before. He caused all the caciques to be summoned and told them that he marvelled that they should not bring food as they had been accustomed to do, knowing that, as he had told them, he had come there by the command of God and that God was offended with them and that on that very night He would show this to them by signs which He would cause to appear in the heavens. And as on that night there was an almost total eclipse of the moon, he told them that God did this from anger with them because they did not bring food. They believed him and were very terrified, and they promised that they would always bring him food.[2] And in fact they did so, until the ship arrived with the supplies which I sent, at which the admiral and all those who were with him felt no small joy. For afterwards in Castile his lordship told me that in all his life he had never seen so joyful a day, and that he had never thought that he would leave that place alive. And in this ship he embarked and came to Santo Domingo and thence to Castile.[3]

---

[1] Anacaona. She was the sister of Behechio, cacique of Xaragua, and widow

frutas, y la envié adonde estaba el Almirante para en que
viniesen él y toda la gente como vinieron allí á Santo Domingo
y de allí á Castilla. e yo me vine delante en las otras dos naos
á hacer relacion al Rey y á la Reina de todo lo sucedido en
aquel viage.

Paraceme que será bien que se diga algo de lo acaecido al
Almirante y á su familiar en un año que estuvieron perdidos
en aquesta isla: y es que dende á pocos dias que yo me partí
los Indios se amotinaron y no le querian traer de comer como
antes; y él los hizo llamar á todos los Caciques y les digo que
se maravillaba dellos en no traerle la comida como solian,
sabiendo como él les habia dicho, que habia venido allí por
mandado de Dios, y que Dios estaba enojado dellos, y que él
ge lo mostraria aquella noche por señales que haria en el cielo;
y como aquella noche era el eclipse de la luna que casi toda se
escurecío, díjoles que Dios hacia aquello por enojo que tenia
dellos porque no le traian de comer, y ellos lo creyeron y
fueron muy espantados, y prometieron que le traerian siempre de comer, como de hecho lo hicieron, hasta que llegó la
nao con los mantenimentos que yo envié, de que no pequeño
gozo fue en el Almirante y en todos los que con él estaban:
que despues en Castilla me dijo su Señoría que en toda su vida
[nunca?] habia visto tan alegre dia, y que nunca pensó salir
de allí vivo: y en esta nao se embarcó y vino á Santo Domingo
y de allí á Castilla.

of Caonabo (cp. *supra*, vol. I, p. 48, note). After the death of her husband and of
her brother, she governed Xaragua: her court excited the admiration of the
Spaniards (cp. Las Casas, i. 114; Peter Martyr, i. 5). For her execution, which is
said to have aroused the extreme anger of Isabella, cp. Las Casas (ii. 9) and Oviedo
(iii. 12). According to Las Casas, Anacaona was a woman of culture and talent, and
a pattern of virtue; according to Oviedo (v. 3), she was a pattern of vice. The
number of the caciques who perished with her is reduced to eighty by Las Casas
and to forty by Gomara (*Historia General de las Indias*, c. 32).

² For the story of the eclipse, cp. Ferdinand Columbus (c. 102) and Las Casas
(ii. 33).

³ During the interval between the departure of Diego Mendez and the arrival
of the ship in which Columbus left Jamaica, Ovando sent Diego de Escobar to
examine the situation and to carry some supplies to Columbus, an action which
has been regarded as indicative of carelessness concerning the fate of the admiral
and even of a wish to leave him to perish. Columbus was also faced at this time
by the rebellion of some of his men, led by Francisco and Diego de Porras (cp.
Ferdinand Columbus, c. 101–7; Las Casas, ii. 32–6).

I have wished to set forth here this brief summary of my labours and of my great and distinguished services. And they are such as never man did to a lord, nor will such be done henceforth in the world. And I do this to the end that my children may know it and that they may be animated to service, and that her ladyship[1] may know that she is obliged to give to them many rewards.

When his lordship came to the court, and was in Salamanca,[2] confined to his bed by gout, and I alone was in charge of his affairs, and endeavouring to secure the restitution of his estate and of his government for his son, Don Diego, I spoke thus to him: 'My lord, your lordship already knows how greatly I have served you and how much I have toiled night and day in your interest. I beseech your lordship to grant me some recompense for that which I have done.' And he answered me joyfully that I should ask and he would do it, since that was very reasonable. And then I told him my wish and asked that his lordship would grant me the office of alguacil mayor of the island of Española for my life. And his lordship answered that he did so with great good will, and that it was little in return for all the service that I had rendered to him. And he commanded me that I should tell this to the lord Don Diego, his son, and he was very glad that the grant of the said office had been made to me, and he said that if his father gave it to me with one hand, he gave it with both hands. And this promise holds good as much now as it did then.

When I had succeeded, not without great labour on my part, in bringing about the restitution of the government of the Indies to the admiral, Don Diego, my lord, his father being dead, I asked for the appointment to the said office. His lordship answered me that he had given it to the adelantado, his uncle, but that he would give me something else equivalent to it. I said that he should give that to his uncle, and that he should give to me that which his father and he had promised to me, the which he did not do. And I was left burdened with services without any reward, and the lord

---

[1] María de Toledo.

He querido poner aquí esta breve suma de mis trabajos y grandes señalados servicios, cuales nunca hizo hombre á Señor, ni los hará de aquí adelante del mundo ; y esto á fin que mis hijos lo sepan y se animen á servir, é su Señoría sepa que es obligado á hacerles muchas mercedes.

Venido su Señoría á la Corte, y estando en Salamanca en la cama enfermo de gota, andando yo solo entendiendo en sus negocios y en la restitucion de su estado y de la gobernacion para su hijo D. Diego, yo le dije ansi: 'Señor: ya vuestra Señoría sabe lo mucho que os he servido y lo mas que trabajo de noche y de dia en vuestros negocios: suplico á vuestra Señoría me señale algun galardon para en pago dello ': y él me respondió alegremente que yo lo señalase y él lo cumpliria, porque era mucha razon. y entonces yo le señalé y supliqué á su Señoría me hiciese merced del oficio del Alguacilazgo mayor de la Isla Española para en toda mi vida: y su Señoría dijo que de muy buena voluntad, y que era poco para lo mucho que yo habia servido ; y mandóme que lo dijese ansi al Sr. D. Diego, su hijo, el cual fue muy alegre de la merced á mí hecha de dicho oficio, y dijo que si su padre me lo daba con una mano, él con dos. y esto es ansi la verdad para el siglo que á ellos tiene y á mi espera.

Habiendo yo acabado, no sin grandes trabajos mios, de negociar la restitucion de la gobernacion de las Indias al Almirante D. Diego, mi Señor, siendo su padre fallecido, le pedí la provision del dicho oficio. su Señoria me respondió que lo tenia dado al Adelantado su tio ; pero que él me daria otra cosa equivalente á aquella. yo dije que aquella diese él á su tio, y á mi me diese lo que su padre y él me habian prometido, lo cual no se hizo ; y yo quedé cargado de servicios sin ningun galardon, y el Sr. Adelantado, sin haberlo servido, quedó con mi oficio y con el galardon de todos mis afanes.

---

[2] Columbus eventually left Jamaica, 28 June 1504. He landed at Santo Domingo, 13 August; sailed for Spain, 12 September, and reached San Lucar, 7 November. After the death of Isabella (26 November), Columbus was at Seville (Feb. 1505), and then followed the king, being at Segovia in May, where he probably remained until 6 October, in order to follow Ferdinand to Salamanca, where the king arrived at the end of the month. In March 1506 the court moved to Valladolid, and it was in that town that Columbus died, 20 May 1506.

adelantado, without having done service, was left with my office and with the reward of all my exertions.

When his lordship arrived at the city of Santo Domingo and assumed the reins as governor, he gave this office to Francisco de Garay,[1] a servant of the lord adelantado, on whose behalf it was to be held. This was on the tenth of July in the year one thousand five hundred and ten. The office was then worth at the least a *conto* a year, and for this my lady, the Vicereine, as tutor and guardian of my lord, the Viceroy, and he are truly chargeable to me and they owe it to me in justice and on the score of conscience. For the grant of the post was made to me, and nothing has been done to compensate me from the day on which it was given to the adelantado down to the last day of my life, for if it had been given to me, I should have been the richest man in the island and the most honoured, and because it was not given to me, I am the poorest in it, so much so that I have no house in which I may live without rent.

And as it would be very difficult to pay me that which the office has produced in revenue, I wish to put forward a compromise and it is this, that her ladyship grant the office of alguacil mayor of the city of Santo Domingo to one of my sons for life, and to the other grant the office of lieutenant of the admiral in the said city. By the grant of these two offices to my sons in the manner that I have said, and by placing them in charge of someone who may hold them on their behalf until they come of age, her ladyship will discharge the conscience of the admiral, her father, and I shall regard myself as satisfied in respect of the pay due to me for my services. And on this I will not say more than that I leave it to the consciences of their lordships, and let them do in the matter that which they think best.

Item: I leave as my trustees and as executors of this my testament, here in the court, the bachiller Estrada and Diego de Arana, jointly with the Vicereine, my lady, and I ask her ladyship to accept this charge and I command them that they do likewise.

Another clause. Item: I command that my trustees buy a great stone, the best that they can find, and set it above my

Llegado su Señoría á la Cibdad de Santo Domingo por Gobernador tomó las varas dió este oficio á Francisco de Garay, criado del Sr. Adelantado, que lo sirviese por él. esto fue en diez dias del mes de Julio de mil quinientas diez años. valia entonces el oficio á lo menos un cuento de renta, del cual la Vireina, mi Señora, como tutriz y curadora del Virey, mi Señor, y él me son en cargo realmente y me lo deben de justicia y *de foro conscientiae*, porque me fue hecha la merced de él, y no se cumplió conmigo dende el dia que se dió al Adelantado hasta el postrero de mis dias, porque si se me diera yo fuera el mas rico hombre de la isla y mas honrado; y por no se me dar soy el mas pobre della, tanto que no tengo una casa en que more sin alquiler.

Y porque haberseme de pagar lo que el oficio ha rentado seria muy dificultoso, yo quiero dar un medio y será este: que su Señoría haga merced de Alguacilazgo mayor de la Cibdad de Santo Domingo á uno de mis hijos para en toda su vida, y al otro le haga merced de su Teniente de Almirante en la dicha Cibdad: y con hacer merced destos dos oficios á mis hijos de la manera que he aquí dicho, y poniéndolos en cabeza de quien los serva por ellos hasta que sean de edad, su Señoría descargará la conciencia del Almirante su padre, y yo me satisfaré de la paga que se me debe de mis servicios: y en esto no diré mas de dejallo en sus conciencias de sus Señorías, y hagan en ello lo que mejor les pareciere.

Item: Dejo por mis albaceas y ejecutores deste mi testamento, aquí en la corte, al Bachiller Estrada y á Diego de Arana, juntamente con la Vireina, mi Señora, y suplico yo á su Señoría lo acepte y les mande á ellos lo mismo.

Otra cláusula. Item: Mando que mis albaceas compren una piedra grande, la mejor que hallaren, y se ponga sobre mi sepultura, y se escriba en derredor della estas letras: 'Aquí yace el honrado caballero Diego Mendez que sirvió mucho á la Corona Real de España en el descubrimiento y conquista de las Indias con el Almirante D. Cristobal Colon, de gloriosa

---

[1] According to Oviedo (iii. 10) this Francisco de Garay built at Santo Domingo the first stone house in the Indies.

tomb, and that around the edge of it there be written these words : 'Here lies the honourable gentleman, Diego. Mendez, who greatly served the royal crown of Spain in the discovery and conquest of the Indies with the admiral, Don Christopher Columbus, of glorious memory, who discovered them, and afterwards by himself with his own ships at his own cost. He died, &c. I beg of your charity a Paternoster and an Ave Maria.'

Item: In the middle of the said stone, let there be carved a canoe, which is a hollowed tree in which the Indians navigate, for in such a one I navigated three hundred leagues, and above it let them set just the letters which read, 'Canoa'.

My dear and beloved sons, born of my very dear and beloved wife, Doña Francisca de Ribera, the blessing of God Almighty, the Father, the Son, and the Holy Ghost, and my blessing, descend upon you and encompass you, and make you Catholic Christians and give you grace that you may ever love and fear Him. Sons ; I earnestly desire you to keep peace and concord and that you be very obliging and not proud, but very humble and courteous towards all with whom you have to do, that all may feel love towards you. Serve loyally the admiral, my lord, and may his lordship make you great rewards, being that which he is, and because my great services merit it. And above all, I command you, my sons, that you be very devout and hear very devoutly the divine offices, and so doing, may Our Lord God grant you long life. May it please Him, of His infinite goodness, to make you as good men as I desire that you may be and may He guide you always with His hand. Amen.

The books which I send you from here are the following:

The Art of Well-Dying of Erasmus.
A sermon of Erasmus in Castilian.
Josephus, *De Bello Judiaco.*
The Moral Philosophy of Aristotle.
The books which are called *Lingua Erasmi.*
The Book of the Holy Land.
The Colloquies of Erasmus.
A treatise on the Complaints of Peace.

memoria, que las descubrió, y despues por sí con naos suyas á su costa: falleció, &c. pido de limosna un Pater noster y una Ave María.'

Item: En medio de la dicha piedra se haga una canoa, que es un madero cavado en que los Indios navegan, porque en otra tal navegó trescientas leguas, y encima pongan unas letras que digan: 'Canoa'.

Caros y amados hijos mios, y de mi muy cara y amada muger Doña Francisca de Ribera, la bendicion de Dios Todopoderoso, Padre y Hijo y Espíritu Santo y la mia descienda sobre vos y vos cubra y os haga catolicos cristianos, y os dé gracia que siempre le ameis y temais. hijos: encomiendoos mucho la paz y concordia, y que seais muy conformes y no soberbios, sino muy humildes y muy amigables á todos los que contratáredes, porque todos os tengan amor: servid lealmente al Almirante mi Señor, y su Señoría os hará muchas mercedes por quien él es, y porque mis grandes servicios lo merecen; y sobre todo os mando, hijos mios, seais muy devotos y oyais muy devotamente los Oficios Divinos, y haciéndolo ansi Dios nuestro Señor os dará largos dias de vida. a él plega por su infinita bondad haceros tan buenos como yo deseo que seais, y os tenga siempre de su mano. Amen.

Los libros que de acá os envio son los siguientes:

Arte de bien morir de Erasmo. un sermon de Erasmo en romance. Josefo de Bello Judaico. la Filosofía moral de Aristóteles. los libros que se dicen Lingua Erasmi. el libro de la Tierra santa. los coloquios de Erasmo. un tratado de las querellas de la Paz. un libro de Contemplaciones de la Pasion de nuestro Redentor. un tratado de le venganza de la muerte de Agamemnon, y otros tratadillos.

Ya dije, hijos mios, que estos libros os dejo por mayorazgo, con las condiciones que estan dichas de suso en el testamento, y quiero que vayan todos con algunas Escrituras mias, que se hallarán en el arca que está en Sevilla, que es de cedro, como ya está dicho: pongan tambien en esta el mortero de mármol que está en poder del Sr. D. Hernando, ó de su mayordomo.

Digo yo Diego Mendez que esta Escritura contenida en

A book of Contemplations on the Passion of our Redeemer. A treatise on the *Avenging of the death of Agamemnon.* And other small tracts.

My sons, I have already told you that these books I leave to you as heirlooms, under the conditions stated above in my testament, and I desire that they be placed with certain writings of mine, which will be found in the chest which is at Seville, which is of cedar, as has already been said. Let them also place in it the marble mortar which is in the possession of the lord Don Fernando[1] or of his majordomo.

I, Diego Mendez, declare that this document, contained in thirteen sheets, is my testament and last will, for I have ordained it and caused it to be written down, and I have signed it with my name, and by it I revoke and annul any other wills whatsoever made by me at whatsoever time and place, and I wish that this only be valid, which is made in the town of Valladolid on the nineteenth day of the month of June, in the year of Our Redeemer one thousand five hundred and thirty-six. Diego Mendez.

And I, the said Garcia de Vera, clerk and notary public, was present at all which has been herein said, wherein I am mentioned, and by order of the said lord, the lieutenant, and by request of the said bachiller Estrada, this testament in these twenty-six leaves of paper, a complete document, as here appears, I have caused to be copied as it was presented and laid before me, and as it originally was left in my possession. And accordingly I here affix this my seal (*here it was sealed*) in witness of the truth. Garcia de Vera. (*Signed.*)

---

[1] Ferdinand Columbus.

trece hojas es mi testamento y postrimera voluntad, porque yo lo ordené é hice escribir, y lo firmé de mi nombre, y por él revoco y doy por ningunos otros cualesquier testamentos hechos en cualesquier otros tiempos ó lugar; y solo este quiero que valga, que es hecho en la villa de Valladolid en diez y nueve dias del mes de Junio, año de nuestro Redentor de mil quinientos treinta y seis años. Diego Mendez. e yo el dicho García de Vera, Escribano Notario público, presente fui á todo lo que dicho es, que de mi se hace mencion, é por mandado del dicho Sr. Teniente é pedimento del dicho Bachiller Estrada, este testamento en estas veinte é seis hojas de papel, pliego entero, como aquí parece, fice escrebir como ante mí se presentó é abrió, é ansi queda originalmente en mi poder. e por ende fice aquí este mi signo tal en (*está signado*) testimonio de verdad. García de Vera. (*Está firmado.*)

INDEX

Augustine, St., bishop of Hippo, authority of, opposed to assertions of Columbus, xvi, liv, lviii, lx; on antipodes lxix, lxxviii; on relation of land to water, 42 and n.

Aurea, the, 104.

Avenruyz, *see* **Averroes.**

Averroes, of Córdoba (Avenruyz), Moorish philosopher, lxxx; on distance from Spain to Indies, 40 and n.

Azores, islands, lxviii, lxxxiii; change of temperature westward of, 10, 26 and n., 30 and n.; boundary fixed beyond, 108.

Azoa, *see* **Azua la Compostella.**

Azua, *see* **Puerto Hermoso.**

Azua la Compostella (Azoa), Diego Mendez reached, 132 and n.

Bacon, Roger, on unknown quadrants of land beyond the seas, lxxviii; views of, supported by d'Ailly, lxxix, lxxx; on extension of India, lxxx; on Aepagan's degree, lxxxi.

Ballena, Golfo de la, *see* **Paria**, Gulf of.

Barcelona, Capitulations of Santa Fé confirmed at, 54 n.

Barra, 100 and n.

Barranco, Diego Martin, 72 n.

Barros, João de, on literacy of Columbus, lxxii.

Basil, St., lxxxi.

Bastimentos, *see* **Nombre de Dios.**

Bear, Lesser, lxxxii.

Beata, island, position of, 76 n.

Behaim, globe of, lxxx.

Behechio, cacique, 134 n.

Bede, on situation of Earthly Paradise, 36 and n.

Begare, 100 and n.

Belem, Rio (Belén, Betlen, Santa Maria de Belen), 86 n.; Columbus shut up in harbour of, 88 n.; native names for (Yrebra, etc.), *ibid.*; *Gallega* abandoned at, 94 and n.; course taken by Columbus from, 94 n.; Diego Mendez on his services to Columbus at, 114; Bartholomew Columbus sent on expedition from, 114 n.

Belén, Rio, *see* **Belem**, Rio.

Belpuerto, *see* **Puerto Bello.**

Beragna, *see* **Veragua.**

Beragua, *see* **Veragua.**

'Bermuda', the, ship, *see* **'Santiago de Palos'.**

Bernáldez, Andres, cura of Los Palacios, xxvi, lvii, lxxxii, 2 n., 64 n., kindness of, to Columbus, lxii; 'book' alluded to by, lxvii.

Berwick y de Alba, Duque de, lxxxviii.

Berwick y de Alba, Duquesa de, lxxxviii.

Betlen, Rio, *see* **Belem**, Rio.

Blanco, Cape, 32 n.

Bobadilla, Francisco de, Columbus refused to acknowledge, xxiv; grievances of Columbus against, xxxi; arrested Columbus, xl.; released Guevara, 54 n.; account of, 56 n.; arrived at Santo Domingo, 56; actions of, 56 and n., 64; new light on relations between Columbus and, 56 n.; royal letter sent to Columbus by, *ibid.*; fuller royal letters produced by, 58 n.; malicious character of, 64; Columbus possibly intended to arm natives against, 64 n.; Santo Domingo handed over to, *ibid.*; plans of Columbus at time of arrival of, *ibid.*; no evidence that he possessed the knowledge Columbus claimed for him, 66 n.; discretion of, 68; Ovando sent to replace, 74 n.; death of, *ibid.*

Bocas, I. de las, *see* **Pozas**, I. de las.

Bonaca (Guanaja), island, Columbus reached, 76 n.

Boto, Cabo, named by Columbus, 18 n.

Brasil, Puerto del, *see* **Puerto del Brasil.**

Brazil, wood, found in Española, 6 and n.

Brazil, coast of, reached by Pinzón, 52 n.

Bueno, Puerto, 96 n.

Buil (Benil, Boil, Boyl, Bruil, Buyl), Fray, lxi, 4 n.

Burgos, Bishop of, *see* **Fonseca**, Juan de.

Burgos, Laws of, lxv.

Caonabo, cacique, xxix, 134 n.

Cabrera, Diego Martin de la, 94 n.

Cabrero, Juan, Columbus on assistance he received from, lxx.

Cabresse Point, height and identification of, 18 n.

Cadiz, Columbus left, on fourth voyage, 72 and n.

154 INDEX